An Introduction to
MODERN
ARAB CULTURE

Bassim Hamadeh, CEO and Publisher

Seidy Cruz, Senior Field Acquisitions Editor

Gem Rabanera, Project Editor

Alia Bales, Production Editor

Jess Estrella, Senior Graphic Designer

Trey Soto, Licensing Coordinator

Natalie Piccotti, Director of Marketing

Kassie Graves, Vice President of Editorial

Jamie Giganti, Director of Academic Publishing

Printed in the United States of America.

ISBN: 978-1-5165-2629-1 (pbk) / 978-1-5165-2630-7 (br)

An Introduction to
MODERN
ARAB CULTURE

BASSAM FRANGIEH

 cognella® | ACADEMIC PUBLISHING

إرضاء النـاس غايـة لا تـدرك

Pleasing People is an Impossible Task

_____

ARABIC PROVERB

BRIEF TABLE OF CONTENTS

DETAILED TABLE OF CONTENTS

CHAPTER 7   Music in the Arab World   135

CHAPTER 8   Modern Arabic Poetry   158

PREFACE

———

MARY JANE PELUSO, YALE University Press publisher, once suggested that I write a book about Arab culture. She was surprised at the lack of comprehensive studies in the English-speaking market about modern Arab culture despite the great geopolitical importance of this region and the attention given to the Arab world following the tragic events of September 11, 2001. The idea of writing a book on Arab culture is frightening, a formidable task that carries great responsibilities. The first challenge that came to mind was: How could I capture and embrace Arab culture, so massive and multifaceted, in a single volume? How can any writer, for that matter, hope to capture a people's rich culture in one book? I began my work, and Mary Jane Peluso graciously continued to be my advisor on the project.

Early on, I decided the book should serve as a wide-ranging yet comprehensive introduction to Arab culture's rich, distinct, and sophisticated aspects for general readers and students alike. It is my wish to provide a deeper understanding of what Arab culture is and how recent events have shaped it. My hope is that *An Introduction to Modern Arab Culture* will help readers to better understand the main characteristics of the Arab people, their culture, and society. This book neither intends to praise Arab culture nor to condemn it. It presents Arab culture from a point of view based on my knowledge of the region in which I was raised, and from my experiences on many personal levels. This book examines Arab origins, identities, values, family, thought, and language, as well as the tremendous developments taking place in poetry, music, and the novel.

An Introduction to Modern Arab Culture also looks closely at subjects that some readers may have some familiarity with, but not a deeper understanding of how these topics are shaping the region and impacting the world. These include the Arab Spring, the Syrian refugee tragedy, and contemporary social, intellectual, and political issues connected to modern Arab culture and thought. The book covers Islam and Islamic communities throughout the ages in an effort to connect and highlight the most significant aspects and features of Arab culture.

It is my sincere hope that this book will be helpful for several different audiences: students of Arab thought, politics, history, and literature; those who are interested in languages, anthropology, sociology, and cultural issues; and general readers who recognize the value and importance of being better informed about the Arab world and its culture. Specialized or non-specialized students of Arabic or the Arab world in the context of Middle East Studies programs may also find this book useful. Finally, this book may benefit people residing in the Arab world who want a broader understanding of the region.

———————

I am indebted to many individuals who helped me in producing this difficult and comprehensive project. Their contributions have greatly improved the quality of this book. Nachy Kanfer, a graduate of Yale University and a dedicated young man, was the first person to help with this project. He enthusiastically provided research and editorial support for the manuscript.

Edward P. Haley, professor of government and international relations at Claremont McKenna College (CMC), read the entire manuscript and offered useful comments; Jamel Velji, a professor of Islam at CMC, read the chapters on Islam and offered helpful comments; the Gould Center for Humanistic Studies at CMC supported the book with a summer research grant; Pomona College alumnus Jake Scruggs read the chapter on the origin of the Arabs and offered comments and editorial assistance; and David White, my research assistant at CMC, provided useful research, particularly on the Arab Spring and the Syrian refugee tragedy.

Retired US diplomat Christopher McShane provided essential support throughout the project, proofreading, editing, and conducting research for the manuscript. I have known Chris since we met in Cairo over twenty years ago, and I am thankful for his dedication and contributions. We had many lively discussions about the book until its completion. He was one of my closest collaborators who shares my love and respect for the Arab world. Chris served at US embassies in Tunisia, Egypt and Bahrain, and currently teaches at the Middlebury Institute of International Studies at Monterey in California.

I must also thank Nick Owchar, who was extremely helpful in proofing the final draft of the manuscript. The former deputy book review editor of the Los Angeles Times, Nick carefully polished and edited the manuscript prior to its production. I am grateful to him and to many other individuals whose names are included elsewhere in this book for spending time with me, and agreeing to lengthy interviews on certain aspects of Arab culture.

At Cognella Academic Publishing, this project was met with great enthusiasm by Seidy Cruz and Bassim Hamadeh. They are delightful and dynamic publishers, and I appreciate how hard they work to keep in close contact with their authors and offer help and support.

Leah Sheets is a hardworking young editor who provided quick support; senior editor Jamie Giganti was supportive and thorough. Jess Estrella, senior graphic designer, produced a beautiful cover for the book. Gem Rabanera, a conscientious project editor and a pleasure to work with, strived to ensure the quality of the manuscript. Alia Bales, a bright and gifted production editor, was a guiding light throughout the production process; she worked hard to support the project and coordinated its conclusion with perfection. Licensing coordinator Trey Soto tracked all third party content with precision. It has been a joy to work with the highly qualified and motivated team at Cognella.

Professors Patricia W. Cummins of Virginia Commonwealth University, Suheir Abu Oksa Daoud of Coastal Carolina University, Shakir Mustafa of Northeastern University, Mostafa Ahmed of Emporia State University, and Mohamed Esa of McDaniel College read the final manuscript and offered useful comments.

To them, and to all those mentioned above, I offer my salutations, gratitude, and love. Any shortcomings in this work are my responsibility alone.

INTRODUCTION

————

MY SINCERE HOPE IS that *An Introduction to Modern Arab Culture*, the first extensive book published in the United States about modern Arab culture written by a single author, will help readers better understand the main characteristics of the Arab people, their culture, and their society. This book closely examines Arab origins, identities, and values as well as the importance of family and language. It examines many other things, including: classical and contemporary poetry, music, Arab thought, and the novel. I also include discussions of the Arab Spring, the Syrian refugee tragedy, and the contemporary crisis of Arab culture, including the social, intellectual, and political issues connected to modern Arab culture and thought. In addition, an understanding of Islam and Islamic communities is necessary to fully appreciate this region of the world and its peoples. Consider this book a moveable feast—moving from one vital aspect of Arab culture to the next but without forgetting that they are all interconnected.

Exploring these interconnections does not require total comprehensiveness: The culture of the Arabs, or of any nation, is too vast to be adequately captured by a single volume. Entire books have been written on some aspects to which I have had the audacity to assign a single chapter (and not a very long chapter at that). Encyclopedias have been compiled about others, such as Islam and the Qur'an. Ultimately, this book makes no pretense to compete with these works. Instead, what this book hopes to address are the gaps existing between generally excellent academic scholarship and ill-informed popular approaches to Arab culture.

It is my sincere hope that this book will be received with interest by several different audiences: students of Arab history, thought, politics, literature, and religious studies; those who are interested in languages, sociology, and cultural issues; and general readers who wish to better understand the Arab world and its culture. Specialized or non-specialized students studying Arabic or the Arab world in the context of Middle East Studies programs may find this book useful, too. A final group who may benefit are the expatriates and ever-more serious individuals residing in the Arab world who want a broader understanding of the region.

It is sad—and understandable—that much of the considerable interest and curiosity that the West currently displays toward the Arab world stems from the attacks of September 11, 2001, and from the emergence of extremist radical movements such as ISIS in recent years. The vast Arab world, spanning Morocco to Oman, with millennia of history and deeply-ingrained cultural values, is more complex than the simplistic reporting that many have used to form their judgments and opinions of this region of the world. What is most often overlooked is the fact that the vast majority of Arabs themselves feel threatened by, and reject, the militant fundamentalist movements threatening their region.

Arabs are warm, sociable people. They express their feelings and reveal their affections for each other easily and simply. They do not hide their emotions; they consider hiding emotions to be misleading to others and untruthful to themselves. Instead, they look for signs of emotion in verbal expressions and in non-verbal cues in the course of normal human interaction. When they don't find them, they feel puzzled or even hurt by the reserve that many Westerners maintain with people they do not know well, interpreting this as coldness and unfriendliness. By the same token, Arabs can be easily misunderstood by non-Arabs unprepared for the familiar warmth and friendliness so openly displayed upon a first meeting. Warmth and friendliness are default settings for Arabs in their social interactions; it is a value that Arab children receive from their families early in life.

Politics is a more complex cultural phenomenon in the Arab world than in many other places. It is rare for Arabs to decline to discuss politics, and the Western idea of politics making for impolite dinner conversation is not widely held in Arab society. This is especially visible during the holidays when multi-generational Arab families stay up late in the night eating, talking, and laughing, with politics traditionally making up a large part of their conversation. On such occasions, even small children get into the act, staying up past their bedtimes and listening to their family members argue about politics. This is a deeply-rooted cultural pattern in Arab society. The book explores how a sense of political exclusion combined with the desire for openness and participation have been at the very heart of most Arab political movements—one hears these themes openly and passionately discussed in many Arab homes.

Along with politics, this book addresses the important role that Islam and the Qur'an play in Arab culture. Arab culture is undeniably a Qur'an-centric culture. Regardless of their own personal religious beliefs, Arabs regard the Qur'an as a book of exceeding literary beauty and power. It has informed, influenced, and inspired Arab poetry, literature, and music, and Islam itself has been the primary shaping force of Arab society and culture for more than a millennium. For that reason, *An Introduction to Modern Arab Culture* includes a chapter about basic Islamic political history throughout the ages. The book would be incomplete without it: For Arabs, the historical weight of their civilization is an indivisible component of their culture.

There is a need for a book based in the respectable academic traditions of Western and Arab scholarship and providing accessibility to readers who are not specialists and who desire a comprehensive overview of the Arab world. Mindful of that, this book examines fundamental aspects of Arab culture and their development over time and brings them up to the present. In the process, it also includes the perspectives of respected intellectuals in the Arab world, many of whom do not have a single work translated into English. In that sense, then, this work seeks to serve both Arab and Western scholarly traditions in a spirit of humility and respect.

The 1967 defeat of the Arabs by Israel cannot be overlooked by this introduction. Many chapters in this book deal with the aftermath of that defeat, a military and political phenomenon that may seem, at first glance, to hold only tangential historical significance. But that defeat's effects have been widespread and lasting: It exposed the profound failures of the political, economic, military, social, and technical systems of the modern Arab world. It also revealed, to the humiliation of Arabs everywhere, the bankrupt, hollow nature of the slogans used extensively by Arab governments prior to the defeat.

Events triggered by the 1967 loss produced a significant rupture in the lives of Arabs at all levels. The course of modern Arab reality and thought shifted; these events overshadowed Arab intellectual communities and left their mark on every form of intellectual expression—not only poetry, novels, and plays, but political, social, and cultural debates as well. A defeat of this magnitude put an end to Arab hopes for a better future, a vast Arab revival, and dreams of Arab nationalism and broad Arab unity. It also strengthened Islamic ideologies and movements in the Arab world, thus triggering the emergence of radical movements existing in Arab culture today.

To fully appreciate the impact of the defeat, first consider Arab sentiments in the decades leading up to 1967. At the end of the Second World War, after the emergence of newly independent Arab states, political national movements developed and focused on the themes of Arab nationalism, Arab unity, and Arab glory. The Egyptian revolution in 1952 further generated and inspired powerful nationalist sentiment throughout the Arab world (discussed in the chapter about modern Arab thought). That revolution stirred Arab hopes for a brighter future. Following the 1956 nationalization of the Suez Canal and Egypt's political victory against a tripartite military attack by France, Britain, and Israel, that hope grew stronger. National and political inspirations led to grandiose visions of a region-wide rebirth of power and a new promising Age. Arab secular, nationalist, and socialist ideologies saw their influence grow; Arab populations believed they could truly unite and expand their influence. Serious and expensive economic and social development projects were launched around the region.

Egypt played a central role in these years of hope supported, in large part, by the vision of its president, Jamal ʾAbd al-Nasir. Born in 1918, he ruled Egypt from

1952 until his death in 1970. He was a charismatic visionary, an ideologist who set the tone for Arab popular nationalism. Fueled by the assumption that the Arab states would unite and emerge to take their rightful place in the world, he promoted genuine social revolution. Nasir called for social democracy as a prerequisite for political democracy, social reform, and secular policy, and he became a symbol of Arab unity and revolution. The 1950s and 1960s in the Arab world were marked by social and economic progress, although disparities and corruption created friction. These years also saw a flourishing of arts and culture—from poetry, prose, and music to cinema and theater—as nationalistic themes became more common and embraced.

The Arab world's renewed sense of itself was further inflamed by the Ba'th nationalist political party, which seized power in Syria and Iraq in the same year, 1963, under the slogan of "unity, freedom, socialism." In Syria that party is still in power today; in Iraq it was dissolved in 2003. The Ba'th Party promoted the formation of a united Arab nation based on nationalistic and socialist politics, and economic and cultural principles, and it theorized that the creation of one progressive and harmonious Arab nation could achieve social justice through a redistribution of wealth and the nationalization of industry and economic development throughout the Arab world. Together, with Egypt, these ruling parties in Syria and Iraq formed the most significant Arab nationalistic sentiments ever found in modern Arab history.

On June 5, 1967, the Six-Day War broke out, ushering in the collapse of the collective hopes of the entire Arab world. The military forces of the Arab states bordering Israel suffered complete defeat in a matter of days. In the months leading up to the war, Egypt under Nasir's leadership took a number of dramatic steps, including expelling the United Nations Emergency Force from the Sinai Peninsula and building up military forces along the Israeli border. Israel responded by launching a preemptive attack on the Egyptian and Syrian air forces—between June 5 and June 10, Israel defeated Egypt, Jordan, and Syria and occupied the Sinai Peninsula, the Gaza Strip, the West Bank, East Jerusalem, and the Golan Heights. In the aftermath, the governments of Egypt, Syria, and Jordan lost credibility in the eyes of their people and the world.

Nasir (as well as the leadership in Syria and Iraq) had promised the Arabs a great victory against Israel, proclaiming that the Egyptian military was the strongest and most effective force in the Middle East. Instead, he led the Arabs into an embarrassing defeat that scarred the spiritual and moral psyche of the Arab world.

The 1967 defeat was followed by a period of soul-searching and resentment as the Arab peoples came to view the promises and proclamations of Nasir and leaders in Syria, Iraq, and other Arab states as false illusions and empty words. Arab populations struggled with a range of emotions and responses as they realized that their leaders had been feeding them propaganda, cover-ups, and misleading reports about the grim reality of their situation. For the Arab world, the defeat of 1967 created an open wound from which it has never recovered.

But the Arab sense of humiliation, helplessness, and anger also stems from other causes in addition to the 1967 defeat. Ironically, after the defeat, Arab leaders remained in power and became more brutal against their own citizens, increasing censorship, suffocating freedom, and employing terrifying tactics with secret police to silence them. Deprived of democracy, economic development, and basic freedoms, Arab populations have come to realize that the greatest obstacles to moving their society and culture forward are the leaders themselves and their authoritarian governments. If the leaders of a country are corrupt, brutal, and unjust, how can change come about?

Conditions in the twenty-first century do not bode well for Arabs, either. This book includes narratives and information about the Iraqi invasion of Kuwait, the subsequent war against Iraq, and the signing of the Oslo Accords by Israel and the PLO in 1993. I also review the American invasion of Iraq in 2003, the Arab Spring from 2010 to the present, the emergence of ISIS and other extremist organizations, and the attack of September 11, 2001, on the United States. Historical, political, and international events are threaded throughout the book's narrative.

An Introduction to Modern Arab Culture begins by tracing the emergence of the people who became the Arabs, defined by a common language, culture, and identity. It introduces one of the book's central themes: With the emergence of Islam and its subsequent religious, cultural, and political power in the Arab world, Arab culture became inextricably linked with Islamic culture. The two are not identical; Arabs enjoyed a unique culture before Islam ever existed, and other forces have also shaped Arab identity. However, inside the Arab world, it is impossible to speak of Arab culture without acknowledging the role Islam has played in defining it, even for Christians, Jews, and other groups in the religious minority.

Chapter 1 concludes with a brief overview of the many religious and ethnic minorities that exist in the Arab world and discusses their contributions over the centuries to Arab-Islamic civilization and heritage. The chapter also describes some of the values and attitudes that define Arab society from a cultural perspective. On several occasions, I contrast an element of Arab culture with an element of American or Western culture; this is certainly not meant as a critique of the latter but simply as a way of highlighting and enhancing the comparison. I dedicate a section of this chapter to a set of Arab beliefs that I feel Western readers will find interesting: The chapter catalogues the many incidents and trends that have combined to fashion Arab views of themselves and others.

Chapter 2 discusses the Arab family and the fundamental role it plays in the Arab world, supplemented with a series of interviews I conducted with Arab individuals on the role that family plays in their lives. The importance of family to Arab culture and identity cannot be exaggerated; not only do most Arab cultural conventions, traditions, and values originate within the family, the structural phenomenon of the Arab family also closely mirrors and influences the structure of Arab society at large. As crucial as rituals and customs of marriage and divorce are to Arab culture, equally important is the extent to which the close-knit nature of Arab families influences the psyche and outlook of individual members.

Chapter 3, on the Arabic language, is also intended to serve as an introductory chapter, and its material informs much of the rest of the book. Arabs are probably more conscious of their language than any other people in the world. The chapter starts by explaining the origin of the Arabic language and some of its most prominent linguistic characteristics. It moves to a discussion of the successful attempts to modernize and reform the Arabic language over the last two centuries and its current vibrant, living form. The differences between colloquial Arabic and Modern Standard Arabic are examined, along with the critical role that each plays in contemporary Arab culture. The chapter concludes with a survey of the current criticism and anxiety in the Arab world and abroad over a perceived, measured decline in general Arabic proficiency, from schools and educational facilities to everyday life.

Chapter 4 introduces classical Arabic poetry, one of two chapters on Arabic poetry in this book. I emphasize the centrality of poetry to Arab culture and identity throughout its history, dating to the very emergence of the Arabs as a people. The chapter opens with a description of the role that the poet and his craft played in pre-Islamic and early Islamic society and examines the evolution of poetic content and form in the Arab world. Though no translation of classical Arabic poetry can capture the unique structure that lends it power and rhythm, I have included some of the best translations to illustrate for the reader the formulaic nature of the poetry of this era. The chapter concludes with a look forward to the nineteenth century and the Arab renaissance, when a group of poets and writers set out to revive this great classical art form.

Chapter 5, on Islam, constitutes a brief guide and introduction to this essential part of Arab identity. Founded by the Prophet Muhammad in the early seventh century, Islam now counts more than 1.6 billion followers, representing nearly all races and nations of the world. The chapter discusses how the Qur'an for Muslims is the word of God revealed in the Arabic language to the prophet Muhammad through the angel Gabriel. The chapter explores the importance of the Islamic *umma*, which established a new social order, and how the Prophet Muhammad asked his followers to unify as one group in order to bind and connect all believers. The idea of the Islamic *umma* was demanding and revolutionary because, prior to its introduction, Arab society was highly fractured—divided into tribes whose members were fiercely loyal to one another. The chapter also offers a short biography of the Prophet Muhammad's life and the early years of the growing Islamic polity.

The chapter also discusses the Qur'an, the first book of prose in the Arabic language. Though it is a great source of pride and inspiration for Muslims and Arabs alike, for Muslims it is also a source of spiritual strength. The Qur'an is relatively brief, approximately four-fifths the size of the New Testament. Muslims believe Arabic is the language of God and that the Qur'an was created by God, and thus the Qur'an is perfect, eternal, and unchangeable. In other words, the Qur'an is inimitable in its language, style, and ideas. I also introduce the five pillars of Islam and discuss the structure of Islamic belief and practice. The chapter concludes with a section on Islam and the West, providing an analysis of how Muslim intellectuals and academics have frequently disputed the West's description of Islam as a fanatical and violent religion.

Chapter 6, on the Islamic community throughout the ages, begins with the Prophet Muhammad's death in 632, which brought about an instant political crisis within the Islamic community. At that time the community consisted of three main groups: the prominent men in Medina who had entered into a treaty with the Prophet; the leading Meccan families; and the Prophet's earliest companions, who had followed him from Mecca to Medina in 622. The chapter discusses how the influential Rightly-Guided Caliphs developed the cities of Mecca and Medina, strengthened the Islamic communities, and concentrated on continuing to unify the *umma*. With their combined military efforts, all of Arabia came under Muslim control. The Umayyad caliphate (661–750) established in Damascus was characterized by secular leaders who developed an effective administrative system of government similar to that of the Byzantine Empire. The chapter discusses the Abbasid caliphate (750–1258) and continues with a history of the final caliphates.

The chapter traces Islamic history and communities from Muhammad to the present day, including eras of great scientific and cultural innovation and achievement, including the Arab expansion to the Iberian Peninsula. The material in this chapter and the preceding one on Islam are crucial for an understanding of the long development of Arab culture, from the days of the tribal Bedouins in the Arabian desert to the twenty-first century. It also covers the distinctions between Sunnism and Shi`ism in Islam, the religious and legal Sunni schools of thought, the political differences between Shi`ites and Sunnis, the revival of Islamic identity, and the emergence of ISIS.

Chapter 7, on Arab music, explores the history of Arab music from pre-Islamic times to today, and shows the intertwined connection between music and poetry. Music was based on song, and song formed the core of meters, rhythm, and melody. The Arab poets of pre-Islamic time were compared to singing birds and their verses to birdsong. The chapter discusses how Arab music possesses significant differences from Western music and explains the essential notion of *maqam*—"scale" or "mode." The chapter highlights Arab instruments, including perhaps the most well-known, the *oud*. It also explains the notion of *tarab*, "trance" or "ecstasy," which is also fundamental to Arab music. Regional variations of Arab music, including *Ma`louf, Rai* and *al-Andalus* are explored. After highlighting a few of the Arab world's most famous and influential composers and singers from the twentieth century, including Umm Kulthum and Fairuz, the chapter concludes with a look at the increasingly diverse contemporary Arab music scene.

Chapter 8 introduces some of the main figures of modern Arabic poetry and discusses their political, social, and cultural influence. Poetry has not lost the status and influence it enjoyed in the pre-Islamic world. But in the modern era, its role has shifted: Poetry now questions, challenges, and provokes the status quo. The chapter explores both political activist poetry and love poetry, the two most prominent genres of the modern age. It is difficult to overestimate the influence of modern poets in both these fields; political poets have inspired the Arab people to desire political change, while love poets have stimulated a reexamination of traditional views on love and sexuality. In this chapter, I also discuss how Arabic poems and songs inspired and motivated protesters during the Arab Spring. Finally, the works of leading Arab poets of modern times, including Adonis, Mahmoud Darwish, Nizar Qabbani, Abdul Wahab al-Bayati, and others, are discussed and reviewed.

Chapter 9 details how the modern novel mirrors modern culture and the close connection existing between the novel and society. More can be learned about the Arab world through the novel than through all of the other studies combined. This chapter traces traditional narration styles in ancient Arabic literature and covers the biography genre, folkloric narration, and travel literature. I explain the development of the *Maqamah* (picaresque tales) genre in the ninth century, the *Saj`* style of rhyming prose, and delve into the pioneers who revived the classical Arabic narrative in the 19th and 20th centuries. The chapter traces the birth of the Arabic novel in 1914 and its development in the hands of Nobel Prize winner Naguib Mahfouz more than two decades later. The chapter traces the novels of Mahfouz post-1945, analyzing six of his great masterpieces, including the three comprising *The Cairo Trilogy*, which established him as the 'master *par excellence* and the chronicler of twentieth century Egypt, and its most vocal social and political conscience.'

Chapter 9 also introduces, after Mahfouz, a second literary giant, the novelist Abd al-Rahman Munif, and discusses two of his greatest works. His masterpiece, *Cities of Salt*, is a remarkable work that tracks the evolution and transformation of Arabia after the discovery of huge petroleum reserves. The works of other leading novelists also analyzed in the chapter include: Ghassan Kanafani, Al-Tayyib Salih, Hanna Mina, Halim Barakat, and Mohamed Choukri. Leading Arab women writers examined in this chapter include: Nawal El-Saadawi, Ghada al-Samman, Hanan al-Shaykh, Ahlam Mosteghanemi, and Joumana Haddad.

Chapter 10, on modern Arab thought, explores the chronological journey into the Arab renaissance, which started in the early nineteenth century, a time coinciding with the European colonization of the Arab world. The Arab renaissance was a time of vigorous attempts to simultaneously revive the Arab past's cultural glory and innovate in areas in which Arab culture lagged behind Europe's advances. The chapter describes the many schools of thought that occurred during the two centuries after the Arab renaissance and discusses the most significant intellectuals, pioneers, and scholars of this pivotal era. I review the developments of the leading schools of Arab thought in the twentieth century with a focus on Arab thought following the Second World War. This includes social and political ideologies, modern political Islam, the rise and fall of Arab popular nationalism, and, finally, the vision of modern Arab intellectuals for contemporary social and cultural change.

Chapter 11 introduces the Arab Spring with a look at the historical background leading up to the events that shook the foundations of oppressive dictatorships and ruthless regimes in the Arab world. The Arab Spring protests began in Tunisia in 2010 when dissent and frustration fused into a new sense of power and possibility to create changes that no one thought possible. The chapter analyzes how, within a year's time, dictators fled, resigned, or were caught and beaten to death by their own citizens in Tunisia, Egypt, and Libya. The chapter follows the uprisings in Yemen, Syria, Jordan, and the Arab Gulf States, and examines a sad reality—that many of these countries are now worse off than they were before the uprisings. Still, this seminal event in modern Arab history has led to positive results. The Arab Spring destroyed the legitimacy of the Arab dictators' regimes and shattered the walls of fear and submissiveness that fostered decades of passive silence. The genie has been released from the bottle; people will not forget that their voices can be heard and will continue to demand freedom along with social and economic opportunities.

Chapter 12 covers a difficult subject, the Syrian refugee crisis. This tragedy, a result of the civil war in Syria following the Arab Spring, presents the most challenging crisis in the region. Syria, which had served as a beacon for refugees across the region since the Second World War, today has become one of the world's leading sources of refugees scattered across the world. In this chapter, I discuss how the Syrian refugee crisis has created, by far, the largest mass migration in the region in modern history. Its implications extend far into the future, with serious consequences not only in the Middle East but throughout the entire world.

This chapter highlights the suffering of Syrian children under the age of eighteen who represent more than half of the Syrian refugee population. These innocent children lost parents, siblings, and friends and saw their homes, schools, and entire communities destroyed by warfare. The refugee experience is a bleak one: They suffer miserable living conditions and have little hope for the future. I also explore the strain of Syrian migrants on neighboring countries, impacting Turkey, Lebanon, and Jordan. The economic and financial repercussions are serious for the countries that host them; they also present severe political threats in some of these countries. The chapter also discusses the impact on European countries and explores several possible solutions to this crisis.

Chapter 13, on the crisis of modern Arab culture, serves as the culmination and conclusion of *An Introduction to Modern Arab Culture*. The chapter opens with a discussion of the role of the Arabs in history and their contributions, including the genius of their language, the majestic and inimitable Qu'ran, and how they brought the religion of Islam to the world. They emerged from the deserts of the Arabian Peninsula and became kings and leaders of a civilization that shone brightly while Europe was plunged in the gloom of the Dark Ages. The chapter lists the contributions of the Arabs to the world in science, literature, and other fields that reflect the diversity and sophistication of the region.

The chapter also identifies the deficiencies and related predicaments facing the Arab world today—taken together, these challenges constitute what I regard as the crisis now confronting Arab culture. These challenges include governance, cultural modernization, the role of Arab media, class inequality, the conditions of youth, and education reforms. The Arab people are still fighting in political, social, and cultural arenas to create a better future. The generation rising during the Arab Spring has unleashed a strong new sense of possibility; that generation now possesses new tools and the knowledge that change is, in fact, possible.

It is my humble aspiration that this book serves as a helpful guide for everyone wishing to better understand the most important features, and challenges, of Arab culture today. In addition, it is my modest goal that this book bridges the gap between specialized and popular scholarship and supplies readers with an accessible, accurate picture of a complex, vibrant, and endlessly fascinating region of the world.

———————

I am indebted to the late Oxford historian Albert Hourani's writing on Arab thought and to the late Princeton historian Philip Hitti's writing on the origins of the Arabs before Islam. I draw from Hitti's work on Arab origins and from Hourani's work for a chapter on modern Arab thought that examines the Arab renaissance of the nineteenth century. It is also important to me to recognize and pay respects to the many authors I have drawn from for their learned reporting and insightful analysis of the many facets of Arab culture covered in these chapters.

CHAPTER ONE

Arab Origin, Identity, and Values

ARAB ORIGIN AND IDENTITY

WHO ARE THE ARABS?

The Arabs are those who speak the Arabic language and feel Arab in their hearts, regardless of race, religion, or background.

The origin of Arab identity lies in the hands of the Bedouin nomads of the Arabian Peninsula. Even though this book is about the modern Arabic-speaking peoples and the populations of the many diverse Arab states, before we talk about the modern period it is essential to trace the history, place, ways of life, and traditions of the original Arab Bedouins.

The origin of Arab peoples begins in the desert of the Arabian Peninsula, a place with significant importance to the Bedouin. The Bedouin had an intimate sense of belonging to this place, to this desert. This place is an enormous wide-open land, which stretches from the coasts of the Persian Gulf and the Arabian Sea in the east to the seashore of the Red Sea in the west. The territory of the ancient Arabian Peninsula includes the modern-day nations of Saudi Arabia, Yemen, Oman, the United Arab Emirates, Bahrain, Qatar, and Kuwait.

The Arabian Desert is certainly hot and dry, but parts of it include plants, palm trees, grapevines, fruit, frankincense trees, coffee plants, and blends of spices. The Arabian routes were essential for trade caravans of the ancient world, and many pilgrimage routes used carved Arabian valleys and roads. Prior to Islam, these trade interactions provided the principle link among the Arabian tribes. When Islam emerged in the seventh century, the religious pilgrimages became the main phenomenon that linked Arabia to the outer world.[1] The existing valleys formed the routes for the caravans on their path in the holy pilgrimage.

The Arab Bedouins were the effective and natural adjustment of human life to the circumstances and conditions of this harsh Arabian Desert. They lived in tents made of goat or camel hair and watched their sheep and goats in the same pastures. They raised camels and sheep, bred horses, hunted, and raided. Their food was mainly dates, milk, and occasional camel flesh. The camel and the horse were the most important animals for their survival, which in such harsh conditions formed the basis for a people and its culture.

Without the camel, the desert could not be "conceived of as a habitable place. It is the nomad's nourisher, his vehicle of transportation, and his medium of exchange. The dowry of the bride, the price of the blood, the profit of gambling, the wealth of a sheikh—all are computed in terms of camels."[2] The camel is the Bedouin's ship of the desert. The Arabic language is said to include "about a thousand names for the camel in its numerous varieties, breeds, conditions, and stages of growth, a number rivaled only by the number of synonyms for the sword."[3]

The horse was certainly of great value to the Bedouin because it provided the required speed for sport, competition, running, and hunting. It also provided the needed success for his raids, which were motivated by difficult economic conditions of the life in the desert. In the desert land, "where the fighting mood is a chronic mental condition, raiding is one of the few manly occupations. Christian tribes, too, practiced it."[4]

ORGANIZATION OF THE EARLY ARAB SOCIETY

The organization of Bedouin society was based on the structure of clans and tribes. Every tent represents a family, a group of related families in one encampment form a clan, and the relatives of several clans make a tribe. All are blood-related. Members of a tribe share water, pasture lands, and livestock. They submit to the authority of one *sheikh*. The *sheikh* is the senior member of a tribe. He must possess excellent personal qualities such as courage and generosity; he rules by a process of democratic consultation with the heads of clans and families. Traditionally, the Bedouin is hospitable, generous, courageous, and loyal to his clan and tribe.[5]

Historian Philip Hitti emphasized that the original home of the Arabs is Arabia and that Arabia was also the original home of all Semites. And it was in Arabia that the ancestors of the Semitic peoples originated, including the Babylonians, Assyrians, Aramaeans, Phoenicians, Hebrews, and Arabs. And it was in Arabia that all proto-Semitic peoples lived at one time as one people. Some Semites of Arabia migrated to the Fertile Crescent and established civilizations as early as the mid-fourth millennium BCE. Arab Muslims were the heirs of the ancient civilizations that flourished in the land between the Tigris and the Euphrates, in the Nile valley, and on the Mediterranean's eastern shore. In present-day Yemen, on the southern edge of Arabia, many states and kingdoms date back to the twelfth century BCE. Hitti states that the famous Queen of Sheba was of south Arabian origin. The Arabians founded rich civilizations all across the area that is now known as the Middle East.[6]

Originally the term *Arabian* did not mean the Arabs alone. Historian Hitti explains that the word *Arabian* was used to refer to all inhabitants of the Arabian Peninsula, including all the Semites of Arabia. South Arabians were the first to develop a civilization of their own; northern and central Arabia stepped onto the international stage with the advent of Islam in the seventh century. The Arabians focused on the trade necessary for a successful maritime civilization. In the south, they linked India with Africa. In the north, they built the two great cities of Petra and Palmyra on the main trade routes.[7]

Arabia was made of nomads and urban dwellers, trade routes and permanent markets, and was a major center for trade. Prophet Moses "married an Arabian woman; the daughter of a Midianite priest,"[8] and the wise men of the East who followed the "stars to Jerusalem were possibly Bedouins from North Arabian desert rather than Magi from Persia. The Jews were geographically the next door neighbors of the Arabians and racially their next of kin."[9]

Christian and Jewish communities were established in Najran, a city in ancient south Arabia. Jewish tribes flourished in Yathrib, a city in the Hijaz region of Arabia that was later named Medina. Christian traders and slaves came from Syria and Abyssinia to the market of Mecca.[10]

Historian Bernard Lewis wrote that near the year 530 BCE. the term *arabaya* began to appear in Persian cuneiform documents. Herodotus and other Greek and Latin writers expanded the term *Arabian* and *Arab* to the entire peninsula and all its inhabitants, including the southern Arabians. The term *Arab* seems to cover all the desert areas of the Middle East inhabited by Semitic-speaking peoples.[11]

Linguistically, the word `*Arab* originates from the Arabic verb `*abbara*, meaning to "express oneself clearly and eloquently." This is a derived verbal form based on the root form `*abara*, originally meaning to "cross over" or "pass through the desert." Supporting this theory is the fact that Bedouins were known for their ability to express themselves and converse with others at the highest level of eloquence in the Arabic language. Bedouins were also known for genuinely preserving their language and original speech patterns. This linguistic culture extends to the overarching concerns of maintaining their traditions and values.

In any case, by the early years of the Islamic era, the term `*Arab* had come to "apply to all those who spoke Arabic."[12] And the Historian Ibn Khaldun, of the fourteenth century, used the term "Arab" to refer to the Arab Bedouin.[13] Arabic has continued as the official language of Arab culture as a whole; the civilization was diverse, yet it was "Arabic in language and tone."[14]

THE ARABS TODAY

The Arab world of the twenty-first century is composed of twenty-two independent states, with a population that exceeds four hundred million individuals who speak the Arabic language and share a common Arab culture and history. By the end of World War II, most Arab countries had achieved their independence from Western colonizers in the form of modern nation-states. The national boundaries that carve apart the Arab world, however, do not separate Arab populations from their shared historical memories, common backgrounds, and beliefs of both past and present.

Arab peoples today are connected by important and powerful elements: the Arabic language and the cultural heritage. Muslims would include the Islamic faith. Despite the geographic distance that separates the Arabs, they share an Arab identity based on common characteristics, traditions, and values. Arabs are also united by shared experience and perceived destiny, as well as other historical, social, linguistic, and religious bonds.

The past is always alive in the collective memory of the Arabs. The empire that conquered the ancient world in the seventh and eighth centuries and created a great civilization bears little resemblance to the current disunited and autocratic Arab states. But the memory of those ancient civilizations lives on for modern Arabs. Although today's Arab world is politically divided, all Arab states use Arabic as their official language. The Arab world today extends over two continents, from the Atlas Mountains of Morocco in the west to the Arabian Sea and the Persian Gulf in the east. It includes the west Asian states of Qatar, Bahrain, United Arab Emirates, Oman, Kuwait, Yemen, Saudi Arabia, Iraq, Lebanon, Jordan, Palestine, and Syria. The Arab world also includes the North African countries of Morocco, Algeria, Tunisia, Mauritania, Libya, Egypt, and Sudan.

RELIGIOUS SECTS AND ETHNIC GROUPS

Islam is the major religion of the Arab world, but the presence of other religions as well as sectarian differences within Islam combine to make parts of the Arab world quite religiously diverse. Altogether over 90 percent of Arabs are Muslim; the remaining population is composed of religious minorities, mostly various Christian groups. Christians are concentrated mainly in Lebanon, Syria, Jordan, Palestine, Egypt and Iraq. A small Jewish minority exists, concentrated primarily in Morocco, Tunisia and Yemen, with token representation in Syria and Egypt. Very small numbers of other religions are also found in the region, including the Baha'i religion.

Within the Islamic religion exist several religious sects; the largest of these is of course the majority Sunni community, followed by the Shi`ite sect. Shi`ites, who account for about 15 percent of the total Muslim population, are concentrated in Iraq, Lebanon, Bahrain, Yemen and the eastern part of Saudi Arabia, and have significant presence outside the Arab world, such as in Iran. The differences in these sects is further discussed in the chapter on Islamic Communities throughout the Ages.

Other Islamic sects include the Druze in Lebanon and Syria, the Alawites in Syria and Morocco, and the Zaydis or (Zaidis) in Yemen. The Arab Christian world also features considerable sectarian diversity. Of all Arab Christian communities, the largest are the Copts in Egypt and the Maronites in Lebanon.

The Arab world features a plethora of ethnic groups, as well. The two largest non-Arab ethnic groups are the Kurds, concentrated mostly in Iraq, Syria and the non-Arab states of Turkey and Iran, and the Berbers, prevalent across North Africa. Smaller groups of ethnic minorities also exist, such as the Circassians in Syria and Jordan, the Assyrians in Syria and Iraq, and the Armenians in Syria, Lebanon and Palestine. South Sudan became independent in 2011, reflecting its significant religious and ethnic differences from the more cohesive north. Each of these ethnic groups has its own distinctive rituals, values and traditions, including unique customs with marriage ceremonies and managing social interactions. Some preserve their original ethnic social costume or dress. By far, the most important aspect of identity for ethnic minorities in the Arab world is the preservation and use of their own languages and dialects, as many groups still use their own native languages in addition to Arabic.

Most ethnic minorities who have preserved mother tongues other than Arabic do not self-identify as Arabs, such as the Berbers, Kurds, Armenians, Circassians and some ethno-linguistic groups of South Sudan.[15] But speaking Arabic does not always guarantee a feeling of Arab identity. Religious sects such as the Maronite Christians in Lebanon have some members who, despite speaking Arabic as their native language, feel they are more Lebanese than Arab. At the same time, of course, some other Maronites have been widely recognized as prominent Arab nationalists; in fact, several of the Arab world's nineteenth century pioneers in language, literature and thought were Maronite Christians.

Similarly, some Egyptian Copts feel they are more Egyptian than Arab, but other Copts have been leading Arab nationalists and intellectuals who greatly contributed to Arab culture and national identity. Finally, sectarian groups such as the Druze and Alawites speak no national language besides Arabic, and while they have preserved their own values, rituals and religious practices, they completely identify ethnically as Arabs. All in all, the diversity of ethnic and sectarian affiliations within the Arab world forms an integral part of Arab culture.

ARAB IDENTITY AND SENSE OF BELONGING

A wide array of cultural, religious, linguistic and social factors make up the Arab national identity. In addition to the Arabic language, many believe that a key element of Arab identity is the Qur'an, a text revealed in the Arabic language to an Arab prophet who spoke in Arabic to an Arab audience. Solidarity in the early days among the Islamic *umma*, and community of believers, was particularly strong among Arabs. Since then, Arab identity has encompassed the two indivisible constituents of language and Islam. These two shared and living artifacts kept Arab culture cohesive and unified throughout the centuries. Recent revolutions and wars in Syria, Iraq, Yemen, and elsewhere are challenging notions of Arab cohesiveness in the twenty-first century. Nonetheless, underlying concepts of Arab identity and identification are important in understanding the contemporary Arab cultural scene.

Even before the appearance of Islam, tribal solidarity and the Arabic language combined to create a strong feeling of belonging to a particular group and a particular culture. The subsequent Islamic conquest then added a religious element to Arabism: speakers of Arabic who were also adherents to Islam became linked more closely than those merely of common tribal solidarity, political allegiance, or economic interest. Individuals who professed belief in Islam through the medium of the Arabic language shared a sense of belonging to an enduring world that was created in the aftermath of the Qur'anic revelations. This world manifested itself in the Qur'an, in the *Hadith* traditions of the Prophet, in different forms of social and intellectual activities, and in systems of ideal social behavior. All this helped to preserve the Arab sense of belonging to one culture and one identity, strengthened by the two powerful constituents of language and religion.[17]

ARABISM AND ISLAMIC IDENTITY

Though challenged and transformed by Islam, the concept of Arabism did not fade. Numerous scholars and expatriates who spent their lives in the Arab world have written about the strong Arabist bonds that still exist. British diplomat Mark Allen, for example, described Arabism as the "mission of being self-consciously true to the Arab identity."[17] Princeton scholar Bernard Lewis further depicts Arabism as the pride of the Arab and his "consciousness of the bonds that bind him to other Arabs past and present."[18] Arabism has allowed Arab non-Muslims to view Arab nationalism as a secular alternative to the Islamic Caliphate. Halim Barakat noted that some of the early Muslims, Christians and Jews were Arabs before they were members of their respective religious communities.[19]

The ethnic and religious combination of Arabism and Islam constitutes the main driving force of Arab identity, but the presence of other religions and ethnicities has contributed in its own way. Non-Arab and non-Muslim groups, by maintaining their distinctive rituals, customs, social practices and traditions, have added a rich diversity to the Arab world and have come to form an integral piece of Arab culture and societal fabric. All Arabs, both Muslim and non-Muslim, share a common heritage that is deeply steeped in the Islamic tradition.

Writing about his own experiences as an Arab Christian raised in the Arab world before emigrating to the United States, the late cultural critic Edward Said emphasized the relevance of Islam to the identity of Arab non-Muslims: "Islam is something all Arabs share, and is an integral part of our identity ... I have never felt myself to be a member of an aggrieved or marginal minority."[20] Other religious and ethnic minority groups also feel part of this common culture, regardless of their affiliations. Some accept the use of the term *Arab and Islamic culture*, because the word *Islamic* is used within a cultural, not religious, context. Examples abound of present and past experiences shared by Arab Muslims and Arab non-Muslims alike, all contributing to the formation of Arab identity.

It is difficult to draw the line between Arab and Islamic identity; the two cannot really be separated. The Islamic ideal of the *umma* was based on pre-existing Arabism as well as the Arabic language and culture. This was why the medieval Arab historian Ibn Khaldun used the term *umma* to mean "nation" as opposed to "religious community." As an early concept, the *umma* was intended to shift the loyalty of Arab tribes away from Arabism toward the religious unity of the Islamic community.

However, over the last decade, Islamic identity has grown much stronger, and some Arab Muslims have begun to describe themselves as Muslims first and Arabs second. Some intellectuals maintain that Islamic identity has attained priority over Arab identity in recent years. The reasons they give include the increased attacks against Islam, oppressive corrupt political and social situations in the Arab world, and the influence of Islamic movements that believed only Islamic ideology and practices are remedies for the weakness and stagnation of Arab society and culture.

However, the line is blurred for most. Arab nationalists, communists, and non-Muslims emphasize their Arabism, while other groups emphasize their Islamism. The majority of the population, whether consciously or unconsciously, does not see any separating line. Arab non-Muslims stress their identity as Arabs, but they are nevertheless aware that Arab and Islamic culture and identity are interconnected and integrated.

Furthermore, Arab awareness of their role in history is very important to their identity, as witnessed by their pride in their contribution to world civilization. Arabs also share the collective memory of defeat, decline, foreign intervention, internal strife, and occupation and domination, but this has unified them culturally.

Today, Arabs join in feeling oppressed, angry, and mistreated, as well as saddened by the disunity displayed among Arab states, including absence of democracy, squandering of wealth and resources, a widening gap between rich and poor, and relentless conflict and hostility. Even the degrading experience of traveling from one Arab country to another is a common experience of humiliation. Westerners are often treated better than Arab nationals when traveling in the Arab world. Upon arrival at an airport in a Middle East capital city, Arabs are more likely to be questioned by immigration authorities, while warm welcomes are extended to Westerners. Americans and Europeans usually do not need visas to enter an Arab country, while citizens of Arab League states do. Furthermore, visas and documents needed to enter an Arab country can be difficult to obtain for some Arab nationals. This common sense of degradation and embarrassment contributes to a feeling of connection to fellow Arabs, and emotional and psychological unity among the Arab peoples.

Above all, though, the most important of the elements that combine to form Arab identity is the Arabic language, discussed in detail in chapter 3. Arabs maintain great respect for their language, "seeing it not only as the greatest of their arts but also as their common good."[21] Arabic has always been the national language of Arabs, not only serving as a medium of daily expression but as the language of culture and progressive thought throughout the civilized world for many centuries. Between the ninth and the twelfth centuries, there were more works estimated in philosophy, medicine, religion, astronomy and geography produced through the medium of Arabic than through any other tongue.[22]

In fact, the concept of Arab nationalism itself is based on the Arabic language. Most Arabic speakers, regardless of race, religion, tribe or region, feel they belong to one Arab nation. Nationalists see the Arabic language as an instrument of communication, a container of ideas and feelings, and an embodiment of the entire Arab culture. Many Arabs even reject the notion that Arab national identity includes the previously described non-linguistic elements such as religion, economy, geography, regionalism, and responses to external challenges, believing instead that the Arabic language and the spirit of feeling connected to Arab origins and their preceding empires represent the only foundation of the Arab identity and Arab nation. The late Egyptian President Jamal `Abd al-Nasir, often described as the "hero of Arab nationalism," was the most prominent advocate of this language-based Arab nationalism.[23]

WHO ARE WE?

Arabs have been united for centuries by their shared religious, linguistic and cultural qualities, but the modern concept of identity did not come into being until the nineteenth century, with the dawn of the Arab renaissance. The question of "who are we?" could not be asked without the implied addition of "as opposed to them?" Syrian writer George Tarabishi noted that this "them" was the West, newly emerging in Arab consciousness as an invader and oppressor. And after defining themselves against the West, another question soon emerged: "Are we Arabs or Muslims or Easterners, or a combination of the three?" Tarabishi wrote that many of the varied attempts to answer these questions have led to conflicting ideologies.[24]

TRIBAL, RACIAL, REGIONAL AND SECTARIAN AFFILIATIONS

A major sectarian tension within Islam began quickly after the death of Prophet Muhammad in 632, when conflict revolved around the leadership of the Islamic community. Disagreement on the rightful successor to the Prophet and on his political and spiritual authority led to the initial split between communities that eventually became known as Shi`ites and Sunnis. This tension created a profound and lasting division throughout Islamic history, maintained through both sharp words and swords, and actively impeding the coagulation of true pan-Arab and pan-Islamic unity.[25]

Tribal affiliations and divisions that remain within the Islamic *umma* and among Muslims today are part of an even older story. Various sects, tribes and ethnicities existed in Arabia before the coming of Islam. Jewish and Christian communities flourished in certain parts of the Arabian Peninsula, together with numerous tribal communities, urban centers like Mecca and Medina, and nomadic clans. When Islam emerged, the Prophet made covenants with various tribes and clans, including the Jewish tribes, shortly after migrating to Medina. From the beginning, Islamic converts were instructed to be loyal to the new established Islamic *umma*, but it was not easy for the population to completely rid themselves of loyalty to their tribes and clans. During the formative period of Islam, and indeed throughout all of Islamic history to the present day, tension has persisted between tribal and Islamic affiliations. At certain points in history, tribal affiliations also helped the Arabs to defend themselves during conflicts with other peoples. The tension between Sunnis and Shi`ites, however, has been largely destructive. And it has prevented the establishment of any genuine Arab unity within the *umma*, thus endangering the stability of the whole Islamic dominion.[26]

After the downfall of the Umayyad Caliphate in the middle of the eighth century, Islamic political life became "an arena of conflict between Arabs, Persians, Turks, Kurds, and Berbers."[27] All of these various ethnic groups are Muslim, but their shared religious identity did not prevent them from fighting for influence in the central government of Baghdad and other seats of the Caliphate. Similarly, conflict between nomadic Arab tribes and urban Arab communities has persisted throughout Islamic history, as well. Tension has also traditionally existed between Muslim and non-Muslim tribes, though Christians and Jews were regarded as "People of the Book" and therefore allowed to keep their property and practice their religious rites in order to maintain their unique religious identities within Arab-Islamic culture. In return, the "People of the Book," also known as *zimmis*, paid taxes that early Islamic rulers demanded from their non-Muslim subjects. Chapter 5 on Islam discusses the evolution and effects of Islam in the Arab world in greater details.

STATE AND NATIONAL IDENTITY

Modern Arab national identities, akin to citizenship, such as Iraqi, Lebanese or Moroccan (not to be confused with the broader Arab national identity) play a further role in complicating the idea of Arabism. Historically, some Arab countries, as with the case of Egypt, had for centuries cultivated their own state identities separate from a pan-Arab identity. When Jamal `Abd al-Nasir took power in 1952, he began to emphasize his country's role in pan-Arabism rather than Egyptianism. After his death in 1970, however, Egyptians began again to think of themselves more as Egyptians than as Arabs. More Arab countries developed unique state identities as well. Following the military defeat of 1967 and the end of the dream of Arab unity, state identities became much more accepted. By the twenty-first century, Syria, Jordan, Egypt, Lebanon, each Gulf State, and others had all fashioned separate state identities. Compared with previous generations, who considered themselves Arabs first, today's residents of the Arab world now define themselves as Egyptian, Qatari, Syrian or Tunisian. Every successive regional crisis, such as the 1990 Iraqi occupation of Kuwait, has seen the pan-Arab national identity lose more ground to individual state identities.

The pre-Islamic tribal identity has not disappeared altogether, even now. Tribal affiliations in many Arab countries are still strong and play an extremely important role in determining the structure of governments, domestic policy, and the direction of foreign relations, especially in Saudi Arabia, the Gulf States, Yemen and Iraq. In these countries, loyalty to the tribe is perhaps the most important loyalty of all. This has been most evident in post-war Iraq, as levels of representation in the Iraqi Parliament have almost exactly mirrored the numerical strength of each sect in the population. The scenario of the country splitting into two or three separate states remains a possible outcome. The Kurdistan referendum held in September 2017, with 93 percent in favor of independence, is a strong example. Since 2011, regions and cities inside Syria have been seized by various groups and factions. Libya also has strong tribal affiliations playing out to this very day.

Still, although the conflicting affiliations of the Islamic community and smaller ethnic and tribal communities have worked against the political unity of the Arab world, its cultural and spiritual unity largely remains whole. The pan-Islamic identity in particular, which is based on the commonality of faith and destiny, has transcended all specific ethnic identities.[28] This tendency has made Islamic society remarkably open throughout history. Muslims would travel through North Africa, the Middle East and other Muslim countries, and find themselves at home and welcomed. In traveling from Morocco to Baghdad or Cairo to Damascus, Muslims feel connected to one culture despite differences in dialect and custom, and this phenomenon creates the feeling of belonging to one united community, albeit a diverse one. The essential bonds of the Islamic community of the past have not been broken, but new political tensions and challenges have emerged today, including sectarian conflicts. Yet the Islamic identity remains strong and alive.

ETHNIC AND SECTARIAN IDENTITIES

As previously mentioned, various minority ethnic and sectarian religious groups in the Arab world assert their identity on the basis of their language, race, origin, religion and history. The largest minority groups of the Arab world are either non-Arab or non-Muslim, possessing their own ethnic characteristics or their own religion. When Islam expanded outside Arabia beginning in the seventh century, some ethnic groups converted to Islam but kept their own languages, like the Kurds of Syria and Iraq and the Berber peoples of North Africa. Some groups, on the other hand, opposed conversion to Islam but adopted Arabic as their language, like the Maronites of Lebanon and the Copts of Egypt. Others resisted both Islam and Arabic, such as the Aramaic-speaking, Christian Assyrian populations of Syria and Iraq. Newer religious sects such as the Druze have also risen within Islam itself.

Many of these ethnic groups were indigenous peoples before the expansion of Islam, having lived on their lands for centuries before the arrival of the Arabs. Berbers, for example, have lived in North Africa since the year 1000 BCE. Arabs brought them the Islamic faith, and Islamic culture has grown to dominate North Africa, while the Berbers have managed to preserve their languages and traditions. Many non-Muslim minorities successfully preserved their religions, as well. These ethnic and sectarian communities lived as part of Arabic and Islamic culture and society, not in isolation from it. Over the centuries, a rich pattern of social and cultural interactions, as well as intermarriage, has played out between Arab and non-Arab minorities, and Muslim Arabs and non-Muslim Arabs.

ETHNIC MINORITIES

The largest ethnic minority in the Arab world is the Berbers, or *Amazigh*, meaning "the free" or "the noble." They speak a common language, which has different regional dialects. Some say they have Bedouin origins. Berbers are concentrated in Morocco and Algeria, constituting at least forty and 30 percent of the population, respectively. Small Berber communities also exist elsewhere in North Africa, in Tunisia, Libya, Egypt, Western Sahara and Mauritania. The Moroccan government has integrated the Amazigh language into public schools, and Algeria has designated it an official language on the same level as Arabic. Although Berbers speak their own language and have largely preserved their identity and traditions, most speak Arabic as well. Berbers constitute an important force inside Arab society and culture, and are gaining more recognition throughout North Africa and the Arab world.

After the Berbers, Kurds form the second-largest ethnic group in the Arab world. Their population is more than eight million in Iraq and more than two million in Syria. In 2003, Kurdish become an official language of Iraq, along with Arabic. Kurdish has several dialects, and many Kurds also speak Arabic, Farsi or Turkish. Kurds form a local majority in northern and northeastern Iraq. Most, but not all, are Sunni Muslims. Though Kurds have kept their customs, traditions and language, they interact with and live among Arabs. Intermarriage between Kurds and Arabs is very common.

Many nationalist Kurds aspire to establish Kurdish self-rule in northern Iraq and create an independent state of Kurdistan, which they aspire to include parts of Iraq, Syria, Turkey and Iran. Historically, Kurds lived within the boundaries of the Ottoman Empire in the province of Kurdistan. After the collapse of the Ottoman Empire in World War I, the Allies created several independent states within the empire's former boundaries. Kurds expected Kurdistan to be one of these new states, but this was not to be. Instead, historic Kurdistan was divided by the Allies among several neighboring countries. Since then, Kurds have not ceased to struggle for self-rule. After the first Gulf war in 1991, with the help of the Americans, *de facto* Kurdish self-rule was established in northern Iraq. After the fall of Baghdad in 2003, Kurds gained even more power. In 2005, for example, Kurdish leader Jalal Talabani became the President of Iraq, succeeding Saddam Hussein, who was a Sunni Muslim.

It is worth mentioning here that the famous Islamic leader Saladin (d. 1193), who recaptured Jerusalem from the Crusaders in the twelfth century, was a Kurd from the city of Tikrit in Iraq. Kurds today represent a major political force in Iraq and enjoy the support of the American government. During the past twenty years, the Kurds have been working hard to establish an independent Kurdish state in northern Iraq. In September 2017, the Kurds voted for independence, but the neighboring countries strongly objected. Establishing an independent Kurdish state has many strategic implications; thus, the United States and the European Union also objected the Kurdish referendum, and the situation continues to evolve.

Circassians constitutes a tiny but distinct ethnic group in the Middle East. They are Muslims but not Arabs. Among the oldest indigenous peoples of the Caucasus region of western Asia, Circassians fled the Caucasus in the nineteenth century after the Russian conquest. Settling first in the Balkans, they then moved to Turkey, and then to parts of Syria, Jordan and Iraq. Their population in the Arab world numbers fewer than two hundred thousand people, who previously were mostly concentrated in the Golan Heights of Syria. When Israel seized the Golan Heights in 1967, most of its inhabitants, the Circassians, left. They lost their homes, and villages, and scattered across cities. A large number also migrated to the United States. Circassians speak their own language but also Arabic; they are mostly Sunni Muslims who have preserved their traditions and folklore. They have no political aspirations, and are well-known for their loyal participation in the national order of each country in which they reside. In both Syria and Jordan they hold modest government positions and are well-integrated into Arab society.

Armenians are another distinct ethnic community, and their existence in the Arab world is deeply rooted. The Armenian community of Jerusalem has existed there since the first century of Christianity, and Armenian churches in Syria date back to the twelfth century. The old Armenian quarters of cities in Syria, Jordan, Iraq, Palestine and other places are distinctive and unique. Armenians have numbered over two hundred thousand in Lebanon and one hundred and fifty thousand in Syria, including Aleppo, Damascus and the north of the country. Armenians are Christians who belong to either the Armenian Orthodox Church or the Armenian Catholic Church. Although most also speak Arabic, they have their own language and keep independent schools, events and social clubs.

Armenians are not very well integrated into Arab society. They associate closely with themselves and retain their own traditions and customs. Some Armenians are against assimilation and integration in Arab culture and society. In Lebanon, Armenians have a strong political presence. Most Armenians in Syria, particularly from the city of Aleppo, migrated to Armenia and other countries including Europe and the United States after the civil war began in 2011.

The Assyrians are descendants of the ancient Assyrian empire, one of the earliest civilizations of northern Mesopotamia, and live today in Iraq, Syria, and Lebanon, as well as Turkey. They number about a million and a half in Iraq and up to half a million in Syria. Assyrians live in Christian communities where the ancient Aramaic language known as Syriac is still spoken. Syriac is also the liturgical language of the Assyrian church and several other eastern Christian churches. Similar to most other ethnic groups, Assyrians have preserved their own customs and traditions inside the larger Arab culture. Many Assyrians left Iraq after 2003, and following the emergence of ISIS in 2006, almost all Assyrians in Iraq migrated out of the country.

SECTARIAN MINORITIES

The Druze community is an Arab religious group concentrated mostly in Syria and Lebanon, estimated at around eight hundred thousand people in both countries. An offshoot of Islam, the Druze religion contains other doctrines in addition to Islamic ones, such as belief in the transmigration of the soul. Druze have strong religious and social rituals; intermarriage is forbidden, and although they form an integral part of Arab culture, the Druze have maintained quite closed communities within larger Arab society. In Lebanon they wield significant political power, and in Syria they are considered leading nationals. When Syria came under the French Mandate after World War I, the Druze launched a revolt against France known as the Great National Syrian Revolt. This revolt, which is well-known in modern Arab history, was under the leadership of the Syrian Druze political leader Sultan Pasha al-Atrash. Memory of the 1925 revolt has allowed the Druze to maintain much respect and admiration as Arab nationalists within Syrian society, and they have since been active in politics in both Syria and Lebanon. Many Druze in Syria hold high positions in the government and in the ruling Ba`th political party.

Long before Islam, Jews lived in Arabia as tribes of great respect and influence. When the Prophet migrated to Medina, he immediately signed a treaty with the Jews, a testament to their high position and influence in the society of the time. After the Islamic conquest, Jews successfully preserved their religion and property, continuing to practice their rituals. Jewish tribes also persisted in Yemen, Sudan and North Africa. Classical Arabic literature features many stories of the famed Jewish Arabian warrior-poet *al-Samaw'al*, who was known for his astonishing faithfulness and loyalty to his friends. In Muslim Spain, Jews and Muslims lived together in harmony, and Jews made contributions to the Arab and Islamic civilization in Spain and elsewhere throughout Arab history.

Today, a few Jews remain in the Arab world as a religious minority, with specialized, skilled professions. After the establishment of the state of Israel in 1948, most Jews moved to the United States or Israel, but some remained in their Arab countries of origin. In Morocco, Jews enjoy a respected status; they speak Hebrew dialects and are a successful, influential and wealthy community. Tunisia also has a small, respected Jewish population. In Bahrain, a very tiny Jewish community has its own public places of worship and a representative in the Bahrain Parliament. The Ambassador of Bahrain to the United States from 2008 to 2013 was a Bahraini Jewish women. In Syria, Jews were unable to travel out of the country after 1948, but this restriction was lifted early in the 1980s by President Hafez al-Assad. As a result, most of the Jewish community in Syria has departed, with only a few remaining in the country. By 2018, there were no Jews left in Syria or Iraq.

The Copts are native Egyptian Christians, constituting the single largest Christian community in the Arab world. According to the Gospel of Matthew, Christ and the Holy Family came to Egypt fleeing from Herod. Thus, Egypt is the only country outside of Palestine in which Christ lived. Though a sectarian minority, Copts by large are not culturally or ethnically distinct or different from Egyptian or Arab society. They are Arabs and speak Arabic. Ancient Coptic is used only as the liturgical language of the Egyptian Coptic Church, but it is taught as a language inside Egypt and in some universities around the world. The number of Copts in Egypt used to be around ten million, and they have been well-integrated in society. Leading Coptic intellectuals have greatly contributed to major aspects of Arab culture throughout the centuries, particularly in modern times. In recent years however, conflicts, sometimes violent, have erupted in Egypt, reflecting the social and political turmoil in the region. Following the American invasion of Iraq in 2003, the emergence of ISIS, and the execution of the former Sunni president Saddam Hussein in 2006, the Copts in Egypt became a target. ISIS has bombed Coptic churches and monasteries in Egypt, resulting in hundreds of deaths. In 2015, ISIS militants in Libya rounded up and slaughtered dozens of Egyptians Copts who worked in construction there.

The Coptic people are descendants of the ancient Egyptians whose history starts with King Mina, the first king to unite the northern and southern kingdoms of Egypt around the year 3050 BCE. Some Copts have always felt they are Copts first, Egyptians second and Arabs third, but other Copts, as mentioned, are Arab nationalists. In addition to the Copts, Egypt also contains a small minority of Shi`ites, and was even ruled by a Shi`ite Caliphate during the Fatimid era in the tenth, eleventh and twelfth centuries.

The Maronites make up the second-largest Christian community in the Arab world, after the Copts, and Arabic is their mother tongue. Concentrated mostly in Lebanon, they constitute about 25 percent of the Lebanese population of approximately six million, and are estimated to number about five million spread across the globe. Some Maronites identify themselves as Lebanese descendants of the ancient Phoenicians, not as Arabs. Others pioneered the Arab renaissance of the past two centuries. Maronites are well-represented in the ranks of Arabic language, literature and thought; famed poet and author Gibran Khalil Gibran is a Maronite, to give one example. Other Maronites are known for their devotion to Arab national issues.

The history of the Maronites goes back to the fifth century, at which time the inhabitants of Mount Lebanon were converted to the Christian faith by several disciples of Saint Maron (d. 410). Arabs then dominated the region in the seventh century with the spread of Islam, but the Maronites were able to preserve their religion. Most Maronites speak French in addition to Arabic. Syriac is the liturgical language of the Maronite Church, but the Gospels are read in Arabic.

Lebanon came under the French mandate after World War I and achieved its independence in 1943. The Maronites, however, had long-established ties with the West, particularly France, and were supported under Ottoman rule by France since the nineteenth century and earlier. Because of their Western connections, Maronites became the most influential sectarian power in Lebanon, bringing them into conflict with the Druze and other Muslim groups. The Lebanese constitution mandates that the president of Lebanon must be a Maronite, a holdover from French mandate influence. Today, however, the Maronites are beginning to lose their political power, and their feudalistic and aristocratic status in Lebanon is weakening. New political forces have emerged, especially that of the Shi`ites.

The Alawites comprise the largest religious sect inside Syria, with numbers exceeding three million. The term *Alawite* in Arabic means "one who follows `Ali." An offshoot of Shi`ism, Alawism is an independent Shi`ite religious sect going back to the eleventh Shi`ite Imam Hasan al-Askari (d. 874). Alawites are mostly concentrated in northwest Syria on the coast of the Mediterranean, but they also live in other cities and areas, including Lebanon and Turkey. Since 1970, many Alawites moved to Damascus to take up positions in the government, military and intelligence services.

During Ottoman reign, Alawites faced persecution by the Muslim Sunni majority, who considered them heretics. Despite constant oppression, however, they have been able to maintain themselves for centuries as a distinct community, preserving their religion and traditions. Alawites are similar to the Shi`ite minority of Lebanon in their historical experience of neglect, poverty and marginalization. They are also similar to the Druze in their belief in dissembling about their religion; they meet in secrecy and privacy and keep their doctrines and texts to themselves.

In the 1950s, many Alawites joined the political socialist Ba`th Party, which had encouraged the poorer classes of society to join. Hafez al-Assad, an Alawite military officer and a member of the Ba`th ruling party, eventually took over the government in 1970 and declared himself president in a bloodless military coup.

Assad, although a dictator, was an Arab nationalist, but elements of the Sunni majority did not like to see an Alawite ruling Syria. In 1982, Assad's secular regime crushed a Muslim Brotherhood revolt in the Syrian city of Hama, and thousands were killed. Hafez al-Assad continued ruling until his death in 2000, and was immediately succeeded by his son, Bashar al-Assad. Alawites have thus ruled Syria since 1970.

Although the Alawite regime practices absolute rule, minority groups in Syria were traditionally treated equally, including the Druze, Circassians, Armenians, Jews and Christians. The current president, Bashar al-Assad, continued his father's policy that sought to bring Syria into stronger alliance with the Shi`ites of Lebanon and Iran and the monarchic Alaouite dynasty that rules Morocco. See chapters 11 on the Arab Spring and chapter 12 on the Syrian refugee crisis.

The Isma`ilis form a branch of Shi`ite Islam distinct from the main Twelver branch (see chapter 6 on the Islamic Communities throughout the Ages), taking their name from Isma`il bin Ja`far (d.760), who was the son of the sixth Shi`ite Imam Ja'far al-Sadiq. The Isma`ilis believe that Isma'il should have been the seventh Shi`ite Imam instead of his brother Musa al-Kazim. For this reason, Isma`ilis are sometimes known as Sevener Shi`ites. Small communities of Isma`ilis can be found across the Arab world, especially in Lebanon, Syria, Palestine, Yemen, and Saudi Arabia. Isma`ili dogma differs in several respects from other Shi`ite doctrine, but like the Alawites and Druze, Isma`ilis traditionally hid their religious beliefs to avoid persecution. In the modern day, Isma`ilis have contributed to the social justice and development causes in the world, largely through the work of the Aga Khan Development Network.

The Baha'i have their own independent religion, based on the teachings of Baha' Allah, who founded the religion in Iran in 1863 and is considered by his adherents to be a Messenger of God. About six million Baha'i exist worldwide, with a large concentration in Iran, and very small communities in Syria, Tunisia and Egypt. Adherents to the Baha'i faith believe in the one and only God, but they cannot practice their religion publicly in many Arab countries because of one major incongruity with Islamic doctrine: Islam considers Prophet Muhammad to be the last of all prophets. Thus, the Baha'i faith, founded by a prophet in the nineteenth century, is not accepted by Islamic teaching.

It is difficult to know the exact number of Baha'i in the Arab world, but there are not very many, and they are represented primarily in the upper-middle social class. During the Shah's regime, Baha'i constituted the largest minority group in Iran, but following the Islamic revolution in 1979, most either left the country or learned to practice their faith in secret. The Baha'i have no religious rituals; believers gather at certain times of the month for prayer and congregation. In Tunisia, the Baha'i have been given much more freedom to openly practice their religion than in any other Arab country. The Baha'i in the Arab world are Arabs, with no distinct culture or language of their own. Some are of Persian origin.

MINORITY INTEGRATION

Still other smaller ethnic and sectarian minorities exist in the Arab world in addition to those covered above, such as the Turkmen of Syria, Lebanon and Iraq. South Sudan features a plethora of different ethnic and religious groups. Some minorities feel they are not Arabs, and some have not even accepted the Arab presence. But proponents of these views are very rare.

Most ethnic and sectarian groups in the Arab world share common memories and culture. The experience of their participation and involvement in Arab society has been universally enriching, and many scholars and activists now call for wider appreciation of their roles. The great Arab civilization of the past was able to flourish thanks in part to the contributions of diverse ethnic and sectarian groups. Today, leading intellectuals, poets, novelists, politicians, activists, and scholars come from non-Arab or non-Muslim backgrounds. The involvement of Druze, Kurds, Berbers, Alawites, Copts, Maronites, Armenians, Turkmans, Assyrians, and others, in all aspects and disciplines of Arab life—social, political, national, literary and artistic—have blurred the lines of ethnic and sectarian identity. Their presence and contributions have enabled the formation and continuation of a rich and diverse Arab and Islamic culture.

Arab culture has been greatly enriched by the existence of ethnic and sectarian minorities, and there are calls for more dialogue, interaction and recognition of their rights.

ARAB VALUES AND VIEWS

Arab culture is traditional, and centers on the Qur'an and family. The values that prevail are, in general, a combination of Islamic precepts and the accumulated traditions of Arabs from pre-Islamic times. These include the values of loyalty, generosity, genuine warmth, honoring parents, and caring for the elderly. As discussed in the chapter on the family, the Arab family is the focal point of Arab social life and plays a pivotal role in preserving all received cultural values. Inside the family, the example is set for adhering to religious and social ethics, ideals and principles.

Children are taught to respect their parents and not to talk back to them, raise their voices, or be disobedient. The importance of caring for, helping and respecting grandparents is also taught at an early age. Loyalty to family and friends is paramount, and generosity with time, money, services and hospitality are important qualities that are emphasized within the family. Children learn to be warm to guests, offering them the best food, and presenting all possible support. Sons are taught responsibility from early childhood and how to deal with family affairs and the community. Both sons and daughters, but especially daughters, are taught the importance of abstinence until marriage. Daughters are encouraged to be successful in school and business, and learn how to manage a home, be a mother and raise children. Arab women usually live with their families until marriage, unless they are studying or working outside of their community.

Arabs involve themselves deeply in the political and cultural issues of their society; intellectuals, cab drivers, bakers, barbers, students, tailors and teenagers all hotly debate important issues of the Arab world. Many nominally public issues are treated as deeply personal, especially issues of religion and politics, nationalism, and social topics.

WARMTH AND EMOTION

Arabs are warm and tend to express their emotions honestly and sincerely, similar to those living in regions bordering the Mediterranean. It is said about some peoples that they hide nine-tenths of their emotions, but Arabs usually translate their feelings into words. Arabs do not understand and can feel misled when people, for whatever reason, conceal their feelings about certain things. Their emotions are reflected clearly in their faces and voices, making dissembling a physically impossible phenomenon.

Foreigners who are used to the natural reserve and privacy of their own cultures can misunderstand the natural warmth and friendliness of Arabs. Strangers to Arab culture can sometimes feel uncomfortable if invited to a gathering for no apparent reason or by someone they hardly know. Rather than any ulterior motive, the truth in these cases is usually that the Arab individual is simply trying to express the generosity, friendliness and warmth that is natural to him and his society.

REPUTATION

It has always been an important value in Arab culture, like most cultures, for an individual to enjoy and maintain a good *sum`a*, or reputation. Arab men and women work very hard to establish good reputations, and they work even harder to maintain and protect them. Individual reputations affect the reputations of their families and communities. It should not be understood from this that Arabs are obsessed with pleasing others. Rather, Arab individuals simply endeavor to behave in an appropriate and dignified way in society that reflects the values of their community.

GENEROSITY AND HOSPITALITY

The value of generosity has been entrenched in the Arab psyche since before the coming of Islam. The harsh climate, continual nomadic traveling and peculiar demands of life in the desert all made the value of generosity not only an appreciated nicety but also a necessary adaptation to ensure human dignity and survival. Demonstrated mostly by hospitality toward others, generosity meant more than simply offering a meal to a guest. It implied supporting and ensuring the guest's survival by providing the most basic needs of life, including shelter, food and refuge in a merciless environment. The occasionally perilous ramifications of fierce tribal competition and warfare, moreover, meant that by accepting an unknown traveler, the host was also accepting that a horde of angry horsemen might be half an hour behind. From this reality came the idea that a host is bound, by unwritten social law, to defend his guest's life at all costs, and if necessary with his own. This sort of selfless generosity and hospitality is an integral part of the Arab character.

Arabs are also generous with their time. They go out of their way to make themselves available to their friends and feel hurt when people say they are too busy to see them. Being too busy to see friends seems like a contradiction in terms. Arabs often host banquets or present unexpected gifts to others. These are gestures of generosity that reflect a deeply rooted value in Arab cultural tradition, and has no other meaning or hidden intention. In their homes, offices and restaurants, Arabs usually consider others to be their guests, and automatically insist on paying for the meals or drinks of others.

FRIENDSHIP

Arabs are open, simple, and direct in expressing their emotions and thoughts. Because of their innocence and willingness to trust, many Arabs seem rather naïve in the eyes of other cultures. They usually develop quick friendly relationships, expressing their inner emotions with intimate facility and genuine sincerity, and find it strange when others are not open to them in the same way. Arabs believe that friendships based on strong bonds and loyalty are very important in life. It is natural for an Arab to do favors for his friends and to expect favors from them. This is seen as a manifestation of strong friendship. Arabs also value and appreciate when others do them favors, and they always try to find ways to reciprocate. Life is considered a difficult journey through which all must pass; if two friends sat together for a meal and it transpired that one needed help the other could provide, it would be expected that the latter would offer to do a favor for the former, and this offer would be gladly accepted.

In Arab culture, a person who does not come through when needed is considered a "useless" friend, and Arabs strongly believe that people should help others and not prove unhelpful in times of need. It would be very strange if, after years of friendship, someone did not volunteer to help in a time of need even before being asked. Indeed, supporting each other and sacrificing not only gives Arabs great pleasure and satisfaction, but also strengthens the bonds among friends. When arriving from another town, for example, it is expected that a visitor's friend will show up at the airport or train station to pick him up instead of asking him to take a taxi. The visitor will stay in his friend's house, as a hotel would be unthinkable, not because of the expense, but because of the lack of warmth and intimacy.

PRIVACY AND CONFIDENTIALITY

Because friendship is based on trust and openness, it is quite normal for Arabs to share many personal matters with their friends, including details of their salaries, incomes and financial situations. There are also well-understood limitations on what to reveal to friends, such as when discussing the personal issues of family members, particularly mothers and sisters. The identity of a woman in a romantic relationship is never revealed to others. In Arab culture, all aspects of a relationship between a man and a woman are very private and not to be discussed, whereas the price of a car or the size of a raise at work are considered too trivial to be private.

This means that the concept of privacy, as understood in the Western sense, is alien to Arabs, who are generally very open and sociable. They do not like to be alone, and feel uncomfortable with drawn-out silences. A prolonged silence will be broken with a question such as 'how are you' or 'how's everything going,' even if this question has already been asked and answered several times. Arabs also habitually drop in on people to say hello, showing up at the door without prior warning. Although this is now changing, a considerable number of people still do not have telephones in their homes, especially in villages and rural areas; even if they do, they still visit each other without calling ahead. It would be odd indeed for an Arab to call his brother or friend in order to ask what would be a good time to visit. This system means of course that people may have several unexpected visitors all at the same time; this is not only normal, but very much enjoyed. Because all working and non-working members of the family usually live together, it is rare to find no one at home.

When friends and family are sick, Arabs regularly visit them in the hospital or home in order to express their love and support. While members of some other cultures prefer privacy from all but their closest family members when sick, Arabs seek the warmth and company of their friends and acquaintances. When someone dies, Arabs visit the friends and family of the deceased several times a day for at least a week after the death, simply dropping in to commiserate and offer support.

The house of the deceased is opened to anyone in the community or nearby communities to visit and give condolences. Many Arabs attend funerals without even knowing the deceased or their families.

The concept of personal space in public places, elevators or parks is an alien concept in the Arab world, due to the uninhibited and expressive warmth Arabs typically display to each other. Keeping a physical distance from people is even considered a sign of coldness and artificiality. Arab men hug, hold hands, and kiss each other on the cheek; this is normal for both sexes. Men hold hands and walks for hours in the streets discussing issues. Women also hold hands while walking and talking in public places.

FEMALE CHASTITY

For the Arab woman, chastity is part of identity, and remaining a virgin until marriage is a matter of self-esteem and pride. Arab culture, like other certain cultures in the world, affords the virgin female a kind of special holiness and considers her a major source of honor for her family. Although premarital sex by either gender is not permitted in Islamic law, even the term "virginity" itself is almost exclusively used for women. As in many traditional cultures, men are not held to the same standards as women in this regard, partially because the loss of virginity leaves no physical evidence on men. In recent years, the double standard applied to female virginity has been opposed and rejected by certain elements of Arab society, particularly intellectuals and women's rights advocates. They argue that the honor of women should not be determined by the status of her virginity and call upon society to be more open-minded.

CONCEPT OF FATALISM

Most Arabs are believers in God; piety and devotion to any of the three divine religions of Islam, Christianity and Judaism are considered excellent personal traits in Arab society. Arabs harbor a strong fatalistic tendency, feeling that humans are powerless over the inevitable events of life. No one knows the day of one's death, for example, or what the future may hold, including events such as an automobile accident, or a disastrous fire or flood. In planning future events, therefore, Arabs believe that everything depends on God's will and that most of life's experiences are intended, fated and predestined.

Some view Arabs as a people that accept destiny out of total surrender to God's plan and rejection of individual agency, deriving support for this claim from out-of-context literature and Qur'anic verses. One oft-quoted verse is: "Nothing will happen to us except what God has decreed for us. He is our protector, and upon God let the believers rely."[29] To bolster the same argument, Westerners also invariably note the popular phrase *In Sha'Allah*, or "God willing," that is often repeated in Arab society. This does not mean that Arabs do not place a high value on free will.

It is true that Arabs tend to be prepared to accept their fate, because God pre-destined their fate and the fate of all humans.[30] But the Qur'an, Arabic literature and Arab proverbs, while they feature sayings to the effect that many things in life are predestined, also include passages that emphasize the free will of humans and one's ability to completely determine his or her own fate. One strong Qur'anic statement of this sentiment is this verse: "God will never change the condition of a people until they change what is in themselves."[31] While the Qur'an and Arabic literature do include expressions of fatalism and a lack of free will, these come mostly in response to the undeniable fact that humans are indeed powerless in the face of death or unexpected tragedy. This does not mean, however, that Arabs are submissive or resigned or refuse to take personal responsibility.[32]

FOREIGN CULTURAL INFLUENCES

A growing multicultural mix is permeating the Arab world, particularly in the Gulf, where people speak combinations of Arabic, English, Hindi, Urdu, Filipino, Turkish, and Persian. Even the names of stores in markets are often written either in colloquial Arabic or incorrect standard Arabic. In Lebanon and North Africa people speak combinations of French and Arabic. Growing numbers of individuals particularly among the upper class groups in Egypt, Jordan, and other Arab nations are eager to boast and brag about their Western education through the way they speak. These groups often intentionally use Arabic mixed with English or French in order to show that they are highly educated. During interviews on Arabic television programs, this social class makes great efforts to include a few words in English or French. They use this conversational tactic to give the impression that their ideas are too deep to be expressed solely via the Arabic language.

Some television channels, especially in Lebanon, promote Western programs and shows, with imitative music videos that feature provocative dancing and cloth-ing. With an eye to these and other phenomena, many believe that Arab culture is being invaded by Western culture, supported by secular Arab "liberals" and some media officials who are paid to promote programming that diverts attention from the serious problems facing the Arab population.

Several years ago, I took fifteen undergraduate students from the U.S. to Amman, Jordan for a summer cultural immersion program. To my surprise and dismay, many local restaurants were playing loud American music and songs, and the waiters kept insisting on taking our food orders in English. My students were clearly disappointed, as they wanted to practice their Arabic language skills. Even the food was not authentic Jordanian cuisine. While it was not a surprise that these restaurants did not feature classic singers like the Lebanese Fairuz or Egyptian Umm Kulthum, but shocking that they were not playing contemporary Arabic music in the background.

Today in the Arab world, one finds McDonalds and Kentucky Fried Chicken on every corner. The local population seems to think highly of these places, which are often more expensive than eating at a local restaurant. On a similar trip to Kuwait the following year, we found Starbucks and other fast food restaurants filling the streets. This applies also to other Gulf Arab states. In some Arab countries, it is possible to shop and make purchase with the U.S. dollar instead of the local currency. In Lebanon, people use the dollar for almost everything, including hotel reservations, restaurants, taxis, and shops.

Sexually provocative music videos and Western soap operas and shows played on Arabic television stations are condemned by Arab conservatives, nationalists and Islamists, all for different reasons. Many Arabs fear that Western cultural invasion aims to weaken the integrity of Arab family-based values. Traditionalists call for strengthening Arab values and protecting Arab culture from Western influence. This is one reason that Arab culture is becoming more conservative in many parts of the Arab world, and another reason why adherence to traditional Islamic values is growing even stricter.

ARABS IMAGE OF THEMSELVES

Arabs are all too aware of the reality of their social, economic and political situation. They understand that their image diminished, as is their hope of becoming a united Arab nation. Arabs lack democracy and self-determination. Only once in modern times have Arab countries tried to reach out to one another since the disaster of 1967, and that was during the war against Israel in 1973. Soon after the 1973 war ended, however, isolation and disconnect was exacerbated. Following the Iraq war in 2003, sectarianism and regionalism have increased. There is no vision today for an Arab strategy that could link Arab heritage with a political or economic plan. Arabs believe that their cultural unity, which held strong against the Mongols, Ottomans and European imperialists, is "unable to stand against regional conflicts and foreign intervention".[33]

Arabs know the extent of the damage inflicted upon their culture and the extent to which it is distant from the glorious past. A strong sense of cultural suffocation inhibits creativity. Arabs first hold themselves accountable for their own short-comings. They blame themselves for their disunity. But they also blame the West for its continual meddling and interference, especially with respect to the support for Arab rulers who have represented the primary obstacles to freedom, and to economic and social advancement.

Arab populations blame their rulers for the under-development of society. The leaders should have borne responsibility for the defeat of 1967, a defeat that revealed the ills and complete powerlessness of Arab society. Yet all retained power, and almost all of those who rule today, up to the Arab Spring, are either the offspring or the associates of this former generation of rulers. Many have been supported, and others still are supported by foreign powers. While Arab governments fight and repress their own citizens, the main function of most Arab armies is to defend the regime against their own population.

Thus, sixty years after the defeat of 1967, the same political, economic and cultural deficiencies still exist in Arab society. Scientific and technical capability is exceedingly limited in the Arab world, and there is no heavy industry to speak of. Most universities still graduate students with limited critical thinking or creativity. In spite of strong rhetoric about the importance of implementing education reforms, most academic curricula are still very weak, and pedagogy is even weaker. In a new introduction to the 2007 reprint of his book *Critique of Religious Thought*, originally published after the defeat of 1967, philosopher Sadiq Jalal al-`Azm calls for modernization and secularization with an emphasis on science and knowledge acquisition, and labels the liberation of women as a necessary condition for the liberation of society.[34]

To critic Faysal Darraj, it seems as if Arab regimes have settled in their powerlessness to the point that they cannot change or transcend their weakness. Even the mentality that justified the Arab defeat in the past remains the same. The national struggle has become a struggle for power and control among rivaling factions, consisting only of daily drama and marginal redundancy. Darraj said that Arab intellectuals and their continuous "criticism" are the only remaining tools of Arab resistance.[35]

Other intellectuals disagree with the self-criticism of al-`Azm and Darraj, emphasizing that foreign intervention and pressure have always been the primary reasons for Arab under-development, by continually working to keep Arab society disenfranchised and backward. But whatever the cause, Arabs are aware that all the ideologies of the nineteenth century Arab renaissance, including the ideology of Arab nationalism, have failed. This is why Islamist ideology, before the Arabic Spring in 2010, had come to dominate the Arab world in such short order: it was the only ideology believed able to battle undemocratic Arab regimes. Therefore, Islamists views remain appealing to the Arab population, and Islamic ideology remains the dominating ideology spreading across the Arab world today.

MISUNDERSTANDING THE ARABS

Arabs in general have felt for years that they are misunderstood and their actions misinterpreted by the West. A major Syrian writer, Muhyi al-Din Subhi, commented back in 1978 that every few months, someone seems to come up with another book about the Arabs. Imagine what he would write in the post-9/11 world if he saw the plethora of misleading books written about the Arabs. According to Subhi, while these works claim to be objective, comprehensive, and friendly, in actuality most of them deliberately and negatively depict Arabs "from one angle, which ultimately leads to poisoning the minds of Western youth about Arabs."[36] Arab-American activist James Zogby also notes that countless books, articles and television documentaries have been written about the Arab world, but that in most cases, Arabs did not participate in the discussions or presentations. As a result, instead of closing the gap, the biased information produced by those efforts served only to deepen misunderstanding.[37] Negative stereotypes of Arabs in textbooks derive mostly from "mainstream perceptions of Orientalism." A sociological study conducted on this issue shows that Arabs are the objects of significant slander.[38]

Contemporary popular perceptions of Arabs are negative not only in the United States but also in Europe. M. Najib Butalib remarked that the same negative image formed of Arabs during the Middle Ages of a backwards, desert people that dwells in tents and travels by camel, lives on in the minds of Europeans today. This negative stereotype is repeated and spread through the media; deeply rooted in Western minds, it is "subjective, unrealistic, and deformed, yet [manages to] reemerge and resurface with every new event."[39] Among Europeans who have never seen Arabs nor dealt with them, the negative image of Arabs is especially prevalent. Tunisian social scientist al-Tahir Labib writes that in Poland, although the small population of Arabs consists mostly of scholars, physicians and students, Arabs are still characterized in general as "aggressive, disrespectful to women, vicious, harsh, fanatical, backward, and scary."[40] In France, even school textbooks present unfair images of Arabs and Muslims in style and compositions.[41]

Arabs have suffered from negative stereotyping, even years before the emergence of al-Qaida and ISIS. Not only in textbooks, but also in American media, film, fiction and scholarship, to the extent that most Americans do not even perceive the stereotyping unless they are specifically reminded. The deep bond of intimacy between novelist and reader contributes to the racism that is prevalent in fiction literature and can be much more dangerous than racism in television or film. Suha Sabbagh points out that in novels, the Arab world is openly discussed as a "place filled with Islamic fanatics, terrorists, sex maniacs, and affluent but totally uncultured individuals."[42] This trend in Western literature goes back to the Europeans who visited the eastern world during the eighteenth century and returned home to write about their experiences. The Orientalist literary tradition that persists today is "characterized primarily by an attitude and a tone of cultural superiority and racism."[43] The books and articles published today on the Arab world and Islam are not fundamentally different from the virulent anti-Islamic polemics of the Middle Ages: "In films and television the Arab is associated either with lechery or bloodthirsty dishonesty. He appears as an oversexed degenerate, essentially sadistic, and low."[44]

WESTERN IMAGE OF ARAB VALUES

Anti-Arab serotypes and negative characterizations even appear in academic courses and scholarship. Many scholarly books claim objectivity and fairness while actually profiling and judging Arabs with subjective, broad statements. These sources have presented misleading information to predominantly Western audiences. The premier example of such books is Rafael Patai's *The Arab Mind*. Not only is Patai's book written in a clearly biased way, it has unfortunately been used for many years as a primary source and one of the chief textbooks in United States military academies. Unfortunately, this biased book has led senior U.S. military personnel to form misleading perspectives about the Arabs and the Arab world.

The Arab Mind has been widely read in US military and diplomatic circles since it was first published in 1973. Colonel Norvell B. De Atkine, director of Middle East Studies at the JFK Special Warfare Center in Fort Bragg, North Carolina, writes in his foreword to the 2002 revised edition: "*The Arab Mind* forms the basis of my cultural instruction, complemented by my own experiences of some 25 years living in, studying or teaching about the Middle East."[45] The Colonel adds that "[o]ver the past twelve years, I have also briefed hundreds of military teams being deployed to the Middle East."[46] For decades, Patai's book was distributed to Pentagon officials and military officers inside the United States, and to those already stationed in the Arab world, as a manual on how to understand and deal with Arabs. It became one of the Pentagon's go-to sources on Arab culture. As revealed by Pulitzer Prize winner Seymour M. Hersh, Patai's book was considered "the bible of the neocons on Arab behavior."[47]

The Arab Mind, however, is neither truthful nor accurate. It is condemnatory, misleading and degrading. Written to explain to the West how Arabs "think," the book has guided American policymakers poorly in their multifarious interactions with Arabs. For example, Patai proclaimed that Arabs are particularly vulnerable to sexual humiliation. As Hersh writes in *The New Yorker*, this idea became "a talking point among pro-war Washington conservatives," and provided the intellectual background for the sexual abuse and torture of Iraqis by American soldiers at Abu Ghraib from 2003 to 2004. Hersh reports that two themes emerged in discussions with an unnamed academic source about Patai's book: "One, that Arabs only understand force, and, two, that the biggest weakness of Arabs is shame and humiliation."[48]

Among the most damaging claims this book makes is that Arabs do not understand the value of guilt, but they do understand shame. This sort of thinking led to the concept that personal honor dictates that Arabs do absolutely anything to avoid shame in their sexual conduct.[49] Hersh quotes a government consultant as saying that the US military took this advice to heart: "It was thought that some prisoners would do anything—including spying on their associates—to avoid dissemination of shameful photos to family and friends ... I was told the purpose of the photographs was to create an army of informants, people you could insert back in the population."[50] The U.S. military was convinced that sexually humiliating prisoners during the Iraq war and threatening to publish these photographs would lead to better results in interrogations.

Certainly, following Patai's instructions to the letter did not result in American military success in Iraq. Harvard Law Professor Emran Qureshi attributes this to the fact that Patai's work is no more than a set of sweeping generalizations about the personality of an entire people, and his methodology is "based on a fatally flawed set of assumptions."[51] Anthropologist Dale Eickelman described *The Arab Mind* as useful only as an example of what not to do: "I used it in an introductory class as an anti-text to indicate the pitfalls of using psychological projections to elicit the characteristics of society and nation."[52]

The negative images of the Arabs widely circulated by Western writers contradict and deny the Arabs of their good values, and insult the entire Arab peoples. The Arabs feel sad, angry, and uncomfortable, as they see the world unfairly viewing them in horrible and harmful ways.

CHAPTER TWO

The Arab Family

"Your lord has decreed that you worship none but Him, and that you be kind to your parents. Whether one or both of them reach old age in your life, say not to them a word of contempt, nor repel them but speak to them noble words. And lower to them the wing of humility out of kindness, and say: 'My Lord, have mercy upon them as they cherished me when I was small.'"

The Qur'an 17:24–25

AS THE RICHEST RESOURCE of Arab culture, the Qur'an teaches that the family is the cornerstone of Arab life and society. It strongly reinforces the interconnection and cohesiveness of the family and instructs children to take care of their parents, offer them support and respect, and provide them with dignity in their old age. The Qur'an never ceases to stress the importance of solidarity between family members, even in an extended family. One scholar draws a meaningful analogy: if the Qur'an could be said to be the soul of Islam, the Muslim family as an institution is the body of Islam.[1] Many Qur'anic verses emphasize the ideal bonds that exist between family members; it is considered a sin to sever connections with relatives, and forgiveness and unity are necessary attributes for any Arab family.

Not only does the Qur'an provide a model for the family, the Prophet Muhammad is quoted in endless sayings about the family. Muhammad gave the mother the highest importance of all, saying those who honor their mothers will end up in Paradise. In another instance, the Prophet describes Paradise itself as lying at the feet of mothers. Arab Christians also embrace the mother in highest honor and hold the Virgin Mary, mother of the Lord Jesus Christ, to be a saint. Arab Jews hold the mother with the greatest respect of all family members. No matter the religious affiliation, the mother of an Arab family is held in the same esteem as saints and martyrs. She enjoys a kind of holiness both within her family and in society as a whole.

Islam considers the family the most essential component of Arab social organization and the most solid of all social institutions. Even in pre-Islamic times, the family served as the basis of Arabian tribal society; this ancient role was adopted and preserved by Islamic tradition, which added a religious aspect and further strengthened the position of family in the Islamic community. Before and after the arrival of Islam, the Arab family has always been the place where an individual finds the basic needs of life, security, emotional support, and a reliable personal and professional refuge. It is the center where Arab values, traditions, costumes, diet, beliefs, and religion are preserved. In addition, the Arab family protects the identity of the individual, his or her religious principles, and social and political affiliations.

This chapter describes the nature and makeup of the Arab family, including its patriarchal structure, close-knit members, and processes of marriage and divorce. The applicability of changes in Arab society to family structure will be addressed, together with personal testimonies from contemporary Arabs on the importance of the family to Arab culture and identity.

THE CORNERSTONE OF ARAB SOCIETY

Because the Arab family is the basic organizational unit of society, Arab social structure is concentrated around the family as a group, not around its individuals. Those in Arab society who for whatever reason are disconnected from their families live in isolation, alienation and insecurity. They lack the protection and personal connections needed in order to survive in a group-centered society. One main reason the family has remained so crucial is because Arab society has proven unable to provide for its citizens any other way, whether through general economic prosperity or government-run social safety nets. In traditional Arab culture, it is the family that supports individuals in need and not the society. The carpenter, the street sweeper, the baker, and the government official all must be connected to families; the alternative is isolation and marginalization. The emotional support that families lend to their members may be the principle reason for the universally low suicide rates among Arabs worldwide.

An individual's need to be part of a family is far more significant to Arabs than his or her economic survival. The social, emotional, and moral resources provided by the family are most important; it is the family that grants social status and connects the individual to ancient Arab principles and traditions. Since pre-Islamic times, the family has been the major institution of Arab culture.

Arab family values developed in the harsh environment of the Arabian desert, where individuals simply could not survive without relying heavily on their immediate families and extended tribes.[2] The interconnectedness and unity of the group was the only way for individuals to secure food, water and security for themselves and their families. It was also the only way to fend off attacks by other tribes. Defending one's family and tribe was a great honor for pre-Islamic Arabs, not only ensuring the survival of their family members but preserving the family's distinct tribal identity. The close bonds among clan members were enhanced by strong feelings of loyalty; individuals did not fight to defend their survival as much as to defend the survival and honor of the group. Individual consciousness was in fact melted into the group, the collective, the community, and the family. When Islam appeared, a new dimension was added to the already tight cohesiveness of families and tribes, as the concept of tribal loyalty shifted to include religious loyalty. In reality, of course, few adopted loyalty to Islam in place of family loyalty. During the period in which Arabia became Muslim, the entire family or clan would convert to Islam at once, thus preserving family and tribal unity but also becoming loyal to Islam. This made the family even stronger.

History does record some individuals who abandoned their tribes and families for the sake of the new religion, as the Prophet Muhammad himself did. Sooner or later, however, the entire clan would inevitably convert to Islam. With Islam, the same family structure persisted, with the addition of a new religious identity. Tribal solidarity and family organization remained essentially the same, but Islam further defined the regulations and laws of the family, especially those regarding marriage, divorce and inheritance. Marriage was already practiced for social and economic reasons at an early age, but Islam reinforced marriage and made it a religious duty. In the words of the Prophet, "marriage is half of the Islamic faith." Arab society consists of families, groups and clans. It is this network that provides for individuals in all aspects of life, from finding a job to finding a wife or husband. Most importantly, the family provides unquestioned solidarity and total involvement in solving any crisis an individual might encounter. It is a close-knit system of inter-reliance and interdependence; the family shelters aged parents and serves as center for the welfare and safety of all individuals associated with it.[3]

Families mediate with other families to locate and secure access to careers for their members. Job opportunities across the Arab world rely heavily on family connections. The family provides all the social needs of its individuals, particularly when public social services are lacking or absent. Because Arab society is unable to provide the economic, social, professional and psychological support needed for its citizens to cope with life, only the family can fill this role. While offering physical protection, it also imparts emotional warmth and love. Traditionally, members of a single family or several related families have worked together in the same profession or service for generations. This practice is the origin of such common Arabic surnames as *sabbagh* (one who works with dyes), *najjar* (carpenter), and *khayyat* (tailor).

Members of Arab families routinely deprive themselves of comfort in order to provide for the needs of other family members. Men, for example, delay their marriages or even cancel them in order to look after aging parents. Similarly, girls may delay or cancel marriage in order to care for their younger brothers and sisters, if no one else can fulfill this role. A brother might work long hours away from home, or work a second or third job at night, in order to pay for schooling for his siblings or health care for his parents. Each person's salary is typically shared by the entire family; those who work provide for and support those who do not have jobs. Everyone within the family unit depends on each other for survival and success in life.

Of course, self-denial and self-sacrifice for the family's sake is not peculiar to Arab culture. But it is one of the unique and defining features of the Arab family. The deep level of inter-attachment among family members, their openness with each other, and their strong sense of belonging and unity are amazing and admirable qualities. An Arab individual could be alienated from his society—and many are—but not from his family. Individuals carry not only the tribal identity of their families, but also their religious and political affiliation, social class, and status in society. To preserve the family's reputation is a collective responsibility of all family members; the family is honored inside the community if one of its members acts honorably, and feels ashamed if one of its members commits misconduct or acts in a dishonorable way.[4]

SELF-SUPPRESSION AND SELF-CENSORSHIP

The Arab Human Development Report notes that Arabs seek refuge in the family and other narrowly defined loyalties because of the general lack of freedom and absence of civil and political institutions that protect the rights of individuals.[5] The report also points to a wide phenomenon of "submission" created in Arab individuals, apparent in educational institutions and curricula. Once children enter school, pedagogical methods and evaluation tend to focus on dictation and submissiveness. In this, the report is slightly off the mark, because the observed submission is not the result of family loyalty and connections, but rather due to the patriarchal structure of the Arab family. This will be explored in greater depth later in the chapter.

It is certainly true, however, that the educational environment in the Arab world does not tend to permit free dialogue or active intellectual exploration, contributing to the restriction of free thought and criticism from an early age. This environment weakens the cognitive competence of individuals and discourages them from entertaining contrasting opinions and points of view. It is a learning method designed to reproduce and regenerate control over its subjects, beginning early in children's elementary school education. The lack of freedom and constant prevention of free thought create "internal constraints on the self," and as a result, Arabs learn to practice censorship upon themselves. This process of constraint causes citizens to live in a state of fear and submission marked by the "denial of their subjugation."[6]

Leading Arab poets and writers have always depicted the Arab in such a psychological state of siege, profoundly penetrating the conditions of fear, submission and resignation of the Arab individual in society. They have written continuously on this subject. Arab novelists offer a comprehensive understanding of the Arab family in their novels. Their writing richly describes the Arab family and its relationships, structures, values, beliefs, conducts, patterns of marriage and divorce, links with society and, finally, its social transformation. This will be explored in greater depth in chapter 9 on the modern Arabic novel.

MARRIAGE PATTERNS IN THE ARAB FAMILY

Even the process of marriage in the Arab world becomes a mass family project in which all members involve themselves. Though marriage technically consists of a union between a single man and a single woman, an Arab marriage is, culturally speaking, a union between two families. Individuals rarely act independently from the family in arranging their marriages; in fact, the family is traditionally more influential than the bride and the groom themselves in making the selection. The family of the potential bride or groom must be approved as the very first step in endorsing a proposed marriage. This is a cultural phenomenon that complements Islamic religious practice but is not derived from it, and thus applies to all religions and all sects in the Arab world.

Usually, the most successful marriage is the one that reinforces family ties. The selection of the bride is usually made inside the extended family, both to maintain group identity and for other considerations as well. After all, any marriage means two families have to decide on issues of inheritance and maintenance of the property and business of the extended family, clan and tribe. But marriages between two individuals from different families and tribes also occur; these are usually arranged for political or economic reasons, and traditionally are also very common, as they strengthen interconnections between tribes and families. Even in the twenty-first century, Arab tribes are still very strong, particularly in the Arab Gulf states, Saudi Arabia, Iraq, Yemen and Jordan. It is common practice in these countries for an important person of one tribe to marry a woman from another tribe, for the sake of political alliance or personal interest. Sometimes, individuals from certain tribes marry several women, each from a different tribe, to multiply the political benefits. Marriages of this type still take place in the Arab Gulf states, Saudi Arabia, and other Arab countries.

Usually, however, individuals are encouraged to marry within their tribe or clan; it is very common for first cousins to marry. In certain tribal and peasant traditions, in fact, it is obligatory for a man to marry his first female cousin. The time-honored pattern of arranged marriages is still strong in Arab culture, though society is changing rapidly on this point. But arranged marriages are still very common, despite the increasing number of opportunities for single men and women to meet and mix in the workplace and school.

Many marriages also take place today based on love and mutual admiration, especially in large urban areas. Even during pre-Islamic times, and throughout Islamic history, the phenomenon of marriage based on love rather than family connections has always existed. In ancient Arabia, men used to see unmarried women in groups at springs of water, as it traditionally fell upon single, young girls to bring home water from the wells. These springs would serve as a meeting place where men could talk to girls, although such conversations were usually brief and took place in the presence of others. After an innocent relationship of love or mutual admiration was established, the man would seek the girl's acceptance of his marriage proposal. If she accepted, he would discuss his marriage intention with his parents and other family members. Then his father, along with a delegation of tribal dignitaries, would pay a visit to the girl's family and ask her father for her hand. After consulting with his daughter to verify her approval, the girl's father would accept the proposal, and the marriage would be arranged shortly thereafter.

Still, the arranged marriage is very common in Arab culture, simply because men and women do not usually mix in social circumstances. This long-established policy of gender segregation is now declining in certain areas. Because Arab society is currently undergoing rapid change due to the spread of university education, the employment of women in mixed-gender workplaces, and many other societal innovations, arranged marriages have declined somewhat in urban areas. Even in cities, however, they are still frequent.

Ultimately, whether or not the marriage is an arranged one, the families of the bride and groom are heavily involved in the process. Permission from the father or guardian of the girl is the first essential and legal step in any marriage process. If a woman gets married without obtaining the permission of her father or guardian, she would be acting against the will of her family. In some Arab communities, especially Arab villages, such a girl would likely be punished by a male member of her family, either her father or one of her bothers or cousins.

In some extreme cases, she could be killed, though mainstream Arab society rejects such measures. Similar punishments could be brought to bear for running away with a man or marrying a man from a different sect or religion. Arab culture does not encourage marriage between a man and a woman from two different religions or sects. According to Islamic law and tradition, a Muslim woman is not permitted to marry a non-Muslim. Any potential non-Muslim bridegroom must first convert to Islam.[7]

The custom of providing dowry, or an amount of money or property given by a man to his bride when they marry, is practiced by many cultures around the world, including those of South Asia and the Arab world. It is a powerful ritual tradition and forms an integral part of the marriage arrangements. Dowry is practiced by all sectors of Arab society and is a long-established cultural component in many marriages, especially arranged marriages. The size and type of dowry can sometimes be very important, as it reflects the social status of the groom, the social class of the bride, the prestige of the bride's family in society, and the degree of closeness in kinship between the two families. The age and physical beauty of the bride can also be important factors in determining the size of the dowry.

Dowry is traditionally given to the bride by the groom in two installments, an advanced portion and a deferred portion. Payment of the advanced portion is legally required for endorsement of the marriage contract. The amount of both installments is usually determined by negotiation between the two families at an early stage in the process. The family of the groom presents the advanced portion of the dowry on the day the marriage contract is signed to the father or guardian of the bride; this part of the dowry may consist of money, goods, or real estate. It is usually spent on the bride and for household and wedding needs before the marriage even takes place. The deferred portion of the dowry is given to the woman if her husband dies or if the marriage ends in divorce.

If the groom's family does not present the advanced portion of the dowry on time, or if its value turns out to be less than what was agreed upon, this is considered an insult to the bride and her family. Such a thing rarely happens, but when it does, it constitutes grounds for the cancellation of the marriage contract by the bride's family. The advanced portion is a basic requirement for the legality of the marriage, and is intended not only to empower the marriage but also to strengthen and consolidate friendship between the families. Many Arabs, especially among traditional tribes, spend extremely generous amounts of money in dowry to the bride and her family out of respect and appreciation. Some also carry out gigantic and profligate wedding ceremonies; this is very common among the influential and wealthy, particularly in Saudi Arabia and the Arab Gulf states. Meanwhile, an enormous number of young men across the Arab world delay marriage indefinitely due to their inability to afford a dowry, even if their intended brides and families of brides accept the marriage proposal in principle. This contributes to widespread feelings of frustration in the Arab world, as the inability to get married strikes a blow at the cornerstone of Arab society, the family unit.

THE MARRIAGE RITES

Other rites and rituals precede the actual wedding in addition to the dowry; a very important one is the official engagement of the man and woman. After the groom's father and other family members and friends officially ask for the hand of the bride, and after her father and family approve, they all agree immediately on a certain day for an official engagement. On that day, families, relatives and friends gather in the bride's house for the engagement ceremony, when the proposed day of marriage is announced publicly to the guests and relatives in attendance. The period of engagement is meant to prepare the couple for the actual marriage. The man and woman are allowed to visit each other's homes during that period, but only in the company of others, and they are not allowed to be alone or go out by themselves. These precautions are meant to protect the woman's reputation and the reputation of her family in case the marriage does not go through. Some families, particularly in Saudi Arabia, Yemen and the Gulf States, do not allow the man and woman to meet or see each other during the engagement period. In these cases, the couple remains separate until the day the marriage contract is signed, usually no more than a few months later.[8]

On the day of the marriage contract, the groom, the bride, their fathers or guardians, and two male witnesses all attend a religious ceremony conducted by a certified religious cleric, or *sheikh*. The *sheikh* verifies the acceptance of the woman and man to the marriage, and the bride's family acknowledges receipt of the advanced portion of the dowry, essential for the legality of the marriage contract. The deferred portion of the dowry is also specified at this time.

Upon signing the contract, the *sheikh* declares the man and woman lawfully married and affirms the completion of all legal marriage processes. After the religious ceremony has been completed, of course, sexual intercourse between the bride and the groom becomes legal and permissible. But this is not usually the end of the story. The marriage now enters another phase, and the date of sexual consummation is postponed for another ceremony, to be mutually decided between the families. This is the wedding ceremony, which follows the contract signing within a few weeks or months at the most.

The wedding day is like a festival, full of excitement, song and dance in an enormous feast and celebration. Some weddings last for three days. All the friends and relatives of the bride and groom are invited, and even people who are not invited often come and participate, as the wedding is traditionally open to all. At the end of the wedding night, the last and most important ritual of all is performed. While the guests continue celebrating, the bride and groom consummate the marriage with sexual intercourse to prove that the bride remained a virgin until the moment of consummation. This is done in private, of course, but all soon know the news.

A close relative, usually the new bride's mother-in-law, waits with associates outside the bridal chamber while the bride and groom consummate the marriage. Eventually the groom emerges and hands her a sheet of the marriage bed stained with the blood of the bride's hymen, proof of her virginity and virtue. Upon verifying that the sheet is stained with blood, the mother-in-law passes along the good news to all the guests, relatives and participants in the marriage ceremony. Proof of virginity brings great pride and honor to the bride and her family.

Conversely, a non-virgin bride is considered to be disgraced, bringing shame and disrespect to her and her family and causing a scandal inside the community. Technically, the lack of virginity constitutes legal ground for the groom to dissolve the marriage immediately. He is entitled to ask the bride's family to return the advanced dowry in full, and he may also demand compensation for all marriage and wedding expenses. As a result, the bride and her family suffer not only dishonor but also financial ruin, eliminating the woman's chances of receiving another marriage proposal in the future. Because the wedding has ended in total disaster and the bride's family is humiliated, some families punish the girl, perhaps severely. In rare cases, the father or brothers of the girl might even kill her to restore the family's honor within the community.

THE *MISYAR* MARRIAGE

In the last two decades, a controversial new type of marriage known as *Misyar* has emerged, authorized by religious authorities because of worsening economic conditions in the Arab world. Widespread unemployment and increased inflation have resulted in an increase in dowry amounts for traditional marriages, and real estate prices have increased with inflation while wages remained stagnant. All these circumstances have made it increasingly difficult for Arab youth to live, work, and marry. Two new phenomena have emerged to facilitate marriage by reducing cost. One is the group wedding; some people, in order to save on expensive wedding ceremonies, arrange for several weddings to be held in one day at one place and time. Up to twenty marrying couples can all share the expenses of weddings in this way. These arrangements are encouraged because they provide opportunity for men and women to get married, even during harsh economic conditions. Some group weddings are even fully sponsored by wealthy individuals.

A more controversial development has been the new *Misyar* marriage of the past two decades. Also known as the religiously sanctioned temporary marriage, the *Misyar* is simply a marriage contract between a man and a woman who propose to continue to live separately but get together for sexual relations. It is a legal and alternative marriage arrangement for men and women for whom marriage costs are unaffordable. *Misyar* has been authorized by religious authorities in Saudi Arabia, Egypt, Qatar, and the United Arab Emirates, among other Arab countries. Like regular marriages, it requires the consent of the two parties involved, the approval of the woman's father or guardian, the presence of witnesses, and the officiating of a religious cleric. Very little cost is involved, if any. The husband is not required to provide a home for his wife or be financially responsible for her. Nor does the *Misyar* even require that the man and woman live together. The wife usually lives with her parents or guardians, while the husband visits her regularly or at scheduled times.

The *Misyar* marriage was officially authorized by some Egyptian Sunni author-ities in 1999, followed by religious figures in other Arab countries. Some see the *Misyar* marriage as perfectly acceptable because it is legal and meets all religious regulations. The *Misyar* is also seen as helping women who are unable to find husbands. Indeed, most women who choose this type of marriage are divorced, widowed, or beyond the customary marriage age, and many men who take on such marital arrangements are unemployed with little or no money. Critics point out that some men are already married but take advantage of *Misyar* to get an extra wife that costs them nothing. For this and other reasons, many Islamic scholars in the Arab world oppose these types of arrangements.

Sociologically, there are advantages and disadvantages to *Misyar* marriages. It was originally justified by religious scholars intending to help those who are financially unable to get married. Just because it is abused by some does not cast doubt on the good intentions behind its creation. However, the *Misyar* does de-prive women of the rights they would normally enjoy in a traditional marriage. It is arranged and conducted in secret, and the husband acts as a guest who pays only occasional visits to his wife. The wife also cannot participate with her husband in public life or social activities. Some men and women, therefore, are faced with the difficult choice of remaining unmarried or marrying according to *Misyar*.

Traditionally, Arab women used to marry at a very young age. Today, marriage in Arab countries is occurring significantly later in life for both men and women. Algeria, for example, has a large percentage of unmarried women; and in the Arab Gulf states and Saudi Arabia, about 30 percent of women have passed up the opportunity to be married. In addition to the high costs of marriages and harsh economic conditions, a new factor has emerged that slightly contributes to the rising percentage of unmarried Arab women. In many places throughout the Arab world, particularly in the Gulf, women are completing higher education degrees more often than men, holding higher positions as a result. Many therefore refuse to marry men who are less educated and thus of lower social status. As the gender difference in education increases, so does this phenomenon.

POLYGAMY IN ARAB SOCIETY

The pattern of polygamy in Arab culture traditionally existed to help fix the demographic balance between men and women during the times of early Islam. Constant war and the resultant death of Arab men caused the number of females to rise above the number of males in society. Polygamy emerged to prevent the prospect of a large number of women being deprived of marital life. It is possible that the concept of dowry itself comes from the practice of polygamy, when the dowry was considered a central value of the bride to her family. Since then the dowry has remained an essential ritual of marriage, but instead of representing a price, it has come to symbolize respect and appreciation toward the bride and her family as well as the husband's commitment toward his wife.

Polygamy in Arab culture was established for many reasons, including the provision of single women with husbands and the prevention of adultery. Islam allowed one man to marry up to four wives at a time; legally, a man cannot marry a fifth wife unless he divorces one of his previous four. Polygamy is legally recognized among all Muslim sects, and is still practiced today, particularly in villages and among Bedouin tribes and peasants.

Although the Qur'an permits a man to marry up to four wives, many restrictions and conditions apply to such a practice. Islamic scholars confirmed that the Qur'an meant to make it so complicated to marry more than one wife that polygamy would become practically difficult. The Qur'an commands the husband to be fair and treat all wives equally, and if the man cannot meet the conditions of fairness, he is not permitted to marry more than one wife. Many argue that it is essentially impossible to treat two or more wives in a truly equal and fair way, establishing a *de facto* prohibition of polygamy. In some Arab countries, polygamy is governed by state law as well as religious law. A potential husband needs to appear before a judge to prove his suitability and financial ability to support a second wife. The man must also prove his legal reason for seeking a second wife; if his first wife is unable to have children or if she has a prolonged illness, he must submit such proof before a judge. Only if his request is approved can the judge then grant permission to marry a second time. In some Arab countries, it is very difficult to have a second or a third wife. Tunisia, for example, has strictly forbidden polygamy. It is much easier to marry multiple wives in Saudi Arabia and the Arab Gulf states than in Syria, Iraq, or Jordan.

In the Arab world, religious law governs all cases of marriage and divorce, as well as issues of child custody and inheritance. A Muslim woman cannot marry a non-Muslim man, though a Muslim man can marry a non-Muslim woman as long as the children are raised as Muslims. Marriages are beholden to religious rituals and ceremonies; religious marriages are highly respected in the Arab world and considered to be blessed by God. Most marriages in the Arab world are religious marriages. Civil marriages are permitted in some Arab states, but they are not generally accepted and therefore remain fairly uncommon. All Arab religious sects, including Christians and Jews, generally marry according to religious law and traditional practice.

ARRANGED MARRIAGES

Due to the traditional separation of men and women, the matchmaker has always played an important role in Arab society. A woman who possesses wide knowledge of the families in her geographic district, the matchmaker has a wide network of friends and relatives who help her collect information. She may work on behalf of a man in search of a wife, or vice versa. This ancient practice is still used in the Arab world today, and it will continue as long as young women and men lack the opportunity to meet. In fact, the arranged marriage is not only perfectly respectable, but seems very appealing in traditional societies. Refusing an arranged marriage could limit for many the chance to marry at all, as the opportunity to interact with the opposite sex in a conservative society is quite slim.

In some Arab countries, and particularly in the cities, the pattern of arranged marriages has declined over the last two decades, as new social and economic factors have emerged. Often, women who achieve higher education no longer accept marriage to arranged husbands, or even men they meet in person who are not their educational, social or professional equals. For men and women who are unable to marry for economic or other reasons, or those who do not use the arranging services of a matchmaker, marriage is often delayed. Sociologists note that Arab society has today a high percentage of celibacy, particularly among women.[9] All this has made the *Misyar* marriage seem a more attractive option for few.

According to the Arab Human Development Report, Arab women enjoy increasing opportunities socially and economically, and have also achieved important success in education.[10] Many women hold high positions in government and the private sector, and others have been recognized in science, literature and other academic fields. Growing numbers of educated women squarely reject arranged marriage, and would not even consider polygamy or the *Misyar*. This is a sign of the growing liberation and self-confidence of women across the Arab world. At the same time, however, this contributes to the high and growing percentage of unmarried women in the Arab world, as well.

DIVORCE

Divorce traditionally was not as common in the Arab world as it is today. Although Islam does permit it, the Qur'an strongly discourages men from divorcing their wives, calling divorce the most hateful of all permissible practices in Islam. Divorce cases in Arab society have increased over the past few decades, however, and continue to rise. Divorce is most common during the first few years of marriage.[11]

The right to divorce a spouse is not exclusive to the man. In pre-Islamic Arabia, women could divorce their husbands if they presented good reason; in certain communities and tribes, the woman could even marry more than one man. In the modern Arab world, however, it is much easier for a man to divorce his wife than vice versa. While a man can divorce his wife for any cause or even no reason at all, a woman must present very serious reasons for divorce, such as the sexual impotence of the husband, severe physical abuse by the husband, or the husband's indefinite absence. She cannot file for divorce because she does not like him or because their relationship is unbearable. If a wife leaves without going through the legal divorce procedure, her husband has the right to order her to return and resume her marital duties. If she refuses to return to him, the husband can file a lawsuit against her as a disobedient wife, forcing her to return.[12]

In Islamic law, a "disobedient" wife is deprived of any financial support from her husband, and she cannot marry another man because she is still legally married to her first husband. Of course, these excessive divorce cases are rare, particularly among the educated class. Once a divorce is granted, child custody law demands that the husband receive custody of the children. Children in these cases remain with their mother until a certain age before moving to live with their father, age seven for boys and age nine for girls.

Over the last few decades, progressives in the Arab world have demanded reform in divorce and child custody laws. These men and women activists advocate for women to be given the same rights to divorce as their husbands, taking the power of divorce out of strictly male hands. They also have demanded that all divorce procedures be processed inside courts and before judges of law. Women have achieved several victories in legal reform; Jordan has passed a law granting the wife the right to divorce her husband, and other countries are in the process of passing similar reforms. The child custody law has undergone change, as well, raising the age of children in their mother's custody from seven to nine for boys and from nine to eleven for girls.

Demands are also afoot to reform inheritance law to ensure that men and women are treated equally. Islamic law differentiates between men and women on the issue of inheritance, entitling women to half the inheritance of men. Islamic reformers, however, argue that law was applied under social circumstances when men, not women, were the only source of family income, and that as circumstances have changed, the law should change as well. Islamic law also requires inheritance to remain within the same family, by not permitting individuals to leave more than one-third of their property to a beneficiary outside the legitimate family. The idea behind such law was to preserve family property. With increasing activism, however, and the ongoing transitions of Arab society, it is inevitable that changes in family law will eventually be made.

THE PATRIARCHAL STRUCTURE OF THE ARAB FAMILY

The Arab family is extended and patriarchal in structure and organization, following genealogically the male figures that represent family identity and preserve the family members' connection to past generations. Today, it is still common for several generations within a family to live together in the same house, run one business, and share profits and property.

The father stands on the top of the Arab family pyramid as master and undisputed authority of the house. Traditionally, the father served as sole protector of his family, taking care of his wife and children and providing for their survival and safety. From this position he naturally assumed control of daily family affairs, and his is the final word in all family decisions. In keeping with his role of authority, he expects respect and obedience by his wife and children. In Arab culture, children take their father's last name as a patronymic and use his first name as their common middle name, so all the family's children have the same middle name. Not only does this practice preserve the family genealogy, it also has value for legal reasons during inheritance procedures. The Arab woman keeps her last name even after marriage.

It was traditionally expected that the eldest son in a family would name his own firstborn son after the grandfather in order to keep alive the grandfather's first name, and this practice continues today. After a man gets married, or even before, the community addresses him by the name of his (actual or anticipated) firstborn son; if the man's father's name had been *Shadi*, for example, his firstborn son would be named *Shadi* as well, and the man himself would be nicknamed *Abu Shadi*, or "the father of Shadi," throughout the community. The same applies to the woman; she would be called *Umm*, or "the mother of," *Shadi*.[13] It is the community itself that encourages individuals to drop their personal identities in favor of the family. This is considered a very positive value in Arab culture, and anyone who did not follow such tradition would be defying powerful norms and conventions. There are exceptions, of course; in fact, this tradition is not as commonly practiced in Algeria, Tunisia, and Morocco.

While the father provides for the family financially, the mother assumes the role of the housewife and takes care of the husband and her children. The Arab family follows a traditional hierarchical structure: the young subordinate to the old, females to males, and everyone to the father. Behind the scenes, however, the mother controls the family in reality. She makes most of the decisions, supervises the children, and above all manages the affairs of the family in the way she sees fit. In many cases, decisions are made by the mother but announced by her husband, in order to maintain the father's image of being the ultimate decision maker. The wife is not as powerless as she seems from the outside: she makes most important decisions, manages the family's finances, and generally wields most influence within the family.

The father often spends most of his time outside the home, a largely absent figure who works all day, comes home after work to have dinner, then leaves again to spend the evening with men in cafés and other places.[14] His habitual absence further strengthens the role of the mother in handling all family matters. Along with other economic and social transitions in the Arab world, however, fathers are now spending more time with their children and families, due in part to the increased employment of women. The patriarchal family structure is changing, as well; the wife contributes financial support along with the employed children, with everyone cooperating to overcome economic difficulty. The father has thus begun to lose his controlling power and absolute authority over the family.

The Arab woman is emerging from her previous seclusion. Many Arab women today are highly educated, hold important positions in government and the private sector, and provide for their families financially. Traditionally, of course, Islam has always given women the right to education and work. Muhammad's wife, Khadijah, was a successful entrepreneur who owned her own business and even employed the Prophet himself. In general terms, women are not as oppressed, powerless and marginalized within Arab and Islamic culture as they are often depicted and portrayed. It is true that Muslim women inherit half the sum of Muslim men, but this religious law is rooted in the economic and cultural context of the bygone era in which it was formulated. Today, there is a wide range in the status of women's rights among Arab countries.[15]

Patriarchy in Arab society involves both the father who sits atop the social structure of the family and the leader who sits atop the social structure of the nation. Some commentators see the father's archetypal influence in any source of societal authority, hence children's fear of the policeman, security guard, army officer, teacher and government official. The Arab child is inflicted from an early age with the fear of authority and domination, an embodiment of the father's authority and domination at home. His is the force of authoritarianism that represents overwhelming power, and it is he who metes out punishment. The entrenched fear of father figures is therefore one reason Arabs are so obedient to their rulers.[16]

As a result of these fear-based relations of obedience, originating in the patriarchal Arab family structure, all relations in Arab society have become based on authority, domination, and dependency. The only concern of the Arab child is to be obedient and to behave appropriately and politely toward the father. As a result, these values are now reflected in the society as a whole, including the values of dependence, repression and authoritarianism. The Arab individual is oppressed within the family as well as within society. He or she is fearful of any authority and is concerned only with satisfying and pleasing the authority. As a result, individuals live in closed horizons, dominated, oppressed and terrified.[17]

Sociologist Halim Barakat noticed that an analogy can be drawn between the Arab family microstructure and the macro institutions of Arab society; to a certain extent, the same relationships that define the family are duplicated in educational, religious and political institutions. Arab political leaders, teachers and employers all act and behave as authoritarian fathers, even commonly referring to citizens as "children." This oppressive relationship is reinforced by a general repressive ideology, based on either terrifying the citizens or using methods of simple enticement and reward. Society as a whole lacks the phenomena of discussion and persuasion. And the educational system in the Arab world, from elementary school to university, is based on memorization rather than on understanding and analysis.[18] Cultural critic Hisham Sharabi emphasized that the obedience since early childhood, along with the strong cultural value of self-sacrifice, led to such widespread dependency in the Arab psyche.[19]

HOW ARABS FEEL ABOUT THEIR FAMILIES

These general observations about the family are certainly true. The Arab world of course has its share of dysfunctional families and serious intra-family feuds. Also, the family's powerful domination of individual lives can be seen as negative.

But most Arabs have very positive opinions of the connections and values their families provide. From my own personal experience and observation, as well as from dozens of interviews I have conducted with individuals from various national, social and educational backgrounds, I have found that most Arabs still consider their families among the dearest aspects of their lives. Not even religion comes before family in terms of importance. Christians, Jews and other non-Muslim Arabs tend to feel the same way.

In conducting research for this book, I met and conversed with youth from many different Arab countries, including Bahrain, Qatar, Syria, Lebanon, Tunisia, Jordan and Egypt.[20] Some of the men and women I met were college graduates, had studied in the West, traveled to many countries, and spoke several foreign languages. Others had not continued their education and found work in various skilled or non-skilled professions. Strikingly, all emphasized that their families are among the most important aspects of their lives, certainly more important than any job, wealth or opportunity in the world. They all agreed the entirety of Arab culture is concentrated around the family. All of those who were unmarried still lived with their families. All of those who now had wives and husbands had also lived with their families until their marriage day, and even some married individuals I spoke with still lived in the same houses as their families.

When asked why the family is important, all told me their families allow them to feel loved and protected, thanks to a strong emotional attachment between family members. Some had lost their fathers at a young age, but were raised by other family members. One man told me he could not imagine life without his family, and, in his words, would certainly commit suicide if he lost them. I cannot reproduce all and every single interview in full; here, I present a number of my conversations with some nationals of diverse backgrounds.

Fatima, whose friends call her Fifi, is a young woman from the Gulf with a master's degree from the United Kingdom. Fatima told me her family is the most beautiful thing in her life, offering real personal connections and strong relationships. Her family provides a peculiar warmth beyond description: a supportive group of individuals who are all related by blood or marriage, who live and break bread together, and who celebrate each other's joys and condole with each other in times of sadness. Fatima does not want to see her family change, and she suggested that any loosening of family ties in general would cause Arab culture to lose its cohesiveness, strength and uniqueness. Family relationships, Fatima said, represent the most honest, pure and wonderful human connections in the world; if this strong family honesty were lost, Arabs would lose the most beautiful part of their culture.[21]

Fatima did describe some negative aspects of the Arab family, such as its control over her independence and personal life. For example, the marriage or divorce of a family member becomes a project for the entire family, all of whose members get involved. A marriage or divorce becomes a family, rather than an individual, decision. No breathing space exists between an individual and his or her family: even if a woman and man love each other, if the woman's family does not like the man's family, the marriage cannot take place. If a woman decides against the will of her family to marry whom she loves, her family may reject or disown her. Because of the segregation between men and women in many Arab countries, especially the Arab Gulf states and Saudi Arabia, Arab women cannot meet Arab men outside of the family, for fear of acquiring a bad reputation. And finally, Fatima affirmed that retaining virginity until marriage remains a very important issue both for girls themselves and for their families.

Hadiya is another young woman from the Gulf who has received degrees in the United States and the United Kingdom; after living and studying overseas for several years, she returned to Bahrain. Hadiya told me that Western values can be very destructive to the Arab family. Western technology is the channel through which western ideas and values reach the Arab world, but Arabs misunderstand the West through this filter and therefore adopt only bad Western values, harming Arab culture and identity. Hadiya described Arab culture as full of beautiful and fascinating rituals, including those of weddings and funerals, whose traditions embody closeness and warmth. For Hadiya, there is a purity in these rituals that does not exist anywhere else, making Arab individuals feel they are part of a group and participants in a community larger than themselves. Family-based communication and ritual is beautiful, meaningful and important, both for the individual soul and for society as a whole.[22]

Finally, Hadiya added that belonging to a family and tribe also means belonging to a particular political party, ideology or national identity. Even within the Arab Gulf states, for all their cultural similarities, there is a strong sense of belonging to a certain country. A Bahraini woman may not want to marry a Kuwaiti man, because this means her children will be Kuwaiti citizens; this further applies to a Kuwaiti woman who does not want her children to be born Bahraini. The issue of citizenship and nationalities is perhaps more sensitive in Saudi Arabia and the Arab Gulf states than the rest of the Arab world. The Bahrainis, for example, do not want non-native Bahrainis to become citizens, even if they were born in Bahrain. Hadiya described predominant Bahraini sentiment toward other nationalities thus: they are very welcome to reside and live in Bahrain, but not to become Bahraini.

Majda is a Syrian Christian woman from the city of Latakiyya, who works at Yale University. Majda described the family as "wealth", to the extent that a person feels she is an emperor when living with her family. There is no joy similar to the joy of spending time with family, especially extended family. Moreover, Majda said, the family provides individuals with security. Strong family ties lead to improved social health. Problems with the Arab family certainly exist, but they seem insignificant when compared to the strong, loving bonds that family members provide.[23]

Majda, whose family immigrated to the United States thirty years ago, has two grown sons. Her relationship with her children is based on love and respect: "I am very close to them. I am very proud of them. They still come to me when they have problems. They ask my advice and my opinion on personal matters. My children have always lived with us." However, Majda did not like the fact the Arab family generally favors boys over girls, and the older over the younger. She remarked that the Arab family should give individuals more freedom in making their own decisions, such as what to study in college or when and whom to marry. For example, when a family decides it is best for someone to study medicine in college or to marry from a certain family, this is very harsh on the children.

Among the most positive aspects of the Arab family for Majda is how friends and loved ones gather around the sick or the person who is in need, but even these admirable qualities can sometimes become negative. Visiting the sick is a great thing, but it does not leave the sick person alone for a minute, as he or she is constantly showered by unlimited visits. All in all, however, Majda would feel very depressed and extremely ill without her family. She lives in Connecticut with her children and husband, but calls her parents every day.

Finally, from her own experience of being raised in the Arab world and raising her children in America, Majda downplayed the cultural differences between Arab society and American society:

> "I think the American woman is like the Arab woman. She takes care of her children, and she takes her children to places of worship. My children are Arab-American; they are integrated into American life and society, but I see them every day and they call me up to several times a day. My youngest son, who found a job recently in Delaware, comes every week to spend the weekend with us, and he takes back with him Arabic food that I prepare for the entire week."

Ibrahim, a young Bahraini university graduate who has worked as a journalist for a daily Arabic newspaper, told me the family represents Arab tribal heritage. Ibrahim has visited the United States and believes that Arab culture in reality is a tribal culture, and this is something about which Arabs feel very proud. The family represents belonging, an extremely important concept in Arab culture. Ibrahim described the feeling of real belonging, whether to the family, religion or tribe, as powerful as nuclear energy, and that which remains when everything else is left behind. The feeling of belonging, for Ibrahim, is the only thing that protects Arab culture and identity.[24]

In the Arab Gulf states, Ibrahim added, there is a concept called *faz`a*, which means to be united with your family and fight for it against others, whether your family is wrong or right. Particularly common to the Arab Gulf states, Saudi Arabia and Iraq, the concept of *faz`a* is based on an ancient Arab tribal proverb: *my brother and I against our cousin, my cousin and I against the stranger.* Such a practice could be wrong, Ibrahim said, but it is an immutable part of Arab life, and it reflects the spectrum of an individual's loyalty—first to the immediate family, then the extended family, then the tribe, and finally the society. Ibrahim does not want to see the Arab family change, despite its drawbacks. And he described Western influence over Arab culture as an invasion that, if not stopped, will harm and spoil Arab culture.

Rashid and Ja`far are two young Bahraini journalists with university degrees and extensive travel experience in Europe and the United States. Like others I interviewed, these individuals confirmed that the Arab family represents Arab identity and vice versa: The Arab individual carries the name of the family, the family carries the name of the tribe, and the tribe rules the country. The two young nationals spoke the same on the concept of *faz`a*, saying this still represents reality for many Arabs. The individual feels he belongs first to his immediate family, then to his extended family, then to the tribe or religious sect, and only lastly to the country at large.[25]

Shadi, a Syrian who works in the private sector, describes his family as his treasure. He notes that in Arab culture, individuals stay and live with their families far beyond the age of eighteen. This arbitrary year in which children leave their families in other cultures has no meaning for Arabs. Arabs are very attached to their families, and therefore children stay with their parents long after they turn eighteen. Shadi himself is thirty years old, and he plans to live with his parents until he gets married.

Like the others, Shadi notes that the positives of the Arab family outweigh the negatives:

> *"One of the negative things is that everyone gets involved in everyone else's business. Decisions are mostly made by the group, not by individuals. Family members never leave the individual alone. Despite this, I cannot live without my family. When I get married I plan to move out, but will continue to be very close. I must see or call my family daily, especially my mother and father. I could wait*

to see or talk to my brothers and sisters every few days, but I have
to see or talk to my parents every day. I cannot live without Arabic
food, especially the food that my mother cooks. Even when I am
in the U.S., I always eat Arabic food. Also, I prefer to marry an
Arab woman because I feel she would understand me better, coming
from the same culture. Girls in the Arab family are not oppressed
at all. On the contrary, the girl in the family is spoiled, because
all her brothers take such good care of her. She certainly does not
have the personal freedom that the American girl has, but she is
still very spoiled and loved by all her family. And everything I have
said applies to Arab families regardless of their religious or ethnic
affiliations."[26]

All of the young adults that I spoke with criticized the educational system in the Arab world and rejected methods based on memorization and repetition rather than critical analysis. Without free thinking and criticism, they stressed, schools do not teach anything useful. The educational curriculum is imposed. Students can only receive ideas, not initiate them. They also described family traditions and values as getting even more conservative.[27]

The Arab family remains a mirror for Arab culture and lends Arab culture its positive and distinct character. Through their families, individuals are united in times of happiness and misery alike. The solidarity and special care given to the elderly is particularly admirable: nursing homes rarely exist, for lack of customers. In recent years, a handful of nursing homes have been established for the elderly in large Arab cities, but it is not widely accepted to have elderly parents sent there. The new nursing homes in the Arab world are for those elderly people who either have no families, or whose families are small and unable to provide the care they need.

Sending an elderly person to a nursing home is against the traditions, values and the customs of Arab culture; it is a severe social stigma, and the family who resorted to such a measure would lose the respect of the community. The Arab family is known for taking very good care of the ill and elderly, cooking for them, bathing them, giving them medication, and most importantly, paying attention to them and entertaining them. Aged and ill individuals are never left home alone. Not only do family members take turns to cater to their needs, relatives and friends also join in to offer services. Those close to the family increase the frequency of their visits. All this is guided by family traditions, social conventions, steadfast personal relationships, and the encouragement of the religions.

Finally, it is due to this intense association and warm openness among family members on a daily basis that individuals feel free to consult with their families about their private concerns and worries in truthful and frank discussions. This practice is emotionally rewarding and often touted as more effective and useful than psychiatric visits. Many Arabs attribute the popularity of psychological treatment in the West to the fact that individuals there have no one with whom to share their deep personal problems save during one weekly hour in a therapist's office. A common impression in the Middle East is that Westerns lack the time to make warm, personal connections. In Arab culture, as well as many other cultures worldwide, it is the family that sits, listens, supports, consults, and consoles. It is the family that happily walks the extra miles needed.

CHAPTER THREE

The Arabic Language

THE ARABIC LANGUAGE SITS at the heart of Arab culture and identity. The collective memory of the dramatic process that gave birth to Islam as a faith and to the Arabs as a nation revolves around the centrality of the Arabic language to the people who speak it. As a language, Arabic has been preserved and maintained nearly intact for more than fifteen centuries. Some changes and innovations have certainly taken place, but the differences between classical and modern Arabic are far less than the differences between twentieth century Italian and fifth century Latin or between eighteenth century French and third century Gallic. An Arab today would have no trouble understanding the Prophet Muhammad's sermons or the public recitations of pre-Islamic poets. This astonishing linguistic fidelity is due to the power of the Qur'an, among other things, to continually cause admiration and awe among its readership in any era. Arabic is dominated by the presence of the "Qur'an, which is both origin and model for everything linguistic that comes after it."[1] Since the beginning of the Islamic era, writers have found the Arabic language to be a perfect instrument for dealing with any topic, whether religion, science, philosophy or poetry.

Moreover, the core of Arab nationalism is linguistic. Regardless of sectarian or ethnic affiliation, all Arab nationalists feel strongly that their language is the most important element of their identity. Arabs, who are probably more conscious of their language than any other people in the world,[2] have considered Arabic the only medium of their culture, from literary expression to daily communication, since before the Islamic era. Qur'anic Arabic resembles the prevailing Arabic dialect of the Hijaz region of Arabia around the year 600. Because Hijazi Arabic was chosen for use in the Qur'an, it immediately stood above all other Arabic dialects of the time.[3] The Qur'an itself repeatedly stresses the centrality and indispensability of the Arabic language to Islamic revelation, reiterating in verse after verse:

> *"We have sent it down as an Arabic Qur'an."*

> *"Thus We have sent it down as an Arabic Qur'an."*[5]

> *"It is an Arabic Qur'an without any deviance."*[6]

In addition to being the native language of more than four hundred million Arabs, Arabic is also the holy language and language of daily prayer for more than 1.6 billion Muslims worldwide. Muslims believe that Isma`il, the son of the Prophet Abraham, was the first person to speak this holy language.[7] Because of the special role Arabic has played both in the revelation of Islam and the formation of the nation, Arabs see preserving their language as both a religious and a national duty. Arabic has not only produced a major religion and a great civilization, it has retained its relevance as the language of modern Arab culture and the pillar of modern Arab nationalist identity.

To Westerners, the nature of the Arabic language is often confusing. It seems that Arabs have three languages: the classical language (the language of the Qur'an and classical literature), the modern standard language (MSA, or *Fus-ha*, the modernized version of the classical language), and the daily spoken language (with its many local colloquial and regional dialects). This is true, but does not seem strange to native speakers. The classical Arabic of the past would be developed and modernized yet preserved separately on its own merits, and it is natural that spoken dialects of Arabic would have regional variations.

ABOUT THE ARABIC LANGUAGE

Arabic belongs to the Semitic language family, with Hebrew, Aramaic and Amharic. It reads from right to left, and its script is cursive, meaning most letters within words are connected. Arabic is also the sixth official language of the United Nations. In the last two decades and especially since the events of September 11, 2001, the 2003 invasion of Iraq, and rapid sociopolitical changes in the Arab world, interest in learning Arabic within the United States has increased dramatically. To native speakers of Indo-European languages like English or French, the Arabic language's grammar and morphological and syntactic systems can be complex and difficult to master. The Arabic language has been classified by the US Department of State as one of the most difficult languages in the world to master, along with Japanese, Chinese and Korean. Although many American students and professors have achieved respectable levels of proficiency in the Arabic language, they (with a few exceptions) tend to lag in understanding Arab culture.

The Arabic alphabet has 29 letters including consonants and vowels. Strict rules govern the pronunciation of words. Arabic has no silent letters like English and French, so the correct spelling of a word is fundamentally necessary for its correct pronunciation. Words are pronounced the way they are written and are written the same way they are pronounced. Arabic in general is a more systematic and consistent language than English, particularly with respect to spelling and pronunciation.

Arabic is very rich in vocabulary and highly derivational in word formation, meaning that words are formed according to a regular system of roots and patterns. Like other Semitic languages, Arabic is built on a collection of word roots, each consisting of three consonants. A few roots have four consonants, but these are rare. By means of adding prefixes, infixes and suffixes, the roots can be built into patterns that express a great range of related concepts. For example, the tri-consonant root K-T-B, which carries the idea of "writing," can form patterned words such as these: KĀTIB or "writer," KITĀB or "book," MAKTAB or "office," MAKTABA or "library," KUTUBĪ or "bookseller," KUTAYYIB or "booklet," MAKTŪB or "written," etc. Thus, the Arabic language has a perfect system of the three consonants (known as radicals), the derived verb forms with their basic meanings, and the precise formation of the verbal noun and the participles. As one linguist observes, "everything is clarity, logic, system, and abstraction. The language is like a mathematical formula."[8]

Vowels, prefixes, infixes and suffixes can all be added to the root to create new words whose patterns have fixed meanings. This process, known as analogical derivation, lends Arabic great regularity and historically has been the most important source for the development of the language. In other words, there are uniform families of words that follow the same patterns yet differ in sound and structure, while at the same time, roots of three consonants each are at the heart of every word's meaning. The high level of regularity and harmonious pattern of creating words aids the rich production of rhymes and rhythms that are essential ingredients of Arabic style; such rhetorical effects "could never be achieved in any European language." For this reason among many others, Arabs consider their language a "perfect instrument of concision, clarity, and eloquence."[9]

The system of verbal conjugation in Arabic is by and large regular, though some irregularities can be found in the "weak" and "defective" verbs. Arabic has a perfect tense, formed by adding suffixes, and an imperfect tense, formed by adding prefixes and sometimes also suffixes to determine the subject of the verb. Arabic also has a future tense, formed by adding a particle or letter before an imperfect verb. Imperative forms, active and passive participles, and verbal nouns all exist in Arabic, and several methods of communicating the passive voice are used. Verbs are inflected to determine their gender and number, which can be singular, dual, or plural. And finally, there are three cases of nominal declension: nominative for the subject, accusative for the direct object, and genitive for the object of the preposition.

REFORMING CLASSICAL ARABIC LANGUAGE

Classical Arabic is the language of pre-Islamic poetry and the Qur'an. It is the linguistic medium for all literary writing of the Arabs since pre-Islamic times, including poetry, prose, commentaries, and interpretations of religious texts, grammar, history, linguistics, morphology, medicine, literary criticism, philosophy, and science. Each of these fields of knowledge was established and flourished in classical Arabic, particularly during the Abbasid golden age of Arab civilization.

The Abbasid caliphate (750–1258 AD) disintegrated and crumbled in the thirteenth century when the Mongols sacked Baghdad, the Abbasid capital (See chapter 6 on Islamic Communities throughout the Ages). This event marked the beginning of a long period of decay that would last until the nineteenth century. The Ottoman Empire began to dominate the Arab world during the sixteenth century and Turkish replaced Arabic as the official language of administration, even further weakening the Arabic language. During this period of decay, Arabs lost the power of the language used in classical poetry and other realms of knowledge. It became common for written Arabic to be full of mistakes and flaws, while imprecise colloquial Arabic made gains. By the end of the eighteenth century, even the language of some religious scholars had become almost colloquial.[10]

When the Arab renaissance of the nineteenth century began, Arabs tried to reconstruct and resurrect their linguistic past. Indeed, the idea of resurrection was at the very heart of the Arab awakening, designed to regain political power and revitalize Arabic language and poetry. Intellectual pioneers of the renaissance exerted great effort to recapture the power and glory of the Arabic language, determined to rid the language of the weaknesses and deficiencies it suffered during the age of Arab decline. Poets and writers returned to classical Arabic literature, particularly golden age Abbasid literature, and reconstructed as much as they could of the classical Arabic language in diction, style, vocabulary, expressions, composition and structure. The Arab renaissance will be explored in greater depth in in subsequent chapters, especially chapter 10 on Modern Arab Thought.

The modern literary renaissance began by stripping out the linguistic triviality and dullness suffered during long centuries of Arab decline and transcending the banality in Arabic literature by imitating great classical works of the past.[11] Jurji Zaydan (d. 1914), a leader of the Arab literary movement of the time, attacked the inferior colloquial Arabic that could not express scientific terminology or complex ideas: "If it were not for the language of the Qur'an, the Arab countries would have been divided into separated states, each speaking a different language not understood by the others."[12] Zaydan called for the modernization of classical Arabic.

He invoked Arabs to use their language correctly and to avoid the use of ancient or irrelevant words and expressions.

The flexibility of today's Arabic is the result of a process of rejuvenation begun a century and a half ago by writers who prepared the ground for a successful modernization of the language. Writers like Farah Antoun (d. 1922), Mustafa Lutfi al-Manfaluti (d. 1924), and Gibran Khalil Gibran (d. 1931), among many others, all gradually and steadily contributed to the process. Although remaining faithful to Arab cultural and literary heritage, they brought new ideas to the development of the language. Other factors also contributed, such as the growth of liberal and intellectual forces in society, the active movement of translation from Western science, culture, and literature, the spread of education, and the increased publication of books and periodicals.

Pioneers of this period published essays and novels on a variety of themes. Al-Manfaluti, for example, wrote a series of adaptations from western novels in a beautiful, modern Arabic style. Al-Yaziji adapted the language to express new ideas and forms of artistic sensibility. Lebanese writer Butrus al-Bustani (d. 1883), used a new kind of expository prose, not departing from the basic rules of Arabic grammar but with simpler modes of expression and new words and idioms developed either from classical Arabic or adapted from English or French.[13] Other pioneers wrote historical novels in order to revive the language, focusing on Arab society in high literary style. The historical novel was indisputably a crucial development for the progression of the Arab renaissance, with its rediscovery of the classical past and reassertion of Arab national identity.[14]

Contributions of these early prose writers are valued highly by modern literary criticism; it is they who prepared the ground for the emergence of the modern Arabic novel, developed later at the hands of Tawfiq al-Hakim (d. 1987) and Naguib Mahfouz (d. 2006). The first novel in Arabic, published in 1914, represents the true beginning of the new literary genre. It employs simple vocabulary and uncomplicated structures, using Arabic as the "language of life and the language of the people."[15] At the same time, Gibran Khalil Gibran had written *The Broken Wings*, a novel-like work charged with dynamic lyrics and departing from traditional Arab style. The Arabic novel will be discussed in more detail in the chapter of Arabic novel.

Soon, other writers were using new, experimental language and modes of writing. The critical analyses of Taha Hussein (d. 1973) on prose, essays, and cultural criticism have contributed enormously to the development and modernization of the Arabic language. Hussein called upon writers to use language that people could understand, and held that authors should write clearly and in modern language. He argued that Arabic must be shared between those who write it and those who understand it.[16]

Meanwhile, Arab poets joined the revival movement of the literary Arab renaissance by consciously imitating the past to free the Arabic language from the weaknesses it developed throughout the past decades. This neoclassical movement in poetry, led by Nasif al-Yaziji (d. 1871), Mahmoud Sami al-Baroudi (d. 1904), Ahmad Shawqi (d. 1932), Ma`ruf al-Rusafi (d. 1945), Jamil Sidqi al-Zahawi (d. 1936), Hafiz Ibrahim (d. 1932), and Muhammad Mahdi al-Jawahiri (d. 1999), revived the language of the past through imitation and reproduction. Its leaders were able to recreate the language of great classical poets in form, content, vocabulary, and expression, drawing from both classical Abbasid and pre-Islamic classical poetry. This was expressed through artistic verse that communicated national sentiments. The efforts of the neoclassical school of poets in strengthening and reviving the Arabic language laid the groundwork for new generations of writers to pursue further modernization.

After World War II, Arab poets further explored the language from within. Modern poetry was a new mix of vocabulary and expressions, employed using new techniques that sought to merge the inner self of the poet with the outer self of the world. This poetic innovation was another enormous contribution to Arabic linguistic modernity. As with the novelists, it was neoclassical pioneers who first revived Arabic poetry, but revolutionaries who modernized it. At the hands of poets and novelists, the Arabic language thus moved into experimentation and revelation.

The most important positive lasting result of the Arab renaissance was the across-the-board achievements made in Arabic language and literature. Throughout the renaissance, Arabic poetry and prose acted as a cultural compass calling for resistance and independence on Arab social, political and national issues, and this role continues. Since the 1950s, Arab poets were able to recreate a new Arabic language. Poets have connected this modernized language with daily life. As a result, the entire Arab region went through a revolutionary linguistic process. Over the centuries of Arab decay, Arabs had lost their powerful language and poetry at the same time that they had lost their political power. During the renaissance, Arabs tried to regain these three essential elements of their civilization, but they succeeded only in regaining their language and their poetry. Chapter 8 on modern Arabic poetry examines this point in more detail.

To strengthen the language, literary pioneers of this period established language academies, held regular meetings and conferences, and translated or adapted prolifically from the corpus of world literature. The spread of education in the nineteenth century also allowed the Arabic language to continue to gain strength. Writers, poets, and academics began to publish periodicals, books, and journals in Arabic. Scholars began to compile modern Arabic language dictionaries. Bustani, a great Lebanese scholar of Arabic, founded four journals and wrote an Arabic encyclopedia of several volumes.[17] He also produced the first modern Arabic dictionary known as *Muhit al-Muhit*, in which he added new vocabulary, idioms, and expressions to the Arabic language from many different fields of knowledge.

Al-Bustani's *Muhit al-Muhit* encouraged others to write and publish their own dictionaries. Among the most important modern Arabic dictionaries of this era were *Aqrab al-Mawarid* by Sa`id al-Shartuni (d. 1912), *al-Bustan* by Abdullah al-Bustani (d. 1930), and, most importantly, *al-Munjid* by Jesuit priest and Arab scholar Luis Ma`louf (d. 1947). The first edition of *al-Munjid* was published in 1908 and has since been reprinted more than fifty times. It remains one of the most frequently used dictionaries of modern Arabic until this very day because of its ease of use. One of its most valuable features is a set of biographical entries on the most important literary, political, social and religious figures since the Arab renaissance. Many other modern Arabic dictionaries are widely available today as well.

Early in the twentieth century, academies were founded in Damascus and Cairo along the model of the *Académie Française*. The goal of these Arabic Language Academies was to preserve the integrity of Arabic by protecting it from dialect and foreign influence and facilitating its adaptation to the needs of modern times. The Damascus Academy was established in 1919, and the Cairo Academy in 1932; another was established in Iraq in 1947, and another in Jordan in 1976. The language academies work through a complicated process of consultation and careful deliberation when deciding to introduce new terms and incorporate new vocabulary into the language.[18] Schools of translation, several of which were established in Egypt, Syria, Iraq, and Lebanon in the nineteenth century, have also played an important role in modernizing the Arabic language. However, individual scholars' efforts on translations have continued to be very much useful and productive in modernizing the language.

The second half of the twentieth century witnessed a further strengthening of the Arabic language. Computer languages and technical jargon and terminologies have been Arabicized and accepted into Arabic systems of phonology and morphology. There have also been efforts to reform grammar, keeping its rules intact while simplifying its use. Many scholars, among them a Syrian intellectual `Afif Dimashqiyya, have concentrated on facilitating the easy use and understanding of Arabic grammar while preserving Arab heritage.

Perhaps the most important force that has strengthened and modernized Arabic has been the development of the modern Arabic novel. The Arabic novel, alongside modern Arabic poetry, has greatly revolutionized the language. The novel has revitalized Arabic into a dynamic and creative language capable of capturing detail and expressing all themes with lively, powerful, and artistic

techniques. The novel has transformed all the structure, style, spirit, and application of the Arabic language. The emergence of the modern Arab novel in Arabic
literature has achieved great stature in the past few decades. The modern Arab
novel reached a high maturity at the hands of Mahfouz, who won the Nobel Prize
for Literature in 1988.

The Arabic novel has developed to the extent that it describes Arab society and
culture with more accuracy and meaning than any philosophical or sociological
study is able to. More can be learned about the Arab world through the novel
than through "all the other studies combined."[19] The Arabic novel has had great
influence not only on the Arabic language, but also on Arab culture and reality. See
chapter 9 on the Arab novel for more detail.

MODERN STANDARD ARABIC

The classical Arabic language that underwent modernization during the Arab
renaissance is now called Modern Standard Arabic, or MSA. This is the modern
classical Arabic language, and it is continually evolving in vocabulary, styles, idioms and expressions. It includes borrowed words such as *sekretair*, or "secretary,"
and is influenced by foreign languages and idiom. Although Modern Standard
Arabic includes new vocabulary and is more flexible, simpler in structure, and
easier to use, it strictly follows the rules of classical Arabic grammar, morphology
and syntax.

Often called *fus-ha* (literally "most eloquent") MSA is the language of contemporary written publications and Arabic media. It is much easier and certainly
more practical than the classical language, which has intricate structures, difficult
expressions and outdated vocabulary and idioms. MSA reflects a new spirit in
a time of intercultural media communications. It also reflects the international
influences of modernist literary style, new journalistic techniques, foreign and
borrowed words, and recent concepts and terminologies. Like the classical language it replaced, Modern Standard Arabic constructs a national Arab identity and
a united Arab culture. The successful emergence and adaptation of MSA proves
that the ancient, ever-developing Arabic language has never died.

Today, Modern Standard Arabic is the official language of twenty-two Arab
countries. It is used in its oral and written form on all formal occasions and is
understood throughout the Arab world. As the formal medium of communication
among Arabs, MSA is the language of contemporary Arabic literature and other
fields of scholarship and publication. Schools and universities teach in MSA, and
newspapers, journals, books, textbooks, lectures, news broadcasts, documentaries
and discussion programs use MSA.

Arab writers worked to bring the classical Arabic language into the modern world by modifying its syntax and introducing new words (such as *sayyara*, or "car") that could not have existed during the classical period. They also succeeded in excavating the language's immense resources through the technical grammatical process of *qiyas*, or "analogy," and forced an entirely new vocabulary onto the classical language, which now makes up roughly sixty percent of MSA.[20] Some Arab writers have excelled in mixing classical Arabic and MSA together in a creative and provocative way, digging deep into powerful, ancient semantics and using them in their modern writing.

COLLOQUIAL ARABIC

Colloquial languages and spoken dialects have always existed in Arabic history, and continue to develop every day. Today, Arabs read and write in Modern Standard Arabic and speak it in formal circumstances, but they use colloquial language to communicate with each other on a daily basis at home and in the streets. The dialect is informal, less complicated, and easier. In fact, the mother tongue of every native speaker of Arabic is actually colloquial Arabic, while MSA is a second language acquired through education and training. The educated native Arabic speaker is thus bilingual, born with a local dialect and acquiring the official formal language at school.

Arabs naturally communicate in their local dialect regardless of their levels of education or literacy; it is their native tongue and the language in which they feel greatest comfort. A man would carry out a conversation with his wife in colloquial Arabic but would write to her in the formal language. There is no need, nor would it be socially acceptable, to speak in formal, literary language with complex grammar and structures just to order a *falafel* sandwich in a crowded market, especially given that most people working in that market would likely be uneducated, and thus be unfamiliar with the most formal Arabic.

Each Arab country has its own dialect, but in many cases, each city or region within the same country has its own dialect, as well. The Syrian dialect, for example, is different from the Egyptian dialect. Additionally, within Syria the dialect of Damascus is different from the dialect of Aleppo, a city located 220 miles to the north, and the dialect of Aleppo is different in turn from another Syrian city farther to the east. None of these dialects is taught in the Arab world. Dialects of certain Arab countries are taught in Western institutions and universities, however, especially the Egyptian, Iraqi, and Levantine dialects.

Despite the plethora of local variations, several distinct and major regional dialects exist in the Arab world and share general linguistic features and similarities.

Each major general dialect covers a region of a group of several Arab countries. The Egyptian dialect covers Egypt and some parts of Sudan; the Levantine dialect covers Syria, Lebanon, Jordan, and Palestine; the North African dialect covers Morocco, Algeria and Tunisia; the Gulf dialect covers Saudi Arabia, Qatar, Bahrain, the UAE, Kuwait and Oman; and Iraq has its own dialect. Each dialect has general characteristics and linguistic features in common, though each country within the group has its own peculiarities in word choice, sentence construction, idioms, expressions, greetings, pronunciation and accent.

The most widely understood dialect in the Arab world is probably the Egyptian dialect. Though the dialect is specific to Egyptians, almost all Arabs are familiar with Egyptian films, radio programs and television shows that are produced in colloquial Egyptian language. During the 1950s and 1960s, Egypt led the Arab world in production of movies, music, and films, exporting its culture and language to other Arab states. In addition, two legendary Arab personalities of the twentieth century are Egyptian. The first, Umm Kulthum (d. 1975), is the most celebrated Arab singer of all time. Beloved by the entire Arab world, she and her records dominated radio and television for several decades, and her songs remain popular today. Although Umm Kulthum sang in classical Arabic, many of her recordings were sung in the Egyptian dialect. The second personality was Egyptian President Jamal `Abd al-Nasir (d. 1970), the pioneer of Arab nationalism. Nasir was a charismatic and compelling speaker, and his addresses used to be beamed to every corner of the Arab world via radio. Although he used Modern Standard Arabic every now and then, most of his speeches were in the Egyptian dialect. When Nasir came on the radio, Arabs used to gather round in their living rooms, enchanted. Years after his death, people continued to listen to his recorded speeches. In the twenty-first century, a new generation of contemporary Egyptian singers and musicians is beloved for their songs and music. Egyptian movies and television soap operas are also hugely popular and viewed all over the Arab world.

Yet another reason Egyptian Arabic is universally understood is that Egypt is the most populous country in the Arab world, and many Egyptians work and live in other Arab countries. Many of these expatriate Egyptians, including teachers, bankers, lawyers, and laborers, have resided for long periods of time outside of Egypt, and even married into the local population.

In general, countries that are geographically contiguous retain common linguistic features and dialectical similarities. For example, Algeria, Morocco, and Tunisia share common linguistic features, and it is therefore easier for the populations of those countries to communicate with one another than with the populations of the countries of the Fertile Crescent region. The Arab Gulf states also share common linguistic features; even using their local dialects, they can still communicate with each other with clarity. When educated Arabs from different geographical regions meet in a social setting inappropriate for the use of Modern Standard Arabic, they usually speak with one another drawing many words from MSA in order to minimize misunderstanding. This is a routine solution for individuals who meet at conferences, business meetings, or any social, cultural, or religious gatherings.

When Arabs speak in colloquial Arabic, they speak it spontaneously, naturally and without effort. They do not need to pause and think about the correct structure or grammar of the sentence, as they do when using classical Arabic. The dialect is a powerful and practical way to communicate, which is simple but contains an extraordinary wealth of semantics, original idioms, and even metaphors. Dialects are lively and very dynamic: when situations change, so do the linguistic tools of dialects to describe and manage them. Dialects are difficult to acquire or learn by people who are not native speakers, because they are not written and do not always follow systematic rules. The best way for a non-native speaker of Arabic to learn an Arabic dialect is to live among the population of a particular region for a long period of time. Some creative idioms exist in colloquial Arabic, but are unknown to non-native Arabic speakers, as they do not exist in any other language.

Jokes in the Arab world are created and told in dialect. There is also a wonderful body of poetry composed in colloquial Arabic, especially on the subjects of love, sadness, and the philosophy of life. This poetry is powerful, passionate, and sincere; it is composed and transmitted orally, and recited with beautiful rhythm and rhyme. Drama, theatre, and film are mostly performed in dialects, as well. Some advocates of colloquial Arabic have called for the use of dialect in writing. But there is a reason that the poetry composed in colloquial Arabic is not written down. Recited orally and often composed spontaneously, this poetry of dialect is natural, beautiful, musical, and close to the heart. Its spontaneous and oral nature suggests it would lose value if transcribed or read from a hard copy. The beauty and effectiveness of colloquial poetry is in its transient, verbal essence; once transcribed, it would lose its uniqueness and resemble only a poor, broken language.

THE DIFFERENCE BETWEEN STANDARD AND COLLOQUIAL ARABIC

There is certainly a difference between the literary, formal, standard Arabic and spoken Arabic dialects. Everyday Arab culture simply has two languages: the informal language that is spoken colloquially and the formal language that is written and used for official and formal business. This *diglossia* is natural for almost all cultures, though the gap between colloquial Arabic and Modern Standard Arabic is perhaps bigger than for most other languages. This gap has narrowed slightly because of several reasons. One reason is the spread of education in which the default medium of instruction is MSA. Another factor is the revolution in Arab media, represented by satellite television channels like *al-Jazeera Satellite Channel*, *al-Arabiya*, and *MBC* (Middle East Broadcasting Center), most of which broadcast solely in Modern Standard Arabic. Some believe this unprecedented media revolution will cause viewers in the near future to realize that standard Arabic is a cultural compass and linguistic landmark, bringing Arabic colloquial dialects closer to MSA and the Arabs closer to each other.

It is widely acknowledged that something must be done to bridge the gap between MSA and colloquial Arabic; a related but more serious problem, though, is that many Arabs do not know Modern Standard Arabic very well. This, not the existence of colloquial dialects, lies at the heart of the problem. The difference between the dialects and standard Arabic is exaggerated in the discourse, mostly by non-native speakers of Arabic. Additional voices inside the Arab world press this issue in order to further a specific agenda: promoting, for various reasons, the use of colloquial Arabic at the expense of Modern Standard Arabic.

Despite the quite different varieties of Arabic that a Moroccan and Syrian, for example, may speak, Arabs always find ways to communicate. They simply use familiar vocabulary and expressions in order to eliminate any lack in mutual understanding. And as more Arabs travel, visit, reside and work in different Arab countries, and decide to marry locally, they learn to understand the dialects of others and assist others to understand theirs. What is needed is not to impose written colloquial Arabic on the unsuspecting masses, but to eliminate the gap through effectively widening the use of Modern Standard Arabic. Edward Said observes that the familiarity of Arabs and Muslims with the Qur'an leads the difference between the classical and the modern to be quite thin. Educated Arabs actually use both the modern and the classical language, which is a common and unsurprising practice as the "two languages are porous and the user flows in and out of one into another."[21]

THE ROLE OF ARAB SATELLITE TELEVISION CHANNELS

The emergence of Arabic satellite television channels has led to the beginning of another much-needed linguistic revolution in the Arab world. More than two decades ago numerous satellite stations launched, broadcasting throughout the Arab world and beyond. The most popular and influential, as mentioned above, are *MBC*, *al-Jazeera*, and *al-Arabiyya*. Others, including the *Lebanese Broadcasting Corporation* (LBC) and *Future TV* in Lebanon, and the *Abu Dhabi Satellite Channel* and *Dubai Satellite Channel* in the United Arab Emirates, are popular as well. All of these stations broadcast news as well as cultural, social, religious and political programming in Modern Standard Arabic, and there are even a few programs and regular series that use classical, non-modernized Arabic, especially those that air during the holy month of Ramadan and other religious holidays.

The veritable explosion in popularity of these channels has wide ramifications in Arab society; its influence on non-linguistic aspects of Arab culture will be discussed later in the chapter on the Crisis of Arab Culture. The relevance here lies in the fact that the greatest contribution of these channels may ultimately be the role they play in an unintended and unexpected linguistic revival. Spreading MSA to the entire Arab population twenty-four hours a day is far more critical and influential than it might seem. Listeners not only appreciate the language used, but they learn from it as well; as the level of language used is superb. On the many live programs, moreover, the *public* participates and converses in Modern Standard Arabic. This constant broadcast of MSA over a period of years has succeeded in spreading the standard language throughout the Arab world more effectively than any other means imaginable.

The high level of eloquence on these shows is striking. Most stations use Modern Standard Arabic even when discussants are hotly disputing major issues such as regional politics or religion. The entire Arab world eagerly watches news and other programs conducted in flawless MSA without using colloquial language. For the first time in history, these stations are thus laying the foundation for MSA a viable means of communication among the entire Arab region. Moreover, most participants on these shows are communicating effectively, and naturally. All follow-up questions and comments from the worldwide audience are made in MSA as well. This proves that MSA is capable of penetrating the houses and the streets of the Arabs, where it was previously considered burdensome and snobbish. Despite its adherence to grammatical rules and structure, it is a dynamic, flexible and practical language.

Regardless of their level of education, Arabs can understand the news broadcasted in Modern Standard Arabic, together with all related commentaries, programs and debates. Not everyone can read or write it, but no native speaker of Arabic has difficulty understanding MSA when spoken aloud. Even the uneducated in the Arab world have some exposure to and are familiar with both the classical and modern standard languages. Those who never went to school know classical Arabic through having memorized parts of the Qur'an, and the *Hadith* of the Prophet Muhammad. Arabs who cannot read and write still memorize lines and verses of classical poetry. They all understand the language of the Qur'an, perform their prayers using formal Arabic, and are perfectly capable of deriving meaning from the language of religious sermons in mosques, at funerals, on the radio and on television. Additionally, uneducated Arabs can understand modern Arabic poetry written in plain and direct language, composed by modern poets, who wrote with the specific intention of reaching out to larger Arab audiences rather than just the educated, urban elite.

A few voices from among the Arab population, but mostly from non-native speakers of Arabic, claim Modern Standard Arabic is lifeless, dysfunctional in communication, and incapable of dealing with real-life situations. Their argument is based on the fact that Arabs speak one language at home, write in a second language, and read the Qur'an and classical literature in a third. But most Arabs do not consider this to be a problem. Even with English, there is the spoken colloquial English that one speaks with friends and family, the formal English of scholarly articles, government documents, and business meetings, and the archaic but highly valued English of William Shakespeare, Edmund Spenser, or Thomas Paine. To arbitrarily eliminate any of these three versions of English would be unnecessary and ridiculous; all three "languages" are part and parcel of the same culture, and are indivisible.

ARABIC TODAY

Literary pioneers of the Arab renaissance in the late nineteenth and early twentieth centuries, modern Arab poets and novelists in the last seven decades, and contemporary Arab media, particularly satellite TV channels in the last two decades, have all impacted the Arabic language in positive ways. However, the Arabic language today faces severe challenges to its identity and future.

Even with all the improvement made, Arabic is still undergoing a dilemma in both the Arab world and in the international community. The quality of Arabic teaching, learning, speaking, and writing is weak, and Arabic language proficiency suffers as a result. Authorities on the subject testify that many Arabs do not know how to read, write, and speak Modern Standard Arabic well due to a poor standard of language instruction and the lack of effective pedagogical methods and curriculum development. Despite great progress in reviving and strengthening Arabic over the last century, this subject is of major national and religious concern.

There have been many calls, particularly from religious and national figures and Arabic language academies, to protect the classical Arabic language tradition from the threats it faces. Advocates are working to find ways to preserve and strengthen the language against three main challenges. The first is the promotion of the spoken colloquial dialects; the second is the spread of foreign languages in national schools to the detriment of Arabic language instruction; and the third is the all-too-common misuse and mangling of standard Arabic by some writers, news broadcasters, and public speakers.[22] This includes Arab rulers and government officials.

One of the major problems that MSA faces is the strong campaign by certain groups to promote colloquial Arabic at the expense of MSA in Arab culture. A battle has been waged between Arab nationalists allied with religious intellectuals, who promote MSA, and some Arabs and minority groups, who promote colloquial Arabic.

One pan-Arab newspaper reported that a Moroccan news announcer was forced to leave his position when he refused the demands of the station owner to broadcast the news in colloquial Arabic instead of MSA. Earlier, the station had begun broadcasting colloquial news twice a day; this new development came in response to the owner's decision to broadcast all the news in colloquial. The station owner argued that forty percent of Moroccans are illiterate and unable to understand MSA despite the fact that Moroccans and other Arabs have listened to news broadcasts in MSA up to this point with no problem.[23]

The newspapers further reported that the effort in Morocco to broadcast the news in colloquial Arabic comes in part from a campaign by the francophone class of Moroccan society to promote colloquialism. Some in this group have been calling for the use of the Moroccan dialect instead of standard Arabic for many years. This position favoring colloquial Arabic is not solely confined to elements of Moroccan society, but has also been supported by some researchers and experts who promote the use of spoken dialects in the media and schools. The colloquial language has been used in advertisements, business commercials and banners throughout the country. Some Moroccans have begun working on a colloquial dictionary, and others are establishing a newspaper in the spoken Moroccan dialect.[24]

Morocco is not the only country to face these internal struggles over language. The use of foreign languages instead of Arabic in advertising and business circles is so widespread throughout the Arab world that many feel it has become an insult to Arab culture. French is commonly found on the streets of Lebanon, Tunisia, and Morocco, and English is widely used all over Jordan, Egypt, the United Arab Emirates, Bahrain, Qatar, Kuwait, Oman and Saudi Arabia.

Abdulwahab al-Misairi and other Egyptian writers filed a lawsuit against the former Egyptian President Hosni Mubarak, demanding that Mubarak uphold the Egyptian constitution, which affirmed that Arabic is the official language of the state. The lawsuit alleged that the plethora of advertisements and company names written in foreign languages constitutes a constitutional violation, and sought an injunction against the Egyptian President to protect the Arabic language. In a press conference, Misairi said that Arabic in Egypt had been exposed to "Westernized hallucination." He presented photographs of commercial advertisements and storefront banners inside Egypt using only the English language, and showed selected Egyptian newspaper advertisements that do not include one single word of Arabic.

In a recent article, founder and editor of the Lebanese *As-Safir* newspaper, Talal Salman, lamented the disrespect shown by Arabs towards their classical language. In Lebanon, not only do private and commercial business companies use colloquial

Arabic in their marketing and advertisements, some government ministries have begun to use colloquial Arabic as if it is the official language of the government. They argue that colloquial Arabic is easier for the public to understand, as if the public is ignorant, illiterate, and does not understand classical Arabic. Salman contends that Arabs today have abandoned their language, claiming it is too difficult. Worse yet, they rely on foreign languages, French and English, as the languages of education for their children. Thus, they intentionally and deliberately continue to discount their mother tongue. They ignore the fact that classical Arabic represents their national identity, and has always been the language of Arab culture, the Qur'an, poetry, and the source of Arab civilization. In Salman's view, it is embarrassing and disgraceful when parents give their children foreign names or Arabic names but tailor and change them to be easy for foreigners to pronounce.[25]

In a similar article, writer Abdulla Al-Nimri observed that at the time when foreigners all over the world are learning and mastering Arabic, we find Arabs in the Arab world "disrespecting their own Arabic language." Al-Nimri wrote that during a conference held in Rabat, Morocco in October 2017, the Russian ambassador to Morocco gave a talk in Arabic while the Moroccan government officials gave their talks in French. The Russian ambassador was shocked three years earlier when he was asked to speak at another conference in French in a country where Arabic is the primary language. Al-Nimri concluded that the Arabic language had become marginalized inside Arab countries.[26]

Faisal Al-Qasim, the well-known and hugely popular host of Al-Jazeera's 'Crossfire,' wrote in a recent article that every time he listens to a speech by certain Arab leaders, he gets the chills. Not because of the flow of their ideas, or the magnificence of their statements, but out of anger because they abuse, insult and harm the Arabic language. Few Arab leaders are able to speak Arabic correctly, and he wonders why the advisers of these leaders do not let them know after their speeches that their use of the Arabic language is scandalously incorrect. Al-Qasim addresses a question to the Arab leaders: "When will you, our dear rulers, learn and respect your own language? When will you realize that your 'broken language' hurts your image and makes you look ignorant? Is not the language the container of thought? So where is your thought if its vessel contains your defective and wrecked language? How can people understand your strategies, your economic and political policies, if your Arabic language is not understood?"[27]

The Arab world is clearly and undeniably suffering in language fluency and proficiency. The quality of Arabic education in the arts and sciences is poor in both private and public schools, causing students to graduate with serious deficiencies in Arabic language. The private schools that dominate the Arab world are international schools: American, British, and French, and they apply Western curricula, concentrating on their own languages, histories, and cultures. As a result, the Arabic language is sidelined, and elite Arab students graduate from these schools with sub-standard Arabic language skills.

Arabic is poorly taught in public schools as well. The low standards and outdated pedagogical techniques in public schools constitute main obstacles to student proficiency in MSA. This problem of poor teaching is due to the lack of qualified teachers, which sparks a general failure in the Arab educational system. The lack of good schools, curricula and competent teachers means that most Arab children cannot read and write in Arabic adequately after graduating from high school.

Writer Noel Abdulahad emphasizes that the level of Arabic language teaching is in a very sad situation. Most students are learning English and other foreign languages, but their knowledge in Arabic remains shallow and insufficient. He adds that, while the Arabic language is the most dynamic and influential factor in unifying Arab culture, schools do not teach Arabic well. Arabic instruction in public schools is a complete failure, and Arabic in private schools is ignored because the foreign languages are preferred. Teachers of foreign languages get better salaries, more respect, and better privileges than teachers of Arabic.[28]

There are other ways in which foreign presence and influence in the Arab world threatens the Arabic language. Much of the upper class in Arab society believe that national public schools do not offer a high level of education, so they send their children to foreign private schools. They are not taught Arabic history, but rather learn foreign languages and Western history. Arab children educated in foreign schools are thus living inside Arab society but are not an integral part of it because they do not fully comprehend their history or identity.

The growing presence of foreign companies in the Arab world is likewise threatening Arabic language proficiency. The foreign companies ignore the Arabic language completely, choosing to impose their own languages onto the work place. A few years ago, Islamic scholar Yusuf al-Qaradawi quoted an acquaintance on *al-Jazeera* program, 'Shari`a and Life,' who told him that after visiting one of the Arab Gulf states, he was surprised to find that people did not speak Arabic in the airport, hotels, or markets, "I was surprised at the airport that people do not speak the Arabic language. Nor do they speak Arabic at the hotels. I went to the market to shop but I did not find anyone who spoke Arabic ... ."[29]

Prominent figures in the Arab world are beginning to sound the alarm about the encroachment of foreign languages on Arabic. The Egyptian newspaper *al-Ahram Weekly* has written about the regression in Arabic proficiency in Egypt. The paper writes that, even though Arabic is Egypt's official language, Egyptian students enrolled in private schools in Cairo possess flawless American accents while their Arabic is weak. According to the paper, the vast majority of university students studying in English departments, "do not master the Arabic language and are incapable of completing a single sentence without throwing in a few English words."[30] Egyptian writer Ni`mat Ahmed Fu'ad also published a lengthy article in *al-Ahram* calling for the re-establishment of the *Katateeb*, or the religious Qur'anic schools, where children memorize the Qur'an and learn to read and write. Fu'ad wrote that this is the best way to strengthen and preserve the Arab language.[31]

One way to strengthen Arabic language teaching could be to conduct the curriculum solely in Arabic at all stages of the educational system, and have all students be required to take a minimum of Arabic grammar lessons per week, along the lines of a suggestion by Egyptian scholar Shawqi Dayf. It seems clear that if no corrective action is taken, the next generation may witness the emergence of an entire social class that belongs neither to Arab society nor to the Arabic language, but rather to foreign languages and foreign culture. Not counting universities, approximately 250 schools in Egypt do not use Arabic at all in their instruction. The vast majority of Arab universities no longer use Arabic in teaching medicine, engineering and other scientific fields because they believe that Arabic is somehow unable to grasp and express the language and vocabulary of science and its recent advances. Strong systems of public education with accurate and serious Modern Standard Arabic instruction is certainly needed within the Arab world itself.[32]

Additionally, Arabic language materials and computer software in Arabic are severely lacking throughout the Arab world. Jaber `Asfour, former head of the Higher Cultural Council in Egypt, criticizes the widespread tendency in society to believe the ability to speak foreign languages is a guarantor of higher social status.[33] It is inconceivable that whatever deficiencies might exist in Arabic for modern technological concepts could not be faithfully integrated with the language. Some scholars have called for an international conference on the Arabic language, where all societies and organizations can meet in order to rectify the situation.[34]

Many Arabs, especially Islamists and nationalists, believe that mastering the classical Arabic language is a duty. Above all, Arabic is the language of the Qur'an and of Arabs from before Islam. The Qur'an and *Hadith* cannot be studied and understood without knowing the classical Arabic language. Islamic intellectuals feel that it is the absolute duty of every Muslim to study classical Arabic in order to understand the first sources of Islam. Studying the secrets of the Arabic language, from linguistics to morphology and grammar, is a prerequisite for grasping the holy text.

During the Islamic golden age, Arabic was the language of the civilization that was the center of human knowledge in the world. Many Arab intellectuals think that the power of language is a representation of the power of the people who speak it: English is strong today not because it is the best language, but because the United States is a leading power. During the height of Arab and Islamic civilization, Arabic was the language of medicine, physics, chemistry, astrology and mathematics beyond the region. Scientific articles were written in Arabic. But when Arabs became weak as a state and nation, sciences began to be taught in English and French instead. Today, in Syria medicine is taught in Arabic, which proves it can be done.[35]

Recently Qatar University switched its primary language of instruction back to Arabic from English in most fields of studies. Arabic will be Qatar University's official teaching language, and the faculties of law, international affairs, mass communication, and management will shift to teaching in Arabic rather than in English. Some departments, however, such as engineering and pharmacy, will continue to teach in English.[36] In a modest step and long overdue decision, Saudi Arabia, according to Gulf News, has prohibited the use of English in answering telephone calls in hotels, private companies, and government offices.[37] Thus, recent developments indicate a minor but needed move by some governments to reinforce the instruction and use of Arabic in their countries.

ARABIC IN THE UNITED STATES

Before September 11, 2001, the Arabic language was taught in American universities to only a handful of students, whose motivation for studying the language was primarily for its beauty and importance to the study of world civilization. Students and their teachers concentrated on the linguistic, grammatical, philological, religious, literary and aesthetic aspects of the Arabic language. Motivations and goals were primarily centered on gaining knowledge and understanding for the sake of knowledge and understanding. After September 11, the situation changed abruptly. Arabic language study suddenly became a strategic need and an issue of national security. By 2005, the United States had classified Arabic a "critical language" and began a series of well-funded programs and grants that encouraged students to learn the language.

Protecting national security and career aspirations began to dominate the reasons for learning Arabic. The market strengthened for jobs in private companies dealing with the Arab world, or in the US government. A high demand remains for government and military positions that require knowledge of Arabic. Arabic also enhances business expertise, especially for the petroleum and financial sectors. Many talented American students have learned the language and became excellent examples of serving themselves and their country.

The United States has prioritized the field of Arabic language instruction as a necessary part of its higher education system. The number of students learning Arabic totaled five thousand in September 2001 and jumped after one year to more than twice that number. In 2013, the number of American university students studying the Arabic language was more than thirty thousand, and has grown in the years since then.[38] The US government provides financial and administrative support to create new programs and to strengthen existing programs in Arabic language studies at universities, educational institutes and centers of Middle East Studies. Critical Language Scholarships, Fulbright exchange programs, and various university programs now provide students with the opportunity to learn Arabic through intensive and immersive programs, including short and long-term training in Arab countries.

The US government contributes significant financial support to a number of universities to promote Arabic language instruction, and to conduct research on the Arab world and the Middle East. These universities have robust programs that include teaching Arabic language and dialects such as Egyptian, Iraqi, and Syrian. The US Department of Education provided support to establish several centers to focus on a broad range of Middle East languages, with Arabic the most important.

Most teaching, however, has focused only on the simplest and practical aspects of the language in order to prepare students for the opportunity to get jobs quickly and to receive grants so they can continue in the field. The serious problem of finding and training qualified teachers remains a hindrance to the desired outcomes of fluency and understanding the region, its history and culture. Arabic regional dialects have become important, thus competing with classical and MSA. Issues of learning dialects and colloquial Arabic at the expense of MSA remain unresolved. Focusing on the language of the press, media and newspapers, as well as emphasizing political and economic vocabulary at the expense of literature, religious and historical texts further limits a true understanding of the region and its people. The escalation of interest in learning Arabic has also extended to Arab-Americans and Muslim students across the United States from many communities. Arabs and Muslims in America also embarked on learning the language in order to be able to read and understand Islamic texts, know their culture of origin, and compete for jobs in government, academia, and business.

Beyond a doubt, the efforts of the pioneers of the Arab renaissance followed by the achievements of the neoclassical poets, novelists and literary intellectuals have resulted in reviving, strengthening and modernizing the Arabic language. Even with the neglect and abuse by many parts of society, the Arabic language today, as written and articulated by leading Arab poets, novelists, journalists, and scholars, is strong, sound, powerful, innovative, dynamic, revolutionary, and exceedingly attractive.

Despite the complex issues discussed above, Arabs are regaining their powerful language, the most essential element of Arab culture. Arabs today have a moral duty to learn, master and preserve their mother tongue.

CHAPTER FOUR

Classical Arabic Poetry

POETRY IS AT THE very essence of the Arab people. It represents a mirror of Arab social values, a key to understanding the Arab mind, and the core and substance of Arab culture. A highly developed and sophisticated art form, poetry was deeply rooted in the psyche and history of the Arabs long before the appearance of Islam. Arabic poetry originated in the same place as the Arabs themselves, the heart of the ancient Arabian Peninsula, and has existed as long as the Arab people have existed. Pre-Islamic poetry contains the record of Arab history, tribal genealogy, and social, political and intellectual developments from before the written Arabic language was widespread. It is called *diwan al-arab*, or the "Register of the Arabs," because it chronicles the contents of Arab memory. Through poetry, the Arabs' deeds, activities, ways of life and civilization have been consecrated and preserved.[1]

Without understanding Arabic poetry, understanding true Arab culture is impossible. Poetry is the authentic witness that truthfully reflects Arab mentality, thought, norms and beliefs. One observer describes it as the "political, social and ethical compass of Arab culture."[2] Poetry has represented Arab identity throughout the ages of history, using the Arabic language in its most majestic form to preserve this identity. The complex and refined poetic arts have eloquently expressed, reported and documented the news, events and wars of the Arabs, in victory or defeat, glory or decline. Poets have also revealed the Arab character and intelligence. Above all, poetry is a great manifestation of artistic creativity, engendering the formidable emotional and spiritual power that made Arabs a nation long before Islam. Through their poetry, Arabs confront life, themselves and others. Adonis, a major contemporary Arab poet, remarks that poetry is a conscious application of speech and a willful participation in the act of existence.[3]

Through their poetry, Arabs embraced history and mankind. Poetry was the first artistic attempt to explain, in the Arabic language, that which the Arabs are. Thus, Arabic poetry is not only the first memory of the Arabs, but also the first wellspring of their imagination. It is the authentic Arab literature that, in addition to its artistic value, provides a historical record of Arabs and their world, including histories of individual countries, cities, and an incessant stream of biographies.[4]

Arabic poetry began with the Bedouins, the original Arabs, who lived in a collective society with little room for individuality. When a poet appeared in an Arab family, other tribes would gather to express their joy for that family's good fortune. The poet was so highly valued in Bedouin culture because he defended the honor of his clan and tribe. R.A. Nicholson, an esteemed scholar on ancient Arabic poetry, observes that in this society, the phrase "the pen is mightier than the sword" represented literal truth; poetry the weapon Arabs used to "ward off insult from their good name, and a means of perpetuating their glorious deeds and establishing their fame forever."[5]

It was the task of the poet to positively reflect his tribe's best qualities. Arabs had no other art except for poetry, the sole medium of their literary expression, though poetry was by no means the only product of Arab culture. It was most representative of their originality and genius, however. Throughout Arab literary history from pre-Islamic times until the first half of the twentieth century, at which time other literary genres emerged, the term 'Arabic literature' has really just meant poetry.[6]

At first, all poetry was composed, transmitted and preserved through oral tradition in the Arabian Peninsula. Arab scholars begin to collect and collate the odes that had survived purely through memory only in the eighth century. This orally transmitted poetic tradition is the repository of Arab culture and history and has played a most important role in preserving the collective memory of the Arabs. The task of the poet was to defend his people and preserve their honor in verse. If the poet concentrated on himself rather than his people, he would have lost his valuable position in society.[7]

THE POSITION OF THE POET IN SOCIETY

The Arabian poet enjoyed an extremely high position in society. He was not only his people's defender, but their oracle, a guide in peace and champion in war. He also served as spokesman, political representative and community ideal. The degree of importance that Arab society afforded poets is rare elsewhere in human history; their cultural significance could perhaps be compared to that of Homer among ancient Greeks.[8] However, the themes and forms of Arabian poetry are very different from those of its Western counterparts.

Furthermore, unlike even ancient Greece, the Arab poet has remained extremely influential in contemporary Arab society. The cultural link between the past and the present has not been broken in this respect. Just as the Arabian warrior defended the people of his tribe by sword, the Arabian poet defended the honor of his tribe by immortalizing their glorious deeds and defaming their enemies.[9]

Adonis further elaborates that the Arabic poem can be considered a dialectic of mutual invitation between the poet and the group; the aim of the poet was to invite response by the group, which would listen and react as if there were no difference between poetry and life. Life meant poetry, and poetry meant life. The poem thus created correspondence, involvement and communication between the poet and his society.[10]

The root of the Arabic word shi`r, or "poetry," is derived from the verb sha`ara, meaning to 'know, understand, perceive.' Poetry and knowledge are inextricably linked in the Arabic language: the poet is one who knows, understands and perceives what others do not. The poet's special knowledge and insight is tempered by strict meter and rhyme, which allows communication of intense and inspiring feeling. The poet thus has a dual role of imparting knowledge and inspiring others.[11]

ANNUAL POETIC COMPETITION

Poets from all over Arabia used to meet and compete annually, gathering for their poetic contest at the Fair of `Ukaz, near Mecca, for rivalry and competition. During the fair, poets would recite their best poems before judges; a special tent would be erected for each poet and his band of reciters and supporters. The winning poem of the year, called the Mu`allaqah, would be announced at the end of the festival. Its words would be transcribed in gold letters upon fine Egyptian linen and hung—hence mu`allaqah, literally "suspended"—on the door of the Ka`ba in Mecca, a place of great honor. The winning poem would be heard and repeated all over Arabia by the next day.[12]

The winning ode thus brought honor to the poet and his clan, adding merit to their position among the tribes. The poet was a leader, savior and healer, never ceasing to bear witness to the most prestigious and unique qualities of his people. He was the singing witness of their heroism, bravery and generosity, inspiring zeal, strong emotions, and high morals through his powerful verses.

The poet was obsessed with the effect he could have on the souls of his listeners. What the poet said was not as important as the way he said things. There were also poetesses in pre-Islamic times; women were regarded as equals and companions, and they provided inspiration for the "poet to sing and the warrior to fight." Both male and female poets of the era used to recite their poetry while standing up and would gesture using their hands or whole bodies. The poetess al-Khansa' used to rock and sway, looking down at herself as if in a trance. Some poets dressed up to perform, as if the occasion were a wedding or feast.[13]

ORIGINS OF ARABIC POETRY

Arabic poetry was born in the sands and oases of ancient Arabia before Islam, the product of a common Arabic poetic language. This was a very formal language, refined in grammar and vocabulary, that evolved by the "elaboration of one particular dialect or perhaps by the conflation of several."[14] The same poetic language was used by poets from all different tribes for at least two centuries before the emergence of Islam.

The origin of this rich poetry, with its sophisticated metrical schemes and rhymes, is obscure. Earlier forms of Arabic poetry could have been fountain songs, love songs, hymns to idols or war chants. The particular environment of Arabia shaped the peculiarity of this poetry, and therefore its content and form were determined by physical Arabian life.[15] Arabic poetry may also have begun with the rhythmic and rhymed language used for incantations and magical spells, later developing into a refined art. The end result, of course, is certainly not primitive; it is the sophisticated product of a long, cumulative tradition. In addition to its significance in Arab tribal life, Arabic poetry was also a crucial element in the courts of great dynasties and empires.[16]

Two primitive types of ancient poetry existed in pre-Islamic Arabia. One was the *saj`*, or "rhymed prose," which had no meter, and consisted of rhymed lines of different lengths. *Saj`*, which has a beautiful rhythm, was originally used by ancient soothsayers in their maledictions, incantations and other kinds of magical sayings.[17] The second earlier type of poetry was called *rajaz*, made up of a single hemistich, or half-line of verse, but with no rhyme. Later, a new poetic form called the *qasida* appeared, replacing these two types of poetry and becoming the only complete form. Synthesizing and replacing *saj`* and *rajaz*, the *qasida* includes meter, rhyme and rhythm.[18]

Arab poets have now been imitating this *qasida* form for over sixteen centuries. It is a long poem built of verses, usually not shorter than twenty-five lines and not longer than one hundred. A constant meter—one of sixteen possible poetic meters in Arabic—runs throughout the poem, as does a single, constant rhyme that ends each line. A line consists of two hemistiches, or halves, of equal length, and each hemistich carries the same number of metrical feet as the other. The rhyme is carried in the first two hemistiches of the first line, then repeated in the second hemistich of every single line until the end of the poem in the form AA BA CA DA EA FA, etc. A hemistich is roughly equivalent in length to a standard line of European poetry.[19]

The two halves of each line comprise a single unit of meaning, and the continuity of thought and feeling is maintained from one line to another throughout the poem. The entire *qasida* thus follows one rhyme and one meter, and is unified in theme and style. The effect of this repeated rhyme and combination of meter is very striking, with verses "falling on the ears of the listeners like magic."[20] Many scholars believe that rhyme was the basic element that distinguished Arabic poetry from the poetry of other peoples. Rhyme in the *qasida* might have originated with earlier forms of ancient Arabian poetry, founded in the chant of the camel-driver to his beasts or in the shouts and cries of war. Arabic rhyme is made up of words and sounds whose rhythmic patterns developed into poetic musical units, leading to the discovery and use of meter. Having existed in earlier types of poetry, rhyme was more ancient than meter, and lent poetry its song-like nature.[21]

Arabic poetry has been described as a song. Classical Arab literary critic Ibn Rashiq, who lived in the eleventh century, once said that song originates with rhyme and meter: "Meters are the foundation of melodies, and poems set the standards for stringed instruments."[22] The response of the Arab audience to poetry is determined by the ability of the poet to make all parts of the musical instrument work together in performing his song.

The poet must co-ordinate the various elements of the poem in order to accommodate its special rhythmic requirements. Through its rhythmic structure, which forms the basis of pre-Islamic poetry, the poet becomes a "living energy binding the self to the others." The *qasida*'s rhythmic strength and fascinating musicality increases its suitability for memorization and repetition.[23]

There are seven, or some say ten, odes that are considered the greatest representations of ancient Arabic poetry. These poems, the *Mu`allaqat*, have survived among other accumulated bodies of ancient literature, and Arabs view them as supreme examples of the greatness of Arabic poetry. Translator and poet Omar Pound describes these poems as a "string of beads on which images are accumulated and juxtaposed one after the other," which psychologically and poetically links the poet with his audience.[24] The best known of these outstanding 'golden poems,' or literally 'suspended poems,' is the ode of Imru' al-Qays, son of a king and undisputed master of poetic verse.

> *O Friend – see the lightning there! It flickered, and now is gone,*
>
> *As though flashed a pair of hands in the pillar of crowned cloud.*
>
> *Nay, was it its blaze, or the lamps of a hermit that dwells alone,*
>
> *And pours o'er the twisted wicks the oil from his slender cruse?*
>
> *At earliest dawn on the morrow the birds were chirping blithe,*
>
> *As though they had drunken draughts of riot in fiery wine,*

And at even the drowned beasts lay where the torrent had borne them, dead,

High up on the valley sides, like earth-stained roots of squills.[25]

Because of its formal structure of meter, rhyme, and rhythm, classical Arabic poetry is very difficult to translate into other languages. Throughout the ages, almost the entire body of Arabic poetry has been composed in conformity with the strict rhythmic patterns of the *qasida*. Many scholars agree it is almost impossible to render a successful translation of poetry from Arabic into English or another tongue without losing the essential quality of the ode: "Neither the rhythm nor the mono-rhyme that occurs as the last syllable of each pair of half lines throughout the poem can be successfully imitated in Western languages."[26] Most translations of classical Arabic poetry into English or into other languages have not been very successful. Translating modern Arabic poetry is more successful, because modern poetry puts a greater emphasis on content than form.

CONTENT OF PRE-ISLAMIC POETRY

The Arabian poet's job was to provide a new treatment to subjects that his audience already knew, focusing on customary themes of elegy, praise and glorification of the tribe, as well as descriptions of battles, bravery, honor and other outstanding qualities. Other common themes included the community's love for dignified life, or courage in challenging death. Poets discussed victories, love affairs, and the hardship of life in the harsh environment of Arabia, describing sandstorms and desert scenes. They also recorded events and interpreted them, revealing their philosophy about life and death. The content of this genre of poetry is thus predictable. Mastery of the form lay in presenting such conventional and limited content with a new and innovative spirit, applying a practiced eye toward aesthetics and musicality, and leaving the audience with moral support and psychological strength.

The *qasida* generally follows a standard outline that contains several major thematic divisions. The poet starts with a descriptive opening scene on the sands, staring at the empty traces of the deserted encampment of his beloved, who had departed before his arrival. He reveals his love aloud to his absent beloved, and describes his powerful emotions and the long, difficult journey he had undertaken to see her. Standing in her deserted encampment, he is saddened by the little things that remain of her tent and weeps at her departure. He talks of her astounding beauty and her great moral qualities, but never reveals her true name to the audience. The poet wants to protect the identity of his beloved.

Alas! She set firm her face to depart, and went:

Gone is she, and when she sped she left us with no farewell.

Her purpose was quickly shaped—no warning she gave her friends,

Though there she had dwelt hard by, her camels all day with ours.

Yea, thus in our eyes she dwelt, from morning to noon and eve—

She brought to an end her tale, and fleeted, and left us lone.

So gone is Umaymah, gone, and leaves here a heart in pain:

My life was to yearn for her, and now its delight is fled.[27]

The love theme is a conventional opening, but there is real love behind it. The lyrics of the prelude reveal the sincere human emotions and personal experiences of the poet, using imagination, imagery, description and metaphor. Love is a human theme shared by all mankind, which is the reason Arab poets used it as a traditional opening.[28] The beginning of the poem had to be lyrically beautiful in order to draw the attention of the listeners. By sincerely opening his soul and emotions to the world, the poet showed the Bedouins' appreciation of love. In the words of the ancient Arab critic Ibn Qutaybah, the love poem "touches men's souls and takes hold of their hearts."[29]

My eyes turned back,

The camp was no longer visible—

My heart turned back.[30]

From the love scene, the poet smoothly moves into his second theme, a detailed description of his hardship and burden during the exhausting journey to search for his beloved. This section usually includes realistic descriptions of sandstorms, dunes, hunger and thirst, thunder and lightning, and other desert scenes. The poet may describe specific dangers he faced, including encounters with wild beasts or enemies, and his fight against all odds, survival and victory. He never neglects to praise his only companion, his horse or camel, with a loving tribute to the beast's endurance, steadfastness and selflessness. The images of this section are concise and intense, and the poet's words are carefully selected. Even if taken out of the poem, some individual lines could stand on their own, with a self-contained idea and imagery that transcends the poem's larger content.[31]

The third and main theme is devoted to glorifying the poet's tribe and deprecating his enemies. He praises his own virtues and the virtues of his tribe, most importantly its courage, loyalty, generosity, hospitality, reliability, solidarity, sense of justice, protection of the weak, struggle against the oppressor, and defiance of death. In this selection, the poet avows his undying loyalty to his tribe:

> *I am of Ghaziyya: if she be in error then I will err,*
>
> *And if Ghaziyya be guided right, I go right with her.*[32]

The emotional involvement of the poet results in highly charged and astonishingly beautiful verse. Because the thoughts and themes of the poem are connected to the desert environment, a physical setting that imposes conventional values, concepts and philosophy, these ideas might seem restricted in scope from the outside. To an Arab listener, however, all is realistic; the thoughts and aesthetics expressed in the poem are not only highly appreciated, but strengthen the human spirit.[33] The poem is like a ritual that celebrates the values of the tribe, such as its physical courage and endless hospitality, asserting life's pulse in the hostile physical environment of the desert.[34]

THE RECITERS

Poetry was composed to be recited in public, either by the poet himself or by a reciter. Each poet had his own *rawi*, or reciter, to commit his verses to memory and accompany him to his poetic recitations. A poet could have even several reciters. The fact that poetry was meant to be heard, not read, has certain suggestions and implications. A single line or number of words would be forced to convey a meaning that could be easily comprehended by his listeners. Additionally, this meant that poetry was usually experienced only in a performance setting, and that every performance of poetry was unique.[35]

Poetry was usually transmitted orally through recitation, but this does not mean that writing did not exist in pre-Islamic times. Arabic inscriptions pre-dating Islam have been found, including inscriptions in the languages of southern Arabia, that go back to the fourth century. During the early stage of writing, poems were written on whatever material could be found: flat stones, palm leaves, or even the bones of camels or donkeys. However, writing was expensive and therefore used rarely, and the system of oral transmission worked for the pre-Islamic Arabs. In addition to the poets themselves, professional reciters or narrators knew the poems by heart and were masters of the fine art of poetic recitation. Johannes Pedersen, a noted theologian and scholar of ancient Arabic manuscripts, writes that the *rawi* was a living "edition of the great poetry collections."[36]

Non-transcribed Arabic poetry reached a very developed stage, bound by fixed rules, rhythm and construction. Yet the poems were only handed down orally. Similarly, the Qur'an was transmitted orally until it was written down; throughout the history of Islam, oral transmission in many cases has proceeded alongside the written. Even if every copy of the Qur'an were to be burnt, it would still be alive, dwelling in the hearts and the memories of Arabs. This also applies to the poetry that preceded the Qur'an. However, because no poem could survive intact and unchanged after a few generations of such transmission, scholars have decided to accept as authentic only those poems dating from 150 years before Islam.[37]

POETIC ORALITY OF THE ARABS

The voice of the poet, as Adonis writes, consisted of "energy replete with signs." Arabs have always considered the recitation of poetry a talent and art in itself. The act of listening was essential to the comprehension of words and musical ecstasy. The better the recitation, therefore, the more profound and effective the poetry. The poets who recited their work were compared to singing birds, and their verses to birdsong, emphasizing the organic link between poetry and song. The Arab Bedouin was called the "essence of perfect eloquence." Alternatively, poetry formed a body whose joints were meter, rhythm and melody.[38]

The strong connection between poetic orality and the act of listening was reflected by the relationship of the poet to his audience. Poets composed for their audiences and others, not for themselves. For this reason, classical Arabic poetry avoids remote allusions and ambiguous suggestions, favoring realistic metaphor to abstract suggestion. Historian Jawad `Ali stresses that the Bedouin is a man of extraordinary memory, who "preserves things and never forgets them."[39]

The encounter between the poet and listeners was an act of participation in life. The poem was effective as a means of communication, and a recitation of poetry was similar to a spiritual gathering or communion.[40] Poet and critic Jamal Eddin Bencheikh writes that three overlapping rhythms take place during the encounter between poet and listener: the rhythm of the poem, the rhythm of the voice of the poet, and the rhythm of the body of the poet. Through these rhythms, the poem flows out warm, passionate, joyful and unique.[41] To be effective in recitation, the poet had to use great enthusiasm and passion. Arabic poetry was meant for loud declamation, featuring its pronounced rhetorical and musical features. The Arab poet has always pursued such an ideal, and several diverse and subtle innovations in poetry have since occurred within the framework of the classical forms.[42]

THE EVOLUTION OF ARABIC POETRY

The poetry of pre-Islamic Arabia has continued to be imitated as the model for writing poetry across the ages. It was the expression of a stable culture with common agreement on fundamental issues, and set the values of its own time as well as for all subsequent times. Pre-Islamic poetry reflected the spirit of its age; it was poetry of great simplicity, originality, purity and power. New themes developed with the emergence of Islam, as the art form began to reflect a more complex and sophisticated era. In the periods that followed the Islamic conquest, different sources of inspiration emerged. The themes of Arabic poetry became richer, and its modes of expression grew more refined. The nature of its audience changed as well, in taste, sensibility and expectation.[43]

New political motifs materialized after the death of the Prophet and his companions, as new trends appeared in politics and religion. As the Umayyad dynasty wrested political control of the still-growing Islamic empire in the seventh century, poetry began to reflect the ideologies of different political and religious parties struggling over the succession to the Caliphate. Some poets wrote revolutionary verse, calling for martyrdom for the sake of justice. They were influenced by the tragic death of Husayn bin `Ali at Karbala (an event whose significance will be more fully examined in chapter 6 on the Islamic Communities throughout the Ages). Pious poetry also emerged, incorporating vocabulary and ideas from the Qur'an into verse. The simple, desert life of the Arabs had changed, as cities were built, wealth increased and the Islamic empire expanded. An independent trend of love poetry also materialized. Although the theme of love had existed in the pre-Islamic poem and was built into the ode, Umayyad love poetry became an independent genre entirely devoted to love and romance. Two different trends of love poetry soon appeared: one of sensuous love, and the other of idealized, pure love, exemplified here by Jamil bin Ma`mar, known as Jamil Buthaynah:

> *I loved you before you were born*
>
> *And when we die, I shall hear your echoes.*[44]

A more famous example of the poetic genre of idealized love, which came into being during the Umayyad era, is the story of Qays bin al-Mulawwah, who immortalized his love for a girl named Layla through a series of passionate love poems. Layla's father, however, denied them permission to marry, sending Qays into madness; for this reason, Qays is often referred to as Majnoon, or "the crazy one":

My love-sickness is beyond all cure

When I pray I turn my face toward her,

Though the right direction is the opposite.[45]

During the Abbasid era, the golden age of culture for Arabic and Islamic civilization which spanned from the eighth to the thirteenth centuries, ethnic and sectarian communities worked together and contributed to the cultural output of the empire. Throughout this time, all sects were mostly integrated in cultural unity, with this 'spiritual mixture' of ethnicities contributing to the glory of Arabic and Islamic culture. Baghdad, the seat of the Abbasid dynasty, was the greatest cultural center of medieval Islam, and poetry from this age represented the highest levels of artistry and sophistication.[46]

Abbasid poets contributed greatly to the magnificence of their age, and they also influenced the European Renaissance in diverse ways. Two poetic schools emerged, the modernist and the neoclassical. Other themes and trends developed as well, including sensuous love lyrics, introspective and analytical poetry, didactic and religious poetry, and special poetry devoted to wine, panegyrics, philosophy and mysticism. The tenth century neoclassicist Abu al-Tayyib al-Mutanabbi is widely considered the greatest Arab poet of all time. Another giant, Abu al-ʿAla' al-Maʿarri, is described as the philosopher of poets and the poet of philosophers. Some Western critics believe that Maʿarri's *Risalat al-Ghufran*, or 'the Epistle of Forgiveness,' was one of the sources that inspired Dante to write his Divine Comedy.[47]

In Muslim Spain, poetry flourished as well. Although it began by imitating the great neoclassicist poets of the Abbasids, by the eleventh century it had acquired its own, unique character. Andalusian poetry was of peculiar importance to the West because, as Mounah Khouri observes, "Arabic and European literatures merged with a resulting influence on Western styles and modes of feeling." The most important form of poetry that emerged in Muslim Spain was the *Muwaššaha*, a complex love poem whose verses were made of rhymed strophes or stanzas, joined by a recurrent two-line envoi. Meant to be sung, it was usually composed in colloquial Arabic:

Will time

See us united even if only in sleep?

Or will my eye

See the face of one who thins my body

In night trips?

O my two guides riding on a night trip

> *Sickness in*
>
> *My heart recalling a meeting, ill!*
>
> *Dismounting*
>
> *At death, hail to the camp of death!*[48]

Music also became very popular in Andalusia, with European and Arabic popular songs contributing to the cross-fertilization of cultures. In the eleventh century, Ibn Hazm of Cordoba wrote the well-known masterpiece *The Dove's Necklace*, an essay on the psychology, anatomy and manifestations of love in joy and sorrow. Ibn `Arabi, of the thirteenth century, was the greatest Sufi poet of Muslim Spain.[49]

Along with the rest of Arab civilization, Arabic poetry began to decline in the thirteenth century, and reached its nadir in the sixteenth century, at which time the Ottomans rose to power and imposed their rule over the Arab world. After conquering Syria and Egypt and then dominating the entire region, the Ottomans would remain in power until the end of the First World War. With the end of the Abbasid Empire in the thirteenth century, and the Arab presence in Spain ending by the fifteenth century, what followed was a long period of decline in the poetic sphere and other aspects of Arab culture, as well. With few exceptions, the Ottoman rule was a period of literary and cultural decline, marked by an absence of originality, a "loss of vigor and an exhausted, inward-looking culture."[50]

It was not until the Arab awakening of the nineteenth century that Arabic poetry began to regain some of the aesthetic, semantic and traditional conventions of its past heritage, after it had suffered weaknesses caused by the harsh conditions "inflicted on the Arab world by the domination of the Ottoman Empire." The four centuries of Ottoman domination were the least culturally productive period in Arab history. Arabs grew disconnected with their intellectual and literary past and a cultural vacuum resulted. In the words of a major Arab critic, Arabic poetry, during the period of decline, "focused on trivial themes, becoming repetitive, artificial and completely lacking in substance.[51]

MOVING INTO THE TWENTY-FIRST CENTURY

During the Arab renaissance, a few decades into the nineteenth century, Arabic poetry began to develop anew. Its first phase of evolution lasted from 1834 until the beginning of World War I and is known as the period of neoclassicism. During this period, Arab poets imitated classical Arabic poetry of the past, particularly the Abbasid period, in form and content. This imitation was necessary to strengthen and revive Arabic poetry in a first step toward modernism.

The neoclassical period also featured adaptations and translations from Western and Eastern literatures.

The second phase, stretching between World War I and II, is known as the period of romanticism and nationalism. This was a tumultuous time for the Arab world, with some new Arab states being created and others waiting for independence. Political parties were formed, and the idea of Arab nationalism grew stronger. In 1948, the State of Israel was created, which had a massive impact upon Arabic literature. Since Israel came into existence, modern Arabic poetry has never since been entirely free from social or political commitment.[52]

The third and current phase of development began at the end of World War II. Immediately, the trend of romanticism in Arabic poetry was replaced by political and revolutionary themes. Poetic awareness of Arab social and national causes increased. Poets called for change, and poetry reflected the harshness of Arab reality. As a result, a sort of radicalism emerged in poetry, together with a debate over the nature and function of literature and the task of the Arab poet. Demand rose for literature written for the people, about the problems of the people, and in language the people could understand. Called the period of conflicting ideologies, this third phase had its own divisions and sub-phases. One sub-phase was marked by the Arab defeat of 1967, and another by the Gulf war in 1991. A third sub-phase began after the fall of Baghdad in 2003, and the age of cultural fragmentation continues.[53]

THE MODERNIST TREND

Early in the twentieth century, Many Arab poets began to abandon the content and form of conventional Arabic poetry, in a modernist movement that remains vigorous and dynamic. This was a radical movement that rebelled against cultural and literary conventions; modernist poets refused to imitate ancient Arabic poetry or regard it as the eternal model for imitation. Instead, they felt it was fixed, rigid, static, and did not reflect the spirit of the contemporary age. In fact, until approximately one hundred years ago, Arabic poetry was in an isolated state, having fallen way behind its glorious medieval achievements. Arab poets therefore experimented widely in an attempt to catch up with contemporary trends in world poetry. Poets also realized it was impossible to create a revolutionary Arab culture without making use of a revolutionary language.[54]

At this time, Lebanese writer Gibran Khalil Gibran (d. 1931) was emerging as a new cultural modernist voice. Along with other Arab poets who migrated to North America, mostly from Syria and Lebanon, Gibran was a real force in breaking with classical Arabic poetry. Perhaps the single most important influence on Arabic poetry in the first half of the twentieth century, Gibran released the art form from its conventional restrictions. Though he mostly wrote prose poetry, he influenced all poetic genres, using unprecedented imagery to open the windows on a new world. At the same time, a group of poets and critics in Egypt joined the forces of modernity and forged an important connection with the North American group. Without Gibran, poetess Salma Khadra Jayyusi wrote, "the development of modern Arabic poetry, would have been unrecognizable."[55]

Leading Arab poets of the free verse movement, which began in 1949, succeeded in pushing Arabic poetry further. Although certainly true that Gibran and other poets from all over the Arab world had paved the ground for such an innovation, the poets of the free verse movement more than anyone else, led Arabic poetry beyond the constraints of classical poetic forms. The pioneers transcended the traditional rhyme schemes and conventional metric patterns that had prevailed for over sixteen centuries, and departed from the substance and structure of classical Arabic poetry.[56] More details will be discussed in chapter 8 on modern Arabic poetry.

Since 1950, Arabic poetry has undergone constant experimentation. It has explored new realms of obliquity and metaphorical adventure, reflecting a sharp awareness of the political and social difficulties facing the Arab world. Today, many Arab poets are among the best in the world, such as, Adonis, Mahmoud Darwish, and Abdul Wahab Al-Bayati. Their poetry is extremely sophisticated and embraces all the themes of the human condition. Details will be discussed in chapter 8 on modern Arabic poetry.

CHAPTER FIVE

Islam, Muhammad and the Qur'an

ABOUT ISLAM

Islam is the fastest growing religion in the world. Founded by the Prophet Muhammad in the early seventh century, Islam now counts more than 1.6 billion followers, representing nearly all races and nations of the world. Islam is also the second largest religion, after Christianity, across both the United States and the world. A Muslim who accepts Islam as his or her faith believes the Qur'an is the word of God as revealed in the Arabic language to the Prophet Muhammad through the angel Gabriel. The basic principle of Islam is the Muslim's submission to only one God. Muslims accept the revealed texts of Christianity and Judaism as divine, and believe in prophets, justice, equality and the Day of Judgment. As a global whole, albeit a complex and diverse one, Muslims comprise a highly spiritual and powerful community that is growing increasingly important in the world's political and economic affairs.

When Islam appeared in the Arabian Peninsula in the year 610, the area was already rich in religious traditions, including Judaism and Christianity. Islam then spread over the peninsula to the north, east and west, creating a new Arabic and Islamic state throughout and beyond the domains of the two greatest empires of the time: the Byzantine Empire in the west and the Sasanian (or Persian) Empire in the east. The growth of Islam can be read as a new religious and political movement, born in the arena of world history.[1]

The word *Islam* in the Arabic language is the verbal noun from the verb *aslama*, meaning "to surrender and submit to the will of God," but this is not the only meaning of the word. *Islam* also conveys the idea not simply of surrendering before God, but of feeling a sense of greatness through becoming close to God and a sense of gratefulness toward the Creator who elevated man to Himself. In this sense, *Islam* implies a relation of love and gratitude between the Creator and the believer. *Aslama* also means to "hand something to someone," and in this sense, the believer hands himself or herself over entirely to God. Mohammed Arkoun, a leading Islamic scholar from Algeria, writes that *Islam* also means "challenging death," meaning the believer would challenge death by giving up his or her life for a noble cause or divine purpose. In the Qur'an, the prophet Abraham is called a Muslim, though he predates Muhammad, because he "obeyed God with great passion when he offered to sacrifice his own son for the sake of God." In this case, Abraham's sacrifice represents a testament to his faith.[2]

Islamic commentators insist that in order to fully understand Islam, it is necessary for the student or adherent to study both the Qur'an and the *Hadith*, a body of texts that relate the words and practices of the Prophet Muhammad.[3] Together, the Qur'an and the oral and written teachings of the Prophet constitute the nucleus of Islamic civilization.[4] Muslims consider the Qur'an to be the last divine revelation that completes and perfects all previous divine revelations. They believe Islam was sent not only to the Arabs but to all of humanity. And the Qur'an provides a textual basis for this belief: "We have sent you to all mankind as a bringer of good tidings and warning against sins."[5]

In practice, Islam provides moral guidelines for virtuous deeds and behavior that must be followed in daily life. Like other divine religions, Islam forbids evil deeds such as the bearing of false witness, arrogance to others, backbiting and the making of assumptions: "O believers! Avoid suspicion and negative assumption. Some suspicion is sin. And do not spy on each other or backbite."[6] Islam also forbids bad manners and indecency, both apparent and concealed: "My Lord has forbidden immoralities."[7] It is a way of life based on strong moral, religious and spiritual values that guide its laws and policies of ethical behavior and correct conduct.[8]

Also like other religions, Islam has developed over the centuries to encompass and embrace multiple sects and schools of thought. However, there is certainly a strong sense of unity among all Muslims. Islamic history has produced many schools of thought in philosophy, law, art and science, and its vast geographic reach includes many local social and religious customs that did not originate in Arabia. For example, the various unique methods of chanting the Qur'an, the fascinating varieties of Islamic calligraphy, and the diverse Islamic architectural forms and literatures worldwide are all encompassed by Islamic tradition. Islamic scholar Seyyed Hossein Nasr has written that, despite the diversity of Muslim peoples across the globe, every generation of Muslims is linked through time to the origin of the religion itself: "Islam is like a tree whose roots are in its revelation, and its entire tradition is linked to the roots and to the tree."[9]

Islam is seen by those who study it as not merely a set of beliefs. It is an all-encompassing way of life that includes codes of ethics, religious and civil practices, a legal system, and schemes for political and social organization. The Islamic system embodies the full range of "principles and precepts by which the believer should order his life."[10] Because Islam is based on both doctrine and practice, a believer cannot choose to follow only one. The broad reach of Islam into aspects of life not previously governed by religion, and Islam's declaration of the existence of only one God, were revolutionary concepts that marked a radical departure from pre-Islamic life in the Arabian Peninsula.[11]

THE PROPHET MUHAMMAD

Muhammad was born in the city of Mecca in the year 570, into the major Arabian tribe of Quraysh. Mecca, a city of cultural, geographical, and political importance, was also a commercial center, by virtue of its convenient location at a major crossroads of the ancient Arabian trade routes that linked the Mediterranean to the Indian Ocean. Ibn Hisham (d. 833), a biographer of the Prophet,[12] wrote that Muhammad was an orphan whose father, `Abdullah, died before his birth and whose mother, Aminah, died when he was six years old. After the death of his parents, Muhammad lived in the care of his grandfather, `Abd al-Muttalib (d. 578); upon his grandfather's death, Muhammad was sent to live with his paternal uncle Abu Talib, who took him on many caravan journeys to Syria.[13]

Within Meccan society, Muhammad enjoyed great respect. The people called him *al-Amin*, or "the faithful," as he was trustworthy and honest. The name *Muhammad* in Arabic is the passive participle of the verb *hammada* and means "one who is highly praised." His name appears in the Qur'an numerous times: "Muhammad is not the father of any of your men, but he is the messenger of God and the seal of the prophets."[14] Muhammad is also identified by the name Ahmad. In the Qur'an, Jesus said: "I am the messenger of God, sent to you confirming the Torah which came before me, and bringing good tidings of a messenger to come after me, whose name shall be Ahmad."[15]

At the age of twenty-five Muhammad married Khadijah, a highly respected and wealthy widow from the tribe of Quraysh. Muhammad then became a merchant and handled Khadijah's business while working in the caravan trade. Khadijah herself was to play a critical role in the coming of Islam, standing at Muhammad's side; as long as Khadijah lived, Muhammad married no other woman. Muhammad lost three sons before infancy and had four daughters, only one whom survived. This daughter, named Fatima, eventually married `Ali bin Abi Talib, a cousin of Muhammad. To Sunni Muslims, `Ali would become the fourth Islamic caliph, and to Shi`ite Muslims, he would become the first legitimate imam, and the most important figure in the history of Islam, after the Prophet Muhammad.[16]

Even prior to receiving the divine revelations, according to the biographies written of him, Muhammad had always been a spiritual man. He used to retreat into a cave called *Hira'* on a hill north of Mecca in order to meditate in isolation. There he would shelter himself for long periods in solitude, mulling over his life and his society, in search of meaning and wisdom.[17] It was inside this cave during the month of Ramadan when Muhammad received his first revelation. He was forty years old at the time. The night of this first revelation became known as *Laylat al-Qadr*, or "the night of power," taking place on the twenty-seventh day of Ramadan. In the words of the Qur'an itself: "We have indeed revealed the Qur'an in the Night of Power. The Night of Power is better than a thousand months. Therein come down the angels and the Spirit by God's permission on every errand."[18]

This first revelation terrified Muhammad. While inside the cave, he suddenly heard a voice commanding him to "recite in the name of the Lord who has created, created man out of a clinging substance. Recite! And your Lord is the most generous, who has taught by the pen, taught man that which he knew not."[19] The spirit Gabriel, or *Jibril* in Arabic, was the bearer of this commanding revelation, which was repeated three times. Muhammad panicked, rushed home in fear, and asked his wife Khadijah to cover him with blankets for warmth, pleading with her to shield him from this divine presence. But the revelation persisted, and more verses were revealed: "O, you who wrapped up with a garment. Arise and warn, and your Lord glorify."[20]

While the voice Muhammad heard during his revelations varied, sometimes sounding like echoing signals, in the later chapters of the Qur'an it grew constant, identified as that of the angel Gabriel.[21] As on the first occasion, when the Prophet received these divine revelations, he would enter an unconscious and trancelike state: he would "sweat profoundly, even on a cold day, and [feel] an interior heaviness."[22] In his later years, the Prophet spoke of his revelations and said, "Never once did I receive a revelation without feeling that my soul was being torn away from me."[23]

Muhammad's revelations lasted for twenty-two years until 632, during which time the Qur'an was revealed gradually to completion. During those years, the Prophet had to listen to the divine words with great attention in order to interpret the meaning of the visions, as they did not always materialize verbally or with clarity.[24] The Prophet explained that "the revelation sometimes comes unto me like the reverberations of a bell, and that is the hardest upon me; the reverberations abate when I am aware of their message."[25] Armstrong noted that the effort of listening to and interpreting the revelations was an enormous strain on Muhammad, as he was not only working through an entirely new political solution for his people, but composing one of the great spiritual and literary classics of all times. Because Muhammad was in fact illiterate, he is considered only an instrument of God: the transcriber of divine revelation, but not the author of the Qur'an.[26]

THE MESSAGE OF ISLAM

The message of Islam is simple and straightforward: It is to believe in and worship God. Islam stresses to its followers that there is only one God, who is the all-powerful creator of the universe, and that Muhammad is His Messenger. Muslims believe in angels, all previous divine Scriptures, all prophets from Adam to Jesus, the Day of Judgment and the Decree of God. The Qur'an tells its followers of the rewards in Paradise for those who carry out God's commands, and warns of punishment in hell for those who disregard them. This message is summarized in a clear and direct verse: "O believers, believe in God and His Messenger, and the Book that He sent down upon His Messenger, and the Scripture that He sent down before. And whoever disbelieves in God, His angels, His books, His messengers, and the Last Day, has certainly gone far astray."[27] This verse also illustrates the Qur'an's recurring emphasis that Islam is not a wholly new faith, but rather represents a return to the true faith of Abraham: "We revealed to you to follow the religion of Abraham, the true in faith."[28]

The pre-Islamic world did not accept Islam immediately or easily. As Islam developed, so too developed a clash between Islam and the old pre-Islamic beliefs and practices of ancient Arabia. Islam, as noted by scholar Constantine Zurayk, was a continuer and "preserver of earlier traditions, yet essentially it represented a discontinuation and revolt against the past."[29] For one, Islam demanded that ancient Arabians abandon their long-held traditions and practices, such as idolatry and the worship of many gods, in addition to their tribal loyalties, in favor of the One and Only God and the Islamic nation, or *umma*. Suddenly, Arabs were being asked to worship only one God and to be loyal to only one community, a community that now included members of rival tribes. Esposito noted that the message of Islam posed a serious threat to the existing social, political and economic interests of the powerful ruling authority of the city of Mecca, the legitimacy of which was based on the ancient traditions that Islam explicitly rejected. Many Arabians rejected the Prophet's teachings because he brought revolution and turmoil into their lives.[30]

Muhammad was indeed a revolutionary, preaching against the superstitious ideas of ancient, polytheist Arabia with its entrenched rituals, conventions and practices. He also challenged social convention by reaching out to the oppressed and poor, calling for social justice and equality. Crucially, Muhammad demanded the transcendence of tribal bonds for the sake of the Islamic religion. Among the early converts to Islam in Mecca were Muhammad's wife Khadijah, her cousin Waraqa bin Nawfal (who had been a Christian), `Ali ibn Abi Talib (Muhammad's cousin, who converted to Islam at a very young age and later married the Prophet's daughter, Fatima), and Abu Bakr (one of Muhammad's closest companions, a merchant from the tribe of Quraysh, who would become the first caliph).[31] These early converts proved very valuable personalities to Muhammad. He needed the support and sympathy they provided during that critical time of early Islamic history, especially while the powerful and influential tribal aristocrats of Quraysh remained uncompromisingly aggressive and hostile to his message.[32]

After suffering persecution in Mecca, the Prophet Muhammad decided to leave Mecca in 622 and travel to Medina, the native city of his mother, where he was accepted with respect and honor and where his divine revelations continued. This proved a successful decision as well as a turning point in Muhammad's life, and is considered more important to Islamic historians than the date of Muhammad's birth or the date he received his first revelation. This particular day of migration from Mecca to Medina on September 24, 622 is known as *al-Hijra*, or "the migration." The *Hijra* marks the beginning of the Islamic era, when Islam became a political reality.[33] Seventeen years later, `Umar bin al-Khattab, the second Islamic caliph, designated the lunar year in which the *Hijra* took place as the "official starting point of the Muslim era."[34]

Muhammad and his initial followers had to struggle for survival, first in Mecca and then in Medina, against those who opposed Islam and who were prepared to use force against the Islamic *umma*. In her foundational book, *A History of God*, religious scholar Karen Armstrong wrote that Muhammad is often presented in the West as a warlord who imposed Islam on a reluctant world by force of arms. The reality was quite different: it was Muhammad who was fighting for his life, trying to teach a new religion without imposing it, and thus Muhammad "evolved a theology of the just war in the Qur'an with which most Christians would agree, and never forced anybody to convert to his religion."[35]

During Muhammad's time in Medina, another important event occurred: during a dream, the Prophet took a mystical journey to Jerusalem and ascended to heaven. The Qur'an relates that Muhammad was miraculously transported at night from Mecca to the site of the Temple of Solomon in Jerusalem, at or near the location where now stands the Dome of the Rock: "Glory be to God who did take His Servant for a journey by night from the Sacred Mosque to the Farthest Mosque whose district We did bless, so We might show him some of Our signs."[36]

According to the story, the angel Gabriel ascended with the Prophet during his journey, through the seven heavens to the Divine Throne, where Muhammad was greeted by all the great prophets including Moses, Jesus and Abraham. Muhammad "preached to them and took their advice" and all the Prophets recognized Muhammad, honored him, welcomed him, and listened to his insights.[37]

This story has become the "archetype of Muslim spirituality because it symbolizes the ascent all Muslims must make to God's level and the Source of

Being."[38] After Muhammad's dream, Jerusalem—a city already sacred to both Jews and Christians—became the third holiest city in the Muslim world (after Mecca and Medina), as it served, in the words of historian Philip Hitti, as the terrestrial station for this dramatic nocturnal journey. The journey, which remains a powerful, living, and moving force in Islam, forms the basis for the profound connection that Muslims feel toward Jerusalem, a connection begun some fifteen centuries ago.[39]

Once the Islamic state had succeeded in Medina, the Prophet concentrated his efforts once again on Mecca. Mecca was not only the political, economic and intellectual center of Arabia; it had also become the designated *qibla*, or the direction for prayers for Muslims. In 628, the Prophet signed a treaty with the Meccans, ending his conflict with his own powerful Quraysh tribe. A number of powerful personalities within Quraysh converted to Islam at this time, among them Khalid bin al-Walid and `Amr bin al-`As. These converts were to provide great support to the Prophet, contributing to the success of the Islamic cause. In the year 630, Muhammad entered Mecca and smashed the 360 idols in the city, declaring: "Truth has come and falsehood has vanished." Remarkably, Muhammad entered Mecca and took control of the city without any resistance or bloodshed. He treated all the Meccans, even his former enemies, with fairness, granting a general amnesty to Quraysh and all other tribes, regardless of whether or not they converted to Islam, "[h]ardly a triumphal entry in ancient history is comparable to this."[40]

Once re-established in Mecca, the Prophet took steps to consolidate his gains. He declared the territory around the *Ka`ba*, the first temple built by Abraham and Isma`il, as sacred.[41] He forbade the polytheists from approaching the *Ka`ba* during the annual pilgrimage, and one year later reached peace treaties with the Jewish and Christian tribes. By Muhammad's orders, local Jews and Christians were protected within the new Islamic community. And the year following Muhammad's re-conquest of Mecca is known in Islamic history as the "year of delegation," in which tribes from all over, including Oman and Yemen, sent delegates to Mecca to offer their allegiance to the Prophet. And Arabia, which throughout its entire history "had never before bowed to the will of a single man, was now under Muhammad's control and integrated into the new Islamic empire."[42]

Islam soon spread to Western Asia and North Africa. And for the first time in Arab history, Islam became the "basis of social organization and structure, replacing the old bonds of kinship and tribal affiliation."[43] The Prophet Muhammad was now the chief of the state, and all the people within the new community of Muslims were brethren, regardless of race or color. This new Islamic community "changed the entire social and political life of the Arabs, as well as the Arabic concept of loyalty."[44] Faith became more important than tribal kinship. The new community had no hierarchy or priesthood, and the mosque became the public forum of the community and its place of worship. Muslims began to protect one another against the perceived hostility of the non-Muslim world. Muhammad was able to unite people who "had never previously united, in a country that had not until that point constituted more than a geographical expression. He had laid the social foundation for empire."[45]

THE ISLAMIC *UMMA*

The creation of this new social order was perhaps the most novel of all the Islamic precepts: the Islamic *umma*, or the pan-Islamic community. Muhammad insisted that his followers unify as one group in order to bind and connect all believers. Albert Hourani said that this concept of *umma* has always been of great importance to Muslims, as it provides not only social unity, but a strong feeling of belonging to a well-defined religious society that transcends the often divisive human characteristics of race, gender and class. And that the *umma* creates social, political and religious bonds among Muslims who see themselves as a group with unique characteristics.[46] The Qur'an itself defines the Islamic *umma* as "the best of peoples evolved for mankind: enjoining what is right, forbidding what is wrong and believing in God."[47] Islam reinforces this unity by teaching that through understanding and obeying the commandments of God, all men and woman will create not only the right relationship with God, but also with each other.[48]

John Esposito wrote that the *umma's* purpose aims higher than the simple unification of Muslims. According to the Qur'anic vision, the *umma* is a 'community of mission,"[49] aiming to create a new and ethical social order. In other words, the Qur'anic mandate to the *umma* was to become a nation that should "enjoin what is right and forbid what is wrong," exemplifying these ideals for other nations. The Qur'an also envisions the Islamic *umma* as arbitrator of the people,[50] serving as a "'just witness" in order to ensure justice for all: "We have made you a community so that you will be witnesses over the people and the Messenger will be witness over you."[51]

Zurayk stated that the idea of the Islamic *umma* was difficult and revolutionary because, prior to its introduction, Arab society was highly fractured, divided into tribes whose members were fiercely loyal to one another. In contrast to the then-existing piecemeal social structure, thus the creation of the *umma* required all Muslims to join as one community. Muhammad counseled his followers that Islam commands the "primary loyalty of all believers."[52] Zurayk emphasized that this is not surprising, because this new idea of *umma* was introduced to an Arab society filled with complex and pre-existing loyalties to tribe and clan, such loyalties were not so easily shed. During Islam's formative period and throughout its history until today, tensions between tribal and Islamic affiliations have persisted.[53]

THE FAREWELL SERMON

At the height of his glory, after the re-conquest of Mecca and the establishment of the Islamic *umma*, the Prophet Muhammad led a humble and unpretentious life. He had no wealth and regarded the small amount of property he possessed upon his death as state property. He lived in a clay house and was often seen mending his own clothes, remaining at all times within the reach of his people.[54] The Prophet's modest way of life and his straightforward daily behavior constituted a canon that millions of Muslims around the world still observe with deliberate imitation. Prophet Muhammad is considered by Muslims to be the "perfect man," and his recorded behaviors and deeds are emulated to minute detail.[55]

By the end of Muhammad's life, most Arabian tribes had become part of the Islamic *umma*, and all of Arabia was under his control. In the year 632, the Prophet led the annual pilgrimage to Mecca and gave a sermon in which he summarized the state of the Islamic *umma* and the "essence of Islam." This was to be his last visit to the city as well as his last public sermon, now known as the Farewell Sermon.[56] In this sermon, the Prophet proclaimed the ancient Arabian pagan rites of *hajj*, or the annual pilgrimage, to be Islamic. He also articulated the beliefs and practices of Islam, stressing the importance of equality and justice:

> "O men! Hearken unto my words and take them to heart. Know that every Muslim is a brother to every other Muslim, and that you are now one brotherhood. It is not legitimate for any of you, therefore, to appropriate unto himself anything that belongs to his brother unless it is willingly given him by that brother. Worship your lord and Sustainer. Perform your five daily prayers. Fast the month of Ramadan. Make pilgrimage to Mecca and the Ka`ba. Pay alms on your property willingly and obey what I command you. Then you will enter the Paradise of your Lord. All of you descend from Adam and Adam was made of earth. There is no superiority for an Arab over a non-Arab nor for a non-Arab over an Arab, neither for a white man over a black man, nor a black man over a white man, except the superiority gained through consciousness of God. Indeed, the noblest among you is the one who is most deeply conscious of God."[57]

Soon after his Farewell Sermon, the following Qur'anic verse was revealed to Muhammad: "On this day I have perfected for you your religion, and completed my favor upon you, and approved for you Islam as religion."[58] Three months later, the Prophet went to Medina for a visit, where he fell ill and died on June 8, 632. By all accounts, religious or secular, traditional or historical, Armstrong said, Muhammad was a man of exceptional genius who managed to bring nearly all the tribes of Arabia into a new, united community. Also, more information is known about Muhammad than about the founder of any other major religion.[59]

ISLAM AS THE RELIGION OF ABRAHAM

The Qur'an clearly and repeatedly denies that Islam is a new religion, instead proclaiming it the culmination of all existing religions and the religion of Abraham (*Ibrahim*). Esposito noted that Islam teaches that the three divine religions of Judaism, Christianity and Islam are all branches of the same family, as all three stemmed from the children of Abraham. Jews and Christians are descendants of Isaac (Abraham's son from his wife Sarah), while Muslims are the descendants of Isma`il (Abraham's firstborn son from his Egyptian concubine, Hagar).[60] The Qur'an contains an entire chapter on Abraham, entitled *Surat Ibrahim*. The Bible also mentions Hagar as Abraham's concubine who gave birth to Isma`il, while Sarah, Abraham's wife, bore Isaac. Though Isaac and Isma`il were brothers, Sarah insisted out of jealousy that Abraham get rid of Isma`il and Hagar.[61, 62]

Under this pressure from his wife, Esposito wrote, the Prophet Abraham took Hagar and Isma`il to the valley of Mecca, where he left them on their own.[63] The Qur'an relates that, though abandoned, God protected and cared for them: when the child Isma`il began to die of thirst, a well of water was revealed. This well became a sacred spring to Muslims, who named it *Zamzam*. Moreover, years later when Abraham returned to visit Isma`il, together they built the *Ka`ba*, the first temple of the One God, on the same sacred ground of *Zamzam*.[64] Muslims also believe it was at the location of the *Ka`ba* in Mecca where Abraham sacrificed Isma`il. Though the Bible narrates a story in which Abraham's son Isaac was sacrificed near the site later to be Jerusalem,[65] the Qur'anic account relates that it was Isma`il who was chosen to be sacrificed, and in Mecca. Similar to the Biblical account, however, the Qur'an explains that God saved Isma`il from this sacrifice through divine intervention.[66]

Armstrong stated that God's act of saving Isma`il's life in Mecca helped define Islam's independence from all other religions and greatly influenced the practice of Islam. Afterwards, God promised Isma`il he would be the father of all the Arabs; in commemoration of this, in 624, the Prophet Muhammad commanded Muslims to change their direction of prayer, the *qibla*, toward the now-holy site of Mecca rather than Jerusalem. Muslims ever since have prayed facing downward in the direction of the *Ka`ba* and declaring they belong to an independent, established religious faith.[67] By praying to Mecca in this manner, they honor the "primordial religion of Abraham, who had been the first Muslim to surrender to God and who built his Holy House."[68] Despite its declaration of independence from Judaism and Christianity, however, the Qur'an emphasizes that Islam, like Judaism and Christianity, is the religion of Abraham: "We shall follow the true religion of Abraham, who joined no gods with God."[69]

THE QUR'AN

> *"Had We sent down this Qur'an upon a mountain you would have*
> *seen it humbled and coming apart from fear of God."[70]*

The Qur'an is the first book of prose written in the Arabic language. While it is a great source of pride and inspiration for Muslims and Arabs alike, for Muslims it is also a source of spiritual strength. In physical size, the Qur'an is approximately four-fifths the size of the New Testament. It was revealed to Muhammad over a period of twenty-two years, and consists of 114 chapters, 6,239 verses, 77,934 words and 323,621 letters.[71] Each *sura*, or chapter, in the Qur'an begins with the *basmala*, the formulaic phrase "in the name of God, the most merciful, the most compassionate." Though it is among the most widely read book ever written, and has been translated into almost every language, only the Arabic language fully captures its religious power and literary beauty, as the Qur'an itself acknowledges: "We have made it an Arabic Qur'an that you might understand."[72]

While most non-Muslims are aware that the Qur'an is the religious text of Islam, many are unaware of its significance to more aspects of Islamic life than just religious philosophy. Practically every young Muslim, for example, learns to read Arabic by studying the Qur'an. In its original Arabic text, the Qur'an demonstrates and proves the remarkable depth and richness of the classical Arabic language: there are ninety-nine Arabic names for God, as represented by the ninety-nine beads in a full Muslim rosary.[73] The Qur'an has also served as the textbook for Muslim students beginning their study of science, theology, and jurisprudence. Hence, the Qur'an represents the heart of the Islamic religion, or a "guide of a Kingdom of Heaven," but is also very much a scientific and political document, embodying a code of laws for a kingdom on earth.[74]

Twenty years after the Prophet's death, Muslims became aware of an urgent need to compile a final and official version of the Qur'an, as the number of individuals who had memorized the Qur'an straight from Muhammad's lips steadily decreased. Muhammad used to recite out loud each segment that was revealed to him. During The Prophet's lifetime, the Qur'an was committed to memory by his closest companions, and some parts were written down. The earlier text of the Qur'an had been constructed and compiled in unofficial versions, both from memory and from passages written on "ribs of palm-leaves and tablets of white stone and from the breasts of men."[75] Islamic historians agree that the finalized, canonical text of the Qur'an was completed during the reign of the third Islamic caliph, ʿUthman bin ʿAffan (d. 656). According to Majid Fakhry, a scholar of Islamic philosophy, the authorized version of the Qur'an was called *Mushaf ʿUthman* in honor of this caliph, and has been called *Mushaf ʿUthman* ever since.[76] After completing the official version, ʿUthman ordered that all other existing copies of the revelation be burned and destroyed.

Perhaps surprisingly, the chapters of the Qur'an are not arranged in the order in which they were received, but rather in reverse chronological order; the earliest chapters, revealed to Muhammad in Mecca, appear at the end of the Qur'an, and the later verses, revealed to him in Medina, appear at the beginning. This order of the Qur'anic chapters is not arbitrary, Armstrong noted, because the Qur'an does not present a purely chronological narrative or a sequential series of arguments. The Meccan chapters were revealed to Muhammad during a period of struggle; correspondingly, they are short, fiery and powerful, focused on the "Oneness of God" and his divine attributes.[77] In contrast, the chapters revealed to Muhammad in Medina were revealed during a time of victory, during the building of the Islamic state. Consequently, these longer chapters contain theological dogmas, legislation, and fiscal and military ordinances, as well as civil and criminal laws that govern topics such as marriage, divorce, and how to treat enemies and prisoners of war. Armstrong also notes that throughout the revelations, God "seems to comment on the developing situations," answering questions from the Prophet about the significance of a battle or a conflict.[78]

The first and greatest of the Qur'anic dogmas is *la ilaha illa Allah*, meaning "there is no god but God." Because there is only one true God, the sin of *shirk*, often translated as "polytheism" or "associating other gods with God," is unforgivable. This concept of only one true God stands supreme in the Qur'an;[79] Hitti estimates that over 90 percent of Muslim theology centers around this principle alone. The second Qur'anic dogma is *Muhammad rasul Allah*, meaning "Muhammad is God's prophet and Messenger," which means that Muhammad is "the last of a long line of prophets of whom he is the seal." In addition to proclaiming only one God whose messenger is Muhammad, the Qur'an also tells of the Day of Judgment, the day of resurrection and the afterlife, hell, reward and punishment, depicting the afterlife as involving bodily pains and physical pleasures and describing the resurrection of the body.[80]

THE INIMITABILITY OF THE QUR'AN

Muslims believe Arabic is the language of God and the Qur'an was written by God, and thus the Qur'an is perfect, eternal, and unchangeable. In other words, the Qur'an is inimitable in its language, style and ideas. One verse in the Qur'an proclaims: "If the whole of mankind and *jinn* gathered in order to produce the like of this Qur'an, they could not produce the like of it, even if they backed up each other with help and support."[81] The language of the Qur'an is unusual and extraordinary; it is neither poetry nor prose, relying on neither meters nor rhymes. It is believed to be a mix of something supreme and inexplicable. In the words of scholar John Esposito, the Qur'an constitutes the divine, "transmitted to the Prophet through angelic mediation."[82] Furthermore, the Qur'an is written in very dense and highly "allusive, elliptical speech," and the chapters of the Qur'an are composed of a "human language crushed and splintered under the divine impact."[83]

Perhaps due to the beauty of its language as well as its message, the Qur'an has played a significant role in the proliferation not only of Islam but of the Arabic language itself. The Qur'an exemplifies the finest and most elegant literary Arabic style with language that is powerful, rich, and highly sophisticated in morphology and syntax—all the while retaining its clarity and splendor. Scholar Munzir Al-Kabisi noted because of the Qur'an, the Arabic language throughout history has maintained its strong, correct, and dynamic character through the foundation it provides for understanding Arabic philology and grammar, resisting corruption and distortion despite numerous foreign intrusions.[84]

The Qur'an does not translate well into other languages; its beauty, complexity and sophistication simply cannot be recreated in a language other than Arabic. When reading the Qur'an in a language other than Arabic, therefore, Muslims feel they are reading an entirely different book. Armstrong comments that reading the Qur'an is a spiritual discipline that Christians "may find difficult to understand," because "Christians do not have a sacred language."[85] The Arabs of Muhammad's era, famous for their love of poetry and poetic skill, were amazed by the language of the Qur'an. Many converted to Islam because they believed only God could create such astonishingly beautiful language. There are many Islamic stories, including one related by Muhammad's first biographer, Ibn Ishaq, detailing such conversions. For example, `Umar bin al-Khattab, an authority on Arabic poetry and prose who would ultimately become the second Islamic caliph, immediately converted to Islam when he heard the miraculous verses from the Qur'an recited. Ibn Ishaq reports that the beautiful words were like magic penetrating `Umar's soul and changing his consciousness: "When I heard the Qur'an, my heart was softened and I wept, and Islam entered into me."[86]

The beauty of the Arabic text of the Qur'an is most fully expressed when recited verbally. Literally translated, the Arabic meaning of the word Qur'an is "recitation." Indeed, when hearing the Qur'an recited, those literate in the Arabic language feel enveloped in divine dimensions, captivated by its voice and significance. The Qur'an itself counsels the reader to experience it through recitation, stressing the power of its sounds: "Say, it has been revealed to me that a group of jinn listened to the Qur'an and said: we have really heard an amazing recitation."[87] Qur'anic scholar Muhammad Mahmoud `Abd al-`Alim, is also of the opinion that only through verbal recitation can people understand the meaning of the Qur'an, as the words "penetrate the hearts, the souls and the minds of the believers."[88] Thus, the Qur'an is not a "book to be read simply to acquire information; it is meant to yield a sense of the divine and must not be read in haste."[89]

To properly emphasize its sanctity, there is a ritual attendant to the verbal recitation of the Qur'an that Muslims have always considered as significant as the meaning derived from the words themselves. When verbally reciting any of the Qur'anic chapters, the reading is preceded by the phrase "I take refuge with God from Satan, the accursed one," followed by the basmala that begins each sura. Then the chapter is recited, ending with the phrase "God almighty has spoken truly." Scholar Malise Ruthven noted that this opening and closing formula establishes a "sort of verbal ritual enclosure or sanctuary around the recital text, preserving it from evil promptings or insincerity."[90] It is also required that Muslims be in a state of ritual purity when they read the Qur'an, as none but those who are "clean in body, mind, thought, intention, and soul can achieve real contact with its full meaning."[91] To achieve the proper state of ritual purity, Muslims must perform ablution, discussed below.

THE PILLARS OF ISLAM

The structure of Islamic belief and practice, including the act of worship, rests upon five pillars (though some believe the duty of Jihad constitutes a sixth). The first pillar is the Shahada, or Declaration of Faith, which is summarized in a formulaic phrase:

"I bear witness that there is no god but God and Muhammad is the Messenger of God."

This absolute belief in the Unity of God and Muhammad's status as His Messenger is fundamental, and any person who declares it to be true in this manner is considered a Muslim.[92]

The second pillar of Islam is the Salat, or "prayer," which the Qur'an declares to be a fundamental trait of a believer: "Establish prayer ... and obey the messenger of God, so that you may receive mercy."[93] The *Salat* is considered the best method of forming and strengthening a relationship with God; as with other divine religions, Muslims believe that constant consideration of God can not only purify the spirit but restrain and prevent the commission of sins. One verse in the Qur'an summarizes this belief: "Prayer prohibits immorality and wrongdoing, and the remembrance of God is greater. God knows that which you do."[94]

Muslims are required to perform *Salat* five times daily, based on the position of the sun. The first prayer of the day is at dawn *(fajr)* and ends just before sunrise. The noon prayer, *zuhr*, starts after the sun has crossed its zenith and begun its decline. The third, mid-afternoon prayer, `asr, starts when the sun begins to decline in the late afternoon; the fourth prayer, *maghrib*, begins immediately after sunset and lasts till dusk. The fifth and final prayer of the day is called `isha', and starts after dusk has disappeared and given way to the darkness of night. The *Salat* is performed in a ritual prostration, with a combination of physical movements and mental concentration.

Prayer must be performed in a state of spiritual purity, accomplished by ritual ablution, or *wudu*. To perform ablution in preparation for prayer, the Qur'an requires the Muslim to wash his or her whole face, particularly the mouth and nose, as well as his or her hands and arms to the elbows, and feet to the ankles.[95] A complete ritual of ablution, in which the entire body is washed and cleansed, must be performed before prayer in certain circumstances, such as following sexual intercourse or the flow of blood from any part of the body, including menstruation. The washing is accompanied by uttering words that glorify God. In situations where water is unavailable or when illness or travel impedes ablution, the Qur'an grants latitude: "If you are ill or on a journey, or one of you comes from the place of relieving, or if you have contacted women and do not find water, then seek clean earth and wipe over your faces and hands with it. God does not intend to make difficult for you, but He intends to purify you and complete His favor upon you, that you may be grateful."[96]

Salat can be performed in any place but must be performed while facing Mecca. The *imam*, who is the leader of the Friday prayers, delivers a sermon every Friday at noon in the mosque, where all members of the Muslim community gather. Women worship in a special section of the mosque behind the men.

In addition to the daily *Salat*, Muslims devote an entire month to prayer. Ramadan is celebrated throughout the Islamic world as a month of profound worship, during which Muslims focus on the study of the Qur'an. Religious and social events are observed, and it is obligatory for each healthy, adult Muslim (though exceptions exist) to fast the entire month, every day from dawn to dusk. This fasting during the month of Ramadan, called *Sawm* (or *Siyam*) in Arabic, constitutes the third pillar of Islam and, like *Salat*, is a very important form of worship. The Qur'an states: "O believers, decreed upon you is fasting, as it was decreed upon those before you, that you may become righteous."[97] Throughout the fast, Muslims are forbidden to eat, drink, smoke or engage in sexual activity. While providing certain health benefits, such as allowing the digestive system to rest and the body to break down its reserves of fat and accumulated toxins, fasting also creates a sense of equality between rich and poor, as all feel the hunger of poverty. This shared experience is intended to teach tolerance, patience, and virtue, while simultaneously creating an ideal time for meditation to strengthen faith. For Muslims, fasting expresses obedience to God and adherence to His teachings. Ramadan thus plays an important role in instilling compassion for others and strengthening the spiritual bonds between Muslims around the world.

In addition to *Sawm*, Muslims observe other rituals during Ramadan, such as on *Laylat al-Qadr*, the twenty-seventh day of Ramadan that marks the date on which Muhammad received the first Qur'anic revelation. Muslims commemorate this occasion by staying awake throughout the night, praying and reading the Qur'an. In Jerusalem, for example, tens of thousands of Muslims on *Laylat al-Qadr* attend prayer services at the Dome of the Rock, for the Qur'an promises that prayer on this night will not go unheeded.[98] There is also a nightly prayer during Ramadan called *Salat al-Tarawih*, which is very popular with large numbers of believers and done in a group setting before dawn.[99] Ramadan ends with a feast called `*Eid al-Fitr* or breaking of the fast.

Muslims also increase their charity and the giving of alms during Ramadan. This alms-giving is the Islamic concept of tithing, constituting the fourth pillar of Islam, known as *Zakat*. The Qur'an obliges Muslims to pay a certain percentage of their wealth for the benefit of the needy. Though the payment of *Zakat* is left to the believer's conscience, those who are wealthy pay a set amount of their wealth based only on assets that generate revenue and surplus funds. *Zakat* is part of the Islamic concept of social justice, which helps establish social solidarity and unity among Muslims. The Qur'an describes those who do not give *Zakat* as "disbelievers" in the hereafter.[100]

The fifth pillar of Islam is the *Hajj*, or the annual pilgrimage to Mecca. The *Hajj* takes place in the last ten days of the lunar month *Dhu al-Hijjah*, reaching its climax with `*Eid al-Adha*, or the Feast of Sacrifice. At this time, Muslims come from all corners of the earth in a collective religious festival to pray in groups, seek repentance and worship the one God together. While ancient Arabs participated in an annual pilgrimage to Mecca that was unrelated to Islam, Islam adopted the ritual as its own, subsequently requiring all adult Muslims—financial and physical circumstances permitting—to make the *Hajj* at least once in their lifetime. While

Muslims may make similar pilgrimages throughout the year to visit the holy sites of Mecca, this lesser pilgrimage—called `Umra, or visitation—cannot replace or substitute for the *Hajj* obligation that all Muslims are to fulfill.

During the *Hajj*, Muslims visit the holy sites of Mecca to commemorate important Islamic events and people. They visit the *Ka`ba*, the House of God built by the Prophet Abraham, which the Qur'an states is the first place of worship ever built on earth.[101] The *Ka`ba* is a large black cubical structure located in the center of the Grand Mosque in Mecca, and is the direction Muslims face during their prayers. It is also the focal point of the *Hajj* ceremony, as it holds the secret black stone given to the Prophet Abraham by the angel Gabriel as a symbol of God's covenant with Isma`il and the Muslim community.[102] To commemorate Muhammad, Abraham, Hagar and Isma`il, pilgrims also stand in the same place near Mount Arafat where the Prophet Muhammad gave his last sermon in the year 632. The act of standing in the holiest places of Islam leaves an "everlasting mark on the spiritual life of Muslims, connecting them in a magical way."[103]

Though the *Hajj* involves the visitation of Meccan holy sites, it is not simply a sightseeing tour. The physical demands put on the pilgrims are significant, as they participate in numerous symbolic rituals. One such important ceremony is the circumambulation, wherein the pilgrims walk seven times around the *Ka`ba* while wearing traditional white garments that erase, at least visually, all differences in race, class and rank. Before they begin the circumambulations, the *Hajj* pilgrims cry in unison, "Here I am at your service, O God." Iranian religious philosopher and sociologist `Ali Shari`ati wrote vividly of this rich spiritual experience:

> As you circumambulate and move closer to the Ka`ba, you feel like a small stream merging with a big river. Carried by a wave, you lose touch with the ground. Suddenly you are floating, carried on by the flood. As you approach the center, the pressure of the crowd squeezes you so hard that you are given a new life. You are now part of the people; you are now a Man, alive and eternal.[104]

Other *Hajj* rituals are reenactments of significant events that occurred in Mecca. For instance, after their circumambulation of the *Ka`ba*, the pilgrims run between the hills of *Safa* and *Marwa*, located a short distance from the *Ka`ba*, to commemorate Hagar's act of running between those same two hills in search of water for Isma`il. In her desperation, she was saved by God who commanded her to strike the ground with her feet, causing water to gush forth miraculously from the spring *Zamzam*. Water from this spring is treasured, and the pilgrims store water from the spring in bottles to take to their relatives and friends.[105] Another ritual reenactment of *Hajj* is "Stoning the Devil." This ritual takes place just outside of Mecca in the desert plain of *Mina* to commemorate Abraham's obedience to God and defeat of the *Shaytan*, or "Devil." Tradition has it that during Abraham's own pilgrimage to Mecca, the Devil appeared to him three times, attempting to dissuade him from sacrificing his son in fulfillment of his duty to God. Each time the devil appeared, Abraham stoned him with seven stones, rejecting his temptations and driving him away. To honor this event and openly declare their enmity to the Devil, the pilgrims also "stone the Devil."

The stoning of the Devil takes place on the plain of *Arafat* at the place on the hill called the Mount of Mercy, where Muhammad gave his last sermon. The night preceding the ritual, the pilgrims sleep on the plain of *Muzdalifah* and collect between forty-nine and seventy pebbles. For the next three days, they throw seven stones at each of the three pillars of *Mina*, which represent the devil and mark the places where the failed temptations occurred. It is a particularly emotional experience for many of the pilgrims, some of whom become so entranced at the thought of physically confronting the Devil they can be heard screaming, "Because of you, I did."[106] After the ceremony, many male pilgrims may shave their heads, symbolizing rebirth and the cleansing of their misdeeds; women, in turn, may trim a lock of their hair. The stoning of the Devil, along with a final circumambulation of the Ka`ba, completes the ceremonial rituals of the *Hajj*.

The *Hajj* concludes with the feast of sacrifice called `*Eid al-Adha*, which is celebrated by Muslims worldwide simultaneously with the pilgrims in Mecca, and commemorates God's demand that Abraham sacrifice his eldest son Isma`il. The feast begins with communal prayer, followed by the ritual sacrificing of sheep, cattle, goats or camels, symbolizing how Abraham was finally permitted to sacrifice a ram instead of his son. The celebration lasts for three days, and many pilgrims take the opportunity to visit the mosque and tomb of the Prophet in Medina before returning home.[107]

ISLAM AND THE WEST

Many Muslims and Arabs believe that the people of the West hold a generally negative view of Islam. Acceptance of this idea has broadened and deepened in the years following the attack on the World Trade Center in September 2001, and the emergence of extremist groups claiming to be inspired by Islam such as al-Qa`ida and Da`ish (ISIS).

Belief in a cultural war waged by the West on the Middle East is widespread. Some scholars argue this perceived cultural war began after the fall of the communist threat, while others trace it to a much earlier time. Most, however, agree that September 11 and the rise of certain groups brought a new intensity to the "global war" against Islam and to popular anger, hatred, and distrust of Muslims in the West.

Some historians and scholars in the Muslim world trace the West's hegemony to the Napoleonic invasion of Egypt in the late eighteenth century. Since that time, in their view, the West has treated the Islamic and Arabic world with a certain arrogance, often conspiring to control and even prevent its development. Philosopher Muhammad Jabir Al-Ansari, and other intellectuals believe the West was biased against Islam from the very beginning, waging a political, economic and military war against Islam before any dialogue between them had taken place. Due to the lack of communication and interaction, the political equation was imbalanced from the start.[108] And still other scholars believe the relationship between Islam and the West has simply always been one of mistrust.[109]

Other Muslim intellectuals and academics have frequently disputed the West's description of Islamic culture as fanatical, violent or terrorist.[110] It should be remembered that all ancient and static texts, including the Old and New Testaments of the Bible, can be, and often are, interpreted at will by the observer, depending on his or her judgement, background and education. Both scholarly and popular Muslim readings of the Qur'an conclude that Islam neither promotes nor aims to create a world consisting of only one culture. In the Qur'an, society is envisioned as a system of human interactions between many varied cultures, civilizations and races, and between many different nations and languages. In fact, Islamic thinker Muhammad `Imara advises that in order to achieve happiness in this world and the afterlife, the Qur'an calls for coexistence and cooperation among all peoples. In this and many other verses, the Qur'an emphasizes this universal vision of Islam: "Of His signs is the creation of the heavens and the earth and the diversity of your languages and your colors. In that are signs for those of knowledge."[111]

Compare `Imara's inclusive and universal description of the ideal Islamic worldview with the Clash of Civilizations theory propounded by the American political scientist and scholar Samuel Huntington, who argues that the post-Cold War era would be marked by civilizational conflict. Huntington writes that cultural differences, such as religion, history, language and tradition, are beginning to divide people, and that, as these divisions deepen, confrontations and conflict between cultures will correspondingly increase. This cultural conflict, according to Huntington, will infect global and international politics. He warns that Western civilization should be concerned about Islam because it is a different civilization, with a population convinced of its cultural superiority while obsessed with its inferiority. Islam has "bloody borders," in Huntington's view; furthermore, he sees the global war on terror as not a modern phenomenon, but rather the culmination of a millennium-long history of conflict between the West and the Islamic world, beginning the day Islam entered Europe for the first time in the eighth century.[112] Muslim intellectuals, for their part, tend to believe that the very foundations of Islam, as interpreted by the world's Muslims, neatly repudiate Huntington's argument, along with other social theories that are premised on the idea of unavoidable conflict between cultures and religions.[113]

This discourse ties in neatly with many observers' critiques from within the Islamic world of the current course of globalization, which they see as overly capitalist, greedy, out of control, and bent on cultural as well as economic domination of Muslims worldwide. `Abd al-Salam al-Masdi, for example, an Arab intellectual and linguist, reasons that Islam forbids "globalization"—whose ultimate endpoint he defines as creating a society without significant diversity—because Islam demands a world filled with a variety of cultures, civilizations and ethnicities.[114] Similarly, Arab intellectual Muhammad Mahfouz also rejects Huntington's notion that the world can only function in a paradigm of clashing civilizations, though he does believe there is a "project of globalization" afoot, by which the West intends to make the entire world one huge consumer market for its goods.[115]

The Western public has been ill-served by the majority of its experts, academics and media sources on the issue of Islam and violence; the complexities of the topic do not make for satisfying sound bites or thirty-second informational slots on cable news shows featuring the opinions of certain people about Islam especially those who have spent little time in the region. Islam does not condone physical violence as a method of dealing with others, though it does not deny its followers the right to self-defense. Crucially, the Qur'an states: "Fighting has been enjoined upon you while it is hateful to you."[116] Muslims are counseled by the Qur'an to fight only out of self-defense or when resisting oppression: "Permission has been given to those who are being fought because they were wronged. God indeed will give them victory."[117] Such verses of the Qur'an were revealed for reasons in the past and for particular historical circumstances, or when the Islamic expansions faced difficulties. In the modern world, this distinction clearly relies on how to define "oppression" and "resistance." Many Muslims have come to feel militarily and/or culturally oppressed, and believe fighting has become a necessary reaction to the confrontation from the West.

According to Muslim intellectuals, however, an important distinction is that these Muslims do not seek to "reduce the West or to dominate its civilization and culture," but rather wish only to protect themselves from a similar end.[118] Even though Islam is based on diversity, tolerance and the acceptance of others, this argument goes, it does not require acceptance of its own destruction. Ideally, the Qur'an teaches its followers to try to repel evil with good: "Not equal are the good deed and the bad deed. Repel evil by that which is better. He who between you and him is hatred will become as a devoted friend."[119]

Years before the World Trade Center bombing, Islam overall seemed a distant and alien culture to many Westerners. Edward Said once characterized the modern Western world's impression of Islam as "part fiction, part ideological label, part a minimal designation of a religion called Islam."[120] This impression is still the same. It goes without saying that there exist gross inaccuracies and factual errors about Islam in the West. Ultimately, the negative terms by which public discourse in the West tends to define Islam has prevented the true and mainstream nature of Islam, as a peaceful, non-violent religion, from being seen. Even President George W. Bush, who is known for his questionable policies in the Arab world, repeatedly described Islam as a peaceful religion. The West has perceived the Islamic world as antipathetically troubled. The Western media has done little to dispel the negative stereotypes; as a result, many of these stereotypes have now become ingrained in Western culture. The perception has been reinforced by the emergence of al-Qaʿida and ISIS and the new phenomenon of suicide bombing and killing of innocent civilians in Europe, the United States, and elsewhere practiced by extremist groups. These militant groups are what appear on Western media outlets, but they represent neither the mainstream view of Arab people nor the true religion of Islam.

Not surprisingly, therefore, a correspondingly strong belief exists within the Arab and Islamic worlds that Westerners are ignorant of, and prejudiced toward, the religion of Islam, and that the West acts in negative and unfair ways in their dealings with Muslim societies. Many Muslim intellectuals believe it is the Arab world's duty to educate the West about the profound and complex cultural and intellectual dimensions of Islamic tradition in order to change these negative views of Islam. These intellectuals indict the media for the damaging role they played over the last decades, even before the emergence of al-Qaʿida and ISIS, portraying killings, assassinations, and explosions as the only worthwhile news from the Middle East.[121]

Mohammed Arkoun points out that such violent acts are a relatively new phenomenon in the Muslim world, and it is unfair to generalize these historically recent events as representative of the entirety of Arab and Islamic history.[122] Interestingly, unlike most of his peers, Arkoun had believed that the negative image of Islam as a "violent and terrorist" religion would be corrected in the near future, heralding the reemergence of the spiritual, intellectual and cultural aspects of Islamic and Arabic heritage. Western and Islamic societies are experiencing a period of transition: as people are now preparing themselves for this "coming horizon," the violence still exists on both sides of the cultural divide. These painful events cannot last long, as societies "cannot live continuously in a state of conflict and violence."[123] Such vision of an improved image of Islam would have been hopeful. But the developments following the emergence of ISIS and other militant Islamist groups after the invasion of Iraq in 2003 have left little doubt that this vision may not soon be fulfilled.

CHAPTER SIX

The Islamic Community throughout the Ages

THE PROPHET MUHAMMAD'S DEATH in 632 brought about an instant political crisis within the Islamic community, which at that time consisted of three main groups: the prominent men in Medina who had entered into a treaty with the Prophet; the leading Meccan families; and the Prophet's earliest companions, who had followed him from Mecca to Medina in 622.[1] Among the latter group was the Prophet's father-in-law Abu Bakr, and it was Abu Bakr who announced the news of Muhammad's death to the *umma*, stating "O men, if you worship Muhammad, Muhammad is dead. If you worship God, God is alive." Abu Bakr stressed the urgent need for the *umma* to immediately select a successor, and the Prophet's companions convened a meeting for this purpose. Despite some who believed the Prophet would have chosen `Ali bin Abi Talib, his son-in-law and relative, as successor, the *umma* elected Abu Bakr instead.[2] The leaders of the *umma* also chose this time to define the political structure of the Islamic community. Because they wanted to preserve the *umma* as it existed during the life of the Prophet, united under a single leader, they decided the new leader would assume all of the Prophet's duties and follow his exact model, excluding of course the receipt of prophecy.

The English word *caliph* is derived from the Arabic word *khalifa*, an abbreviation of *khalifat rasul Allah*, or the "Successor to the Messenger of God." In this way, Abu Bakr became the first Islamic caliph and leader of the *umma*.[3] All of the first four caliphs were among the Prophet's earliest and closest companions: Abu Bakr, `Umar bin al-Khattab, `Uthman bin `Affan, and `Ali bin Abi Talib. They strictly adhered to the original conception of the caliph as continuing in the Prophet's footsteps and, as such, they are known as *al-Khulafa' al-Rashidun*, or the *Rightly-Guided Caliphs*. These four caliphs steered the *umma* from 632 to 661, assuming all the Prophet's responsibilities: leading the Friday prayers, delivering the sermons, and commanding the army. They succeeded in expanding the Islamic state beyond Arabia, and each played a significant role in Mecca and Medina. Their combined period of rule is widely considered to be as "formative as that of the Prophet himself."[4]

The Rightly-Guided Caliphs developed the cities of Mecca and Medina, strengthened the Islamic communities, and concentrated on unifying the *umma*.

They built armies, expanded the Islamic State, and maintained the alliances Muhammad had made with the Byzantines and others. With their combined military efforts, all of Arabia came under Muslim control. During the rule of ʿUmar, the second caliph, Muslims conquered Iraq, Syria, Palestine and Egypt; during the rule of ʿUthman, the third caliph, Muslims reached North Africa and Cyprus. Though they spent most of their time in the Islamic capital of Medina, the Rightly-Guided Caliphs were never cut off from Mecca and traveled there often with their families and associates.

One advantage that the Rightly-Guided Caliphs lacked, according to Islamic tradition, was of course Muhammad's personal divine link; God had provided direct guidance to the Prophet on all matters facing the Islamic *umma*, from military strategy to jurisprudence, and upon his death, the "door of Divine revelation was closed."[5] The subsequent caliphs, who became responsible for promulgating Islamic law and settling disputes, therefore used the Qur'an and the oral tradition of the Prophet's personal practices and sayings, known as the *Sunna*, in place of Muhammad's direct instructions from God. Those who accepted these practices and teachings became known as *Sunni* Muslims. Promulgating laws for the community was no easy task, although Muhammad's teachings and examples contained an implicit universalism. And as the Islamic community grew, so did the complexity of the issues it faced. Abu Bakr, like all who would succeed him, faced greater and more complicated issues than the Prophet himself had ever confronted.[6]

THE FIRST ISLAMIC CALIPH

Abu Bakr (d. 634), who lived an extremely simple life as caliph, led the *umma* from 632 to 634. During the first six months of his rule, Abu Bakr traveled daily back and forth from his home in *al-Sunh*, where he lived in a modest house with his wife Habiba, to the Islamic capital of Medina. He received no stipend for his work. Over his two years as leader, Abu Bakr worked aggressively to maintain the unity of the *umma* and continue the Prophet's work. In the years just before Muhammad died, for example, Muhammad had sent military forces to the Byzantines, as well as emissaries to the rulers of other states, and these alliances seemed likely to dissolve after his death. Yet Abu Bakr maintained these alliances and succeeded in consolidating central Arabia under Muslim control, ultimately uniting Arabia by defeating tribes that tried to break away from the *umma* in the Wars of *Riddah*, or "apostasy".[7] Through his efforts and leadership, Abu Bakr created an Islamic army and expanded Muslim territory, while maintaining peace among the Arab tribes.[8]

COMMANDER OF THE FAITHFUL

The second caliph, `Umar bin al-Khattab (d. 644), ruled from 634 to 644, and was known as *Amir al-Mu'mineen*, or the "Commander of the Faithful." Due to the merciful manner in which he treated those he conquered, Muslims and Arabs revere him as the paragon of fairness and justice.[9] During his rule, the Arabs came to control Iraq, Syria, Palestine and Egypt. They defeated the Persian forces at the famous battle of *Qadisiyyah* in 637, and the following year, they succeeded in conquering Jerusalem. As the Islamic empire grew to include the provinces of the Byzantine Empire and part of the Persian/Sasanian Empire, the political frontiers of the entire Near East changed. The Arabs evolved into a structured society, no longer resembling a disorganized tribal horde but rather a unified, professional force.[10] They neither compelled nor encouraged those they conquered to convert to Islam; the Jews and Christians of the new Muslim lands simply acquired *dhimmi*, or "protected," status, and were permitted to continue practicing their own faith, in exchange for paying a poll tax. In fact, Armstrong said that the Roman Christians, who had long suffered persecution by the Greek Orthodox Church, greatly preferred Muslim to Byzantine rule. All the lands Muslims conquered were left to the original inhabitants, in return for a rent paid to the Muslim state. Further, the Muslim troops were not permitted to live among the conquered people; instead, the Muslims lived in garrison towns (*amsar*), according to the ascetic virtues of the Prophet Muhammad.[11]

Like Abu Bakr before him, `Umar lived an unpretentious lifestyle as caliph. He supported himself by trade and was idolized as the embodiment of piety, justice and simplicity, all the virtues Muslims believed a caliph should possess. He owned only one shirt and one mantle, both of which were "conspicuous for their patchwork."[12] He slept on a bed of palm leaves and, as tradition has it, concerned himself only with safeguarding the purity of Islam, maintaining justice, and preserving the security of Islam and the Arabs.[13] Despite his great success, however, the Commander of the Faithful was assassinated in 644 by a Persian man who is said to have harbored a personal grudge against `Umar.

Less than a century after the death of the Prophet, the Islamic Empire extended from the Pyrenees to the Himalayas, the Muslims having achieved great military victories over the two world empires, Persia and Byzantium. Muslim forces had accomplished this territorial expansion and occupation of non-Muslim communities without forcing non-Muslims to convert to Islam.

THE THIRD ISLAMIC CALIPH

After `Umar's assassination, a committee of people whom he had personally select-
ed for this task named `Uthman bin `Affan (d. 656) as the third caliph. `Uthman, a
successful merchant who had amassed great wealth, ruled from 644 to 656. He had
been a close friend of Abu Bakr, and like Abu Bakr and `Umar, `Uthman was pious
and unassuming. He spent part of his nights in prayer and fasted every second day.
`Uthman was known for his generosity, as he donated a good portion of his wealth
to the welfare of the Muslim community and the supply of the Muslim armies. In
spite of his wealth, he lived very humbly, sleeping on bare sand in the courtyard of
the mosque.[14]

`Uthman's first few years as caliph were outwardly marked by great success:
the Islamic army conquered additional territory, including Cyprus and Tripoli,
extending the boundaries of the Islamic empire as far as Afghanistan, the River
Oxus in Iran, and the Sind in the Indian subcontinent.[15] An Arab fleet was developed, which achieved the first great naval victory over the Byzantines in 655.[16]
However, `Uthman's actions as ruler did not please the entire Islamic community.
As a member of the inner core of the tribe of Quraysh, `Uthman followed a policy
of appointing members of his own clan as provincial governors. This practice angered many Muslims, particularly the sons of the Prophet's early companions, the
Prophet's wife, `A'isha, and tribes in Kufa and other regions who resented Meccan
domination. `Uthman also alienated the Muslims in Medina by giving the most
prestigious official posts to members of his own Umayyad family. He appointed
Mu`awiya bin Abi Sufyan, whose father had been an enemy of the Prophet, as
the governor of Syria. The tension created by these acts eventually caused a split
within the Islamic community; `Uthman was eventually murdered, ushering in an
era of civil war between Muslims.[17]

THE LAST OF THE RIGHTLY-GUIDED CALIPHS

After `Uthman's assassination, the office of the caliphate remained vacant for
several days until `Ali bin Abi Talib (d. 661) was finally elected the fourth Islamic
caliph. `Ali would rule for only five years, from 656 to 661. The first cousin and
son-in-law of Muhammad, `Ali had been very close to the Prophet. He grew up in
Muhammad's own household, married his daughter Fatima, and was the second
person to convert to Islam after the Prophet's wife, Khadijah. `Ali was also a great
soldier, who fought with great distinction in all the early Islamic battles. It is said
the Prophet gave him the title of "The Lion of God."[18] Furthermore, `Ali was a
gifted writer and scholar of Arabic literature, grammar and rhetoric. His sermons

and letters are esteemed as models of great prose, and many of his epigrammatic sayings have been preserved. His creative works are collected in the book *Nahj al-Balagha*—"The Peak of Eloquence"—an eloquent work capturing ˋAli's wisdom, philosophy and thought.

Although the vast majority of Muslims accepted ˋAli as caliph, he faced opposition soon after his election. The relatives of ˋUthman and ˋA'isha, among others, disputed the validity of ˋAli's election. In response to his dissidents, ˋAli moved the Islamic capital from Medina in Arabia to Kufa in Iraq. He fought the rebels and dissidents in Basra and discharged the governors ˋUthman had appointed, replacing them with those loyal to him. Muˋawiya bin Abi Sufyan, however, refused to obey ˋAli's order discharging him. Muˋawiya who was appointed by ˋUthman as the governor of Syria, had the support of the wealthy Meccan clans who were fellow members of the Quraysh tribe. In an act of further defiance, Muˋawiya demanded that ˋAli avenge ˋUthman's murder by punishing those who were guilty of killing him. Others joined Muˋawiya's demand for revenge, including ˋA'isha and some of the Prophet's early companions. ˋAli was unable to discover the identity of ˋUthman's murderers. Thus, the resulting civil strife within the Islamic *umma* lasted for five years.[19]

By 657, the conflict between ˋAli and Muˋawiya intensified to the point of armed conflict. Their armies met at the Euphrates River near the present-day Syrian city of Raqqa in the Battle of *Siffeen*, but the fighting ended when both sides agreed to arbitrate the issue of who would be caliph. This arbitration ended with Muˋawiya deposing ˋAli and declaring himself caliph. Meanwhile, a radical group of ˋAli's followers had refused to participate in the arbitration; they believed ˋAli, as the rightful caliph, should never have submitted to arbitration or accepted compromise. In their view, arbitration was tantamount to surrender, an act the true caliph should never abide. This group became known as the *Kharijites*, derived from the Arabic verb *kharaja*, meaning "to come out or leave the hold." The Kharijites repudiated ˋAli for his surrender, yet refused to recognize Muˋawiya's claim to the caliphate, as they considered it illegitimate. However their call for *Jihad* went unheeded by the mainstream, which considered it a diversion from the Islamic *umma*.[20]

After losing the caliphate, in 661, ˋAli was assassinated by a Kharijite in Kufa.[21] ˋAli was believed to have inherited some of the Prophet's extraordinary qualities, and his betrayal by both friends and enemies has made him a "symbol of the inherent injustice of life" for millions of Muslims ever since.[22] Those who remained loyal, or partisan, to ˋAli became known as *Shiˋite* Muslims, derived from the Arabic word for *partisan*.

UMAYYADS SEIZE THE CALIPHATE: 661–750

His rebellion complete, Mu`awiya bin Abi Sufyan moved the Islamic capital from Kufa to Damascus, where he ruled from 661 to 680 as the first Umayyad caliph. The term *Umayyad* refers to those descended from Umayya bin `Abd Shams, the great uncle of Prophet Muhammad and great grandfather of Mu`awiya. Though `Uthman had also been a descendent of Umayya, as well as a cousin of Mu`awiya, the Umayyad dynasty officially begins with Mu`awiya because he was the first to assert the Umayyads' right to rule based on a dynastic principle. The death of `Ali, the last Rightly-Guided Caliph of Islam, thus brought an end to the first phase in the history of the Islamic *umma*. Mu`awiya assumed the caliphate and thereafter turned succession into an inherited right based on bloodline rather than election by the community.

The Umayyads had been planning to take over the caliphate even during `Uthman's reign, and as soon as Mu`awiya seized power, the Islamic *umma* fell under the rule of the elites.[23] The Umayyads according to Moroccan historian Abdallah Laroui practiced coercive ideology and exploited religion purely for overt political purposes. And that Mu`awiya and his successors, propagated the "pre-destination doctrine" in order to absolve themselves of guilt for the many injustices they perpetrated. By claiming all acts were simply "fated acts ordained by God under their rule in the name of God," the Umayyad caliphs avoided the need to further justify any of their actions.[24]

`Ali's elder son Hasan accepted a pension from Mu`awiya in return for agreeing not to pursue his claim to the caliphate, and while the Umayyads rose to power, he withdrew from Islamic politics. A year later, he was murdered in Medina. After his death, the Shi`ite followers of `Ali called upon Husayn, `Ali's younger son, to claim the caliphate. So in 680, when Mu`awiya died and his son Yazid became caliph, Husayn led a small group of supporters, along with their children and wives, to Kufa, where they planned to join their Shi`ite comrades in confronting Yazid and reclaiming the caliphate.

THE MASSACRE OF HUSAYN

Although the Shi`ites of Kufa encouraged Husayn's uprising and intended to fight with him, the local Umayyad governor forced them to withdraw their support. Husayn, his family and the seventy others with him were thus met outside the city of Kufa, on the plain of Karbala, by the caliph's army of thirty thousand men. In spite of the overwhelming force against him, Husayn refused to surrender, and he and his group were slaughtered. Yazid's army first beheaded Husayn's child, whom he held in his arms, and then Husayn himself. Husayn's other infant son, `Ali bin

Husayn, somehow survived the melee. Yazid's army carried Husayn's head on the tip of a spear all the way to the Sunni caliph in Damascus, six hundred miles away.

The massacre of Husayn and his followers by the Umayyads solidified the division between the Shi`ite and Sunni sects, and the issue of the rightful succession of the Prophet would divide them forever. Both sides disagreed not only on who should lead the Islamic community, but also on what role the leader should assume.[25] Like the murder of `Ali himself, the Battle of Karbala came to "symbolize the chronic injustice done unto the Shi`ites by Sunni hands".[26] Shi`ites all over the world now celebrate the holiday of `Ashura` in honor of the martyrdom of Husayn at Karbala. His death is viewed as a voluntary sacrifice made for the good of the community, an implicit promise that God will one day restore the right order of things.[27]

The day of `Ashura` falls on the tenth day of *Muharram*, the first month of the Islamic lunar calendar. It is a solemn day of mourning. Shi`ites dress in black and march through the streets while chanting and slapping their chests, and some imitate the suffering of Husayn by whipping themselves with chains.[28] The mourners also form processions symbolic of Karbala and recite moving poems about the tragedy. The theme of martyrdom recurs throughout Shi`ite history; eleven of the twelve Shi`ite imams (`Ali and his direct descendants) all died as martyrs.[29]

DEPARTING FROM THE WORLD OF THE PROPHET

With Damascus as the new capital of the Umayyad caliphate and power concentrated in one family, the *umma* appeared to be moving away from the world and political order envisioned by the Prophet. The Umayyads were secular leaders who developed an administrative system of government similar to that of the Byzantine Empire. They expanded the territory of the Islamic empire by replacing the Muslim Arab troops who had reached North Africa with regular paid forces.[30] They then took Kabul and Bokhara in central Asia, while simultaneously pressing westward toward the Atlantic in North Africa. Once they controlled the Mediterranean and North Africa, they crossed into Spain.

Despite the apparent progress of conquest, many Muslims believed the Umayyads were rejecting the ways of the Prophet and sought to bring the *umma* back to a righteous, divinely-ordained path. Opposition to the Umayyads was widespread, though especially intense in Persia, where the heavy-handed Umayyad domination was resented. The Persians would later ally themselves with the Abbasids, or descendants of `Abbas, the uncle of the Prophet; the Abbasids eventually overthrew the Umayyads in 750.[31]

However their subjects and contemporaries viewed them, the Umayyads made several important and lasting contributions to the history of Islam during their rule. They erected the first great building of distinction in the Islamic civilization, namely the Dome of the Rock in Jerusalem, built on the Temple Mount in Jerusalem. This building encircles a huge rock located in its center from which, according to the Qur'an, the Prophet Muhammad ascended to heaven during his Night Journey. The Dome of the Rock has survived intact since its completion in 691 by the Caliph `Abd al-Malik; it is the "most enduring Islamic architectural treasure and the first major Islamic monument."[32] The dedicatory inscription reads: "This dome was built by the servant of God `Abd al-Malik bin Marwan, emir of the faithful." It was created to assert the supremacy of Islam in the holy city of Jerusalem, which had a large Christian majority at that time. As such, it carried the message that "Islam had come to stay."[33]

The Umayyads also built the Umayyad Mosque in the old city of Damascus, one of the largest and oldest mosques in the world. The construction of this mosque took eight years, and its roof and dome are coated in gold. The mosque contains a prayer niche that faces Mecca, lined with precious stones and illuminated by the sunlight filtering through its seventy-four windows. The shrine of Saint John the Baptist and the tomb of Saladin are both located inside, and the structure itself is a masterpiece of architectural originality. Some believe that on the Day of Judgment, Jesus Christ will descend on one of its spires. Considered by Muslims to be one of the holiest mosques in the world, the Umayyad Mosque serves as a symbol of a splendid period of Islamic civilization. It became an architectural model after which other Islamic mosques were patterned, and its beauty and majesty draws visitors from all faiths. Pope John Paul II visited the Umayyad mosque during his visit to Syria in 2001.

In spite of these contributions to the glory of Islamic tradition, the rule of the Umayyads featured chronic controversy and opposition. In addition to their old Shi`ite foes, who organized many revolts against them throughout their reign, during the last decade of the dynasty the Umayyads were forced to contend with the Kharijites, as well. The Kharijites believed that `Ali and his descendants were the only legitimate imams, and that one day one of the Shi`ite imams would arise to inaugurate the rule of justice. This expectation of the coming of a *mahdi* (Arabic for "he who is guided") arose early in the history of the *umma*, and would become a recurring theme throughout Islamic history.[34]

THE ABBASID CALIPHATE: 750–1258

A group of descendants from a different branch of the Prophet's family, the Abbasids, opposed the Umayyads and organized a coalition of Shi`ites and Kharijites against them. These opposition forces, after numerous battles, eventually defeated the

Umayyads in the years 749 and 750, and the last Umayyad caliph, Marwan II was pursued to Egypt, where he was killed. In fact, all members of the Umayyad ruling family were massacred except those who escaped to Spain; one of these was `Abd al-Rahman I, who fled to Cordoba and ruled there as an Umayyad prince in 756.[35]

After defeating the Umayyads and claiming the caliphate, the Abbasids named Abu al-`Abbas al-Saffah as caliph, who ruled from 750–754. Abu al-`Abbas relocated the Muslim capital from Damascus to Kufa, Iraq, and it was in Kufa that he was proclaimed leader of the *umma*. He wore the Prophet's sacred mantle as a symbolic gesture to show that he represented the time and eternity of the Islamic community.[36] In return for the Shi`ites' help, Abu al-`Abbas had promised them that their spiritual leader, Imam Ja`far al-Sadiq (d. 765), the great grandson of Husayn, would succeed him as caliph. However, when Abu al-`Abbas died in 754, his son Mansur murdered Imam Ja`far and seized the caliphate for himself, crushing the disappointed Shi`ite wing of the movement that had brought the Abbasids to power in the first place.[37]

After murdering Imam Ja`far, Mansur ruled as caliph from 754–775. He moved the capital from Kufa to Baghdad, where one hundred thousand men labored for over four years to create the powerful center of the Abbasid dynasty. In Baghdad, court officials guarded access to the caliph, and the important position of *wazir*, or "top minister," emerged within the caliph's office. This position, which had begun as an adviser to the caliph, soon evolved into the head of the caliph's administration, and the term would be later adopted by the Ottoman Turks as *vizier*, chief adviser to the sultan.

The Abbasids concentrated their power in the caliph's office and developed a powerful intelligence system, wherein administrators reported to the caliph on developments in the outlying provinces. In addition to a centralized government, the caliph and his governors hosted public sessions at which citizen complaints were heard and resolved. The Abbasids ruled for five hundred years until the fall of Baghdad to the Mongols in 1258, making a vast contribution to the world in both knowledge and culture.

The importance of the Abbasids' overthrow of the Umayyad Dynasty in 750 cannot be overstated; one observer calls it a "revolution in the history of Islam, as important a turning point as the French and Russian revolutions in the history of the West."[38] Under the Abbasids, Islamic civilization reached its zenith: a golden age of literature, arts, music, science, theology and philosophy. Harun al-Rashid (d. 809), the fifth and most famous Abbasid caliph, generously supported writers, artists, musicians, philosophers, scientists and scholars. And during the reign of al-Ma'mun (d. 833), the famous *Bayt al-Hikma* was founded, a prestigious institution of learning and center of translation from Greek and other ancient texts into Arabic. This golden age of Islamic culture had a great influence on the European Renaissance. Not only did Islamic culture flourish under the Abbasids, the geographic boundaries of the empire also grew. By the time Harun al-Rashid started his first of twenty-three years as caliph in 786, the empire of Islam included southwest Asia, Asia Minor and North Africa. In addition to occupying these lands, Rashid established diplomatic relations with China to the east and Charlemagne to the west. The Islamic Empire maintained a strong organized army as well as a police force, postal service, mobile medical units, and recreation centers along the post roads. [39]

After the reign of Harun al-Rashid, civil war erupted when his two sons Amin and Ma'mun both vied for power. This turmoil was to give a lasting and distinctive shape to the political life of the world of Islam, resulting in a weakening of the caliph's power. This enabled the governors of the remote provinces to grow more powerful, to the extent they eventually became practically independent from the empire. Thus, after Rashid's time, the Abbasid caliphs only held power in the cities of the empire, while the provincial governors ruled the outlying areas. These governors preserved their power by creating local dynasties, such as the Saffarids in eastern Iran (867–1495), the Samanids in Khurasan (819–1005), the Tulunids in Egypt (868–905), and the Aghlabids in Tunisia (800–909). [40]

THE UMAYYADS IN SPAIN: A RIVAL CALIPHATE

Despite their defeat by the Abbasids in the Middle East, the Umayyads remained in power in Spain throughout the Abbasids' rule. In 699, while still in power in the Islamic empire proper, the Umayyads had named Musa bin Nusayr, an Arab Muslim from Syria, as the governor of North Africa. Musa drove the Byzantines from the territory west of Carthage and gradually pushed his conquests all the way to the Atlantic, acquiring for Muslim forces a pressure point for the invasion of Europe. [41] In 711, Musa dispatched his Berber lieutenant Tariq bin Ziyad with seven thousand men, mostly Berbers, to *al-Andalus*, or Spain. Tariq landed near the mighty rock which has ever since borne his name: *Jabal Tariq* or "Mount of Tariq," known in English as the Rock of Gibraltar. These first Arabs and Berbers in Spain were later joined by a second wave of soldiers from Syria, who played an important part in supporting the Umayyads.

When the Umayyad prince `Abd al-Rahman I (d. 788) escaped massacre by the Abbasids and fled Damascus in 750, he eventually landed in al-Andalus, where he became known as *al-Dakhil*, or "the Immigrant." Upon arriving, he assembled forces loyal to the Umayyads from among the Syrians and Berbers already in Spain, and defeated Cordoba's governor in May 756, just outside the city walls of Cordoba. His successors would rule Cordoba for the next century and a half. In al-Andalus, he helped establish an independent Umayyad dynasty and seriously influenced European history and culture.[42] His grandson, `Abd al-Rahman III (d. 961), eventually established Umayyad control and authority over all of al-Andalus, and even expanded its territorial reach. In the year 929, `Abd al-Rahman III changed his title from Emir to caliph. Thus, a new Umayyad caliphate was created.[43]

The Islamic culture of medieval Spain was in many ways the greatest culture of all medieval Europe, reaching its height in the mid-tenth century. Cordoba declared itself the center of the Islamic world and the ornament of the world. In Spain, the Umayyads developed new irrigation techniques previously unknown to Europe and made Cordoba the most important medical and philosophical center in Europe. They created prestigious educational institutions and universities where scholars from elsewhere in Europe came to study such subjects as medicine, philosophy, music and science. The sciences of astronomy and astrology flourished, and the existing body of theological philosophy expanded.[44] Medieval astrologer Michael Scot, born in Scotland in 1175, traveled to Cordoba to study Arabic, in order to read the Arabic translations of Aristotle's writings and those of other Arab scholars. Scot brought the works of the Arab philosophers Ibn Rushd, or Averroës, and Ibn Sina, or Avicenna, to Italy, where they were translated into Latin and became a major contribution to the European intellectual Renaissance. Scholar María Rosa Menocal elaborates that similarly, Muslim Spain was a center for Jewish scholarship and culture; during this period, Jewish poets and writers flourished in al-Andalus and contributed not only to the cultural life of Spain but to the development of Jewish philosophy as well. Ibn Ma'mun, or Maimonides, was born in Cordoba in 1138 and became one of the most significant intellectuals of the Middle Ages. A rabbi, physician and philosopher, the influence of Maimonides spread well beyond the Jewish world.[45]

Throughout this period, Berbers from North Africa continued to migrate to al-Andalus, and by the end of the tenth century, some of the indigenous Christian population had converted to Islam. With them lived many who did not convert, both Christians and a considerable Jewish population. Jews, Christians and Muslims lived side by side in Muslim Spain despite religious and cultural differences, and they nourished a complex culture of acceptance held together by the cross-religious spread of the Arabic language and by the Umayyads' tolerance toward Jews and Christians.[46] A considerable portion of the non-Muslim population accepted the language of the rulers, and by the eleventh century, the language and religion of the majority population were Arabic and Islam, respectively. But this Andalusian society differed from contemporaneous Islamic society in the Middle East by virtue of its geographic separation and ethno-religious diversity; Menocal notes that "[t]oleration, a common language and long tradition of separate rule all helped to create a distinctive Andalusian consciousness and society."[47]

The reign of `Abd al-Rahman III represented the apex of the independent power the Umayyads held over al-Andalus. Cordoba, which was located at the intersection of several different regions, remained a market for the exchange of ideas as well as commerce during his rule. In the eleventh century, however, the united Islamic rule of al-Andalus ended, when the Umayyad dynasty broke into a number of small, fragile, independent Islamic states called *al-Tawa'if*. This process of political fragmentation swept through Muslim Spain, dividing the Umayyad state into a series of petty kingdoms and princedoms whose rulers were known as the "party kings," belonging to Arab or Berber dynasties. This phenomenon was similar to what would eventually occur with the Abbasid Empire, as well. The Andalusian caliphate ultimately collapsed and was abolished as a result of a final civil war.[48]

Despite the glorious Arab history of Muslim Spain and the great Umayyad civilization, traditional Arab historians do not spend much time in Spain. Menocal noted that even though Islam was both present and influential in Europe for over seven hundred years, most Arab scholarship looks upon Andalusian history with more of a nostalgic curiosity than anything else, because Islam did not survive as the dominant religion or political institution in Europe. By the late fifteenth century, the Muslims— along with the Jews—were driven out of al-Andalus. Nevertheless, by the time the Islamic polity of medieval Europe disappeared altogether in 1492, it "had left behind a transfigured world."[49]

THE END OF ABBASID RULE

Back in the Middle East, the Islamic Empire reached its height during the Abbasids' rule: geographically, it stretched over a vast area, incorporating culturally and ethnically diverse groups all united by the religion of Islam and the Arabic language. The Abbasids presided over a remarkable civilization for approximately five hundred years, uniting many countries in a single empire composed of different groups that possessed different interests and traditions. They created several Islamic centers of culture and knowledge, which produced distinguished scientists, mathematicians, poets, philosophers, and astronomers. It was a golden period of high intellectual activity in all fields of knowledge, and Islamic legal, religious and political thought flourished along with the science of the Qur'an, linguistics, literature, medicine and chemistry. The Abbasids also built and governed a strong economic infrastructure. In spite of increasing political conflict due to rival dynasties and emerging political change, the cultural unity of the Islamic world flourished and deepened as more of the population became Muslim and as the Islamic faith articulated itself into systems of thought and institutions.[50]

Ultimately, it simply was not possible for the Abbasids' military and administrative resources to maintain political unity, caught as they were between various Arab rivals and other emerging powers, including the Persians and migrant Turks. New independent states materialized, ruled by sultans who used the Abbasid caliphs as puppets and established rival caliphates: the Fatimid dynasty emerged in the tenth century; the Saljuks of Turkish origin in the eleventh century; and the Ayyubids in the twelfth century. The Fatimids, an offshoot of the Shi`ite sect whose rulers claimed to be descendants of the Prophet's daughter Fatimah, established a caliphate in Egypt and North Africa, with Cairo as its capital. The Kurdish general Salah al-Din al-Ayyubi, known in English as Saladin, became the sultan of Egypt in 1171 after defeating the Crusaders and eventually founded the Ayyubid dynasty, reestablishing a Sunni regime and putting an end to the last Shi`ite Fatimid caliph.

The Ayyubid dynasty, in turn, was short-lived and quickly toppled by the Mamluks, whose dynasty by the thirteenth century reached Palestine. The Mamluks, rulers of slave origins who succeeded in uniting Syria with Egypt, were powerful enough to prevent the Mongols from invading Syria. The central Islamic Empire, however, was not; in 1258 the Mongols, led by Hulagu, sacked the capital city of Baghdad, burned its libraries and killed the last Abbasid caliph, Al-Musta`sim. While the Mongolian invasion precipitated the end of the Abbasid dynasty, the empire's collapse had begun long before. The gradual fragmentation of the empire over the centuries had resulted in the decline of the Abbasids' power, with their rule becoming largely symbolic as various sultans and rulers traded the real military and political power back and forth. Thus, by the time the Mongols sacked Baghdad, the rival dynasties were either claiming the caliphate or offering token obedience to a powerless caliph.

Eventually, in the sixteenth century, most of the Arab world fell under the power of the emerging Ottoman Empire, based in present-day Turkey. The Ottomans conquered Cairo, Syria, Jerusalem and the holy cities of Mecca and Medina, becoming the most powerful rulers of the Islamic world. The Islamic caliphate continued to exist under Ottoman rule, but it was primarily a symbolic gesture; Ottoman Turkish sultans even adopted the title of Islamic caliph themselves. The last to do so was Abdülmecit II, who held the title until 1924. This was the year Kemal Ataturk, the first President of the new Turkish Republic, constitutionally abolished the Islamic caliphate as an institution. The Ottoman Empire remained in power until 1918, when it was defeated during the First World War. This defeat brought a conclusive end to the last Muslim Empire, as Turkey was declared a secular state in 1928.

SUNNISM AND SHI`ISM

Though Islam is based on one essential faith, it comprises different sects, the two largest of which are the Sunnis and the Shi`ites. Shi`ites constitute only about fifteen percent of the global Muslim population, while Sunnis constitute approximately eighty-five percent. While some differences exist between the two in custom and practice, there is also much commonality. Both Sunnis and Shi`ites believe in the five essential pillars of Islam, though the Shi`ites tend to combine the five prayers into three sessions and fast only half a day while traveling during Ramadan. The real difference between the two is not found in religious practice but rather in political theory, primarily stemming from the two groups' historically diverging views on the rightful leader of the Muslim community.[51] Additionally, Sunnis and Shi`ites tend to disagree about the form of government the Islamic *umma* should follow, the direction of Islamic affairs, and the necessary traits and qualities a caliph should possess, as well as the political and spiritual authority a caliph should exercise. These issues have created the deepest and most lasting divisions within Islam, with major political and historical ramifications for the *umma*.[52]

The Shi`ite population today is concentrated mostly in Iran, southern Iraq, southern Lebanon, Bahrain, and the eastern province of Saudi Arabia, Yemen, and Syria. Adherents of this religious sect believe that `Ali bin Abi Talib, who was married to the Prophet's daughter Fatima and was the fourth Islamic caliph, should have been the first caliph instead of Abu Bakr. Based on this belief, most Shi`ites refuse to recognize the first three caliphs revered by Sunnis: Abu Bakr, `Umar and `Uthman. And because `Ali should have been the first caliph, it follows that `Ali's son Husayn should have been the caliph in place of Yazid bin Mu`awiya, the very man who ordered Husayn's death at Karbala, and so on down `Ali's bloodline. Fatima, `Ali, and their two sons Hasan and Husayn are the key figures in Shi`ite Islamic tradition. Shi`ites view the Prophet Muhammad, his daughter Fatima, and the Shi`ite imams as the spiritual guides on the path to the knowledge of God.[53]

While Sunnis believe that caliphs should be chosen by election, Shi`ites believe their leaders, the imams, must be descended directly from the Prophet and `Ali, this bloodline providing them with infallible authority. For Shi`ites, the imam is both a religious and political leader who himself is divinely guided. The imam has the ultimate authority by Shi`ite doctrine to interpret God's will, and therefore the imam has unlimited power.[54] The religious authority of the imam is far more important and significant to Shi`ites than any political power a leader may possess. According to the Shi`ite imamate theory, which began to develop in the tenth century, God's plan was to establish the imam in the world as *hujja*, or proof, in order to govern humanity with justice and authoritatively teach religious truths.[55]

As such, remarks Moojan Momen, `Ali should have become leader of the Islamic community not only as caliph, a merely temporal head position, but as imam, a spiritual head position, as well.[56] It should be mentioned that some Islamic scholars date the developments of the Shi`ite imamate theory to the eighth century.[57]

`Ali bin Abi Talib was thus the first Shi`ite imam, followed by his two sons, Hasan, the second imam (d. 669), and Husayn, the third (d. 680). Husayn's surviving son `Ali Zayn al-`Abidin then became the fourth Shi`ite imam (d. 714), followed by his son, Muhammad al-Baqir, the fifth imam (d. 731).[58] Muhammad al-Baqir had contested his brother, Zayd bin `Ali, being named imam, believing he alone received from his father the special characteristics and esoteric lore that empowered him to uncover and grasp the sacred meanings of scripture. And so Zayd was not chosen; rather, Baqir chose his own son, Ja`far al-Sadiq (d. 765), to be the sixth Shi`ite imam. Sadiq shared his inherited "divine knowledge" with his followers, guiding them to understand the hidden meaning of the Qur'an. He instructed them to practice *taqiyyah*, or dissimulation, for their own safety, as it was often dangerous to be a Shi`ite in the midst of the Sunni caliphate.[59]

Despite their practice of dissimulation in dangerous political climates, every single Shi`ite imam was eventually murdered by whatever happened to be the established governmental authority at the time. During the ninth century, when hostility between the established Abbasid government and the Shi`ites arose once more, the Abbasid caliph al-Mutawakkil summoned the tenth imam, `Ali al-Hadi (d. 868), from Medina to Samarra, where he was placed under house arrest. From his imprisonment, the imam was forced to secretly communicate with his sect through the use of agents. And when the eleventh imam, Hasan al-`Askari, was killed in 874, Shi`ites believe he left his young son hidden in order to save his life. This *hidden imam*, whose name was Muhammad al-Mahdi, went into occultation, the state of being miraculously concealed by divine intervention. Persecution of Shi`ites has been intense through Islamic history; it was not until the tenth century that Shi`ites were able to publicly mourn Imam Husayn on `Ashura`, the anniversary of his death.[60]

The largest branch of Shi`ites is known as the Twelvers, those who believe in the legitimacy of all twelve imams. This main branch of Shi`ism is practiced by the majority in modern Iran. Twelvers, as mentioned above, believe the line of descent from `Ali ended with the twelfth imam, Muhammad al-Mahdi, who disappeared in the year 874. According to Twelver doctrine, Mahdi, literally "he who is guided," will reemerge in the future to usher in an era of justice to the world.[61] (The hidden imam has a large number of titles, including: *al-Qa'im*, or "he who will arise," and *al-Imam al-Muntazar*, or "the awaited Imam," among others.) Twelvers to this day blame the Twelfth Imam's occultation on the hostility of the imam's enemies and the resulting danger to his life.[62] This notion of the hidden imam strengthens Shi`ites' devotion and loyalty to the house of `Ali.

Twelver Shi`ites believe mankind needs guidance until the lost imam returns. For this guidance, some rely on the Qur'an and the *Hadith* of the Prophet as previously interpreted by the Shi`ite imams, while others believe there is a continuing need for Qur'anic interpretation and leadership beyond the teachings of the first twelve imams.[63]

Other sects besides the Twelvers exist within the Shi`ite community, such as the major Shi`ite groups of Zaydis and Isma`ilis. The differences between these Shi`ite groups can at some times be confused; Shi`ite scholar Akbar Ahmed explains that while it is difficult to understand the origins of the divisions between some of the Shi`ites, these divisions reflect the different interpretations of the principles governing succession, the concept of which is central to Shi`ites' belief. So while the Twelvers restrict the imamate to the descendants of `Ali by his wife Fatima, the Zaydis believe *any* descendant of `Ali can become an imam. Those who believe that Zayd bin `Ali (Husayn's grandson) was the true fifth imam—they are sometimes called Fiver Shi`ites. The Zaydi (Zaidi) dynasty was founded in Tabaristan on the Caspian Sea in 864. And a Zaydi state was formed in Yemen in 893; this state actually continued to exist until 1963, when it was destroyed in the modern Yemeni civil war.[64] Yemen's northern highland region has been the heart of the Zaydi community since that time. See details on the Zaydis in endnotes.[65]

The Zaidi community in northern Yemen came to international attention following the Arab Spring. An armed revolutionary group called the Houthis unified in northern Yemen, also known as *Ansar Allah*, or "Supporters of God." They advocate a version of Zaydi ideology calling for imamate leadership and receive backing from Iran. The Houthis were active in the 2011 revolution that deposed the president of Yemen Ali Abdullah Saleh. Since that year the Houthis with the help of varying and new alliances including the deposed president Saleh, acted to take political control of the country. Several actors are struggling for control of Yemen, including al-Qa`ida in the Arabian Peninsula, the new government administration backed by a Sunni coalition of the Kingdom of Saudi Arabia and the Arab Gulf States, and the Houthis. Thus the conflict between the Shi`ites and the Sunnis has continued. Further discussion of the situation in Yemen can be found in the chapter on the Arab Spring.

The Isma`ilis, on the other hand, are sometimes called Seveners, as they believe `Ali's line ended with the seventh imam, Isma`il (d. 760). Seveners believe that the sixth imam, Ja`far al-Sadiq (d. 765), designated Isma`il to be his successor, but Isma`il died before Ja`far, thus becoming the seventh and last imam. They do not recognize the legitimacy of Ja`far al-Sadiq's second son, Musa al-Kazim (d. 799), whom the mainstream Twelver Shi`ites consider the seventh imam. Like all other Shi`ites, the Isma`ilis believe the Qur'an must be understood on two levels, both literally and figuratively, as its meaning is hidden and opaque to those who do not possess inner knowledge.[66] In 909, the Isma`ilis seized control of Tunisia and then took Egypt from the Abbasids in 969, establishing the rival Fatimid caliphate in Cairo. Isma`ilis also live in Syria, Iraq, Iran and Yemen. In recent years, foundations such as the Aga Khan Development Network have raised the profile of Isma`ilis and their faith, due to substantial investment in charity and economic development across the Muslim and non-Muslim worlds. Aga Khan claims direct descent from Ali.[67]

According to most Shi`ites, in the absence of the imam, any distinguished religious scholar can act as guide or authority on Islamic law. The *Ayatollahs* are of higher rank, with the highest being the *Ayatollah al-Uzma*, or the "Grand Ayatollah." Imam Ayatollah Khomeini (d. 1989) held the rank of *Ayatollah al-Uzma*, and the additional title of *Faqih* (jurist) was granted to him, as well. Ayatollah Ruhollah Khomeini was a great scholar and a revolutionary leader, who embraced both spiritual and political power. The Iranian Revolution was intimately connected to the Shi`ites' interpretation of history and their religious structure, with its emphasis on the supremacy of the imam.

Scholar Akbar Ahmed argued that such a revolution as the one that took place in Iran in 1979 would be unlikely to occur in Sunni-dominated countries such as Egypt, because in those countries, there could be no central religious figure like the Ayatollah Khomeini; there are no *Ayatollahs* in Sunnism.[68] Though the recent Arab Spring revolutions have occurred under different dynamics than those of 1979 Iran, the argument that such uprisings would not take place in Sunni-majority populations is ultimately incorrect. Revolutions have taken place in Egypt, Libya, Syria, and other Sunni-majority countries since 2010.

Throughout history, tension has existed, and the Shi`ites have rejected all succeeding Sunni caliphs and remained loyal only to the Shi`ite imams, the descendants of `Ali. This rejection of Sunni authority and belief has often escalated into sectarian strife.[69] The Iraqi cities of Najaf and Karbala are sacred to Shi`ites because they contain the land where `Ali and his son Husayn were martyred. The brutal death of Husayn in the Battle of Karbala, the manner in which he was killed, and the injustice done to him and to his followers have created a historical identity for Shi`ites as dedicated believers in strict principles of justice, to the extent that most Shi`ites are prepared to martyr themselves for their just cause.[70]

FOUR RELIGIOUS AND LEGAL SUNNI SCHOOLS OF THOUGHT

Sunnism, which is more straightforward in both doctrine and practice, is perhaps simpler to understand than Shi'ism. Every Muslim who adheres to the mainstream traditions of Islam as practiced by the early Islamic community is considered a Sunni. In Arabic, the Sunni tradition is known as *Ahl al-Sunna* (the People of the *Sunna*). This tradition is based on a literal interpretation of the Qur'an and the Sunna, or the traditions and the practices of the Prophet Muhammad. The Sunna serves to complement the Qur'an by providing concrete answers to difficult Qur'anic principles, as well as essential details to the practice of Islamic law. Sunnis seek to preserve the unity of the Islamic community and the authoritative practices of the first generation of the Islamic *umma*, stressing the need for solidarity among Muslims. Unlike Shi'ites, Sunnis believe the first four Rightly-Guided Caliphs were the legitimate rulers of the early community, whose teachings must be followed. And they also believe in the doctrine of pre-destination, which posits that everything happens according to God's plan.

Sunnism was first defined in the ninth century during the Abbasid era, when non-Shi'ite Muslims began to follow the teachings of four distinct Islamic schools, each founded by a well-known Islamic jurist: the *Hanafi* school, founded by Imam Abu Hanifa (d. 767); the *Maliki* school, founded by Imam Malik bin Anas (d. 796); the *Shafi'i* school, founded by Imam al-Shafi'i (d. 820); and the *Hanbali* school, founded by Imam Ahmad bin Hanbal (d. 855). These Sunni orthodox schools are both religious and legal schools of thought, and though each promulgates different legal theories and general principles, all are based on a literal reading of the Qur'an and the Sunna. Of the four jurists, Ahmad bin Hanbal was the most prominent, and it is he who is credited for creating the mode of religious thought known generally as Sunnism, which is practiced today by the majority of Muslims. The most far-reaching of the four, however, was the Hanafi school, which was less severe than the strict Hanbali school and was favored by the Ottomans. The modern-day adherents of the Hanbali school are primarily located in Saudi Arabia, Qatar and other Gulf States.

The four Sunni schools are not different religious sects. All exist within the larger Sunni Muslim community and Muslims may freely decide which school of thought they prefer. Most Sunni scholars believe it is not necessary for a Muslim to adhere to a certain school; all that is required is a belief in God and the Prophet. When a *fatwa*, or formal legal opinion, is needed, Sunni Muslims may consult with any Islamic scholar regardless of affiliation. In fact, many Sunnis do not follow any of the schools. The fundamentalist *Salafi* movement, for example, strictly follows the ancestors of the first generation of the Muslim community and rejects adherence to any particular school of thought, relying only on the Qur'an and the Sunna as sources of Islamic law.

All Sunni schools are based primarily on the Qur'an and the Sunna, but when these sources cannot provide clear guidance in a specific matter, Sunni jurists often turn to two additional sources for Islamic law: *ijma`*, or the consensus of the community, and *qiyas*, the attempt through analogical reasoning to determine how the principles of the Qur'an and the Sunna could be applied to a situation. (The *qiyas*, in turn, is based on *ijtihad*, the process of making a legal decision by independent interpretation of the various legal sources.) Each school differs on the permissible degree of reliance on these two additional sources; in general, however, Sunnis consider both principles legal and valid. All four schools of thought are widely regarded as orthodox and base themselves on *shari`a*, a system that contains rules of procedure for the application of laws to particular legal cases and life in general.

SUNNI SOCIETY: ISLAMIC LAW WITHOUT CENTRAL RELIGIOUS AUTHORITY

Religion and politics are inseparable in Islam. Sunnis rely on *shari`a* not only as a basis for their religious practices, but also for their government. The evolution of this reliance on Islamic law can be traced to the end of the era of the four Rightly-Guided Caliphs, when the religious and political leadership in Islam was left without unity and centrality. In response to this lack of leadership, the `ulama', or Sunni religious scholars, turned to the *shari`a* to implement, execute and govern all matters of Islamic society, including marriage and divorce, inheritance and ownership, investment, debts, and all non-legal issues, as well. Muslims have used the legal and religious principles of the four Islamic schools to determine the framework for their interactions with other cultures, and when divisions have begun to form within their own Islamic community, they have used *shari`a* to guide the interactions between themselves, as well.

Because there is no central religious authority in Sunnism, theological and legal interpretations vary from country to country, region to region, and even from one mosque to another. Most Sunni Muslim clergymen use the title *sheikh* instead of *imam*. The term *sheikh* especially applies to heads of religious orders or institutions and distinguished religious scholars. Any pious Muslim who leads the prayers at a mosque may also be called an imam, but unlike an imam in Shi`ism, a Sunni imam has no absolute authority. In Shi`ism, only `Ali and his descendants are recognized as imams and only one imam can exist at one time. By contrast, all great religious Sunni authorities are called imams, like Imam Ibn Taymiyya and each founder of the four Sunni schools of religious jurisprudence. The term *imam* is also synonymous with *caliph* in Sunni Islam, as both are used to refer to the leaders of the Islamic community, particularly the four Rightly-Guided Caliphs. Thus, only `Ali was ever recognized by both Shi`ites and Sunnis as an imam.

A major institution of higher learning for Sunni Islam is al-Azhar mosque, which is also the oldest degree-granting university in the world. Located in Cairo, it has served as the greatest center of Islamic education since it was built by the Fatimid Dynasty in 971. Though the Fatimids were Shi`ites and built al-Azhar as an institution to propagate the teachings of the Isma`ili sect, the Ayyubids converted al-Azhar into a school for Sunni Islam when they took control of Egypt. The head of al-Azhar is considered the highest Islamic Sunni source, though even he has no absolute religious authority. He is also called *Shaykh (Sheikh)* of *al-Azhar* and the Grand Mufti, due to his significance in issuing *fatwas*. Traditionally, al-Azhar was an independent religious institution, whose head was appointed by a committee of top religious scholars. Now, the appointment is made directly by the Egyptian government.

Sunnis believe that maintaining power and order sufficiently legitimizes a political leader's authority. As a litany of Sunni thinkers and jurists have proclaimed, even a bad Muslim ruler is preferable to anarchy, and the Sunni religious tradition provides only limited circumstances in which revolution or rebellion is permitted, though it is a religious duty for Muslims not to obey a command that is contrary to God's law. Since 2010, however, popular Sunni revolutions throughout the Arab world have overthrown entrenched, autocratic and exploitative dictators who had ruled Arab nations for decades.

The lack of clerical hierarchies and centralized religious authorities in Sunni Islam means that Sunnis must approach God directly, without reliance on human intermediaries. Today, in many locations around the Islamic world, some government-appointed religious leaders abuse their significant social and political power by asking people to accept the unsatisfactory status quo. It is these appointed Sunni religious leaders who often justify the wrongdoings of their government and who contribute to the absence of revolution in the Islamic Sunni world. This lies in stark contrast with the role of Shi`ite religious authorities in the Iranian revolution of 1979, who encouraged the Iranian people to rise up and oust an oppressive ruler.

SUNNI CONSERVATISM FROM HANBALISM TO WAHHABISM

As previously mentioned, Ahmad bin Hanbal was the most prominent of the four Sunni jurists whose schools of thought ultimately came to define Sunnism. Born in 780 to Arab parents in Central Asia, Ibn Hanbal moved to Iraq after his father died, where he became a student of Imam al-Shafi`i. In Baghdad, he concentrated on the science of the *Hadith*, and after studying with Imam al-Shafi`i, he traveled through Arabia and Iraq to collect the *Hadith* of the prophet. Devoutly religious, he was known to have recited the entire Qur'an daily. He was also steadfast in his beliefs: when the Abbasid caliph al-Mu`tasim imprisoned him in an attempt to force his support for the Mu`tazilite ideology, which promoted the theory the Qur'an was created rather than revealed, Ibn Hanbal refused. The conservative school of thought named after him was based on the principle of literal interpretation of the Qur'an and the *Sunna*.[71]

One of the most devoted disciples of the strict Hanbali school was Imam Ibn Taymiyya (d. 1328), who became an extremely significant conservative Sunni jurist and whose influence on Sunni conservatism ultimately surpassed even that of Ibn Hanbal himself. And like Ibn Hanbal, Ibn Taymiyya's refusal to yield his political and religious positions resulted in his persecution and imprisonment. He eventually died in a Damascus prison. During his life, Ibn Taymiyya ardently defended Sunnism against Shi`ism and attacked the Sufis and philosophers. He opposed visitations of the tombs of saints and refused to condone the idea of *intercessions*, or religious imams serving as intermediaries between Muslims and God. The *Encyclopedia of Arabic Literature* describes the doctrine of Ibn Taymiyya thus:

> "conservative reformism, stressing the need for communal solidarity. One of the lasting influences on contemporary political Islam; cherished in contemporary Saudi Arabia as the predecessor of Muhammad bin `Abd al-Wahhab on whose doctrines Saudi religious policy is based."[72]

His influence is particularly seen among *Wahhabis* and *Salafis*, the latter of which advocate a return to the authoritative practice of the first generation of the Islamic *umma*.

WAHHABISM

Wahhabism is the continuation of the ideas and practices of these two most conservative Sunni imams, Ibn Hanbal from the eighth century and Ibn Taymiyya from the thirteenth century. Today, the Wahhabi religious scholars in the Kingdom of Saudi Arabia represent the fundamentalist positions of the conservative Hanbali school. As a form of Sunnism, Wahhabism is centered on the need to return to the religious principles gleaned from a strict and literal interpretation of the Qur'an. Hanbalism, upon which Wahhabism is based, mandates that the Qur'an must be understood literally—without question or interpretation—as it is believed to need none.[73] Thus, Wahhabism forbids any reliance on *qiyas* and *ijma`*. The movement further stresses opposition to material possessions and luxurious lifestyles, instead advocating a return to the idealized purity of early Islam with its plain attire and modest behavior.

Muhammad bin ʿAbd al-Wahhab (d. 1792) was a radical conservative follower of Ibn Taymiyya. His father was a *qadi*, or judge of Islamic law, who had applied Islamic law in accordance with the Hanbali practices that were traditional to the region.[74] Due to his disappointment with the moral decline and laxity of his society, Ibn ʿAbd al-Wahhab left the Ottoman Empire and established a state in central Arabia, where he denounced many popular beliefs and practices as un-Islamic. By the early twentieth century, ʿAbdul ʿAziz bin Saʿud had succeeded in uniting the tribes of Arabia and, in the process, building the Saudi kingdom and spreading the Wahhabi movement.[75]

The Islamic societal conversion in Arabia to Wahhabism began only in 1932, yet today it exists as the dominant religious school of thought in the Kingdom of Saudi Arabia and Qatar. It counts Osama bin Laden as a follower. Wahhabi Muslims believe Ibn Taymiyya's ideas are the only correct principles for the practice of Islam. They prefer the title *Ahl al-Tawhid*, or the "Asserters of the Divine Unity," to *Ahl al-Sunna*, the mainstream Sunni epithet.[76] In Wahhabism, shaving the beard and smoking are forbidden. Mosques must be simple and plain, and the attendance of public prayers is mandatory. It is also prohibited to celebrate the Prophet's birthday or make offerings at the tomb of the Prophet's family.

DIFFERENCES BETWEEN SHIʿITES AND SUNNIS

Shiʿites and Sunnis share the main articles of Islamic belief and most consider themselves brethren in faith. Most Muslims do not identify themselves as belonging to a particular sect, instead feeling part of one large and diverse *umma*. Key differences between the Sunnis and the Shiʿites lie not in the practice of their religion but in their political beliefs. These stem primarily from their different accounts of who was the rightful leader of the Islamic community upon the death of the Prophet, and how such a leader should have been chosen. As discussed earlier, while Sunnis believe Muhammad's successors should have been elected, the Shiʿites believe the leader must have been a direct descendant of ʿAli and his wife Fatima, because the authority to guide the *umma* comes directly from God. Throughout history, therefore, the Shiʿites have refused to recognize the authority of the elected Muslim leaders, which has had vast ramifications for the unity of the Islamic political entity. It has also resulted, as mentioned previously, in the historical persecution of Shiʿites, which in turn has supported the motif of martyrdom of Shiʿite leaders. Understanding these core issues is essential to understanding key events in the region up to the Syrian revolution in 2011 and the subsequent and ongoing civil war.

While Sunnis and Shiʿites agree on most fundamental Islamic beliefs, differences exist in some religious practices like the performance of their prayers and ablution. The Shi`ite call to prayer, for instance, consists of a different formulation than the better-known Sunni version. While prostrating, a Shi`ite will place his or her forehead on a piece of hardened clay brought from the holy city of Karbala, while a Sunni will simply use a runner or mat on the floor. Sunnis pray five times a day, while the Shi`ites usually combine the five prayers into three. Furthermore, because the Shi`ites dislike some of the companions of the Prophet, particularly the first three caliphs (Abu Bakr, `Umar, `Uthman) and Muhammad's wife `A'isha, they make no reference to their testimonies or traditions in their religious practice, instead referring only the sayings of `Ali and Fatima. Sunnis include the sayings of the Prophet and all his companions in their practice.

Shi`ites and Sunnis also disagree on the permissibility of certain social conventions. In Shi`ism, temporary marriages are lawful, while in Sunnism they are not. A temporary marriage is called *Mut`a*, or "marriage of enjoyment," and differs sharply from a conventional marriage, whose permanence is designed to produce and raise children. The temporary marriage consists of a contract between a man and a woman for an agreed-upon, short, fixed period of time. When the time expires, the marriage is dissolved. The ceremony may require the permission of a guardian and the presence of two witnesses, and it may not. Historically, temporary marriage was practiced in pre-Islamic times and even during the Prophet's life; Shi`ites argue it is not forbidden under Islamic law because it was Caliph `Umar, whose legitimacy they reject, who forbade it. To Shi`ites, the legality of temporary marriages is established in the Qur'an and the *Hadith* because it was practiced during the Prophet's time. They believe temporary marriage preserves purity and saves people from sin by insulating them from having sex outside of marriage. It should be mentioned that while Sunnis do not approve of the practice of temporary marriages, and indeed consider it forbidden, some religious Sunni authorities have recently begun to permit the *Misyar* marriage, which has many similarities to the Shi`ite version (see chapter 2 on the Arab family).

While Sunni Muslims hold the Prophet's family and his descendants in great respect, they regard Shi`ites' worship of them as excessive, ungodly or heretical.[77] This plays out in the differences between Sunni and Shi`ite imams. In Shi`ism, only `Ali and his descendants are recognized as imams, whereas Sunnis recognize any religious authority as an imam. Therefore, for Shi`ites, there can be only one imam alive at a time. The imam in Shi`ism carries a special and great significance as the mirror image of the Prophet, sinless and infallible. He acts as an intercessor with God and boasts supernatural knowledge and absolute authority. With the exception of `Ali, however, none of the twelve Shi`ite imams ever ruled an Islamic state. The Twelfth Shi`ite Imam disappeared from the world in 874, though the Shi`ites believe he is still alive and will return.

Sunnis have often repressed Shi`ites because they regard them as religious deviants, wrongfully equating their imams to the level of the Prophet himself. While the Sunnis reserve the performance of circumambulation during their pilgrimage to Mecca to honor God, the Shi`ites make a pilgrimage to the tombs of the imams as well, where they practice the circumambulation in honor of them. Out of disapproval of this Shi`ite practice, the Wahhabis demolished the gilded or silver grills around the tombs of the Prophet's family in 1920. The strong Shi`ite motif of worldly suffering is linked with the promise of Paradise, which helps many Shi`ites cope with their historical persecution by Sunnis. However, out of fear, some Shi`ites continue to practice dissimulation of their true beliefs whenever they live on Sunni territory.[78]

Sunnis' and Shi`ites' very different views of Islamic history lead to occasional disagreement. Sunnis view Islam's early military, political and religious success as God's reward, while Shi`ites view it more as the beginning of an oppressed and disinherited minority community's struggle to restore God's rule on earth. For Shi`ites, the martyrdom of the imams such as `Ali and Husayn epitomizes their struggle, while Sunnis reject such symbolism. Akbar Ahmed notes that Sunnis do not condone the use of intermediaries such as the imams, believing there can only be a direct relationship with God. Shi`ites, on the other hand, believe intercession is necessary for Muslims' salvation, and that all imams, including `Ali, served as intermediaries between God and the believers.[79]

Sunnis, furthermore, do not share Shi`ites' belief in the divine authority of the imams. The `ulama', Sunnism's traditional legal scholars, believe it was the Prophet who revealed God's laws in the Qur'an, so any possible interpretation of those words ended with Muhammad's death. This demands a literal interpretation of the Qur'an's text for orthodox Sunnis. Shi`ites, however, believe God would not leave his people on earth without proper guidance. For this reason, according to Shi`ite doctrine, God sent the sinless imams to earth with the divine ability to interpret the Qur'an.

Likewise, Sunnis do not consider the martyrdom of Husayn, the third Shi`ite imam, at Karbala in 680 to be an incident of great importance. To the Shi`ites, however, Husayn's death has tremendous significance, as it remains representational of the need for Shi`ites to continue on the path of martyrdom. It was Husayn's emblematic martyrdom, among other moving religious symbols, that rallied the people of Iran to revolt against the Shah in 1979.[80]

Unfortunately, the conflict between the Shi`ites and Sunnis often leads to violence. The situation in Iraq, following the fall of Baghdad in 2003 and the American occupation, resulted in clashes between the two sects, which spread to other areas such as Syria, Yemen, and Bahrain. From 2011 until the present there has been a civil war in Yemen between the Houthis (Shi`ites) and the Sunni government, supported by Saudi Arabia and its Arab allies (see chapter 11 on the Arab Spring). In Pakistan, where Shi`ites comprise a minority of the population, clashes occur often between the two sects. This is particularly true on `Ashura', the tenth day of the month of Muharram, when all Shi`ites mourn the death of Husayn. In recent years, `Ashura' has become a day of violent clashes between the two dominant sects of Islam across the Islamic world.[81]

REVIVAL OF THE ISLAMIC IDENTITY

During the nineteenth and twentieth centuries, the Arab and Islamic world fell under the control of European imperial powers. Throughout the twentieth and into the twenty-first century, questions surrounding Islamic identity and political authority have increased. The West's ever-increasing interests and interventions in the political, economic and cultural aspects of the Arab world have contributed to the revival of the Islamic identity, as many Muslims and Arabs feel threatened by globalization and Western domination over their economy, resources, traditions, and national and political interests. Many Muslims aspired for Islamic political and religious leadership in the twentieth century, and profoundly felt the loss of their religious connection to the past when the last Islamic caliphate was abolished in 1924. The caliph was seen as the guardian of Islamic faith and law and was a symbolic figure for both the religion and the government of the Islamic community, and this loss has been keenly felt by many all over the Islamic world.

After World War I, the remnants of the Ottoman Empire were distributed among the European powers as protectorates, and new independent Arab States thereafter emerged. The lack of even a symbolic Islamic caliphate, combined with the oppressive political, social and economic reality of the Arab world, has led to the strength of the Islamic revival movement within Arab society.

The loss of the caliph figure prompted the formal establishment of the Islamic revival movement and the search for a practical institutional alternative to the caliphate. In 1928, an Egyptian social and political reformer named Hasan al-Banna founded the Muslim Brotherhood. Other Islamic organizations were similarly established throughout the Arab and Muslim world by those who had tired of their puppet-like, Western-controlled governmental leaders. These organizations advocated a return to early Islamic lifestyles and practices in the search for ways to change the unfortunate reality. Due in part to these organizations, the pan-Islamic identity has been strengthened despite the absence of the caliphate and a just rule of law. Muslims organize Islamic symposiums and conferences, attended by Islamic organizations, political parties and religious groups, to discuss ways to return to Islamic unity. Some Muslims debate the legitimacy and effectiveness of a caliph who lacks political authority, but many others believe the existence of the office of the caliph is necessary for Islam to flourish.

Islamist revival movements, fueled by widespread discontent with the political and cultural realities of the Arab world, have grown in strength. Some have even succeeded in wresting the issue of Palestine from the Arab nationalist discourse, claiming it is more of a religious issue than a national one. The goal of these Islamic movements is to re-establish an ideal Islamic community, following the example of the Prophet and the four Rightly-Guided Caliphs. Their adherents, far from considering themselves radicals or dreamers, possess the solid conviction and strong belief that this goal will be achieved. For example, the Islamist party Hizb al-Tahreer, or the "Liberation Party," was founded in 1953 in Jerusalem but now boasts a presence in many Arab countries. Khalid Sa`eed, a spokesman for Hizb al-Tahreer, affirms the group's commitment to bringing back the caliphate. He pronounced this goal to be not just a possibility, but a promise that must be delivered according to the will of God. And he observed that the present seems to offer more promise than ever before for re-establishing the Islamic caliphate. Such an endeavor does not come without risks or difficulties, but he urged Muslims to start somewhere and then expand.[82]

Islamic movements like Hizb al-Tahreer have no preferences where to start such a pan-Islamic state. Many believe it could start anywhere, then expand and spread virally to other countries. Obvious candidates seem to be Syria, Iraq and Gaza. Others favor the Arabian Peninsula, the birthplace of Islam and the land where Muhammad and the first four 'Rightly-Guided' Caliphs presided over an ideal Islamic community.

THE EMERGENCE OF ISIS (*DA`ISH*)

The political developments after the fall of Baghdad in 2003 have paved the ground for the emergence of militant Islamist movements including ISIS (Islamic State of Iraq and Syria), also known as ISIL (Islamic State in Iraq and the Levant). This movement, which calls itself the State of the Islamic caliphate was fueled by the discontent populations of Syria and Iraq. Economic and political disenfranchisement, sectarian divisions and overall stagnation led many citizens to turn to any promise of change. ISIS, a militant radical terrorist group, represents a corruption of Sunni Islamic ideology and has openly declared its intention to forcibly create a new Islamic caliphate. *Da'ish* is far more dangerous than Osama Bin Laden's al-Qa`ida.

Da'ish emerged in 2006 from the political power vacuum following Baghdad's fall. The political changes that put Saddam Hussein (d. 2006) out of power also resulted in the dismissal of large numbers of his former government. These Ba'thist Sunni officials, many of whom were trained members of the Iraqi military and excluded from participating in the new American-led Iraqi government, joined the ranks of radical organizations and destabilized the new government. Thus, ISIS quickly benefitted by immediately gaining well-trained and experienced fighters into its ranks.

Since 2011, *da'ish* has taken over large regions in Iraq and Syria and has captured civilians and kept them under its ruthless control. Its propaganda and effective use of social media has attracted converts and fighters from across the Middle East and outside of the region. *Da'ish* creates fear and exercises brutality against Arab civilians beyond its strongholds in Syria and Iraq, extending to Libya, Yemen and elsewhere in the Middle East and North Africa. Acts of terrorism and the indiscriminate killing of innocent people in Europe, the United States, and on the African continent indicate its global reach.

Da'ish has exacerbated the continued suffering of people in Syria, Iraq, and other Arab and Western countries. Torture, violence and mass executions are cornerstones of its methods as it expands its territory. Notably, the movement has also destroyed many significant archeological sites and artifacts in ancient cities from the Islamic Golden Age and earlier, especially in Palmyra, Syria.

The vision of a caliphate put forward by ISIS does not represent the true political or social aspirations of today's Muslim communities. Its militant and radical tactics and goals are born out of the political and cultural suffering that has existed in the Arab world throughout the modern era. The vision of ISIS to establish a new Islamic caliphate will not transpire, and ISIS was militarily defeated in 2017. Unfortunately, its ideology will continue to be a very powerful force inside the Arab world for many years to come.

CHAPTER SEVEN

Music in the Arab World

Sing in every poem you compose

Singing is the domain of poetry

Hassan Ibn Thabit (the poet of the Prophet, d. 674)[1]

THE EMERGENCE OF ARAB music in the Arabian Peninsula predates Islam. A variety of distinct forms of music existed. Oral poetry was the most important of these forms. Recitation of poetry is considered a form of song and "Poets who recite their work are often compared to singing birds and their verses to birdsong. Song is the leading-rein of poetry."[2] These poetic verses were also accompanied by a drum or *rabab* following the poetic meters. In Arab musical tradition, there is "hardly any music without song. Music and poetry are so closely woven together that to this day it is difficult to discover the names of the composers of classical Arab music. We often only know the names of the singers and poets."[3] Thus, the Arabic language and poetry are at the very core of Arabic music's originality, development and expression.

The development of Arab music has deep roots in pre-Islamic Arabic poetry. These poets used to recite poems with a high musical rhythm and tone. Adonis (b. Ali Ahmad Said, 1930), a leading Syrian poet and cultural critic wrote that pre-Islamic poetry was born as a song. It developed "as something heard and not read, sung and not written, the voice in this poetry was the breath of life "body music." It was speech and something which went beyond speech."[4] A rich and complex relationship existed between the poet and the physical actuality of the voice. In this style of music, when we hear "speech in the form of a song, we do not hear the individual words but we hear what goes beyond the body towards the expanse of the soul."[5]

Arab musical tradition is fused by religion, history and culture, and it also has outside influences. Individual countries have retained their own musical heritage, now often blended with other forms from other regions and the West. The melodic songs, styles and interpretations continue to tell the stories of the Arab people, with some musical pieces having been part of the popular consciousness for thousands of years.

HISTORICAL CONTEXT

Mecca, a holy shrine before Islam, was the great cultural center for Arabia, where traditional music, classical poetry, and dancing songs were performed. Competitions of poetry and musical performances were held periodically including the Fair of `Ukaz, which attracted the most distinguished poet-musicians from all over Arabia. There was also cultural contact with Byzantium and Persia, as well as the music practiced in Mecca, which was more sophisticated than the music practiced in the nomadic encampments of Arabia. This included singing girls that performed songs of their homeland in noble households, and in scattered taverns.[6]

After the emergence of Islam in the seventh century, the recitation of the Qur'an developed through its captivating melodic harmonious musicality. The Prophet Muhammad had tolerated functional music such as war songs, pilgrimage chants, and public or private festival songs. In addition, he himself instituted in 622 the `Azaan (call to prayer), chanted by the Mu`azzen (muezzin), a man who calls Muslims to prayer from the minaret of a mosque. For this task he chose the Abyssinian singer Bilal, who became the patron of the Muezzins and their guilds throughout the Islamic world.[7]

A decade after the Prophet Muhammad's death, the Islamic empire expanded and came into contact with the other cultures, and "in spite of the austere regime of the four orthodox caliphs (632–661), joy of life dominated the two holy cities of Mecca and Medina". Musicians were brought in and became the pillars of musical life. There were concerts held in houses, and sophisticated literary and musical salons."[8] The city of Medina in Arabia became one of the wealthiest cities in the empire when Islam expanded and pilgrims began visiting from beyond the Arab world. The city became a cross-cultural nexus as languages, cultural traditions and musical instruments created new forms of artistic expression. Habib Touma notes: "most of the great male and female singers in the days of Islam were Persians, Ethiopians, or black Africans."[9] Popular poems provided the words for musical compositions, and the resulting music would accompany dancing, often by women in palaces and private homes. The broader region of Hijaz, Arabia's western province where Medina is located, produced some of the Arab world's finest musicians.[10]

Arab music reached a golden age during the Abbasid Caliphate (750–1258) when the heart of the music world shifted to Baghdad, and Persian influences, including poetry and new melodies, were incorporated. By the ninth century Arabic music was already highly developed. At that time, the Arabs already had an extensive musical repertoire, a musical history recorded in writing, and well-trained musicians and singers who enriched the musical life of the courts.[11] Muslim scholars translated Greek music principles. The word *musiqa* was introduced into Arabic. Scholars published encyclopedic collections of poems and music.

Arab musicians in this Golden Age established what is known as "The Great Arab Musical Tradition."[12] Schools and conservatories were established and music was a central part of secular and ceremonial life. The musical styles were preserved by Al-Farabi (d. 950) in his notable work *Kitab al-Musiqa al-Kabir*, the "Great Book of Music."[13] He documented the Arab tone system, *maqam*, which governs styles of rhythm and scales unique to the Arab world. These qualities form the very core of Arab music tradition and are still used today and will be discussed later in the chapter.

During this time, the first written records of songs were preserved in Baghdad by literary scholar Abu al-Faraj al-Isfahani (d. 967) in his *Kitab al-Aghani*, the "Book of Songs," an encyclopedic work on Arabic, composers, poets, musicians and songs, as well as notes on the rhythm and mode of the songs.[14] Even today traditional Arab music is not written or scored as we are familiar with in the West. The elements surrounding it— the stories, the poetry, the musicians and the instruments—form an organic style of music that embodies each piece. Al-Isfanhani captured how the interplay between these elements comprises the core of Arab musical traditions.

When Islam expanded onto the Iberian Peninsula beginning in the eighth century, Arab cultural forms followed, including music. Touma cites the influence of a young, talented music student, Ziryab (b. 789), who left Baghdad, traveled to Syria and Tunisia, and arrived in Cordoba in 822 where he founded a music school. He also brought fresh perspectives and interpretations of music from his travels, which formed the nucleus of what would become Al-Andalus music.[15] Andalusian music spread to Northern Africa and remains a part of contemporary culture in the *Maghreb*. It also influenced European music, especially through the introduction of Arabic instruments.

From the thirteenth through the nineteenth centuries during the Age of Decline; Ottoman, Byzantine and Persian forms played a greater role in Arab music. Despite these outside influences, Arab music did retain the antecedents of the formative ninth century and earlier years. In the thirteenth century Al-Isfahani's *Kitab al-Aghani*, was translated into Spanish by Ibn Aqnin (d. 1226), validating the importance of the Great Arab Musical Tradition, and fermenting the role of Arab music in Iberian culture.[16] *Kitab al-Aghani*, which consists of "twenty-one volumes and took fifty years to comply, is the most striking proof that poetry in the Pre-Islamic period was synonymous with recitation and song."[17] The central role of poetry in traditional Arab music cannot be underestimated.

By the end of the nineteenth century, given the long rule by the Ottomans, Turkish modes and the Turkish language continued to blend into the Arab canon.

Turkish composers were known through the Arab world and instruments from Turkey and Persia were integrated into Arab musical performances. But the influences were mutual; Turkey adopted the Arabic *maqam* modal system and Arab songs made their way into Turkish music. The cultural, political and social domination under the Ottomans to some extent quelled natural development of Arab music. However, it always remained more vocal than melodic, retaining the key characteristic that most identifies it today. A revived sense of Arab nationalism and inevitable influences from the West would combine to generate a new golden Age of Arab music in the twentieth century.

ENCOUNTERS WITH EUROPEAN CULTURE

Throughout the late eighteenth and nineteenth centuries, European powers expanded their influence across the region as the Ottoman Empire weakened and eventually collapsed after World War I. As quickly as European colonial armies permeated their land, so too did European social and cultural influences. "Very quickly, nationalist movements emerged in Arab countries, which wanted to break free from the bonds of stagnation and return to the splendor of the past in all cultural areas, including music. Arab Music, which was still rooted in The Great Arab Tradition and was already influenced by Ottoman and Persian culture, now acquired new influences from the encounter with European culture."[18] The differences in Western music were more significant than those in Turkish and Persian music, creating more room for exploration and experimentation. Arab music did not lose its emphasis on tradition nor were its unique characteristics lost. But a shift did occur and "the new terms *qadeem* (old) and *jadeed* (new) were formed in order to distinguish between traditional and modern styles of music."[19] Arab music entered a new century and a new era.

After World War I, the infusion of Western styles and forms continued, especially with the predominant British and French influences across the region. Greater exposure to new and foreign styles excited some and threatened others. In 1932 an International Congress of Music was held in Cairo. This marked one of the first times that Arab experts and musicians met with counterparts from Turkey, Persian and Western Europe to discuss in detail Arabic music, engaging in intercultural dialogue and exchange.[20] Although Arab music remained rooted in its indigenous traditions, more musicians started to embrace different music and instruments. Some musicians and composers decried the loss of "pure" Arabic music that had survived for so many centuries. Others continued to explore how to incorporate the new genres into traditional Arab music, adopting and adapting foreign instruments such as the violin, cello, double bass and accordion. Radio began in the Arab world in the 1920s and Egyptian State Radio first broadcast in 1934. Demand began to grow for Arab-inspired and Arab-produced music.

WESTERN INFLUENCE ON ARAB MUSIC

The Western influences that surrounded the International Congress of Music in Cairo actually produced an Arab music renaissance that lasted into the 1960s. Classic and contemporary poems were set to new styles of music that celebrated a rebirth of Arab culture and nationalism. Musicians incorporated foreign instruments and sounds without sacrificing the essential Arab nature of their works. It featured a new golden age of Arab music, with renowned artists including Egyptian singers Umm Kulthum and Abdel Halim Hafez and Lebanese singers Wadi` al-Safi and Fairuz. During the 1950s and the 1960s classical orchestras blended Western instruments and compositions into traditional Arab forms, generating new audiences. Arab film and television production increased, especially in Egypt, and scoring for these media outlets offered musicians additional audiences for their music. Arabs traveled abroad to study Western theories of harmony and learned to play different instruments. Western musicians traveled to the Arab world to perform, listen and collaborate.

By the 1970s a new generation of singers, many from or based in Egypt, were creating songs increasingly based on Western sounds and rhythms, giving birth to the genre of contemporary Arab pop. Freedom and creativity came with Western-Eastern cultural exchange, but at some cost to Arab norms. Arab pop usually consists of Western-styled songs with Arab instruments and lyrics. Many debate whether the influx of Western song content, musical styles and video dominance have irreparably damaged Arab music. Even with the inflow of outside pressure and influence, both classical and popular Arab music remain cherished, vibrant, and accessible across the region.

An appreciation for the history of Arab music requires thoughtful consideration not only to its origins in poetry and the Arabic language, but also in its embrace of musical cues from its neighbors, both near and afar. The fabric of the new Arabic music is best described as an interweaving of new and old, language and tone. It is in this vein that we will delve deeper into the myriad elements of Arabic music—encompassing its storied history with the exploration of instrumental, cultural, religious, performance, and style components that make Arabic music unique.

TRADITIONAL ARAB MUSIC

Characterizing Arab music, which spans millennia, is no easy task. In his seminal work, *The Music of the Arabs*, Habib Hassan Touma identifies five key components that help to understand the unique qualities of Arab music:

1. The Arab tone system (*maqam*), a musical tuning system that relies on specific interval structures.
2. Rhythmic-temporal structures that produce a rich variety of rhythmic patterns, known as *awzan* or "meters," that are used to accompany metered vocal and instrumental genres, to accent or give them form.
3. Musical instruments that are found throughout the Arab world that represent a standardized tone system, are played with standardized performance techniques, and exhibit similar details in construction and design.
4. Specific social contexts for the making of music, whereby musical genres can be classified as urban (music of the city inhabitants), rural (music of the country inhabitants), or Bedouin (music of the desert inhabitants).
5. A musical mentality, that is responsible for the esthetic homogeneity of the tonal-spatial and rhythmic-temporal structures in Arab music whether composed or improvised, instrumental or vocal, secular or sacred.[21]

This chapter considers some of these concepts in more detail, beginning with the very essence of Arabic music, *maqam*.

THE *MAQAM*

Arab music is based on a tone system, unique to the region, which falls under what is called *maqam*, (pl. *maqamat*) "mode" or "scale." The concept also covers variations in tone and pitch. This foundation is shared across the entire region and underlies sacred and secular music as well as vocal and instrumental music. Like in the West, the scale consists of tones and semitones but Arab music can also move in quartertones; thus it can have far smaller tonal steps and more variations. This is the root of the familiar sound to Arab music: "it repeatedly plays around the notes in slight variations, without the musician losing sight of the keynote."[22] It can be compared to some extent to jazz, when one musician plays a central line and the other musicians play above, below and around it. Melody, rhythm and improvisation become the central part of the *maqam* musical experience. In terms of pitch, classical Western music has two: flat and sharp. Arab music has more than seventy.[23] Thus the nuances in the melodies can be extremely varied.

Songs incorporate *maqam* to provide the underlying framework. Each *maqam* conveys a specific mood or emotion with an intricate network of other *maqamat*, which create interplay between them. For example, one *maqam* is connected with a feeling of power, health and strength; another inspires joy, vitality and femininity; a different *maqam* is for the size and eternity of the desert; and another represents sadness and pain.[24] With over seventy of these set modes, emotion, mood and intensity can be extremely varied. But the true genius of the music comes from what is played around the core *maqam*, which the musician never loses sight of.

The lack of fixed meter creates an environment guided by emotion, which may run from lament to liveliness to ecstasy and everything beyond and in between. For some it is hard to tell if a song has a beginning or end. Every piece is created by the musicians; there is no written score: "Arab music does not measure itself in terms of technical perfection, but by the degree of intensity and emotion in the tone, feeling, ornamentation, performance and singing. The Western musician repeatedly practices a piece as it is written in the sheet music until he is able to play and interpret it perfectly. The classical Arab musician, on the other hand, is only able to access the music through its 'soul' and what it stimulates within him."[25] An Arab musician can play the same piece at the Cairo Opera House, at a local music festival, at a wedding or a funeral, and it will sound entirely different each time, as if they are different pieces. The experience comes from the poetry of the words, the shifting melodies, the instruments and the voices. Interpretation is the essence.

MUSICAL INSTRUMENTS AND PERFORMANCE

Arabs have preferred performing music in small ensembles, known as *al takht,* for thousands of years. These are small groups, traditionally between three to five musicians, most often on a raised platform. Larger groups of eight or more musicians are known as *al firqa*, or orchestra. Classical Arab music concerts can have up to one hundred musicians in a *firqa*.[26]

As early as the tenth century Arab scholars in Baghdad classified instruments as percussion, plucked, bowed and wind. [27] The same instruments mastered then are played today. Mastery in the art of producing instruments is highly regarded. The three Arab musical instruments that form the heart of *maqamat* expression are:

Oud: Arab short-necked lute. This is the best-known and most important instrument in Arab music. It is fretless with a body shaped like a half pear made from wood. It is the central instrument, providing both the rhythm and melody. Arabs call the *oud* "The Sultan of the Musical Instruments."[28]

Qanoun: Pluck boxed zither with between sixty-three and eighty-four strings. It has movable bridges that allow for numerous micro-intervals and is played on the lap. As far back as the ninth century, al-Farabi in his "Great Book of Music" (Kitab al-musiqa al-Kabir) "already discussed the tuning of the forty-five stringed instrument of the time."[29]

Nay: Wind instrument similar to a flute, open at both ends. Unlike the Western flute, there is no mouthpiece. Instead, a player holds the *nay* at a 45-degree angle and blows across the top of the long, hollow tube. *Nay* players manipulate the pitch through subtle adjustments of their fingers over the holes. Originally made from wood with seven holes, this instrument has been played for some five thousand years.[30]

Rhythm and percussion instruments often include: *Daf*, a large frame drum, often made of wood; *Darbouka* (or *Tablah*), a goblet-shaped hand drum played by both women and men. Made from wood or clay, it can be played standing, tucked under the arm, or sitting; *Riqq*, a type of tambourine, traditionally with a wooden frame, cymbals and a thin, translucent membrane made of fish or goat skin; *Rabab*, the most common string instrument, a one-stringed fiddle, which usually has a rectangular frame covered on the front and back with skin and a bow made of horsehair. A *rabab* player rests the instrument vertically on his or her knee and bows across the string in a similar fashion to a cello player. Numerous other instruments are played across the region with rich variances, especially in the *Maghreb*, but these are the ones that have formed the core of traditional Arab music for over a thousand years.[31]

Song is the most essential element to Arab music, and poetry forms the basis for the songs. The composers may not be remembered over time but poets and singers are venerated. The chapter on Arab poetry explains how the rich traditions, union of meter and rhyme, and measured verses lend themselves to being recited and sung. Muallam explains how the poems form the music: "a composer who wants to write a melody to a certain poem checks firstly the poetic rhythm and meter of the sound, then examines which musical patterns are suitable for the poem, and only later decides about melodic aspects, such as *maqam*. This means that when composing poetry into a song, the decisions concerning rhythm precede those that concern melody. The composer may decide about a certain *maqam* in order to stress the emotional character of the song—happy, sad, emotional, or grave, but ultimately, poetry is more strongly connected to rhythm than with melody."[32]

By comparison, in the West, the lyrics most often are tied to the melody. In Arab songs, the words form a more hypnotic effect with the melodies going around them. Rhythmic structures in Arab music produce a rich variety of rhythmic patterns, known as *awzan* (meters), which accompany metered vocal and instrumental genres, to accent or give them form. Arab singers must have strong and beautiful voices that can represent a counterpart to the musicians. Singers create *tarab*, which signifies "exhilaration, ecstasy, or euphoria." This mood is created by intertwining the song and the music to transport the entire audience, whether bringing them to tears, inducing strong romantic feelings, or causing them to rise to their feet cheering. The style and performance of the singer determines the intensity of the *tarab*; both the musicians and listeners are united in a direct association that binds their thoughts and emotions. The term can also be used to describe transcendent Sufi music and the music of mystics who practice *wajd*, or religious ecstasy.[33]

Arab music provides entry to the audience's deepest emotions; the melodies emote feelings across the spectrum of a human being. Al-Ghazali's (d. 1111) *The Revival of the Religious Sciences*, widely regarded as the greatest work of Muslim spirituality, wrote of the power of music over the human heart: "There is no entry into the heart except through the antechamber of the ears. Musical tones, measured and pleasing, bring forth what is in the heart and make evident its beauties and defects ... whenever the soul of the music and singing reaches the heart, then there stirs in the heart that which preponderates in it."[34] Arab music's transformational power captivates mentally, emotionally and physically. The combination of poetry, song and voice applied on top of the evocative *maqamat* remain the foundations of Arab music twenty-two centuries after they were first recorded in writing in the Great Books of Music and Songs.

RELIGIOUS MUSIC

Religious music in the Islamic world is "sung text" that glorifies God, the Prophet Muhammad and the Prophet's family (*ahl al-bayt*). It is performed in mosques during the *Zikr* (remembrance) ceremonies, during the *mawlid al-Nabawi* (celebrating the Prophet's birth) festivities and other religious occasions.[35] Melodic musical instruments are not played. However, Islamic music, including the *Tajweed* or recitation of the Qur'an, is structurally equivalent to secular music in the Arab world. Islamic legal scholars and theologians have debated the value and function of singing and instrumental performance in either religious or non-religious contexts for over a century. Nonetheless distinctive Islamic musical styles have developed.[36] One who presents the Qur'an would never be known as a *mughanni*, (singer), but rather as a *muqri`*, *tali*, muratti, or *mujawwid* (reader or reciter). The Qur'anic reciters are revered for their strong and beautiful voices. They maintain high status and devote their lives to their craft. Another important form of this genre is the mu`azzin (Muezzin), who recites the call to prayer.

SUFI MUSIC

Sufi music is most highly developed in Syria. The Sufi musical brotherhood known as *Mawlawiyya* created chants and songs based on sacred forms from the ninth century. Sufi pieces are deeply rooted in religious texts and themes. The vocalists "extract from the repertoire of the mosque the naming of God (*zikr*) and the birth of the Prophet (*mawlid*) in a serene expression that has a rigorously organized rhythm. Thus the vocalist leads the assembly into a trance or a state of meditation (*ta'ammul*). The music inspires the lifting of the soul."[37] Leading Syrian Sufi singer Sheikh Hamza Shakkur (b. 1947) describes seven languages Sufi musicians use to explain Sufism to Westerners:

> First, the Arabic language, the language of the Qur'an and poetry.
>
> Second, the universal language of music.
>
> Third, the language of the eyes.
>
> Fourth, the language of silence.
>
> Fifth, the expression of feelings.
>
> Sixth, physical expressions; and
>
> Seventh, the language of the soul.[38]

The Sufi tradition includes *sama*`, listening to all forms of music spiritually; thus, music and poetry do not have to be only religious. Shakkur is known across the Arab world and has performed many times in the West. Other notable Sufi musicians from Syria include Husayn Ismail Al-Amzi (b. 1952) and Bachar Zarkan (b. 1962), who has shifted his repertoire to Sufi traditions and sounds.

FOLK MUSIC

Hundreds of local folk traditions are found throughout the Arab region. Some carry traces of the musical practices of peoples with whom Arab populations have traded, or travelers from afar who have made pilgrimages. The rich drumming traditions of the Arab Gulf states are believed to result from extensive contact with African traders. The *Gnawa* tradition of Morocco takes its name from Guinean slaves brought to Morocco from West Africa. Nubian music in Egypt draws upon a distinctive melodic system that incorporates tones and distinctive rhythms more common further south in Africa. Folk traditions have evolved over many centuries. Some have been integrated into popular music, adopting new instruments and even Western styles.[39]

Arab folk music incorporates religious chants, poetic song forms, and dance for performances at weddings and other social events. Music is performed by both amateurs and professionals, depending on the style and the locale. Like traditional music, folk music is dominated by vocal repertoire, in part due to the transitory lifestyle of many of the Arab's nomadic ancestors. In general, while men both sing and play instruments, singing is the main musical activity for women.[40]

The *qasida* is one of the most ancient forms of folk music, and it spans across the Arab world. This style presents a poem that can be 100 lines long arranged in couplets. Each couplet is self-contained and is often improvised, so that a singer is lauded for creative verses. There are also many other forms of traditional music including shorter forms such as the *ataba* (found in Lebanon, Palestine, Jordan, Syria, and Iraq), sung at weddings or festivals, which follow specific rhyme schemes, rhythms, and line lengths.[41] Vocal storytelling accompanied by compelling, intricate rhythms formulate the root of this folk music.

Folk music in most of the region is based on *maqam* and improvisation is an essential feature. Although there are variations by region, the instruments used are common across the region. In addition to the aforementioned *nay, daf, darbouka* and *riqq*, wind and percussion instruments are especially utilized due to their portability. These include bright, double-pipe instruments like the *arghul* and the *mijwiz*. The *arghul* has one long pipe, which carried the scale, while the melody is played on the shorter pipes. The *mijwiz* is comprised of two short pipes, which a player will often bring in close pitch to create sonic beats. These and other wind instruments are played with circular breathing to create a continuous melody.[42] Drums of all sizes can be used, but unique to the region is a percussion instrument that doubles as a coffee grinder. The mortar and pestle creates a rhythm in combination with the scraping of the beans against the bottom.[43] The music tends to be lively and celebratory, appealing to broad audiences.

TRADITIONAL MUSIC OF THE ARABIAN PENINSULA

Al-ardah, meaning "display" or "performance," is one of the Arabian Peninsula's enduring styles that incorporates folk music with dancing. Saudi folklore is a blend of Bedouin practices and Islamic beliefs enriched by historical interaction with different civilizations that crossed the peninsula. Bedouin oral poetry is known as *Nabati* poetry. When performed, either solo or collective songs are played. This genre prospered in pre-Islamic Arabia and relayed many universal themes such as romance, tribal glories and spiritual devotion. *Nabati* music generally begins with a single line accompanied by drumbeats and a sword dance by the group. The music of *nabati* poetry becomes more melodious when it is accompanied by *rababah*, a common Bedouin string instrument, which belongs to the *oud* family, but is played with a bow.[44] This music is still performed today, and remains very popular with school children and youth.

Bedouin traditions influence the poetry, song, music, rhythm and dance of *al-ardah*, venerating the past while celebrating events of the present. *Al-ardah* is an essential component at weddings, religious festivals, and to mark other special occasions; it also is Saudi Arabia's national dance. Most Saudi folk songs follow a pattern of repeating a melody that is sung back and forth between a soloist and a chorus. In *al-ardah* performances, musicians play the three central Arab traditional instruments, *oud*, *qanun* and *nay*. Even these most basic folk traditions follow esthetic principles of *maqam*. Poetic lyrics drive the performance; many of the songs reflect age-old stories, accounts of battles and celebrated love stories. Sung poetry may represent three main forms: camel drivers' music; warriors' songs, and love songs. The term *al-ardah* refers to both songs of battle and the overall performance that incorporates both singing and dancing.[45]

Regional variations are common across the peninsula with the greatest musical differences found along the coast, where the Bedouin influence was not as strong. Here, popular songs are derived from seafaring, pearl diving, and trading. Each pearl diving ship had a boat singer, who sang to the crew throughout the day and as the ship returned to port with different songs for different stages of the sailing and diving. Kuwait, Bahrain, Qatar and the United Arab Emirates each have local folkloric styles derived from their location along the gulf. *Khaleej*, (meaning "Of the Gulf") music has strict five-tone scales and rapid rhythms. Music comes from the *oud*, various forms of drums, which has a deep full sound, and hand clapping.[46] This music has retained its form; songs that have lasted many centuries are still performed at celebrations and taught in schools.

Although known all along the Gulf coast but performed mostly in Kuwait and Bahrain, the *sawt*, which translates as "sound," is salon music. Some in a *sawt* group play the *oud* and *rabab* and sit at the far end of two lines of men who kneel, facing each other. After a short improvisation on the *oud*, "they start into song, and some of the men in the lines begin to play a small, cylindrical hand-drum, called the *mirwas*, in a percussion pattern that lightly punctuates the melody."[47] The interplay between the musicians and singers is similar to the improvisation and rhythmic innovation found in all traditional Arab music. Folk music of the Arabian Peninsula reflects a musical heritage that has lasted from pre-Islam to modern time. Sung poetry and music have been the popular forms that represent ideal cultural expression.

MA`LOUF MUSIC

Ma`louf music developed in Tunisia, and has its roots in the Spanish conquest of the thirteenth century. The genre also incorporates Turkish influences from the

Ottoman era, especially in the eighteenth century. *Ma'louf* means "familiar" or "customary." Songs are about commoners, reflecting people's lives and struggles, and lyrics could be provocative and coarse. Libya also has an indigenous Ma'louf music, as does Algeria, where it is called *Gharnata*. Ma'louf is rooted in a traditional *maqam*, known as a *nuba*, which is like a two-part suite. Each *nuba* lasts about an hour, and contains varied instrumental and vocal pieces in a traditional sequence. Originally, Ma'louf was performed in small folk ensembles with simple instrumentation: usually an *oud* (lute) and a *rabab (one-stringed fiddle)* accompanied by *bandir* (frame drum), *tar* (tambourine), *darbukka* (goblet-shaped drum) and *naqqara* (small kettle drum). Pieces are sung by soloists or small groups.[48]

Following the International Conference of Arab music held in Cairo in 1932, Tunisians moved to preserve this indigenous form of classical music, to some extent by modernizing it. A cultural preservation association, the *Rachidia*, was formed in 1934 to preserve the Ma'louf. The Rachidia revised offensive lyrics and constructed two performance spaces in Tunis to provide a venue for musicians. Instead of only using traditional instruments, new works incorporated foreign instruments and symphonic pieces inspired by Western classical music. Egyptian musical forms also influenced the modernization of Ma'louf. Today Ma'louf has become Tunisia's best-known classical music, performed in large ensembles of formally dressed, highly trained musicians. The music flows from powerful melodies that are enhanced by the number of musicians. Smaller groups still play at local festivities such as weddings.

ANDALUSIAN MUSIC

Al-Andalus, or Andalusian music is one of the oldest genres of North African music. Developed as a fusion of Iberian-Arab musical styles around the ninth century in Cordoba, Spain, Andalusian music spread across North Africa in the early sixteenth century, following the expulsion of Muslims from Spain. Andalusian music is found today across North Africa, but most notably in Morocco and Algeria. The music is extremely structured and performed by Andalusian orchestras. The traces of original Andalusian music have been passed through generations and still inspire performers and audiences.

The beginnings of Andalusian music can be traced to 822 when Abu Al-Hasan Ali Ibn Nafi (d. 857), known as Ziryab (Blackbird), arrived in Cordoba, Spain. Originally, from Baghdad, he also lived and performed in Tunis. Cordoba was a cosmopolitan center of learning and the arts. He was a famous singer, talented *oud* player and "is said to have known 10,000 songs and their melodies by heart."[49] In Cordoba, Ziryab founded a music school and codified classical music performances. These suites of vocal and instrumental music are now known as *nubah* (pl. *nubat*)—"turn." The form contains pieces composed in a single mode, and grouped according to rhythmic structure. The twenty-four nubat—seven established by Ziryab—are the basic structural elements that created early Andalusian music. It inspired contemplation and transformation: "each of the twenty-four *nubat* supposedly corresponded in quality with an hour of the day, and with different temporal, seasonal and emotional characteristics. Together they formed what is called "a symbolic tree of temperance." The performance of each nubah is said to have served a therapeutic function by keeping various body humors in balance."[50]

The traditional nubah structure is divided into five movements. Each has a corresponding rhythm that progresses from slow to fast over the course of its performance. Performing any single nubah could take between five and nine hours; consequently, the suites are rarely performed in their entirety today.[51] Orchestras use musical instruments including the *oud*, the *darbuka*, the *rebab*, and the *tar*, a North African name for a *riqq*. Instruments and musical forms from ninth century Levant and Iberia still provide avenues of musical expression in Andalusian music.

Notions of Andalusia are romanticized in the Arab world as a period of artistic flourishing, religious expansion and intellectual gains. The music of the era was founded by Ziryab, "a man who was exiled from his homeland in the East to find wealth and success in the West, a figure to whom the modern Arab can easily relate ... much of the original repertoire is lost, and the music as it actually sounded in Ziryab's time is probably gone forever; yet the spirit and vibrancy of Andalus music lives on in a number of Arab traditions."[52] The music remains an integral part of Moroccan and Algerian heritage. Several northern Morocco cities including Fes, Tetouan, Tangier and Chefchaouen are home to respected Andalusian orchestras. Today, to conserve the musical style and historical roots, both Fes and Essaouira in Morocco, and Algiers, Algeria, host annual Andalusian festivals.

RAI MUSIC

Rai is a newer form of Arab music that originated in the small Bedouin community in the city of Oran, Algeria in the 1930s. But like *Ma`louf*, it has foreign roots. In the sixteenth century, Oran was occupied by the Spanish, who divided it into four sections: Jewish, Spanish, French and Arab. Each community had its own musical style. These varied influences colored the musical scene of the city and other cities in Algeria into the twentieth century.

Traditional Bedouin instruments and rhythms form the heart of the music. Rai singers are referred to as *cheb* (f. *cheba*) or "youth." Older singers are known as *cheikh*, (f. *cheika*). As opposed to other forms of traditional music in the Arab world,

Rai has a long tradition of incorporating female singers. Rai music concerns issues of social justice, economic issues and identity. From its beginning, Rai countered established traditions and sought to modernize traditional Islamic ways.[53] The language of Rai can be rough and the lyrics often refer to struggle. The word *rai* means "advice" or "opinion" and the music is a form of asserting the musician's views of issues facing them personally or representing a community.

Following Algerian independence from France in 1962, Rai became popular throughout the country, especially among youth. In the 1960s and 1970s, musicians Bellemou Messaoud (b. 1947) and Belkacem Bouteldja (d. 2015) incorporated Western influences, including Reggae music and electronic instruments, to transform the music into what some call *pop-Rai*. Rai has always been a fluid musical form, incorporating foreign influences and responding to changes in the political landscape. Woods reflects that "the local and the global intersect in Rai."[54]

Rai reached its greatest popularity in the 1980s. Singer Khaled (b. 1960), formerly known as Cheb Khaled, became Rai's most famous and best-selling singer, popularizing the music within Algeria, throughout Europe, and internationally. He became known as the "King of Rai." With openness to Western influences, Rai deconstructs Arab-Islamic traditions and reinterprets them in a Western rock-pop context. Rai music was officially banned on the radio by the Algerian government in 1988, and by the 1990s political unrest led to further crackdowns on Rai production and performances. By its very nature, Rai had the power to criticize regimes and generate opposition to the increasingly brutal governments, especially after the Algerian army rejected the result of the elections in 1991.

In the coming years, Rai musicians were targeted, jailed, and worse. In 1994 one of Algeria's most famous Rai artists, Cheb Hasni (b. 1968), was killed by an Islamic extremist group in front of his parents' residence in Oran. By this time many Rai stars and musicians had left the country, mostly to France. Rai music remains popular internationally, especially among Algerian and other immigrant populations in France and neighboring countries. Cheb Mami (b. 1966) gained international success performing with Sting on the album *Desert Rose*. In Algeria, the Festival du Rai d'Oran originated in 2007. Oujda, Morocco also hosts an International Festival of Rai.

MUSIC VENUES AND FESTIVALS

In addition to the festivals mentioned above, other international music festivals occur throughout the Arab world and provide outlets for many forms of Arab music. The Ba`albek International Festival, the Middle East's longest-running and best-known music festival, celebrated sixty years in 2017. Held in the Roman Temple of Bacchus in Baalbek, Lebanon, it has hosted Lebanon's most famous artists as well as leading singers and musicians from the region and across the globe. The Kingdom of Jordan's Jerash Festival for Culture and Arts began in 1991, has brought musicians from around the region, and international performers, to Jerash. Jazz festivals are held in Cairo and the Gulf, especially Dubai, and Sharjah.

The Wanas International Folk Music Festival, organized in Cairo by El-Mastaba Center for Egyptian Folk Music, highlights traditional Egyptian music including Bedouin, Sufi, Delta, and Nubian. Morocco's Master Musicians of Joujouka is a micro-festival held annually in the village of Joujouka in the Rif Mountains where musicians play *rhaita* (the name of a two-stringed reed instrument), along with pipes and percussion. They are best known for Sufi trance songs. Tunisia hosts numerous music festivals, including the International Festival of Carthage, the International Festival for Symphonic Music in El Jem, and the International Festival of Testour, which highlights *ma`louf* music.

POPULAR FIGURES IN TWENTIETH CENTURY ARAB MUSIC

Cairo emerged as the center of the Golden Age of Arab popular music in the 1930s, lasting until the 1970s. Lebanon was, and remains, an important source of composers, singers, musicians and production studios. A few of the leading artists of this era include:

Sayyed Darwish (1892–1923), born in Alexandria, Egypt is known as the father of new Egyptian music and the leader of the renaissance of Arab music. He rejected Turkish styles of music, creating new music under the principle that genuine art must be derived from people's aspirations and feelings. He was known for his strong, melodic voice and most of the songs he performed were *taktuka*, usually short songs played for amusement and entertainment.[55] The people around him and the events in their lives inspired his music. His works blended Western instruments and harmonies with classical Arab styles and Egyptian political and popular themes. He appealed to the entire population, wealthy and poor, across all of Egypt. He composed the music for Egypt's national anthem. Darwish is credited with liberating Arab music from its classical style, modernizing it and opening the door for future development, while not losing Arab sensibilities.

Muhammad Abdul Wahab (1902–1991), the "Father of Modern Egyptian Song," reshaped Egyptian traditional songs as a successful singer, composer and musician from the 1930s until the 1970s. In the years of independence and nationalism, he inspired Egyptian and other Arabs to reassert their national heritage. His lyrics were often poems from the Golden Age of Arab Poetry; he composed over one thousand songs and was a renowned *oud* player. Although he championed classical Arab musical styles and themes, he also enriched his music by bringing in Western themes and instruments. His enduring legacy is cemented by his scoring the national anthems of Egypt, Oman and the United Arab Republic.

**Wadi` al-Safi** (1921–2013) is known as Lebanon's eternal voice. He appealed to crowds with a powerful voice that had both strength and sweetness. He was also a skilled musician, versed in traditional Lebanese folk music, and participated in the first Ba`alback International Festival in 1957. He spent periods of time abroad, first in Brazil, then Europe, and finally in other Arab countries during the 1975–1990 Lebanese civil war, popularizing his interpretations of Lebanese folk songs for expatriates, including Arab and European audiences. Upon returning to Lebanon, he began to develop a new Lebanese urbanized folk style, performing with Fairuz and other leading Lebanese singers.[56] Like Darwish and Abdul Wahab, Al-Safi was open to experimentation with Western instruments. He also performed religious, nationalistic and romantic pieces, and was known for his ability to help audiences to reach *tarab*, a state of ecstasy and rapture.

Riyad al-Sunbati (1906–1981) was a well-known Egyptian composer and musician who composed and wrote dozens of songs for Umm Kulthum, including some of her greatest pieces. His composition of *Al-Atlal* (The Ruins), sung by Umm Kulthum, is perhaps the most famous piece of music he produced. He was well known for his performances on the *oud* based on *maqam* forms, which influenced many musicians who followed him. By incorporating foreign styles such as tango, rumba and waltz, he modernized the Egyptian music. Al-Sunbati took the Arabic classical music to new innovative levels.

Sheikh Imam (1918–1995) was an influential Egyptian composer and singer known for his songs of protest. He was well versed in Egyptian folk and traditional music. He is best known for collaborations with Egyptian poet Ahmed Fouad Negm (1929–2013). Their music, based on traditional forms, celebrated the lives of the poor and working classes and called for social change and empowerment. During the 1960s and 1970s their songs, often critical of government policies, were banned from Egyptian radio, but remained extremely popular with audiences. Imprisoned by both President Nasir and President Sadat, he became an icon of dissent. Some of his works have been reinterpreted in electro-pop and hip-hop styles, giving him lasting influence. He was blind, "but, as his fans would have it, saw the world more clearly than anyone."[57]

Umm Kulthum (1898–1975) is widely regarded as the greatest Arab singer of all time. Born in the rural Nile Delta, she was a child prodigy and her powerful voice inspired others from an early age. Her father was the head of a village mosque, and as a child, she learned to recite the Qur'an. In her twenties, she moved to Cairo and from then on captivated Egyptian and Arab audiences with her powerful emotions, immense singing voice, and stage presence. Throughout her career she was known for inspiring *tarab* ("ecstasy") through her voice, interpretations and emotion. By the 1940s she had assembled the very best *takht* ("ensemble"), comprised of Egypt's leading musicians. She also began to perform songs written by twentieth century composers such as Mohammed Abdul Wahab, with more contemporary themes. She also had a career as a celebrated actress portraying Egyptian heroines in hugely successful films.

It is hard to fathom the level of Umm Kulthum's popularity from the 1940s until her death in 1975; she was the most famous and popular artist in the Arab world. She put poetry to music, and "achieved the unimaginable; she brought fine literature to the masses, many of whom were illiterate. Because of her broadcasts, young and old, rich and poor now hummed the words to intricate Arab poetry that was previously inaccessible to most. In her monthly Thursday night concerts, her voice flooded the radio waves across the Middle East ... She had earned herself the title, 'the voice of Egypt.'"[58] Her songs of love, devotion, loss and triumph resonated with her audiences, linking human emotions and uniting the countries sharing the Arabic language. She performed live and on radio throughout the 1950s and 1960s and became a figure of Egyptian and Arab nationalism, especially following the defeat in the 1967 Six-Day War. She remains the centerpiece of the Golden Age of Egyptian music, and her songs continue to be reinterpreted by contemporary singers. Her funeral in 1975 was legendary; four million mourners flooded the streets of Cairo.

Fairuz was born Nuhad Haddad in 1935 in Beirut, Lebanon. She is the most famous living Arab singer. She first gained attention in her native Lebanon appearing in musical plays in Ba`albek that had roots in Lebanese folklore. She first performed at the Ba`albek International Festival in 1957 and famously returned after a twenty-five-year absence in 1998. In her vocal training she studied the art of chanting the Qur'anic verses, giving her a mastery of the Arabic language, whether for traditional Arab songs or Christian liturgy. She found success and popularity in all forms of music: "art songs, classical language, Lebanese dialect, pop, dance, Eastern *tarab*, Western classical (even a Mozart tune with Arab lyrics), children's and patriotic songs. She excelled in all."[59] Her fame spans the Arab world, to Europe, South America and the United States, where a Las Vegas concert drew over ten thousand fans.

Fairuz's serious formal reputation underlies her commitment to perfectionism and putting the song above all. She has performed in nearly every Arab country, receiving accolades from leader after leader. She also has been a fierce supporter of Lebanon and its people. Her husband, Assi Rahbani (d. 1986) and his brother, Mansour Rahbani (d. 2009), known as the Rahbani Brothers, were composers and producers with whom she worked throughout her career. Her son, Ziad Rahbani (b. 1956), is also a composer.

Marcel Khalife (b. 1950) is a traditional musician who embraces Lebanese traditional and folk music, but includes instruments such as the piano and other Western imports, including electronic instruments, into his performances. He has been an influential teacher at the Beirut Conservatory and other musical institutions in the Arab world. He is a renowned *oud* player known for interpreting the lyrics of Palestinian poet Mahmoud Darwish (d. 2008). Khalife has been the target of attacks from critics who have accused him of insulting religious values and remains an outspoken critic of censorship and injustice, championing humanism and tolerance. His son Rami Khalife (b. 1981) is also a gifted and accomplished composer.

Mohamed Munir (b. 1954) one of Egypt's best-selling popular musicians, is also known as *al-Malik* (The King). He continued the trend of earlier twentieth century icons by infusing Western styles and instruments, yet retaining a distinctive Egyptian-Arab sound. His songs address contemporary social and political concerns. In the 1970s he became Egypt's first bona fide pop star, with his charisma, appealing voice and popular charm. In the 1980s, he began a successful film career. He also has released an album of Sufi devotional music.

CONTEMPORARY ARAB MUSIC

Arab music in the twenty-first century has reflected the region's turmoil politically, socially and culturally. To some in the Arab world, the influence of Western values has ruined Arab culture. To others, the interchange between Western and Arab music remains fertile ground for experimentation and collaboration. Contemporary music attracts youth, especially with music videos. Some performances are characterized by revealing clothes and provocative dancing. The satellite revolution makes it impossible for governments and religious authorities to censor or ban the videos, which have transplanted the traditional live nature of Arab music.

In some contemporary music, for a certain audience, the physical attraction of the performers with its provocative sexual content has become more important than the music itself. Many lament the decay of Arab music, citing negative influences from the West as the cause. Yet music has retained its power over Arab audiences in its ability to provoke strong emotions and has become an important vehicle for people to vent their frustrations and demand social and economic changes. Music mixed with poetic verses played a powerful role forcing out the leaders of Tunisia, Egypt, Libya and Yemen during the Arab Spring revolutions.

THE ROLE OF MUSIC IN THE ARAB SPRING

Although musicians in Tunis, Egypt and elsewhere helped to drive the Arab Spring, their music of dissent had a huge impact on the people. Before the events broke out in December 2010 in Tunisia, artist Hamada Ben Amor (b. 1990), "El General," had protested against the Ben Ali government and voiced his generation's dissatisfaction with unemployment, the lack of opportunities for youth and the corruption of the Ben Ali regime. His song "Rais Lebled (President of the Country)," a scathing personal attack on President Ben Ali, became the anthem of the revolution and allowed people to have a shared expression, channeling their desires for a different way of life. Topics that were taboo even in private were now sung in mass in public. The song's calls for change were later adopted in Egypt and other Arab countries. Immediately after Mohammed Bouazizi set himself on fire in December 2010, El General released several other songs including "Tunisia Our Country."

In an interview with journalist Lauren Bohn in the summer of 2011, El General explained his dissatisfaction with the government and his generation's concerns: "We were guests in our own country. We weren't landlords. The suffering of the people made me speak. And I chose rap to do this ... I'm ready to sacrifice my life for what I'm thinking, for the ideas I'm transmitting. I see one thing. Only the truth."[60] This commitment extended to all of the singers, composers and musicians who played a part in Arab Spring protests. By immediate spreading on social media, his call to action inspired Tunisians around the country to rise in protest against the Ben Ali regime. El General's compatriot, Emel Mathlouthi (b. 1982), became known as the "Voice of the Revolution." Her songs, "Ya Tounis Ya Miskina (Poor Tunisia)" and "Kilmiti Hurra (My Word is Free)" also spurred people to demonstrate, and gave a voice to their aspirations. With the revolution in Tunisia, music became a social instigator wielding the power to inspire the masses, especially youth, and not just call for change, but force change to happen.

Ramy Essam (b. 1987), one of the leading voices in Egypt's revolution, created music during the protests in Tahrir Square and was arrested, but his impact did not diminish. His song "Irhal (Leave)" celebrated the refusal of the protesters to leave despite violent police attacks. The song incorporates protest chants that the crowd used. Another Egyptian, Maryam Saleh (b.1986), reworked Egyptian folk tunes, challenging the established social order and pointing out injustice and hypocrisy.[61] Egyptians effectively utilized social media to release protest songs, which attracted international attention. Even foreign-based and non-Egyptian singers such as Syrian-American Omar Offendum (b. 1981) and Iraqi-Canadian Yassin Alsalman (b.1982, known as the Narcicyst or Narcy), joined the protests.[62] Easily spread though social media, their songs provided motivation and a unifying effect for those in the uprising. The popularity of the songs also drew attention to the cause.

Khaled M. (b. 1985, Khaled Ahmed, Libyan-American) was a key player in the Libyan revolution, stressing common values of Libyans at home and abroad to rise up against the Gaddafi regime. The Yemeni protest song "Mu`tasimeen (The Protesters)" was popular throughout the country, addressing President Ali Abdullah Saleh directly: "There is no power in the world that can stand against the Yemeni people/Are you sane or insane?/There are 20 million of us."[63] The protest songs were effective by appealing in local Arab dialects to the aspirations and demands of the people. They emerged from each country's traditions, amplified by being sung in crowds of thousands of people across all strands of society.

A cultural movement in Morocco known as *Nayda*—"get up on your feet"—was popular before the Arab Spring and continues to express the political frustrations of youth. Algerian rappers released protest songs as early as the 1994 during the Algerian civil war; Issa Ghandour sang about the lament of Lebanon's suffering during the Cedar Revolution in 2005 (a series of demonstrations against Syrian presence in Lebanon),[64] the protest music in the Arab world "invokes deep collective memories. It reminds its audience that the protesters are of the people, and that they are fighting for their own heritage. It reminds them of the power and grandeur of Arab music, that the heritage of their past is what they are calling for in the present."[65] Music not only accompanied the revolutions, it created a form of revolution in and of itself, the music and lyrics gave rise to self-expression and empowerment for young Arabs responding to both their own situations and a global digital age.

ARAB POP AND CONTEMPORARY ARTISTS

From the end of the twentieth century to the present, the genre known as Arab pop refers to the music popular across the region heavily influenced by Western sounds. Music videos have been an important facet of this music's success, as there are over forty Arabic satellite music channels. Beirut and Cairo are both lucrative music and video production centers, and a number of the corporations controlling the music industry are extremely profitable. With the population of the Middle East and North Africa estimated to be approximately four hundred million, and increasingly under 25 years of age, the market is enormous.[66] Digital technology advances have made music and video production possible virtually anywhere, and social media platforms made distribution easy, precluding government censorship.

Arab pop targets mainstream audiences, and the music is meant to appeal to large populations across the region. Exposure, sales and profit drive the industry.

One of the first Arab pop styles, the Egyptian *Sha`bi* (popular) music, emerged from working class neighborhoods. Although sometimes political, the music tends to be humorous with many double entendres. Singer Ahmed Adawiya (b. 1942) was one of the first modern Arab pop stars; like many to follow, he had a successful film career. Hakim (b. 1962) and Sha`ban Abdel-Rahim (b. 1957) have followed Adawiya as best-selling Egyptian *sha`bi* singers.

Amr Diab (b. 1961) is Egypt's leading pop star and one of the few also well known in the West. His popular films have enhanced his fame. He is known for his diverse repertoire, singing traditional Egyptian pieces, soulful ballads and fla-menco-tinged songs. Singer and composer Tamer Husny (b. 1982) has performed many varieties of Egyptian pop music as well as an album of Islamic-based and Ramadan-themed songs. He has appeared in numerous music videos and is a popular film star. Sherine (b. 1980, Sherine Ahmed Abdel Wahhab) is a best-sell-ing Egyptian singer and media personality, known for upbeat songs that present strong images of women.

Charismatic Palestinian singer Mohammad Assaf (b. 1989) became famous after winning the second season of *Arab Idol.* He has gone on to record popular albums and is Palestine's leading singer. His background growing up in the Khan Younis refugee camp in Gaza inspires Palestinians throughout the world. Syrian Assala Nasri (b. 1969) became famous with her recordings of classic Egyptian songs in the *tarab* style. She recorded 26 albums between 1992 and 2017 and is one of the best-selling Arab recording artists. More recently, she has campaigned extensively against the Assad regime in Syria.

Lebanese female pop singers have become the most famous stars of Arab pop. Nancy Ajram (b. 1983) rocketed to fame because of her sexually provocative videos. Elissa (b. 1971) is also known as a risk-taking performer with suggestive videos. Nawal Al Zoghbi (b. 1971) emerged in the late 1990s with clever pop songs and provocative videos, which attract millions. She is prolific, releasing her eleventh studio album in 2018. Model-turned-singer Haifa Wehbe (b. 1976) is another Lebanese singer in this genre who has become more famous for her appearance and sultry manner than her singing.

Some artists are taken more seriously and respected for cultivating the roots and styles of traditional Arab music. Yasmine Hamdan (b. 1976) is a Lebanese-born singer who represents Arab music's growing international side. She has lived in Lebanon, Kuwait, Abu Dhabi, Greece and currently resides in France. She is committed to bringing Arabic singing into the musical mainstream and out of the "world music" box. She gained recognition in Beirut with the electro-beat duo Soap Kills, which garnered a cult following for its innovative mix of Western sounds and Arabic lyrics. In 2009, she produced an album in

Paris called *Arabology* which gained attention for being a cutting edge, dynamic Arab-rooted album. Hamdan has a deep interest in traditional Arab songs as sources of inspiration. Her 2013 album *Ya Nass* (Hey People) incorporates many different dialects and forms of Arabic, including songs in Lebanese, Egyptian, Palestinian and Bedouin dialects. She is inspired by both contemporary singers and former stars such as Umm Kulthum and Sayyed Darwish.[67] Her 2017 solo album, *Al-Jamilat* (The Beautiful Ones) explores Arab traditions in a contemporary way. The title song is from a poem by Mahmoud Darwish; the album incorporates Arab melodies and styles mixed with contemporary instruments and electronic mixing.

Iraqi Kazem Al-Saher (b. 1961) is popular throughout the Arab world for his songs and performances that use traditional Arab instruments and orchestrations. He revived classical sequences and infused his music with traditional Iraqi sounds and styles. More recent music has incorporated Algerian Rai rhythms, and he has collaborated with artists as diverse as Lenny Kravitz (b. 1964) and Sarah Brightman (b. 1960). He is known as a humanitarian, both for Iraqi and global causes.

Although Tunisian artist Emel Mathlouthi (b. 1982) fled Tunis and settled in New York, her music has become emblematic of contemporary Arab music's classical foundations infused with Western electronic sounds and world beat percussions. She is first and foremost a musician as opposed to a protest singer. As she explained in a recent interview: "Music is so immediate it shouldn't need translation ... I have the opportunity to carry many struggles ... it's important [for me] to be out there as a creative, Tunisian, Arab woman from a Muslim culture, but completely free."[68] She represents a new generation of singer-songwriters who may live abroad, but are committed to incorporating Arab musical forms and are inspired by past singers and composers.

One of the most dynamic and influential groups performing today is made up of Egyptians Maryam Saleh (b.1986) and Maurice Louca, with Palestinian Tamer Abu Ghazale (b. 1986). Their last names give the group its name, and their most recent album *al-Ikhfaa* was released to critical praise in 2017. Rhythmic yet dissonant, it uses the *ney* (an open-ended flute), percussion and keyboard to create a modern yet distinctly Arab sound. Saleh grew up in an artistic family that frequently hosted legendary singer Sheikh Imam; his music has influenced hers and she has performed his music. The group creates alternative Arab music that incorporates many forms of Egyptian music. Continuing a long tradition of Arab songs being inspired by the words of poets, their recent album ʿal-Ikhfaa sets to music the poems of their contemporary poet Mido Zoheir (b. 1974), one of the young talented poets in Egypt today.

TRADITIONAL ROOTS AND MODERN INFLUENCES

Arab music is decidedly unique. Its storied journey riding the line between adhering to its rich and deep roots while also embracing the influence of other styles and genres sets it apart from other music. Formed out of poetry originating in the Arabian Peninsula, traditional Arab music mixed with poetic verse is respected and celebrated as an independent and lively creation. Between the spoken word and the complex tonal forms of *maqam*, Arab music is a mix of simplicity and sophistication.

Sung mostly in dialects understood across the Arab world, Arab lyrics continue to reflect the heritage of long tradition with poetry-infused feeling. Folk music of the Arabian Peninsula reflects a musical heritage that has lasted from pre-Islam to the modern time. *Khaleeji* music has retained its form and includes songs that have lasted many centuries and are still performed at celebrations and taught in schools. Sung poetry and music continue represent the ideal cultural expression.

That said, while the traditional musical forms continue to exist independently, new styles have been integrated. Adaption of Western influences after World War I actually spurred a modern renaissance in Arab music, which has had a lasting influence. Arab peoples throughout the Arab world still listen to the traditional twentieth century music and songs of Fairuz, Umm Kulthum, Marcel Khalife, and many others. Whether incorporating Persian, Ottoman, Iberian or other influences, "relatively quickly, Arab ears became accustomed to the new music."[69]

Rap and hip-hop have become popular in the Arab world, embracing the Arabic language, incorporating national themes and valuing individual interpretation. Arab poets, composers, musicians and singers are incorporating musical influences from their neighbors and across continents, adding new instruments and modern technology into new and often very Arab forms of collective expression. Both Arab traditional and contemporary music are now available throughout the world, often marketed as ethnic music or world beat.

The ever-changing form that is Arabic music will continue to play an important role in Middle Eastern life and culture. Music has most recently proven to be a strong vehicle for political change in the Arab world during the Arab Spring. In its ability to bring its people back to their roots while also exposing them to new ways, Arab music possesses the profound power to shape its own sphere of influence. History and tradition notwithstanding, Arab music will undoubtedly remain at the foundation of Arabic culture and life.

CHAPTER EIGHT

Modern Arabic Poetry

EMERGENCE AND DEVELOPMENT

What we now call modern Arabic poetry first surfaced after the Arab renaissance at the end of the eighteenth century, shortly after the French invasion of Egypt in 1798. Many believe the modernity in Arabic poetry was the product of indigenous Arabic language literary tradition meeting the cultural forces of the West,[1] but this theory is not entirely accurate. Modernism in Arabic poetry has existed in every historical era and is as old as the language itself. In fact, although it has followed conventional forms and structures for fifteen centuries, Arabic poetry has undergone continual innovation as well.

In Arabic poetry there has always been a tension between the old and the new, between imitation and innovation, between the classicist and the modernist. Modernity, as an artistic movement, has been less about the *when* of artistic creation and more about the *how* of it: a poem written a millennium ago, then, can just as easily be considered more modernist than a poem written a year ago. Modernity in Arab poetics was not the result of its encounter with the West, either, even though this has been demonstrably influential over many aspects of Arab culture, including poetry. Great modernist poets existed in the Arab world long before the nineteenth century, particularly during the Abbasid and Umayyad periods. This chapter, however, focuses on the latter half of the twentieth century and treats the poetry of this period as a testimony to contemporary culture and life in the Arab world.

At the beginning of the Arab renaissance, poets began imitating classical Arabic poetry in form and content, particularly focusing on the great Abbasid poets. This neoclassical movement became a necessary first step in the rebirth and modernization of Arabic poetry and culture after a period of stagnation dating to the thirteenth century. After centuries of decline, however, it was no easy task to recapture the genius and magic of the earlier traditional poetic conventions.[2] To eliminate the creative weaknesses inflicted on the classical art during long centuries of Ottoman domination, poets set poetry free from old linguistic tricks and addressed its lack of gravity, originality, and overall power. They revived old poetic forms and content that would pave the way for modernization of the poetic art.

When we talk about modern Arabic poetry, we are talking about a poetry of vision. Poets in the modernist school took it upon themselves to create a new culture, a new society, and a new way of thinking. They played the roles of redeemers, saviors, and visionaries, and they believed they were leading the Arabs away from cultural stagnation toward the creation of a new Arab World.[3] From the early twentieth century on, modern poets rejected the traditional forms of poetry and began, especially in the last half of the century, to bring new insight and awareness to political and social predicaments that were suffocating the Arab world, especially those involving the issues of freedom, liberation, and justice. Poets were the ones who openly opposed the oppressive and reactionary conditions of Arab society and became personally involved in its growth. Their poetry is complex, aesthetically sophisticated, and original; it is also filled with anger, rejection, and a longing for Arab rebirth. In short, poets of this age are poets of revolution. They insist on destroying the existing order and rebuilding a new one, which is, at once, both their "greatest aspiration and most arduous task."[4]

Since the 1950s, modern Arabic poetry has exhibited a deep commitment to the national, social, political, and cultural struggles of the Arab world. This poetry can often seem angry, especially in its insistence on creating a dignified future and continuing the struggle until justice and freedom flourish in society. When the political realities of the Arab world changed suddenly and drastically after World War II, the political commitment of its poets also changed. Poetry began to focus on issues of national independence, economic conditions, and corruption's various shapes and forms in the modern world—the indignities of unemployment, poverty, and the non-existence of public services and health care. After the loss of Palestine in 1948, Arab poetry tackled censorship, police terror, foreign intervention, and the dictatorship of Arab rulers. In the modern era, Arabic poetry has become a literature of commitment that concentrates on the major issues of our time. It turns its back on the rigid structures and formulaic content of past poetic traditions and aims instead at creating a new future for the Arab world.[5]

Poetry remains one of the most incisive tools in modern Arab society. The twentieth century has witnessed the emergence of new literary genres—the novel, short story, dramatic play—in the Arab world, but poetry remains by far the most effective weapon in its cultural arsenal. Though poets today occupy an important space just as they always have, their function has changed. Ancient Arab poets defended the honor and values of the tribe but did not question the tribal system itself. Modern Arab poets neither support their political and social systems nor glorify their groups and communities. Instead, they hold themselves in eternal opposition to, and conflict with, the system, attacking its stagnation and calling for its immediate replacement.

That conflict with prevailing culture is a far cry from ancient Arab poetry's effort to depict a stable and harmonious culture; modern Arabic poetry instead reflects a more complex, sophisticated situation. Its sources of inspiration and modes of expression are different from earlier traditions, too. Audiences no longer expect poets to praise and glorify the positive aspects of society; in fact, they are now expected to use poetry to inspire social and political change. As a result, new themes and schools have emerged, including the nationalist, socialist, realist, surrealist, and existentialist schools, that use innovative metaphor, intense poetic imagery, and complex style.

Revolutionary ideals have dominated Arabic poetry since the early 1950s as poets called for self-determination and a rejection of colonization and occupation. An enormous poetic corpus has been written that speaks against foreign intervention and in support of independence and freedom. The Algerian revolution against France, the Palestinian struggle, the Egyptian revolution of 1952, and the nationalization of the Suez Canal in 1956 have all provided abundant grist for the mill of poetic inspiration. Palestinian poetry, which emerged after 1948, shifted by the early 1960s from romanticism to themes of resistance, revolution, and defiance. Arab nationalism also dominated as a motif with the rise of Jamal `Abd al-Nasir of Egypt. Nasir's eloquence and dream of a strong, united, and independent Arab world inspired poets and the population at large. The dream of re-creating a great Arab civilization in the image of the glory from centuries past seemed real once more; poetry expressed these desires and hopes of the Arab people. A strong demand emerged for a literature written for everyday people in accessible language.

INNOVATORS IN VERSE

By most accounts, Gibran Khalil Gibran (d. 1931) gave birth to modernist Arab poetics. Gibran and other Arab-American writers, joined by a spontaneous movement of poets and critics in Egypt, Syria, and Lebanon, all broke away from the traditional poetry of the classical era. Their poetry used new language and images, radical ideas and beliefs, and fresh structures and forms.

By the late 1940s and early 1950s, another pioneering group emerged as well: the Iraqi poets, who led a movement toward free verse in Arabic poetry. Their innovative movement discarded conventional content and form in order to avoid verse they considered rigid, fixed, and static. Poets from across the Arab world soon welcomed free verse, and the movement is still undergoing active evolution in form, content, and technique.[6] The Arabic free verse movement was born in 1949 with Nazik al-Mala'ika (d. 2007), Badr Shakir al-Sayyab (d. 1964), and `Abdul Wahab al-Bayati (d. 1999). Although other poets paved the way for the movement's emergence, these three Iraqi poets led the effort to guide Arabic poetry beyond the constraints of its classical structures. This involved learning to transcend traditional rhyme schemes and conventional metric patterns that had prevailed for more than fifteen centuries and departing from classical poetry in substance and configuration.[7]

Since the beginning of the free verse movement, poets from across the Arab world, particularly in Iraq, Syria, Egypt, Lebanon, and Morocco, have conducted continual poetic experimentation. They have employed the deliberate obscurity of words and metaphorical exploration to create a new consciousness about the lack of freedom and justice in the Arab world. Many gifted Arab poets have emerged in their wake, earning great acclaim within the Arab world and on the international stage, including: Muhammad al-Maghout (d. 2006), Adonis (b. 1930), al-Bayati, Nizar Qabbani (d. 1998), and Mahmoud Darwish (d. 2008), to name a few. Their poetry draws on complex, symbolic systems and enjoys universal appeal, criticizing Arab realities and inciting optimism for social, political, and cultural change in Arab society.

DEFENDERS OF THE PEOPLE

Deeply involved in the issues of the day, some leading Arab modern poets have acted as martyrs or saviors of their people and society. The Palestinian `Abd al-Rahim Mahmoud (d. 1948) was the first Arab poet-martyr of the modern era. He "carried his soul in the palm of his hand," he writes in one verse, and "threw it into the caravan of death" at the age of 35, dying in the fight to keep Palestine free from foreign occupation. His verses merge with his death, eliminating the gap between words and action; Mahmoud is regarded as a poet of purpose who turned vision into reality and reality into myth.[8]

It is not a new concept in Arab society for the poet to be defender of his people, or, as in Mahmoud's case, to die for them. In pre-Islamic times, Arab poets were warriors besides being the voices and representatives of their people. The ideal hero of Arab culture has always been the warrior-poet, wielding sword and pen against injustice and oppression. This aspect of the poet's role in society has not changed in modern times, either. Hafiz Ibrahim, Jamil Sidqi al-Zahawi, Ma`ruf al-Rusafi, Ibrahim Tuqan (d. 1941), and Muhammad Mahdi al-Jawahiri, to name a few, are regarded as fighters for social and political justice—their activities reaffirm the continuing involvement of Arab poets in this struggle. Tawfiq Zayyad (d. 1994) wrote verses extolling the efforts of the Palestinian people to overcome their

difficulties, and he was heavily involved in many aspects of the Palestinian struggle. Samih al-Qasim (d. 2014) and Darwish have continued to fight for a Palestinian
homeland with their verse—in a sense, they have both served as the unofficial
spokespersons for the Palestinian people.

Probably nowhere in the modern world are poets more actively engaged in the
cultural, social, and political realities of their societies than in the Arab world. Arab
poets are considered by the general population to be visionaries and creators of
ideas and awareness, and many Arab governments have grown to fear them for this
reason. With intensified challenges, most poets have grown even more involved in
society—and increasingly critical. Today's Arab poet has become a "fighter against
his time," to use Nietzsche's formulation. As fighters, many prominent Arab poets
have also been imprisoned, tortured, or forced outside the borders of their homelands over the last few decades.[9] Al-Maghout, Muhammad `Afifi Matar (d. 2010)
and Abdellatif La`bi (b. 1942), and others suffered imprisonment. Al-Bayati died
outside of Iraq; Muzaffar al-Nawwab (b. 1934) lived underground; and Saadi Yousef
(b. 1934) lived in exile. Other poets, such as Adonis and Qabbani, have chosen to
live completely outside the Arab world.

FACING TRAGEDY WITH A NEW VOICE

As their world experienced a series of tragic events in the political, social, national,
and cultural spheres, Arabs faced complicated issues associated with foreign intervention, harsh economic conditions, and threats that were both internal and external. After World War II, newly independent Arab states became quickly corrupted,
mostly ruled by foreign-backed dictators or monarchies. Along with the loss of
Palestine in 1948, these realities caused demoralization across the Arab world and
deeply affected the collective Arab psyche—but it also marked a turning point for
modern Arabic literature on a pan-Arab scale. Poets confronted these events with
a bold, new attitude of defiance. The romanticism that dominated Arab literary
circles between the two world wars was quickly discarded.[10]

To reflect these developments in their world, the poets had to effect a revolutionary (and rapid) change in their verse. Their poetry needed new linguistic
resources to meet the needs of modernity. They found new symbolism and imagery
in ancient Arab culture, classical mythology, and modern European poetry, and all
of it was given a vibrant, local resonance. The rigid constraints of classical poetic
forms, traditional rhyme schemes, and conventional metric patterns were rejected
in favor of free verse poetry without restrictions.[11] Badr Shakir al-Sayyab, who was
hunted by Iraqi authorities and forced into exile, used free verse and symbolism
to describe the many tragic aspects of political and social oppression. Swept by

homesickness and longing for his country, he describes the injustice of the Iraqi situation in "Song of Rain," composed during his exile in Kuwait in 1954.[12] Gazing at Iraq from across the border as the rain falls, the poet writes that ravens and locusts, symbols of the corrupt Iraqi government and social system, have eaten the growing crops. The rain, a life-giving force and symbol of fertility, serves only to perpetuate the hunger and misery of the people, who cannot even reap the harvest of their own slave labor.[13]

Critics would have been hard-pressed to find a major poet who did not use his voice as a weapon for political and social change. The concept of *iltizam* (commitment) became a key term in the Arab critic's vocabulary;[14] it was a direct translation of the term *engagement*, coined in 1948 by French philosopher Jean-Paul Sartre. The importance of *iltizam* was driven home by the influential Lebanese periodical *al-Adaab* (Literatures) which was founded by Arab writer Suhail Idris (d. 2008). This pan-Arab publication, established in 1953 and devoted to emphasizing the need for literature to have a societal message, played an important role in shaping the course of modern Arabic literature.

Likewise, the literary periodical *Shi`r* (Poetry), was extremely influential in the social development of modern Arabic poetry.[15] Founded in Beirut in 1957 by Yusuf al-Khal (d. 1987) and Adonis, *Shi`r* featured poets who were extreme in their rejection of traditional values and radical in their uses of language. The content and form of their poetry demonstrated metaphysical and mystical dimensions and showed the clear influence of contemporary Western poetry, especially French symbolism and surrealism. Soon another important intellectual and cultural journal called *Dirasat `Arabiya* (Arab Studies) was founded in Beirut by Basheer Daouk (d. 2007), a leading Arab intellectual, and focused on maintaining modern Arab culture's political, national, and social commitments.

The emergence of these journals coincided with several new political movements seeking to achieve independence, freedom, justice, and unity within the Arab world. The pan-Arab movement attracted the support of large communities, particularly in Syria, Lebanon, Jordan, Iraq, and Egypt, and its message resonated in the hearts of poets as well as the general public. Socialist movements including the Ba`th, Syrian Nationalist Party, and National Progressive Socialist Party were formed, counting poets among their ranks. Prominent intellectuals of Marxist and communist leanings also joined the fray. Another response to the tragic events of the twentieth century came from the Islamic movement, which emerged as a major political force, particularly in Egypt and Syria.[16]

SHATTERED DREAMS AND DESPAIR

By 1961, the political unity between Egypt and Syria which had been established in 1958 at the height of the popularity of ʿAbd al-Nasir's pan-Arab vision, had disintegrated. Leading Arab nationalist poets responded with frustration and disappointment. A further blow to Arab nationalism was their sudden, unexpected defeat in 1967, which shattered all hopes for an immediate restoration of Arab glory. The promises made by Nasir and other politicians were suddenly broken; all their proclamations came to be viewed as false illusions. What followed in the Arab world was an intense period of profound depression and, in the words of Jabra Ibrahim Jabra (d. 1994), a "complete spiritual impotence."[17] Arab poets began to express intense anger, resentment, and alienation in verses echoing the bitterness of the Arab population.

After the collapse of the United Arab Republic of Syria and Egypt, the Lebanese poet Khalil Hawi (d. 1982), a great modernist and fervent champion of Arab nationalism whose poetry was dominated by the idea of a resurrection of Arab civilization, fell into despair. In 1962, Hawi wrote the prophetic and tragic poem "Lazarus," which predicted the disaster of the June war that would befall the Arab world five years later. The poem is inspired by the Gospel story of Lazarus, in which Jesus raises him from the dead and demonstrates his true divine identity. In Hawi's version, though, Lazarus symbolizes the dead Arab man who does not want to be resurrected. Hawi portrays him as being in love with his own death and asking the gravedigger to make his hole deeper:

> Deepen the hole, gravedigger,
>
> Deepen it to an unfathomable depth
>
> That extends beyond the orbit of the sun
>
> Into a night of ashes.[18]

In Hawi's poem, the character of Lazarus's wife—who symbolizes the lust of Arab civilization for life—has long been awaiting her husband's resurrection. But her burning desire to reunite with him is crushed by the tragedy of his deformed return. She is shocked and devastated by what she sees—the cold body and dead spirit of her exhumed husband:

> He was a black shadow
>
> Looming over the mirror of my breast
>
> And in my eyes the shame of a woman

Undressed to a stranger.

Oh! Why did he return from his grave

A dead man?[19]

The wife of Lazarus longs for an existential renewal to satiate her body and soul, but her husband, the modern Arab, fails her. Indeed, as a consequence of Lazarus' dark resurrection, his wife loses faith in her husband and in the God who brought him back.

Hawi's "Lazarus" foretells the impossibility of Arab recovery from the setbacks of the twentieth century. The poem opens at Lazarus' grave and closes at the grave of his wife, whom he ultimately drags with him into the world of the dead. She is too weak to resist and, having lost her lust for life, she follows him into the abyss. In this prophetic vision, Hawi suggests that the Arab nation, like Lazarus, is too broken to restore itself, and that Arab civilization, like Lazarus' wife, is too weak to avoid being dragged into the grave. Many Arab intellectuals today would say that Hawi's tragic prediction has been realized to its utmost.[20]

The Iraqi poet al-Bayati, a pioneer in the free verse movement, was also obsessed with the resurrection and revival of Arab civilization. Though Hawi's vision of the future is grave, al-Bayati's poetry generally reveals hope and confidence in an ultimate victory and positive change. Nonetheless, in his collection *Death in Life*, written after the 1967 defeat, al-Bayati depicts the Arabs in a state of, to use literary critic Northrop Frye's phrase, "refrigerated deathlessness." Al-Bayati expresses great despair born from the death of Arab civilization. In his poem "Elegy to `A'isha," written in 1968, the poet communicates his sense of utter shame and suffocation. He stands before `A'isha, who represents Arab civilization, and finds that her hands have been cut off, symbolizing her powerlessness and disability. But that is not all. Corruption and decay surround and cover her: In the darkness of her braided hair he sees rats scuttling about, and worms devour her eyes. `A'isha can neither fully live nor die: She goes to her own grave not quite dead. Al-Bayati's poem reflects the inability to achieve rebirth and revival, thus implying that the resurrection was false and that the Arabs were waiting in vain for one. In the words of Syrian literary critic Muhyi al-Din Subhi, `A'isha represents a "false pregnancy."[21]

In his moving poem "Lament for the June Sun," which was written immediately after the 1967 defeat, al-Bayati condemns the deficiencies in Arab society and its death-in-life state. He bitterly attacks the corruption of Arab rulers for deceiving the people with propaganda, and blatantly false news broadcasts about the grim reality of their situation. The poem ends on a note of optimism, however; al-Bayati insists that only the Arab leaders have been defeated, not the people.[22]

To convey the state of psychological siege permeating the Arab world, al-Bayati's poetry turned surrealist and highly symbolic. "The Nightmare of Day and Night" from his 1970 collection *Writing on Clay* reveals the transformation of a disillusioned dream into a nightmare. In the poem, the proverbial Arab man is unable even to find a place to bury his own corpse. "The Nightmare of Day and Night" demonstrates al-Bayati's sharp awareness of the complexities of Arab life in a confused time of defeat and absurdity and the sharp contradictions between the reality and the dream.[23]

The same complexities of the post-1967 Arab world are reflected in the works of Adonis (Ahmad `Ali Sa`id), a Syrian poet deeply committed to cultural and poetic change. His landmark 1974 book *al-Thabit wa al-Mutahawwil*, or "The Static and the Dynamic," is a provocation; he wrote it to stir immediate and radical change in modern Arab culture. In a poem penned after the 1967 defeat, published in his 1969 collection *This Is My Name*, Adonis touches upon the same theme as al-Bayati in "Lament for the June Sun" and portrays the broken, defeated Arab nation as a corpse wrapped in shrouds. "This broken jar is a defeated nation," the poet writes, and "only madness remains."[24]

THE STRENGTH OF THE PALESTINIAN SPIRIT

The defeat of June 1967 may have shattered the dreams of the Arab people, but in Palestine it strengthened the will and determination of its people to resist Israeli occupation. Al-Qasim and other Palestinian poets emerged as powerful voices in the Arab world who showed an unwavering determination to continue the struggle while non-Palestinian Arabs were reeling in shock. Not only did their earlier poetry play a formative role in mobilizing the Palestinian people to revolt, it also tried to help restore and strengthen the spirit of the Arab people by calling for renewed resistance and dedication to the Arab national cause.[25]

The poets of Palestine have long described themselves and their countrymen as victims of history. The underlying tenets of Palestinian poetry are resistance and defiance, determination in their struggle, and continuing faith in the ultimate justice of their cause. Palestinian poet Zayyad used simple language and expressions of daily life, often mixed with colloquial dialect, to transform his verses into weapons of defiance in support of the Palestinian liberation movement. Many of his verses were put to music and became national emblems of the Palestinian struggle—powerful language and enchanting musicality created an enduring source of inspiration and spiritual strength for the Palestinians. Children even chanted some of his works during the *Intifada*, or "popular uprising," in Palestine in 1986. As such, Zayyad's song-poems have become an integral part of Palestinian resistance ideology.[26]

The poetry of Mahmoud Darwish, one of the best-known modern Arab poets internationally, focuses on the Palestinian homeland and resistance to Israeli occupation. Darwish's work, which has been extremely potent in mobilizing the Palestinian people, has turned him into a symbol of defiance, and his verses are widely recited throughout the Arab world. Darwish left Israel in 1971 and joined the Palestinian diaspora, maintaining a high profile and presence as one of the greatest Palestinian poets. He continued to draw attention to the struggles of the Palestinians for a homeland as well as the internal and external problems that were suffocating this effort. Darwish died in 2008 and was buried next to Ramallah's Palace of Culture, a shrine erected at the summit of a hill overlooking Jerusalem on the southwestern outskirts of the city of Ramallah.[27]

DREAM OF RENEWAL

To rescue Arab society from its prolonged spiritual death, Arab poets have often resorted to employing myths and archetypal images of the "savior" and the "redeemer" in their efforts to keep dreams of renewal and resurrection alive. Poets have drawn from a wide variety of myths and mythic figures from the ancient Near East such as *Ishtar*, a Babylonian and Assyrian goddess, and *Tammuz*, *Baal*, and other variations. They have also invented their own symbols and assumed the persona of archetypical figures from history, the Bible, the Qur'an, and Greek mythology. Some poets wear the mask of Noah as they attempt to express the possibility of building a better world after their hopes drowned in the flood. Others have inhabited the personae of Ulysses and Sinbad to express the restlessness of the archetypical Arab man on an endless quest. Poets have invoked Prometheus, Sisyphus, Job, and Husayn Mansur al-Hallaj, the Sufi martyr and exemplar of heroism and courage who was accused of heresy and crucified for compiling what Carl Jung would later refer to as the archetypes of the "collective unconscious."

The very fact that Ahmad ʿAli Saʿid chose early in his career to write under the pseudonym "Adonis" reflects his deep belief in the myth of resurrection after death. In his poetry Adonis has used several different variations of the myth of eternal return, including that of the Phoenix, a legendary Arabian bird who, when faced with imminent death, would consume itself in fire and rise renewed from the flames. In a poem entitled "Resurrection and Ashes," Adonis begins with a dream of holding an ember in his hands that came to him on the wings of the Phoenix. This dream unites the poet with the Phoenix myth, implying that Arab society, like the bird, must burn its corruption and stagnation away before a new beginning can rise from the ashes. Adonis also links the myth of the Phoenix with that of the ancient Mesopotamian god *Tammuz*, whose blood fertilized the entire country. In this sense, it is the poet's sacrificial words that will fertilize his nation and bring new life to the Arabs.

Arab poets also have employed the life of Jesus and his crucifixion as a myth of resurrection, lending a national dimension to the story of Christ. In the modern corpus of Arabic poetry, Christ is a symbol of the sacrifice and martyrdom that is necessary for national resurrection. Al-Sayyab liked to Arabicize almost all myths that he used in his poetry, and even the nearly-universal image of Christ and his crucifixion became, in al-Sayyab's poetry, part of Arab heritage as well.[28]

In his poem "Christ after Crucifixion," al-Sayyab speaks in the voice of Jesus, drawing a parallel between Jesus and the archetypal Arab: Both are victims of tyranny, injustice, and corruption. Both are tortured, beaten, and murdered. Al-Sayyab thinks of himself as Jesus, as a redeemer and life-giver to his people. In his poetry, therefore, Jesus comes to symbolize the revolutionary Arab fighter who martyrs himself for his cause.

What these poets have suggested to their readers is that the birth of the Arab nation can begin only with a significant sacrifice. In this regard, Hawi also saw himself as a Christ-like figure, carrying the sufferings of his nation as a burden on his shoulders. With a boundless love for his people, Hawi metaphorically describes stretching out his body as a bridge, just as Jesus stretched out his body on the cross in order to save humanity. In Hawi's case, the ribs of his body become a solid bridge upon which revolutionaries can march toward a brighter future.

OVERWHELMED BY REALITY

The criticism—often vicious—that has been vented by a number of modern Arab poets on their society actually stems from its opposite: from a deep love of their people and culture. Rejecting the slow death of the Arab nation, poets took on the roles of saviors, redeemers, and prophets of change and used the mythology of death and rebirth as an expression of hope for the resurgence of the Arab spirit. Unfortunately, those Arab poets who saw themselves as prophets and saviors did not see their vision achieved. Some grew disillusioned and lost faith in their ability to inspire societal change, thinking that their struggle was futile.

Al-Sayyab was one of these, believing that his vision of hopeful change amounted only to failure. Though always retaining its revolutionary spirit, his poetry began to express a sense of uselessness about the struggle.[29] In *Jaykur wa al-Madina*, or "Jakur and the City," al-Sayyab associates oppression and political corruption with spiritual death. It is a dark vision: He writes of "ropes of mud" wrapping around his heart and "cables of fire" devouring the fields, leaving only ashes of hate. When he looks at the city, he sees high walls and locked gates. Unable to enter, unable to return home, the poet has no other choice: He surrenders.

It is the same for Al-Bayati. When he considers the Arab world's bleak reality, it causes him to plunge into deep despair. In his poem "The City," he depicts the reality of life in the Arab world as harsh and full of confusion and contradictions:

> When the city undressed itself
>
> I saw in her sad eyes:
>
> The shabbiness of the leaders, thieves and pawns,
>
> The gallows, the prisons, and the incinerators,
>
> The sadness, the confusion, and the smoke.[30]

Al-Bayati likens the Arab in this age of defeat to a postage stamp, affixed to everything but with control over nothing. In the meantime, the orphaned children of society wander about searching in garbage dumps for a "moon dying upon the corpses of houses," while the Arab man is for sale:

> I saw: the man of tomorrow
>
> Displayed in the storefronts,
>
> On the coins and in the chimneys,
>
> Clothed in sorrow and blackness
>
> The policemen, the sodomites, and the pimps
>
> Spitting in his eyes
>
> As he lay shackled.[31]

A similarly dark vision of Arab civilization's future haunts Hawi's work, too. Remember his Lazarus, who drags not only his wife into death but also the entire Arab nation. For Hawi, Arab society can no longer be revived, and the Arab man can no longer be saved. What we find in his work and the work of other modern Arab poets is a loss of faith in the future. All of these poets look around and see that heroism has been defeated, that streets are filled with the dead. Fields are barren, and leaders are brutal and corrupt.

Even the myths they employ to inspire the Arab world have, like the *Sayf*, a sharp and unexpected edge. The figure of Christ mentioned earlier, who symbolizes the need for sacrifice in order to bring about renewal, can be used for other meanings, too. In despair, al-Sayyab also writes that Christ was not resurrected—that extreme hunger and starvation caused people to hallucinate that he was rolling back the stone from the tomb, curing the leper, and making the blind see. He says that Christ never brought Lazarus back to life, but rather left him asleep until his flesh dried up, later to be sold in the cities of sinners. The poet sees only bones, daggers, and dogs in the country—no water or green fields. Even the moon has disappeared. Only Judas is active, serving as a symbol of treachery, deception, and the secret police.

Another prominent poet, Lebanese writer Yusuf al-Khal, shares this tragic vision. In his "The Deserted Well," al-Khal describes a well that people pass by, neither drinking from it nor throwing stones into it. They feel apathetic after discovering that their lifetime of toil has been in vain, and their tears from waiting for salvation turn into tears of humiliation and defeat. Al-Khal comes close to calling on the people to resign from the struggle.[32]

For his part, al-Bayati once said that a poet is compelled, at the very core of his being, to be "burned with others when he sees them burning and not to stand on the other side of the bank absorbed in prayer."[33] That bold statement eloquently expresses his commitment to the use of poetry for social and political change. Yet he certainly had his doubts about the ability of poetry to truly affect reality, and his verses are often darkened by this skepticism. His work resembles that of a wounded man who continues to raise intelligent questions about his treatment but is unable to convalesce.

At times, in fact, al-Bayati doubts whether anyone will wear the robe of a martyr. In a 1975 poem, "Reading from the Book of al-Tawasin," he dons the robe of Hallaj, the Sufi martyr and archetype of heroism and great courage. (The *Book of al-Tawasin* is a famous tract of Hallaj.) Speaking through this character permits al-Bayati to lament over Arab reality. The poet sees only a simple wall of stone separating thousands of poor, desperate people from freedom and justice. Approaching this wall, which also separates words from action and truth from falsehood, he discovers that it is surrounded by another wall, and then another wall, rising and rising. The polar star has disappeared, and there is no way out.

In his worst moments of despair, al-Bayati expresses the belief that the Arab has been sentenced to death by leaders who use him as a puppet in a game of death. He describes such a trap in his 1989 work "A Conversation of a Stone":

A stone said to another:

I am not happy by this naked fence

My place is in the palace of the sultan.

The other said: It is no use!

Tomorrow this palace will be destroyed

As well as this fence

By an order from the sultan's men

Who will repeat this game anew.[34]

In comparison, Hawi, as previously noted, is far more pessimistic than this. He retains no hope for change in this contemporary era, seeing only dead fish, rotten fruit, corpses, ghosts, and boats tipping into the sea. He senses a spell of darkness falling over the Arab world and the approach of a slow death. For Hawi, the tragedy of Arab reality has intensified to such a degree that death becomes the only solution. In her introduction to Hawi's poetry, scholar Rita ʿAwad comments that Hawi saw the present reality as no more than the next step in centuries of mounting Arab decline.[35] Hawi himself could protest in verses no longer: He shot himself in the head on June 6, 1982, the day on which the Israeli army invaded Lebanon. This was also the day that marked the fifteenth anniversary of the June 1967 War. There is little doubt as to the symbolism of the date and manner in which Hawi chose to end his life: He shot himself to proclaim the final defeat of the entire Arab nation laid low.[36]

Arabic poetry has always provided a reflection of Arab reality; when that reality is dark, so is the poetry. This is a frightening and alienating age; if at some moment in Arab history there existed a dream of a glowing future, that dream has shattered along with the world. Men are paralyzed and made ineffective by fear, which leaves nothing but absurdity and madness. Critic Kamal Abu Deeb (b. 1942) saw the modern Arabic poetry written in this period as a reflection of the world's collapse, as poetry of conflicts, oppositions, and fragmentations of self and of text.[37]

With the fall of Baghdad in 2003, those who felt the Arab world could not collapse further were proven wrong. Al-Maghout best depicted the multiple disconnections of contemporary Arab culture. He was a torn man, deeply committed in his soul to the battle of progress and unable to accept the misery of Arab reality. Above all, he was a man of honor who never compromised his principles. His death in 2006 was seen as a sort of victory, testifying to the nobility of a poet who never expediently changed his beliefs and who made good on every word he uttered. Scholar Asʿad AbuKhalil (b. 1960) wrote a letter to the poet immediately after his death, saying: "You have died a free man. Congratulations! We will miss you."[38] A few months earlier, Maghout had written verses depicting the disconnection between the world and the self:

The world does not like my nation, and my nation does not like my homeland.

My house does not like my room and my room does not like my pillow.

My pillow does not like my head, and my head does not like my forehead.

My forehead does not like my poems, and my poems do not like my fingers.

My fingers do not like one another.[39]

Although torn and exhausted inside, al-Maghout never ceased to speak out, devoting his life to achieving societal change and dreaming of a new Arab socio-political culture based on freedom and democracy. While the lamp of the Arab world flickered perilously, al-Maghout continued to kindle the Arab future with dreams. His poetry serves as that blue lantern that illuminates Arab society's path into the future:

They all see in me

A steadfast fortress

A towering mountain

In the face of time

But they do not see

The crumbling hut in my depth!

All hear the neighing and screams

The dust of the spurs swimming in the air,

But they do not see

My foot that is stuck in the heels.[40]

Al-Maghout's poetry transcends the temporal boundaries of a world swept by absurdity and irrationality. "The streets I cross reject my steps," he declares. In her introduction to an anthology of Maghout's works, Salma Jayyusi affirms that the poet is always direct, ironic, witty, and hard. There is no poet quite like him: He "satirizes a whole age with images of unexpected, surprising effect, attacking our age with all the tools of the poet."[41] Al-Maghout's verses always explicitly confess his concern that hope may shatter and the possibility of change vanish. In one famous passage, he screams in protest and resignation:

You have defeated me!

But in all this defeated land

I can find no proper hill

On which to plant my banner of surrender.[42]

Other poets are still fighting "against their age" as well. Adonis, among others, has always called for radical change in Arab sociopolitical culture but strongly rejects the idea of change from the outside. He attributes the fall of Iraq in 2003 to its prison-like nature and the lack of real national sovereignty there. Adonis has said that as long as Arab governments remain oppressive, the people will have nothing to rely on and nothing to defend. He described the American occupation of Iraq as "an outer storm that has shaken Iraq. Now, the people must control the storm and get rid of it."[43]

Though a renowned authority on Arabic culture, even Adonis is unable to find a solution. He confesses that he is "unable to interpret the contradictions that exist in the Arab world." Lost, terrified, and trapped in the unsolvable predicament of Arab existence, Adonis writes:

I come from a land with no bounds,

Carried on people's backs.

I was lost here, was lost there,

With my verses.

And here I am, in the terror and withering,

Knowing neither how to stay

Nor how to return.[44]

Another leading poet, the Iraqi Saadi Yousef, refused to abide by Saddam Hussein's rule and has been living in exile ever since. Regarding the American occupation he wrote, "I shall never return to Iraq under American occupation. I left Iraq to protest dictatorship and oppression. I will not return to a colonized and more oppressive Iraq."[45] In a poem entitled "God Save America, My Home Sweet Home," he says:

I, too, love jeans and jazz and Treasure Island

And Long John Silver's parrot and the terraces of New Orleans

I love Mark Twain and the Mississippi steamboats and Abraham Lincoln's dogs

I love the fields of wheat and corn and the smell of Virginia tobacco.

But I am not American.

Is that enough for the Phantom pilot to turn me back to the Stone Age![46]

During the first few days of the military invasion in 2003, when Iraqi forces demonstrated fierce resistance to the American advance, major Arab poets such as Adonis and Darwish published poems praising and supporting the Iraqi resistance. Soon after, however, Baghdad fell, and the poets were silenced. It had become clear to all that the entire region had suffered absolute failure and defeat.

THE WAY FORWARD

In spite of disappointment, despair, and frustration, Arab poets never stopped fighting for social, political, and cultural change. Syrian poet Qabbani, the most renowned love poet in the Arab world, became a powerful voice in the struggle for social and political revolution: "Woman has been my beloved and she still is, but I am now taking a second wife: her name is 'the homeland.' "[47] Qabbani's poem "Marginal Notes on the Book of Defeat" is boldly critical of Arab governments:

O Sultan, O my lord: Twice you have lost the war

Because you cut out the tongues of half your people.

What use are a people who cannot speak?[48]

Iraqi poet Muzaffar al-Nawwab faced dire personal consequences for his political verses; he was forced to live underground most of his life because of his biting satires about corrupt Arab leaders and their establishments. Though his poetry was universally banned throughout the Arab world, it was gleefully photocopied, secretly traded, and memorized by Arabs everywhere. Al-Nawwab spent his life in exile, skipping from one hideout to another to avoid imprisonment and torture. He attacked virtually every Arab leader and major political event in the Middle East—in one verse he even calls Arab leaders "Sons of Bitches." Al-Nawwab became the voice of a silent majority who saw their leaders conspiring against their own people.[49]

In contrast to Hawi's black despair, other poets have refused to give up hope for salvation and reawakening, believing it is still the responsibility of poetry to nurture this vision into fruition. Arab poets have expressed their determination to continue the fight. Adonis wrote: "I am not alone." Al-Bayati always claimed to write for the oppressed and the poor. Muhammad al-Maghout was known as the voice of the voiceless. Nizar Qabbani and Mahmoud Darwish didn't leave the battlefield until they died. Other poets have also continued to dream. Even in moments of despair, leading Arab poets have vowed to continue the struggle, and they have paid a high price for their courage. In spite of the injustice and difficulty of struggle, and in fact because of this injustice and difficulty, these spokespeople for Arab society still fight 'against their age.'

Qabbani criticized the 1990 Iraqi invasion of Kuwait in a poem written immediately after the invasion. A few years later, he wrote another poem entitled "I Am with Terrorism," in which he strongly criticized the 1993 Oslo Accords, particularly because of violent clashes in response to renewed and enlarged Jewish settlements on land to be negotiated with the Palestinian Authority. Drawing a distinction between peace and surrender, he argued that he himself had been accused of being a terrorist many times simply for defending the rights and dignity of the Arabs and speaking out against Arab leaders who had suddenly changed from devoted nationalists to middlemen and agents. In cases such as this, Qabbani wrote, one is compelled to come down on the side of 'terrorism.'

Similarly concerned, Darwish resigned from his position in the PLO after a disagreement with Yasser Arafat about the content of the 1993 peace treaty with Israel. In his 1995 book *Why Have You Left the Horse Alone*, Darwish reconfirmed his complete rejection of the peace treaty with Israel. He expressed a deep sorrow for the victims who died as martyrs, saying their deaths were for nothing. In the years since, his words have echoed this same attitude and tone—quieter, perhaps, but remaining clear and firm.[50]

As opposed to other modern poets who sometimes flaunt their elitism, al-Maghout is humble and real. He composes his verses about the people of the Arab streets, from coffee houses to cheap hotels, bars, and restaurants. He reveals his vision with cries of terror and denounces the unjust world against the freedom of the individual. In al-Maghout's formulation, the Arab is a defenseless individual who is besieged by the forces of contemporary wickedness. From the depth of the destruction of the Arab world, we still hear his "continual screams in the face of all evils."[51]

AGENTS OF CHANGE: POETS AND THE ARAB SPRING

Modern Arab poets have long hoped that their writing and positions on national, social, and political issues of the Arab world would result in significant and positive cultural change. Their verses were not in vain, and the strong presence of poetry in Arabic culture, with its continuous involvement, provocation, and close connection to the people, promoted revolutionary ideals during the Arab Spring, which is discussed in detail in chapter 11 of in this book. Arabic poetry proved to be a force in the Arab world for provocation, contemplation, criticism, and for planting new visions for cultural, social, and political changes. New verses written used to inspire and fuel the Arab public. Popular poems set to music continue to delight listeners, reflecting not only feelings and passions but also forwarding social and political messages.

The Arab Spring started in December 2010 in Tunisia. On the first day of the Tunisian revolution, verses by Tunisian poet Abu al-Qasim al-Shabi (d. 1934) were recited and chanted by thousands of protesters and demonstrators. The protestors derived spiritual strength and moral vigor from the powerful revolutionary verses of their poet, which provoked revolt and uprising, and they sought victory by overthrowing Arab dictators and tyrannical regimes. Among al-Shabi's verses recited in the streets of Arab capitals during the Arab Spring was the following:

> *If the people desire to live*
>
> *Destiny will have to obey*
>
> *Their night is destined to fade*
>
> *Their chains are destined to break*[52]

Demonstrators chanted verses of other poets such as Darwish, Samih Al-Qasim, Zayyad, and Amal Donkol as well. Young poets wrote new protest poems and songs for the occasion, and their verses served as a catalyst strengthening the will and empowering the masses to keep revolution strong and alive.

Poetic expression became central to revolutionary rallying cries, especially when young poets put their words to new music. In Cairo's Tahrir Square, as well as in the streets of Syria, Yemen, Libya, Iraq, Tunis, and elsewhere, music and poetry combined and became politically influential. Arab people set their words to traditional Arab melodies and rhythms; genres like hip hop and rap became important mediums of expression for the protests; and recurring call-and-response songs turned poetic verses into social and political anthems. Poetic expression during the Arab Spring was used as a medium for masses in revolution. The words and rhythms created a unique solidarity among a population of people, uniting them in powerful defiance and strong determination for the successful struggle of the Arab Spring.

New verses, often songs, have used colloquial Arabic. The colloquial language is the language of daily life in the Arab streets, where native-speakers communicate with one another outside of formal or academic settings. The colloquial Arabic language is not constrained by grammar, syntax, and formal vocabulary in the way

that *fus-ha*, ("classical") or MSA, is. This new musical trend and the use of colloquial language have allowed for a much wider audience and have demonstrated a
particular effectiveness. The expanding use of social media has allowed colloquial
Arab poems and songs to become more influential and more accessible. Carried by
social media, poetic expression has greatly increased the quantity of participants
in demonstrations and has intensified mass determination.

In 2010 in Tunisia, rap artist Hamada Ben Amor (b. 1990), under the stage
name El Général, released a track in solidarity with Mohammed Bouazizi's setting
himself on fire in protest of working conditions. The song is angry and directed
at then-Tunisian President Zine El Abidine Ben Ali (b. 1936). El Général's song
Rais Le Bled, or "President of the Country," led to the artist being arrested and
interrogated by state authorities. El Général's song ignited an outcry of frustration
about the corruption of the Tunisian President and his inner circle and about the
injustice and stagnation of Tunisian society.

> *Mr. President, today I am speaking in the name of all the people,*
>
> *Who are suffering and dying of hunger,*
>
> *Our voice is not heard and we became like animals*
>
> *We are suffering, we are living like dogs*
>
> *Mr. President your people are dead. Your people eat from the garbage*
>
> *Misery is everywhere and people cannot find a place to sleep.*

Adapted from https://www.bam.org/music/2013/el-general-lyrics.

Egyptian musical artist Ramy Essam (b. 1987) composed a piece in colloquial
Egyptian called *Irhal*, or "leave." *Irhal* was addressed to then-Egyptian President
Hosni Mubarak (b. 1928) during the revolution. Essam sings with the simple ac-
companiment of a guitar; *Irhal* became a revolutionary anthem. At the height of
Egypt's 2011 revolution, Essam performed the song over loudspeakers in Tahrir
Square as thousands of amassed Egyptian people chanted lyrics back to him in
protest of the Mubarak regime. Essam and his music helped inflame the Egyptian
people in 2011, and Essam was eventually arrested and tortured by the military
near Tahrir Square.

Even after Mubarak left power, Essam composed protest music against
Muhammad Morsi (b. 1951), the man who replaced Mubarak as president. When
Abdel Fattah Al-Sisi (b. 1954) seized power in Egypt in 2013, Essam sang a new
song titled "The Age of the Pimp." The piece represents a powerful attack on the
leadership of Egypt, as well as on Arab leaders throughout modern Arab history.

The Age of the Pimp

...

Our brothers in prison are piles of flesh,

... the pimp rules.

We are stuck with the pimp

We became strangers in our own land

Puppets bring puppets.

Ibrahim Qashoush (b. 1977, d. 2011) was a Syrian singer influential in Damascus, Syria, during the attempted revolution in mid-2011. Qashoush repurposed traditional Arab melodies, including those used at weddings, to create colloquial verses that could be chanted by large crowds in rhythm. Qashoush created the popular song *Yalla Irhal Ya Bashar*, or "It's Time to Leave, Bashar." The chant became a protest anthem early in the Syrian revolution. Ibrahim's voice lifted thousands of Syrian people amassed in the streets of Hama, and his music has continued to do so since. CBS News reported that "Ibrahim Qashoush's lyrics moved thousands of protesters in Syria who sang his jaunty verses at rallies, telling President Bashar al-Assad [b. 1965], 'Time to leave.'"[53]

It's Time to Leave, Bashar

...

Time to leave, Bashar! Get out, Bashar!

Bashar, you're the infiltrator

You and your Ba'th party can go to hell.

We will remove Bashar with all of our strength.

Syria wants Freedom! Syria wants Freedom!

Qashoush died early in the Syrian uprising: His body was found dumped in the Asi River. Syrian authorities had left a large open wound where his Adam's apple and vocal cords had been ripped out. This represented a clear message by Assad's Syrian government that those who dare to raise their voices against the regime would be severely punished. *The Guardian* reported on 5 July 2011 that "[one] of many grim videos to emerge from the Syrian city of Hama purported to show the body of protester Ibrahim Qashoush after his throat had been cut by the security forces."[54] Artists and demonstrators across Yemen, Libya, and other Arab states continued to use poetic protest songs with the word *Irhal* during social and political uprisings.

The old dreams of the Arab poets for freedom and dignity were renewed, and poets are continuing to provoke the people until real progress takes hold. But the tools of poetry seem limited, though—while the ancient Arab bards, who had the freedom to speak, could use the *qasida* effectively to praise and defend their tribes, the challenges facing modern poets are much more complex. Because of the lack of freedom, and the oppression facing poets by their governments, poetry alone is not sufficient to create a successful and lasting popular revolution, or to overturn the political regimes of the Arab world and create real progress and reorganization. Poetry, along with other forces in society, has indeed joined the Arab Spring and succeeded in toppling dictators' Arab regimes. Modern Arab poets will continue to fight and will never lose faith or abandon their roles as visionaries and leaders. As scholar Hisham Sharabi (d. 2005) once profoundly remarked, "[t]o fight the pessimism of the intellect, one must hold fast to the optimism of the will."[55] This is the role of the modern Arab poet: to provoke, inspire people, and give them hope, and to participate in the revolution through the power of the word.

THE THEME OF LOVE IN MODERN ARABIC POETRY

Although the passage of time has transformed the Arab poet's role into something more political, the theme of love continues to exist in Arabic poetry. In the contemporary Arab world, poets continue to write about love and romance: Some devote entire poems to love, while others mix romantic and non-romantic themes together.

Until very recently, because of the conservative nature of Arab society and a long tradition of male domination, Arab women in general could not express their romantic passion in poetry. Syrian poet Nizar Qabbani, the most prominent male romantic poet of the modern era, thus took upon himself the task of openly articulating women's love and passion. Qabbani acted as the champion of women's rights, urging women to take control of their lives, bodies, and destinies. A proponent of women's liberation after centuries of male chauvinism in the Arab world, Qabbani succeeded in initiating a change in attitudes surrounding sexuality, erotic freedom, and the right of women to celebrate ecstasy. He asserted that women's freedom of the body would lead to everyone's freedom of the spirit, and he called for liberating the new generation from repression to help women erase the guilt and embarrassment associated with sex.[56] As early as 1944, Qabbani published poems full of sexual imagery. In his poem "Your Breast," the poet implores a woman to:

> *Unlock your treasury*
>
> *Lay bare your burning breast*
>
> *Don't smother your imprisoned fire!*[57]

Qabbani sought to break the entrenched walls of silence around love and sex and to normalize contemporary and liberal love poetry. His efforts caused disturbances in Syria and other Arab states. Conservatives who had vested interests in traditional lifestyles attacked Qabbani, but he did not cease attempting to propel poetry into an era of greater freedom, movement, and transcendence.

THE POET WHO "PUT ON THE CLOTHES OF A WOMAN"

For the first time in Arabic literary history, with Qabbani, a male poet expressed himself in the Arabic verbal conjugations linguistically reserved for the first-person feminine, as would a woman. This was an important aspect of Qabbani's poetry, through which he tried to give a voice to what was previously a hidden, silent world of women. He elaborated further on the societal pressures placed upon Arab women in his collection *Diary of an Indifferent Woman*:

> *"This is the book of every woman sentenced and executed before she could open her mouth. The East needs a male like me to put on the clothes of a woman and to borrow her bracelets and eyelashes in order to write about her. Is it not an irony that I cry out with a woman's voice while women cannot speak up on their own?"*[58]

From the very beginning of his career, Qabbani sided with women and held male-dominated Arab society to be mostly responsible for the inequality and injustice they faced. He tried hard to understand most women's problems from their perspective, and his radical positions on women's rights remained unchanged throughout the fifty-six years of his writing career. There is little doubt that Qabbani's poetry and activism, with its social and aesthetic dimensions, has made a difference in public perceptions of women's issues. Allying himself with liberal forces already at work in the Arab world, Qabbani courageously produced vivid and provocative poetry and helped to create an atmosphere in which women could gain the right to express themselves without facing universal calumny.

Of course, not all of Qabbani's poetry was meant to provoke women to break out of silence. He wrote about everything related to the female world—but sometimes from an extremely male perspective. His poem "Musical Variations of a Naked Woman," from the collection *Poems Against the Law*, depicted himself lying before a naked woman, his senses expanding to transfer the movements of the woman's breasts into voices, scents, tastes, flames, and colors:[59]

> *Two beautiful roosters*
>
> *Crow on your chest and sleep*

I remained sleepless

The hand-embroidered sheet

Was covered with birds,

Roses and palm trees ...

Your breasts were two unbridled horses

Drinking water from the bottom of mirrors.[60]

Though the subject here is a passive recipient of the poet's adulation, Qabbani always tried to incite women to reject their society-imposed passivity in love. He refused to accept the silence of women on the topic, believing their silence was based on structural oppression in society. His verses therefore were mostly directed to women, encouraging them to liberate themselves from constrictive social convention.[61] In one of his most famous lines, he writes: "Love me and say it out loud; I refuse that you love me mutely."[62]

For most poets, women are an important source of inspiration. Bayati, Adonis, and Darwish, for example, talk about lovers by equating them with the homeland and mothers in a highly symbolic and metaphorical way. It could certainly be said that these poets' passions for women are deeper and more powerful than that of Qabbani's even if they pertain less explicitly to the female form. Their verses delve into profound mystical and spiritual dimensions that Qabbani's verses do not approach. Qabbani's writing is valuable for communicating simply and clearly to a popular audience, and no poem of his is free of female presences. There is nothing about women that Qabbani cannot transform into subject matter for his writing: "I become ugly when I don't love, and I become ugly when I don't write."[63] The supreme importance of women to Qabbani is indicated in another verse, which hints at a supernatural power that women hold over him: "Nothing protects us from death except women and writing."[64]

Qabbani's simplicity and fluency are the most important characteristics of his poetry. The secret of his lasting success is a constant ability to express what the reader holds in his or her own mind. No literate person exists in the Arab world, at least among the young (or young at heart), who has not read at least one book of poetry by Qabbani. All of his poems are written in the first person; many, as previously mentioned, speak in a female voice and tackle the perennial problems women have faced in their relationships with men since time immemorial. His poetry pays a great deal of attention to the emotional life of women, and he is fond of addressing the minute details that shape how women think and feel. Qabbani uses the female voice to reveal the way a woman feels when she is in love. He describes her love, relishing in the details of her rich imagination, and conveys her passion, warmth, and innocence:

> Little things which mean the world to me
>
> Pass by you without making an impression
>
> From these things, I build palaces,
>
> Live on them for months
>
> And spin many tales from them.
>
> But these little things mean nothing to you.
>
> When the telephone rings
>
> I run to it with the joy of a small child
>
> And wait for your warm voice to come to me
>
> Like the music of fallen stars
>
> I cry because you have thought of me.[65]

To Qabbani, the female figure is a haven who gives the poet life and provides him with bread, water, and strength. He links the struggle for her rights with the war for social liberation in the Arab world as a requisite of emancipation for both men and women. Qabbani always maintained that there could be no social revolution in the Arab world until women are viewed as active participants in, rather than passive objects. He claimed that of all the problems in the Arab world, sexual repression is the biggest: "Sex should be considered a normal part of life and not be exaggerated or made into a nightmare."[66] The poet called for an end to the game of love behind closed doors, proclaiming he would set an example:

> "I have moved my bed to the open air and written my love poems on trees in public parks in order to make love legitimate and put an end to the secretive and martial laws imposed on the body of the Arab woman."[67]

Qabbani found that, due to the deep conservatism of Arab culture, even Arab leftists and revolutionaries avoided discussing issues of sexuality in their society. He concluded that leftist discourse on women in Arab society did not vary significantly from traditional discourse. Qabbani's poetry therefore holds a very important place in modern Arabic literature and culture. As he himself proclaimed: "I am the first Arab poet to introduce the details of everyday love in poetry, and the first one to try to record the romantic relationship in my time and in my own way." His task as a poet was to take poetry from the lips of individuals and return it to them; his words were directed to innocent, simple people, those who could not find clothes to wear so they wore a poem instead.[68] His poetry remains exceedingly popular in the Arab world because it depicts accessible emotions in realistic colors without makeup or masks. In fact, more than any other contemporary Arab poet, Qabbani's poems have been set to music and recorded by talented Arab singers. Since popular music in the Arab world has a massive audience, these recordings have broadened Qabbani's popularity and appeal.

VOICES OF ARAB WOMEN

Since the 1940s, Arab women have written poetry about love and romance. Nazik al-Mala'ika was a pioneer of the free-verse movement, along with al-Sayyab and al-Bayati. She wrote love poetry as did Salma Jayyusi (b. 1926) and Lamia `Abbas Amara (b. 1927). Fadwa Tuqan continued to write poems about love and other themes until she died in 2003. Women's offerings in the genre of love poetry were generally shy, restricted, and very conservative. These poets are therefore remembered mostly for their considerable contributions to social and political discourse.

Bold female voices on the theme of love have not emerged until recently, but that is not a surprise: Women writers have been scarce in the Arab world until very recently. Joseph Zeidan observes that female-produced writing in the Arab world was usually an imitation of norms "established by the existing male-dominated literary tradition."[69] Due to these circumstances, as mentioned earlier, Qabbani took on the task of speaking in women's voices. But there would have been no need for this sort of pretension by a male poet if women had been permitted to express themselves to their own satisfaction.

By the 1980s, however, Arab women were producing distinguished and personally assertive literature, not only demanding equal rights but also addressing all aspects of Arab society, including previously taboo topics. Women have also emerged as distinguished, first-class poets. Over the last thirty years, and particularly in the last two decades, Arab culture has been blessed with an increasing number of female poets and writers, and the Arab world now boasts outstanding female novelists, journalists, scholars, and intellectuals of great distinction.

Qabbani genuinely worked to prepare the ground for women's voices to emerge; this certainly would have occurred without him, but it would probably have taken longer. Through his activist campaign to force issues of sexuality into the public sphere, Qabbani expedited and smoothed the path for authentic women's voices to enter the field, and his contribution cannot be denied or underestimated. When most Arab women were forced into silence, Qabbani spoke for them. Over the past three decades, the Arab world has finally witnessed the expressions of women about their experiences of love and sexuality, along with their individuality, identity, and sense of romance. Today, there is no longer a need for an Arab male poet to cry out in a woman's voice.

Syrian writer Ghada al-Samman (b. 1942) is a well-known poet and novelist as well as a distinguished woman's voice over the past forty years. She joined Qabbani in the battle for women's liberation and represented the voice of the revolutionary Arab female, calling upon her fellow women to speak freely about their sexuality. She also urged women to join the battle against restrictions placed on them by society. Al-Samman is "hailed as the most rebellious poetess against the unjust ruling system of Arab society."[70] She called upon women to quickly abandon their stagnant tribal traditions and affiliations and to join the modern world. (More about Samman as a novelist is discussed in the chapter of Arabic novel.)

Al-Samman is an Arab intellectual who is deeply invested in the liberation of women and men alike. But her verses also reveal a strong call for Arab women to rebel against the patriarchal system of Arab society:

> *"I am an Arab woman laden with a thousand years of wars, of plunders, of sorrows, and tragedy. I am a woman whose tribe's males wage their wars against me, and buried me alive for centuries. But I rise up from my ashes. I am tired of the civilization of death, of wars. I want to embrace life, to embrace joy."*[71]

Al-Samman is an acknowledged liberal force in society seeking freedom and justice and fighting a battle for social and political change in Arab culture. She writes:

> *I am tortured by my great love.*
>
> *For my lover's sake,*
>
> *I abandoned my home and deserted my country*
>
> *My great love is 'freedom.'*[72]

In her poetry, prose, and journalistic columns, al-Samman stresses the need for Arab women to gain social equality. She calls for their liberation, independence, and equality with men. As an early leader in the feminist struggle, she wrote "[a] lone, I stand against all forces that are against me." She also wrote:

Here I am running alone in the rain

Without a man or a nation

I weave the threads of my freedom

Far from the path of the flock.[73]

Al-Samman has constantly provoked women to speak about themselves. Her poetic themes range from love and romance to freedom and social liberation. She is defiant and rebellious, and her writing is a "cry for individual liberty"[74] through political involvement. In an interview with intellectual Ghali Shukri (d. 1998), al-Samman stressed, as Qabbani did before, the desperate need for sexual liberation in Arab society:

> "Sexual liberation is a part that cannot be separated from the re-volt of the Arab individual against what restricts freedom in all spheres, including economics, politics, free speech, expression, or thought. There is no way out but through struggle against all reactionary thought, which includes our understanding of sex."[75]

Al-Samman believes that the taboo nature of sex is hypocritical, leading to the repression of women's sexuality and to male domination. Although she is influenced by Western literature on this topic, she does not imitate previous scholarship in her writing: "I am influenced by my Western education, but that doesn't mean that I am simply a shadow of it. I am learning how to polish my tools in the light of the literary endeavors of others." Scholar Pauline Homsi Vinson notes that al-Samman's creative writing, particularly her devotion to the liberation of Arab women, functions as "literary wake-up calls for those willing to listen:"[76]

When I die

These letters will still carry me to you

When I die, search well inside the paper

Go to the depth of my words

And you will see me on the lines

If you are sad and burn the edge of my book

I shall come to you

Like the genie in my grandmother's Damascus stories.[77]

Al-Samman has played an important role in modern Arabic culture, having fought for cultural change since the early 1970s and continuing her mission with great devotion. She is an authentic part of the very texture of the Arab culture she has been trying to weave anew.

Both al-Samman and Qabbani called for sexual liberation in modern Arabic poetry and society, and their efforts have paved the way for a female-driven movement along those lines. Qabbani dressed himself in woman's clothes, wrote linguistically and grammatically in the female voice, and tried to reveal the inner emotions, passion, and sexuality of the Arab woman. Although his accomplishments are appreciated, there are many who see his role as abnormal, particularly women who believe that a man cannot accurately penetrate their inner world or their emotions surrounding love and sex. But Qabbani did what he could during a period when women could not express themselves.

Lebanese poet Joumana Haddad (b. 1970) has liberated herself beyond Qabbani's wildest imagination, and expresses her passion and sexuality in powerful and challenging artistic style. Haddad puts her naked body in the open through her poetry. With great confidence she melds herself with her words in a poetic, yet real, sexual intercourse. She has exceeded the degree of independence and freedom that Arab society expects of a woman, taking full control of her life, her body and her destiny. Haddad strongly expresses sexuality, erotic desires, and the right as a woman to celebrate ecstasy. Most significantly, she has changed feelings of guilt and embarrassment at breaking societal taboos into enjoyment and delight at rebelling against the Arab world's most deeply held societal constraints. With intense passion, warm emotions, and fervent sexual desire of the liberated woman, Haddad lays herself before her audience in relating her desire for the body of a man.

Though the adjectives *courageous* and *brave* have been heaped upon her, she rejects such notions, saying it is not an act of courage for a woman to express herself. "The truth is women make love and practice sex and desire the body of man. Woman has so much to say about the body of man; she knows the points of weakness and the points of strength of his body, and she loves it."[78] Haddad is a poet who takes her readers into her bedroom to reveal to them how the woman expresses the deep secrets of femininity in her love and personal, intimate sexuality. She rhythmically moves her body and soul, using words to build up her sexual delight:

> My poem is a man's sex draped with desire
>
> Bridge stretched between the universe and me
>
> Marvelous fruit that lives on my body
>
> Eye which slakes my thirst and snatches me up in its whirlwind
>
> I never want to come out of its rainy tunnel.
>
> My poem is a road, it walks within me.[79]

Confident in both herself and her femininity, Haddad believes that women should not abandon their femininity and should seek to complete man, not to compete with him. "I am against women who act as men. I am against the woman who abandons her femininity and who seeks equality out of hate and out of aggression against man. The poetry I love is the poetry of men."[80] Just as male poets write about woman's beautiful breasts, desirous lips, and body that makes them blaze, Haddad similarly writes: "I write about my own body, and I write not to be courageous but to be truthful to what is boiling inside me as a woman:"[81]

> *I have a body waiting at the ocean's bottom*
>
> *I have a body which is like a volcano*
>
> *Whose crater the water licks*
>
> *Lest it should emit pleasure before love comes*
>
> *I have a body which I do not know*
>
> *But I will discover its taste*
>
> *With two lips which will burn*
>
> *And a tongue which will take in*
>
> *And with a lava which has a sound*
>
> *Like entering Paradise!*[82]

To further express her complete freedom and liberation as a woman, she declares: "I drink from the river that I desire regardless of what everyone says. I am responsible for my words, for my truthfulness. My freedom is my love." Haddad's body is the focal experience of her love, closely connected not only with her soul but with her very existence as a woman and poetess: "My body is the earth that receives the rain, the sun, the moon, the wind, the birds and my lover. When I write, I write with my own body upon my own body." To her, love is an endless learning experience that cannot be reached, an unattainable yet constantly-attained dream: "My femininity needs a lover who spoils me, strokes my hair with his hand, a lover for whom I would invent every day a new madness."[83]

Haddad, who is discussed further in chapter 9 on the Arabic novel, is a fine example of the new generation of Arab women who have recently begun to express sexual liberation through poetry. Another poetess is the Palestinian Suheir Daoud (b. 1969), who has joined Haddad in writing openly about her experiences of love and sexuality. Daoud courageously reveals her sensations of femininity as she describes passionate kisses with her lover. The reader can feel the body of the poetess trembling beneath extreme passion, and can hear her words in moments of sexual excitement mixed with lust and tenderness.

Like Haddad, Daoud reveals her true experiences, writing about a secret love affair with a married man. Her verses tell the story of a woman in very private moments of passion, confessing her personal life in public in order to assert her independence and individuality as a free woman.

> *I loved you in secret*
>
> *I met you in hiding*
>
> *You turned my days into wildly hot*
>
> *Shameless nights*
>
> *And weeping rites.*[84]

For some reason we do not know, the poetess could not continue her affair. But she made it known that her love was sincere and her passion strong, depicting her private ecstasy with her lover in a moment of intimacy as a "holy secret of joy," while melting her soul and body in his.

> *Our secretive gatherings were*
>
> *Extreme, lustful and violent*
>
> *Every time there was madness.*[85]

Years later, she falls in love with another man. She is as freshly excited about this new love affair as she was with her first, and again she falls madly in love. But this time, deep into her romantic involvement, she begins to realize that her lover is cold, arrogant, and dominating. The poetess begins to protest her lover's selfishness, slowly but strongly rebelling against him. Despite her strong love for him, she can no longer continue in such an unequal relationship.

> *I am sorry that I cannot be*
>
> *What you have always wanted me to be:*
>
> *A robot*
>
> *A heart made of ice.*[86]

Realizing she is afflicted by her passion and plagued by an addiction to her lover, she suffers sleepless nights, great anxiety, and extreme yearning for a warm and compassionate heart. Yet she still resents the unequal reciprocation of love, and certainly resents her lover's domination:

For all the time I have known you

I always needed your permission

To utter a shameless moan

To make my ecstasy known

To reveal my lustful desires

And to rejoice.[87]

Despite her repeated attempts to change the man she loves into a better person, she fails. The man remains unchanged. Feeling trapped and frustrated, she decides to end this incompatible love affair:

I write to you today to say

I am no longer able to be with you

And that your lifeless face

In the casket of your backward belief

Makes me sad

But will not change me.[88]

While Haddad expresses her anticipated sexual ecstasy, Daoud describes her sexual ecstasy and climax after lovemaking, which lasts in her body for a number of days. Not only is her body eternally suspended in delight, but so is her whole existence:

Your body cast a spell on me

It suspended me in a moment of time

And kept me on hold.[89]

Such frank, bold expressions by Arab women about their sexuality is a current phenomenon in the region, and this would not have been possible even four decades ago. At least among literary elites, liberation has been partially achieved for Arab women. This has developed more quickly than Qabbani and other intellectuals expected; Qabbani would have been pleased to know that the complete silence of women has ended, a mission he had imagined to be extremely difficult to achieve. He and other liberal forces in society always maintained that without the sexual liberation of women, Arab society would not develop, and without the right of women to free expression, there would be no progress. Furthermore, Qabbani was convinced that sexual repression played a major role in the economic backwardness and political disintegration of the Arab world. As he said more than once, "any revolution concerned solely with an individual's thoughts and not with his or her body is half a revolution."[90]

LANTERN FOR CULTURAL CHANGE

Many intellectuals, such as al-Samman, agreed with Qabbani that women's sexual liberation was vital to the development of Arab society. Some Arab women writers have not only ended their long silence but have also liberated their bodies, expressed their sexual feelings and passions, and celebrated their ecstasy by openly discussing desire for men's bodies in the same way that men express their desire for women's bodies. Arab women are now speaking and writing about love and their sexual feelings, more so in fact than men. Women writers have also been more articulate and expressive than men in conveying their inner feelings and emotions.

It is clear, however, that in order to achieve true development and progress, Arab culture needs more than the sexual liberation of a few brave women who live in certain large cities among intellectual elites. The steady process of sexual liberation in both women and men is a positive trend, but it will not be enough to effect cultural and social change. Sexual liberation is meaningless without the political, economic and social liberation of all Arab citizens. Democracy and political freedoms, especially freedom of expression, are necessary to achieve real progress. Poets will continue to guide societies forward with reflections on the realities people face and expressions of what might be possible for them to achieve.

Arab poets have a long tradition of pointing out the ills of their societies, reflecting the malaise among citizens who feel powerless to change. Arab poets also have a compelling history of calling for change and urging their compatriots to fight for their causes and themselves. Sadly, any optimism often has been met with the harsh reality of the stagnation and repression in their societies. Between government tyranny, lack of freedom, and bitter events such as the 1948 Palestine war, the defeat of 1967, the Lebanese civil war, the crumbling of Iraq after 2003, and the 2011 civil wars in Syria and Yemen, Arab poets have had to reflect upon and react to these bitter realities of their world. However, in pointing out the ills that they lament, they also are calling on people to recognize these realities. By expressing their views, poets in the Arab world illuminate new ideas and can spark people to move forward, even toward revolution.

Poets reflect the souls and aspirations of their society. They also speak on behalf of their people, opening the doors of inquiry and showing new possibilities. Arab poets have played these roles for millennia, sometimes with more success than at other times. Today Arab poetry has been revitalized with the mass movements of the Arab Spring and the ability to transmit poems and songs across social media. Poets have become true agents of change, even if progress is slow and may seem futile with the outcomes of the Arab Spring. The ideas, passion, and commitment have not abated, and the voices of contemporary poets will be heard. There is no doubt that modern Arabic poetry will continue to be the needed lantern on the road to a better future. In the words of French poet René Char, poetry is needed not only to enrich the human soul and spirit, but also to keep dreams alive; this is very pertinent to the Arab people. Their poetry is the lamp that enlightens a path that has seemed impossible to traverse. Throughout this struggle, though, the voices, verses, and visions of Arab poets, both women and men, have not been in vain.

CHAPTER NINE

The Arabic Novel

POETRY, IN ARABIC SOCIETY, has always held a preeminent position, but today that position is being challenged. In the opinion of several major writers and critics, the novel has become *more important* than modern Arabic poetry, because the novel form has clear advantages over poetry: the form allows for more details and precision, resulting in a more comprehensive depiction of Arabic society and culture. That is why many writers consider the novel as the "mirror" of the modern age. A leading Arab writer has explained that, through the novel, we are better able to "read, see, and understand what is happening inside our closed and secretive society."[1]

Although modern Arabic poetry exposes Arabic society's problems, the novel possesses more accurate means for examining these problems and closely chronicling the daily lives of the people inside that society. Novelist Abdelrahman Munif, looking at Arabic society, has said that reading novels will enable the people to understand their broad universal existence and help them to predict the future. The novel, he wrote, is like "a camera that observes, records, and reads the pulse of society and its situations and conditions. It has become the compass and the scope; if we read it wrong, then we will pay a very high price for our mistake."[2]

Throughout history, Arabic poetry has been called the "register" of the Arabs for registering their most important social and political developments, events, cultural values, and beliefs. Now, however, major novelists argue, the novel should take over that title and role. For many writers, it is becoming the "new creative register" of the Arabs. Further, some intellectuals believe that the novel has not only surpassed poetry but has also "hammered" all other genres (including theater, criticism, and short stories) and is now "ahead of everything, and has succeeded in becoming superior to poetry, and the dominating literary genre of the present."[3]

Hanna Mina, a Syrian novelist, strongly supports the claim that the term "register" in Arab literature should now belong to the novel. A major "shift" has happened and occurred inside literary circles, he has explained, and that shift is in favor of the novel. Today's age, he writes, is the "age of the novel. The novel concentrates on the sufferings of the people, the way they live and experience life.

Novelists through their education and mastery of the language do break the taboos of society."[4]

PRE-MODERN ARABIC NARRATION

The Arabic novel is a newly-developed literary genre even though there are scholars and writers who insist that it has existed for as long as poetry in Arabic literature. Their claim is based on the argument that the art of narration has always existed in Arabic prose literatures, such as fables, autobiographies, travel stories, tale stories, and vernacular and folk literature. Because the Arabic novel relies on the same narrative mechanics and practices, explains Egyptian novelist Gamal Al-Ghitani, that means the genre of the Arab novel has existed since early Arab history, and this art of narration tells our history and our early existence.[5] Edward Said wrote that Arabic literature before the twentieth century possessed a rich assortment of narrative forms—including qissa, sira, hadith, khurafa, ustura, khabar, nadira, maqama—but none of these ever became, as in the case of the European novel, the major narrative type. That said, Said still extolled the virtues of "a modern Arabic novel which, during the twentieth century, has undergone numerous and interesting transformations. Today it has produced a very wide variety of talents, styles, critics, readers, all mostly unknown outside the Middle East."[6]

Certainly Arabic literature in the past enjoyed a rich variety and a mixture of narrative forms and traditional fiction-writing. The familiar narrative structure essential to all storytelling existed in Arabic literature, centuries before the developments of the modern novel. That traditional form was used to record important historical happenings, occurrences, and incidents, and narrated significant aspects and facets of the lives of the people. This rich body of narrative writings includes beautiful popular and oral narrative and is based on the oral tradition that was composed and transmitted over centuries before it was captured in written forms. That includes Arabic folklore, biographies, autobiographies, epistolary works, travelogues, and historical, social, and cultural stories and events.

BIOGRAPHY AND FOLKLORIC NARRATION

There are two celebrated biographies of the Prophet Muhammad's life. The eighth-century biography by Muḥammad Ibn Isḥāq (d. 767), known as *Sirat Rasul Allah* (*Life of God's Messenger*), is an important source for the biography of Muhammad and for the history of early Islam. It is the earliest record of Muhammad's life and a valuable resource on the life of Muhammad and the history of Arabia during the rise of Islam that records the Islamic historical events in chronological order.

The other biography was written in the ninth century and was composed by Ibn Hisham (Abu Muhammad Abd al-Malik, d. 827). Ibn Hisham's biography is an edited and annotated version of the same biography of the Prophet that was composed a century earlier by Ibn Isḥāq. But Ibn Hisham's biography, which is known as *al-Sirah Al-Nabawiyyah (The Biography of the Prophet)*, is considered the standard biography of the Prophet and the source for most subsequent works on the subject. It is assembled into a historical, lengthy narrative known as *al-Sirah (The Biography)*, which refers to its being an exclusive narrative history of the Prophet's life.

Prior to these biographies, much earlier in history, there were traditional narratives of folkloric traditions about tribal and national heroes; among these *Sirahs* of the folklore narratives is the *Sirah* of the pre-Islamic knight poet and Bedouin hero, *Antarah bin Shaddad Al-Absi* (the Son of *Shaddad* of the tribe of *Abs*) was the son of a slave mother; therefore, his father denied him. The tale says that *Antarah* had "erased" the disgrace of his birth by the great courage he demonstrated against the enemies of his tribe, showing extreme bravery in wars and battles. His poetry represents the ideal of manhood and genuine Bedouin morals. Prophet Muhammad said: "No Arab was described to me that I wanted to see save *Antarah*."[7] He died in 615.

Antarah is also famous for his profound love for his cousin, *'Ablah*, and his verses about his beloved *'Ablah* are still recited today by lovers of poetry and documented in books of classical Arabic literature. "I felt like kissing the swords," one of his verses for his beloved *'Ablah* says, "because their glimmer reminded me of your smile."[8] The *Sirah* of *Antarah* is only one example of the rich Arabic folklore narration that includes many other stories and tales, including *Abu Zayd al-Hilali* in the eleventh century and, perhaps the most well-known of all, the tales of the *Arabian Nights*, which will be discussed later in this chapter.

TRAVEL LITERATURE

Another classical genre relying on narrative mechanics similar to what a novel uses is the genre of autobiographical travel narration, which is also present in earlier Arabic literature. One of the most popular is the travel narration of the Moroccan *Ibn Battutah* (d. 1368), who went on a journey from his city of Tangier and traveled for twenty-four years before returning home. *Ibn Battutah* traveled through Muslim and non-Muslim countries, learning a great deal during his journeys from scholars and theologians in major centers of learning in cities including Cairo, Damascus, and Baghdad. *Ibn Battutah* voyaged around the Mediterranean, North Africa, Andalusia, Central Asia and Anatolia, South and Southeast Asia, China, and West and East Africa.

His book on travels, which is abbreviated as *al-Rihlah* (*The Journey*), includes detailed descriptions of his adventures and the countries he visited during his twenty-four years of continuous travels. These accounts were recorded when he was an old man, back in his home city of Tangier, and were reported to a secretary who wrote them down. His book is one of the most important works of the travel literature genre and a major source of historical, social, cultural, and religious information about the medieval period. He gave us an invaluable document containing his observations, comments, and details of the world during that period in history. Another example of this genre in Arabic pertains to the tales of Sinbad or *Sindbad al Bahri* (Sinbad the Sailor) in *One Thousand and One Nights*.

THE *MAQAMAH* (PICARESQUE TALES) GENRE

The *maqamah* genre is a traditional prose genre that originated in the tenth century with Badi` al-Zaman al-Hamadani (d. 1008). His stories don't pretend to be factual, but instead they give us entertaining accounts often about rogues, tricksters, and beggars, and he presents them in a thrilling narrative style that displays the narrator's eloquence, fluency, humor, literacy, and knowledge. This genre first established by al-Hamadani was revived by Al-Hariri (Abu Muhammad al-Qasim ibn Ali, d. 1122), who was also a great scholar of Arabic grammar, style, and verse. The tales of the *maqamah* (plural *maqamat*) are filled with humor and adventure, and they display linguistic and poetic skills. Al-Hariri's *maqamat* were a "popular subject for book illustrators during the eighteenth century and the basis for lively depictions of scenes of everyday life."[9] The *maqamah* contains alternating rhyming verses about two imaginary characters, and its basic form consists of a picaresque narrative that exploits the "antics of a narrator and rogue (in al-Hamadani's case, *Isa ibn Hisham* and *Abu al-Fath al-Iskandarani*, respectively) to provide both social commentary and, mostly through inverse implication, moral enlightenment."[10]

THE *SAJ*` STYLE IN AL-MAQAMAH

Saj` is Arabic that means "rhyming prose"—a style that involves rhyme, rhythm, and cadence. It makes full use of the musical and morphological potential of the Arabic language. This type of rhyming prose had existed in the magical utterances of soothsayers in the pre-Islamic period and is also used in the Qur'an. This rhythmic prose style was particularly connected with the *maqamah* genre, and with its two most famous practitioners al-Hamadani and al-Hariri, in the tenth and eleventh centuries, respectively.

What is important about these narrative forms for this chapter is the fact that the *maqamah* genre was revived and imitated late in the nineteenth century by the Egyptian writer Muhammad al-Muwaylihi (1858–1930) in his book *Hadith Isa ibn Hisham* (*The Words of Isa ibn Hisham*). Before its publication in 1907, his book was serialized from 1898 to 1902 in newspapers in Cairo. This book, as well as the books and writings of other pioneers of the Arabic cultural awakening, serves as a link and a bridge between classical Arabic literature and the newly evolving forms of modern Arabic literature. With his popular book, firmly planted in the twentieth century, Al-Muwaylihi looked back and imitated the form and content of the *maqamah*, even naming the main character *Isa ibn Hisham*—the same name used in Badi` al-Zaman al-Hamadani's *maqamah*.

Roger Allen notes that "we are dealing with the deliberate revival of the past heritage, and its application to the present, a fully conscious neoclassicism."[11] Al-Muwaylihi used *saj`* at the beginning of each serialized episode, and he explored many of the problems, inconsistencies, and ironies of life in Egypt—especially aspects of modernization and Westernization, the British occupation of Egypt, and the chaotic Egyptian legal system—that would become familiar ground for later Arabic novelists. He also added another lens to his narratives by contrasting these elements with life in the countryside. Thus, the work of al-Muwaylihi serves in itself as a major precedent—as a bridge and landmark in the development of the novel in Arabic from its early phase of "transition, imitation, and adaption to the phase of creation and experimentation, which led to the creation of the first Arabic novel at the hands of Muhammad Husayn Haykal in his novel *Zaynab*."[12]

REVIVING THE CLASSICAL ARABIC PAST

The history of the Arabic novel's development involves many pioneering works— more than the limited space of a single chapter will allow. This chapter's primary task is confined to giving a general idea about the classical heritage's revival in the works of selected pioneers who serve as a connection between the classical past and the modern present. As mentioned in the chapter about the Arabic language, Arab writers in the second half of the nineteenth century and in the first few decades of the twentieth century tried to revive Classical Arabic and classical Arabic literature by reconstructing and resurrecting the excellent literary past. Poets and prose writers alike returned to the past and reconstructed and revived the classical language's phraseology, vocabulary, and structure, which had deteriorated after the collapse of Arab civilization in the thirteenth century.

As mentioned earlier in this chapter, the novel as a modern literary genre did not exist in ancient Arabic literature. Its emergence as a new genre was the result of a progression made by Arab writers who prepared the ground for a successful modernization of language and thought. This gradual and steady process, which would transform the Arabic language, consequently led to the creation of the modern Arabic novel.

The Arabic writers who led these efforts in the nineteenth and twentieth centuries published essays on a variety of themes and adapted popular Western novels for Arabic audiences using a beautiful, modern literary style. They also adapted Arabic to express new ideas and embrace new forms of artistic sensibility. Other factors that emerged at the same time and helped pave new paths and routes to modernism include: the growth of the translation movement, the spread of journals, the establishment of Arabic publishing houses, and the creation of schools of foreign languages. Where the translation of scientific works for Arabic readers was concerned, journalism played a decisive modernizing role because it "helped gradually to change the style of Arabic prose, ridding it of excessive rhetorical devices, making it a simpler and fitter vehicle for conveying ideas as well as for sustained narrative."[13]

Writers critical during this period of convergence, which contributed to the Arab cultural awakening of the late nineteenth and early twentieth centuries, include: al-Muwaylihi (1858-1930), who was mentioned earlier; Nasif al-Yaziji (1800-1871), Farah Antoun (1874-1922), Jurji Zaydan (1861-1914), Mustafa Lutfi al-Manfaluti (1876-1924), and Gibran Khalil Gibran (1883-1931), to mention only a few. They produced innovations that were truly revolutionary for Arabic literature. Lebanese scholar and writer Butrus al-Bustani (1819-1883), for example, used a new kind of expository prose that didn't depart from the basic rules of Arabic grammar but used simpler modes of expression and new words and idioms that were developed from Classical Arabic and adapted from English or French.[14] Other pioneering figures wrote historical novels that focused on Arab society and employed a high literary style. The historical novel was indisputably a crucial development for the progression of the Arab renaissance, with its rediscovery of the classical past and reassertion of Arab national identity.[15]

THE BIRTH OF THE ARABIC NOVEL

The contributions of the early prose writers to the formation of the modern Arabic novel are highly valued by modern literary criticism; without the accumulated efforts of these thinkers, the modern novel's emergence in Arabic culture and society would certainly have been delayed. That novel could not have been born without its forerunners in historical, autobiographical, biographical, translation, and adaptation narratives. The first modern novel is considered to be

Zaynab, which was authored in 1914 by Egyptian writer, politician, and journalist Muhammad Hussein Haykal (1888-1956). Most Arab critics agree that *Zaynab* represents the true beginning of the new literary genre and the first developed Arabic novel.

Haykal's novel, which he composed while studying in France, encompasses many facets of Egyptian society: the country's rising national consciousness, what love and romance were like in a restrictive society, manners and social behavior, scenes of the countryside and village life—all of it rendered in Egyptian dialect in an effort to give readers a realistic depiction of Egyptian society. Haykal also employs simple vocabulary and uncomplicated structures. The novel uses the language of "ordinary people, reflecting the beauty of nature and the beauty of the Egyptian women of the village."[16] Nevertheless, critics also have recognized the novel as having many "serious shortcomings that are inevitable in all pioneering works."[17] Two years earlier, Gibran Khalil Gibran wrote *The Broken Wings*, a novel charged with dynamic lyricism that departed from traditional Arab prose style. Though *The Broken Wings* precedes Zaynab and also addresses a range of social issues—the overwhelming power of love in conservative social traditions, the lack of women's rights, the tyranny of the clergy—*Zaynab* is considered by Arab critics to be more developed than Gibran's novel.

Along with the appearance of *Zaynab*, the short story genre grew and found a suitable home in a surge of new journals. Many writers have preferred to concentrate on the growth of the short story genre, that is the reason why there is a "temporal gap between the publication of *Zaynab* and the appearance of a whole host of novels in the 1930s."[18] The second most significant work after *Zaynab* is *al-Ayyam* in 1929 by Taha Hussein (1888-1973). This autobiographical novel was translated into English as *An Egyptian Childhood* in 1932. Hussein's second novel was *Du`a' al-Karawan* (*The Call of the Curlew*) in 1934. Hussein also wrote critical analyses on Arabic literature and culture; his writing contributed enormously to the development and modernization of the Arabic language and style. Hussein called upon writers to use language that people could understand and held that authors should write clearly and simply and use standard Arabic language.

Other writers who have made significant contributions to the development of the Arabic novel include Yahya Haqqi (1905-1992), Abdel Rahman al-Sharqawi (1920-1987), Ibrahim al-Mazini (1889-1949), and Youssef Idris (1927-1991). Substantial progress in the development of the Arabic novel took place in the hands of Tawfiq al-Hakim (1898-1987) and by Naguib Mahfouz (1911-2006), who advanced the growth of the modern Arab novel and brought it to its highest level of maturity and development in his work during the second half of the twentieth century.

Meanwhile, as Arab prose writers worked to develop a modern Arabic novel, Arab poets were also engaged in reviving the Arabic language and consciously imitating the classical past in order to free the language from weaknesses that had developed over several centuries. This neoclassical movement, led by the pioneering poets of the Arab renaissance, recovered the language of the glorious past through imitation and reproduction as well as recreating form, content, vocabulary, and expression. Drawing on both classical Abbasid and pre-Islamic classical poetry, these poets gave powerful expression to Arab national sentiments. Their pioneering efforts, along with the efforts of writers in prose, set up the conditions that would allow new generations of writers to pursue further modernization and transformation with vibrant, innovative language capable of fully articulating ideas with lively, powerful, and richly aesthetic techniques. Among the pioneering neoclassical poets are: Mahmoud Sami al-Baroudi (1839–1904), Hafiz Ibrahim (1872–1932), and Muhammad Mahdi al-Jawahiri (1899–1999).

After the end of the Second World War, two important forces in modern Arabic literary history emerged to reinforce and support renovation and modernization of language and style: the mature advancement of the Arabic novel and the rise of the free verse poetic movement. Both forces revolutionized the Arabic language and transformed it into a dynamic and creative language capable of capturing a wide range of details and themes that created new structures, style, spirit, and application. This new modern Arabic language significantly accelerated the rising stature that the Arabic novel and poetry achieved in the past several decades.

The Second World War served as a significant landmark in the history of Arabic literature besides being a turning point in the social, economic, political, and cultural life of the Arab world. It marked the fading of elements of Romanticism in prose and poetry. After the war's end, Arab poets and prose writers continued to explore the language's grammatical and syntactical structures. They used a new mix of vocabulary and expressions, utilizing new techniques to merge the inner self of the writer with the outer self of the world. This poetic/prose innovation had an enormous impact on Arabic linguistic modernity. The generations of writers that followed the pioneers succeeded in moving the Arabic language into a new phase of writing skills, experimentation, exploration, and revelation.

THE ARABIC NOVEL AND SOCIOLOGY

It is Naguib Mahfouz, awarded the Nobel Prize for Literature in 1988, who has produced the greatest impact on the development of the Arabic novel. In his hands, the novel form reached its zenith, and many other Arab novelists have followed his example, producing fascinating modern novels that effectively capture the vagaries and contradictions, beauty and ugliness, harmony and confusion of modern Arab reality, drawing on their high intellectual talents and individual skills at deploying various themes, techniques, allegories, and styles.

Today the Arabic novel has successfully described Arab society and culture with more accuracy and understanding than any competing philosophical or sociological study. In fact, sociologist and novelist Halim Barakat even insists that more can be learned now about the Arab world through the novel than through "all of the other studies combined."[19] The Arabic novel has influenced not only Arabic language but also Arab culture and reality. Furthermore, the novel creates a bond between the novelist and his reader, involving the reader in the complex and rich process of writing.

Arab novelists, like poets and other intellectuals, use their ideas to inspire and move the Arab world to create a better one. Their visions inject a new consciousness into society as they observe the stagnation of life and expose society's corruption and deception for their readers. Their writing offers a realistic image of life and a picture of the possible future. By reflecting on reality, they transcribe the biography of a nation. They monitor and illuminate the social, economic, political, and cultural aspects of the Arabs. Their novels show us the conflicts and contradictions, crises, and defects of society with techniques and lyricism normally reserved for poetry. In the modern Arabic novel, language, technique, and narration reach their fullest potential.

ARAB NOVELISTS OF MODERN TIMES

Though the contributions of Arab novelists as a group are considerable, the artistic contributions of two giants in particular, Naguib Mahfouz (1911–2006) and Abdelrahman Munif (1933–2004), have been greater than all other writers in contemporary times. Until their deaths more than a decade ago, both novelists guided the novel into the very heart of modernism and post-modernism with their astonishing abilities to describe in profound detail all of the social, political, and cultural realities of Arab life and society in modern times.

NAGUIB MAHFOUZ

Naguib Mahfouz, also spelled Najib Maḥfuẓ, was born and raised in an old quarter of Cairo, which is also the setting of many of his novels. He received a degree in philosophy from Cairo University and began publishing his short stories and articles on the history of ideas and philosophy in journals in 1934. He worked in the Egyptian civil service; his last position was as a consultant on Cultural Affairs to the Ministry of Culture, from which he retired in 1972. He began his career as a novelist by writing historical fiction and published three novels in this particular genre between 1939 and 1944, in which he implicitly criticized the tyranny of King Faruq of Egypt and expressed his explicit feelings of nationalist resentment against the British occupation of Egypt. The first of his published historical novels was `Abath al-Aqdar (The Mockery of Fate) in 1939.

Mahfouz would later shift his attention to the realistic novel in Khan al-Khalili (1945), followed in 1947 by Zuqaq al-Midaqq (Middaq Alley). Mahfouz narrated the development of modern Egypt in a body of work that includes 33 novels, 13 anthologies of short stories, several plays, and 30 screenplays. When he received the Nobel Prize, his work was hailed by the Swedish Academy of Letters as "an Arabian narrative art that applies to all mankind."[20] The generation of novelists following Mahfouz produced excellent novels influenced by and benefiting from Mahfouz's achievements.

These characters are the city's ordinary people, shopkeepers, thieves, prostitutes, grocers, public servants, and peasants. He wrote about Egyptian women abused by others, the contradictions of life in Egyptian society, and the suffering and problems of the Egyptian people in daily life. In Egypt, each new book published by Mahfouz was understandably regarded "as a major cultural event and his name [was] inevitably among the first mentioned in any literary discussion from Gibraltar to the Gulf."[21] The New York Times wrote that Mahfouz has often been referred to as the "Egyptian Balzac for his vivid frescoes of Cairenes and their social, political and religious dilemmas. Critics compared his richly detailed Cairo with the London of Charles Dickens, the Paris of Émile Zola and the St. Petersburg of Fyodor Dostoyevsky."

ZUQAQ AL-MIDAQQ (MIDAQ ALLEY)

Midaq Alley, 1947, is considered one of Mahfouz's most significant novels. Set in Old Cairo, the novel shows the changes of Egyptian society through the lives and interactions of the people living in the alley. Mahfouz describes that alley in loving detail: the inhabitants, their work and spare time, their complex social relationships, and their close community. M.M. Badawi wrote that Mahfouz gives a vivid picture of the sights, sounds, and smells of the alley, and that he paints a gallery of colorful characters: "The novel deals with the pressure of life in Egypt shortly before and during the Second World War, [and] shows the tragic impact the outside world has upon this community, as well as the destructive effect the presence of the British occupation army has upon Egypt during the war."[23]

Written in 1941-1945, the novel reflects the rupture between two worlds—the traditional and the modern—in 1940s Egypt. It documents important historical years from the perspective of the individuals living in the narrow, ancient streets of

Cairo's old city. The main character is the beautiful young Hamida, who is engaged to Abbas al-Hilu, a barber in the alley. In order to save money for their marriage, Abbas decides to join the British army camp and work there for a year. Shortly after he leaves, Hamida's adoptive mother encourages her to break her promise and accept a marriage proposal from a rich older married man who owns a grocery store in the alley. After Hamida agrees, the old man develops a serious illness, and the marriage does not take place. Later, another man—a handsome young man who seems rich to Hamida—seduces her, and she later discovers that he is a pimp for the British army. His job is to find prostitutes to entertain the British soldiers, and Hamida moves out of the alley and lives in an upper class neighborhood as a professional prostitute.

When her fiancé, Abbas, finds Hamida, he learns the story of her disappearance and is determined to punish her seducer. Hamida arranges to meet him at a bar and to show him her seducer. When Abbas arrives at the bar earlier than Hamida expected, he finds her in a revealing dress, entertaining some drunken British soldiers. He's unable to control his rage and throws a bottle of beer in her face. The British soldiers beat him to death. This, Mahfouz writes, is "only one of many sad changes in the lives of the inhabitants of the alley."[24]

Mahfouz depicts many characters to capture the character of the Midaq. Among these are Mu`allim Kirsha, a café owner, who spends his money on hashish and homosexual pursuits; Uncle Kamil, who is always dozing off with a flywhisk in his lap as flies swarm around him; and Shaykh Darwish, a former schoolteacher ousted by national changes to the education system who spends most of his time at a local café. There is also Faraj, the pimp who convinced Hamida to leave the alley for a top-quality life in the world beyond. Mahfouz also shows us the social stratification of the world of the Midaq with characters such as Salim Alwan, a wealthy older merchant with business in the alley who does not actually reside in it. In Mahfouz's portrait of a fat and stagnant shopkeeper, he embodies what Rasheed el-Anany calls the "past that has overstayed its time, a past that is only clinically alive."[25] One of the characters says that "everything in this alley is dead, and as long as you live in it, you won't need, one day, burying."[26]

Mahfouz shows the great differences existing between the worlds of Hamida and Faraj. Faraj, in order to lure her away, tells Hamida more than once that the alley is a "graveyard of decaying bones," and that life in the Zuqaq is a life of hardship, a place where beauty fades away while life in the world beyond the alley is full of light, wealth and happiness."[27] Faraj even asks Hamida to change her name to Titi and to change her attire.[28] Hamida leaves the alley and Abbas behind, and the contrast "between the two worlds can be seen through the changing relationships between individuals."[29]

When Abbas met Hamida during his visit, Hamida realized the huge gap that occurred, and separated them. She told him "we are complete strangers now, I cannot go back and you cannot change me."[30] Even Abbas, who greatly loves Hamida, is aware of the strange distance that separates their two worlds. But Hamida isn't forced into becoming a prostitute; it is her choice and desire to leave the alley, Abbas, her mother, and everything else behind. Abbas's search for Hamida ends in his being beaten to death by the British soldiers. The world has shifted, and it cannot be reversed.

Hamida symbolizes Egypt at a certain time in history, and she represents the conflict between past and present, old and new, tradition and modernity, East and West. Her decision to follow her self-interest at the expense of tradition and dignity has far-reaching consequences. This novel is not, as some would think, simply about "a poor girl dazzled into a life of sin by her ambition and her lust for life—it is as much a novel about a nation at the crossroads, torn between a cultural past that is her very identity, and a modern world" that "does not accept you unless you abandon your values."[31]

AL-THULATHIYYA (THE CAIRO TRILOGY)[32]

About ten years after the publication of *Midaq Alley,* Mahfouz published *al-Thulathiyya* (*Trilogy*) in 1956–1957 and followed it with a series of eight powerful novels. Soon after, Mahfouz emerged as the "master par excellence of the Egyptian realist novel, the chronicle of the twentieth century Egypt, and its most vocal social and political conscience."[33]

The trilogy, which is about 1500 pages, was published in three separate volumes taking their titles from the street names in old Cairo where most of the characters actually lived: *Bayn al-Qasrayn, (Palace Walk), Qasr al-Shawq (Palace of Desire),* and *al-Sukkariyya (Sugar Street).* The first volume was published in 1956 and was followed a year later by the other two volumes. The trilogy deals with three generations of the family of Abd al-Jawad and begins in 1917 with the growth of the nationalist movement, the Egyptian revolution of 1919, and extends into 1944 just before the end of the Second World War. The trilogy calls to mind the major national transformations of Egypt in the first half of the twentieth century and expresses them through the experiential perspective of a family living in the heart of Cairo.

The three books capture the important historical events in Egypt's modern history and its struggle for national independence from British rule. They describe in detail the daily events of a middle class Cairene family over three generations. Mahfouz's work is more than fiction; since there are no books in modern history that record life there during that period, he records the impact of Western influence and the pressures of life on the city's population.

Critic Sabry Hafez wrote that the trilogy is one of "those rare works which provides its reader with a deep insight into the culture which produced it. Reading this monumental yet highly enjoyable book enriches one more than any number of textbooks about Egypt's modern history, society, and culture."[34] Mahfouz captures all of the political happenings during a twenty-eight-year period and intertwines and interconnects them into the lives of the characters of the protagonist family.

The characters represent three main trends in the political life of Egypt: the political national movement formed in the aftermath of World War I, which led to the revolution of 1919 against the British occupation; the growing socialist movement; and the beginnings of a fundamentalist Islamic movement "for the newborn is the son of the Islamist, a portent that is still relevant to the Arab reality of the present day."[35]

The trilogy is an incredible achievement, especially considering that the modern Arabic novel was still in an early stage of its development when it first appeared. The trilogy is predictive: Each novel ends with a death and a birth. The birth in the trilogy's final novel, *Sugar Street*, is especially significant. Denys Johnson-Davies wrote in *The Guardian*, of the trilogy's rapid success, that it has quickly become a bestseller in the Arab world, and those who could not read it came to know its characters through the films that were made of it; that it could also be appreciated outside its own cultural confines is shown by the fact that in the United States the trilogy achieved sales of more than 250,000 copies.[36]

Mahfouz gives us enormous amounts of information about the daily life of the members of his protagonist family, the Abd al-Jawads. He portrays their interactions with each other and with the city of Cairo as the transformation of Egypt as a nation is taking place. Throughout the trilogy, Mahfouz observes and explores the connections and communications of the families, their behavior, thoughts, and activities in Cairo, and he observes the "mutation of values across generations, the time gap between contemporaneous social classes, and the changing lifestyle concomitant with the changing value system."[37] The characters live through a series of major historical events in Egypt: the revolution of 1919, the British occupation during World War II, the national struggle of Egypt for independence, and the establishment of different political movements and their influence and impact on individuals, families, and the entire nation.

Mahfouz's trilogy mirrors the social, political, and cultural development of Egyptian society in a state of instability under British occupation. In addition, the novels capture the inner lives of the characters, their intellectual and political preoccupations, as well as serving as a "political allegory, and a reservoir of social custom, folk tales and songs, popular tunes, common proverbs, and the whole undercurrent of urban culture in Egypt in the first half of this century."[38]

For M. M. Badawi, the trilogy stands as "a unique monument, covering such a huge canvas, offering a panorama of Egyptian society, keenly sensitive to the passage of time, and recording the minutest changes in social and political life that testifies to Mahfouz's admirable architectonic sense and reveals his ability to design almost in epic dimension."[39]

CHILDREN OF GEBELAWI AND THE THIEF AND THE DOG

After the trilogy's publication but before the 1961 appearance of *al-Liss wa al-Kilab* (*The Thief and the Dog*), Mahfouz wrote *Awalad Haratina* (*Children of Gebelawi*), which was first serialized in 1959 in the daily newspaper *Al-Ahram* and received strong opposition and condemnation from Islamic conservatives and religious authorities in the country. As a result, the novel's publication was banned in Egypt and Mahfouz was disheartened by this reaction to his novel, which portrays "in allegorical form a man's struggle for comprehension and solution of the problem of existence."[40] Mahfouz responded to the situation by refraining from writing; he was too discouraged by "the furor the novel caused in traditional and religious circles."[41]

The cause of the furor, according to the Nobel Prize committee's notes on Mahfouz's career, is the approach Mahfouz takes in writing "a history of human-kind up to the 1950s, starting with the Dawn of Creation. At the same time, it is a story about children in a Cairo suburb and their difficulties. For his narrative, he has drawn on, or sometimes paraphrased the *Qur'an* and the traditional Islamic *Hadith* literature for many figures and events, freely transforming them and insert-ing them into a new historical and completely fictional context."[42] Critics claimed that the main character in the novel, Gebelawi, represents God even though Mahfouz rejected that claim.

M. M. Badawi suggested that the novel's over-arching theme is, in fact, the whole of human history and "man's quest for religion from Adam and Eve, Cain and Abel, Moses, Jesus, Muhammad, right down to the last of prophets, the modern man of science. Mahfouz here is giving modern man's view of the stories of prophecy narrated by the Qur'an."[43] Roger Allen noted that this novel represents the opening of what was to be an ambitious and controversial literary undertaking by Mahfouz, that is, the "role of religion in modern society."[44] Eight years after the ban in Egypt, the novel was published finally in Lebanon in 1967. Mahfouz would have to wait until 2006, the year of his death, before its publica-tion in Egypt.

Three years after that novel's original newspaper serialization, Mahfouz pub-lished *The Thief and the Dogs* in 1961; the novel was well-received and was soon followed by several more impressive novels. That novel marks a new phase in

Mahfouz's career as he concentrated on writing shorter novels that focus mainly upon a single protagonist. *Thief* employs dramatic and lyrical language, stream of consciousness, inner monologue and a combination of political and psychological narrative.[45] *Thief* registers the rage and disillusion of the Egyptians after Nasser's revolution in 1952. Egyptians had cheered and applauded that revolution and its promise, but they were soon disappointed and "disenchanted, frustrated, and alienated by the turn the revolution took, it imposed military rule and banned political parties, suppressed freedom, and crushed all opposition. This resulted in the rise of a new cynical class of self-seeking opportunists who paid only lip service to the revolution's social slogans."[46]

Thief's central character is the thief Said Mahran, who grows up in poverty and later falls under the influence of Rauf Ilwan, a revolutionary and idealist who tells him it is morally justified if the poor rob from the rich. Said falls in love with a girl in his neighborhood and marries her, and they have a daughter. Soon after, the police catch him and send him for four years to prison. While there, Said's wife divorces him and marries his best friend, and Said suspects this friend of being the one who informed the police about him and caused his imprisonment.

When he is freed, finally, Said is understandably a very angry man and wants revenge. He goes immediately to see his old mentor and supporter, Rauf Ilwan, but his mentor has changed under the new revolutionary regime; Said encounters a rich, obese man, an opportunist living a luxurious life in an exclusive area that Said once targeted. Rauf Ilwan turns his back on him and makes it clear that he no longer can help him. Before he does, however, he gives Said some money and tells him to go away and look for an honest job.

Frustrated and angry, Said burgles his former mentor's house, but Rauf Ilwan catches him and humiliates him before letting him go. Said moves from one cause of his misery, Rauf, to another: his unfaithful wife and her lover. He obtains a gun and goes to their house to punish them, and doesn't realize that they have moved out. When he enters and fires a shot, killing the new occupant, Said goes back to kill Rauf Ilwan and misfires again, this time killing the doorkeeper. Pursued by the police, he finds refuge with a prostitute he knows in her flat, which is adjacent to a cemetery. The novel ends with Said's death at the hands of the police and their dogs inside the cemetery. *Thief* is a tragic novel about the hopelessness and failure of man, betrayed by the revolution, friends, wives, and mentors. It is about the absurdity of life and the alienation of the individual from his own society. Said is a "lost soul who has been abandoned by God ... a hapless victim of fate, and this among other factors makes us feel that in some ways he is more sinned against than sinning"[47]

THARTHARA FAWQ AL-NIL (CHATTERING ON THE NILE)

Mahfouz's 1966 novel *Tharthara Fawq al-Nil* (*Chattering on the Nile*) shocks readers with its bold representation of defeatism and escapism in Egyptian society right before the 1967 Six-Day War. Set on a houseboat on the Nile, a group of intellectuals and representatives of the middle class—a lawyer, actor, journalist, literary critic, student, housewife, and civil servant—get together for drug- and sex-filled evenings. These gatherings provide them with an escape from reality, and they temporarily lose themselves in a haze of hashish, alcohol, sexual promiscuity, and nonsense political chats and mockery.

When the group leaves the houseboat and takes an evening drive, their car hits and kills a peasant woman. No one reports or acknowledges the accident; instead, the group responds with apathy and neglect. In his analysis of the novel, Rasheed El-Enany notes that the group's collective killing of a fellow citizen is a wakeup call; that the experiences on the houseboat are "symbolic of a society on the verge of sinking, and the car accident is a prophecy, pointing at the other catastrophic incident awaiting the nation around the corner of history, that is, the 1967 defeat in the war with Israel."[48]

Mahfouz highlights the absurdity of Egyptian life, a life without meaning or purpose. He presents a sharp criticism of society, of its moral crumbling and lack of commitment, which are the result of a "lack of political power and suppression of freedom."[49] These negative qualities persist and become even more pronounced in Mahfouz's next novel, *Miramar*.

The defeat of the Arabs in the Six-Day War of 1967 registered a massive blow to the foundations of Arab society. That stunning defeat affected every aspect of Arab life, including literature. Writers in Egypt and elsewhere in the Arab world responded to the defeat in a variety of ways. Some fell silent, others grew angry; Mahfouz reacted by writing a series of symbolic, cynical short stories published in collections in 1969 and 1971. These short stories "all reflect the sense of question, challenges, and recrimination which were so characteristic of this period."[50] These stories aside, though, Mahfouz would not write another novel until 1972, when he published *al-Maraya* (*Mirror*).

AL-MARAYA (MIRROR)

Al-Maraya, a name of a pension in Alexandria, narrated through its characters staying in the same pension. It represents the gloomy picture of the Egyptian society, totally lacking in values, the shortcomings of the leaders, and reflects twentieth century Egyptian history over 50 years: from the 1919 revolution through the 1952 revolution and 1967 defeat—a period Mahfouz himself experienced as an eyewitness.

The novel covers five decades of historical, political, social, economic, and cultural changes in Egypt, its political movements, its leaders, wars, and the changes that the Egyptian people and their society endured during these turbulent years. Mahfouz shows us these changes, and their impact, on the lives of people whom Mahfouz himself knew and loved. The accounts of the characters in the novel are observed with "extreme frankness about politics, including the Egyptian revolution, international relations, and the continuing dilemma regarding the fate of the Palestinian people ... this particular phase in Egypt's history was certainly one of looking back in anger."[51]

ABDELRAHMAN MUNIF

After Naguib Mahfouz, Abdelrahman Munif is the most significant Egyptian novelist in modern times. The son of a Saudi father and an Iraqi mother, Munif was born in Amman, Jordan, then moved in 1952 to Iraq to study law. He worked in Iraq as the editor of the Iraqi journal *Al-Naft wa al-Tanmiyah (Oil and Development)* and received a doctorate in oil economics from the University of Belgrade. He lived in France for five years and moved to Syria in 1986. Though he was stripped of his Saudi citizenship for his opposition to the Saudi royal family, Munif is celebrated as one of the greatest novelists in the Arab world. He wrote fifteen novels, many of which were banned in Saudi Arabia and other countries for their political content. His masterpiece is *Cities of Salt* (1984–89), a quintet (a group of five novels) that begins with *Mudun al-milh (Cities of Salt)*, *Al-ukhdud (The Trench)*, *Taqasim al-Layl wa-al-Nahar (Variations on Night and Day)*, *Al-munbatt (The Uprooted)*, and *Badiyat al Zulumat (The Desert of Darkness)*.[52]

AL-NIHAYAT (ENDINGS)

In 1978, Munif published *al-Nihayat (Endings,* 1988), which is one of his most original novels. It describes a small desert village in the Gulf during a severe drought and how the drought drives the inhabitants to hunt in the desert. When "drought seasons come," Munif writes, "things begin to change, life and objects change, humans change too."[53] A group of visitors from the city descend on the village for a pleasure hunt, despite the growing shortages of wild life because of the drought. Regardless, the visitors are still welcomed according to traditional Bedouin hospitality. They are guided by Assaf, an outsider living in the village who is a master hunter and who hunts birds with his dogs for the hungry inhabitants of the village. Roger Allen has noted how the emphasis on the desert, intense heat, the danger of travel, the search for food, and other elements set this novel apart from other Arabic novels, and that Munif's attention to depicting "this particular segment of contemporary Arabic society takes the Arabic novel to previously unexplored venues."[54]

When Assaf leads the visitors into the desert, the excursion culminates in his own death during a sandstorm. The protagonist's death occurs at the novel's mid-point: Munif divides the story into two distinct sections—the first during Assaf's life, and the second after his death as the village grieves for him. Stefan Meyer has noted that such structural innovation is significant to the development of the Arabic novel. Munif, he explains, is primarily concerned with "developing an innovative style that is not imitative of the West."[55] Munif warns in the novel of over-extracting natural resources and of the greed of man, which parallels human extremes with regard to another resource Munif understood well, the exploitation of oil. M.M. Badawi has commented that during Assaf's funeral, he is transfigured into a mythical hero whose death inspires the villages to call for the city authorities to build a dam that has been promised to save them from future droughts.[56] The novel is rich in themes, highlighting the tension between town and desert, and it "dramatizes the primordial balance and near mystical affinity between man and nature. It is yet another manifestation of Munif's originality"[57] that "possesses the momentousness of myth."[58]

MUDUN AL-MILH (CITIES OF SALT)

Cities of Salt is a remarkable work that tracks the evolution and the transformation of Arabia by the oil surge. It is an enormous work, consisting of five large volumes that run to more than 2,400 pages. This "marathon work has no parallel in modern Arabic fiction: not even Mahfouz's trilogy is comparable in length and epic breadth."[59] It deals with the most significant historical event in modern Arab history, the discovery of oil in Saudi Arabia and the Gulf, and the impact of oil on the individual, social, cultural, and environmental life of societies in the region, in particular the psychological disruptions and distortion brought by the discovery of oil. Edward Said has described Cities of Salt as the "only serious work of fiction that tries to show the effect of oil, Americans and the local oligarchy on a Gulf country."[60] In the pages of The Guardian, we find a similar overview of this five-part novel as an examination of "Munif's theory that the Arabs were the subjects of injustice, deprivation and oppression. A work saturated in symbolism, its message can be applied to any and each city in the Arab oil countries, where Arabs have been the victims of their rulers and the foreigners. This was the central theme of his writing, particularly the most celebrated of his 15 novels."[61]

During a period when Gulf monarchs and Arab elites relied on Western oil companies, Munif's Cities of Salt served as a very threatening portrayal of the oil boom's negative effects on local Arab populations and the "destruction of traditional values and customs."[62] *Cities of Salt* shows how a desert oasis was altered and then destroyed by the arrival of Western oil companies, and how reserved, traditional communities were interrupted and complicated by the arrival of foreigners and their endless geographical surveys and questions.

Munif's story covers the period from 1933, the beginning of the search for oil by Americans, until the year 1975. The novel opens with a description of Wadi al-Uyun, an Arabian village, and its dignified people, whose peaceful existence is suddenly disturbed by arriving American companies. Villagers are forced to relocate to make room for various oil installations; trees are taken out, and agriculture is replaced by new industrial projects. The Emir and his circles also begin to upset and contribute stress to the peaceful and harmonious atmosphere of the community. By the end, the oil profits will go only to the Emir and his inner circles. The novel is a "moving lament of the destruction of the traditional society and its replacement by the 'cities of salt', i.e. ephemeral artificial creation, lacking any roots, and bound to dissolve into nothingness once the oil is exhausted."[63]

OTHER NOVELS AND ARAB NOVELISTS

GHASSAN KANAFANI: *MEN IN THE SUN*

Ghassan Kanafani is a leading Palestinian writer, born in Akka (Acre) in 1936. His family fled Palestine in 1948 and settled in Syria. After graduating from Damascus University, he worked as a teacher and journalist, first in Damascus and then in Kuwait, later moving to Lebanon, where he became a spokesman for the Popular Front for the Liberation of Palestine and the founding editor of the weekly magazine *Al-Hadaf*. He wrote short stories, plays, and five novels which have been translated into many languages. Kanafani was killed in a car-bomb explosion in Beirut in 1972.

Kanafani's 1963 novel *Rijal fi al-Shams* (*Men in the Sun*, 1978) depicts the powerlessness and the plight of Palestinians and their misfortune in 1948; the novel illustrates their miserable search for jobs and places to accept them and their exploitation, including their mistreatment by Arab states. *Men in the Sun* is a brilliant masterpiece, and no modern Arab novelist "has been able to project the tragedy of the Palestinian people in fiction with greater impact than Ghassan Kanafani."[64]

Kanafani's heartbreaking story of the Palestinian refugees follows the death journeys of three men from three different generations: Abu Qais, As'ad, and Marwan, all trying to leave their harsh lives in the refugee camps and hoping to find work in Kuwait as laborers during the oil boom. Now an old man, Abu Qais hates his life in the humiliating refugee camps and wants to support his family with whatever work he can find. As'ad is fleeing from the oppression and brutality of the Jordanian police. Marwan needs to find a job to support his mother because his father has abandoned the family. The three men arrive at *Shatt al-Arab*, the confluence of the Tigris and Euphrates Rivers in the city of Basra, Iraq: This is the transit point through which they will illegally cross the desert into Kuwait, and these three men "come together as any group of people might convene to execute an illegal escape plan."[65]

In Basra, they negotiate a deal with a fellow Palestinian smuggler, Abu al-Khayzuran, who agrees to smuggle them to Kuwait. He fought for the Palestinian cause in 1948, and now he drives a lorry with a water tank between Iraq and Kuwait. At the first border checkpoint, the men remove their clothing and hide inside the lorry's empty water tank. They endure the intense heat inside the tank for seven minutes as Abu al-Khayzuran rushes to the office of the border control to complete the paperwork necessary for the crossing. He is successful, and they pass the first checkpoint. Exhausted and fatigued by their hiding place inside the tank, the three men ask Abu al-Khayzuran for a different strategy to avoid hiding there again. But Abu al-Khayzuran says that there is no other way, and he warns them that they will be caught if they try something else. He pleads with them to follow the same procedure: There is a final checkpoint ahead, and beyond that checkpoint, they will find new opportunities to help their families.

What else can they do? The three men realize they have no other choice and climb inside the empty tank. Stopped at the second checkpoint, Abu al-Khayzuran goes into the border patrol office to get papers signed. But this time there are more delays: The officials are bored, and they want to gossip about his alleged sexual adventures in Iraq. They joke and waste precious time. What is ironic about this situation—aside from the three refugees waiting inside a burning tank—is the fact that Abu al-Khayzuran is sexually impotent as the result of a surgical operation that saved his life. The officials ignore his repeated appeals for urgency. Finally, after they sign his papers, he rushes off and drives away to a safe distance to open the tank. To his horror, he finds that the three men are dead—suffocated to death from the heat that turned the tank into a furnace.

Abu al-Khayzuran continues into Kuwait and dumps the bodies in a garbage heap in Kuwait City. He drives away, then turns the lorry around and goes back to the garbage area to shout at the corpses. The novel ends with his shouting as he gazes at their dead bodies: "Why didn't you knock on the sides of the tank, why, why, why?!" The novel shows us "the futility of the quest for individual salvation pursued by fleeing Palestinians, and condemns the tragic passivity of their sufferings, as well as their betrayal by unsympathetic Arab authorities."[66] The three Palestinian refugees die silently and passively inside the oven-like tank, killed as much by the officials' indifference as by the heat of the desert.

"Kanafani lived and died according to his ideals," explains critic Hilary Kilpatrick. "Yet, unlike many committed writers, he refused to impose an ideological scheme on his fiction in any but the most general terms ... although his plays, novels, and short stories were written to serve the cause of Palestine, they have a universal appeal, thanks to his literary talents and his tenacity in preserving that freedom without which art is stifled."[67] *Men in the Sun* is, in the words of Edward Said, "his finest work and one of the most powerful of modern novellas."[68]

AL-TAYYIB SALIH: *SEASON OF MIGRATION TO THE NORTH*

Al-Tayyib Salih (1928–2009) was born in Sudan and studied at the University of Khartoum before traveling to England and studying at the University of London. He worked for the BBC's Arabic Service and UNESCO and produced three novels. His 1967 novel *Mawsim al-Hijrah ila al-Shamal* (*Season of Migration to the North*) is among the most accomplished works in modern Arabic literature that deal with "cultures in contact, and particularly with the confrontation between traditional and modern values."[69] Because of its many layers of meanings, this novel has been subjected to varied interpretations.[70]

Season of Migration to the North tells the story of a man who returns to his village after years abroad, only to discover that another man has taken his place in the village. A strange, elliptical work according to *The Guardian*, the novel "reads like a series of theatrical monologues which map out the distance between the rural countryside of northern Sudan and cosmopolitan London of the 1920s."[71]

There are two main characters: the narrator and Mustafa Saeed. The narrator is a Sudanese who returns to his village after seven years of study in London. The narrator notices a stranger in the community, Mustafa Saeed, a man from Khartoum, who moved into the village and married a local woman. The narrator and the stranger became friends, and Mustafa (who is also a Sudanese) reveals to the narrator how he grew up without a father and with a horrible mother, and how he went to England to study in the same country that dominated his homeland for many years. In England, Mustafa says he wanted to avenge the wrong done to his colonized people by means of his conquest of the women of England: "[T]o his African friends he used to say he was going to liberate Africa with his penis."[72] Three women who had affairs with him have committed suicide; a fourth, with whom he was besotted, became his wife.

But she was unfaithful to him, and he ended up killing her: "It was a ritual murder, mixing sex and violence: at her invitation, he plunged his knife between her breasts, while she lay naked in bed, ready for him."[73] Mustafa says he was sentenced to seven years in prison, and after his release he returned to Sudan and settled in the village. Mustafa's strategy of "seducing English women by posing as the fulfilment of their Orientalist fantasies" represents "one of the most remarkable encounters of its kind."[74]

Of Mustafa's strategy with the women, Roger Allen says he acts as a conqueror and an invader from the South. But his relationships with them are complex, and the love-hate relationship with the fourth English woman "symbolizes the absolute clash of these two cultures within a Western context."[75] For M.M. Badawi, however the novel is not really only about the perennial theme of opposition between East and West, it is "also about the question of identity. The relation between conscious and unconscious self, the alienation, the imbalance of heart and mind, and the nature of evil."[76]

Badawi elaborates further that Mustafa is not just an African intellectual in Europe; he is an individual with a specific history, and his character comes alive through a skillful use of his own words, thoughts, and memories, shreds of words said at the murder trial, and his conversations with his various women victims—all of which cumulatively contribute to building a vivid portrait of a tragically torn man whose attitude to women has been determined in part by the absence of a father and the lack of a mother's affection. And his evil outlived him."[77]

The novelist's works, according to the *New York Times*, "reflected the Arab and African quest for identity, especially in the 1960s, which saw the end of colonialism and the rise of nationalism across the region ... The story is about intellectuals torn between the culture of their native Sudan and that of Europe, where they lived for a time. A main character describes his time in the West, where he seduces and then leaves a succession of British women before finally marrying one in a stormy love-hate pairing that ultimately results in her murder at his hands."[78] Mustafa commits suicide in the Nile, and the novel ends with the narrator also committing a suicide in the same river. The novel is devastating in its effect, rich in theme, complex in structure, and relies upon devices such as "parallelism, juxtaposition, and contrast, sophisticated in narrative techniques, with brilliant use of stream of consciousness."[79]

HANNA MINA: *SUN ON A CLOUDY DAY*

Hanna Mina was born in 1924 in Lattakia, Syria. A self-made man who worked as a stevedore, sailor, barber, and journalist, Mina has spent time in exile and in prison due to his political views and is highly regarded as one of the premier Arab novelists. He has published more than 25 novels, including *Blue Lamps (1954)*, *Sail and Storm (1966)*, *Snow Comes through the Window (1974)*, *Picture Fragments (1974)*, and *The Swamp (1977)*.

The 1973 novel *Al-Shams fi Yawm Gha`im (Sun on a Cloudy Day)* takes place during the French Mandate period in Syria, prior to Syrian Independence in 1946, and tells the story of a young Syrian man struggling for an identity in a country riven by class distinction. The man rebels against a father grounded in the tradition of the landowning aristocracy, aligned with French politics and culture. The young man joins ranks with the poor, the simple, and the deprived; he refuses to associate with the Casino, where his family members dance the tango and socialize with the French colonizers. The young man serves as the novel's narrator, and we understand many aspects of his personality: his love of music, his friendship with a tailor who is a musician and with a nationalist who lives in a poor part of the city. The tailor understands the narrator's philosophy and his opposition to the ruling class and French domination, and he becomes the young man's mentor.

It is the tailor who teaches him the dagger dance, an intense and dangerous dance performed in public for ordinary spectators. His father, mother, and sister only dance the Tango in a fancy private casino, and they are horrified when they learn that their only son is participating in an underclass form of dancing (the dagger dance symbolizes rebellion and revolution). Another of his acts of defiance is his attraction to a black-eyed woman who happens to be a prostitute. Like the tailor, she is also an underground radical. As the young man dances, he becomes more enchanted with this mysterious black-eyed woman who comes to watch him dance and who lives, he later discovers, in the tailor's basement.

Once, during the dagger dance, the narrator is seriously wounded, and she rushes up to help him. She removes the dagger from his knee and then she disappears. Later, she visits him in his home while he is bedridden with his stab wound. The narrator's family, understandably, is outraged to find her there. They insult and slap her before kicking her out of their home. Before leaving, however, she reveals to them that the touted "respectable" fiancé of their daughter (the narrator's sister) visited her brothel and left his underpants in her room. This episode brings the narrator into greater conflict with his family and strengthens his connections with the lower social class.

Thinking that he can save his son (and their family) from this dismal insult to their social status, the father pays someone to kill the tailor. The young man confronts the cruelty and hypocrisy of his father, who doesn't care because his loyalty is with the French occupiers. Enraged, the young man calls his father an "assassin," and the novel ends with an enormous rift existing between father and son. But not only between them: That rift signifies the one existing between the elitists (and their collaborators) and the oppressed class. Mina through this main character accurately portrays the political conflicts and social contradictions that beset Syria during the French mandate. Mina's novel is considered one of his "strongest portrayals of feelings in the context of class conflict intertwined with anticolonial struggle during the French Mandate in Syria."[80]

Najah al-Attar has said that Mina's vision in this novel goes beyond class struggle and political conflicts: The dagger dancer in *Sun on a Cloudy* Day seeks to show us what lies beyond the horizon—the justice that is as inevitable as the sun rising despite the thick black clouds blocking its rays.[81] The novel presents a "portrayal of the pressures that impinge upon the individual and society as a result of internal and external forces"[82] as well as a "powerful glimpse of the passion, which allows humans to revolt" against the most unjust oppressive circumstances. Poet Kim Jensen has written that because the seed of the narrator's awakening is the seed of music, poetry, passion, and love for the underground woman, "we can read *Sun on a Cloudy Day* as an attempt to reconcile revolutionary principles with their origins in the human desire for spiritual satisfaction."[83]

HALIM BARAKAT: *SIX DAYS*

Born in 1933 in Kafrun, Syria, and raised in Beirut, Lebanon, Halim Barakat is a novelist and sociologist. He received his doctorate in Social Psychology in 1966 from the University of Michigan, Ann Arbor, and retired from Georgetown University after many years of teaching. His novels include *Six Days (1961), Days of Dust (1969), A Journey between the Arrow and the Cord (1979)*, and *The Crane (1988)*. He has also published numerous sociological studies.

His 1961 novel *Sittat Ayyam (Six Days)* depicts the struggle of a fictional city under siege. The inhabitants of the city of *Dayr al-Bahr* (which represents Palestine) are confronted with an ultimatum to surrender or be wiped from the face of the earth. They choose to defend the city, knowing very well that they will be defeated. Their desperate struggle is sustained by a strong determination to be free. Fierce battle rages for six days and ends in the burning of their city.

Prophetically titled, *Six Days* appeared six years before the Arab defeat in 1967— as mentioned earlier in this chapter, that defeat was a shattering and resounding blow for the Arab world. The Arabs lost enormous amounts of land to the Israeli victors, and thousands of people were displaced and forced to flee. *Six Days* also serves as a prelude to his later 1969 novel *Awdat al-Ta'ir ila al-Bahr (Days of Dust)*, which dramatizes the events of the Six Days War and gives us a realistic account of the war and an accurate reflection of Arab society at the time. Barakat's work, Roger Allen has explained, stands out as one of "the most effective commentaries on the 1967 debacle and its implications, and, one may say, almost *ipso facto*, it will thereby remain a reference point for Arabic fiction."[84] Both novels stress the problems and ills within Arab society.

In *Six Days*, the main characters depict the stagnation of Arab society by referring several times to a large clock that has stopped working for a long time but it is still placed in a prominent spot in the city's downtown. For these people, time has stopped: Barakat uses this as a vivid, resonant symbol of the stillness in their society. The main character Suhail describes the contradictions of Arab society through his vision of the city: "Dayr al-Bahr is a mosaic, what draws him to it? What binds him to its fear, ignorance, poverty, feuding, disorder and greed? Oh a torn city! A woman wearing pants stands next to a veiled woman wearing a thick black robe. One ignores the other. They lived in separate worlds ... the jails stand between the school and the house of God."[85]

Suhail is a national Christian intellectual who recognizes the illnesses of Arab society and wants to turn this stagnation into progress and advancement. He wants the clock to start moving again. Suhail joins the resistance to fight against the enemy knowing that the resistance has decided to fight until death and never surrender. But his efforts are complicated by the fact that he is in love with a Muslim woman, and this affair shocks the people around him. Barakat describes the love affair between Suhail and the Muslim woman, Nahida, with passionate, physical details. One of the novel's clear messages is that we cannot fight the enemy without until we crush the enemy within: "The enemy is not the only problem. Our enemy is inside as well. We are failing against the enemy out there because we are ignoring the enemy within ourselves. We have to throw off our heritage first."[86]

The city refuses to surrender, and eventually the enemies outside are successful and destroy the city. The novel describes the deceit, fear, and panic that sweeps over the population. All of Suhail's friends are killed, but he is captured. His interrogators show him, through a window, the smoke arising from the burning buildings. The novel ends with this exchange between the interrogating officer and Suhail:

> -Do you see the fire over there? Soon it will be ashes.
>
> -Ashes will fertilize the land.
>
> -But we will reap it for ourselves.
>
> -Only for a short time.[87]

Barakat has said that one of his intentions with this novel is to identify with a society in a state of national crisis, and that the hero of *Six Days* is the "society itself, symbolized by Dayr al-Bahr, the name of an imaginary town, embodied in individual characters, and the problems of these characters are intricately and genuinely connected with the plight of their threatened society."[88]

Six Days both predicts the future defeat of the Arabs and calls for immediate societal and cultural change before it is too late. And his 1969 novel *Days of Dust*, has dramatizes the events of the Six Days War "Hanging over all the writing produced after 1967 is, nevertheless, the sense of profound disappointment," Edward Said has explained, "This is true of Mahfouz's work, of Halim Barakat's fiction ... and indeed, of all those works either portraying or explaining the sudden speed of the disaster, is astonishing surprise, and the catastrophic lack of Arab resistance."[89]

MOHAMED CHOUKRI: *FOR BREAD ALONE*

Mohamed Choukri, also spelled Muhammad Shukri (1935–2003), is a Moroccan author and novelist best known for his autobiographical writings and the close friendships he established in Tangier with international writers including Paul Bowles, Jean Genet, and Tennessee Williams. Choukri's father sold him as a boy to a hashish addict; Shukri ran away and lived on the streets of Tangier, begging, eating from the garbage, finding occasional jobs, committing petty crimes, and smuggling. He did not learn to read and write until the age of twenty. His works include *For Bread Alone*, the first in an autobiographical trilogy, followed by *Time of Mistakes or Streetwise* and *Faces*. He also wrote a play and collections of short stories including, *Violence on the Beach* and *The Tent*.

His novel *Al-khubz al-Hafi (For Bread Alone)* is a major work in modern Arabic literature. The American writer Paul Bowles translated the novel into English in 1973 before it was published in Arabic in 1982. The novel was banned in Morocco for its frank depiction of sex, homosexuality, and alcohol and drug use. Thanks to Bowles' enthusiasm for the novel, and his conviction of its greatness, the Arabic version was published nearly a decade after it first appeared in English translation.

An autobiographical novel, *For Bread Alone* begins with the author's earliest childhood, as the member of a poor, dysfunctional family in rural northern Morocco, before moving to his youth and adolescence as a fugitive and outlaw around the city of Tangier. The novel portrays Moroccan society there on the eve of independence, and Choukri "combines personal narratives with references to the wider struggle for national liberation without turning his characters into mere representatives of a political ideal. These experiences inspire a lifelong hatred of injustice in the author and a determination to resist oppression. While he rages against the beatings meted out by his father, Choukri clearly identifies the underlying cause of oppression as the everyday brutality and humiliation of colonial rule in North Africa."[90]

Choukri's story is a heartbreaking one. He narrates the misery of life on Tangier's streets, living in dark and dangerous alleys, searching for food in the rubbish heaps, searching for a place to sleep at night, surrounded by drug addicts, alcoholics, and criminals. It is a life lacking in everything, especially bread and love. Described by the author as a communal autobiography, the book draws from Choukri's personal experiences as well as the lives of countless other people like him: "When I said that my autobiographical *Al-Khubz Al-Hafi* is more of a social document than a work of art I meant that I actually attempted a semi-documentary endeavor about a social group that included myself and my family."[91]

In the introduction to his English translation of *For Bread Alone*, Bowles writes of his friend: "Choukri grew up under conditions of poverty excessive even for Morocco. Eight of his brothers and sisters died of malnutrition and neglect. Another brother was killed outright by Choukri's father in an excess of anger and desperation. Mohamed and one or two others managed to survive, even under these worst possible circumstances."[92]

Both Choukri and Bowles collaborated on the translation, and Choukri describes how he went to see Bowles with the first chapter, written in Classical Arabic, and how "it took us, Paul Bowles and I, two or more days to translate one chapter into English. Meanwhile, I would finish the following chapter."[93] Bowles elaborated on their collaboration this way: "*For Bread Alone* is a manuscript, written in classical Arabic, a language I do not know. The author had to reduce it first to Moroccan Arabic for me. Then we used Spanish and French for ascertaining shades of meaning. Although exact, the translation is far from literal."[94]

Narrating explicit and painful details drawn from the first twenty years of his own life, Choukri also includes fictionalized details about his family—how his mother was forced to sell vegetables while the father was useless, abusive, and cruel. The family was driven by famine from their hometown and forced to walk to Tangier for survival. Life was not better there, as Bowles relates in the quote above. That is how Choukri came to live on the streets. He also spent time in a filthy Moroccan prison and met an inmate who influenced his life and opened his eyes to the concept of reading.

Choukri decided to commit himself to becoming literate and taking control of his life. After prison, he attended a primary school and learned how to read and write; eventually he became a schoolteacher. Choukri is an honest writer, and his ingeniously realistic fictions make his stories attractive to both readers and critics. There is a profound vitality, and a spirit of political strength that "lies in his use of realist representation of the urban experience of the figure of the street boy, who embodies the extreme poverty of 'natives' in the colonized African city."[95] Choukri writes not only the history of his life and of the suffering of the neglected, but also the history of a large, entirely marginalized social class in Morocco. His writing is a reflection, and a tribute to, the daily life of the poor, and the unfortunate, the depressed and the deprived in Tangier.

ARAB WOMEN WRITERS

NAWAL EL-SAADAWI: *WOMAN AT POINT ZERO*

Nawal El-Saadawi, who is one of the Arab world's most widely-known feminist writers, is also an activist, physician, and psychiatrist. Born in 1931 in a small village outside of Cairo, she was educated at Cairo University (M.D., 1955), Columbia University, NY (M.P.H., 1966), and then worked as a physician at Cairo University and in the Egyptian ministry of health. In 1966, she became the director-general of the health education department and in 1968 founded *Health* magazine. But the magazine was later shut down, and she was expelled in 1972 from her position in the ministry of health because of her book *Women and Sex*, which was condemned by the religious and political authorities. In 1981 she was jailed in Egypt for her political views. Her works include *Women and Sex (1972)*, *The Hidden Face of Eve (1977)*, *Memoirs from the Women's Prison (1983)*, and *God Dies by the Nile (1976)*.

Her 1975 novel *Imra`a 'Inda Nuqtat al-Sifr* (*Woman at Point Zero*) is a real story. The novel's first line announces: "This is the story of a real woman, I met her in *Qanatir* prison a few years ago."[96] In an introduction to the novel, the author confirms that her protagonist is based on a real person and that "she stood out amongst the others, vibrated within me, or sometimes lay quiet, until the day when I put her down in ink on paper and gave her life after she had died. For, at the end of 1974, Firdaws was executed, and I never saw her again."[97]

When she first encountered the heroine of her novel, El-Saadawi was a psychiatrist conducting research on the subject of neurosis and women in prison. The doctor of the prison provided the author with information about the inmates, including a young woman named Firdaws, who had killed a man and was sentenced to death. The author conducted interviews with many inmates, but meeting Firdaws and interviewing her was difficult. Firdaws was unlike any other inmates in the prison—she refused to accept visitors, rarely talked or ate, and hardly slept. She even refused to sign an appeal to the president asking that her death sentence be commuted to life in prison.

In the novel, Firdaws also declines to talk to the narrator. The narrator tries to persuade her and gives up. As she is leaving the prison, the warden gives her a last-minute message that Firdaws has agreed to meet with her. Inside the cell, the narrator sits on the cold ground and listens to Firdaws, who tells her story just before her execution. Her story is sad, distressing, and horrifying. Without any interruption from the author, Firdaws describes how she grew up in a poor family in the countryside. Her father was abusive and regularly beat her mother. When Firdaws met a boy in the field, her mother had her circumcised and forced her to stay home. After her parents' deaths, she lived with her uncle and endured his regular sexual assaults. When he marries, finally, she is sent off to a boarding school.

After Firdaws' graduation, her uncle and his wife plan to marry her off to a man who is forty years older than her and has a disgusting skin condition. But like every male in her life, he is abusive, too, and she runs away and encounters a coffee shop owner, who seems sympathetic and offers to take her home, but he abuses her, too. He keeps Firdaws locked up during the day and allows his friends to abuse her, also. When she escapes from him, she falls into other traps: She becomes a prostitute and suffers continual rape and abuse from a pimp and wanders the streets. She tries to change her life and takes a job in an office, falls in love with a coworker who uses her, and returns to a life of prostitution.

We are approaching the "point zero" of the title, but we haven't reached it, yet. This time her new pimp demands a larger percentage of her earnings, and when she decides to leave him, he beats her, and she stabs him to death. This is the story of this woman who is awaiting execution in a Cairo prison. El-Saadawi gives us the story of a beautiful young woman victimized by her society, living in the streets, hammered by men and pimps. There is nothing for her to live for, and nothing for her to lose. After a lifetime of misery, murdering her abuser is her only choice.

In her foreword to the English translation of the novel, Miriam Cooke writes that "it does not matter if this story is true or made up, or a bit of both (which it is). What matters is, that it unfolds a universal tragedy, as great as any of Sophocles, even if without the epic heroes ... readers cannot but be drawn into the catastrophe of Firdaws's life in such a way that her hope and disappointment become theirs ... you do not have to be a sex worker to understand how circumstances threw her into the pit of prostitution and how the demons drove her to murder her pimp."[98]

GHADA AL-SAMMAN: *BEIRUT NIGHTMARES*

Ghada al-Samman is a distinguished novelist born in Syria in 1942. She studied at Damascus University, the American University of Beirut, and London University and worked as a journalist. She has published more than 40 works in a variety of genres, including poetry, short stories, and novels, and today she lives in Paris. Since the early 1960s, al-Samman has been a prominent public intellectual and a strong voice in the battle for women's liberation and cultural change in Arab society (See chapter on modern Arabic poetry). Her many works include *Beirut 75*, *The Night of the First Billion*, *No Sea in Beirut*, and *Squared Moon*.

Her 1976 novel *Kawabis Bayrut* (*Beirut Nightmares*) is a powerful account of the cruelties of the Lebanese civil war. It describes the ugly dreams and nightmares of the days and nights during the war. The plot is simple: The narrator is a female journalist (and a Marxist) who is trapped during a rigorous bombing of Beirut for about two weeks in her apartment, located behind the Holiday Inn hotel, which was also hit by a bomb and set on fire. The narrator describes her nightmarish experiences, including what happened to her lover, a schoolteacher from another religion, who was shot and killed by the street militia.

The narrator is a virtual prisoner inside her flat, unable to go out for fear of being caught in the crossfires of ongoing battles or shot in the street by a hidden sniper. The narrator sometimes takes shelter with her downstairs neighbors because safety isn't guaranteed even at home; at one point her flat is struck by a rocket and her most valuable possessions, her books, go up in flames.

Early in the story, her brother goes out to find food and never returns. The narrator tells us about him—how he escaped from the war zone and was arrested for possessing an illegal firearm. One of her ensuing nightmares is about how he transforms himself in prison from a shy man into a criminal who is taking advantage of the war and people's suffering to make money. The narrator tells us about other characters as well who find opportunities in the war to make a fortune while others turn to crime in order to survive. The narrator rejects the act of violence, but she recognizes that same capacity for violence in herself when she takes a pistol and shoots at a figure from a window at night. Even though she tells us that "the figure turns out to be a dog and not a human being, her reaction is the same; she was willing to pull the trigger."[99]

Nightmares in this novel vary in intensity, shifting from surrealistic images born of the narrator's imagination to stark scenes of absolute terror. Sometimes the nightmares blend into each other, merging reality with imagination, showing readers the intensity of the narrator's psychological disturbances and her inability to see things clearly. This provides us not only with an account of social and political collapse in a time of war, but also with a reflection on the confusion setting in during times of isolation and crippling horror. Near the novel's end, the narrator is finally rescued by the army, and what does this rescue mean for her? She is deposited in front of another hotel, in a different part of the city. She reflects on the utter "helplessness of the intellectuals and writers in the face of this outbreak of violence."[100]

HANAN AL-SHAYKH: *THE STORY OF ZAHRAH*

Hanan Al-Shaykh was born in Beirut, Lebanon, to a conservative Shi`ite Muslim family in 1945, and received her primary education in Beirut. Later she attended the American College for Girls in Cairo and returned to Lebanon to work as a journalist for the Lebanese newspaper *An-Nahar.* She left Beirut again and moved to Saudi Arabia before settling in London in the 1990s. Her novels often depict female characters confronting conservative religious traditions against a background of political tension and instability created by the Lebanese civil war. Her novels include *The Story of Zahrah (1980), Women of Sand and Myrrh (1988), Beirut Blues (1992), I Sweep the Sun off Rooftops (1998)*, and *Only in London (2001)*.

Her 1980 novel *Hikayat Zahrah (The Story of Zahrah)* was banned in most Arab countries and is one of the most accomplished novels in contemporary Arabic literature. The novel tells us about the narrator Zahrah, a Shi`ite girl from southern Lebanon, during the Lebanese civil war. Zahrah grew up in a lower-middle class family in which her father is a tyrant, who frequently beats her mother. Even with this brutal treatment, he is incapable of controlling her: Zahrah's mother engages in a love affair with another man and takes Zahrah along when she goes to meet him. Zahrah watches as her mother makes love to another man.

Zahrah is dominated and seduced by one of her cousins, and she fears that if her father finds out about this, and about her loss of virginity, her life will be in danger. This causes her to have a nervous breakdown, and it is in this low point that something good finally comes: an invitation to go and see her uncle in Africa. He fled Lebanon for political reasons, and Zahrah accepts his invitation as a chance to escape her stressful circumstances. But in Africa, she is no better off: Her uncle starts to harass her sexually. To escape him, she marries a lonely Lebanese emigrant who lives in Africa, and that marriage is a disaster, too.

After her divorce, Zahrah returns to Lebanon; during the civil war, she develops a relationship with a sniper using a rooftop near the building where she lives. At first, her intention is only to stop him from killing people. But after she climbs to the roof and meets him, he seduces her (though "rape" is perhaps a more accurate word than "seduce"). With the sniper, though, for the first time she experiences sexual fulfilment and continues to see him—and becomes pregnant. Angered by this news, the sniper still comforts her and promises to marry her. Zahrah leaves the roof, happy, thinking of her future and the life of her child, and the sniper fires several times and kills her.

The Story of Zahrah presents us with Lebanese society during a period of intense crisis. Zahrah experiences more than a single mental breakdown just as her society does: al-Shaykh uses illness as a metaphor for Zahrah's world. "The overreaching subjects of this novel: mankind's violence towards his fellow creatures, the complexities of sexuality, the agony of exile, are not confined to Lebanon," Roger Allen explains. "Hanan al-Shaykh's novel thus carries a message that is both continuing and universal."[101]

AHLAM MOSTEGHANEMI: *MEMORY IN THE FLESH*

A popular Algerian writer, Ahlam Mosteghanemi was born in 1953 in Tunisia and is the first Algerian women to publish a novel in the Arabic language. Her novels have been translated into several languages (including English and French) and include a trilogy (*Memory in the Flesh, Chaos of The Senses, Bed Hopper*) as well as *Black Suits You So Well* and *The Art of Forgetting*. Mosteghanemi grew up during the Algerian struggle for independence and has used the Arabic language as a challenge and a form of resistance against French cultural domination.

Her 1993 novel *Zakirat al-Jasad* (*Memory in the Flesh*) won the Naguib Mahfouz Medal for Literature in 1998 and was praised as "the most successful Algerian novel in the Arab world and one of the most profound and original creations of contemporary Algerian culture in any language."[102] The novel is based upon her personal experiences and the national experience of Algeria, covering fifty years of Algerian history from 1945 to 1988, including the social and political struggles of the Algerian people before and after the revolution. She also talks about the corruption of the post-revolution, national elitist class. The writer dedicated her novel to both her father, a fighter in the national liberation struggle, and to the Algerian writer Malek Haddad (1927–1978), who after Algeria's independence in 1962 refused to write in French. Her novel was written in Paris between 1984–1988, and it is full of nostalgia for her homeland. Though the author focuses on modern Algerian history, her novel also includes important events and issues of modern Arab history such as the Palestinian problem and the Israeli invasion of Lebanon in 1982. In her 2006 novel *Their Hearts With Us and Their Bombs On Us*, she talks about the American invasion of Iraq in 2003.

The narrator of the novel is Khaled, who writes his memoir in the form of a novel. Khaled is in love with Ahlam and served as a fighter in the Algerian revolution along with Ahlam's father, who was Khaled's commanding officer. Living in exile in France, Khaled now works as a painter, and Algeria's history is told by Khaled. After Ahlam matures into a beautiful young woman and a successful novelist, she shows up in Paris at one of Khaled's art exhibitions. He falls in love with her, but it is a one-sided love—except for a single passionate kiss, his feelings aren't reciprocated.

It shouldn't be surprising; he is too old for her. They live at opposite ends of the spectrum. She is a much younger woman whose father lost his life fighting for the revolution; Khaled is an old warrior who lost his arm during that same struggle against the French. Nevertheless their meeting arouses in Khaled a yearning and nostalgia for his Algerian past. Ahlam does not reciprocate his strong sincere love, and instead marries a corrupt military officer who is a member of the post-revolution Algerian class elites—a corrupt class that abuses and exploits the revolution and that embodies the failures of that revolution. In this book, as in her others, Mosteghanemi finds a unique way of conveying the impact of events on individual lives by combining love stories with political and social history and fusing them together in the present.

In an interview with Nuha Baaqeel, she explains that Khaled sees Ahlam as a symbol of the Algeria he loves and that he sacrificed himself for—an Algeria that betrayed him. The betrayal lies in the fact that Ahlam marries a corrupt opportunist officer of Algeria's post-revolution period. The military came and took her away by force.[103] In the same interview, Mosteghanemi says her novel is not autobiographical, and that no single character represents her; instead, she explains, she distributes her personal experiences across all of her characters who, together, portray the Algerian people's collective history. "I have narrated the entire history of the Arabs over the past halfcentury, with their disappointments, complexity, victories, poetic power and naivety," she says of her trilogy and other novels.[104]

Poet Kim Jensen has said that the novel is not about love but "remains much more than a love story. It is an allegory about the tortured fate of Algeria and perhaps the whole Arab world in its struggle for freedom … the narrative serves as poignant sociopolitical commentary, telling of the distorted relations between man and woman in a society destroyed by war and colonialism … and that Khaled and Ahlam's unfulfilled love becomes symbolic of the abortive experience of post-revolutionary Algeria, which gives birth to corruption, alienation, and violence, a terrifying progeny."[105] Using Arabic in her literary work is of fundamental cultural importance to Mosteghanemi—nearly all Algerian writers composed in French, the language of the colonizers. But Arabic was first for Mosteghanemi and her family, and her decision to compose in Arabic serves as a "statement of independence from the Eurocentric homogenization of language and discourse, and as a feminist political statement."[106]

Of Mosteghanemi's *Memory in the Flesh*, poet Nizar Qabbani has said "this novel is a poem written with many poetic patterns and rhythms, rhythms of love, sex, ideology, and the rhythm of the Algerian revolution, which included: fighters and opportunists, heroes and killers, angels and devils, prophets and thieves. This novel does not only summarize the memory of the flesh, but it also summarizes the history of the Algerian pain, the Algerian grief, and the Algerian ignorance that should end."[107]

JOUMANA HADDAD: *I KILLED SCHEHERAZADE*

Poet, journalist, translator, and women rights activist, Joumana Haddad is the chief editor of the cultural page of the Lebanese daily *An-Nahar*. Born in 1970, she grew up in Beirut, Lebanon during the civil war period. When she was twelve, she read *Justine* by the Marquis de Sade and Vladimir Nabokov's *Lolita*—both served as inspirations for breaking down taboos and conventions in her society.

The founder and editor-in-chief of *Jasad* magazine, a controversial Arabic magazine specializing in the literature and arts of the body, Haddad aims to challenge the sexual taboos of the Arab world and to empower women. *Jasad* is the only magazine of its kind published in Arabic. Haddad's works include *Invitation to a Secret Feast (1998)*, *The Hands of the Abyss (2000)*, *I Have Not Sinned Enough (2003)*, *Lilith's Return (2004)*, and *Cage (2016)*.

Her 2011 book *Hakaza Qataltu Shahrazad: I`tirafat Imra`ah `Arabiyyah Ghadibah (I Killed Scheherazade: Confessions of an Angry Arab Woman)* is not a novel but a collection of essays, autobiography, and testimonies reflecting the dilemmas of women in Arab societies. Haddad refuses the submissive attitude of *Scheherazade* and wants Arab women to object, resist, and rebel. Haddad relies on her ability to convey personal experiences and the experiences of the women around her, to communicate a message that "attacks the sexist system, but not men themselves."[108]

Haddad told an interviewer that she wrote *I Killed Scheherazade* for two reasons: because she was fed up with the clichés and generalizations made about Arab women in the West; she wanted to write something for Arab women because they fall into the trap of victimization and do not do enough to emancipate themselves.[109] Haddad also sets about to "deconstruct and analyze what it means to be an Arab woman writer"[110] and "affirms that egalitarianism is not a demand, but an assertion that every woman must feel free to make."[111]

The book's title refers to the narrator of *The Arabian Nights* (discussed later in this chapter). Scheherazade was the narrator and victim of a vengeful king who would marry a young virgin at night and kill her in the morning, but Scheherazade was able to delay her death and gain the King's love by telling him a new story each night but not finishing the tale until the morning. Many have seen Scheherazade's character as an inspiring champion of women, but for Haddad the character is not an inspiration. "I attack the image of Scheherazade," she writes, "because she negotiated with the man, the king, and told him: 'I will tell you a story each night, and you let me stay alive.' The woman is sometimes the worst accomplice against herself."[112] In Haddad's eyes, Scheherazade is the symbol of the submissive Arab woman whose false liberation is only possible through entertaining and gaining the favor of the man who holds power over her. For Haddad, Scheherazade represents a figure inherently privileged and ultimately saved by an upper middle-class education, not a "resourceful, brave, and determined young heroine."[113]

"Correct me if I am wrong," Haddad writes in *I Killed Scheherazade*, "but it seems obvious that this method puts the man in the omnipotent position and the woman in the compromising, inferior one. It does not teach women resistance and rebellion, as is implied when the character of Scheherazade is discussed and analyzed. It rather teaches them concession and negotiation over their basic rights."[114]

Haddad seeks to end this continuation of woman as an archetypal damsel in distress whose rescue comes only through a more powerful male hero's will: *I Killed Scheherazade* is the literary product of her effort do to this.[115] In Haddad's own words her book is "a call to Arab women, and the entire Eastern and Western worlds to rethink their idea of what an Arab woman is."[116] She says her book draws on her own experiences and the entire history of women's rights issues around the world; she sheds light on Arab women alive today whose appearances and actions counteract the image of an Arab woman as veiled, subdued, and lacking choice or control in a patriarchal society.[117]

Though written as a call for Arab women to change their lives, *I Killed Scheherazade* has been seized upon by Western women and has been translated into thirteen languages. Haddad has said this is a "strange, strange thing, I'm writing about my own society and experiences. But when I travelled around the world, women in France, Germany, Italy and Latin America came to me and said they were feeling the effects of this macho, patriarchal society, too. That's the beauty of literature, isn't it? You think your problem is specific but, perhaps, it's universal."[118]

Haddad describes her efforts, in this book and others, as an ever-expanding attempt to understand and to express her thoughts on the position of women in global social structures. That attempt, she says, "soon became a small text; the small text developed into a long piece; the long piece then grew to become an exposé; the exposé combined with other texts I had produced around the same subject on various previous occasions; it all merged with some pertinent and revealing autobiographical notes I had written over the years; and the result was a book: this book."[119]

Let the final word go to Lebanese-American poet and artist Etel Adnan (b.1925), whose forward to Haddad's book describes its importance in a biblical context: "She speaks of the Arab woman, of what is familiar to her, but what she says concerns all women, throughout history, especially those of the Mediterranean region; where they are told with sacred authority that they are a sub-product of Creation, God having created Adam whereas Eve merely emerged from his rib. But Haddad brings the good news that woman comes only from herself, and that she must make herself, must create herself, just like man."[120]

THE INTERNATIONAL PRIZE FOR ARABIC FICTION (IPAF)

In 2007, a literary prize was established and funded by the Tourism & Culture Authority of Abu Dhabi in the United Arab Emirates. The International Prize for Arabic Fiction (IPAF) promotes excellence in contemporary Arabic fiction writing; an appointed committee gives the prize every year to a novel written in Arabic. Each year a newly-appointed panel of five judges (consisting of literary critics, writers, professors, other academics) read novels that have been submitted for consideration. IPAF aims to bring recognition to outstanding writers in Arabic and to bring recognition and prestige to the prize's sponsor and organizer. Each year the event receives wide media coverage from around the Arab world.

The winner's announcement takes place each spring in an Abu Dhabi ceremony—publishers and journalists are invited to attend—with the winner receiving a sixty-thousand-dollar cash prize along with the commitment to pay for the cost of translating the novel into English and increasing world audiences for the Arabic novel. Shortlisted authors each receive ten thousand dollars, and the prize encourages the translation of their novels into non-Arabic languages, too. IPAF represents an important effort to increase the publication, and visibility, of Arabic novels in the world of letters.

FOLKLORE LITERATURE: *THE ARABIAN NIGHTS*

When Western readers are asked about Arabic literature, *The Arabian Nights* is frequently the example most are familiar with, and that is due to many reasons. *Alf Layla wa Layla*—literally "Thousand and One Nights"—is not considered literature *per se* by Arabs. They treat this popular narration of Arabic folklore as part of the Arabic oral tradition that was composed and transmitted through several centuries, mostly between the tenth and fifteenth. Some scholars believe *The Arabian Nights* were born as early as the ninth century.[121] The stories and events are set in various places and times, and they are the product of several cultures, including Persian, Indian, Turkish, and Arabic.

The collection of oral tales begins with the story of the King Shahrayar, who discovers that his wife is cheating on him with men working in his palace. After executing her and declaring all women unfaithful, he decides to marry a young virgin every night and execute her the next morning. This process continues for several years. When the *wazir*, or "head minister," of the King begins to find it difficult to find a new virgin every day, he reveals his worries and concerns to his daughter Shahrazad. After learning of the situation, Shahrazad decides to offer herself as bride to the King, much to her father's anguish.

Shahrazad is a seductive storyteller; on the first night, she begins to tell the King a tale but leaves it unfinished. In order to hear the end of the story, the King keeps Shahrazad alive for another night. The next night she tells him the rest of the first tale, only to begin (but not finish) another exciting story. The King keeps her alive every night, hoping to hear the rest of each unfinished anecdote. After one thousand and one nights of tales and stories, the King finds he has fallen in love with Shahrazad and the three children she bore him during that time. Her life is spared.

The stories of *The Arabian Nights* are derived from the original tales that Shahrazad told the King. Some are intertwined with other tales, while others begin and end on their own. The available editions usually contain only a few hundred stories, which are full of fantasy and magic from beginning to end. Some of the best-known are about Aladdin, Ali Baba and the Forty Thieves, the Seven Voyages of Sinbad the Sailor, and the Fisherman and the Jinni. Folklore literature in Arabic, as explained earlier, is not an imitation of classical Arabic literature. It is an independent genre with its own experimentation and vision. *The Arabian Nights* is popular literature that is distinct from urban culture; this folk art was derived from the real daily lives of the people and based on the ancient traditions of several cultures and societies. It is popular, rich, and diverse literature that speaks to ordinary people rather than to the educated élite.

Folklore literature is not new in Arab culture, nor was it born with *The Arabian Nights;* such literature is deeply rooted in Arabic oral tradition and dates its existence to pre-Islamic times. The popular stories of various heroes and tribes have always been a part of the Arabic folk tradition, similar to the already-mentioned tale of *Antarah bin Shaddad*, the pre-Islamic knight and poet. Many of these folklore pieces were later transcribed in books, and *The Arabian Nights* is one of the best-known that grew out of this tradition. When it was translated into French by Antoine Galland, whose version appeared in twelve volumes in the early eighteenth century, its influence spread to European audiences. Galland's was followed by an English translation by Richard Burton in ten volumes in the late nineteenth century. Other translations were produced; the tales have been translated into numerous other languages. It is important noting that *The Arabian Nights* has many editions in the Arabic language, too.

Meant to be narrated rather than read, *The Arabian Nights* are transcribed in a mix of colloquial and classical Arabic. That is one reason why these tales are not considered as an "official" example of Arabic literature. In fact, teaching *The Arabian Nights* has been banned in many schools and universities across the Arab world because of the more risqué story lines. The work has even been considered immoral in some circles since it includes descriptions of sexual encounters considered unsuitable for families, children, and teenagers. For these reasons, Arab literary circles have neglected *The Arabian Nights*—it was only recently that Arabs started to read these stories again.

A GROWING CHORUS OF VOICES

Arabic novels are complex and sophisticated narratives, comprehensive and charged with the social and political upheavals of the Arab world. The novels engage the dominant themes and issues of modern Arab history and culture, in particular: the struggle for national independence, opposition to the domination of the European imperialism, the encounter with the West, the Palestinian question, the plight of the Palestinian refugees of 1948, the Egyptian revolution of 1952, the Arab national movements, and the Arab defeat in 1967.

Novelists have examined the consequences of the Lebanese civil war (1975–1990), the Iraqi invasion of Kuwait (1990), the American invasion of Iraq (2003), the Israeli-Lebanese war (2006), and other major political events affecting Iraq, Lebanon, Palestine, Egypt, Syria, Yemen, Tunis, Libya, and the Arab Gulf States. They also have written about the Arab Spring (2010–the present), its consequences, the aftermath; the massive killings and migrations after the Arab spring, the death and sufferings of the migrants. They have written about life inside the Arab prisons, the miserable treatment of citizens inside detention centers, and the inhuman treatment of political prisoners. They have written about Arab repressive regimes, lack of freedom, lack of democracy, and the sufferings of Arab citizens at the hands of Arab police states. They have written about alienation and exile, the plights, ills, despair, and fragmentations of Arab culture, the shortcomings of Arab societies, the negative effect of Arab petroleum on Arab social, political, and economic independence. Arab female novelists have shown us the plight of the Arab woman, her oppression, her lack of equal opportunities, her lack of freedom, her sexual repression, and other taboos surrounding her in Arab culture.

Since the appearance of the first Arabic novel in 1914, Arabic novelists have opened wide the aperture of the novel genre in order to take in all manner of issues and events, to reveal and examine the fabric of Arab society. Therefore, it is difficult to classify the Arabic novel in categories or divisions, or to mark novels according to certain trends or directions.

The selected novels in this chapter serve only as samples—as an introduction to the rich, complex, and original body of Arabic prose writing. Although novelists differ in their visions, themes, and styles, together they illuminate the major shared features and issues of modern Arab culture. These selected works are meant to suggest that the genre of the Arabic novel is a successful, expansive, vigorous, and significant part of Arab culture today. In addition, the writing of Arab women has introduced powerful new perceptions and insights and a vibrant new dynamism into the genre. The strong courageous voices of these men and women—past and present—are contributing to a flourishing body of work that is finding new audiences not only in the Arab world but in the broader world of letters as well.

CHAPTER TEN

Modern Arab Thought

IN 1974, MOROCCAN SCHOLAR Abdallah Laroui proclaimed that "those who for decades have been eagerly awaiting an Arab springtime are waiting for an event that is today more uncertain than ever."[1] Yet an Arab Spring did arrive and ignited the hopes and dreams of many, although in the end it remains the harbinger of a very uncertain future. Even with the unprecedented movement that started in Tunisia at the end of 2010 and spread throughout the region in varying degrees throughout 2011, the likelihood of the Arab world returning to its past glory has only decreased, as the region continues to fragment and fall further into a state of despair. The Arabs are moving away from the promise of springtime, languishing in a winter that blankets the entire Arab world today. This winter is not perpetual; springtime is not unattainable. But it has not yet succeeded.

Some two hundred years ago, the Arab world was alive with a spirit of renaissance. Today, this Arab renaissance continues, but in regression. The modern Arab world is a region rife with contradictions and turmoil. People live in a state of disintegration, division, and conflict, due largely to the continual domination of Arab governments, lack of development, and foreign control over political and economic life. Most Arab intellectuals see this repression as a serious threat to the very existence and future of the Arab world. There is much irony to be found in the current situation. In some instances, the foreign dominance of the Arab world is supported by Arab governments and maintained by Arab funds.[2]

In a widely-viewed television interview, renowned poet and cultural critic Adonis reflected that the Arabs are in a stage of failure because they have no creative presence in the world. Although Arabs have the quantity, the sheer masses, of people, they "no longer possess the capacity needed to change [their] world." The fact that Arab intellectuals continue to think in the context of such failure is, to Adonis, in fact its clearest portent.[3] Similarly, novelist and cultural essayist Ilias Khouri has observed that while the beginning of the twentieth century featured an Arab nationalist struggle for independence from colonialism, the twenty-first century has begun with the Arabs considerably worse off, suffering foreign occupation, fragmentation and civil war.[4] These are not marginal or exceptional views; the majority of leading Arab intellectuals and scholars today have noted some variation on the belief that the Arab world is presently in a state of fragmentation.

ORIGIN AND DEVELOPMENT OF MODERN ARAB THOUGHT

Awakening and *renaissance* are both terms Arab intellectuals use to describe the process of Arab modernization, which most historians believe began a few years after the 1798 occupation of Egypt by Napoleon. This Arab renaissance can be described not as a spontaneous spurt of cultural awareness, but rather as a reaction to the challenges posed by the West on all levels of existence—social, political, economic and psychological. The Arab renaissance is often called the "Shock of Modernity," due to the influence of the sudden external intrusion onto the centuries-old Arab and Muslim culture. By introducing new ideas and Western modernity, the Awakening led to some transformation and change in Arab society, but also the loss of social cohesion and the growing alienation and self-consciousness of the Arab and Muslim peoples.[5]

The Arab renaissance had begun prior to Napoleon's invasion. Its origins go back to the fifteenth century. Arabs had already begun seeking a resolution to the increasing problem of their society's stagnation following the decline of Arab and Islamic civilization in the thirteenth century. However, it is generally agreed that the Arab renaissance began in earnest around 1800. The Arabs first encounter with the modern West presented a challenge that stimulated various types of responses, often simultaneously accepting and rejecting the new ideas and institutions of Europe. This confused reaction originated from the Arabs' goal of preserving the religion and culture of Islam. While they were impressed by Europe's strength and wanted to adopt their ideas, they did not want to be unfaithful to their own beliefs.

Arab intellectuals of the renaissance consisted mostly of writers in major Arab capitals, especially Cairo and Beirut. They spread new political and social ideas throughout the Arab and Muslim world, ideas whose historical importance to the region cannot be overstated. Since the renaissance, Arabs have continued to study, review and reflect upon emerging and inherited ideologies, never ceasing to voice their views on European influence and modernization or their opinions on what ideas should be accepted or rejected from the West. Modern thinkers have followed their predecessors from the renaissance by trying to identify the social needs of the Arab world and implement change through the promotion of societal awareness.

Intellectuals continue to influence modern Arab thought. For instance, Islamic thinker Sayyid Qutb (d. 1966), who wrote several influential books in the 1930s and 1940s, greatly influenced Ayman al-Zawahiri, second-in-command of the al-Qaʿida organization who became the leader of al-Qaʿida after the death of Osama bin Laden in 2011. Arab intellectuals' connections to each other and their predecessors make it possible to trace the continuity of their thought.[6] In examining modern Arab thought, it is thus necessary to first identify the most important contributions of the Arab renaissance and use this as a foundation to explore Arab thought during the most recent fifty years.

While the Ottoman Empire was collapsing in the late eighteenth century, Europe was on the rise. The Ottomans simply could not compete, lacking European technology and suffering from weak social and political structures. The juggernaut of Europe's ascendancy is, in fact, reminiscent of the original Arab Muslim conquest and their emergence as a major power in the seventh century.[7] With the eventual demise of the Ottomans, Europe came to dominate the world in the nineteenth century; by the twentieth, Europe had directly colonized almost all of North Africa and the Middle East.

Though modernity resulted in autonomy for European and American societies, the modernization of the developing world was inexorably accompanied by domination and loss of independence. These different experiences of modernity represented a fundamental and original dichotomy between the colonizers and the colonized. Karen Armstrong noted that developing countries, instead of pursuing innovation, could only imitate the advances of the West without much hope of catching up to their success. And in comparison with the leadership it enjoyed over the medieval world, the contemporary Islamic world was quickly reduced by the European powers to a dependent and submissive bloc, with a few exceptions. Western colonists generally disrespected Arabs and were often appalled by what they viewed as the "backwardness" of the Muslims.[8] Abdallah Laroui attributes this apparent backwardness to the cultural retardation forced upon Arab and Muslim society by Western colonization.[9] The Europeans simply assumed their culture to be inherently superior to that of the Muslims and Arabs of the East, ignoring the fact that Europe had seemed just as backward only a few centuries earlier.[10]

The process of European colonization of the Middle East was lengthy. France played an enormous role, beginning with Napoleon Bonaparte's invasion of Egypt in 1798, and following with the occupation of Algeria in 1830, Tunis in 1881 and Morocco in 1912. Britain seized its share of colonial plunder as well, including Aden in 1889, Egypt in 1882, Sudan in 1889, and finally the Persian Gulf. Italy, for its part, occupied Libya in 1912. Before this feeding frenzy was even completed, Arab and Muslim society no longer existed as a "stable and self-sufficient system of inherited culture." It was a struggle to barely "survive in a world dominated by the others."[11]

POLITICAL DEVELOPMENTS OF THE TWENTIETH CENTURY

In 1916, Britain and France signed a secret document known as the Sykes-Picot Agreement in which they divided the Arab provinces of the declining Ottoman Empire between themselves. The next year, in what eventually became known as the Balfour Declaration, British Foreign Secretary Arthur James Balfour formally pledged Britain's support for the creation of a Jewish state in Palestine. Some previously-occupied Middle Eastern countries began to gain independence, often after bloody revolutions; however, Western powers continued to control their economy, oil and vital resources, as with Egypt's Suez Canal.[12]

The period following World War II marked great historical change for the Arab world. Perhaps most significantly, Palestine was lost to the Arabs when the Jewish state of Israel was officially proclaimed on May 15, 1948. This event resulted in hundreds of thousands of exiled Palestinians taking refuge in neighboring Arab states, including the Jordanian-administered West Bank and the Egyptian-administered Gaza Strip, with enormous economic, social and environmental ramifications. Moreover, in June 1967, the Arabs suffered a humiliating defeat by Israel, which seized land from Syria, Egypt and Jordan in an extremely short period of time. Six years later, another Arab-Israeli war resulted in another military defeat. In 1978, the Camp David Accords that ended the state of war between Egypt and Israel was signed; peace in the Middle East, however, was far from realized. The Islamic Revolution in Iran resulted in the overthrow of the US-backed Shah in 1979; the following year, Iran and Iraq began a long and costly war, lasting for eight years and sapping the wealth and young lives of both countries. In 1982, Israel invaded Lebanon, and in 1990, Iraq, led by Saddam Hussein, invaded Kuwait.

In the last two decades, unexpected events have further shaped the Middle East, often negatively. In 1991, the United States formed a broad coalition of nations, including many Arab nations, to expel the Iraqi army from Kuwait; while America's intervention restored Kuwait's sovereignty, it also provided America a secure and seemingly permanent military presence in the region, with bases in Saudi Arabia, and Bahrain. The war to liberate Kuwait left the region in strife, causing deepening political rifts among Arabs and Arab states. Civil war, meanwhile, erupted in Algeria in 1991, when the Islamic Salvation Front achieved victory in the first round of the national elections and the secular Algerian army cancelled the second round in response. The second Palestinian Intifada broke out in 2000, causing renewed bloodshed and putting an end to the already faltering implementation of the Oslo Accords. In 2003, the United States invaded Iraq, seizing Baghdad and setting up an occupational authority. Meanwhile, every year in Iraq has seen a further intensification of violence, as American troops withdrew and Iran's involvement intensified. Syria since 2011 has been mired in revolution and civil war, with long-lasting ramifications certain throughout the region.

Even before these most recent developments, the Arab world of the twentieth century was divided as a result of colonization into states, emirates, kingdoms and republics, whose borders were arbitrarily created by their former colonial rulers in accordance with the imperial "divide and rule" strategy. Populations are frequently divided along religious sectarian lines even within the same state. Lebanon, for example, was created with a population divided among three major religious communities—Sunnis, Shi`ites and Maronite Christians— and multiple smaller ones. In Iraq, the population is still intractably divided among Sunnis, Shi`ites and Kurds. The Arab world will almost certainly face still more political transformation over the next few years as new borders could be drawn in Syria, Iraq, Yemen, and Libya.

Arabs had a conflicted reaction to European domination and modernity. First of all, Arab intellectuals gained importance within Arab society, a manifestation of the increasing contact with Europe that brought about a process of education and enlightenment. These Arab intellectuals were both participants in and witnesses to the Arab renaissance, and responded in various ways to the rapid societal changes. Some rejected the West entirely, while others advocated total adoption of Western ideas. Many took a middle path, rejecting only some Western ideas and practices while accepting others. A broad spectrum of intellectual movements was created during this time, promoting the conflicting ideologies of diverse social and political groups. Each group pushed its own ideas regarding the reformation and modernization of the existing social and political order.[13]

The number of nineteenth century Arab writers seems insignificant in comparison with the vast number of their twentieth century heirs, showing that their ideas could be built upon and gain broad acceptance. Religious, political and social writers, poets and novelists, literary essayists and critics—all participated in creating a new collective consciousness for the Arab people. Some writers wanted to modernize the Ottoman Empire, while others wished it to expire. Some admired the European record of achievement and modernization, while others abhorred it. Still others advocated a return to the roots of Islam.

PIONEERS OF THE ARAB RENAISSANCE

The intellectuals examined in this chapter are considered among the most important pioneers of modern Arab thought due to their contributions to its creation and development. Many of these pioneers produced schools of thought that bear their names. Their ideas are embodied in political and religious movements and repeatedly appear in books, newspapers and periodicals. Some organized political parties, religious associations and national societies. Many pioneers lived during periods of time when rapidly transitioning events transformed their viewpoints on certain issues. It is therefore difficult to classify their ideas into neat categories or impose an artificial unity on the diversity of their intellectual output.[14]

The philosophies, theories, and ideologies of the leading Arab intellectuals since the renaissance, particularly in the last hundred years, have shaped contemporary Arab thought significantly. The threads of their ongoing impact can be seen throughout the Arab world today in the social, political and religious trends and movements that continue to evolve and shape the region. As we see today especially in Syria and Iraq, fundamental differences concerning how communities should be led and governed, what rules should guide society and what role religion should play are all influenced by intellectual thought. The following sections discuss how key concepts developed, both from within the Arab world and from outside influences.

ADMIRATION OF FRENCH CULTURE AND SOCIETY

Egyptian Rifa`a Rafi ` al-Tahtawi (d. 1873) was fascinated by early nineteenth century French culture and society, and based much of his writing around its analysis and criticism. Tahtawi was impressed by the Europeans' enlightenment and, though not especially influential, he was among the earliest intellectuals of the Arab renaissance. Tahtawi graduated as an imam from al-Azhar, the world's oldest institution of higher learning, in 1817. After his graduation, Egyptian ruler Muhammad `Ali (d. 1849), who together with his family instituted a dramatic program of modernization in Egypt, sent Tahtawi to Paris with the first Egyptian educational mission. Tahtawi spent five years in France, where he was greatly influenced by French Enlightenment philosophy. He admired many French ideals, particularly the belief that people should be allowed to participate in their government and that laws should evolve according to changing circumstances. Upon his return to Egypt, he wrote a book in which he detailed French customs and characteristics for the Arab reader. He admired the French for their strong work ethic and devotion to their children's education, but criticized their lack of generosity and what he viewed as the subjugation of French men to their women.

After his return to Egypt, Tahtawi founded a school of language and translation in Cairo, held the position of inspector of public schools, and became the editor of an official government newspaper. He preached that all citizens should receive a political education and that women should be allowed to work. He also glorified ancient Egypt and praised the Pharaohs. Tahtawi argued for Arab society to adopt the modern sciences of Europe, as they had evolved from the Islamic sciences.

He also believed that religious scholars should assist the ruler in running the government, a concept of political authority well within the tradition of Islamic thought. Ultimately, Tahtawi failed to offer a well-defined philosophy in his simultaneous welcome of, and opposition to, the West. Despite his shortcomings, however, Tahtawi's writings—like those of intellectual activists Khayr al-Din al-Tunisi (d. 1899) and Butrus al-Bustani (d. 1883)—have endured, paving the way for more original and revolutionary intellectual production.[15]

RETURN TO THE TRUTH OF ISLAM

A pioneer of what came to be known as the Islamic reformation, Jamal al-Din al-Afghani (d. 1897) greatly influenced modern Arabic thought by advocating a return to the original practices of early Islam. Afghani opposed any imitation of the West, considering it a dangerous threat to Muslim society. He promoted a scientific culture to break with the past by formulating new laws and principles. Back in the fourteenth century, Sunni scholars had declared that *ijtihad*, the process of independent analysis or interpretation of Islamic law, could no longer be used to make new decisions, calling instead on the legal system to restrict itself to decisions of past authorities. Afghani called upon Muslims to re-open the gates of *ijtihad* and devise an independent interpretation of Islamic law for application to contemporary situations.

Afghani was a Shi`ite who studied Islamic tradition and philosophy in the cities of Najaf and Karbala, but lived in Egypt for a few years and taught at the Sunni al-Azhar institution. He also studied mathematics and modern European science in India. Some of Afghani's students at al-Azhar would eventually play important roles in Egyptian political life; intellectual pioneer Muhammad `Abdu (see below) was in fact one of his disciples. Afghani opposed European intervention in Arab affairs and advocated resisting the West through national Arab unity. In response to British pressure, Afghani was deported from Egypt to India, where he wrote and lectured to encourage his disciples to remain active within Egypt.

Afghani left India in 1884 for Paris, where he was eventually joined by Muhammad `Abdu. Together they founded a secret Muslim society with branches in several Islamic countries, including Tunisia, and published the Arabic political periodical *al-`Urwa al-Wuthqa* "the firmest bond." This hugely significant publication included ideas on Islamic reform and analyses of Western colonial policy. Muslim countries under British control censored the periodical, whose revolutionary articles would influence Islamic thinkers for generations to come. In 1896, one of Afghani's disciples assassinated Shah Nasir al-Din of Iran.

Afghani feared that any further weakening of the Islamic *umma* would mean the end of its existence. He believed the strength of the *umma* in the past was based in the political institution of the caliphate and the religious scholars who preserved the correctness of the Muslim doctrine, two elements now lacking in Muslim society. In order to 'regenerate' Islam, Afghani believed the religious scholars themselves must return to the truth of Islam. He preached that the gates of *ijtihad* were not closed, and that Muslims have a duty and right to apply the principles of the Qur'an to their time-specific problems.[16]

REFORMATION OF ISLAMIC LAW

Another influential Islamic reformer was Egyptian Muhammad `Abdu (d. 1905) a former student of Afghani. After studying at al-Azhar, `Abdu found a teaching position at *Dar al-`Ulum*, where he edited the official journal *al-Waqa'i` al-Misriyya*. The British sentenced him to exile for three years, during which time he joined his teacher Afghani in Paris. In 1888, he was permitted to return to Egypt, where he became a judge and eventually *Mufti*, or head of the entire system of religious law in Egypt. The formal legal decisions that he issued on questions of public concern, known in Arabic as *fatwas*, helped reinterpret religious law in accordance with contemporary needs. `Abdu admired Europe and was well versed in western philosophy and science; he also appreciated modern European political, legal and educational institutions. Believing education rather than revolution to be society's salvation, he pushed for reform of the Arab educational system. Despite their closeness, `Abdu criticized Afghani for being too revolutionary and rejected Afghani's radical philosophy, advocating instead a reformation of the Islamic law system.

`Abdu concentrated on the problems of decaying Muslim society. He preached for society to regain its virtue by abiding by simple Islamic doctrine for guidance on human conduct and life. `Abdu stressed that individual *ijtihad* is essential and that the *Salaf*, or "Elders", represented the ideal *umma* in the early days of Islam. And although he admired the achievements of modern Europe, `Abdu opposed the transplantation of European laws and institutions to Egypt, proclaiming: "[L]aws planted in another soil do not work in the same way. They may even make things worse."[17]

WESTERN SCIENCE AND TECHNOLOGY

One of `Abdu's disciples, Muhammad Rashid Rida (d. 1935) was a Lebanese scholar with a solid knowledge of Islamic classics and history. He was a very spiritual man, having joined a spiritual religious order as a mystic in his youth. He rejected such practice later in life after being drawn to Wahhabism and the teachings of Ibn Taymiyya, who condemned mysticism (and the Sufis who practiced it) for weakening society and endangering the Islamic religion. In 1897, Rida left Syria for Cairo and began to publish *al-Manar*, a publication that, like *al-`Urwa al-Wuthqa*, became a mouthpiece for the Islamic reform movement; Rida continued to publish *al-Manar*, or 'The Lighthouse', until his death in 1935. Though he was active in Islamic affairs and attended Islamic conferences in Mecca and Jerusalem, as a Lebanese national, he stayed on the sidelines of Egyptian politics, though he did write several criticisms of the governance of Muhammad `Ali.[18]

Rida viewed the Islamic *umma* as the heart of world civilization and believed Muslims were 'backward' only because they lost the truth of their religion, a situation encouraged by poor political leadership. In his view, the great Islamic civilization of the past could be restored with the Islamic *umma* as both a religion and a nation. Rida insisted the Muslim community's authority came directly from God, based on a saying of the Prophet: "My community will not agree upon an error." The truth, therefore, existed only in the teaching of the Prophet and the *Salaf*. Though a Sunni Muslim whose interpretation of Islam was based on strict Hanbalism, he believed in unity between Sunnis and Shi`ites. In later life, he supported the revival of Wahhabism in central Arabia and its leader, `Abd al-`Aziz bin Sa`ud. Rida stressed the orthodoxy of the Wahhabi doctrines and their faithfulness to original Muslim practice, and he implored Muslims to follow the model of the early Muslim community as described by the *Hadith*.[19]

Rida was convinced that, were it not for the Catholic Church and the inner decay of Islam, Europe would have become Muslim. He argued the Muslim community could not become strong unless it acquired the science and technology of the West, and that Europe had progressed only thanks to insights and inventions gleaned from Muslim Spain and the Holy Land. Rida advocated Arab unity with the Turks, believing the two groups shared common interests. He also defended the vanishing Ottoman religious system, as he was concerned about rising secularism in the Arab world.[20]

FREEDOM IN SOCIETY

Another disciple of Muhammad `Abdu was liberal Egyptian intellectual Qasim Amin (d. 1908). Amin studied law in Egypt and France and collaborated with Afghani and `Abdu on publishing the periodical *al-`Urwa al-Wuthqa*. He believed the decay of Islamic society was caused by ignorance, advocating the importance of women's active participation in building Islamic society and maintaining that Islamic law could provide freedom and equality between women and men. As such, he supported the education of women and their right to work. He called for an end to the veiling and seclusion of women in the conviction that such practices increase sexual desire rather than preserve virtue. And he pointed out that the Qur'an only mentions the seclusion of women with respect to the wives of the Prophet, not the Islamic community at large.

Ahmad Lutfi al-Sayyid (d. 1963) was another liberal intellectual in Egypt, whose father and grandfather both served as `umda, or village head. Sayyid was educated in Qur'anic studies and law and was the founding member of the Egyptian People's Party, spending several years in government service. He wrote articles for the al-Jarida newspaper that aimed to shape the moral consciousness of the Egyptian nation. These articles urged Muslims to adopt the western concept of freedom while criticizing British rule for its absolutism.

Indeed, Sayyid's concept of freedom was central to his thinking and perhaps his greatest contribution to modern Arab thought. He considered the old Qur'anic schools to be unsuited to the modern world, and the abstract idea of the umma did not overly concern him compared with the immediate situation in Egypt. During Sayyid's time, Egyptian nationalism did not center on Arabs as a whole and limited itself to the Arabs of Egypt. Therefore, Sayyid rarely mentioned Arabs as an entity, not viewing Egyptians as part of the Arab nation, and he neither condemned nor endorsed the idea of an Islamic state.[21]

NATIONALISM, SECULARISM, AND SOCIAL JUSTICE

Revolutionary Syrian thinker `Abd al-Rahman al-Kawakibi (d. 1902) was one of the most important Arab visionary intellectuals of the nineteenth century. Kawakibi was not only a progressive radical and Arab nationalist, but the first modern Arab intellectual to theorize about democratic, secular and socialist Arabism as an alternative to the Ottoman caliphate. He wanted to destroy the dominant political and social system, which he described as despotic, sectarian and traditional, and in its place he hoped to create a new order based on Arab nationalism, secularism, scientific thinking and tolerance. One of the first thinkers to ever provide a systematic view of Arabism based on culture and geography, Kawakibi argued that national ties are superior to all others and favored a unified Arab polity over the Ottoman caliphate. He also believed the Turks detested Arabs. In his book Umm al-Qura (the Mother of Villages), he declared the need for the caliphate and the umma to return to Arab control. Finally, he called for the separation of religion and state, warning against the negative consequences of mixing the two.

Kawakibi was gripped by what he saw as society's need to be liberated from despotism. In his book Taba'i` al-Istibdad (Nature of Despotism), he strongly attacked tyranny and autocratic rule centered solely on the ruler's own wishes. Despotism, Kawakibi believed, distorts both religion and education. He promoted socialism as an alternative system that could provide social justice and equality in society.[22]

CRITICIZING THE ISLAMIC CALIPHATE

An important and early modernist concerned with the role and nature of the caliphate in Muslim society was Egyptian Sheikh `Ali `Abd al-Raziq (d. 1966), an Islamic judge and graduate of al-Azhar. `Abd al-Raziq ultimately concluded that neither the Qur'an nor the *Hadith* provide for the existence of the caliphate, similar to Christian reformers who point out that there is no basis for the Catholic church and papacy in Scripture. He adopted a secular stance toward politics, supporting the separation of church and state in the Islamic world. His 1925 book *al-Islam wa Usul al-Hukm*, or "Islam and the Principles of Governance," generated great controversy. He insisted that neither the Qur'an nor the Prophet Muhammad promulgated specific rules or forms for Islamic governance, concluding that the caliphate was unnecessary and a 'disaster' for Muslims. The religious authorities rejected his views and `Abd al-Raziq was put on trial, expelled from his position and condemned, and his book confiscated.[23]

`Abd al-Raziq found no evidence of an organized Islamic government existing during the Prophet's lifetime. The authority of the caliphate, he concluded, was harmful to Islam and Muslims and a source of evil and corruption. He noted that the absence of the caliphate would made no difference to the worship or welfare of the people in Muslim countries. The abolishing of the Turkish caliphate in 1924 did not seem to make any difference to the population, at least religiously.[24]

Sheikh `Abd al-Raziq believed the Prophet Muhammad's essential function was to preach the truth to the people and serve as spiritual guide, not to exercise political authority. However, though the Prophet's authority ended at his death, `Abd al-Raziq considered the spiritual community that Muhammad created a fertile space for Muslims to found an Arab nation and Islamic religious community. Most ominous for the contemporary political authorities, `Abd al-Raziq stressed that Islam does not forbid Muslims from participating in revolution and overthrowing government, particularly one that had not ceased to humiliate them ever since adopting it.

Many were bitterly critical of `Abd al-Raziq's ideas. Fellow intellectual pioneer Muhammad Rashid Rida was among those who disliked him, calling `Abd al-Raziq the 'enemy of Islam' and accusing him of trying to weaken Islam from within.[25]

QUESTIONING PRE-ISLAMIC POETRY AND THE QUR'AN

Another leading modernist, as well as one of the greatest Arab intellectuals of the last century, was Egyptian Taha Hussein (d. 1973). Born in a small town in Upper Egypt to a poor family, and blind from an early age, Hussein went at age thirteen to study at al-Azhar, where he came into contact with the ideas of Muhammad `Abdu. His knowledge of the Arabic language and classical literature was superb. He studied in France from 1915 to 1919 and married a French woman. After his return, he became the center of literary and academic life in Egypt, holding several important positions in government, including Minister of Education from 1950 to 1952.

Hussein's 1926 book *Fi al-Shi`r al-Jahili*, or *On Pre-Islamic Poetry*, raised serious questions about the authenticity of pre-Islamic poetry and the source of Arabic oral traditions by applying a method of modern critical scholarship that, if applied to the Qur'an, would cast doubt on its authenticity as well. He concluded that a considerable body of pre-Islamic poetry had actually been composed *after* the appearance of Islam.[26] Immediately after the book's publication, Hussein was labeled a blasphemous infidel, his book was banned, and he was dismissed from his office as Dean of Letters.[27]

In 1938, he published another book entitled *Mustaqbal al-Thaqafa fi Misr (The Future of Culture in Egypt)*. A controversial but enormously important work of social thought, the book concludes that Egypt is culturally affiliated with Western, rather than Eastern, civilization. Hussein argued Egypt had always been part of Europe, and that Egyptians must "become European in every way, accepting both its good and its bad."[28] The Turks' domination of Egypt and other eastern Mediterranean countries, according to Hussein, caused them to fall behind European civilization. But Europe too had its Dark Ages, and even the Islamic Dark Age was less felt in Egypt than elsewhere. Finally, Hussein noted that the European Renaissance began in the fifteenth century, whereas Egypt's awakening had begun only recently. Egypt, then, was "catching up fast."[29]

RATIONALISM AND SCIENTIFIC THINKING

Egyptian thinker Salama Musa (d. 1958), a Coptic Christian, was another modern reformer and socialist who supported the liberal movement. Musa wrote on wide-ranging themes that included socialism, Egyptian nationalism, literature, political democracy, evolutionary theory and secularism. He founded the first socialist party in the Arab world and later joined the Egyptian *Wafd* party, with whose leaders he worked to achieve independence. He also published the weekly magazine *Majallat al-Misri* and edited the monthly journal *al-Majalla al-Jadida*. In all his writings, Musa expressed his admiration of Western culture and science. He was outspoken in at-tacking Arab traditions and calling for complete Arab modernization and adoption of Western civilization, including equality for Arab women. Musa believed in the power of the written word and the ability of literature to create conditions in which freedom can succeed and prevail. His books are still in print today.[30]

Another liberal cultural and literary critic is Zaki Najib Mahmoud (d. 1993). Born in a village in Lower Egypt, he studied at the Teacher Training College in Cairo, and in 1947 received a PhD in philosophy from the University of London. Mahmoud believed authentic Arab culture could be reconciled with modernity. In addition to numerous books written in both Arabic and English, he authored more than one thousand articles on Arab culture, literary criticism, and Islamic and western phi-losophy. Mahmoud encouraged Arabs to choose their own traditions by rejecting those no longer applicable and adopting concepts from the West in order to achieve renewal and rebirth. He instructed Arabs to be open-minded and apply rationality to their construction of modern society. He also warned against ignorance, illusion and myth, and called on Arabs to liberate themselves from the shackles of imperialism and Arab despotism.[31] Mahmoud was the founder and editor of *al-Fikr al-Mu`asir*, or the *Journal of Contemporary Thought*, wrote weekly for the Egyptian newspaper *al-Ahram*, and was recognized for his scholarly contributions.[32]

RESTORATION OF THE ISLAMIC STATE

Inspired by the influential periodical *al-Manar*, Islamic reformer and political ac-tivist Hasan al-Banna (d. 1949) founded the Muslim Brotherhood party in Egypt in 1928. When Banna was thirteen, he participated in demonstrations against British rule during the Egyptian revolution of 1919. Studying later at *Dar al-`Ulum*, an affiliate of al-Azhar, he met prominent Islamic scholars but was disappointed in their failure to voice opposition to the rise of secularism and collapse of tradi-tional ethics. When working as a teacher in the city of *Isma`iliyya*, he preached in mosques and coffeehouses and held nightly classes for his students and their parents in their homes.[33] Banna was an active writer who advocated a return to Islam's origins in order to re-capture Islam's early glory. This could be achieved, Banna argued, only through the restoration of an Islamic state and the application of Islamic law with the Qur'an as the source of world order.[34, 35]

When he was twenty-two, Banna founded the religious organization of the Muslim Brotherhood with his brother and five others. In his most famous book, *Letter to a Muslim Student*, he explained the principles of this movement, which began as a small Muslim youth organization to promote moral and social reform. In 1933, Banna moved the organization's headquarters to Cairo and established branches in other Muslim countries, including Jordan. Soon, his political commitment became a strong religious ideology. In 1948, he proclaimed that the Egyptian government was responsible for the Arabs' weakness in the war against the newly formed State of Israel. Banna was shot and killed in Cairo in 1949 in an action possibly orchestrated by the Egyptian government.[36]

ARAB UNITY IN THE FERTILE CRESCENT

Originating from the nationalist and socialist parties, another emerging trend in modern Arab thought focused on political ideology rather than religion. At their earliest stage, these political thinkers advocated Arab unity based on geographical, cultural and national bonds, but limited themselves to Syria, Lebanon and the surrounding geographic area known as the Levant. Among the leaders of this movement was Lebanese intellectual activist Antoun Sa`ada (d. 1949) who founded *al-Hizb al-Suri al-Qawmi* (Syrian National Party) in 1932. Sa`ada's desire for Arab unity was exclusive to greater Syrian, not Arab, nationalism. Born in Lebanon, Sa`ada worked as a German teacher at the American University of Beirut. He was able to attract several thousand members to his movement, mostly from Syria and Lebanon. Sa`ada conceived of Syrian political unity as including the population of the entire Fertile Crescent. Despite, or perhaps because of, his inclusion of Lebanese territory in this theoretical political entity, the Lebanese government harassed and imprisoned him; as a result, Sa`ada left Lebanon for Brazil in 1938, but returned in 1947 to campaign for a united Syrian nation. He was arrested and executed by Lebanese authorities in 1949.[37]

Sa`ada authored *Nushu' al-Umam* (Evolution of Nations) in 1938, defining his conception of nationalism and his belief that Syria and Lebanon form a distinct nation. He called on people to participate in national loyalty by abandoning all communal loyalties. Sa`ada was convinced that all societal contradictions could be resolved through secularism and the elimination of feudalism; his ideas continued to be very influential for several decades following his death.[38]

ARAB THOUGHT AFTER THE SECOND WORLD WAR

A more expansive Arab nationalism emerged in the aftermath of the Second World War that reached beyond Sa`ada's limited initiative of unifying the Arabs of Syria and Lebanon. This new nationalism, which stressed the ties among all Arabs and their common need for a political community, was immensely powerful and helped to generate strong and lasting bonds between Arabs. The whole world was transformed by the Second World War, and the Middle East was no exception; in the aftermath of this conflict, new independent Arab states were formed, Arab armies were defeated, Palestine was lost, and the new Jewish state of Israel was established. The expulsion of much of the native Palestinian population to neighboring Arab states dramatically affected the course of Arab nationalist thought, leading to a debate on the cause of the Arab failures. The post-war period also produced many Arab intellectuals who focused on the theme of Arab nationalism. Additionally, the Egyptian revolution in 1952 would generate and inspire powerful nationalist sentiment throughout the Arab world.

This Egyptian revolution inspired the Arab masses, giving them hope for a brighter future in the region. The subsequent nationalization of the Suez Canal, together with Egypt's political victory against a tri-partite military attack from France, Britain and Israel in 1956, inflamed the Arab world's passion for national and political thought. During the three decades following World War II, secular, nationalist and socialist ideologies grew in influence while religious voices simultaneously began actively appealing to the Arab peoples. Muslim intellectual giant Sayyid Qutb reactivated the Muslim Brotherhood after the death of its founder Hasan al-Banna.[39]

The Algerian Revolution, which lasted from 1954 to 1962 and succeeded in expelling France from one of its last remaining colonial footholds in the Arab world, helped to give Arabs a sense of pride and inspired further Arab nationalist sentiment. Optimistic feelings of national unity increased among the Arab population, and new ideas emerged in the vein of liberal and progressive movements. Modern political and social parties formed. Communist intellectuals appealed to nationalist ideology in order to stress the need for social justice. Communists opposed colonialism and their ideology was full of nationalist imagery. Liberal thinkers concerned themselves with transcending Arab stagnation through modernization. Postwar nationalism dominated the political landscape of the Arab world.

As they had done throughout modern history, Arab intellectuals began to define the nationalist movement in the wake of these political developments, trying to diagnose the problems and to offer solutions. Constantine Zurayk (d. 2000) was one of the most significant of these Arab nationalist thinkers. In 1939 he published *al-Wa`y al-Qawmi*, or *National Consciousness*, considered by many to be the true birth of Arab national awareness. Zurayk's ideas on nationalism were based neither on Arabs' past glory nor the rejection of other nationalities; rather, he focused on the future of the Arab peoples and the bonds that unite all Arab countries on the basis of geography, history, culture, common natural resources and strategic interests. He concluded that the Arab nation, if united, could achieve liberation, progression and advancement.[40]

Zurayk believed the Arabs' unique characteristics gave them an important position in the world. He viewed Israel's goals of expansion as dangerous, but argued that Israel could be contained if Arabs learned to use their strength for self-defense, which would require a comprehensive societal transformation. As the only solution, Zurayk proposed the creation of a single, unified Arab state with the capacity to initiate serious projects of economic and social development. Finally, he emphasized the need for Arabs to accept secularism and rational, scientific thought for the sake of effecting fundamental change in Arab society and culture.[41]

POLITICAL PARTIES: SOCIAL AND POLITICAL IDEOLOGIES

In 1940, Michel `Aflaq (d. 1989) and Salah al-Din al-Bitar (d. 1980) founded the Ba`th Party in Syria, which became operational by the latter part of the decade. An important and influential nationalist ideology emerged with its creation. The Ba`th Party has played a critical role in the contemporary history of the Arab world, particularly in Syria and Iraq. Its founders `Aflaq and Bitar met as students in Paris; `Aflaq was a Greek Orthodox Christian studying philosophy and history at the Sorbonne from 1929 to 1936. He and fellow Syrian nationalist Bitar, a Sunni Muslim from Damascus, formed the Arab Students Union at the Sorbonne. Later, back in Damascus, they established *Hizb al-Ba`th al-`Arabi al-Ishtiraki* (Arab Socialist Resurrection Party) which seized power and ruled Syria from 1963 until the present day.

The Ba`th Party promoted the formation of a united Arab nation based on nationalist and socialist political, economic and cultural principles, and theorized that the creation of one progressive and harmonious Arab nation could achieve social justice through the redistribution of wealth and the nationalization of industry and economic development. Upon returning from France, `Aflaq taught at a prestigious high school in Damascus before resigning in 1944 to concentrate on political activities. Despite his rather uncharismatic speaking skills, he was quite popular. He held the position of Minister of Education in 1949, and subsequently became Secretary General of the party. In 1966, following internal conflicts with other Ba`th politicians, `Aflaq traveled to Lebanon, Brazil and ultimately Iraq, where he died in 1989.[42]

Through his writings, `Aflaq thoroughly explored ideas of Arab socialism, nationalism and unity. He envisioned an Arab nation consisting of the vast geographical area of the entire Arab world. Stressing Islam as the national culture of the Arabs, he believed it would be dangerous for Arabs to separate religion from nationality. He felt the essence of Islam was in its revolutionary quality.[43]

The Arab Socialist Party, led by Syrian nationalist Akram al-Hawrani (d. 1996), united with the Ba`th Party in 1953. Hawrani was an intellectual who believed strongly in social revolution. He called for radical wealth redistribution and for government control of public resources, as well as the creation of an Arab Union and free trade zone. He also firmly believed that Arab unity could not be realized without first achieving social justice and independence. Socialism for Hawrani was an essential part of Arab nationalism.[44] As both parties felt threatened by communism and shared the common goal of Arab nationalism, the two parties after their merger engineered a political union with Egypt in 1958, creating the United Arab Republic, which lasted until 1961. For a period of time, Hawrani served as Vice President of the new United Arab Republic, under the presidency of Egyptian Jamal `Abd al-Nasir. Syria eventually broke the union between the two countries in 1961. Two years later, the Ba`th Party seized power in Syria. Although the Ba'th party still in Syria, the actual power is in the hand of the intelligence agencies, the military and inner circles of the President.

The Ba`th Party was active in Iraq throughout the early 1950's, and in 1958 Abd al-Karim Qasim (d. 1963), who was the leader of the Free Officers Movement, overthrew Iraq's Hashemite monarchy. Iraq's turbulent politics were influenced by internal Ba'athist divisions, religious and regional differences and ongoing interactions with Syria's Ba'ath party. Ahmed Hassan al-Bakr (d. 1982) led successful Ba'thist coups in 1963 and 1968. Iraq's economy and social system improved significantly under his leadership. Saddam Hussein (d. 2006), a protégé of al-Baker, overthrew him in 1979, and ruled until 2003. Following the American invasion, the Ba'ath party's hold on the government was dissolved and a transitional government was established. The 2005 elections reaffirmed a Ba'ath party ban (with pressure from the United States) and in 2006 the Iraqi National Assembly approved a permanent post-Saddam government. Members of the Ba'th party, including the military officers, were dismissed and persecuted throughout the transitional period. Their exclusion from previous roles in the military and political spheres led many to join radical Islamic movements like ISIS.

THE RISE AND FALL OF ARAB POPULAR NATIONALISM

Without a doubt, the most significant Arab nationalist in modern history was Egyptian President Jamal `Abd al-Nasir. Born in 1918, Nasir ruled Egypt from 1952 until his death in 1970. He was a charismatic leader and a visionary ideologist who set the tone for Arab popular nationalism. This movement owed its existence to multiple factors. One of these was the emerging Third World bloc made up of undeveloped countries committed to neither the Western nor Eastern blocs, and another was strong Marxist ideology emanating from the Soviet Union and leftist parties in Western Europe. Arab popular nationalism was also fueled by the assumption that the Arab states would unite after achieving independence.[45]

Nasir embraced the ideals of nationalism and the call for social justice within the Arab world. He exhorted Arabs to unite in a secular society and expressed solidarity with the peasants. During this period, even al-Azhar began to promote Arab nationalism. Egypt was no longer simply a part of the Arab world; it had become its leader. Although the immediate impetus for the Egyptian revolution of 1952 stemmed from a desire to overthrow the ruling monarchy of King Farouk, the revolution's goals eventually expanded to include a push for Arab nationalism. This became particularly true after 1956, when the Suez Canal was nationalized and Britain, France and Israel joined forces, to attack Egypt. The swell of support for Egypt from the entire Arab world during this time, combined with Egypt's political victory added a nationalist dimension to Egypt's struggles, further strengthening the region-wide Arab nationalist movement.[46] Nasir became the most important Arab nationalist leader of modern times and a living embodiment of the movement.[47]

Nasir believed in social democracy as a prerequisite for political democracy. Following a strong pan-Arab policy, he applied socialist theory in Egypt to improve the social conditions of the Egyptian villages. He diverted Egyptian and foreign capital from land investment to industrial investment and, in 1961, nationalized Egypt's industries in order to bring the entire economic life of the country under state control. His program included public ownership of public services, such as banks and foreign trade, and a provision for health care and education to be provided to all citizens.

Though he successfully instituted various measures aimed at social reform, Nasir was unable even at his peak to resist all of Egypt's complex political forces. Marxists criticized Nasir's socialism as lacking a scientific approach, while the Muslim Brotherhood accused him of using the language of Islam to promote a secular policy. Nevertheless, Nasir's political victories during the crises of 1956, the successful construction of the Aswan High Dam, and his support of the Palestinian cause made him the embodiment of the hope for millions of Arabs. Dreams that a united Arab nation would emerge to take its rightful place in the world, rejuvenated by genuine social revolution, seemed less unlikely. Nasir became a hero throughout the Arab world, a symbol of Arab unity and revolution.[48]

The Six Days War in June 1967, however, was the greatest humiliation of modern Arab history, with the military forces of the Arab states bordering Israel suffering complete defeat in fewer than six days. The sudden military defeat shattered the nationalists' hopes, and other ideologies competed to fill the vacuum, including socialism, communism, and Islamic movements. During the months preceding that June, Egypt under Nasir's leadership took a number of dramatic steps, including expelling the United Nations Emergency Force from the Sinai Peninsula and building up military forces near the Israeli border. Israel responded by launching a pre-emptive attack on the Egyptian and Syrian air forces on June 5, 1967. After only a few days, Israel wrested the Gaza Strip and the Sinai peninsula from Egypt, East Jerusalem and the area west of the Jordan river known as the West Bank from Jordan, and the fertile, water-rich Golan Heights region from Syria. The Arab peoples have yet to recover from the lasting implications and devastating effects of this loss. The governments of Egypt, Syria and Jordan lost all their credibility. Many in the Arab world are still trying to understand what happened.

Nasir, in all his glory, had promised the Arabs a great victory, proclaiming the Egyptian military to be the strongest and most effective in the Middle East. Instead, he led the Arabs into an embarrassing defeat that stunned and deeply penetrated the spiritual and moral psyche of the Arab population. Intellectuals began to concentrate on this shocking defeat in an attempt to understand the perceived deficiencies of the Arab world.

Following the Six Days War, Zurayk published another book, entitled *Ma`na al-Nakba Mujaddadan*, or *Meaning of the Disaster, Revisited*, meant as a deliberate reference to his 1950 book 'The Meaning of the Disaster,' in which he analyzed the original Arab-Israeli problem. This follow-up work discussed the astonishing defeat of 1967 and examined the roots of the failure. Zurayk emphasized the need for the Arab world to transform into a practical, rational and scientific community, concluding the Arab disaster was a result of the scientific underdevelopment of the Arabs. While he conceded the modernity of the Israeli state in the sense of science and rationality, he argued that such attributes alone are not enough. It is also necessary, Zurayk wrote, for a society to include a strong spirit of activism—such as the spiritual strength displayed by the native populations of Algeria and Vietnam—in order to defeat an enemy in the face of scientific superiority. He emphasized that the reason for modern Arab fragmentation and defeat was their lack of spiritual might and cohesiveness.[49]

The 1967 defeat was not the only factor contributing to the dissolution of unity in the Arab world. The actions of Anwar al-Sadat of Egypt and Saddam Hussein of Iraq greatly harmed prospects for unity, as well. In 1977, Sadat shocked Egypt and the rest of the Arab world by his sudden and unprecedented visit to Israel, followed shortly by his hasty signing of the two peace agreements known as the Camp David Accords with Israel in 1978. With only American support, Sadat entered the Camp David Accords independently from and in exclusion of all other Arab countries, creating a unique relationship between Israel and Egypt. His initiative was startling, to say the least, as it was completely out of the historical context of the Arab-Israeli conflict, apparently acted upon without considering the lasting implications for the entire Arab world. Sadat's actions, which threw Arabs into unresolved conflict, confirmed that the ideal of Arab cooperation and partnership was no more than a false dream.

Like Sadat's unilateral peace agreement with Israel, Saddam Hussein's invasion of Kuwait in 1990 created an irresolvable crisis for the entire Arab world. Even prior to invading Kuwait, Saddam had been fighting a Muslim-Muslim war against Iran since 1980 that vastly weakened Iraq, consuming the country's wealth and strength, liquidating its natural resources, and causing the death of one million Iraqi citizens. Many Arabs blame Hussein for subsequently providing the pretext for the presence of American and allied forces in the region, which divided the Arab world. Some Arab states joined the allied forces to fight Iraqis, while other Arab states supported Iraq. Thus the Gulf War of 1991 vanquished any remaining hope for Arab national unity and seemed to leave Islam as the only remaining, and appealing viable ideology, for making change.

RELIGIOUS THOUGHT: MODERN POLITICAL ISLAM

After 1948, meanwhile, the Muslim Brotherhood became a major political power in Egypt and was gaining strength in Syria and other Arab countries, as well. Even after the assassination of its founder Hasan al-Banna, the Brotherhood continued its struggle against the British and Egyptian governments. Following the Egyptian revolution of 1952, the Brothers' hopes of legitimately participating in government ended with their persecution by Nasir's regime. They became instead a clandestine movement ostensibly working for social justice. Sayyid Qutb's book al-`Adala al-Ijtima`iyya fi al-Islam (Social Justice in Islam) provided a powerful definition of the social justice sought by the Brotherhood in the name of Islam.

Qutb, one of the most important Islamic thinkers of the modern era, is considered the founder of Islamic fundamentalism in the Sunni world. He believed Muslims should model their lives on the Prophet Muhammad, isolate themselves from mainstream society, and be always ready to embark upon *Jihad*. A major contributor to the body of thought known as 'radical Islam,' Qutb authored a significant amount of Qur'anic commentary and theoretical writing that stressed the strong connection between religion and politics. For his part, Qutb was influenced by the renowned Pakistani scholar Sayyid Abul A`la al-Mawdudi (d. 1979), who founded the political movement Jama`at-i Islami in Pakistan, led the contemporary Islamic renaissance and was among the most outstanding Islamic thinkers of his time.

Qutb was born in 1906 and raised in an Egyptian village, attending a Qur'anic primary school. In Cairo he received a Western education and, starting in 1948, spent three years in the United States on a scholarship to study the American educational system. He received a master's degree in Colorado. During his stay in the United States, Qutb was highly critical of the racism he witnessed, as well as the mingling of men and women in the schools and workplace. He viewed American society as superficial and focused primarily on material goods. Before he went to the United States he was known as a reformer; ultimately, however, his American experience coupled with his subsequent imprisonment in Egypt drove him to radicalism. He joined the Muslim Brotherhood upon returning from the U.S., and called for an Islamic political system and ideology that rejected all other forms of government.

Many Muslims consider Sayyid Qutb a martyr, hung by the Egyptian government in 1966 for his political beliefs. He was accused of conspiring to assassinate President Nasir in 1954 and was originally sentenced to fifteen years of hard labor, released ten years later only to be rearrested and finally executed. Qutb rejected corrupt Muslim rulers throughout his life and writings and deplored them as enemies of Islam. His fellow members of the Muslim Brotherhood assassinated Egyptian President Anwar al-Sadat in 1981, believing him an oppressive traitor and *Jahil*, or one ignorant of religious truth.

While imprisoned, Qutb honed his philosophy and presented his views on radical Islam in two important works. The first is entitled *Fi Zilal al-Qur'an*, or *In the Shade of the Qur'an*, and consists of thirty volumes of commentary and interpretation of the Qur'an. In his second work *Ma`alim fi al-Tariq*, or *Milestones*, he advocates a modern Islamic theocracy. These two works cemented Qutb's status as initiator of modern political Islam. He has had a powerful and lasting impact on modern Arab thought, especially through his influence over radical groups and individuals such as Ayman al-Zawahiri and Osama bin Laden.

CRITICISM OF ISLAMIC THOUGHT

After 1967, some Arab intellectuals completely rejected Islamic religious thought and severely criticized its proponents. The Syrian philosopher Sadiq Jalal al-`Azm (d. 2016) called the dominant religious thought 'false in itself' and incompatible with authentic scientific thought. He believed the turn to religion represented a dangerous obstacle to the genuine movement of Arab social and political liberation.[50]

Al-`Azm is considered one of the most prominent intellectuals in the contemporary Arab world. After studying at the American University of Beirut and

Yale University, he taught at Princeton and other universities in Syria and the United States. In 1969 he published *Naqd al-Fikr al-Dini*, or 'Critique of Religious Thought,' in which he voiced his rejection of Islamic religious extremism and fundamentalism, leading an academic battle on behalf of progressivism, historicism and modernity. Because of this publication he was jailed and prosecuted, though unsuccessfully. Conservative Muslim clerics bitterly denounced him for defending Salman Rushdie, author of *The Satanic Verses*.[51] `Azm's writing criticized many religious-oriented thinkers for using Islam to legitimize Arab governments without disclosing their political and economic connections to those governments. This legitimization, `Azm argues, enables governments to control religious thought by dominating the religious intellectuals; the intellectuals, in turn, are always prepared to issue a *fatwa* in order to please the government. Ultimately, this *quid pro quo* relationship between the government and religious leaders creates alienation among the Arab population and lies at the root of Arab failures.[52]

Islamic thought has persisted despite such severe criticism, of course, remaining a dominating force in Arab culture. Some writers have combined religious and nationalist sentiment in an attempt to reconcile the two. Egyptian thinker Muhammad `Imara (b. 1931) advocates reconciliation of the religious and nationalist movements, arguing that by joining forces they could more effectively challenge the Western cultural invasion. This invasion, `Imara claims, throws the already complex cultural differences between Muslim society and the West into further confusion. He urges Arabs and Muslims to preserve Arab-Islamic identity, and contends that the end of Arab dependency on the West hinges on the incorporation of Islamic law into Egyptian jurisprudence, as secularism is not an indigenous feature of Arabic-Islamic civilization.

In Morocco, meanwhile, a school of thought inspired by Muhammad `Abdu's reform movement developed during the nineteenth century. Among the founders of this new movement was Moroccan intellectual and political leader `Allal al-Fasi (d. 1974), who believed the separation of religion and government to be a product of Europe and Christendom. Like `Imara, Fasi argued that secularism is a non-native and unnatural system imposed on the Islamic world. Algerian intellectual Malik Bennabi (d. 1975) went a step further by criticizing Islamic thought and society as having acquired the decadence of the modern Muslim people. He believed that religious ideas are the primary movers of history and constructors of reality. Bennabi called for the awakening of the Islamic community from its deep sleep, exhorting Muslims that "religious ideology is the only way to reform civilization." Likewise, Syrian thinker Salah al-Din al-Munajjid explained the Arabs' defeat in 1967 as a cause-effect relationship, occurring because Muslims abandoned their faith in God and God abandoned them in return.[53]

Like Sadiq Jalal al-`Azm, however, prominent intellectuals do exist who criticize Islamic thought and advocate liberation from the dominant religious dogmas. Algerian intellectual Mohammed Arkoun (d. 2010) promoted liberation through "historicity" and application of the "multidisciplinary methodologies" of the social sciences. Arkoun sought to deconstruct the dominant religious ideology by freeing the "first text" (the Qur'an) from the "second text" (the dominant interpretation of the Qur'an). He explained that the second text has overshadowed the first text, creating an obstacle to free thought.[54]

Arkoun believed religion had been turned into an ideological weapon by the ruling classes, and in light of political anthropology, Islamic thought should be secularized. He supported `Ali `Abd al-Raziq's 1925 attempt at secularization and called for its continuation. Some intellectuals consider Arkoun to be one of very few scholars in the Arab world who possessed a genuine intellectual project that reaches beyond academia and goes to the heart of the issues of modernity, enlightenment and the Arab renaissance.[55]

CONSTRUCTING THE PRESENT THROUGH LIBERATING THE PAST

Current Arab cultural identity is inextricably tied up with cultural memories of the past, and this reality has provoked various strong reactions within Arab scholarly circles. Moroccan philosopher Mohammed `Abid al-Jabiri (d. 2010), for example, rejected any fundamentalist ideas that reconstruct the present based on an idealized image of the Arab past. He considered the prevailing Arab discourse to be one of memory rather than reason and examined the cultural hegemony practiced by religious or political movements seeking political control. Jabiri argued for a liberation of Arab thought from the "referential framework of the past." Even though Islam constitutes an essential element of Arab nationalism, the relationship between religion and the state should be studied separately in each Arab country.[56]

Among the intellectuals concerned with redefining the past, present and future of Arab culture is Moroccan scholar Abdallah Laroui, some of whose trenchant observations introduced this chapter. Laroui observes that Arabs must understand the past in all its attributes if they wish to transcend it; this will require a radical criticism and reevaluation of their culture, language and tradition. To Laroui, criticism of the past is a prerequisite for constructing the present. The Arab intelligentsia has failed to develop a realistic and comprehensive theory of history, simply continuing to revive old Arab traditions, instead. Both the religious and westernization movements, in Laroui's view, serve as sources of alienation.[57]

Modern Arab thought, of course, has not been confined to commentary on religion, culture and philosophy within the Islamic world. One cultural critic and economist, Egyptian Samir Amin (b. 1931), has played an important role in the development of contemporary economic theory. Writing in Arabic, French and English, Amin strongly opposes globalization in its current unchecked form. Amin offers a new economic perspective on the process of development by focusing his analysis on the process of how developing countries can become independent. According to his redefinition of the theory of dependency, the Third World, or countries of the "periphery," produce raw materials, while western societies, or countries of the "center," produce industrial goods. This dichotomy between center and periphery is one of domination and exploitation, a relationship that leads multinational corporations to ally with the ruling classes of the Third World. This trend, Amin argues, only further widens the gap between developing countries and the Western world, ending with uneven international development. He concludes that the instability and irregular development of the Third World also diminishes the prospect of a unified Arab nation and culture.[58]

THE VISION OF MODERN ARAB INTELLECTUALS

Arab intellectuals have long grappled with the deficiencies of Arab society at all levels—cultural, political, social, and economic. These thinkers have developed a comprehensive understanding and description of the Arab situation, and they strive to contribute to solutions to the region's problems.

The corpus of modern Arab thought adequately articulates the needs of Arab society, such as democracy, freedom, national unity and secularism, and it accurately identifies many problems, such as those caused by oppressive governments. Yet concrete solutions remain absent. Many Arab intellectuals have been harassed, jailed, exiled, and tortured before they could see any real change in Arab society. Arab governments also persecute their families. Some intellectuals were able to escape from the region, but the majority could not leave or did not want to leave. Those who continue to live inside their own countries often fear for their own lives, and the lives of their family members. Secret police forces and other brutal government agencies clamp down on intellectuals, scholars, writers, and journalists, who advocate for transparency and change, leaving Arab citizens in states of anxiety, fear and dismay.

Although Arab intellectuals have expressed a comprehensive understanding of the Arab situation, they were unable to create a roadmap for actual cultural and political revolutionary change in Arab society. Their ideas and thoughts have remained theoretical. Therefore, the Arab intellectuals themselves were surprised by the sudden massive revolutions of the Arab Spring in 2010-2011. Ordinary people, students, the marginalized, the hungry and unemployed, and the uneducated carried out these revolutions, not the Arab intellectuals.

ARAB SYMPATHY FOR ISLAMIC POSITIONS

The Arab population has witnessed Arab society in a state of stagnation, with no viable solutions, watching the intellectuals unable to transcend mere diagnostic ideation of societal change and remedial action.

People were tired of countless academic lectures, conferences, television programs, books and articles focusing on the problems of Arab society, and impotent rhetoric that cannot deliver actual change. Misery and suffocation define the proverbial Arab street, and the masses have come to regard intellectual thought with apathy. After so much repetition of impractical talk, they have lost faith in Arab nationalism and other socialist or liberal ideas.

The Arab population also has largely learned to ignore the slogans, especially those with a nationalist agenda, that are broadcast daily by Arab government-run media. Rather than inspiring unity and hope, these meaningless platitudes tend to incite feelings of ill will, as they emphatically stress freedom, democracy, justice, and other ideals that do not exist in Arab reality. In fact, the reality for most Arabs is quite the opposite, featuring oppression, disunity, censorship, and domination. Elections are shams. The population became sick of government propaganda and deliberate policies of misleading ideology.

From this position of hopelessness, renewed Islamic religious ideologies have emerged and seemed as credible catalysts for change. This is one reason, even before the Arab Spring, that the religious *Hamas* party won a sweeping victory in the 2006 Palestinian elections against the secular *Fatah* party. In Algeria, the Islamic Salvation Front won the 1991 elections but was defeated by the military, which set up a High Council of State ruled by military leaders and members of the former government.

Were legitimate free elections held in every Arab country today, Islamic political parties would probably win sweeping victories in the majority of them. Following the Arab Spring in Egypt, the Muslim Brotherhood decisively won the 2012 election. The emergence of ISIS in Syria and Iraq imply that Islamist movements continue to play a crucial role in contemporary politics. Islamic thought continually grows stronger as other ideologies offer no real solution for societal change.

Islam has inspired societal action beyond mere rhetoric. The goal of creating a true Muslim society offers 'hope for the world,' as Sayyid Qutb once proclaimed. In 1981, fifteen years after Qutb's execution, his Muslim brethren still believed so passionately in the principles he espoused that they assassinated Egyptian President Anwar al-Sadat. The following year, in Syria, the Muslim Brothers mobilized to overthrow the secular Ba`thist regime of Hafez al-Asad. The Iranian Revolution of 1979 is perhaps the greatest example of mass political action inspired by the vision of an Islamic society.

In general, the Muslim world objects to the use of the term 'fundamentalism,' as the meaning remains unclear to Arabs who do not see it through a Western lens.[59] Nonetheless, what has become known as the Islamic fundamentalist movement has been gaining strength in the Arab world since 1967, reacting to both the outside world and the continuation of poor government regimes within. Islamic fundamentalists consider the Qur'an to be the source of all guidance, containing the necessary rules to provide justice, dignity and a system of morality. They also believe that Islamic thought provides the necessary philosophy, faith and vision for a massive transformation, and a complete concrete plan for change. The current direction of modern Islamic thought advocates revolution similar to the Iranian revolution in 1979. However, ISIS has gone much farther, brutally fighting to establish an Islamist caliphate over the entire Arab world, a caliphate fundamentally different in nature from the real first Islamic orthodox caliphate. These are described in the chapter on the Islamic community throughout the ages.

Countless intellectuals who devoted their lives to enlightened thought and true progression in the Arab world did not live long enough to see the first day of the Arab Spring in 2010. Others have seen their ideas materialized in actions carried out by a new generation of change makers who impassioned Arab masses throughout the region. The students and followers of these visionaries, advocates and true agents of change even if their ultimate goals were thwarted, have continued to work to improve the pressing issues of Arab society and culture. The Arab Spring proved that these forces remain persuasive, active and vital. Details of the Arab Spring will be discussed in a following chapter.

CHAPTER ELEVEN

The Arab Spring

THE LONG WINTER OF the Arab people's oppression did not end in 2010 and 2011. The suddenness of a wave of uprisings and protests in the Middle East and North Africa, which came to be known as the Arab Spring, took the region's writers and thinkers by complete surprise. They were at a loss to explain what happened even though, as previous chapters suggest, they dreamed of overturning the region's authoritarian regimes for a long time. Many of these intellectuals did not live long enough to see their dreams become a reality. Others did, however—they watched as their ideas animated and inspired the pro-democracy actions of the Arab masses.

Ordinary people, students and marginalized youths, the hungry and unemployed, however, and not the intellectuals themselves formed the activist and leadership core of the Arab Spring. The glaring absence of Arab intellectuals at the center of the movement, which would have guided and focused attention on larger, more fundamental issues at play, became problematic. Ordinary citizens exploded into a rage against Arab society's accumulated injustices and picked up the torch—a torch emblazoned with the accumulated thought and insight of past generations. Despite the fervor and energy unleashed by their actions, the long-term results of the Arab Spring remain unclear today; ongoing analysis and observation are needed to fully determine what kind of impact it will produce on the region.

Starting with protests in Tunisia in late 2010, the Arab Spring spread to Egypt, Libya, Syria, Yemen, and other Arab countries throughout 2011. Massive demonstrations swept the streets of their capitals and challenged the tyrannical regimes with calls for their removal in the name of freedom, justice, and democracy. Entrenched and corrupt, these regimes had grown stagnant after long decades of oppressive rule. Risking brutality and violence at the hands of security forces, the demonstrators bravely denounced these regimes and expressed their political and economic grievances.

Other Arab populations joined in, unifying with them in loud, passionate rejections of the repressive autocrats who had been governing the Arab states ever since independence. Public demonstrations erupted in almost every Arab state; some were larger and more violent than others. In some cases, regime leaders quickly made or promised reforms, and public unrest calmed; in others, public unrest grew into full-scale revolutions as entrenched dictators were forced from power. Civil war ensued as some governments struggled to remain in power and suppressed public criticism and opposition.

What was the immediate result of the Arab Spring? As of this book's publication, the outcomes are varied. Winter has returned to some of these states, which have reverted to autocratic systems again with little change in personal or political freedoms, with little promise of building democratic post-revolutionary structures. Other states have fallen into utter chaos with no recognized legitimate leader and many groups vying for control. Post-Arab Spring outcomes have led to disappointment for many: "It often happens that the revolutionaries who sacrificed themselves are then dismayed to see their hopes dashed while a new order that is as bad as, if not worse than, the one they ousted becomes a reality."[1] The region is still coming to terms with what occurred and what lies ahead. One thing is sure, however: The effects of this tumultuous period on the younger generation will give insight on what may happen in the future.

BEFORE THE SPRING: HISTORICAL BACKGROUND

Some argue that the Arab Spring ended a period of stability that the region enjoyed for decades and replaced it with widespread instability, chaos, warfare, and more conflict and uncertainty than ever existed before. Others regard this so-called stability as nothing more than stagnation, oppression, and a lack of progress. They contend that the superficial stability and economic growth of the region's elite class were only made possible by the brute power of autocratic governments finally defied and challenged in 2010 and 2011. Unrest across the region may have started with events in Tunisia, but the true roots of this period of political and social mobilization stretch much further back in history.

To understand the significance of the Arab Spring, it is necessary to briefly consider aspects of sociopolitical history of the Arab world, in particular: the development of modern Arab states, the influence of the Ottoman Empire that collapsed with the end of World War I, the following decades of European colonization, and the modern dictatorships born of these imperial relationships.

During the sixteenth century, the Ottoman Empire expanded, gaining political control of an area stretching from North Africa into the Arabian Peninsula and through all Arab lands from the Mediterranean Sea to the Persian Gulf. For the next three centuries, Arab lands would remain divided into various Ottoman provinces. With the defeat of the Empire and its eventual collapse after World War I, a new world order emerged. The Arab lands that had previously existed under the

Ottoman umbrella were divided up by the victors of the Great War. A period of colonization and division emerged as France, England, and Italy arbitrarily drew lines in the sand to plunder and exploit this land for its resources. The Arabs were given no say in the matter and had no viable path to sovereignty and self-rule. Instead, they segued, almost seamlessly, from Ottoman rule to European colonization. At the end of the Second World War, when the Arab states finally gained political independence, another segue took place: This time the states and their populations fell under the rule of oppressive Arab dictators who occupied the power vacuum.

It was at this time, during the 1940s and 1950s that the region saw growing political movements calling for independence from foreign control. Political and military leaders emerged in the new Arab States and received credibility by mobilizing the public, and promising economic reform. Populist movements of the 1950s fueled hopes of Arab unity, freedom, democracy, broad economic opportunities, and stronger national and regional identity even though, as scholars of the period note, "none of those democratization initiatives ... led to lasting transitions and ended in the ruthless consolidation of authoritarian rule across the region."[2]

Despite efforts to achieve emancipation from foreign rule, the goal of establishing true self-determination as new-formed independent states proved to be elusive. Most of this period's leaders were tyrants who opened their countries to military and economic control by foreign powers and as a result, the economies of these Arab states grew and enriched the military and political elites. The marginalization of Arab populations continued as these governments enjoyed the support of Western powers that valued stability in the region over the development of democracy. Ultimately, France, Britain, the United States, and other Western countries ignored human rights violations, destructive domestic policies, and tyrannical dictators for the sake of prioritizing stability, which better suited their interests.

In turn, Arab populations came to see themselves as betrayed once again. Rather than gaining self-determination, the Arab people found themselves ruled by dictators they saw as either in-league with Western interests or harmful to their own states. These autocratic leaders suppressed political opposition and freedom of expression, which produced an era of sociopolitical and cultural stagnation. Unable to express themselves, unable to determine their own futures, the populations of these countries sank into utter helplessness.

By the eighties, however, circumstances were gathering that posed real challenges to the region's dictators. The long-term effects of economic stagnation, demographic shifts toward a younger population, migration from regional areas to large cities, and increased accessibility to print, broadcast, and (later) social media all grew into powerful threats to their leadership. Dissent spread as networks demanding political change, especially regime change, became more active. Nevertheless, authoritarian leadership across the region "had perfected the art of pervasive social and political surveillance and control," thwarting any serious challenges throughout the decade.[3] Populist anti-regime movements were crushed by well-developed security forces in Syria, Jordan, Egypt, Tunisia, Morocco, Iraq, and Algeria. Totalitarian control, repression, and restrictions on political expression remained the norm. Leaders also played internal and external cards to reinforce their legitimacy. Many allowed Islamist political groups to operate within their borders and then treated their threats as a justification for heightened security. Other external pressures, especially the Islamist revolution in Iran, economic and political pressures from the West, and the ongoing Israeli-Palestinian conflict, also helped these leaders to justify their use of severe state controls to maintain order and security.

In the nineties and early years of the new millennium, some countries began to allow limited freedoms to civil society organizations "which could not openly mount political challenges but helped carve out spaces for independent political action," explains Mark Lynch in *The Arab Uprising*. "But soon after these governments, again, cracked down on these organizations. All of that laid the groundwork for the seismic transformations that began to take hold in the 2000s."[4] "Seismic" is an appropriate term to describe what was taking place—internal forces were building that would eventually topple these regimes. In addition, this period was marked by ongoing economic challenges and failed promises for reform. Criticism of the excesses of the elites (often connected to government leaders) mounted as dissatisfaction spread to all levels of society. As domestic economic problems worsened, "the middle class disappeared, the poor scrambled for survival, and youth found all doors closed to them."[5] It is no surprise that government credibility in the region plummeted as living conditions and job opportunities deteriorated and as citizens witnessed a widening of the economic chasm separating them and the elite classes.

During this period the rapid growth and influence of pan-Arab news sources (such as *Al-Jazeera*) and social media platforms helped anti-government groups across the region to learn what was taking place outside their immediate communities and to connect and communicate in ways that eluded governmental control. Such technology, which was not available to earlier movements and calls for reform, "created a virtual space for deliberation and anti-regime organization."[6] It was now possible, despite the best efforts of various regimes to obstruct it, for decades of mounting resentments to finally be shared; thanks to technology, a renewed sense of purpose coalesced among the peoples of the region and united their voices. Technology not only assisted them, of course. Innovations led to significant governmental efforts to monitor, control, and censor[7] access to electronic media outlets with mixed results—by comparison, protesters were able to utilize satellite and social media outlets with great success.

The Arab Spring's development and progress in the region is described in the following sections, which describe country-specific factors and other details related to the places affected most: Tunisia, Egypt, Libya, Syria, Yemen, Jordan, and the Gulf.

TUNISIA

From their independence in 1956 until the Arab Spring in 2010, Tunisians knew only two leaders. Habib Bourguiba, the founder and head of the country's Neo-Destour party, which led the drive for independence from French rule, assumed the presidency in 1957. In 1987 Bourguiba was succeeded by his prime minister, Zine Al Abidine Ben Ali (b. 1936). Ben Ali, according to Michele Penner Angrist in the *Middle East Journal*, "attempted to legitimize his autocratic rule largely through rational stewardship of the Tunisian economy that would lead to general prosperity, but he did not succeed."[8] By the 2000s, increasing income inequality, restricted political freedoms, and resentment toward his ruthlessness and corruption led to increasing challenges to his control. What emerged was a dynamic of contentious politics, which according to Sidney Tarrow, posed considerable dangers for his regime.

> Contentious politics [emerge] in response to changes in political opportunities and constraints ... Building on these opportunities, and using known repertoires of action, people with limited resources can act contentiously—if only sporadically. When their actions are based on dense social networks and connective structures and draw on consensual and action-oriented cultural frames, they can sustain these actions in conflict with powerful opponents. In such cases, we are in the presence of a social movement; when contention spreads across a society, as it sometimes does, we see a 'cycle of contention'; when such a cycle is organized around opposed or multiple sovereignties, the outcome is a revolution.[9]

That last sentence is especially true of what happened in Tunisia. A well-established base of political opposition (both above- and below-ground), an increasingly urbanized youth population under the age of 25 and savvy at social media, and a bloated, unsustainable regime all contributed to a perfect storm and a "cycle of contention" that produced the first revolution of the Arab Spring.

It was on December 17, 2010; the precise beginning of the Arab Spring is traced to that winter day when a young Tunisian, Mohamed Bouazizi (b. 1984), immolated himself in front of a government building. Bouazizi was a 26-year-old seller of roadside fruit and vegetables in the rural town of Sidi Bouzid.[10] Before Bouazizi's death, local authorities had harassed him, because the produce cart he used did not have a government permit. His harassment and death fueled widespread protests in Tunisia against the unfair treatment of Bouazizi and against the broader societal problems of unemployment, a stagnant economy, a lack of political freedoms, and the general corruption associated with the 28-year regime of President Ben Ali.[11]

After Bouazizi's death, citizens demonstrated for several weeks across Tunisia; some of these demonstrations were more confrontational than others. Ben Ali made minor concessions to calm his population; he even announced that he would not seek reelection in 2014 and that he would invest ten million dollars in an employment program. But it didn't matter; the masses across every social and economic line sustained their protests, and Ben Ali's regime was unable to effectively counter and repress them. Faced with greater violence and destruction, Ben Ali left the country on January 14, 2001, and was granted safe haven in Saudi Arabia. It was a stunning moment for Tunisia and the region. Public protests, in less than a single month, had removed one of the most entrenched, autocratic leaders in the Arab world and his corrupt den of crony capitalism. This inspired new sentiments of hope and opportunity across the region in many other long-silenced Arab populations.[12] In a matter of weeks, similar public movements began brewing in other Arab nations with autocratic leaders who had held office for decades, including Hosni Mubarak's Egypt (in power since 1981), Muammar Gaddafi's Libya (in power since 1969), and Ali Abdullah Saleh's Yemen (in power since 1978).

There were several reasons why the Tunisian revolution was so successful so quickly. The country's civil society institutions, including a robust labor party organization (RTTD), professional groups, and journalists, all enjoyed some degree of autonomy. In addition, a history of constitutionalism, developed in response to French colonial rule, created a legacy of political activism and a sense of national identity. The Tunisian military also did not belong to Ben Ali's security apparatus and remained outside the political realm so that "when the revolution came, it did not support him."[13] The military would play an influential role—both positive and negative—in all of the countries that experienced revolutions in the Arab Spring.

After Ben Ali's forced exile, the full reins of power were not ceded immediately. Instead, an interim government was formed that included many high-level officials in the Ben Ali administration, in particular former Prime Minister Mohammed Ghannouchi (b. 1941) and former Speaker of Parliament Fouad Mebazaa (b.1933). Many in the Tunisian public were disappointed with this new government because it too closely resembled the Ben Ali administration, and public protests continued. The ministers of the interim government severed their ties with Ben Ali's political party and stayed in office until special elections could be held. These elections did not settle the matter. In fact, they demonstrated the shortcomings of a revolution without the guiding influence of the country's intellectuals. Tunisia did not have unified, well-organized opposition parties with governing experience; this outcome of their revolution would also characterize uprisings taking place in other Arab countries.

The media's impact on the success of the uprising in Tunisia was considerable. Qatar-based *al-Jazeera* dedicate its coverage of the unfolding events in Tunisia, and this attention emboldened the demonstrators with a new sense of credibility. The people in this small North African country suddenly found themselves at the center of the world's attention. By February 2011, "virtually every city in the Arab world marched to the same beat, chanting the same slogans, watching each other, and feeding off a shared energy within a shared narrative. Al-Jazeera became the primary televised home of revolution both in Arabic and in English."[14]

Ben Ali's fall was unprecedented; a populist movement had publicly and relatively peacefully uprooted a ruthless leader who had sustained his corrupt regime through fear and intimidation. The news network played varying roles in subsequent uprisings with its far reach, open debates, guests with a broad range of political views, and relatively limited censorship. Satellite coverage encouraged movements that were gathering in nearby Libya, Egypt, and elsewhere in the region.

Other electronic media platforms, which had been developing in a relatively well-wired Tunisia since the nineties, also shaped the movement. That is why the Arab Spring in Tunisia is sometimes referred to as "The Social Media Revolution." Facebook, Twitter, internet sites, and blogs did not cause the revolution itself, but protesters did utilize social media against the regime's attempts to block the flow of communication and coordination. News from Tunisia traveled quickly to France, where some leading Tunisian dissidents had relocated. New technology "opened up greater spaces for public debate and contestation—necessary conditions for the emergence of a kind of collective action that can withstand the coercive nature of repressive regimes."[15] By 2010, Tunisians were able to employ sophisticated and coordinated techniques to share information, develop a following, and use media platforms for mobilization that circumvented government control. They also broadcast these events to eager audiences of viewers throughout the Arab world.

Social media and satellite channels helped disseminate something else that was important for the Tunisian uprising: music. Popular songs inspired the protesters and gave words and momentum to their movement. Musician Hamada ben Amor (b. 1990, known as "El General"), who was considered the "Voice of the Revolution," released his controversial hit 2010 song "Rayees Le Bled" ("President of the Country") in December as demonstrations were building in strength. In this song, he speaks directly to Ben Ali about his failures as president (such a gesture risked imprisonment or worse). His lyrics stirred the protesters' hearts:

Today I speak fearlessly on behalf of the people

crushed by the weight of injustice

Mr. President

Your people are dead

Your people eat garbage

Look at what is happening in your own country![16]

Protest singer Emel Mathlouthi (b. 1982), who moved to France after her songs were banned in Tunisia, returned to Tunis in 2011. One of her videos, in which she sings "Kilmiti Hurra" ("My Word is Free") to protestors on the streets of Tunis, went viral in Tunisia and throughout the Arab world. (More on the role and impact of music on the Arab Spring can be found in chapter 7, "Music in the Arab World.")

For some scholars and analysts, Tunisia is regarded as the lone success story of the Arab Spring, a country that still possesses a relatively peaceful, stable democratic government. The country's stability and peace today is an outcome few could have expected in the early months after Ben Ali's exile. In October of that year, the moderate Islamist party *Ennahda* (or al-Nahda; "The Renaissance") won a majority of votes in new elections. (This initial victory by an Islamist party would be mirrored in Egypt in the following year when the Muslim Brotherhood won elections there.) But unrest and uncertainty still continued in Tunisia because of dissatisfaction with the new ruling party's decisions and an ongoing struggle over issues of governance. By 2013, two opposition political leaders had been killed, heightening tensions and calling into question the possibility of lasting democratic reform.

Despite these tensions, rival factions were able to negotiate in late 2013 for new elections that would take place in the following year. The Tunisian National Dialogue Quartet, which made this critical negotiation possible, received the Nobel Peace Prize in 2015. The Nobel Peace Prize underscores just how important this negotiation was: The peace that ensued allowed Tunisia's new democratic governing system to remain legitimate and keep Tunisia from falling into the chaos experienced by other Arab states. The prize citation notes that the group averted a civil war by creating an alternative political process that established "a constitutional system of government guaranteeing fundamental rights for the entire population, irrespective of gender, political conviction or religious belief."[17]

In January 2014, a new, progressive constitution was ratified; in elections held that same month, the secular-nationalist party *Nidaa` Tunis* won a majority while the *Ennahda* party remained politically active and involved, thus representing a successful transition of power and peaceful cooperation between parties within a democratic system. Radical militants still exist in Tunisia, and the highly-publi-cized shooting of seventeen tourists at a beach resort in March 2015 demonstrates the challenges still facing the country. This ultraconservative *Salafi* movement continues to threaten the transition process; many worry that their numbers are growing.[18] This unsettling situation, along with an uneven post-revolutionary landscape, high unemployment, poverty, and few economic opportunities (espe-cially for the young), have left many Tunisians doubting the new government's effectiveness. For some, that doubt has opened the doors to radicalization.

Nevertheless, the revolution in Tunisia can be regarded as a success. Other countries in the region have failed to bring about lasting democratic governments with their revolutions, but in Tunisia today a democratic government and a large measure of political freedom and freedom of speech still exist. The government re-mains secular, and the national dialogue is represented by more than one hundred political parties and civil society organizations. One finds good examples of part-nership and pluralism between the government and citizens[19] even as the country still struggles to solve divisions and inequalities related to the initial unrest.

EGYPT

Inspired by events in Tunisia, large public demonstrations started on January 25, 2011, in Egypt. Similar grievances about socio-economic conditions, especially unemployment, and the corruption of President Hosni Mubarak's thirty-year reign sparked mass protests with a speed and ferocity that surprised many inside and outside the country. In eighteen days, Mubarak and his entrenched political party were forced out of office, initiating a period of uncertainty and transition in Egyptian politics that persists to this day. With a population of more than ninety million, Egypt retains its position at the heart of the Arab world as its most influ-ential player. The uprisings received more attention than any other in the region, and its outcome continues to be monitored throughout the world.

Before considering the many factors behind the uprisings, it is important to examine an Egyptian-born movement that has no parallel in the Arab world. The Muslim Brotherhood, established in 1928, is a Sunni Islamist religious, political, and social movement that promotes traditional Islamic *Shari`a* law and has chapters across the Arab world. From its beginnings, it has been an influential institution in Egyptian political and civic life. Throughout the years the Egyptian government has alternated between allowing its members limited political freedom and performing excessive, brutal crackdowns on them. An uneasy truce developed during the twentieth century between the government and the brotherhood, whose legitimacy and effectiveness countered the government's ongoing failures:

> The Muslim Brotherhood spread its ideas and exerted its position in Egyptian society by providing a wide range of social services such as food, jobs, health care, schools, and banking services. The Muslim Brotherhood has a reputation for providing services in areas where the state has either failed or has shown considerable weakness. One widespread saying in Egypt about the Muslim Brotherhood summarizes some peoples' attitudes toward its services: "When the Muslim Brothers are asked, they open the drawer and give you something. When you ask government officials, they open the drawer and they ask you to give something."[20]

The Egyptian government's banning of the Muslim Brotherhood as a political party but still allowing its existence as a social movement has had powerful repercussions for the country. By being able to maintain its structure and cohesiveness while expanding its social and political clout over many years, the Muslim Brotherhood has emerged as a powerful political force in the immediate aftermath of the Egyptian revolution.

In the 1950s and 1960s, Egypt was the leader of Pan-Arab nationalism. President Gamal Abdel Nasir (d. 1970) overthrew the corrupt regime of King Farouk in 1952. Despite his charisma and popular support in Egypt, Nasir ruled with an iron fist, consolidating power with the military (he had been in the Free Officers movement) and limiting political parties and dissent. Following an assassination attempt in 1954, Nasir banned the Muslim Brotherhood, imprisoning and torturing many of its members. As his control of all aspects of the nation-state expanded, the government bureaucracy ballooned, and a ruling bargain "emerged in which the state promised to provide for the prosperity and security of citizens in return for their acquiescence."[21] The promises of state-sponsored benefits and social stability gave way to economic disenfranchisement and social inequality, both exacerbated by Egypt's population growth and incessant poverty. The loss of Gaza and the Sinai in the Six-Day War in 1967 weakened Nasir's standing domestically and internationally, but his offer to resign the presidency was not accepted by the nation. Ongoing military expenditures diverted resources from economic and social reform; by the end of the 1960s, Nasser's socialist vision for Egypt had not been achieved.

Anwar Sadat (d. 1981), another army officer, took power after Nasser's death and became the country's president in 1970. He reoriented Egypt's foreign policy toward the West, established peace with Israel, and began a program for economic liberalization, the *infitah*, or open-door policy. Sadat established the National Democratic Party (NDP), which consolidated the regime's power both at the governorate and national levels and limited any possibilities of political liberalization. Sadat allowed the Muslim

Brotherhood to operate as a social institution. Its precarious relationship with the government continued until the peace accords with Israel were signed in 1979. The movement turned against Sadat. At that time income inequalities in the country had widened, with some benefitting from the *infitah* and its Western orientations while others continued to suffer from poverty and a lack of economic opportunities.

In 1981 Sadat was assassinated by Islamic radicals and succeeded by his vice president, former air force commander Hosni Mubarak (b. 1928). Mubarak continued to serve as an ally of the West, particularly the United States, and broadened Sadat's economic reforms, especially privatization programs that increased his support from private sector leaders. Middle East expert Mehran Kamrava notes that Egypt under Mubarak represented an "exclusionary state," one that tries to exclude from the political process social actors who are not already part of or affiliated with the state."[22] To many observers two Egypts existed at this time—one belonged to the *fallaheen* (peasants) living not so differently from their ancestors thousands of years ago, the other to a flashy elite with imported cars, European vacations, and summer villas along the Mediterranean. Propping up the latter became Mubarak's purpose. With official political expression suppressed, Egyptians maintained their cautious criticism of the government with the use of clever cartoons. These cartoons appeared in the national and local press and appealed to all Egyptians, educated and uneducated alike. Limited media freedom was allowed for the exchange of ideas and debate in a controlled but lively Egyptian press and broadcast media, which operated under a red line of what was permissible by the government. Government-approved NGOs (non-governmental organizations), some with foreign funding, also promoted positive social change.

Such openings in the nineties created a budding Egyptian civil society, which called for economic, political, and social reform. By 2004, the *Kifaya* (Enough) protest movement challenged Mubarak's rule with well-organized campaigns. The broad-based movement attracted participants from across Egypt's regions and social classes. Its popular appeal "pioneered protest methods, organizational forms, and communication tactics that were adopted by later Egyptian and wider Arab protest movements."[23] The *Kifaya* movement signaled to a new generation that perhaps the government did not have as much control as the people had thought. In 2005, the Muslim Brotherhood also demonstrated publicly against the regime, the first time since the 1960s.[24] Egyptians were beginning to see that even though their calls for reform might be squelched, they were still being heard. Many became adept at knowing how to skirt authoritarian interference and use social media more effectively with each new available platform and device.

Mubarak, with a constitutional referendum, allowed parties other than his NDP (National Democratic Party) to run for office in 2005. Although the November elections were rigged by the NDP, members of the Muslim Brotherhood gained 88 of the 454 seats in the People's Assembly.[25] Reflecting an ongoing contradiction between asserting authoritarian control and allowing some degree of political expression, Mubarak in 2007 again reformed the constitution to limit opposition parties as well as the judiciary's independent ability to monitor elections. Alarmed by the Muslim Brotherhood's potential political strength, Mubarak made sure the new amendments banned political parties with a "religious framework," thus effectively excluding the movement from any political participation.

Essentially, Mubarak was "de-democratizing Egypt's political system."[26] The stops and starts of political reform were further exacerbated when it became clear that Mubarak was grooming his son, Gamal, to become the next leader of Egypt. Public discourse predicted that he would run for president after his father's term expired in 2010. Egyptians, fed up with neo-pharaonic rule, had a new figure to resent in Gamal. The parliamentary elections in 2010 were regarded as the "most fraudulent and restricted of any in Egypt's history."[27] False promises from the president's office, NDP leaders, and bloated ministries led to more and more public frustration. By 2010, underlying dissatisfaction with every aspect of the Mubarak government angered opposition leaders, the struggling middle class, urban youth, and the emerging group of savvy technology experts.

The events of 2010 and early 2011 in Tunisia fueled Egypt's opposition movement. Ben Ali's stunningly quick fall from power emboldened a broad and loose network of Egyptians. If a public uprising could topple an entrenched dictator nearby in North Africa, it was time for change at home. *Al-Jazeera* and other media outlets, as well as social media, brought Tunisia's uprising to Egyptians in real time. Protesters from both countries were exchanging information, slogans, and strategies (music provided an inspiration for the movement, too). Electronic media reminded Arab peoples across the region of the common links and culture they share. They "identified with each other across borders and saw their struggles as intimately and directly linked. When the Tunisia uprising began, history tells us that it was almost inevitable that it would spread across the region."[28]

Although Egyptians had been resisting the Mubarak regime for three decades, their growing calls for protest on a profoundly different level had to surmount a formidable obstacle. The regime was also watching the events in Tunisia unfold, preparing for demonstrations to erupt in Egypt and making sure its hold on power would not be broken. For the opposition, "the challenge was in persuading potential participants that they could succeed. They needed to persuade ordinary people that it was worth the risks and costs to leave their homes and come into the streets against Mubarak. The example of Tunisia was the single most important thing that changed those minds."[29]

On January 25, 2011, activists flooded Tahrir (Liberation) Square at the center of Cairo. The crowds of protesters, which was larger than anyone expected, denounced the brutality of the regime's police forces. For the next eighteen days, protesters in the thousands, then tens of thousands and eventually hundreds of thousands jammed the streets demanding the overthrow of the Mubarak regime. Social media played a key role, personified by Google employee Wael Ghonim, who helped organize the January 25 demonstrations in Cairo with a network of savvy operatives who were able to get their message out. Ghonim developed a page on Facebook, "We Are All Khaled Said," to commemorate a young civilian beaten to death by Egyptian security forces in Alexandria. The page became a national rallying place for youth fed up with police brutality and their lack of civil liberties. The stated purpose of the January 25 protests in Tahrir Square had been to call for "ending poverty, placing a two-term limit on the presidency, firing the autocratic interior minister, and annulling Egypt's emergency law."[30] Alarmed by the rapid assembly of a large, animated crowd of protesters, on January 26 the government shut off the country's leading mobile phone and Short Message Services (SMS). But the tide was already turning just one day after the protests erupted. *Al-Jazeera*, which became "the unquestioned home of the revolution on the airwaves," was already broadcasting the protests full time, showing the locations and interviewing Egyptians, many of whom seemed startled themselves by the popularity of the movement.[31]

Social media-savvy protesters ensured that everyone stayed connected and knew what was happening whereby circumventing the government's attempt to control digital outlets. Sustained and organized civil disobedience spread throughout the country. The international media televised moving and graphic images of confrontations between Egyptian security forces and Egyptian citizens. As in Tunisia, a successful "cycle of contention" formed through shared understandings, effective social networks, and determined action."[32] A revolution had begun. The entire country was represented in Tahrir Square and the message was clear: Mubarak must go. Egyptian musician Ramy Essam's (b. 1987) Arab Spring anthem "Irhal" ("Leave") declared: "We are not leaving / He will leave / As one / We demand one thing / Leave, leave, leave."[33]

Security forces maintained tight control. During eighteen days of revolution, an estimated 840 protesters were killed, many more were injured and jailed. Mubarak did acknowledge that changes had to be made and initially offered concessions similar to Ben Ali's in Tunisia. Between January 29 and February 1, 2011, he announced changes to his cabinet and a commitment not to seek reelection. The Muslim Brotherhood generally kept out of the protests, adopting a strategy of self-restraint, but they remained a player behind the scenes. On February 7, Mubarak offered to carry out a dialogue with the Muslim Brotherhood as well as enact a small increase in Egyptian salaries and pensions. Four days later, on February 11, as protests arose in response to these inadequate minor concessions, Mubarak resigned from office, and power shifted to Egypt's Supreme Command of Armed Forces (SCAF); the reshuffled cabinet that Mubarak had formed amidst the protests before his resignation stayed in power to oversee the political transition.

Although Mubarak left office less than a month after Ben Ali, the year that began with unbridled optimism deteriorated into despair as the people realized that Egypt was now a police state run by the SCAF. It was a regime far more ruthless than Mubarak's, utilizing violence, torture, and imprisonment. Nevertheless the protests continued, sometimes with fatal results. Recorded acts of violence against women, doctors, nurses, and protesters of every stripe, even against soccer fans, suggest the wide commitment of Egyptians across the board to real change despite the entrenched power of the security forces.[34] Political parties formed and regrouped, maneuvering to gain power. The Muslim Brotherhood "became emboldened and could not reign in its political ambitions" with an outward slogan of "participation, not domination."[35] The beleaguered bureaucracy managed to proceed with elections in this brutally violent and tense stage as the SCAF held the country together.

In November 2011, parliamentary elections began and the Muslim Brotherhood, which had established the Freedom and Justice Party (FJP), won a majority of seats. The party labeled itself a *hizb madani* (civil party), but religion still influenced its platform, which called for "enhancing Islamic morals, values and concepts in individuals' lives."[36] In June 2012, the FJP's candidate, Mohammed Morsi (b. 1951), won the presidential election, a stunning triumph for what was in fact Egypt's main opposition force since 1928. The other finalist was Ahmed Shafik (b. 1941), Mubarak's former prime minister. This was the second revolution, after Tunisia, in which open elections brought to power an Islamist party. In the immediate aftermath of the Mubarak era, the Muslim Brotherhood was well-established and respected by many, though it lacked the necessary experience to govern.

During the transition, the SCAF remained very much in power as the military maneuvered to retain its grip. Once in office, Morsi dismissed Mubarak holdover and de facto head of state Defense Minister Muhammad Husayn Tantawi, replacing him with General Abdul Fattah al-Sisi (b.1954). Morsi consolidated power among his ideologues and "was perceived by many Egyptians as the Brotherhood's man in the presidential palace instead of a President for all Egyptians."[37] Morsi struggled to deal with the many challenges facing Egypt, and although he held power, he was not in control of the state structures that had propped up Mubarak for so long. The Brotherhood faced the resistance of many, especially the Supreme Command of Armed Forces, and was limited by the conservative nature of the movement itself, by the lack of an overreaching plan to address the issues prompted by the protesters, not to mention a glaring lack of governing experience. Morsi proved cautious in limiting the military's powers; a new constitution in 2012 actually granted more authority and powers to the military and kept its budget free from civilian oversight.[38]

Public demonstrations continued throughout Egypt during these years. On June 30, 2013, millions rallied for Morsi's resignation. A quick military coup followed and forced Morsi, whose government proved unpopular to many Egyptians, out of power. After banning the Muslim Brotherhood, Al-Sisi was formally elected as president in an election with low voter turnout in May 2014.[39] Al-Sisi proved ruthless in cracking down on anti-government protests and justifying his actions in the name of stability and order even while images of police brutality were being broadcast around the world. Later that year, during the protests of August 14, an estimated one thousand people were killed, and many more were injured and jailed. These uprisings were more violent than the Tahrir Square events of two years earlier yet they received far less attention. Al-Sisi's military coup broke the legitimacy of Egypt's young democratic system. Morsi was imprisoned along with other leaders of his government. Today the Muslim Brotherhood is banned in Egypt, and has been formally listed as a terrorist organization. Ultimately, the hopes and desires of Egypt's peaceful and swift 2011 revolution have yet to be realized. Al-Sisi has consolidated control of the SCAF, internal security forces, and the civilian police. He also has pursued a pro-Western outlook. The United States has been critical of Egypt's human rights abuses and other issues, but in the end the US has continued providing Egypt with significant military and economic assistance.

The demonstrations in Tahrir Square represented a model of peaceful protest that culminated in a successful, albeit short-lived, revolution in the Arab world's most populous and influential country. Voter turnout reached sixty-five percent in the post-revolution elections and referenda of 2011 and 2012.[40] However, this democracy could not be sustained. If Tunisia is seen as a success story of the Arab Spring, many people regard Egypt as its failure. An initially effective revolution failed to establish a lasting and representative new government. The first democratically-elected leader in the new Egypt was overthrown by his own military elite in a coup after just one year in power. Many observers say that al-Sisi's current government is as autocratic and repressive as the original Mubarak regime, if not more.

Al-Sisi has been generally welcomed by Western states, which see him as a safeguard of stability, and the situation in Egypt is worse than its pre-Arab Spring status quo. An autocratic and repressive leader from the military elite holds a firm grip on power, and he is backed by strong foreign nations less interested in human rights and democracy than in stability. Over half of the Egyptian population is under twenty-five years of age.[41] They know that their collective voice has power; in the years ahead, their insistence on human rights, and having a role in a transparent democratic system will play a crucial part in Egypt's future.

LIBYA

From 1911 to 1943, Libya was an Italian colony, and in the wake of Italy's withdrawal from the country following World War II, the United Nations installed theologian and political leader King Idris I (d. 1983) as the first and only king of Libya. After the discovery of oil in 1959, the country emerged from being one of the world's poorest to one of its wealthiest per capita. Ten years later, young military officer Mu`ammar Gaddafi (d. 2011) became Libya's autocratic ruler in a bloodless coup. During this time, Libya continued to supply massive quantities of oil to developing nations of the world along with the West, and its economy grew with the money received. Gaddafi nationalized most economic sectors, particularly the oil sector. The growing economy, and by extension the fabric of the Libyan sociopolitical structure, depended upon extracting oil and selling it internationally. The financial benefit from the unsustainable oil economy was focused tremendously in the hands of Gaddafi himself along with a minority of political, military, and other elites. The majority of the Libyan people did not share in these benefits and lived repressed and exploited by the Gaddafi regime.

Throughout a reign spanning four decades, Gaddafi was met with frequent opposition in the form of military coup attempts and dissent among the population at large. To diminish the threat of his officers rising against him, Gaddafi deliberately weakened the Libyan Armed Forces by establishing a revolving-door policy for officers and relying heavily on loyal elite troops such as the Revolutionary Guard Corps, the *Khamis* Brigade, and even his personal Amazonian Guard. As a result of sacrificing professionalism for loyalty within Libya's military contingent, the country became vulnerable to opposition during times of crisis, especially in early 2011.

While Gaddafi successfully contained internal military dissension with tact, from early on opposition among the general population was handled through brutal repression. Dissent was declared illegal in 1973, at which time Gaddafi's security forces targeted hundreds of leftists, Islamists, professors, lawyers, doctors, students, and journalists who opposed laws banning political parties and unions, as well as restrictions on free speech. Gaddafi's "overblown security and paramilitary apparatus enforced harsh repression of any form of dissent to his rule. Notwithstanding limited reforms and rhetoric about human rights in the late 1980s and again in the mid-2000s, Gaddafi's repressive security state remained largely untouched."[42] Campaigns of violence and intimidation against opponents of Gaddafi—often described as the "Green Terror"—included highly-publicized hangings of regime opponents. "There were public executions, unforgettably broadcast on national television, and those who fled found little respite as the regime openly adopted a policy in the 1980s of assassinating dissidents in exile, whom Gaddafi infamously called "stray dogs.""[43]

Unsurprisingly, Gaddafi had made many enemies during his years of absolute power, including "bold young activists, exiled dissidents, despondent reformists and businessmen, frustrated lawyers and journalists, unemployed youth, wearied Islamists and their families, and anyone suspected of belonging to any of these groups."[44] By 2009 Libya was considered the most censored country in the Middle East and North Africa, according to the Freedom of the Press Index. Prisons were run without documentation of the inmate population and housed a significant portion of the opposition. Dissent had reached a tipping point by 2011, and the protests that began in Tunisia provided the country with a catalyst for regime change.

Protests in Libya began on February 15, 2011 in front of a police headquarters building after the arrest of a human rights attorney.[45] The National Conference for the Libyan Opposition declared February 17 as a "Day of Rage" against the forty-two-year-old Gaddafi government. Confrontations between demonstrators and government forces became more violent in Libya than in either Tunisia or Egypt. Struggle for control over the country soon came to resemble civil war. Acts of civil disobedience and demonstration transformed into militarized factions fighting a territory war on the ground in addition to a campaign for political legitimacy. While Gaddafi still held power during most of 2011, the anti-Gaddafi faction gained control of the city of Benghazi and used it as their provisional capital. They set up an opposition government in Benghazi called the National Transitional Council.[46] Meanwhile, Gaddafi still ruled from the city of Tripoli.

In the following months, anti-Gaddafi forces aided by the West and some fellow Arab states sought to destroy the Tripoli-based Gaddafi government while creating a legitimate and functioning government of their own based in Benghazi. Gaddafi was attacked by NATO bombers while attempting to flee Tripoli. His convoy was scattered, and he was discovered "hiding in a drainage pipe, by a group of opposition fighters from Misrata, a city hungry for revenge after [Gaddafi's] forces had destroyed most of it over months of intense fighting."[47] On October 20, 2011, Gaddafi was finally captured and beaten to death by a mob of civilians.

Elections were held in July 2012. The General National Congress (GNC) formally and democratically replaced the National Transitional Council that had been set up in Benghazi early in the revolution.[48] However, the GNC did not cede power when its term ended, and elections held in 2014 were influenced by both violence and low voter turnout.[49] A full civil war had broken out by the end of 2014. As the

GNC began to transition power to the newly elected House of Representatives, rifts between political parties became violent and fractured into several entities warring for control of the country. Two opposing governments, the reinstated GNC based now in Tripoli and the House of Representatives based in the city of Tobruk, became the primary actors vying for legitimate control of the country.

Realistically, the absence of the rigid Gaddafi regime and its institutions left a vacuum in which many actors began to vie for power in a chaotic Libya. The country's volatile post-revolutionary landscape has precluded the formation of any legitimate and cohesive new government. With openings in the absence of Gaddafi, the revolutionary side fractured into many opposing factions, each with militias and rebel groups undermining one another. The 'so-called' Libyan National Army (LNA) emerged as a key player vying for control of the country. The chaos and lack of control also contributed to massive arms trafficking into and out of Libya as well as the spread of radical nongovernmental actors. ISIS has emerged, exerting influence in the power vacuum. Libyan borders have remained open and virtually uncontrolled.

For the Libyan people, quality of life has diminished amidst a landscape of warfare, insecurity, and turmoil. Libya presents a humanitarian crisis in which basic services and a normal functioning of economic and civil sectors is lacking. The violent Libyan landscape has led tens of thousands of Libyans to seek refuge outside of the country, contributing to the refugee crisis both in Europe and across the Middle East. In the first half of 2017 alone, 28,886 Libyans attempted to migrate to Italy across the Mediterranean Sea.[50] Displacement of populations within Libya has created challenges that will last for decades. In 2016, a council of nine members of rival political factions came to an agreement to establish a unified government and designated Fayez al-Sarraj (b. 1960) as prime minister, with the backing of the UN. In the summer of 2017, French President Emmanuel Macron convened a meeting between al-Sarraj and Libyan National Army (LNA) leader Khalifa Haftar (b. 1943). Haftar controls many of the militias in the eastern part of the country; the meeting resulted in an agreement to set a cease-fire and hold elections.[51] Given the short and spontaneous nature of Libya's revolution, it lacked an overarching ideological framework to guide a subsequent transition, and the country's political situation today remains tenuous at best.

SYRIA

Following World War II, Syria became independent in 1946, but experienced a number of military coups, and control of the country changed between four military generals between 1949 and 1954. After 1954, the nation's leaders associated themselves with the Ba'ath party. The Ba'ath party stood, on paper, for policies of pan-Arab unity, freedom from colonial rule, and left-wing politics. From 1958–1961, Syria merged with Egypt under a pan-Arab vision to create the United Arab Republic. The union was not a success, however. Following a military coup in 1961, Syria withdrew itself from this union with Egypt and eighteen later, on March 8, 1963, another military coup seized power that was led by the Ba'ath political party. Nour Eddin al-Atassi (d.1992) was put in power though General Salah Jadid (d.1993) became the country's de facto leader.

Hafez al-Assad (d. 2000) became the head of the Syrian Air Force in 1964 and minister of defense in 1966. Syria was defeated in the 1967 Six-Day War, and Syria lost the strategic Golan Heights. Jadid retained immense power within Syria as leader of the Ba'ath Party, but fallout from the military defeat created serious tensions within the country. Disagreement over the direction that Syria would take after the 1967 defeat, and with regard to Syria's alliance with the Soviet Union, put strains on the Ba'ath ruling political party. In November 1970, al-Assad launched a bloodless coup, taking power from Jadid and al-Atassi and imprisoning them.

Assad ruled with a ruthless hand. Examples include the 1982 uprising in the city of Hama, when he sent the Syrian military into Hama, killing more than 25,000 civilian inhabitants to discourage future uprisings. Assad became known as 'the Sphinx' for his enigmatic hold on the country and for his skillful navigation of international relations. Although some economic gains were made during his years in power, political freedom was not allowed. At the time of Hafez al-Assad's death in 2000, a stable but tightly-controlled Syria was handed over to his son, Bashar al-Assad (b. 1965). Since then, the younger al-Assad has been entrenched as an autocratic ruler similar to his father, equally repressive of political expression and exploitative of his people.

Despite the autocratic grip marginalizing the Syrian people for decades, few expected the Arab Spring uprisings to spread to Syria. "Assad felt protected by [Syria's] resistance identity and popular foreign policy."[52] Prior to the Arab Spring, there was not much of an opposition movement in Syria, and any organized political opposition, such as the Muslim Brotherhood, existed only in exile. This suppression of dissent was due in large part to Syria's "particularly intense breed of authoritarianism [which] had eviscerated any form of independent civil society or political opposition."[53] Bloggers, internet activists, and any other semblance of an independent press were non-existent or ineffective in Syria, making the dissemination of opposition news near impossible. "Even internet-savvy middle-class youth, who had had a central role in the mobilization and articulation of discrete social and political groups during the Tunisian and Egyptian revolutions, seemed to be quite peripheral to the Syrian uprising."[54]

Though effectively silenced by the Assad regime, Syrians were just as discontent as their Arab neighbors over their political and socioeconomic situations. Trade imbalances were hurting Syrian businesses, migrations to and overpopulation of the cities added to an expanding lower class desperate for work, and existing social networks and infrastructure were inadequate or poorly integrated. Pervasive corruption and unmet promises of political reforms further undermined confidence in the regime's credibility and the people's ability to enact substantive change. While dissatisfaction among the populace was extensive, the internal divisions of the established opposition had helped the Assad regime to isolate itself even more from the protests. In this regard, the Syrian uprising stands apart from the other revolutions of the Arab Spring because of its local, fragmented nature:

> The relative isolation of the protests made it easier for the Syrian government to repress them through the use of military and paramilitary violence. While the demonstrations and protests did not stop—as soon as one focus of revolt was repressed, another one appeared—they did not manage to occupy in a sustainable way a territory with historical and symbolic significance that could serve as a reference to all protests, such as happened with Bourguiba Avenue in Tunis or Tahrir Square in Cairo.[55]

Technically the first protests to be considered part of Syria's Arab Spring began on January 26, 2011. Initial protests were focused on the treatment of two teenage boys in the small town of Dar`a who were arrested and tortured for writing anti-government graffiti. However, the first signs of popular mobilization appeared in the margins of Syrian society in mid-March.[56] These protests, amid violent responses by government forces to suppress the revolutionary movement, grew into large demonstrations across Syria calling for the removal of Bashar al-Assad from office, for systematic governmental reforms, and for greater personal and political freedoms.

In April 2011, Assad made minor concessions such as repealing a 1963 law allowing the government to suspend constitutional rights, but he also increased violent government responses to public protests, including full use of the military to disband organizations and demonstrations opposed to his role.[57] The situation in Syria devolved into the bloodiest and perhaps least successful outcome of the 2011 revolutionary movements of the Arab Spring. In 2018, Assad still holds onto the presidential office, though his authority and legitimacy have diminished considerably. International actors including Russia and Iran support him. Early in the uprising, and because of the extreme force Assad demanded his army use against protesting civilians, many Syrian military officers left the military to join anti-Assad groups. These former government soldiers became known as the Free Syrian Army and were initially funded by the United States and several Gulf states to continue fighting Assad. The anti-Assad opposition has fractured into several groups, some supported by the United States and its allies, fighting both against each other and against Assad. Meanwhile, ISIS used the landscape of violence and uncertainty to gain control of large portions of Syrian territory.

Other Arab nations carried out 2011 revolutions that successfully removed long-term autocratic leaders from power and began political transitions with varying degrees of success and struggle. Syria represents a case in which the autocratic leader who was supposed to be ousted managed to use force to suppress and fracture the revolution, thus ensuring his continued power. Today the situation in Syria is perhaps the most well-known in the Arab world as the country descended into civil war in the continued effort to force Bashar al-Assad from power.

The current actors can be divided, roughly, into pro-Assad and anti-Assad factions with corresponding bases of foreign support. Both sides, especially the original revolutionary force against Assad, have fractured into several factions warring both with Assad and with each other. The United States and ISIS are ironically both technically fighting against Assad, and US-backed anti-Assad militias and Assad himself seek to defeat ISIS and other radical opposition groups. Meanwhile Assad, with foreign backing from Russia, Iran, and other actors, continues to subdue movements against him with brutal and extreme force, which has created a humanitarian crisis within his own nation as well. The Syrian refugee crisis is discussed in the following chapter.

JORDAN

From the moment of independence [in 1946], Jordan enjoyed a special political sphere. It was this history, unique in the region, which allowed the state to see minimal public unrest and structural change during the Arab Spring. That is not to say that Jordan was without its own history of political repression. In 1957, King Hussein (d. 1999), at age 23, dismissed the country's leftist prime minister, implemented martial law, and jailed dozens of leftist activists and parliamentarians.

However, what is noteworthy about this early period in Jordan's political story is that while protest activities were suppressed during martial law, they never fully went away. Jordan has a lively civil society and has allowed open dialogue and even criticism of government policies.[58] Though this leeway was often reserved primarily for the Muslim Brotherhood during the 1960s as opposed to the more leftist factions, such a willingness to allow some form of opposition ultimately instilled in the country a sense that the government was not unassailable. Thus, while the Brotherhood had fashioned itself as a 'loyal opposition' to the King's government, they still "continued to critique the state, and periodically organized protests, particularly in opposition to the regime's relations with Great Britain and later the United States."[59]

The following decades were characterized by a constant give and take, an easing and tightening of the regime's control over the opposition. That said, with an exception to the violent confrontations between Palestinian militias and the regime that culminated in Black September in 1970 and caused the deaths of thousands of Palestinians (mostly militia members), protest activity was relatively civil. In fact, "the rest of the 1970s were relatively quiet in terms of protest activities, with the exception of labor protests, primarily small sit-ins and strikes at factories outside Amman, which averaged three to four per year."[60] The 1980s brought renewed protest activities due to economic deterioration. By 1989, the king introduced political liberalization "as a means to defuse domestic tensions and channel dissent into debates about political reforms and away from economic grievances"[61] as well as lifting martial law, the liberalization of media, and the introduction of constitutional amendments.

Soon after these impressive reforms were enacted, the regime began reversing these changes. The reason was simple: King Hussein did this to appease parliamentary members whose votes were needed for the upcoming passing of Jordan's peace treaty with Israel. More freedoms were reversed throughout the mid-nineties, resulting, for example, in greater crackdowns on the press. King Hussein's death did nothing to usher in a new era of reform as King Abdullah II (b. 1962) dismissed the parliament in advance of elections in 2001. This was met with a new wave of protests in 2002, and per usual, minor concessions from the government and acceptance of protests: "The regime sought to permit protests while attempting to control the specific locations and dynamics as much as possible."[62]

Such a patterned and unique—at least in comparison to other Arab states—history of easing and tightening control over dissent helps paint a picture of how Jordan managed to survive the Arab Spring with minimal public unrest and structural change. Mark Lynch notes that these patterns were related to negotiations between state and non-state actors and supply a rich background against which we can view how, in more tumultuous periods such as during the Arab Spring, protests began to deviate from known 'scripts' of acceptable behavior, former 'cooperators' with the regime began to refuse to cooperate, and the regime responded to this variety of transgressions.[63]

As such, well before the Arab Spring, the system in place on both sides of negotiations was experienced at maintaining stability. The largest demonstration during the Arab Spring involved 15,000 participants—it was also the largest public demonstration in Jordanian history but significantly smaller than demonstrations elsewhere in the region. Protests in Jordan were almost completely nonviolent, although they were consistent. Citizens continued to gather each Friday in Amman and other cities for multiple years after the initial Arab Spring protests to demand reforms from King Abdullah II.[64] It also helped that most Jordanian demonstrators wanted changes from the government but did not explicitly demand the removal of the king.

There are a number of other reasons why the Arab Spring did not deeply impact Jordan's political structure. The first is quite simply that King Abdullah responded to his population and made reforms. The monarch used the opportunity to blame challenges for reform on entrenched intelligence officials and deep state members in order to build up his own image as a reform-minded king.[65] King Abdullah quickly removed and replaced some ministers to appear responsive to his subjects, who called for the removal of Jordan's appointed prime minister. King Abdullah invested $500 million to raise wages for government employees, including national soldiers, to maintain his support base.[66] Parliamentary elections planned for 2015 were moved up to 2013, and this became Jordan's 17th Parliament—some minor changes were also made increasing women's and minority representation. The government created a new electoral commission to make the voting process more inclusive.[67] The King also established the Royal Committee to Review the Constitution (RCRC). This committee recommended changes to 42 articles in the constitution, nearly all of which were passed by Parliament and signed by the King.[68] King Abdullah made enough changes to quell his population, though time will tell if these changes are superficial or will produce some impact.

In other Arab Spring countries, protests were the emotional, chaotic result of widespread public behavior; in Jordan protests were more calculated, organized manifestations of various established opposition entities. That is why opposition in Jordan was divided. The major groups opposing the Jordanian status quo are Islamists, tribal factions with roots in East Jordan (Transjordan), and neoliberal reform groups. Islamists in Jordan, associated with the Muslim Brotherhood but officially called the Islamic Action Front, focused their demands on democratization. They want a constitutional monarchy. East Jordanian tribal groups focus on unemployment instead and want more public sector jobs offered by the Jordanian government. Neoliberal reformers urge for democratization but also advocate for privatization of industry and better employment opportunities. Opposition parties may share central demands for democratic reform and benefits for exploited groups, but they also have other priorities that are often at odds with one another. During the Arab Spring, these differences weakened the demonstrators' unified call for reform.[69]

The Syrian crisis and massive influx of foreign refugees into Jordan also have impacted how the Arab Spring has played out in the country. Creating space and services for new migrant populations became Jordan's national priority and distracted attention away from the calls for regime change. The Syrian refugee crisis showed Jordanian citizens the immediate and grave possible consequences of a national uprising.[70] As the refugee crisis grew, attention remained focused on that issue, and citizens and King Abdullah could point to that situation for uniting them to solve the nation's challenges.[71]

Jordan relies on international support to cope with Syrian refugees. This steady inflow of foreign money and other resources provide the means for the government to retain a firm hold on the country's political and economic situation. The ongoing crisis and high stakes have given Jordan the opportunity to leverage major international aid into the creation of national frameworks and programs that may ensure Jordan's own lasting stability. Humanitarian assistance from the U.S. directly to Jordan to address the Syrian refugee crisis has totaled more than $900 million since the crisis began.[72] In 2015, the U.S. and Jordan signed a Memorandum of Understanding continuing U.S. economic and security assistance, guaranteeing Jordan one billion dollars per year between 2015 and 2017.[73] In the same 2015–2017 timeframe, the European Union's European Neighbor Partnership (ENP) provided Jordan with EUR 200 million in direct economic assistance and more than EUR 700 million for Syrian refugee-related assistance.[74] Saudi Arabia has also given Jordan well over a billion dollars in grants during these years.[75] Managing these resources has been a challenge and leads to questions of corruption, but the Jordanian response to the overwhelming challenges of having so many refugees with no clear end to their plight has been impressive. Jordan's stability is still holding though the economic situation is worsening there. How long it holds is hard to tell at this point. Today Jordan remains a stable, though overburdened, Arab nation both regionally and internationally important.

YEMEN

During the nineteenth and early twentieth century, much of modern Yemen, especially the southern port city of Aden, was under the influence of Britain and, to a lesser extent, the Ottomans. In 1962, a military coup ended the Zaydi imamate government in northern Yemen, and the Yemen Arab Republic (or North Yemen) was founded. A contemporary independence movement in the south created the People's Democratic Republic of Yemen (or South Yemen) in the same decade. In 1990, the two states united into the modern state of Yemen, and Ali Abdullah Saleh (d. 2017), who had been the leader of North Yemen since 1978, became its president.

Loyalty of key tribal leaders and financial support of Western states were central to the success of Saleh's government. Saleh and his inner circle enjoyed the majority of the economic growth that industrialization and modernization brought to Yemen at the expense of large sections of the Yemeni population, especially in rural areas.

In the two decades after unification, Saleh's regime faced significant internal conflict that precipitated the Arab Spring in Yemen and produced deep social, political, and economic grievances in the south. First, in 1994, South Yemen attempted but failed to secede. Then, between 2004 and 2010, Saleh successfully fought six separate wars against the Houthis, a predominantly Shi`ite religious political movement. During this time, Saleh's "iron-fisted rule went beyond military campaigns; he readily cracked down on his political opponents, and his reign was fraught with allegations of extrajudicial imprisonments, torture, and forced disappearances."[76] Brutal repression, skillful political maneuvering, and manipulated foreign interests enabled Saleh to retain power for more than three decades. That included Saleh's clear intention to ordain his son as his political successor.

As Saleh's repression machine worked to choke substantive opposition movements, discontent simmered on a number of fronts. The Yemenis endured a lost list of grievances and injustices, including: the postponement of parliamentary elections; widespread unemployment, especially among the youth; deteriorating standards of living for all but the upper ruling class. In addition to ecological depredations and acute water shortages; bad educational and medical facilities; censorship, harassment, arbitrary detention, and brutality against journalists, dissidents, and regime opponents; and profound, widespread malaise.[77]

Demonstrations in January 2011 called for Saleh's thirty-three-year-old government to cede power. "Like his counterparts in Libya and elsewhere, Saleh initially responded to his country's [Arab Spring] demonstrations with defiance and violence."[78] But when tens of thousands of undaunted protesters assembled in the Yemeni capital city of Sana'a in late January and early February, Saleh made some concessions, including that he would not run for reelection in 2013 nor pass on the presidency to his son.[79] Like concessions made in Tunisia and Egypt, these were not enough to placate the opposition, which grew to include influential and previously loyal tribes and military commanders. Protests returned and some demonstrations became violent as government forces attempted to control crowd size. Many senior politicians resigned from Saleh's government, and many members of his *Sanhani* clan showed sympathies to the anti-government demonstrators.[80] The General People's Congress, which is Saleh's ruling party, as well as the Gulf Cooperation Council and many international organizations agreed to a plan for a governmental transition, but Saleh himself refused to sign the agreement.[81]

In late 2011, Saleh handed over power to his deputy, Abd-Rabbu Mansour Hadi (b.1945), who won an unopposed election for a two-year presidential term starting in February 2012. The conflict between the central Yemeni government and the Houthis has continued. Houthis formed an alliance with former President Saleh (whom the Houthis had worked to overthrow). This unlikely alliance had some success in a coup in February 6, 2015, which was preceded by the resignation of former President Hadi and his cabinet. Hadi later escaped from house arrest in Sana'a and fled to Aden, where he withdrew his resignation, condemned the Houthis, and declared Aden as the country's capital.[82]

By then the Houthis controlled military bases in *Ta'iz* in southwestern Yemen and were close to taking Aden when Hadi's calls for outside help resulted in airstrikes against the Houthis.[83] The conflict in Yemen has become an international conflict between external actors: Iran supports the Houthi Shi`ite rebels, and Saudi Arabia and its Sunni coalition (the Arab Gulf States, Egypt and Jordan) support the Sunni government of Abdrabbuh Mansur Hadi.

Thus, Yemen has become a warzone. As in Libya, Yemen has not yet moved toward significant national reconciliation; unlike Libya, however, the country has experienced the establishment of an extensive national dialogue.[84] Nonetheless, seven years on, many sociopolitical factors continue to affect Yemen. Only time and attention to the humanitarian crisis will tell the future for its 27 million people—approximately 46 percent of this population is under the age of fifteen, while an estimated 60 percent faced severe food shortages in 2017.[85]

Ironically, Saleh allied with the Houthis against the central Yemeni government, but then suddenly broke ties with the Houthis in December 2017. Two days later, he was killed. The air campaign led by Saudi Arabia and its allies since 2015 is aimed at restoring Hadi's government and defeating the Houthi rebels; it continues in 2018.

THE GULF STATES

Nearly forgotten as part of the Arab Spring story are the protests in Arab Gulf countries—namely, Gulf Cooperation Council (GCC) members Saudi Arabia, Kuwait, Bahrain, Qatar, Oman, and the United Arab Emirates, with Saudi Arabia being the undisputed hegemon among the GCC. Events in the Gulf were mostly left in the background as turbulent events in Tunisia, Egypt, Libya, and Syria dominated the headlines. It is for this reason that the protests and their response have been collectively dubbed 'The Silent Revolution' in academia and the media. Small protests emerged in the Gulf States during the weeks and months after revolutions arose elsewhere in the Arab world—any political dissent quieted quickly, however, and political structures there were mostly unaffected. Faced with these rising political challenges in early 2011, the Gulf States—Bahrain and Saudi Arabia in particular—mobilized sectarianism, played on their strong ties to the West, and utilized robust treasuries to suppress domestic calls for reform and appease the people.[86]

Before examining in more detail how the events and circumstances of the Arab Spring in the Gulf states were different from their neighbors in the region, it is important to understand the historical and cultural complexion of these states and the mitigating sociopolitical forces leading up to their 'Silent Revolution' after 2011. As will be explained later, by virtue of their distinguishing characteristics—predominantly as sectarian monarchies and hosting abundant oil resources, having strong ties to Western powers—the Gulf State governments and regimes reacted differently to the Arab Spring. This does not mean the plights and grievances of its peoples in the years leading up to the Arab Spring were altogether dissimilar from their Arab neighbors. In some cases, they also endured years or decades of discrimination, oppression, and economic degradation.

Of all the Gulf States, Bahrain experienced protests that were the most significant and received the most media attention. Events there reflected longstanding disparities between the Sunni ruling Al-Khalifa family and the Shi`ite-majority population. Religious identity played a part in the interplay of what led to the Gulf Arab Spring revolts in 2011, but geopolitics and socioeconomic concerns are equally important. Following independence from Great Britain in 1971, Sheikh Isa bin Salman bin Hamad al-Khalifa (d. 1999) established a National Assembly, but from the start its makeup and powers were limited. Ongoing nationalist and labor disagreements between the ruling family and its people continued through the 1980s. The government granted limited concessions, but political dissent was never tolerated as "state security courts operated without legal oversight, and torture was widespread."[87] This history of "alternating cycles of struggles and repression" describes the dissension and underlying instability that have formed a pattern in Bahraini politics since the country's founding.[88]

In the nineties, the Bahraini political scene revolved around constant calls for reform met by increasingly harsh crackdowns. A nonsectarian movement known as *al-Haraka al-Disturiyya* (the Constitutional Movement, or CM) emerged in 1994 and called for labor and constitutional reform, bringing Shi`ites, Sunnis, and various leftist parties together.[89] Upon the death of Sheikh Isa bin Salman bin Hamad al-Khalifa in 1999, Sheikh Hamad bin Isa Al Khalifa (b.1950, declared King in 2002) continued the ruling family's repression of any dissent and "consciously pushed the sectarian cards, attempting to foster divisions between Shi`ites and Sunnis, and accused regime opponents of being a fifth column backed by Iran."[90]

By 2010, youth demonstrations had sprouted across Bahrain, taking aim at the issues of discrimination, poverty, and political freedoms. A wave of arrests in August-September of that year detained hundreds of Bahraini activists; even though this repression was primarily intended to weaken opposition in the October 2010 election, an opposition party (the largest Shi`ite organization, al-Wifaq) won a plurality.[91] Thus, Bahrain was facing serious and longstanding challenges as the Arab Spring rounded the corner.

Historically speaking, Saudi Arabia also mobilized sectarianism and Islamism to oppress dissent and crush political opposition looking to relegate the power of the monarchy and liberalize the country. Furthermore, like Bahrain, Saudi Arabia was able to use its considerable economic resources like oil and advantageous relationships with the West to redistribute wealth, create an elaborate social welfare state, and subsequently check the political ambitions of the kingdom's citizens. Demonstrations existed and popular dissent certainly simmered, but this welfare state ultimately maintained stability: "Although Saudi Arabia had endured several episodes of domestic unrest in the previous thirty years, most notably in the aftermath of the 1991 Gulf War, when oil prices collapsed and social services were reduced, it had been mostly stable."[92] Thus, while Saudi citizens had long hoped for more political rights, they had been slow to challenge a system that, for the most part, satisfied their needs. This was the safety net and mindset that the Saudi government would retain as the Arab Spring approached.

Qatar, with the third largest liquefied natural gas reserves in the world after Russia and Iran, has invested for more than two decades in education, health, research, and infrastructure. This activity was ushered in by Sheikh Hamad bin Khalifa al-Thani (b. 1952) following the overthrow of his own father in a bloodless coup in 1995. According to Middle East Researcher Shelly Culbertson, "if we consider the Arab Spring broadly to include replacing ineffective governments with optimistic investments for the future, even outside of the 2011–2013 protests, then the Arab Spring in Qatar might have started twenty years ago, in 1995."[93] Enabled by its energy wealth, Qatar has changed faster and more significantly than almost any other country in history, largely for the better of its population. This has meant limited internal dissent over the years, especially because so much of its population immigrated to the country in the years after liberalization and did not have deeply-seeded grievances. Though opposition was quiet in the years leading up to the Arab Spring, some stones of discontent were overturned in Qatar during the uprisings.

Oman, Kuwait, and the United Arab Emirates have shown little or no social and political upheaval in the last two decades; thus protest movements following in the footsteps of other Arab Spring participants seemed unlikely. These countries, Oman especially, had been quite isolated from the political currents of the region and shared few elements in common with the other uprisings of the Arab Spring. Prior to the Arab Spring, the only recent point of contention in Oman is "what became known as the 'Green March' [that] began in the shadow of an impending transition to the unknown, with a public debate about an aging sultan who had no sons."[94] Even then, Omanis did not call for the removal of the sultanate, but rather protested for ending corruption, lowering inflation, and increasing social spending.

The level and scale of the Arab Spring protests in the Gulf initially differed from state to state. Demonstrations in Bahrain were occurring at the same time as events in Egypt, and groups demanding reform amassed in a large public square called the Pearl Roundabout in Bahrain's capital city of Manama. Over a hundred thousand Bahrainis protested against King Hamad bin Isa al-Khalifa; when measured in proportion to Bahrain's general population, that group of demonstrators was greater than the ones demonstrating in Egypt or Tunisia.[95] Given Bahrain's small size, in one overnight raid in February, 2011, state police violently removed all civilians from the square, resulting in several deaths and hundreds of injuries.[96] Limited demonstrations continued and, on March 14, GCC forces primarily composed of Saudi and UAE soldiers destroyed the Pearl Roundabout so that it would no longer serve as a symbol of hope or revolution. Protesters continued to battle security forces throughout the fall, but the regime never offered any serious concessions or promises. Strong backing from the United States, Great Britain, and Bahrain's GCC allies propped up the regime in the name of geopolitics and, as has been discussed several times already, stability in the region.

Protests in Saudi Arabia centered in the capital city of Riyadh and in the Eastern province. The Saudi government immediately shut down public demonstrations with uncompromising force, including killing some protesters.[97] In Oman, when thousands of civilians protested nonviolently for major political and economic reforms, Sultan Qaboos bin Said (b. 1940), who had been Oman's ruler since 1970, initially tolerated these demonstrations. When violent clashes occurred, he dispersed the crowds with unrelenting force. Protesters did not challenge the sultan's legitimacy or call for regime change; their demands focused on policy change within the Sultan's rule. Omanis' central demands called for more employment opportunities, a free press, an independent judiciary, and real power for Oman's legislative council.[98]

Qatar saw very few protests by its own civilians, and there were no loud public calls for a new government. Though the Arab Spring in Qatar was quiet, the government still took a conciliatory approach by throwing money at the problem: "In 2011, all Qatari national government employees (the vast majority of employed Qataris) were given a sixty percent raise, and the military and police received 120 percent raises."[99] The government also made small changes to assuage concerns about Qatari culture being marginalized by a massive influx of foreigners such as revoking liquor licenses and reinstating Arabic to balance out English-language dominance in schools.

"In Qatar, this was Arab Spring Light ... it was about small changes being made in response to popular sentiments." Though the Arab Spring was calm on the home front, the government did, under Emir Hamad bin Khalifa al-Thani, play a role in other Arab Spring movements. Qatar sent soldiers to Libya to fight against Gaddafi and funded rebels in both Syria and Libya.[101] Though other Gulf States show skepticism about Qatar's association with extremist groups, the state has been an important balancing force in the region and a mediator in previous international disputes. Emir Hamad transitioned power in a natural succession to his son Tamim bin Hamad al-Thani (b. 1980) in 2013.[102]

In Kuwait, protests continued for well over a year, resulting in Prime Minister Sheikh Nasser al-Muhammad Al Sabah's (b. 1940) removal and new parliamentary elections; ultimately these protests changed little about Emir Sabah al-Ahmad al-Jaber al-Sabah's (b. 1929) rule or Kuwait's deeper political structure.[103] In the UAE, revolutionary sentiment among the intellectual class left five men imprisoned, but public protest never took significant form.[104]

HOW THE GULF STATES CONTAINED THE ARAB SPRING

All of the Arab leaders thrown out during the Arab Spring, including Gaddafi in Libya, Mubarak in Egypt, and Ben Ali in Tunisia, belonged to republican military dictatorships. In the Gulf States, some argue, a ruling structure of royal monarchies has created circumstances in which populations are less likely to call for complete regime change. That was also true of Jordan and its ruling monarch, King Abdullah II. Due to the deep roots of Arab cultural history, royal monarchs in the Gulf differ from military dictators elsewhere in the region. Their loyalty structures are rooted deeply in tribal, clan, and family allegiances, which means their support base is stable.[105]

Another influential difference between the Gulf States and the region's other Arab nations involves the oil reservoirs that all Gulf nations have within their territories. This resource places the Gulf nations at the heart of the global oil market, and that translates into significant wealth trickling down into general Gulf society—something that is not true for other Arab nations. Gulf governments are more willing and able to fulfill a social contract with their populations because of oil money; they can provide their citizens with housing, jobs, and services that keeps enough of them above the levels of desperation that lead to prolonged social unrest.[106]

That responsiveness to their populations is also true of how Gulf governments have reacted to public dissent and demands for reform. In the Gulf States where Arab

Spring protests did occur, quick decisions were made to increase financial benefits to populations that helped lower revolutionary fervor. In Bahrain, the King used his nation's limited oil money to maintain loyalty networks through tribal affiliation.[107] The Saudi government gave its population economic handouts and services after silencing protests. These benefits to citizens amount to billions of dollars. Saudi Arabia's government also pledged to increase job opportunities; this was a common tactic among Gulf monarchies because unemployment served as a major point of anger among Arab Spring protesters.[108] In Oman, Sultan Qaboos promised fifty thousand new jobs; he let money flow to his people in the form of unemployment benefits and increased student stipends.[109] Sultan Qaboos also created an institution to regulate prices and gave power to a prosecution department more autonomous from his rule. All of these changes were the result of public demand.[110]

Another reason why the Arab Spring in the Gulf States was different from the rest of the region has to do with their strategic international importance. Military bases, including the US Navy's Fifth Fleet (based in Bahrain), are located in the Persian Gulf. More important, because many societies worldwide depend on oil extracted and shipped out from the Persian Gulf, any incidents of political unrest, revolution, and civil war in the Gulf would almost certainly impact global structures. For that reason, the Gulf States have received more support from international actors than did Syria, Egypt, Libya, and other states.[111]

One final tactic that the Gulf monarchies have used to avoid major political unrest involves manipulating the protest narratives with state-run media outlets. These outlets have revised the nature of the conflict as one existing between Sunni and Shi`ite sects, not a population united against a corrupt government. By inciting hate among easily identifiable groups, Gulf leaders have divided their populations, which is particularly true in Saudi Arabia and Bahrain. In Bahrain, between sixty and seventy percent of the population is Shi`ite, and the country's ruling family is Sunni. More important, Shi`ite citizens disproportionately make up the poorest and most exploited socioeconomic class.[112] For this reason, more Shi`ite Bahrainis called for government reforms than their Sunni compatriots during the Arab Spring. Rather than addressing the rational concerns of this majority of the country's population, the Bahraini government framed the predominantly Shi`ite protest groups as radical Shi`ite actors working with Iran to incite religious conflict. By transforming the story line, the king has distracted and divided his citizens and redirected their attention from calls for regime change to volatile tensions within the population.[113]

Though *al-Jazeera* is available in the Gulf, Saudi Arabia controls the media there and exerts major influence on how political stories are portrayed internationally. Most Gulf citizens, especially Shi'ites, have rational grievances against their political and economic systems, but these grievances have been obscured by Saudi TV and international media's portrayal of political dissent in Bahrain and other states as being based on sectarian tensions alone.[114] *Al-Jazeera's* coverage of the protests in Bahrain was more muted than coverage of protests elsewhere. Within this sectarian narrative, Gulf governments have the ability to treat predominantly Shi`ite protest groups as terrorist threats. They treat the situation militarily, which means that GCC troops have the ability to use force to repress all political dissent.[115] As long as Gulf leaders retain loyalty from a large enough sector of their populations using financial incentives, they retain their power.[116]

This divisive tactic poses dangerous implications for the region. By creating an enemy to distract political anger away from themselves, Gulf leaders are destroying the root impulses among the Arab people to bond and unite, which has been the Arab dream for centuries. The hatred that these monarchs willingly incite to stay in power is critically dangerous for the region's future. The rhetoric that these Gulf leaders use—which vilifies one sect and glorifies another—drives extremist Sunni thought in Syria, Libya, and elsewhere as well as extremist Shi`ite counter-ideology. In this way, sectarian conflict becomes a self-fulfilling prophecy. State-sponsored speech against Shi`ite populations can be used to stir up Sunni sentiment while also radicalizing disenfranchised Shi`ite actors.[117]

THE ARAB SPRING'S LEGACY

The Arab Spring shook the very foundations of the oppressive dictatorships and ruthless regimes that Arab leaders established to control their populations. In the spring of 2011, brewing dissent and frustration fused with a new sense of power and possibility and produced changes no one thought possible.

Who could imagine that Ben Ali would flee Tunisia within weeks of mass protests, Mubarak would be toppled a month later, and that Gaddafi would be dead by the year's end? The Arab Spring presented a blueprint for change in the region—a blueprint, unfortunately, that has not been fully realized. The sad reality is that many of the countries swept up in the demonstrations and protests are now worse off than before.

The protesters who fought and died for better governance, rule of law, and equality have not achieved lasting change; their reforms, for the most part, have not materialized. After winning a democratic and fair election, the Muslim Brotherhood was outlawed in Egypt, where one ruthless dictator has been replaced by another. There are no longer any protesters on the streets of Cairo or Bahrain—they have all been jailed or intimidated. Libya is a war zone. Yemen is a failed state. The Syrian refugee crisis is among the worst the world has ever known.

Certainly there was no roadmap for the protesters to follow. Despite the euphoria and sense of unity sparked by the protests, few groups had formulated concrete plans for governance. There was little or no consensus on what political and economic models should replace existing systems. Beyond calls for government reform and greater social justice, there was no magic cure-all for the ailing economies of the region. Every political party promised more jobs and higher wages, but none came close to developing a program with concrete, far-reaching economic policies. Well-meaning and even well-organized groups did not have a legacy of successful governance to help them. The path ahead may seem dim, but if the Arab Spring uprisings have succeeded in one area, it is that "they have helped to illuminate the profound challenges Arab societies face in the long journey toward civility and a better future." [118]

An Arab expression, *Kharaja al-Marid Min Al-Qumqum* ("the genie has left the bottle"), best explains the passions, visions, and hopes that the Arab Spring released in the region. The dreams and principles for which people risked their lives have not been forgotten, and they cannot be ignored or sequestered anymore. According to two polls conducted in 2016, when asked what they most want for their societies, Arabs prioritized good governance and freer political systems along with an end to corruption and economic reform. [119] Terrorism and regional security issues rank lower. People want good governance, the freedom to determine their own destinies, and to know that there will be opportunities for their families and their communities. Despotic regimes will not be able to get away with the decades of oppression that became the norm of the twentieth century because people know they have voices and that those voices can be heard.

For those who consider the Arab Spring a failure, it is worth bearing in mind what Alfred Stepan and Juan J. Linz wrote about upheavals in another part of the world: "Neither the Hungarian Revolution of 1956, the Prague Spring of 1968, nor Poland's Solidarity in 1981 succeeded in immediately creating a democracy. Yet each of these historic movements eroded forever the legitimacy of the dictatorial regime that it challenged." [120] The Arab Spring did just that: It destroyed the legitimacy of the Arab dictatorships. The Arab Spring made Arab leaders well aware that their brutal rule has repercussions and that such a repressive system of governing is unsustainable. They cannot trust that their people will passively submit anymore. The people have broken down the walls of fear and a long, obedient silence. When those walls collapse, they are gone forever.

———

CHAPTER TWELVE

Syrian Refugee Tragedy

SYRIA, A WELCOMING BEACON for refugees in the region since the Second World War, has now become the greatest producer of refugees scattered around the world. The Syrian people's current movements from their war-torn homeland to surrounding countries has few historical precedents. By far, it is producing the most profound impact of any mass migration today on the region and the international system: Its implications affect the entire world and extend far into the future.

In recent history, North Africa and the Middle East have become homes for Syrian populations displaced for a number of reasons—everything from dire economic conditions and political repression to complete warfare and the destruction of their homes. These refugees have long found safety in bordering states. Though migrant crises have impacted the region for decades, the Arab Spring has contributed to the most recent and alarming refugee movements in North Africa and the Middle East. The resulting population movements have created a crisis for the surrounding states, especially Jordan, Lebanon, and Turkey. Syrian refugees are deeply impacting these nations as well as other institutions across Europe and the rest of the Western world.

Syria is far from the only place in the region with a refugee crisis. Today, forced migrations are originating in a range of countries including Iraq, Libya, Sudan, and Yemen. But the Syrian refugee crisis attracts the most attention world-wide in part because of its civil war, which is among the most extreme militarized conflicts now taking place in the world. Massive migrations in the Arab world, however, are not a recent development. They were taking place long before the Arab Spring—in fact, historically, Syria has given refuge to many forced migrants from across the Arab world. To look at the current crisis requires context: This chapter addresses earlier migration issues in Syria, the situation since 2011, and its impact on neighboring countries as well as what is happening in Libya and Yemen. Taken together, these pieces give us a portrait of a region in turmoil and the tragic impact on millions of lives.

SYRIA: HAVEN OF THE DISPLACED

The land known today as the Syrian state belongs to a much larger area historically regarded as Greater Syria *(bilad al-sham)* or the Levant. After World War I, this expansive region was turned into colonial possessions of Britain and France after being divided into areas of control called *mandates*. France controlled Lebanon and Syria, while Britain controlled Palestine and the territory that would become Jordan. Today a cultural and social bond still exists among the Arab peoples in this region, reinforced by ongoing population movements that are taking place. Traditionally families have crossed borders to conduct business with each other and share cultural communications.

In this dynamic environment of interaction among the region's populations, Syria remained more politically and socially stable than its neighbors (until the Arab Spring), and that stability resulted in the country receiving several forced migrations, mainly from Lebanon, Palestine, and Iraq. After World War II, when leadership in these lands transferred from the former colonial powers to nationalist leaders, internal strife, sectarian division, and political conflict in Palestine, Lebanon, and Iraq significantly impacted and displaced civilian populations of these neighboring countries, and other minorities. For them, Syria offered better opportunities for their lives and futures in the decades leading up to the Arab Spring.

Wars in 1948 and 1967 forced major populations to move from the West Bank and Gaza to Syria. After Syria lost the Golan Heights in 1967, Syrians living there migrated to Damascus and other Syrian cities, creating a large wave of Syrian refugees in their own country. Prior to 1967, the Golan had a population of approximately 130,000 Syrians living in more than one hundred small villages and dozens of farms. Other more recent examples of refugees flowing into Syria include the aftermaths of the invasion of Iraq in 2003 and the Lebanese-Israeli war in 2006, which destroyed both Iraqi and Lebanese communities and pushed many of their inhabitants into Syria. For the most part, these refugees and others from neighboring countries successfully resettled and integrated into Syrian society. In her book *Iraqi Migrants in Syria: The Crisis Before the Storm*, Sophia Hoffmann writes of the country's historical acceptance of foreign refugees in Damascus and other Syrian towns and cities,[1] Hoffmann explains, "as long as they maintained the essential red lines of public loyalty to the government." If refugees would observe these lines, she adds, "they enjoyed substantial freedoms to reside, work, and thrive, despite the absence of official papers (163)."[2]

THE END OF SYRIAN OPENNESS

Syria's history of welcoming refugees ended after the Arab Spring. What began in 2011 as a popular revolution continues today as a civil war waged in both the countryside and cities. For Iraqi refugees living in Syria for a decade, the civil war has spelled "an end to the safe haven … most were forced to migrate further or to return to an unstable and dangerous Iraq—when in 2013 the conflict escalated in Iraq's northeast, thousands of Iraqis again crossed into war-torn Syria."[3] It is no different for Lebanese and Palestinian refugees there who are being displaced again. The Syrian civil war, in fact, has re-displaced more than 80 percent of these Palestinian refugees.[4]

As for the Syrian people themselves, the civil war creates lasting destruction. After the Syrian population's uprising, President Bashar al-Assad retaliated with the might of the national army and suppressed his own people. As of the publication of this book, Assad still clings to power, and his actions have forced the opposition to mount a militarized response. As part of his repression, the Syrian government has killed, imprisoned, and chased into exile thousands of citizens in targeted operations. There is nowhere to escape: For some, the government's destruction of entire neighborhoods has forced populations to leave collectively and become refugees.[5]

Today more than half of Syria's pre-war population has been displaced. The United Nations High Commission for Refugees (UNHCR) officially counts more than five million Syrian refugees abroad—along with more than six million Syrians internally displaced within their country. Together, this amounts to a displacement of more than eleven million of Syria's pre-war twenty-one million inhabitants.[6] UNHCR statistics only record those Syrians who officially register with the international organization upon arriving in an asylum country: Realistically, the majority of fleeing Syrians probably do not register with the UNHCR. Thus the actual number of Syrian refugees around the world is likely much higher than what has been officially recorded.

"As the promise of the Arab Spring metastasized gradually into a bloody civil war," writes mass-displacement scholar Tahir Zaman, "Syrians caught in the cross-hairs of the conflict have been compelled to confront key ontological and existential questions on a daily basis."[7] For those Syrians whom the UNHCR documents as refugees, humanitarian resources are available: In Jordan, for example, hundreds of thousands of registered Syrian refugees live in designated refugee camps constructed by the national government and the UNHCR. But aside from these, many neither live in refugee camps nor are documented by any international aid groups. Instead they enter foreign towns and cities to look for work, food, and housing independently or, if they are lucky, with family and friends.

But there is little luck in the experiences of most Syrian refugees—most experience horror and tragedy in their attempts to flee from the violence and destruction. Many asylum-seekers never reach a destination: They get caught in war zones, die while being smuggled out of the country, or fall into the hands of exploitative traffickers and extremist groups. The refugees who do succeed in resettling in foreign countries may find help with relatives and friends—the truth is, however, many of these refugees become homeless and unemployed in their struggle to survive in foreign communities.[8]

Syrian children are one of the groups suffering the most from war and upheaval. More than half of today's Syrian refugees are under the age of eighteen: These children have lost parents, siblings, and friends and witnessed the destruction of their homes, schools, and communities by warfare. There are children who have gone years without any consistent education, and the psychosocial impact of these circumstances is expected to affect practically an entire generation.[9]

TENSIONS AMONG SYRIA'S NEIGHBORS

The impact of Syrian refugees on European states and institutions is certainly significant, but the circumstances are gravest for Syria's neighbors. Syria shares long borders with Turkey to the north, Lebanon to the west, and Jordan to the south—the vast majority of today's Syrian migrants live in these three bordering nations. Each country hosts higher numbers of Syrians than are found in all of Europe.[10]

A nation hosting such large refugee populations accepts an extra burden on its economic, infrastructural, political, and social systems. For Syrian refugees, that situation is particularly severe in Jordan, Lebanon, and other nations where these systems are already weak.[11] But the systems themselves aren't the only things feeling the strain. Migrants who attempt to integrate into urban society also compete against the lowest socio-economic class of citizens for low-income housing and unskilled jobs—for this reason, tension also erupts between refugee and local populations as they compete for the same resources.[12]

THE SITUATION IN TURKEY

For Turkey, the Syrian refugee situation has been especially significant. The southern Turkish border is the top destination of countless Syrians fleeing from the civil war—more than three million Syrians have crossed into Turkey since 2011.[13] Though many refugees use Turkey as a transit route into Europe, others have decided to settle there. One quarter of Syrian migrants in Turkey today reside in large urban areas such as Istanbul (about 360,000 Syrians) and Izmir (83,000).[14] In smaller towns near the country's southern and eastern borders, Syrian migrants account for between 10 and 20 percent of the local population.[15] This has produced a noticeable effect on Turkey's demographic composition—Syrian migrants already account for nearly 4 percent of Turkey's population of 78.8 million.[16]

The country's immigration policy is relatively generous to refugees: They are able to apply for Turkish citizenship after only five years in the country. That means that Syrians who crossed into Turkey during the Syrian civil war's first years are already eligible to become naturalized Turkish citizens. These demographic changes are having another result as well: a deepening of political divisions over immigration, as there are several opposition parties that do not support foreign migration into Turkey.[17]

The refugee experience in Turkey has resulted in the creation of a semi-coordinated network of international, government-sponsored, and private organizations that provide humanitarian aid to Syrians living in Turkey, especially those near the Syrian border. The network, which is "unruly, complex, and highly contested,"[18] creates cross-border movements of people and products and exists alongside a local smuggling economy. Local traffickers, some of whom are more exploitative of migrants than others, join (or compete with) internationally-funded humanitarian actors to provide services and necessities for migrants.

Tahir Zaman explains the dynamic between humanitarian support and local trafficking economies this way: "In otherwise forgotten border towns such as Kilis and Reyhanli, where until very recently the mainstay of the local economy had been the movement of contraband—cigarettes and diesel fuel—humanitarian actors have set up operations directing food, clothing, and medical supplies across the border. On the Syrian side of the border, erstwhile smugglers in similar local economies (now re-branded as militias) have trained their attention and focus on imposing and levying control over humanitarian supplies into towns and camps where the internally displaced have gravitated toward."[19]

The refugee crisis has given the Turkish government, which wants to join the EU, a bargaining chip with European countries. Turkey is home to many Syrian migrants who do not wish to stay in Turkey: They want to go into Europe and resettle there in the long term. As the major transit area between Syria and Europe, Turkey exerts control over how many Syrian migrants enter Europe. It is important for Europe that Turkey's borders, especially routes from the Turkish coast across the Mediterranean into Greece, remain tight: European organizations need cooperation from the Turkish government to control the flow of refugees. The number of migrants continues to grow in Turkey and, as it does, it imposes a heavier strain on national structures. That situation could be addressed in a simple way: The Turkish government could relax its borders and tacitly allow many of these refugees to flow out of Turkey and into Europe.

LEBANON: THE PRICE OF HOSPITALITY

Bordered by Syria to the north and east, and Israel to the south, Lebanon has a population of roughly six million, which includes approximately 1.5 million Syrians displaced by civil war. These refugees account for a quarter of the country's people—the highest per-capita refugee population of any country in the world. Historically Lebanon has welcomed many—the country serves as home to hundreds of thousands of displaced Palestinians accepted in the past several decades. Its political structure faces many challenges: For years, the government has been deadlocked, and that has made it difficult to address direct aid to its Syrian refugees as well as deeper challenges within the systems that support its population.[20]

Syrian migration has increased the country's pre-existing income inequalities and put further strains on financial, social, and political structures. To survive, Syrians find work in informal and undocumented labor markets, which pay low wages and exploit refugees. While Syrians must take advantage of desperate opportunities to survive, growing low-wage Syrian labor displaces low-income Lebanese citizens for jobs. Since 2011, two hundred thousand Lebanese citizens have dropped into poverty, and three hundred thousand are unemployed.[21] Currently at least 20 percent of Lebanese nationals are unemployed, due in large part to the labor force growing by 50 percent since the beginning of the Syrian civil war. This desperation forces many refugee children to find ways to contribute to their families, ranging from street begging to child marriage and involvement with violent extremist groups.[22]

The migrant crisis has profoundly impacted Lebanon's public health sector as well: Syrian health needs result in overflowing facilities, undersupplied resources, and unrealistic demand for medical professionals and services. Diseases like tuberculosis are becoming more common, and water pollution due to waste from human settlements has increased by 33 percent during this time.[23]

The Lebanese government reaffirms that it will not close borders to Syrian neighbors fleeing war; however, every national sector is impacted by the extreme population growth and widespread need. There are no formal refugee camps for Syrians in Lebanon, and many refugees live in abandoned buildings and in tented settlements.[24] As the crisis drags on and weighs down the daily lives and social structures of the Lebanese population, local sentiment grows against refugees and migrants.[25]

JORDAN: A DIFFICULT AND DELICATE BALANCE

With a long history of accepting refugees, Jordan today hosts nearly 1.5 million Syrian inhabitants—but only about half of these are registered officially as refugees with the UNHCR. For much of its modern statehood Jordan has provided resettlement to Palestinian and Iraqi refugees—today's Syrian migrants add to this group, which accounts for more than a quarter of Jordan's total population.[26] During the Syrian civil war's first years, the rate of refugee flow across Jordan's border was highest—the Jordanian government now controls its border much more strictly, and few people move freely between Syria and Jordan.[27]

Today Jordan serves as the home of three official refugee camps. These camps assist UNHCR-registered refugees and primarily operate in the country's northern region, close to Syria's border. Two additional settlements along the border are the result of Syrian refugees being denied mass entry into Jordan. The first and largest of these is Zaatari, which opened in 2012 and is home to some 80,000 Syrians (half of which are children).[28] Because of government policies that have tightened up Jordanian borders, Zaatari is no longer growing as rapidly as it once was—at its height, Zaatari hosted 125,000 refugees, and as many as half a million people have likely passed through this camp.

The Jordanian government has intended Zaatari and all refugee camps as temporary settlements hosting refugees until they can return home—the reality is, Zaatari is transforming into a semi-permanent city and will likely remain when Syria's war is over. Many refugees are finding employment today in the clusters of small shops set up in the camp's marketplace area. This local economy is innovative—the camp's residents have created a special community that allows them to live with dignity and a measure of self-sustainability.[30]

Compared with Zaatari, Jordan's smallest refugee camp is Mrajeeb al-Fhood, which opened in 2013 near the Jordanian city of Zarqa. Located between the Azraq and Zaatari camps, Mrajeeb al-Fhood's purpose is to absorb overflow refugees from the larger camps. With its current population of more than 7,000,[31] this camp is different from Jordan's other refugee camps because it is funded and run by the United Arab Emirates, not by the United Nations and the UNHCR. As a result, the inhabitants of Mrajeeb al-Fhood have enjoyed better resources such as housing, food, and lighting.[32]

Mentioned above, the Azraq camp was opened in 2014 and is located about one hundred kilometers to the east of Amman. More than 50,000 Syrians live there—as is true of other camps, more than half of Azraq's population is under the age of eighteen. Azraq is also home to an important project that has been made possible by international funders: a field of solar panels built on land near the camp.

This project has allowed almost half of Azraq's inhabitants to have access to sustainable, renewable energy. The camp's current plan is to double the size of the solar field, which will create enough electricity for the entire camp. Azraq refugees receive about twenty-eight dollars each month in humanitarian assistance to buy food, and the camp's primary and secondary schools aim to educate every child—today educational facilities in Azraq enroll more than ten thousand children. The camp also has three primary health care centers and one secondary health care center operating twenty-four hours a day.[33]

The circumstances in Jordan's informal refugee camps is very different: They are in the midst of deep struggles. These camps, which are *not* officially designated by the UNHCR, are generally considered inaccessible to international humanitarian efforts. As mentioned earlier, the creation of these settlements is the result of Jordan's denying entry to fewer migrants at pre-existing border crossings. When that happens, these rejected groups set up makeshift settlements right there at the border-crossing rather than turn back to war-torn Syria. As more of these migrants have flocked to the border, these de facto camps have grown.

An example of the informal refugee camps is al-Rukban, which is named after a no-man's-land area in the east. Al-Rukban is a former border crossing, and refugees were trapped there when Jordan closed its borders. Some 80,000 refugees live in a tented settlement—it is a population as large as the one in Zaatari—but because of border restrictions, humanitarian aid groups are struggling to help them. Jordan's "movement bans" that keep numbers low are intended to control *da'ish* (ISIS) members from entering the country—as many as four thousand (about 5 percent) of al-Rukban's current inhabitants fit this category and belong to militant gangs. These gangs have access to all sorts of weapons, including anti-aircraft machines, and gun battles are common and take place throughout al-Rukban's makeshift streets even as refugees there are struggling to survive.[34, 35] Some within the international community have criticized Jordan's King Abdullah II for keeping these refugee communities outside of Jordan along its northern border. "Part of the problem," King Abdullah II has explained to Western media outlets, is that "they come from the north of Syria, from Raqqa and Hasakah—and Hasakah is the heartland of where ISIS is, as we know that there are ISIS members inside those camps."[36] The number of refugees vetted there, the king continues, is "about fifty to one hundred every day, and we do have our government, our military, and our hospitals, as well as NGOs on the other side looking after them."[37]

But the majority of Syrian refugees do not live even in these camps: Instead, they travel directly to Jordanian cities and attempt to integrate there with the civilian populations. The Jordanian government is not bound to provide them with housing, employment opportunities, public education, or even freedom of movement. Without a legal right to work in Jordan, these refugees do not have access to self-sustaining livelihoods and face homelessness and illegal labor markets. More than three-quarters of Jordan's Syrian refugees are living this way throughout the three northern municipalities of Amman, Irbid, and Mafraq—their attempts to integrate with local populations results in competition for jobs and other resources with the poorest in pre-existing Jordanian communities.[38]

The same structural challenges hampering other refugee-accepting nations in the Middle East also hamper Jordan. The needs of refugee populations exacerbate pre-existing issues involving public education, infrastructure, healthcare, employment, and marginalization of rural communities.[39] Syrian migrants objectively increase job competition, especially in informal labor markets, and overflow the housing infrastructure, physical resources, and other public services such as medical care and education. Jordan's territory is resource-poor, especially with respect to water, and unlike oil-extracting neighbors Jordan has limited internal revenue sources. Regionally Jordan has remained stable in part due to extensive and sustained aid from Western governments and international institutions. Jordan's systems of social services, employment, infrastructure, and macroeconomics have faced challenges in supporting Jordanian citizens alone—now, with larger migrant populations, these structures are being pushed to an existential crisis point.

Because Syrians cannot legally work in Jordan, widespread unemployment has been a central characteristic of the migrant crisis there. An estimated 160,000 Syrians work in Jordan's informal job sector, which includes agricultural labor and construction. Syrians willing to do work that is undocumented and underpaid tend to displace the poorest, most vulnerable Jordanians who might have been considered for these jobs. The International Labor Organization (ILO) estimates that the initial years of the migrant crisis saw Jordanian unemployment rise from 14.5 percent to 22 percent. This has resulted in growing tensions among refugees and Jordanians angered that jobs are being taken away from them. The ILO reports that 98 percent of Jordanians believe Syrian migrants are taking away jobs, while 85 percent believe that Syrians should not be allowed to freely enter into Jordan at all—many believe that Syrians should stay in the camps and not compete with them for jobs, housing, and other resources.[40]

With a scarcity of low-income housing already, rents are increasing by an average of three times in Jordan's six northern municipalities as a result of housing competition between locals and refugees. In the Jordanian towns of Mafraq and Ramtha, which both have very high populations of refugees, rent has increased by as much as six times the average rate. These conditions are detrimental not only to refugees but to pre-existing populations as well. For those Syrian refugees who cannot find or afford housing in this environment of accelerated rents, many choose to live in semi-homeless conditions instead. Those who do manage to afford the rents and settle in homes aggravate the situation by displacing many poor Jordanians.[41] The same problems and displacements in housing are true of public education in Jordan—more than half of all Syrian refugees are under the age of eighteen. As public schools have tried to accommodate the needs of incoming Syrian children, they have become vastly overcrowded and double-shifted.[42]

In the area of healthcare, Jordan once held optimistic development goals for its system—but these now seem far out of reach because of the ways that dramatic population increases have overflowed hospitals and medical clinics. Jordan's healthcare sector made major developments before the refugee crisis—every Jordanian citizen had access to public medical care. In the first years of Syria's refugee crisis, the Jordanian government gave subsidized public medical care to all Syrian migrants—but by 2014, Jordan revoked this policy because its healthcare system was being overwhelmed. Overcrowded public health centers impacts most Jordanian citizens because it forces them to seek quality medical care at private hospitals, which are less accessible and more expensive. Tuberculosis, polio, and measles, all of which were previously eradicated in Jordan, have started to reemerge since the arrival of Syrian migrants. For this reason, supplying vaccinations to incoming Syrians has been a high priority and a true test of the country's health service structures.[43]

Along with jobs, housing, education, and healthcare, Jordan's equilibrium in the region is affected by its environmental circumstances. As one of the world's most water-scarce countries, Jordan's per-capita annual water level is at about a tenth of what the World Bank estimates to be stable and sustainable. The country's water comes from subsurface aquifers, which are extracted twice as fast as they can be naturally replenished. The country's growing population is adding extreme pressures to this situation—refugees often concentrate in areas with poor water infrastructure and supply systems. In response to the country's refugees and water needs, the Minister of Water and Irrigation recently issued a statement that "we are now at the edge of moving from a chronic water problem into a water crisis: the element that will trigger this movement is the number of Syrian refugees."[44]

Understandably, the migrant crisis in Jordan has become a divisive political topic, too. Initially, the arrival of Syrian refugees actually helped to calm Jordan's own Arab Spring protests in 2011. Accommodating new migrant populations became a political priority that distracted from any calls for regime change—the Syrian refugee crisis also served as a warning to Jordanian citizens about what happens when revolutions and protests fail.[45] In addition, as the refugee crisis grew, faulting the government alone for the country's challenges was problematic—Syrian migrants initially served as scapegoats who drew blame away from the Jordanian government for the country's problems. Now, today, Jordanian citizens are putting the blame squarely on both migrants and the government.[46]

In spite of the challenges posed by refugees, the government still shows a willingness to support them with other channels of support. Jordan relies on international assistance to support not only its own population but also the added responsibility of over a million new migrants.[47] The impact of the Syrian crisis on Jordan's national government is well over two billion dollars. Foreign aid to Jordan amounts annually to about one billion dollars, mostly from the United States: This money supports many national operations in the country. Even with this assistance, however, Jordan's plans for sustainable development that integrates migrant populations are chronically underfunded.[48]

OTHER MIGRANT CRISES

Although the focus of this chapter is the Syrian situation, refugee crises elsewhere in the region are having a significant impact in Europe and around the world. Syria may represent the most devastating forced migration in today's world, but the refugee crises of Libya and Yemen are resonating across the Middle East and North Africa as well.

THE LIBYAN FUNNEL

Since the beginning of the Arab Spring protests, Libya has hosted as many as a million internally displaced people. Today, about a quarter of a million internally displaced individuals remain in Libya. After the Libyan people removed President Mu`ammar Gaddafi (d. 2011), Libya slid into a civil war, and today stability remains an elusive, impossible goal.[49] It is estimated that between one and two million Libyans live outside of Libya, but very few are officially registered as refugees.[50]

Since the Libyan revolution and Gaddafi's death, the nation has struggled to unite under a new government, and today the country remains a chaotic and uncertain place torn by civil war. The country has become a smuggling and trafficking epicenter because the central authority (such as it is) is unable to enforce its borders. Weapons, migrant workers, refugees, and militias are all in transit across open borders—enormous flows of migrants from sub-Saharan African nations are moving through Libya in an attempt to get to Europe. Most of these migrants come from Somalia, Sudan, and Eritrea, although the migrant flow also represents several other countries that intermix as they funnel through Libya to Europe.[51]

Movement through Libya is dangerous. As many as 4 percent of the migrant population is currently detained—tens of thousands are held either in Tripoli government facilities or in illegal detention centers that have been created by traffickers and militias. This disorder has created lucrative economic opportunities for smugglers and organized crime groups on both sides of the Mediterranean to exploit desperate migrants. Migrants in Libya are sold on illegal markets for ransom and forced labor, and are physically and sexually abused.[52]

The International Organization for Migration (IOM) estimates that in addition to internally displaced Libyans, more than three-quarters of a million migrants from other African countries live in Libya—this is equal to 12 percent of Libya's prewar population.[53] Other sources say that it is likely that more than a million migrants and refugees from sub-Saharan nations currently live in Libya—most of these have Europe as their hopeful destination and seize the opportunity presented by chaos, anarchy, and unmonitored borders to pass from the northern coast to the southern shores of Italy.[54] These activities lead to countless potential tragedies. In a single boat headed for Italy, hundreds of intermixed migrants who began their journeys across Africa, Asia, and the Arab world finally crowd themselves for a perilous sea crossing that could drown every person aboard. A reported one out of forty migrants en route across the Mediterranean died in 2016, although the true number of fatalities is likely much higher than officially documented.[55]

European institutions rely upon the cooperation of Libyan authorities to restrict the number of people arriving in southern Europe or perishing at sea. Since the beginning of the civil war, though, Libya has not had many stable and capable institutions to effectively control this situation—the country's borders remain open and uncontrolled.[56] Faced with uncertainty and destruction at home, refugees are willing to pay any price and risk everything—even their lives—for the promise of better lives in Europe.

CHAOS IN YEMEN

Like Libya, Yemen is gripped in a civil war that is causing lasting problems—clashes between the government and various rebel coalitions have forced Yemenis from their homes and towns. Naval and land blockades have been in place since the civil war's beginning: the Yemeni people are trapped and about 3.1 million civilians are internally displaced.[57] These displacements are concentrated in the country's northern region where the government and its Sunni coalitions (Saudi Arabia and the Arab Gulf States in addition to Egypt and Jordan) continue to launch airstrikes against the Shi`ite Houthi rebels (a major anti-government opposition supported by Iran). Civilian displacements created by government-military efforts are creating an endless cycle of anger, discontent, more violence, and more displacements. Another cause of displacement and unrest is an environmental issue: Yemen's water scarcity is even more severe than in Jordan. This had led to sociopolitical unrest that is harming Yemeni society in profound ways.[58]

Historically, Yemen has served as a welcome destination for large numbers of refugees and migrants from the Horn of Africa. Even after the current civil war began, Yemen continued to host hundreds of thousands of refugees and migrants, nearly all from Somalia. Yemen also happens to be a transit state for East Africans moving toward the lucrative Gulf States in search of low-skill jobs in the oil industry. About one hundred thousand people per year cross the Gulf of Aden from the Horn of Africa to Yemen in crowded boats. These migrants rely on dangerous and illegal human smuggling systems that subject individuals to assault, trauma, and mistreatment. The UNHCR supports Non-Governmental Organizations (NGOs) that receive and rescue boatloads of migrants traveling this route to Yemen.[59] For these African migrants, Yemen served as a place with more safety and economic opportunity than their home nations; today, the situation has reversed—Yemen is now one of the international community's most unstable and dangerous countries.

EUROPEAN PATHWAYS AND OBSTACLES

The European Union (EU) is a twenty-eight-member union of European countries that is based upon economic and political cooperation. Nearly all EU countries (and some non-EU European states) belong to what is called the Schengen Area, a zone where twenty-six European countries acknowledge open borders with other member nations and where most travelers can move freely from one Schengen country to another without a passport. This cooperative system allows travelers to move easily throughout Europe, but not without consequences: The system has also struggled to control millions of Arab and African migrants entering Europe from the south and hoping to cross into central and northern Europe.

Nearly all migrants from the Middle East and North Africa pass through Europe's Mediterranean-bordering states first. Greece is the first of these to receive most Arab migrants, especially Syrians. The Greek coastline is close to both the coasts of Turkey and Syria, and thousands of migrants arrive daily on boats and makeshift rafts after a journey that has taken them through Turkey and across the Aegean Sea. The EU exerts pressure on Greece to monitor its borders closely, but migrants overflow the nation's ability to register every refugee and enter Greece from Turkey with relative ease.[60]

Macedonia, to Greece's north, accepts far fewer foreign migrants. The government ordered the construction of a razor-wire fence along the Gevgelija-Idomeni border crossing from Greece—in doing this they have blocked a major route from Greece to the north. In desperation and in protest, thousands of Syrians and other refugees have camped along this fence, and tension is understandably high between migrants and the national authorities.[61]

Hungary is another crucial passageway for those traveling toward northern EU countries. Hungary's Prime Minister Viktor Orbán (b. 1963) opposes important EU policies allowing displaced Arabs to have a safe haven in Europe. Orbán, like other national conservative politicians in Europe, is concerned not only about the socioeconomic strain brought on by accepting immigrants—he also expresses a xenophobic fear that Arab immigrants and Islam in particular are disruptive to Europe's Christian heritage. Hungary has not accepted the EU plan to distribute 160,000 migrants from southern Europe across EU countries. Like Macedonia, the Hungarian government has physically fortified its borders, including the use of water cannons and tear gas in clashes with refugees at the border.[62] Many Hungarians support their government's strict immigration stance.

Refugees who manage to pass through Hungary—in spite of the challenges and obstacles—continue into Austria on their way to southern Germany. Because so many migrants are in transit through Austria, the government practices an emergency protocol for border identification checks that results in large groups of migrants at various transit hubs. Besides creating tighter security on public transportation for all Europeans, this situation creates overall congestion in the normally easy-to-travel zones of the Schengen Area. In 2016, Austria was accepting a daily maximum of eighty asylum applications and 3,200 migrants in transit through the country at once.[63]

Germany lies at the heart of Europe's refugee crisis. The country is a top destination for migrants and home to more than one million asylum-seekers from the Arab world—Germany is also a leader within the EU and holds power in shaping important migration policies for all EU countries. The refugees whom Germany already hosts put a strain on local authorities and housing infrastructures—the German government, international institutions, and NGOs all work together to set up emergency camps and supply basic services. German Chancellor Angela Merkel is a leading European political voice who affirms Europe's responsibility to embrace refugee populations: She has made it clear that Germany will continue to accept and support genuine refugees inside its borders.[64] "Many refugees have terrible tales to tell of human smuggling and trafficking in human beings," Merkel has said, "states thus have to work together, we have to create legal options for movement and must not permit people to make money from the suffering of others."[65] Many Germans support Merkel's generous migration stance—they urge other EU nations to shoulder some of the weight of the refugee crisis by accepting migrants redistributed from France, Italy, Greece, and other Mediterranean states. Other political parties oppose Merkel, irrationally fearing the "Islamization of Europe" and blaming migrants for national challenges and problems. What is happening in host countries in the Middle East is true in Europe: Fear and tension is high in these countries, especially in Germany after several recent terror attacks—xenophobic German groups have retaliated by attacking hostels and deserted buildings that are being used to house refugees.[66]

During the Arab Spring's first years, Italy received more incoming migrants from the Arab world than even Greece. As mentioned earlier, many of these migrants to Italy consisted of refugees from Libya and other Arab-African states as well as other sub-Saharan African states. Similar to the sea route from Turkey to Greece, crossings from the North African coastline into Italy on overcrowded dinghies and rafts have resulted in many deaths at sea. Italy, a nation bearing the heaviest burden of the migration crisis, uses facilities on the islands of Lampedusa and Sicily to receive them. For this reason Italy has joined with Germany, France, Greece, and other high-refugee EU nations in calling for the European states to accept plans for dispersing refugees across the EU.[67]

France is a major transit point for migrants from North Africa and Italy with a goal of reaching the United Kingdom. These refugees live in temporary tented settlements for months (even years) along France's northern coast as they wait and hope to cross the English Channel. Many of these refugees originated in sub-Saharan Africa and North Africa rather than Syria—it was the pressure of these waiting migrants that decisively influenced Britain's decision to leave the EU. Conditions are changing in France as well: Since the 2015 Paris attacks, the country has tightened up its border control and urged other nations to do the same.

Xenophobia and anti-immigration sentiments are playing a divisive role in France as they are in other parts of Europe. There is grave concern there over easy travel and access through the zones of the Schengen Area: In fact, two Paris attack suspects traveled into France after arriving in Greece from Turkey. One of the leading voices of anti-immigration and anti-EU sentiment in France is Marine Le Pen of the National Front Party. A major candidate in the 2017 French presidential election, Le Pen advocated a hardline anti-immigration and anti-EU platform influenced by public fear of Arab and Muslim populations. She saw the French election as a choice between "a multicultural society, following the model of the English-speaking world, where fundamental Islam is progressing and we see major religious claims, or ... an independent nation, with people able to control their own destiny."[68] Le Pen ultimately lost the election to a centrist candidate, Emmanuel Macron (b. 1977), who reaffirms France's commitment not only to the EU, but also to the duty of accepting asylum-seekers.

European populations, governments, and institutions are in disagreement over how to deal with the migration crisis. Some understand Europe's moral responsibility and necessity to embrace populations fleeing their homelands despite the strains on structures and resources. Others fear the impact of these refugees and are calling for a closure of the borders. These conflicting views, note immigration scholars Andrew Geddes and Peter Scholten, reflect ideological divisions in local populations: "For many people these changes are viewed as positive and as providing economic, social and cultural enrichment. For others they are viewed more negatively as a cost and burden (2)."[69] This divide leads to tension within the EU and affects major political elections and national policy across Europe.

To rally support during election cycles, some national conservative politicians rely on a narrative that portrays immigrants, especially Arab-Muslim ones, as detrimental to Western society. France's Le Pen and her party are one example: another is the UK's vote to withdraw from the EU—which is a landmark example of policy influenced by public opposition to Arab migration into Europe. Political figures across Europe fear both the structural burden of refugees as well as their cultural differences. In many elections across Europe, in fact, Dutch, French, and German candidates have tried to appeal to voters by prioritizing border closures and opposition to foreign asylum-seekers. Though centrist candidates committed to accepting refugees were ultimately victorious over these candidates in recent elections, immigration will remain among the most divisive topics within European political institutions for years to come.

SYRIA'S "LOST GENERATION"

In every refugee crisis, children are among the groups that suffer most. In Syria's civil war, for example, more than half of its displaced population is under the age of eighteen, and about half of these are even younger—under the age of eleven. Consider another statistic that is even more dramatic: that about three million Syrians are under the age of six, which means their entire lives have been lived in the shadow of the civil war as refugees.[70] The struggles of these children were brought to new international prominence partly because of a photo showing the body of a dead Syrian infant that washed up on a Turkish beach. The child fell from an overcrowded boat of refugees headed for Greece. That photo does not represent an isolated incident but an experience tragically common for many refugee families.

In the longer term, the Syrian civil war is creating what some refer to as "a lost generation of refugees—even for children who survive warfare and dangerous journeys, the refugee experience cuts deep in their lives. Toxic stress and the psychosocial complications of these traumatic formative years may affect them for years to come."[71] The deepest implication for this generation of children, however, is the lack of a stable educational experience which "is creating an education crisis— a lost generation of children without education across multiple countries of the Middle East."[72] These children are missing out on crucial years of primary and secondary education: Half of them are no longer in school, while public education systems in high-refugee states like Lebanon and Jordan are struggling to accept many others. In Lebanon, for example, the public education system can only accept about a third of Syrian refugee children.[73] Even for refugees admitted into public education classrooms, access is not steady. Shelly Culbertson and Louay Constant explain that "while Lebanon, Turkey, and Jordan all set policies that enable Syrian refugees to have access to public education, enrollment is low and actual attendance is unknown. Many children have been out of school for several years because after their education was interrupted in Syria, a lack of stable access in the host countries followed."[74] Educating Syrian refugees also proves difficult because educational access and quality are at odds with one another. Rapid changes to education structures to accommodate new refugee students are burdensome. In Culbertson and Constant's assessment, "accommodating the education needs of a large number of refugees has posed challenges to the quality of education, for both citizens and refugees, as resources are strained, classrooms become more crowded, and public education systems struggle to keep up."[75]

The lack of education among Syrian youth poses ominous implications for the country's post-war future. To rebuild its social and economic fabric, the Syrian state will need young professionals and skilled vocational workers. That pool of workers and the country's future, Culbertson and Constant explain, "will depend on ensuring that school-age children receive the education they need to be resilient to the circumstances they face and to develop the capability to provide for themselves and their families. Lacking the protective environment of education, development of critical thinking skills, and the opportunities that result from education also could make more youths vulnerable to the recruitment of radical groups."[76]

In other words, when Syria finally does emerge from war and regains an element of stability, it may lack a young generation strong and capable enough of rebuilding its society—too many of these children have spent their formative childhood and adolescent years caught between nations in an existential struggle to survive.

IS THERE A SOLUTION TO THE SYRIAN CRISIS?

Long-term answers to this question lie, ultimately, in creating the conditions for a stable society in Syria and in strengthening the public structures in neighboring states to support Syrians who will likely never return home. Humanitarian organizations and NGOs can help by giving direct aid to the refugees, but the root of the situation—and its solution—exists on a much deeper level.

Direct humanitarian aid is essential in the short term, but sequestering refugees in camps and making them rely on resources from NGOs and international institutions without developing their own capacities for post-refugee life is dangerous—that is why the re-integration of refugees into society is essential. Within all asylum countries, giving refugees the authorization to work and giving refugee children access to education must become priorities.

But that is only the beginning—in Turkey, for instance, Syrians are now able to work but have little training in vocational and professional work or in the Turkish language and culture. If Syria's border countries, and truly all asylum states, do not focus on job creation that is aimed at employing Syrian refugees, these countries will witness the growth of a bottom-level class that they cannot sustain. For the youngest generation, less than a third are in formal schools—in some cases that means that these children are being exposed only to an informal education that may come with a radical narrative.[77] For that reason, integrating children into national education systems within each host country is another important way to help the refugee generation.

Syria's neighboring countries with significant refugee populations rely on resources from international institutions. A joint statement issued by the governments of Canada, Ethiopia, Germany, Jordan, Mexico, Sweden, and the United States underscores that reality, identifying the need "to increase international humanitarian assistance funding, offer opportunities for refugee resettlement and alternative forms of legal admissions, and facilitate refugees' access to education and lawful employment."[78] This is a hopeful sign that the international community intends to continue its support for Lebanon, Jordan, and Turkey, but that support must do more than address immediate humanitarian needs: It must also strengthen the systems that support refugee populations in the long term.

In Lebanon, the national government and the United Nations are working together on a crisis response plan for the Syrian crisis: The plan involves both long-term and short-term considerations including humanitarian services supplied directly to refugees and investments in national infrastructure to accommodate as many as 2.2 million refugees—however, this initiative doesn't have nearly the resources it requires.[79] The World Bank has invested hundreds of millions of dollars in projects in Lebanon that address not only immediate humanitarian needs but also the Lebanese state's underlying systematic challenges—these projects work to build stronger public education, social protection, healthcare, transportation, and water and environmental regulation systems that can cope with population surges.[80]

The United States Agency for International Development (USAID), which is the American government's foreign aid agency, has assisted Jordan for more than sixty years. USAID has supplied Jordan with 1.5 billion dollars since 2011 in addition to helping collect billions more from other sources.[81] USAID's money is dispersed with the goal of creating deeper macroeconomic and social stability in Jordan, and much of this money is invested in infrastructure development: this includes expanding and improving the physical infrastructure of schools, hospitals, and other service facilities and the renovation and construction of wastewater treatment facilities in northern Jordan.[82] Jordan's stability and success are international priorities, and the country is a very important ally of the United States, the European Union, and other international institutions—they are the ones who supply most of Jordan's funding and resources. For the Jordanian government, accepting refugees is not only a moral and regional responsibility: It also represents an opportunity to leverage international funding for the refugee crisis that can create structural stability and lasting benefits for the country.[83]

Direct humanitarian assistance to the refugees is essential, of course, but it is unsustainable both financially and socially—in Syria, the conflict that has created the crisis has deep, complex roots and requires something more extensive. At its most simple, the Syrian conflict is a power dynamic between three main actors: the existing Assad government (backed by Russia and Iran), *da'ish* (ISIS), and a nebulous and ever-shifting international coalition of militaries that oppose both Assad and *da'ish* (ISIS). That international coalition comprises, among others, the United States, the United Kingdom, Turkey, Jordan, Saudi Arabia, and local Syrian militias.

But a lasting solution to the Syrian conflict must be diplomatic—though Assad refuses to give up power, dialogue is still ongoing between the international community and state governments supporting him. Right now, the most important of these is Russia, which is at odds with most of the international community, including the United States, the EU, the Syrian people, and neighboring Arab countries. But there is still room for all of these actors to cooperate in regard to *da'ish*. Assad (and his international supporters), the United States-led coalition, and the Syrian people all want to counteract *da'ish*, and for this reason Russia and Assad negotiated brief cease-fires with opposition actors in order to combine forces against this other threat. About his cooperation with Russia's Putin despite the country's backing of Assad, Jordan's King Abdullah in his discussions with Putin, has said they have addressed the need "to move the political process forward as quickly as possible ... the Russians are fully aware that sooner rather than later we have to have a mechanism that allows the process to move forward. And I think we all understand that that does mean the departure of Bashar."[84]

Much of the international involvement in the conflict has been military—but the conflict is not a fundamentally military one. While a focus on liberating *da'ish*-controlled territory is important, a physical and violent end to *da'ish* as an organization will not mean an end to its radical ideology. Organizations like *da'ish* thrive in chaotic and uncertain landscapes in which basic social services and survival resources are absent: These are the desperate structural conditions that push civilians toward extremism, and it is through changing these base conditions that extremism finally loses its power.

A peaceful, stable Levant may seem difficult now, but as earlier chapters suggest, the Arab world is a complex and resourceful place. Its people have endured through eras of immense prosperity and hardship. Despite daunting challenges, Turkish, Lebanese, and Jordanian populations are doing everything in their power to assist their war-ravaged neighbors. Though other countries and international organizations are offering assistance, the current Syrian situation can only be effectively solved after refugees return home and live under a newly-established democratic government that respects its people and provides them with peace, justice, security, dignity, freedom, and employment.

CHAPTER THIRTEEN

The Crisis of Arab Culture

GLORIOUS PAST AND ARAB CONTRIBUTION

To understand the Arab present, which is this book's intent, it is necessary to explore the rich legacies of its history, language, civilization, religion, and defining culture. The glorious Arab past is not past in the minds of the Arab people: It remains vividly alive in their collective memory. Today they still look back to that period, starting in the seventh and eighth centuries, when a glorious empire conquered the ancient world and created a rich, five-hundred-year-old civilization that produced significant economic developments, scientific advancements, and a cultural blossoming. That period is celebrated as a golden era that flourished in North Africa, Asia, Southern Europe, and the Middle East while the rest of Europe was lost in the Dark Ages.

During that era of stability and prosperity, Arabs made enduring contributions to the world and humanity. Extensive trade networks, the high importance of learning, and a respect for tolerance characterized the empire. Arabs created a vital, dynamic, progressive civilization that included diverse ethnic, religious, and racial populations. Jews, Christians, and Muslims all participated in developing this Arab golden age. This era ushered in great advancements in scientific fields, including chemistry, mathematics, astronomy, physics, medicine, and navigation. Philosophy, architecture, literature, and music also thrived. All of these fields were rooted in a framework of stability and strong cultural cohesiveness. Arabs understandably take pride in their glorious past. It is natural that they express nostalgia and a profound longing for a civilization that led the world for five centuries. This glorious past will always live in their minds and hearts.

Arab identity has been shaped by thousands of years of evolution and transformation. Sometimes progress has been expansive; in the eighth and ninth centuries, for example, Arab political control spread from the Middle East to North Africa, the Iberian Peninsula, and the borders of present-day India. At its height, the Arab empire included nearly thirty percent of the world's population.[1] After its collapse, its culture was suppressed and suffocated under the rule of the Ottoman Empire, European colonizers, and Arab dictators.

In the course of describing the history, this book has presented many of the Arab people's cultural characteristics and qualities, including identity, literature, family, language, values, traditions, Islam, Qur'an, thought, history, social and political developments, and music. Language, in particular, has been a central instrument in the development of religion, science, philosophy, and literature. So have the daily discussions and conversations taking place, from Morocco to Oman, in rich and varied dialects based on the classical foundations of this exquisite language.

Poetry, which draws from the same classical foundations, provides the most sublime reflection of the Arab mind, portraying Arab social values and revealing the core and substance of its culture. A highly developed and refined art form, poetry was deeply rooted in the psyche and history of the Arabs long before the appearance of Islam. It originated in the same place as the Arabs themselves, the heart of the ancient Arabian Peninsula, and has existed for as long as the Arab peoples. Through poetry, the Arabs' deeds, activities, ways of life, and civilization have been consecrated and preserved.[2] Poetry is not an art form for only the elites or the well-educated: The spoken words of poetry, often accompanied by music, have been savored by every strata of society.

In the contemporary period, leading poets have held themselves in eternal opposition and conflict with the current socio-political system, attacking its un-productivity and calling for its immediate replacement. New themes and literary schools have continued to emerge, along with innovative metaphors, intense poetic imagery, and complex wording and styles. Poets continue to call for self-determination; the dream of re-creating a great Arab civilization is still alive and well in the words and visions of modern Arab poets.

Notwithstanding poetry's power, the modern Arab novel has become a potent tool for depicting Arab society and culture with a laser-like precision that illuminates key features and issues shared by all Arabs across the region. In addition, female authors have introduced powerful new perceptions and insights and brought a vibrant new dynamism into the genre. Their strong, courageous voices are contributing to a flourishing body of work that is finding new audiences in the Arab world and beyond.

Arab music, which emerged on the Arabian Peninsula before Islam, encompasses a wide variety of beautiful, complex, and distinct forms. One of these is the oral poetry. We have seen how the recitation of poetry was intertwined with songs and melodies; in Arabic musical tradition, language and poetry form the core of Arabic music's originality, development, and expression. The melodic songs, styles, and interpretations of its musical traditions continue to tell the stories of the Arab people, and some of these pieces of music have belonged to the popular consciousness for thousands of years. During the Arab Spring, musicians and singers were the ones who motivated protesters and gave a voice to hundreds of thousands of citizens across the region. Their music adapted popular folk tunes and call-and-response songs harking back to traditional poetic forms; in other cases they drew on the cutting-edge genre of rap music to gain worldwide attention for their cause.

A SUCCESSION OF DECLINES AND FALLS

In spite of a glorious heritage and the many rich, lasting qualities of their culture, Arabs today suffer from many social, economic, political, educational, and developmental dilemmas. Faced with vulnerabilities and fragmentation on many levels, Arab culture is facing a decline that seems all but inevitable.

For the Arab people, the dysfunction and backwardness of the present day are in stark contrast to the once-splendid civilization that led the world for several centuries. What followed that golden civilization was a succession of disastrous events that marked a steady deterioration. The decline started in the thirteenth century after the Mongols invaded Baghdad and burned its libraries in 1258. The Arab empire in southern Spain declined and was abolished in 1492. Much of the Arab world then fell under Ottoman rule for some four hundred years (1516–1918). At the end of the First World War, the Arab people exchanged Ottoman rule for European colonization. At the end of the Second World War, most Arab states gained independence, but they fell victim this time to the internal tyranny of their leaders and, to some extent, were also dominated by Western economic interests.

THE CRISES OF ARAB CULTURE

Centuries of decline and foreign domination have resulted in a modern Arab culture suffering from stagnation and suffocation. Social and cultural growth is frozen because of the continuing obstructions to free expression from Arab governments. Corrupt Arab leaders and their oppressive governments are preventing advancement and have shown themselves to be the enemies of their own people. Look at the Arab world today and you find leaders exploiting their citizens for their own gain or to serve the foreign powers supporting their rule (or both). The power of these corrupt rulers comes at the expense of potential economic, political, societal, and educational development across the Arab world. Thus, the leaders of the present day and their governments are repressing their populations into acquiescence and failure. What follows is a critique of the failure of modern Arab culture, culled from a variety of contemporary Arab cultural critics, intellectuals, and experts representing various views and analyses.

The decline of Arab civilization started in the middle of the thirteenth century and continued with the ascendancy of the Ottoman Empire. The Arab Awakening emerged early in the nineteenth century after Napoleon Bonaparte's invasion of Egypt in 1798, and that sudden encounter with the West is something Arab scholars have traditionally called the 'Shock of Modernity.' More than two centuries later, though, Arab modernity has not been achieved. Some Arab scholars see this as a failed or false renaissance; some believe the genuine process of Arab renaissance and modernity actually started in the fifteenth century, long before the arrival of the West. Others, including prominent Egyptian scholar Mahmoud Amin al-`Alim, emphatically argue that the West permanently thwarted any indigenous process of Arab renaissance with its invasion, domination, and colonization of the Arab world. Al-`Alim prefers the expression 'Shock of Abortion' to 'Shock of Modernity.' In his view, this communicates not only the failure of Arab modernity to come to fruition but also its curtailment from the outside.[3]

Despite competing views, there is a generally common acceptance that a renaissance or awakening started early in the 19th century. Many intellectuals, though, believe it ended with the defeat of the Arabs in 1967. The dream of lasting, real independence faded, and most Arab regimes were left under the influence of foreign powers instead. Even oil-rich Arab states, despite their great wealth, were unable to produce industrial, scientific, social, political, and cultural developments for their people. Instead of producing freedom and democracy, they produced oppression and tyranny. No one in the Arab world could have predicted this outcome back in the 1950s and early 1960s, as it was a time when new feelings of hope for Arab unity, revival, and rebirth were re-emerging. But all of this, as has been mentioned earlier in this book, ended in one disappointment after another. Instead of becoming one great nation again with key power and influence in many areas, economic, military, scientific, the Arab states have given their citizens backwardness, stagnation, tyranny, and suffocation.

Regardless of what the Arab renaissance managed to accomplish, Syrian scholar Muta` Safadi insists that it certainly did not produce modernity—and its failure to achieve this has pervaded Arab thought for the last two centuries. Safadi is troubled by the focus that academics have placed on a single train of thought: the similarities and differences between the Arabs and the West. The emphasis on a gap existing between the 'self' and the 'other' has spawned a deep sense of inferiority in the Arab psyche and a strong sense of superiority in the psyche of the oppressive 'other.'[4] Concentration on this single point has so dominated modern Arab thought that it has prevented thinkers from asking other more important questions about modernity. That focus on either accepting or rejecting the 'other' and reexamining the contextual problem of the 'self' has "handicapped [Arab thought] throughout modern history and since the renaissance."[5]

It must be emphasized that Arab intellectuals since the renaissance faced great challenges trying to revive what they could of the golden age of Arab civilization. The difficulties facing them were seemingly insurmountable, considering the long period of decline, Ottoman rule, Western colonization and Arab dictators who followed.

Despite these major obstacles and hindrances, the Arab intellectuals, along with the political, social, and cultural forces of the society, together with scholars, writers, and critics, were able to revive several important features and key elements of the glorious past of Arab civilization. They revived the Arabic language of the classical era, modernized it, and reestablished its high level of power, beauty and influence. They also revived Arabic literature. Modern Arabic poetry today is exceedingly advanced and sophisticated, standing shoulder to shoulder with any first class world literature. The Arabic novel developed to a high level of experimentation and refinement, taking its place among the great novels of world literature. Arab musicians have revived classical Arabic music, enriching modern sounds and styles. Academics and writers have made great progress in the fields of journalism, media, and translation.

In spite of the progress, intellectuals have been unable to liberate or modernize overall society and culture or pull them out from their long entrenched quagmire and crises. The challenges remain huge and the problems are unsolvable in light of the current unhealthy political, economic, and governing realities of the Arab world.

In order to better understand the challenges facing today's Arab world, this chapter looks at several key crisis areas informed by the views of contemporary Arab academics, intellectuals, and journalists. These areas involve the issues of Arab unity; economic dependence; foreign intervention; Arab thought; sectarianism; authority; leadership and accountability; legitimacy; modernization; the middle class; the Arab media; education reform; and youth. The list is a long one (unfortunately, it still does not include every serious impediment in the way of Arab social and cultural advancement). Unless these dilemmas are reconciled, only sweeping political and economic changes will ever usher in a new Arab renaissance.

ARAB UNITY

When the decisive encounter with Europe occurred at the end of the eighteenth century, Arabs differed in their reactions. Some were amazed by Western progress and technology and considered Europe an ideal to be emulated; others rejected it and glorified the Arab past instead. This tension, which to this day remains unresolved, manifested itself in many facets of Arab culture. It led to an uneven imitation of the West, which generated a sense of inferiority and discouraged critical thinking and independent thought. Even though Arab intellectuals did talk about modernity at length, few had either modern or independent enough minds to produce free ideas. Muta' Safadi contends that most ideas arising from this renaissance were received from the 'other'—Arab thought became solely fixated on what to adopt and what to reject from the West. The Arab mind, he contends, "became a single-function filtering machine. During the renaissance, 'modern' Arab thought served only to justify what the Arabs wanted to accept and receive from the West and what they wanted to deny and reject."[6]

Safadi pointed out that the Arabs, throughout the nineteenth century and until the end of the First World War, possessed no political entity of their own. Instead, they wrapped themselves up in the Ottoman cloak and pledged loyalty to the Ottoman Sultan. Even after the Ottoman Empire collapsed and Arabs achieved independence, they still could not form their own nation in the modern sense. The independent Arab states were not "truly independent, having only transitioned from control by Western colonizers to control by local colonizers, the Arab leaders."[7] Noted scholar Albert Hourani wrote that real Arab unity has not existed since perhaps the fall of the Abbasid dynasty in the thirteenth century, and it seems unlikely to exist again any time soon.[8]

Jamal Abd al-Nasir attempted to unify the Arab world, starting with the political unity between Egypt and Syria in 1958, but that project failed less than four years later. It is certainly true that Nasir's ideology and personality helped stir strong feelings of Arab solidarity and the expectation of a new pan-Arab nation's creation. But these ideas, which the Arab masses believed in and trusted, were proved untrue by the June 1967 war. Many intellectuals trace the comprehensive crisis of the Arab world to June 5, 1967, a date that represents an overall *cultural* defeat as well as a military one. As Arab states tried to strengthen their national sovereignty and cultural identity during the twentieth century, plans were set in motion to establish modern industrial and economic projects. But the 1967 defeat marked the end of the Egyptian revolution and other experiments in Arab modernity, and the Arab renaissance was seen as a failure.[9]

Albert Hourani elaborated that even the war waged by Egypt and Syria against Israel in 1973, which temporarily inspired a revival of solidarity, ultimately furthered Arab disunity. That sudden war ended with an imposed cease-fire and the seizure of more Arab lands by Israel. Months later, it became clear that Egypt had not started the war with the intention of achieving military victory. Rather, Egyptian President Anwar al-Sadat wanted a pretext to start bilateral peace negotiations with Israel and to regain the territories that Egypt lost in 1967. He was "uninterested in a comprehensive Arab settlement, and Syria was not aware of Egypt's strategy; as a result, the two countries suffered a serious rupture in relations after the war."[10] This additional military failure contributed to the weakening of the Arab psyche.

Sadat himself grew close to the United States; it is one of many reasons why American political influence was able to grow in the Middle East. The Americans managed to conclude initial peace agreements between Egypt, Jordan, and Israel, and some Arab states became politically and economically dependent on the United States. Arab cohesion, which was already weak, splintered even more—by the end of the 1970s, the Arab world sank further into the abyss of weakness and disunity.[11]

Sadat was assassinated in 1981 and succeeded by Hosni Mubarak, who continued his policies. Egypt under Mubarak grew even more close to the United States and began to receive a large amount of financial aid through which the United States wielded considerable influence over Egyptian domestic and foreign policy. Hourani noted that during this period, other Arab states moved closer to the United States as well; they include Morocco, Tunisia, and Jordan along with Saudi Arabia and the oil-producing states of the Gulf. During the 1973 war, Saudi Arabia and the Arab Gulf states imposed a short embargo on oil exports to the United States and other Western countries in solidarity with the Arab countries involved in the war; it was "the first and perhaps the last time the Arabs were ever to use their oil as a weapon."[12] The embargo, which managed to disrupt the world oil supply chain, lasted only from October 1973 to March 1974. In the end, the Arabs were unable to exert substantial influence with their most significant resource against the West.[13]

After 1967, for the first time in Arab history, the great cultural centers of Cairo, Beirut, Damascus, and Baghdad lost their capacity for cultural and social leadership as the civil societies of Egypt, Lebanon, Syria, and Iraq were shattered. The civil war in Lebanon lasted from 1975 to 1990. The Arab Spring's promises failed to deliver, except perhaps in Tunisia. The fragmented Iraqi reality and the ongoing civil wars in Syria, Libya, and Yemen are further examples of the sectarian division and fragmentation devastation of Arab society and politics. A large number of Arab intellectuals believe that the political situation of the last four decades has been the worst in modern Arab history. Oppression and repression are spiraling out of control, and the economic situation of the Arab people remains hopeless. According to Ilias Khoury, contemporary Arab culture stands caught between a fundamentalist Islamic culture that wants to return to the past and a Westernized culture that wants to dominate the future.[14]

Moroccan writer Abdallah Laroui reminds us that Arab intellectuals have diagnosed the Arab reality but have not provided any prescription or remedy. The most prominent thinkers of the generation are deeply divided in their search for answers, dissecting every new historical development and every new event. After independence and throughout the years that followed, numerous movements emerged that tried to bring about radical change in Arab society, and Arab intellectuals "had great expectations concerning the movement of Arab liberation or the pan-Arab project."[15] Most Arab intellectuals have supported all possibilities for change. However, because the movements of national liberation, Arab socialism, and international communism have all failed, a change of direction seems prudent.

Regimes do not exercise self-criticism and do not afford to others the right to criticize them, resulting in a manufactured image of imposed tranquility and contentment that the political opposition finds too difficult to challenge. The upshot has been an almost complete blocking of any possible movement toward democracy, unity, and development. Poet Abdul Wahab al-Bayati believes this crisis has reached a level unknown since pre-Islamic times and calls into question the credibility and usefulness of the Arab identity itself, as it has proved unable to unify the present or protect Arab heritage. The Arab renaissance project of the nineteenth century has retreated. What is left today is either "an Islamic fundamentalist project or a project for surrender and defeat."[16]

According to Al-Bayati, the vision of a comprehensive Arab unity has disappeared and been replaced by local, sectarian, and regional political ideologies. No political movements today can propose any form of pan-Arab project to connect Arab heritage with a plan for the future. In fact, some professional politicians make deliberate attempts to separate Arab culture from its past heritage. Though Arab culture remained strong and united throughout history against the Mongol invasion, Ottoman rule, and European imperialism, it is now unable to stand united.[17]

ECONOMIC DEPENDENCY

As the demand for oil has increased in industrialized countries, the Arab oil-rich states have increased their production and grown wealthier as a result. Hourani noted that this increased wealth has been accompanied by an increase in economic dependency on those same industrialized countries. Arab oil states invest their surpluses in developed countries, primarily the United States, although they have been investing in Asia, particularly China and India. Arab governments have traditionally depended on Western technical expertise for their economic development and for building up their armed forces and security operations. Meanwhile, they have also "realized that their oil-derived wealth has generated weakness and dependence rather than strength and autonomy."[18]

In the 1970s some Arab states initiated various programs supposedly to promote economic liberalization. After the 1973 war, Egypt's Sadat initiated the *infitah*, or openness policy, encouraging foreign investment in the private sector. Resulting income inequalities and the belief that the policy enriched the elites led to large-scale riots in 1977. Middle East expert Fouad Ajami summed up the claims that the *infitah*, instead of bringing widespread prosperity, "brought wild rents, land speculations, inflation, and corruption."[19] The focus on private sector investment in Egypt continued during the Mubarak regime and now with current President Abd al-Fattah al-Sisi, and the perception remains among many that today's policies in that country continue to enrich the upper classes at the expense of the poor whose situations have not improved.

One of the most sweeping initiatives that offers a more modern economic system including foreign investment is Saudi Arabia's "Vision 2030," which was launched in 2016 by Crown Prince Mohammed bin Salman Al-Saud. This ambitious long-term plan is intended to wean the country from its diminishing oil revenues and broaden the economy. The government is attracting foreign investment to promote development across many economic sectors with the goal of creating more jobs for Saudi nationals and transferring foreign technology and expertise.[20] One year into the plan, significant adjustments have been made to the projected gains, and expectations have been lowered. Scholar Hilal Khashan has remarked that, "already, contrary to what one might expect from a country that claims to be committing itself to economic liberalization and ensuring the happiness of its people, the Saudi government is further clamping down on the freedom of expression, dismal to begin with, under the guise of promoting religious moderation."[21] Despite constant proclamations that economic liberalization will lead to political liberalization, governments are unable to loosen their grip on power.

After the Iranian revolution of 1979, the United States feared the Islamic revolution would spread into neighboring areas and topple the American-friendly political systems of Saudi Arabia and the Arab Gulf states. Saddam Hussein, then the President of Iraq, started a war against Iran in 1980 to prevent the spread of revolutionary Islamic ideology to Iran's Arab neighbors. The Iraq war against Iran greatly slowed the export of the Islamic revolution to the Arab world, exhausting Iran and draining the Iraqi economy. While Iraq was fighting Iran, the rest of the Arab world experienced other difficulties. A long civil war in Lebanon attracted Arab and foreign military interventions, including Israel's invasion and the occupation of southern Lebanon in 1982. The Iraqi invasion of Kuwait in 1990, the American invasion of Iraq in 2003, and the civil wars in Syria, Libya, and Yemen after 2011 all preclude investment and development. Conflicts in the region and foreign interventions such as these have played a major role in preventing Arabs from attaining their national aspirations and achieving economic independence.

Throughout the region, economic reform initiatives and reliance on foreign private investment have not yielded their intended results. Repressed populations only see limited, if any, opportunities for advancement. Job growth has lagged far behind population growth. The Arab Spring uprisings reflected this lack of any tangible economic gains: "Economic advancement was slowing while political participation was narrowing. In some ways, economic liberalization contributed to 'an upgrading of authoritarianism' but clearly it also contributed to citizens' growing opposition to policies that were not lifting all boats."[22]

Economic growth that creates more jobs and a transfer of wealth to mitigate the vast income disparity in every Middle Eastern country are both necessary in order for citizens to see real change. Lebanese venture capitalist and businessman Fadi Ghandour stated in an interview with Shelly Culbertson: "If the economic elites and rulers do not appreciate that their success requires the proper delivery of services, then all the regimes that changed will not be successful going forward. People will go back to the streets, or the next generation will, if there are no economic benefits or feelings of fairness in the system."[23] By failing to fulfill the demands that erupted during the Arab Spring, authoritarian governments retaining their stranglehold on economic development will likely face more heated protests in the coming years.

FOREIGN INTERVENTION

Since the time before independence, the Arab world has been exposed to exceptional Western pressures and influences, especially in recent years. Some Arab intellectuals believe that Western intervention is aimed at hindering and discouraging the Arab world from ever uniting in productive economic cooperation in order to ensure the continued flow of oil to the West and to guarantee recognition of and support for Israel. They insist that foreign powers have intentionally established and supported certain Arab regimes to control, isolate, and weaken their societies. Western leaders seek to maintain the divisions among the Arabs. Preserving Arab regimes has been the key to ensuring stability for the West's strategic interests and preventing Arab unity and the development of their countries.[24]

For Arab writers and observers today, the so-called independent and sovereign Arab states are fragile. Safadi stated that, even after most Western armies left the Arab world, national governments continued to stagger under the control of foreign powers, starting with the Europeans and followed by the Americans. Most Arab governments today are neither independent nor nationalist: Most resemble "an extension of the imperialist colonialist power." The only difference is the legal legitimacy that they enjoy, which might be recognized by the United Nations but is largely ignored by the Arab peoples.[25]

The strength of foreign intervention is proportional to the weakness of the Arabs. The wealth of the Arab Gulf states, especially Saudi Arabia, should be able to buttress their strength, but ironically, wealth has seemed to only make them weaker. Syrian-French academic Burhan Ghalion, who teaches at the Sorbonne, believes the United States is engaging in a form of blackmail with Arab regimes by threatening to withhold military protection that they need to remain in power. In return, these Arab regimes fully submit to the Americans while continuing to publicly denounce U.S. regional policies. Ghalion further contends that some Arab regimes use patriotic and nationalist slogans in order to legitimize their control and domination over their people. Most Arab leaders are isolated and disconnected from the people they govern. They resort to patriotic slogans and mottos to conceal their efforts to suppress any movements that seek change and reform.[26]

ARAB THOUGHT

The crisis in modern Arab thought has intensified since 1967. Several trends regarding this crisis have emerged, all concerned with dissecting the essential flaws in previous scholarship and finding a useful and actionable prescription for modern Arab society and culture. The Islamist trend calls for reconstruction of society according to Islamic values and law, while the secularist trend calls for separation of religion and the state. Marxists, nationalists, and liberals have all contributed to this discourse. Several ideological directions may also exist within one trend; for example, moderate, traditionalist, and radical Islamist intellectuals all compete with each other at the same time that they compete with their ideological opponents among the secularists and Marxists. Today, the dominating trends are the Islamist and secularist. Both demand the democratization of Arab society as a necessary condition of societal change.[27]

Georgetown University professor Hisham Sharabi has said that the role and nature of the Arab intellectual has also changed in the past fifty years as the cultural crisis has emerged and deepened. In the past, an intellectual would be either a person of important social status, a known writer who fit into certain easily-categorized ideological orientations, or a leader of a particular intellectual trend. The number of thinkers who represented major ideologies and schools of thought, and who innovated with new directions for scholarship, used to be very small. Today, on the other hand, more than two hundred universities are sprinkled throughout the Arab world, contrasted with only a handful of universities fifty years ago. Intellectuals have also acquired a measure of popular and effective influence in society. Today's ideologies, represented by the various nationalist, communist, and Muslim Brotherhood movements, have all become social forces and are led by inspiring and visionary individuals. The Arab world today possesses numerous qualified intellectuals who can build a new critical discourse for all levels of Arab society.[28]

In the past, Arab intellectuals were not only few in number, Sharabi elaborates, but they also tended to come from wealthy or influential families; that was particularly true of the bourgeois class that was closely connected with the political decision-making establishment. At the present time, in contrast, perhaps as many as three quarters of Arab intellectuals come from more popular classes, including the peasantry and the poor. And the role of the intellectual has become intertwined with the project of modernization. The remaining Arab academics from the bourgeois class, with few exceptions, are far removed from the population. Even when they talk about social issues relevant to today's Arab world, they cannot remove themselves from their elite social position. Arab intellectuals hailing from the poor and lower-middle classes have offered much more to Arab society and culture of late. It seems that the thinkers who play significant roles in building a political horizon for Arabs and participating in popular political movements come almost entirely from non-bourgeois backgrounds.[29]

Burhan Ghalioun said that Arab governments used to marginalize and silence the intellectuals, either imprisoning them or censoring their writings. Presenters of ideas and thoughts on the future were expelled, which prompted an "Arab political crisis." Many intellectuals were arrested and imprisoned; some were exiled and their passports confiscated. Others sought political refugee status abroad. At the same time, a number of intellectuals served and supported the authority while the majority remained outside and opposed to this illegitimate authority, living the "agony of the Arab intellectuals." They had little power or voice, and lived "scattered and fragmented and without recognition. They are victims."[30] Sharabi stressed the difficulties inherent in the role Arab intellectuals play in society. Whereas intellectuals in more advanced societies can focus on philosophical pursuits, Arab intellectuals must devote themselves to searching for practical solutions to economic disparities and social problems. If successful, these steps will lead to an active and participatory civil society despite governmental wishes to the contrary.[31]

SECTARIANISM

Acute chaos in the Arab world, stemming from a series of defeats, civil wars, sectarian infighting, and rampant disunity in the aftermath of June 1967 has led to an overall loss of direction and confusion. Lebanese novelist and critic Ilias

Khouri traces the history of this crisis from the Lebanese civil war of 1975-1990 to the Iraqi invasion of Kuwait in the 1990s to the American war and occupation of Iraq in 2003. These tragic conflicts have not only definitively heralded the end of Arab nationalism, he said, but they have proved the impossibility of "transcending sectarian and tribal ties in the Arab world." Of particular concern to Khouri is the sectarian democracy created in Iraq, which has turned out to be a roadmap for civil war and the planting-ground for seeds of ethnic and sectarian fragmentation. This led to creating opportunities for sectarian revenge.[32]

The conflicts resulting from sectarianism present grave socio-economic pressures. The 2016 United Nations Arab Human Development Report notes that "conflicts also are reversing hard-won economic development gains by destroying productive resources, capital and labor within a larger territory, including neighboring countries where they are fought."[33] Internal crackdowns and ongoing battles of attrition within some Arab states have increased. Sectarian pressures continue to emerge, most drastically with the September 2017 Kurdish referendum in Iraq.

Yemen remains split into two separate, warring states. Lebanon, once a model of a unified state comprising diverse populations and political parties, faces constant threats from competing factions. Bahrain's majority Shi'a population remains ruled by a Sunni royal family. Rival groups in Syria have destroyed the country, fighting against each other for more than eight years. Governments have failed to provide adequate accommodation to various groups within their borders, resorting only to oppression and domination. Resentments and anger grow, resulting in violence that prevents reconciliation and impedes socio-economic progress.

AUTHORITY

In addition to civil wars and sectarianism, more subdued contradictions reign. The parliamentary councils, representatives, and institutions of democracy and free expression that manage to exist in the Arab world remain suffocated, suppressed, and controlled. Arab existence features a duality: Though Arabs enjoy some degree of free markets and unrestricted trade, especially on a local level, they are very restricted in most other facets of life. A gap exists between thought and practice and between theory and application. Mahmoud Amin al-`Alim writes that two cultures exist in Arab society: the "culture of authority and culture of the people."[34]

Another aspect of this frustration stems from the tendency of some Arab intellectuals to change allegiances according to shifting political circumstances. Khalid Harb noted some opposition figures have experienced startling transformations in perspective once their political parties seized power and have started to act as intellectuals of the authority rather than as intellectuals of the people.[35] Arab authorities and governments have succeeded on occasion in buying off some of the Arab intellectuals who used to criticize the political status quo.[36]

Over the decades, Arab intellectuals have established and joined social and political movements and parties calling for freedom and democracy. Some of those organized political parties have succeeded in seizing power through military coups or other means. And some intellectuals have begun to work with the new authorities as bureaucrats, thus becoming part of the establishment. From these positions, they begin to defend the interests of the leaders who seized power. Simultaneously, governments eliminate those who oppose the new regime and its authority. Burhan Ghalioun said that many Arab intellectuals have lost their political role and resigned themselves to "shout into the empty desert. That is all they can do."[37] Authority continues to suppress the people's will even though the Arab Spring indicates their voices cannot be silenced forever.

LEADERSHIP AND ACCOUNTABILITY

The crisis of Arab governance stems from individual failures of leadership. No Arab leader took responsibility for the defeat of June 1967. No investigative committees were formed, nor did anyone admit wrongdoing or fault. On the contrary, Ilias Khoury observes, the defeat became an occasion for Arab governments and leaders to grow more oppressive and to terrorize anyone who raised questions. Following the fiasco, only President Nasir of Egypt announced his resignation. Immediately after his announcement, however, millions of Egyptians marched in the streets of Cairo and demanded that he stay in office. Meanwhile, in Syria and Jordan, leaders did not even offer to resign, nor did demonstrations take place. Instead, the leaders pretended they had been victorious and continued to rule in the name of the people until they died. Khouri elaborates that many questions remain unanswered such as: how could the weapons and armies of several independent Arab countries collapse within a few hours? Who ordered the soldiers of Egypt, Syria, and Jordan to withdraw? How was the Egyptian Air Force so suddenly and completely destroyed? Only one fact is known for certain—all Arab leaders remained in their positions.[38]

Certain Arab governments even declared victory, claiming that Israel had failed to remove them from power. The regimes also punished anyone who discussed or talked about the defeat. Before 1967, Arab leaders openly advocated the liberation of Palestine. After the defeat, they talked only of the "elimination of the Israeli aggression of 1967." In 2018, Palestine is no longer a priority for Arab governments, and even new alliances are being established between some Arab states and Israel. Egypt's Nasir, who used to expound at length in inflammatory speeches about Arab nationalism and the liberation of Palestine, had always claimed that Egypt was the greatest military power in the Middle East. This claim, of course, collapsed on the first day of the war. Khouri wrote, "Even Arab historians no longer concentrate on the June defeat: Arabs are reading their history in the books written by the Israeli victors. This is a cultural chaos."

Adonis writes that slogans about Arab unity have resulted in more division and avoidance of responsibility. Rallying cries of freedom and sovereignty have ended in oppression and dependency. Slogans of socialism have led to poverty and unemployment: "[E]verything the Arabs dreamed of and planned for in the second half of the twentieth century has ended with the opposite, this is the time of the great Arab failure."[40] Further, the Arab world has been loaded with disconnection, confusion, and loss of direction. Political regimes are isolated from each other and their own people. Most Arab states consist of two states— one of the oppressors and one of the oppressed, with foreign powers supporting the former against the latter. Islamist radical movements were born from this isolation and chaos.

To most leaders of Arab society, growth, development, and freedom have all been subservient to the goal of terrifying the people and maintaining power. Multiple levels of fear and oppression have been at work in Arab society. Anwar al-Sadat, for example, as president of Egypt, used fear-based governance to transform his country into a "frightened society ruled oppressively by tyranny and starvation."[41] Fear has always been used in the Arab world to play off certain political opposition groups against each other. Sadat used the Islamist fundamentalists against the leftists and Arab nationalists. And when the Islamists threatened to gain the upper hand, the government turned against them once more. Mubarak employed many of the same tactics for internal control, and the current Egyptian President Abd al-Fattah al-Sisi continues in this vein today.

Most regimes rule their citizens with an iron fist and use highly centralized systems of governance, the secret police, the media, and virtually all means at their disposal to maintain their dubious political legitimacy. As a result, the Arab world lives in a serious developmental crisis and lacks necessary projects for growth and development. The Arab Human Development Reports describe the situation in grim terms, noting that the "Arab development crisis has widened, deepened and grown more complex. Partial reforms, no matter how varied, are no longer effective or even possible. Comprehensive societal reform in Arab countries can no longer be delayed or slowed down."[42]

LEGITIMACY

The Arab Human Development Report further states that, in order to continue to remain in power, the Arab regimes justify their legitimacy by presenting themselves as the lesser of two evils: the oppressive but stable status quo versus the prospect of Islamic fundamentalist tyranny and/or anarchic chaos and collapse. This formula is termed by the UN report as the 'legitimacy of blackmail.' In order to protect their survival, Arab regimes claim to be fighting against terrorism because modernization cannot be achieved with the existence of terrorism and fundamentalism.[43]

Some regimes, according to the report, rely on mixed alliances of rural and traditional forces in society along with local bourgeoisie and external forces. This corralling of internal groups is why the existing civil opposition movements in the Arab world, thus far, have been proven weak. Some supposed opposition movements have even been staged by Arab regimes themselves, following yet another paradigm of survival: pretending to open up towards democracy.[44]

This "legitimacy of blackmail" blocks all avenues of political and civil activity and prevents alternatives that might bring about change. In the absence of legitimacy, Arab regimes rely on other paradigms of survival, including the 'black-hole' state. This relies on control, propaganda, and "striking bargains with dominant global or regional powers."[45]

The Arab Spring broke down the fears of the people and succeeded in toppling some leaders (though not their entire regimes). It has been a long-awaited revolution, even if it did not succeed the first time. Nonetheless, the protests did shift the narrative: "The authoritarian bargains of the past that skirted democracy for Arab national causes, industrialization and social welfare, gave way to new demands: *khubz, 'amal, huriyya, wa karama* (bread, jobs, freedom and dignity)."[46] People were able to topple regimes; the growing younger population will not forget that such direct challenges to the legitimacy of their governments can, in fact, happen.

It should be noted here that some minor opposition movements have existed in several places in the Arab world, but they were ineffective and shrouded by fear and intimidation. The walls of fear ensured that these movements were very marginal and did not promote serious change. Among these movements is *Kifaya* in Egypt, which called for democracy and freedom in 2004-2005 when President Hosni Mubarak allowed for some degree of political pluralism. *Kifaya*, the Arabic word for 'enough,' expressed opposition to many of Mubarak's policies, including his plan to hand down the presidency to his son. Like all Arab opposition movements, *Kifaya* was ultimately suppressed. Current Egyptian President Abd al-Fattah al-Sisi has raised the walls of fear anew after the Arab Spring in Egypt, reminding the population of the severe brutality the regime will employ against any revolutions or opposition.

Other Arab regimes, including the Libyan, Bahraini, and Syrian governments, granted limited freedoms to political opposition groups before the Arab Spring as well. Soon afterward, however, these same governments cracked down on these parties, put individuals in jail, and exiled many others. Unfortunately, most Arab regimes hinder the development of civil society by silencing activists and monopolizing the media. All political and civilian activities are monitored and controlled, and secret police forces keep close tabs on all lectures and meetings. Imprisonment, torture, and even death sentences are tools that the authoritarian regimes use to maintain their legitimacy. Individuals are not only beaten and jailed—their family members are also beaten in front of them to create further fear in the population and to frighten individuals and groups in opposition movements. In the end, though, public revulsion at these tactics only further undermines the authority of the leaders.

MODERNIZATION

The crisis of Arab governance is connected with the theory of dependency, which in turn is crucial to understanding the worsening discrepancy between the developed and underdeveloped world. Economic theorist Samir Amin said that the Arabs live now in a period defined neither by post-colonization nor by post-capitalism, but by a "mixture of colonization and capitalism." The basic differences between the center and the periphery of the global economic system—differentials that have existed since the dawn of the industrial revolution—have today grown much more severe. Thus, the center has continued to monopolize the periphery because the process of industrialization that began only after World War Two in many countries of the periphery has failed.[47]

Moreover, Amin elaborates that the center has developed new methods to control the periphery. Even beginning the process of industrialization in undeveloped countries does not portend their catching up with major industrial powers. Countries of the center enforce their monopoly over technology, information, and communications and control the distribution of natural wealth in the underdeveloped world, including Arab oil resources.[48]

In other words, 'Arab oil' is only regarded as 'Arab' when it is deep inside the earth. As soon as it gets extracted, it becomes 'Western oil' paid for in advance with money that is inevitably reinvested in Western banks. The Arab oil is thus removed from Arab lands and transported to the Western industrial world in exchange for large sums of money that do not produce modernization: "money without modernization and consumption without democracy." Amin emphasizes that progress will never transpire without real democracy; this democracy, however, is not limited to the political process—social relationships inside the workplace, schools, universities, and even families all require democracy. When true democracy exists, the center cannot monopolize industry. Democracy negates monopoly. Arab industrialization and political progress cannot be achieved without social progress. So far, as we have seen, such progress has not been achieved.[49]

In contrast with Sharabi, who sees an expansion and improvement in the role of today's Arab intellectuals in their society, Amin maintains that contemporary Arab intellectuals are either silent or withdrawn concerning this issue. Among them are many intellectual opportunists who are invested only in financial gain; these charlatans participate in symposiums and conferences, stay in five-star hotels, and work directly with Arab regimes. The remaining genuine scholars bear great responsibility. Even if they cannot change the present reality, they must prepare for the future with new intellectual ideas and criticism. Arabs must achieve social and political progress as necessary conditions for democracy and modernity.[50]

For this reason, Amin observes, modern socioeconomic models cannot be introduced in the Arab world without understanding the underpinnings of Arab society. He emphasizes that imposing political democracy in the Arab world without social progress, or achieving social progress without real democracy, are both wrong because "democracy and social progress must go together." Imposed democracy would lead to a total social collapse—and, in fact, that has already precipitated such a collapse in Iraq. Democracy can be achieved only when it is linked to central social issues and represented in civil and secular society.[51]

DISAPPEARANCE OF THE MIDDLE CLASS

Another crisis facing Arab society is the growing disappearance of the middle class. This trend accelerated after the ideological Arab nationalist movements collapsed in the 1970s while surpluses in the Arab oil states increased. Arab society now comprises, in essence, just two classes: a ruling class that holds all of the wealth, and a popular class that owns almost nothing. Sharabi has noted that Arab intellectuals used to stand as a bridge between these two social classes, but after the failure of the ideological parties, that bridge collapsed, too. Little remains in common between the elite classes and the people. Arab intellectuals cannot work and hobnob with rulers while at the same time proffering theories about the ills of Arab society; such a position of "luxurious intellectuality," is just not acceptable.[52] Regarding this crisis of class inequality, Georgetown University Sociologist Halim Barakat wrote that extreme wealth inequality defines the Arab world, where the social order is dominated by a few elites.[53]

British academic Adam Hanieh notes that social and economic inequalities remain among "the most pressing developmental issues for the Arab region— these inequalities are indicated by the large and persistent disparities that exist in ownership and control of economic wealth, access to resources and markets, and the exercise of political power."[54] On this issue, economist Elena Ianchovichina further confirms that, across the Arab world, a handful of billionaires in each Arab state controls a far larger share of national wealth than the elite classes in other similarly-developed regions. A few families own as much as a third of the national GDP in some states, and the largest corporations operating in many Arab countries are owned by the ruling elite or by close family members.[55]

Enormous inequality also exists between oil-rich nations in the Gulf and those states that lack strategic natural resources. Hanieh observed that, in the Gulf, oil reserves generate enough revenue for national governments to maintain persuasive welfare programs for their citizens—however, the amount of oil income concentrated in the ruling families and elites of the Gulf regimes accounts for the majority of national wealth. Unemployment and poverty among the poorest classes has grown more severe.[56] Governments will continue to falter unless they create economic opportunities for the increasingly disenchanted younger citizens. Demands for economic opportunity are just as strong as demands for political change were during the Arab Spring.

ARAB MEDIA

The transitioning nature of the Arab media cannot be neglected in discussing an important crisis of Arab culture. The majority of Arab media outlets have been and still are under direct or indirect control by either Arab governments or certain political parties, including most satellite television channels, radio stations, newspapers, journals, and magazines. Arab governments seek to control virtually all media sources inside their own countries, and some have even attempted to control the regional media outlets. Through their power over the media, most Arab regimes dominate the media with monopolies and are able to block voices of opposition and liberalization. Most media sources become mere spigots of propaganda, spewing out only carefully-screened messages and suppressing reality. This was the situation in the Arab world until Al-Jazeera Satellite Channel was founded in Qatar some two decades ago, creating a broadcasting revolution in the Arab world.

Over the past two decades, satellite television stations have been established which broadcast throughout the Arab world and beyond. Some, such as *al-Jazeera Satellite Channel* and *al-Arabiya Satellite Channel*, are very popular and influential, watched by millions for news coverage and programming. Even these new stations, which brought new life to the Arab peoples, are still vastly preferable to their state-controlled predecessors. They are not fully independent: *al-Arabiya* is Saudi-owned and *al-Jazeera* is owned by the state of Qatar. The former, in fact, was expressly established in order to compete with *al-Jazeera*, which for many years was the most popular news source in the Arab world.

Al-Jazeera's vast network of correspondents are based throughout the Middle East, Africa, and Asia, as well as in the United States and Europe, and they broadcast live and often compelling reports from regional trouble spots where Western journalists are sometimes unable to penetrate. The credibility of the station goes back to its history as the first satellite television channel in the Arab world to provide daily 24-hour news coverage. The station was founded in 1996 by the former Emir of Qatar, Sheikh Hamad bin Khalifa al-Thani, who took over the country from his father in the previous year. Interested in quality, the Emir employed a team of highly professional and well-trained individuals, including many former BBC journalists. The idea was simply to launch a trustworthy news station in Doha in part to raise the visibility and reputation of Qatar in the Arab world and beyond.

The young al-Jazeera received an assist from timing and market: Arab viewers had long been desperate for a news channel willing to broadcast the true feelings of the Arab population. In comparison, the controlled Arab media stations were still reporting daily on the endless protocol gatherings, meetings and boring speeches of rulers, followed by mind-numbing hours of national anthems, adoring commentary, and ersatz analysis.

Al-Jazeera appeared in the Arab world during a time of media suffocation and became an outlet for the Arabs after a long period of control and censorship. Despite most government wishes to the contrary, al-Jazeera began broadcasting the news without alteration to the truth-starved populations of the Arab world. It also produced discussion programs in which political and social figures of all stripes, including representatives of political opposition movements, were not only allowed, but encouraged to participate. Guests on al-Jazeera programs have openly criticized Arab leaders and policy-makers, and they have called for democracy, justice, and freedom—a previously unusual, if not altogether unknown, phenomenon for television in the Arab world. Some guests on al-Jazeera have been arrested by their governments after their appearances due to the political views they espoused during the programs.

Syrian writer Hakam al-Baba, in explaining the success of al-Jazeera, notes that Arabs have found no leader in the last thirty years who could give them the right to think and speak freely. Because the level of freedom of expression found on al-Jazeera does not occur elsewhere in Arab society, people have found relief in al-Jazeera's programming, especially in the weekly "Crossfire" program moderated by popular host Faysal al-Qasim. This, like other al-Jazeera features, derives its popularity from its ability to stir the emotions of the helpless, hopeless, and suppressed. People find on al-Jazeera a substitute for the freedom they lack in real life.[57]

The station's record on transparency and independence is by no means perfect. While al-Jazeera is based in Qatar and operates from the country's capital in Doha, it has refrained from criticizing Qatar's foreign and/or domestic policies. Ironically, though al-Jazeera has provided a generally honest venue for popular criticism of the Iraq war, it was unable to report or discuss the fact that Qatar provided the United States with one of the air bases from which Iraq was bombed in 2003, located some thirty miles from the news channel's headquarters. This and related contradictions have sometimes made al-Jazeera seem disconnected from reality, as if broadcasting from outer space and not in the midst of the Gulf. Both the government of Saudi Arabia and the Bush administration repeatedly pressured the Qatari government to order al-Jazeera to tone down its coverage of Osama bin Laden, the Iraq war, and other inflammatory topics. Some believe that the station's tone on these and other issues grew softer under constant pressure.

Non-academic commentators have also noticed the station's political shift. Cable television executive Ned Lamont, for example, observed in *The Nation* that "following the invasion of Iraq, al-Jazeera used the same language it applies to the Israeli-Palestinian struggle: resistance fighters versus occupiers. Today, it has changed the rhetoric, referring instead to military or militia groups and government forces."[58]

Al-Jazeera, however, must be given a huge credit for its coverage of the Arab Spring in 2010 and 2011, particularly in Tunisia and Egypt. Al-Jazeera was the source of information for the popular revolutions in the Arab world and played an important role benefitting revolutionaries by providing real-time coverage when the Egyptian government censored the media there during the uprising. Most recently, al-Jazeera's coverage of the war in Syria has been biased. Because Qatar supports and finances certain opposition militia groups inside Syria, al-Jazeera adopted the Qatari position throughout the civil war in Syria after 2011 and reported with a one-sided point of view. Also, it coverage on the Yemen civil war is biased. Further, due to the most recent crisis between Qatar and the Arab Gulf States, al-Jazeera is taking the position of Qatar and acts as its defender.

Al-Arabiya Satellite Channel, which was launched in early 2003 as a competitor to al-Jazeera and an alternative source of news, reporting in Arabic. Its funding is primarily derived from Saudi sources. *al-Arabiya* has some excellent programs and employs talented anchors and correspondents, some of whom are becoming as popular as those on al-Jazeera. It follows Saudi policy and political agenda in its coverage, and refrains from serious analysis of the governments of Saudi

Arabia and some of its neighbors. Thus, while al-Jazeera avoids discussing Qatar altogether, whether in a positive or negative light, al-Arabiya cannot actively encourage open and critical discussions of Saudi government policies. Its coverage on the Syrian civil war, and on the Yemeni civil war are biased. During the recent political crisis between Qatar and Saudi Arabia, its coverage and reporting on this subject are biased.

In addition to al-Arabiya, the Saudi government and individuals closely associated with it own and control a number of newspapers. These include the two most established daily Arabic-language newspapers, *al-Hayat* and *al-Sharq al-Awsat*, both of which are published in London. The Saudis, among other governments, have unfortunately adopted the practice of financing Arab intellectuals throughout the region and then deploying them as pro-Saudi voices in the media when needed. When governments pay off intellectuals and journalists in this manner, it creates serious obstacles to freedom of expression and democracy. The phenomenon of employing Arab intellectuals on a massive scale by powerful regimes aims not only to silence those intellectuals but also to halt progress toward political, social, and cultural change.

Print media has various degrees of freedom in the Arab world depending on the country. Egyptian journalist Lina Attalah founded an independent newspaper, *Mada Masr*, (*Range* or *Span of Egypt*). Shelly Culbertson notes how Attalah represents those who covered the Tahrir Square revolution as journalists, and who have subsequently continued to push for change. Attalah exists in a domain that includes " those ... physically incarcerated, threatened, out of the country, or grappling with deep depression and despair."[59] The al-Sisi government closed down her publication, but it continues on-line internationally. Atallah refuses to relinquish her reporting, but she is aware of the power of the state to clamp down on free expression: "The state is powerful and will always be more powerful. But we have also been building power." She is a champion of the Egyptians who did not vanish after the revolution but have moved underground and remain dedicated to political liberalization: "At moments of crisis, at times of direct collision with state power, those hundreds of thousands, if not millions, of us have not really drowned in despair, but rather we have been able to craft politics. And in being political, we recognize and grab moments of possibility, even if they come wrapped in crisis."[60] Every Arab country has a legion of committed and savvy journalists who continue to forward the causes of freedom, transparency, and accountability.

Tunisia provides an interesting example of how media reform since the Arab Spring can look on paper but differ in practice. The media was previously fully controlled by President Ben-Ali's authoritarian apparatus. Despite the new government instituting sweeping reforms to liberalize the media and lift censorship, some contend that little tangible progress has been made. Rasheeda al-Neifer, a member of the council charged with establishing and implementing the new reforms, remarked that "on the levels of reform, decrees and legislation, everything seems perfect. However, on the application level things are different. No serious change has taken place on the ground so far."[61] Efforts to liberalize the media are met in the Arab world with intransigence; red lines of which topics can and cannot be discussed remain in place.

Social media presents a myriad of issues. Some feel it portends a real democratic potential that has helped create a new pan-Arab identity. According to this optimistic view, a new generation of journalists creates and conveys news and opinions that are often critical of their countries' leadership. Thus, they are "building the underpinnings of a more liberal, pluralistic politics."[62] Others take a more skeptical view, noting how Arab regimes have proven adept at utilizing social media tools themselves to enhance their authoritarian control. Those who hold this more fatalistic perspective feel the new Arab media "has served to impede rather than promote genuine political reforms and democratization."[63] Social media has in fact empowered both sides of the equation. It remains to be seen whether governments with vast resources at their disposal will be able to suppress journalists who promote more openness and freedom.

However, a significant and lasting shift has taken place throughout the entire region today, as opposed to previous decades in which Arab media was controlled exclusively by autocratic regimes (Lebanon being an exception). Today "the permeability shaped by the new Arab media is driven from below, and expresses a set of common political and socioeconomic demands, ranging from individual freedoms and freely elected and accountable governments, to a fairer distribution of national wealth."[64] Courageous journalists utilize all outlets at their disposal to fight for their causes and to demand accountability from their governments. Perhaps the most notable voice for freedom of expression is Yemeni journalist and Nobel Prize winner Tawakkol Karman: "A free press should be the standard of any country with claims to democracy. It is both the means and the goal of any change: In the absence of a free press, there is no democracy."[65]

EDUCATION

Scholar Vincent Romani notes that even though primary education is available and mandatory in much of the Arab world today, deep-rooted issues plague the Arab education system, especially in urban areas.[66] The irony is that during the Golden Age of the Arabs, cities including Baghdad, Cairo, Fez, Tunis, Damascus, and Cordoba were centers of knowledge for the Arab world and surrounding regions. Institutions of higher learning in these Arab cities, many of which became multi-ethnic cosmopolitan hubs, produced advanced works of philosophy, literature, mathematics, and the physical sciences. Throughout the Medieval Period, in fact, intellectual institutions in major Arab cities devoted themselves to intellectual culture, including preserving and translating ancient Greek and Roman literature, and eventually playing a central role in inspiring European Renaissance thinkers.[67]

Education expert Abdeljalil Akkari has written about how many indigenous Arab peoples were excluded under the colonial education system. This created a wide gap between the educated elite within a society and the illiterate rural masses. Education during the period of colonization was conducted through the colonial language, perpetuating colonial ideas and marginalizing indigenous language, culture, and thought. This had the effect of increasing dependency and drawing Arabs further from their own heritage. The system also focused on modern economic development as opposed to free and critical thought, "restricting modern schooling and especially European-language education to a minimum of students who would simultaneously strengthen the colonial administration and weaken nationalist tendencies."[68] The alternative to Western colonial education during this time came in the form of traditional Qur'anic education in Islamic *madrasas*. This represented an indigenous alternative that was both more accessible to rural populations and was not under foreign influence. However, Qur'anic education focused on memorization and recitation.[69]

Following independence in the Arab world throughout the twentieth century until the present, Akkari observes, national education systems controlled by domestic governments continue to suffer many similar flaws. Post-colonial Arab regimes consist largely of dictators with the primary goal of maintaining their own power. The system of education became a tool for the Arab governments to establish legitimacy and to develop a national workforce. For this reason, post-colonial education became increasingly focused on preparing a population for the skills to join the labor force. In this way the entire education system is considered by central governments to be not a moral or social obligation to their populations, but rather an investment made in order to transform the nation's human capital into national production.[70]

Therefore, there is a void of creative and critical thinking: "Many of the countries of the region have decades of educational centralism combined with little concerns with socio-cultural productivity of schooling—many educational systems in the region suffer from bureaucratic structures that emphasize a top-down approach to learning. Through the production and diffusion of textbooks, ministries of education implement rigid curriculum centered on memorization and dictation as everyday activities."[71]

Thus, in the eyes of the government, the education system is seen through a purely quantitative economic perspective—success is judged by how effectively the education system transforms its students into productive workers who can increase national productivity, even if the process of marginally accomplishing this causes Arab culture and intellectual thought to be stagnant and crippled.[72]

Romani elaborates further that, though public education has grown much more widespread in the Arab world, there is still a huge inequality in access to education. Schools and universities are concentrated in urban areas, where resources and teachers are most abundant, thus: "overvaluation of the general teaching university; poor research; redundancy of the most attractive disciplines, resulting in the demonetization of these disciplines; the related increase in graduate unemployment; the 'brain drain' of the most skilled; and the unavailability of vocational training are among the principal structural problems associated with Arab higher education."[73]

Today, urban areas sorely lack the qualified staff and funds to provide quality education. Akkari has said that in extremely poor areas, especially rural parts of nations, access to education is very low and illiteracy is still widespread. Women are especially underrepresented where education is less accessible. Consequently, the nations with large rural populations like Yemen, Egypt, and Morocco struggle most with implementing universal education.[74]

Most Arab governments control the curricula and programs of study at schools and universities, resulting in a situation in which practically the entirety of Arab culture is controlled and restricted. No truly open dialogue exists on political, economic, social or cultural issues at universities in the Arab world, with the possible exception of the American University of Beirut in Lebanon, due to its unique history and level of independence. Protests and demonstrations are forbidden in most Arab countries, except those organized by the government itself, and meetings of popular organizations and intellectual or cultural societies are not allowed. Instead, military and emergency law is applied in the name of protecting society from terrorists and outlaws. The definitions of 'terrorist' and 'outlaw' are of course arbitrary, tailored to fit government policy and interests. Voices of rationalism, secularism, modernity, and enlightenment have been forced into silence, and Arabs have been left without weapons to defend the peculiarity of their culture and national identity.[75]

YOUTH

In her study on the youth of the Arab world, Emma Murphy notes that the Arab world is home to a disproportionately large youth generation compared to the population at large; about a third of the Arab world population is under the age of fifteen, and this figure is as high as 46 percent in Palestine and Yemen. Arab regimes supported population growth during the second half of the twentieth century, thinking themselves to be increasing potential for national strength and growth. However, as this young Arab generation comes of age today, many Arab nations do not have the jobs to employ this large cohort nor the national resources to support them. Strain is put on public services and national infrastructure, and tension arises between disenfranchised youth and the patriarchal governing regime that the youth are disenfranchised from.[76] This "youthful demographic momentum" presents an enormous challenge to Arab nations on many levels.[77]

Murphy emphasizes that leaders perceived the youth bulge in the Arab world as boding well for society. Governments envisioned a large young generation as an abundance of human capital that could be transformed into a strong labor force and grow national production. The reality is, though, that these youth have not been given a central role in shaping their society at all. Rather than being the force allowing their nation to thrive, Arab youth are marginalized by, and disenfranchised from, their own society. This shows a deep-rooted cultural dysfunction between the Arab ruling elites and the large younger middle and lower classes. Public education institutions have failed. "The promises of post-independence regimes not only remain unfulfilled, but for those who were born too late to play a part in bringing them to power, the gap between rhetoric and reality leaves a deep sense of alienation and exclusion."[78]

Oxford University scholar and author Marilyn Booth further states that the inequality that Arab youth face is extreme. "Many Arab adolescents grow up in cities where rapid expansion far exceeds capabilities of city services and existing housing, and where extreme poverty is juxtaposed with new, conspicuously displayed, wealth."[79] Unemployment disproportionately affects the Arab youth generation. Even in oil-rich Gulf nations, youth unemployment can be over 25 percent; in poorer Arab states youth unemployment approaches 50 percent.

A large uneducated and unemployed youth population, beyond the challenges it creates for the state apparatus and social services, contributes both to cultural stagnation and to rage and tension between the youth and the institutions and elites who control the circumstances of their lives.[80] Development expert Jad Chaaban adds that, ultimately, for the same reasons that youth are disenfranchised from society, they are also left without the ability, skills, or resources to change neither their own situations nor that of their societies.[81]

Murphy further explains that on a more personal, cultural level, the Arab youth generation is experiencing extreme stagnation and frustration in its coming of age. The Arab youth are in a state of waiting. No education means no jobs, and no jobs mean no income to move out of the family house, become independent, and support themselves or a family of their own. Relatively traditional cultural and societal norms tie the ceremony of marriage and family life closely to social position and opportunities. Marriage is the embodiment of becoming an adult in traditional Arab culture, meaning that many Arab youth today are humiliated by being denied the ability to come of age both on cultural and societal levels.[82]

According to Murphy, in recent years youth activism has increased. Traditionally disenfranchised youth have long held very little agency to advocate for themselves within the political system. Most organized youth activism has taken place in urban streets in the form of usually nonviolent, public demonstrations. But in the past decades youth activism has grown even more impassioned.

As we know, youths have been a driving force behind the enormous surge of grassroots political activism across the Arab world since 2010, and their actions quickly removed several entrenched and repressive rulers from power. Murphy writes that the "discussion of existing framings of Arab youth offered thus far indicates that Arab youth as a social category are united not just by age but by shared experiences of political, economic, and social exclusion. This categorization is indeed inclusive of not just those of a certain age conventionally associated with youth, but all those who have been marginalized by the spectrum of failures of the post-independence Arab state."[83]

Engaging these youth populations is essential if any transformation is to occur in the Arab world. The 2016 United Nations Arab Human Development Reports maintain that Arab countries "can achieve a significant leap forward in development, reinforce stability and secure [social and economic] gains in a sustainable manner, if they urgently prioritize adopting policies that ensure the well-being, productivity, self-determination, and good citizenship of their young population."[84]

CONCLUSION

POLITICAL CHANGE: THE KEY TO CULTURAL CHANGE

Arab scholars and intellectuals have analyzed and described the ills of Arab culture, explored ways to move forward, and called for desperately-needed cultural and societal change. Even before the Arab Spring, many academics, poets, writers, journalists, and activists faced exile, imprisonment, and torture at the hands of regimes for expressing these ideas. Yet throughout the twentieth century and the first two decades of the current century, the calls of intellectuals did not translate into sweeping reforms or popular revolution. Their ideas could not change the miserable reality inside Arab society. The popular revolution that was able to change the course of Arab reality came at the hands of the youth, the unemployed, and the marginalized people who started the Arab revolutions in 2010.

Tunisian Mohamed Bouazizi, the twenty-six-year-old sole breadwinner of a family of seven who set himself on fire in the streets in Tunisia to protest the injustice of the regime and the brutality of the police, was the true instigator of change. Soon after, uprisings swelled across Tunisia with people protesting terrible economic conditions, youth unemployment, high food prices, corruption, and the oppressive government. In less than a month, President Ben-Ali was forced out of office and out of the country. The true instigators of change were also the youth in Cairo, Syria, Libya, Yemen, and other Arab countries that marched in the streets of Arab capitals demanding leadership changes and political freedom, chanting "leave" at their rulers. These disenfranchised youths led revolutions that seemed impossible in modern Arab history.

The sudden uprising was a total surprise to the Arab intellectuals themselves. The Arab intellectuals did not predict the revolution. There was a very clear absence of intellectual leaders in the uprising and in the events leading up to it. There was a glaring lack of any scholarly focus. The actual leaders of the revolution were ordinary citizens who exploded in rage and rebellion against the accumulated injustice and harsh treatment by their governments. These ordinary citizens realized and implemented the thoughts and ideals of the Arab intellectuals. Thousands died, thousands were imprisoned, millions were displaced and became refugees outside of their countries. People have paid a high price for their active resistance. The Arab populations have finally spoken with blood not words.

Arabs know that their culture cannot develop or advance without democracy and freedom. They know that democracy and freedom cannot happen without removing the tyrants who stand as obstacles to cultural change. Arabs know that changing their political systems is not achievable without a successful revolution. Nevertheless, for a long time the walls of fear seemed too high.

Finally, not just one but a series of a revolutions took place in the modern Arab world. Four deeply entrenched tyrants were ejected in Tunisia, Libya, Egypt, and Yemen. Bashar al-Assad in Syria continues to face challenges. Even if the revolution in Egypt did not succeed, if Yemen remains in the throes of civil war, if power struggles continue to wrack Libya, and the Syrian civil war approaches its eighth year, people did manage to break through barriers of oppression that kept them restrained for a very long time. Because of the example of these courageous and popular revolutions, the emerging generation will learn how to mobilize, organize, and muster new revolutionary methods. They will discover how to overcome difficulties and setbacks.

The Arabs have realized that they cannot remain marginalized, oppressed, and silent. They know that only a massive revolution can remove the corrupt political systems that stand in the way of social and cultural progress. Now that the walls of fear have collapsed, they shall be collapsed forever.

Iraqi poet Abd al-Wahab al-Bayati best described the struggle of the Arab peoples in the face of adversity and their refusal to succumb:

> They lied.
>
> Happiness is not for sale
>
> The newspapers wrote
>
> That the sky
>
> Rained frogs last night.
>
> They deceived you
>
> Tortured you
>
> Crucified you
>
> In the snare of words
>
> In order to say:
>
> He died
>
> To sell you a place in the sky.
>
> Ah, crying is in vain
>
> I am ashamed
>
> The frogs
>
> Stole happiness from us
>
> Yet in spite of the suffering, I am
>
> On the road to the sun, marching.[85]

Today's tyrants can only fend off future Arab revolutions for a short period. They cannot extinguish the flames of the Arab Spring. The wheels of the Arab revolution have started turning, and they shall continue to move until a true and lasting cultural change in the Arab world begins.

KEY TERMS

———

This glossary provides a list of terms and brief definitions used in the book, and provides transliteration to guide pronunciation.

`Alawites / ʻAlawīyyīn: A branch of Shiʻite Islam the adherents of which are concentrated mostly in Syria, Lebanon, Turkey, and Morocco.

Alf Layla wa Layla / Alf Laylah wa Laylah: Literally *One Thousand and One Nights*, this collection of Arab oral folklore is usually known as the *Arabian Nights* in English.

Arab Spring/ Ar-Rabīʻ al-ʻArabī: The revolutionary uprisings in predominantly Arab countries, starting in December 2010, that sought to overthrow oppressive Arab regimes, and install democratic societies.

Armenians / Arman: A Christian minority living mostly in Syria, Lebanon and Palestine. Armenia is a landlocked country with Turkey to the west and Georgia to the north. Part of the Soviet Union until 1991, Armenia boasts a history longer than most other European countries.

`Ashura / ʻĀshūrāʼ: Shiʻite holiday commemorating the martyrdom of Husayn and his followers at Karbala that takes place on the tenth day of the Islamic month of Muharram. Some worshippers reenact the Karbala scene, recite moving poetry, or even whip themselves with chains to express their mourning.

`Asr / ʻAṣr: The mid-afternoon prayer.

Assyrians / Ashūrīyyīn: A Christian minority group living mostly in Iraq and Syria, Assyrians are native speakers of Aramaic and are also known as Syriacs or Chaldeans.

Ayatollah / Āyat Allāh: High-ranking authority of Islamic law in the Shiʻite hierarchy. ʻGrand Ayatollah' is the highest rank of all.

al-Azhar / al-Azhar: The chief center of Islamic and Arabic learning in the world, Al-Azhar is centered on the mosque of that name in the medieval quarter of Cairo. Founded by the Fatimids in 970, it was formally organized by 988. The oldest university in the world, the basic program of studies was, and still is, Islamic law, theology, and the Arabic language. The head of al-Azhar is informally considered to be the highest Sunni source, though he has no absolute religious authority. In the past, the head of al-Azhar was appointed by a committee of religious scholars; now the position is appointed by the Egyptian government.

al-Qaeda/ al-Qā`ida: A broad-based network of militant Islamist groups, Al-Qaeda was founded in 1988 and associated with the terror attacks on the World Trade Center and the Pentagon in 2001. The name comes from Arabic, meaning literally 'the base.'

Balfour Declaration (November 2, 1917): A statement of British support for "the establishment in Palestine of a national home for the Jewish people." It was made in a letter from Arthur James Balfour, the British foreign secretary, to Lionel Walter Rothschild, 2nd Baron Rothschild, a leader of British Jewry. Though the precise meaning of the correspondence has been disputed, its statements were generally contradictory to both the Sykes-Picot Agreement and the Ḥusayn-McMahon correspondence.

Basmala / Basmalah: Formulaic phrase "in the name of God, the most merciful, the most compassionate" that opens each chapter of the Qur'an.

Bedouin / Badū: A collective name for the original nomadic population living in Arabia. Famous for their poetic expression, nobility, generosity and hospitality, many Bedouin populations still exist today across the Arab world.

Berbers (Amazighis) / Barbar (Amāzīgh): The indigenous peoples of North Africa before Arabs arrived during the Islamic conquest. Berbers have largely retained their own languages and customs in addition to Islam. In Morocco, Berbers recently won the right to educate their children in Tamazight.

Camp David Accords (September 17, 1978): The Camp David Accords are agreements between Israel and Egypt signed on September 17, 1978 that led in the following year to a peace treaty between those two countries, the first such treaty between Israel and any of its Arab neighbors. Brokered by U.S. Pres. Jimmy Carter between Israeli Prime Minister Menachem Begin and Egyptian President Anwar el-Sādāt and officially titled the "Framework for Peace in the Middle East," the agreements became known as the Camp David Accords because the negotiations took place at the U.S. presidential retreat at Camp David, Maryland. Sādāt and Begin were jointly awarded the 1978 Nobel Prize for Peace for their efforts.

Circassians / Sharākisah or Sharkas: An ethnic Sunni minority living mostly in Jordan, Syria, and Palestine, descended from Caucasian peoples.

Copts / Aqbāṭ: A Christian sect mostly concentrated in Egypt, and the largest Christian minority in the Arab world. According to the Gospel of Matthew, Christ and the Holy Family came to Egypt fleeing from Herod. Although integrated in the larger Egyptian nation, the Copts have survived as a distinct religious community forming today between ten and twenty percent of the native population. They pride themselves on the apostolicity of the Egyptian Church whose founder was the first in an unbroken chain of patriarchs.

Dhimmi / Dhimmī: Protected status enjoyed by Christians and Jews in Muslim-conquered lands, involving an extra tax but substantial religious freedom.

Diwan al-Arab / Dīwān al-'Arab: Literally the 'Register of the Arabs,' this is an epithet applied to classical Arabic poetry, which recorded and immortalized every aspect of Arab history, society and culture.

Druze / Durūz: The Druze religion was first promulgated in 1017, during the reign of the sixth Fātimid caliph al-Hakim bi-Amr Allah, (Ruler by the Command of Allah) who ruled over Egypt (996–1021), whom the Druze thought to be an actual incarnation of God. The Druze are publicly open about very few details of their faith. A small religious sect characterized by an eclectic system of doctrines and by a cohesion and loyalty among its members that have enabled them to maintain for centuries their close-knit identity and distinctive faith. The Druze numbered more than one million in the early 21st century and live mostly in Lebanon and Syria.

`Eid al-Adha / 'Īd al-Aḍḥā: The Feast of Sacrifice that constitutes the climax of the annual pilgrimage to Mecca.

`Eid al-Fitr / 'Īd al-Fiṭr: The fast-breaking feast that ends Ramadan.

Fajr / Fajr: The dawn prayer.

Fatwa / Fatwā: A formal religious opinion or ruling.

Fus-ha / Fuṣḥā: Literally "the most eloquent," this refers to either Classical or Modern Standard Arabic (as opposed to colloquial Arabic).

Hadith / Ḥadīth: A body of texts that relate the words and practices of the Prophet Muhammad. Together, the Qur'an and Hadith comprise the essential texts of Islam; unlike the Qur'an, however, the validity and genuineness of various passages of Hadith can be called into question. Throughout Islamic history, thousands of Hadith passages have been examined and rejected as apocryphal by religious authorities, and different sectarian communities may recognize different Hadith texts.

Hajj / Ḥajj: An ancient Arabian pagan tradition of pilgrimage, the hajj was adopted as an Islamic principle by Muhammad in his Farewell Sermon. It is one of the five pillars of Islam.

Hijra / Hijrah: The day of Muhammad's migration from Mecca to Medina, on September 24, 622. This marks the beginning of the Islamic era.

Hira' / Ḥirā': The cave in modern-day Saudi Arabia in which Muhammad spent much time for the sake of isolation and meditation, and where, according to tradition, he received his first divine revelation.

Ijma` / Ijmā`: "Consensus of the community," a source (for Sunnis) of Islamic law in addition to the Qur'an, Hadith and *Sunna*.

Ijtihad / Ijtihād: The process of independent analysis or interpretation of Islamic law.

Iltizam / Iltizām: Arabic for political or social 'commitment,' this became a necessary quality for modern poets in the Arab world.

Imam / Imām: This term means different things to Sunni and Shi`ite Muslims. To Sunnis, an Imam is a respected figure in the community who leads Friday prayers in the mosque, or a prominent religious scholar. To Shi`ites, the Imam is one of twelve hereditary leaders of the *umma* who descended from the bloodline of `Ali bin Abi Talib.

Intifada / Intifāḍah: Arabic for "uprising," two sustained Palestinian Intifadas have erupted against the Israeli occupation, one in 1987 and another in 2000.

`Isha' / `Ishā': The evening prayer.

ISIS / Dā`ish: The Islamic State of Iraq and Syria, also known as ISIL, the Islamic State in Iraq and the Levant. A militant Islamic fundamentalist group active particularly in Syria and Iraq, with followers in others parts of the Middle East and Africa. ISIS emerged in 2006 after the American invasion of Iraq in 2003. The movement also calls itself the State of the Islamic Caliphate.

Jahil / Jāhil: Arabic for "ignorant," Jahil traditionally referred to the Arabs who existed before Islam. Sayyid Qutb reinterpreted Jahil to refer to the insufficiently Islamic society that surrounded him.

Jihad / Jihād: Raised to the dignity of a sixth Pillar of Islam by at least one Muslim sect, the Kharijites. Jihad has many interpretations. Most literally, it refers to waging war in the way of God. Many scholars stress its essentially self-defensive nature. The 'Lesser Jihad', according to the Prophet, represents the armed struggle, while the 'Greater Jihad' should be waged against Muslims' own passionate souls.

Jinn / Jinn: Collective noun encompassing the spirits of Arabic and Muslim tradition, from which the English word 'genie' is derived.

Ka`ba / Ka`bah: A large black cubical structure located in the center of the Grand Mosque in Mecca and, according to Muslim tradition, the first temple built by Abraham and Isma`il. The Ka`ba was used before Islam for pagan rituals.

Karbala`/Karbalā`: A well-known battle in 680 A.D. between Husayn ibn Ali, grandson of the Prophet who was seeking to be Caliph and Yazid, son of Mu`awiya. Husayn was killed with many members of his family. This divided the Muslims into Sunnis and Shi'ites. The Shi`ites are the followers of Husayn and his father Ali.

Katatib / Katātīb: Religious primary schools where children memorize the Qur'an and learn to read and write.

Khalifa / Khalīfah: Arabic for "caliph," and abbreviation of *khalifat rasul allah*, or "successor to the Messenger of God."

Kharijites / Khawārij: Radical group of `Ali's followers who refused to acknowledge the validity of the arbitration between `Ali and Mu`awiya. Kharijites played a major role in early Islamic history.

al-Khulafa' al-Rashidun / al-Khulafā' al-Rāshidūn: The first four "Rightly-Guided" Caliphs.

Kifaya / Kifāyah: Arabic for "enough," the Kifaya movement in Egypt expressed opposition to Mubarak's policies.

Kurds / Akrād: One of the non-Arab ethnic minorities of the Arab world, Kurds are concentrated in Syria and Iraq (as well as the non-Arab states of Turkey and Iran). Many Kurds harbor aspirations for a state of their own. Since the American war and occupation of Iraq began, a *de facto* Kurdish national government has been operating in the northern area of the country.

Laylat al-Qadr / Laylat al-Qadr: The twenty-seventh night of Ramadan, on which Muhammad received his first revelation. On Laylat al-Qadr, Muslims stay awake through the night praying and reading the Qur'an and, in Jerusalem, attend prayer services at the Dome of the Rock.

Mahdi / Mahdī: Arabic for "he who is guided," the Mahdi is the hidden Shi`ite imam who remains in "occultation" but will one day arise to inaugurate the rule of justice on earth.

Maronites / Mawārinah: A Christian sect that forms one of the largest ethnic/religious groups in Lebanon.

**Mu`allaqah / Mu'allaqah:** Literally "hanging" or "suspended," this was a name given to a winning poem at the Fair of Ukaz in pre-Islamic Arabia. After being designated a winner, the poem would be transcribed in gold and hung over the Ka`ba in Mecca.

Mu`tazilite / Mu'tazilī: An ideology promoting the theory that the Qur'an was created rather than revealed.

Maghrib / Maghrib: 1. The post-sunset prayer. 2. North Africa.

Misyar / Misyār: An alternative form of marriage under Sunni law, promoted to address the issue of unaffordable marriage costs, between a man and a woman who propose to continue to live separately but get together for sexual relations. Criticism of *Misyar* marriage includes that it involves a significant curtailing of rights given to women in traditional marriages by Islamic law.

Mujahid / Mujāhid: One who strives or fights in the process of *Jihad*.

Mut`a / Mut`ah: An alternative form of marriage practiced by the Shi`ites, this "marriage of enjoyment" differs sharply from a conventional marriage, which is designed to produce children. It is a temporary marriage with a fixed, limited amount of time specified in the beginning.

Oslo Accords: The Oslo Accords, officially called the Declaration of Principles on Interim Self-Government Arrangements or Declaration of Principles, were finalized in Oslo, Norway in August 1993, and subsequently signed at a public ceremony in Washington, DC in September 1993, with Yasser Arafat signing for the Palestine Liberation Organization and Shimon Peres signing for the State of Israel. In it, the PLO reaffirms its recognition of Israel's right to exist, and in turn, Israel recognizes the PLO as the sole representative of the Palestinian people.

Palestine Liberation Organization (PLO): The Palestine Liberation Organization (PLO) was established in 1964 and has been the embodiment of the Palestinian national movement. It is a broad national front, or an umbrella organization, comprised of numerous organizations of the resistance movement, political parties, popular organizations, and independent personalities and figures from all sectors of life.

Qadi / Qāḍī: Judge in Islamic court.

Qasida / Qaṣīdah: The classical Arabic form of poetry featuring strict rhyme and meter.

Qibla / Qiblah: Direction of Muslim prayers toward the holy city of Mecca.

Qiyas / Qiyās: 'Analogy,' a source (for Sunnis) of Islamic law in addition to the Qur'an, Hadith and *Sunna*.

Qur'an / Qur'ān: The Islamic sacred book, believed to be the word of God as dictated to Muhammad by the archangel Gabriel and written down in Arabic. The Qur'an consists of 114 units of varying lengths, known as *suras* ; the first sura is said as part of the ritual prayer. These touch upon all aspects of human existence, including matters of doctrine, social organization, and legislation. The Qur'an serves as the central religious text of Islam. All Muslims, regardless of religious sectarian differences, recognize the Qur'an as revealed by God to the Prophet Muhammad as a guide for living a moral life. Muslims consider the Qur'an inimitable, written in a language mixed with poetic prose that is inexplicable and divine.

Quraysh / Quraysh: The powerful Meccan tribe, into which Muhammad was born, that resisted Islam until 628, when Muhammad returned to Mecca.

Rajaz / Rajaz: A form of classical Arabic poetry that predates the *qasida*, made up of a single hemistich with no rhyme.

Ramadan / Ramaḍān: The holiest month of the Islamic calendar, marked by Muhammad receiving his first divine revelation. Muslims fast during the whole month of Ramadan, at the end of which is the holiday and feast known as ʿEid al-Fitr.

Rawi / Rāwī: Professional reciter of poetry.

Sajʿ / Saj ʿ: A form of rhymed, meter-less prose that predates the *qasida* form of classical Arabic poetry.

Salat / Ṣalāt: The second pillar of Islam, "prayer," Salat is performed five times daily at times based on the position of the sun. Salat is performed on one's knees while facing in the direction of Mecca. Ritual ablution is required before performing Salat.

Sawm (Siyam) / Ṣawm (Ṣiyām): The third pillar of Islam. Arabic for "fasting," *sawm* is obligatory for most healthy, adult Muslims during the month of Ramadan.

Shah / Shāh: A Persian word originally meaning "king," *Shah* has been adapted by Arabic and other languages to mean 'ruler.' Before 1979, the rulers of the Pahlavid dynasty of Iran used the title of *Shah*, before their ouster in the Islamic Revolution.

Shahada / Shahādah: The first pillar of Islam, the "Declaration of Faith," in which the Muslim proclaims: "I bear witness that there is no god but God and Muhammad is the Messenger of God."

Shaheed / Shahīd: Arabic for "martyr" in any of its various interpretations.

Shariʿa / Sharī ʿah: Arabic term meaning the legal code by which Islamic society should run. Shariʿa contains guidance on every aspect of Islamic life, from personal conduct to the ideal political structure of the Islamic *umma*.

Sheikh / Shaykh: 1. Leader of a tribe. 2. Religious scholar, especially in Sunni Islam.

Shiʿi / Shī ʿ ī: Of or relating to the Shiʿite of Islam. Shiʿite Muslims form a minority of the Muslim world, concentrated mostly in Iraq, Lebanon, Bahrain, Yemen, and of course in Iran. They believe that the first three Caliphs were not the rightful political successors to Muhammad. Unlike in Sunni Islam, there is a central hierarchy of Shiʿite religious authority that hands down decisions; this, in combination with traditional Shiʿite reliance on reason and analogy in jurisprudence, contributed greatly to the conditions that led to the Islamic Revolution in Iran.

Shiʻr / Shi ʻr: Arabic word for "poetry," derived from the verb sha ʻara, meaning to "know, understand, perceive."

Shirk / Shirk: Often translated as "polytheism" or "associating other gods with God."

Sufi / Ṣūfī: Of or relating to the Sufi movement of Islam. The word is derived from the rough woolen cloth that Sufis (Ṣūf means "wool" in Arabic) used to wear. This was a mystic movement that had ascetic tendencies and believed that closeness or Oneness with God could be achieved through dhikr, or "mentioning God," and sometimes religious song and dance. They were vigorously opposed by conservative Sunnis such as Ibn Taymiyya. One of the most famous Sufi figures, Mansour al-Hallaj, was tortured and executed for heresy.

Sumʻa / Sum ʻah: Arabic for "reputation."

Sunna / Sunnah: The exemplary behavior or the personal practice of the Prophet Muhammad.

Sunni / Sunnī: Of or relating to the Sunni of Islam. Sunni Muslims form a majority of the Muslim world; they believe in a literal interpretation of the Qur'an and use Hadith extensively to provide guidance.

Sura / Sūrah: Chapter of the Qur'an.

Sykes-Picot Agreement (May 1916): A secret convention made during World War I between Great Britain and France, with the assent of imperial Russia, for the dismemberment of the Ottoman Empire. The agreement led to the division of Turkish-held Syria, Iraq, Lebanon, and Palestine into various French- and British-administered areas. Negotiations were begun in November 1915, and the final agreement took its name from its negotiators, Sir Mark Sykes of Britain and François Georges-Picot of France.

Turkmen / Turkmān: A Turkic ethnic minority living mostly outside the Arab world, though scattered pockets exist in Iraq, Syria and elsewhere.

ʻUkaz / ʻUkāẓ: Site and marketplace of an annual fair in pre-Islamic Arabia where poets would come to compete in Mecca. Location was tied to the pilgrimage season in pre-Islamic times and served as a place where warring tribes could come together peacefully to worship and trade together.

ʻUlama / ʻUlamā': Sunni religious scholars.

Umayyad / Umawī: A dynasty of Damascus-based Caliphs that succeeded the first four 'Rightly-Guided' Caliphs and was succeeded in turn by the Abbasid dynasty. A second Umayyad dynasty later sprung up in Cordoba, Andalusia, where it reigned for several more centuries.

ʿUmda / ʿUmdah: Village head.

Umma / Ummah: The early pan-Islamic community that binds and connects all believers by transcending differences, providing strong religious social unity, and solidity among Muslims.

ʿUmra / ʿUmrah: A "lesser pilgrimage" to Mecca that does not come at the specific time of *hajj*.

Wahhabism/ al-Wahhābiyya: A strictly orthodox Sunni Muslim sect founded by Muhammad ibn Abd al-Wahhab (1703–1792). It advocates a return to the early Islam of the Qur'an and Sunna, rejecting later innovations; the sect is still the predominant religious force in Saudi Arabia.

Wazir / Wazīr: "Top minister" in the Abbasid and subsequent courts.

Wudu' / Wuḍū': Ritual ablution required before undertaking prayer.

Zamzam / Zamzam: The sacred spring in the valley of Mecca where Muslims believe God revealed a well of water to Isma ʿil as he lay dying of thirst.

Zakat / Zakāt: Fourth pillar of Islam, "alms-giving."

Zaydis / Zaydiyya: A Shi ʿite sect whose adherents today live principally in Yemen. A Zaydi state survived in present-day Yemen until the year 1963.

Zuhr / Ẓuhr: Noon/ The noon prayer.

KEY PEOPLE

───

This glossary contains names of deceased historical, political, and literary figures mentioned in the book, and provides transliteration to guide pronunciation.

`Abd al-Malik bin Marwan / ʿAbd al-Malik bin Marwān (d.705): The fifth caliph of the Umayyad dynasty, ʿAbd al-Malik constructed the Dome of the Rock in Jerusalem.

`Abd al-Muttalib / ʿAbd al-Muṭṭalib (d. 578): Grandfather of the Prophet Muhammad, ʿAbd al-Muttalib looked after Muhammad for a period following the death of his parents, before his own death in 578.

`Abd al-Nasir, Jamal / ʿAbd al-Nāṣir, Jamāl (1918–1970): An influential Egyptian President and prominent advocate of Arab nationalism and pan-Arab thought. ʿAbd al-Nasir was the sole Arab leader to tender his resignation in 1967, though popular demonstrations by Egyptians led him to withdraw the resignation. His funeral in 1970 was one of the largest in history, attended by approximately five million people.

`Abd al-Rahman I / ʿAbd al-Raḥmān I (d. 788): Umayyad prince who escaped massacre by the Abbasids and fled Damascus in 750, arriving in Andalus where he helped establish an independent Umayyad dynasty that would last several more centuries.

`Abd al-Rahman III / ʿAbd al-Raḥmān III (d. 961): Established Umayyad control and authority over all of Andalusia and changed his name from Emir to Caliph, thus creating another Umayyad caliphate.

`Abd al-Raziq, `Ali / ʿAbd al-Rāziq, ʿAlī (1888–1966): Egyptian scholar and Islamic reformer who criticized the Islamic caliphate. See chapter Modern Arab Thought for more details.

`Abdu, Muhammad / ʿAbdū, Muḥammad (1849–1905): Egyptian intellectual and Islamic reformer. See chapter 10, "Modern Arab Thought" for more details.

Abu Bakr / Abū Bakr (d. 634): One of the Prophet Muhammad's closest companions, Abu Bakr was among the first to convert to Islam and then succeeded Muhammad as the first 'Rightly-Guided' Caliph.

Abu Hanifa / Abū Ḥanīfah (d.767): Founder of the Hanafi school of Sunni jurisprudence.

Abu Talib bin ʿAbd al-Muttalib / Abū Ṭālib bin ʿAbd al-Muṭṭalib (d. 619): Uncle of the Prophet Muhammad, Abu Talib is most famous for his son ʿAli, who became the fourth caliph and the most influential figure in Islamic history next to the Prophet himself.

Abu al-Tayyib al-Mutanabbi / Abū al-Ṭayyib al-Mutanabbī (d. 965): A neoclassicist poet of the ʿAbbasid era, widely regarded as the greatest Arab poet of all time.

al-Afghani, Jamal al-Din / al-Afghānī, Jamāl al-Dīn (1839–1897): Pioneering Arab intellectual who called for a return to the truth of Islam. See chapter 10, "Modern Arab Thought" for more details.

ʿAflaq, Michel / ʿAflaq, Mīshīl (1910–1989): A Greek Orthodox Christian studying philosophy and history who, together with Salah al-Din al-Bitar, founded the Arab Students Union at the Sorbonne and later the Baʿth party in Syria.

Ahmad bin Hanbal / Aḥmad bin Ḥanbal (d. 855): Founder of the Hanbali school of Sunni jurisprudence.

Ahmad, Eqbal (1933–1999): Pakistani political philosopher, poet and activist.

ʿAʾisha / ʿĀʾishah: Surviving wife of the Prophet Muhammad who was to play an influential role in later controversies regarding the Prophet's rightful successor.

ʿAli bin Abi Talib / ʿAlī bin Abī Ṭālib (d. 661): The fourth Islamic caliph, ʿAli's rule was marked by controversy and strife within the Islamic community; which led to a division that eventually produced two divergent Islamic movements, Sunnism and Shiʿism. All Muslims respect ʿAli, but Shiʿites especially revere him as the true heir and successor to the Prophet. Shiʿites afford ʿAli certain attributes of the divine.

ʿAli, Muhammad / ʿAlī, Muḥammad (1769–1849): Egyptian ruler who instituted a major process of reform and modernization. ʿAli sent students and scholars to study in the West, including Rifaʿa al-Tahtawi to France as imam.

Amin, Qasim / Amīn, Qāsim (1865–1908): Liberal Egyptian intellectual who sought the freedom and liberation of women. See chapter 10, "Modern Arab Thought" for more details.

`Amr bin al-`As / 'Amr bin al-ʿĀṣ (d. 664): A powerful personality within the tribe of Quraysh who converted to Islam after a treaty was signed between Muhammad and Quraysh in 628. `Amr is known for conquering Egypt on behalf of the growing Islamic empire.

`Antarah bin Shaddad / 'Antarah bin Shaddād (d. circa 600): A pre-Islamic poet, knight and hero who displayed great courage in the famous war of Dahis and al-Ghabra'. `Antarah's love for his cousin `Abla was renowned. His poetry is a mix of the ideal of manhood and genuine Bedouin morals. The Prophet Muhammad said about him: "No Arab was described to me that I wanted to see save `Antarah." His adventurous stories constitute an important part of Arab folklore traditions.

Antoun, Farah / Anṭūn, Faraḥ (1874–1922): Lebanese intellectual, novelist and writer who contributed in a major way to the modernization of the Arabic language.

Arafat, Yasser / ʿArafāt, Yāsir (1929–2004): Yasser Arafat, also spelled Yāsir `Arafāt, also known as Abū `Ammār, president (1996–2004) of the Palestinian Authority (PA), chairman (1969–2004) of the Palestine Liberation Organization (PLO), and leader of Fatah, the largest of the constituent PLO groups. In 1993 he led the PLO to a peace agreement with the Israeli government. Arafat and Yitzhak Rabin and Shimon Peres of Israel were jointly awarded the Nobel Prize for Peace in 1994.

Arkoun, Mohammed / Arkūn, Muḥammad (1928–2010): A leading scholar in Islamic studies from Algeria, and author of books in many languages including English and French.

al-Assad, Hafez / al-Assad, Ḥāfiẓ (1930–2000): President of Syria from 1970 until his death in 2000. His tenure included the 1973 war with Israel and the 1982 crackdown on the Muslim Brotherhood in the city of Hama. He was succeeded by his son, Bashar al-Assad, who has been president since 2000.

al-`Askari, Imam Hasan / al-ʿAskarī, Imām Ḥasan (d. 874): The eleventh Shi`ite imam and father of the "vanished" imam, al-Mahdi. `Askari and his disciple, Nusayr, are often cited in spurring the formation of the `Alawite sect.

Atatürk, Mustafa Kemal (1881–1938): First president of the new Turkish Republic, who constitutionally abolished the Islamic caliphate as an institution.

al-Atrash, Sultan Pasha / al-Aṭrash, Sulṭān Bāshā (1891–1982): Famous and highly re-spected leader of the Druze in the Levant who led the Great National Syrian Revolt against French occupation in the 1920s.

al-Ayyubi, Salah al-Din / al-Ayyūbī, Ṣalāḥ al-Dīn (d. 1193): Kurdish general who became the sultan of Egypt after defeating the Crusaders and eventually founded the Ayyubid dynasty.

al-ʿAzm, Sadiq Jalal / al-ʿAzm, Ṣādiq Jalāl (1934–2016): Born in Syria and a graduate of Yale University, ʿAzm was a premier advocate of secularism and rationalism in the Arab world. His controversial 1969 book *Critique of Religious Thought* has been reprinted several times.

Baha' Allah / Bahā' Allāh (1817–1892): Founder of the Baha'i faith in Iran in 1863, Baha' Allah means "the Splendor of God" in Arabic.

Balfour, Arthur James (1848–1930): British Foreign Secretary who formally pledged Britain's support for the creation of a Jewish state in Palestine in what became known as the Balfour Declaration (see key terms).

al-Banna, Hasan / al-Bannā, Ḥasan (1906–1949): Egyptian political activist and founder of the Muslim Brotherhood who sought a return to the origins of Islam and the restoration of the Islamic state. See chapter 10, "Modern Arab Thought" for more details.

al-Baroudi, Mahmoud Sami / al-Bārūdī, Maḥmūd Sāmī (1839–1904): Neoclassical poet who contributed to the revival of the classical Arab poetry, and the Arabic language.

al-Bayati, Abdul Wahab / al-Bayyātī, ʿAbd al-Wahhāb (1926–1999): A prolific Iraqi poet and intellectual, and one of the pioneers of the Arab free verse movement.

Bencheikh, Jamal Eddine / Jamāl al-Dīn bin Shaykh (1930–2005): Algerian intellectual, poet, and scholar of Arabic literature.

Bennabi, Malik / Ibn Nabī, Mālik (1905–1975): Algerian intellectual who criticized Islamic thought and society as having grown decadent.

al-Bitar, Salah al-Din / al-Bīṭār, Ṣalāḥ al-Dīn (1912–1980): Sunni Muslim from Damascus who met Michel ʿAflaq in Paris while studying at the Sorbonne. Together, they later founded the Baʿth party in Syria.

al-Bustani, Abdullah / al-Bustānī, ʿAbd Allāh (1854–1930): Lexicographer who compiled the modern Arabic dictionary *al-Bustan* and contributed to the modern Arab renaissance.

al-Bustani, Butrus / al-Bustānī, Buṭrus (1819–1883): Lebanese writer who used a new kind of expository prose with simpler modes of expression and new words and idioms. He founded four journals, wrote a several-volume Arabic encyclopedia, and produced the modern dictionary *Muhit al-Muhit*.

Darwish, Mahmoud / Darwīsh, Maḥmūd (1941–2008): The most prominent Palestinian poet, Darwish is well-recognized internationally both for his political activism and his moving verse.

Daouk, Basheer / Dā ' ūq, Bashīr (1931–2007): Founder of influential Beirut cultural periodical Dirasat Arabiya as well as Dar al-Tali`a, a leading publishing press in the Arab world.

Dayf, Shawqi / Ḍayf, Shawqī (1912–2005): A prominent Islamic and literary academic from Egypt, Dayf served as head of the Arabic Language Academy in Cairo and received numerous awards and recognitions for his scholarship.

al-Fasi, `Allal / al-Fāsī, ʿAlāl (1910–1974): Moroccan intellectual and political leader who believed the separation of religion and government was a product of Europe and Christendom.

Fatimah bint Muhammad / Fāṭimah bint Muḥammad (d. 632): The only surviving daughter of the Prophet Muhammad, Fatimah married `Ali bin Abi Talib, the fourth caliph, and holds special significance for Shi`ites.

Gibran, Gibran Khalil / Jubrān, Jubrān Khalīl (1883–1931): A Lebanese poet and author who migrated to North America and provided a crucial modernist voice in literature and culture.

Habibi, Emile / Ḥabībī, Imīl (1922–1996): Prominent Palestinian novelist and politician.

al-Hakim, Tawfiq / al-Ḥakīm, Tawfīq (1898–1987): Egyptian dramatist and playwright, and one of the first true novelists of the Arab world.

al-Hallaj, Husayn Mansour / al-Ḥallāj, Ḥusayn Manṣūr (d. 922): A philosopher, poet and founder of a Sufi order who was accused of heresy and ultimately crucified, decapitated and burned to death.

Haqqi, Yahya / Ḥaqqī, Yaḥyā (1905–1992): Early Egyptian writer and novelist, author of *Umm Hashem's Lamp*.

Hawi, Khalil / Ḥāwī, Khalīl (1919–1982): A Lebanese modernist poet and a fervent champion of Arab nationalism, Hawi shot himself in 1982 on the day the Israeli army invaded Lebanon.

al-Hawrani, Akram / al-Ḥawrānī, Akram (1912–1996): Prominent Syrian nationalist who led the Arab Socialist Party, which united with the Ba`th party in 1953. For a time, Hawrani served as Vice President of the United Arab Republic under Jamal `Abd al-Nasir.

Haykal, Muhammad Hussein / Haykal, Muḥammad Ḥusayn (1888–1956): Egyptian intellectual, novelist and author of *Zaynab*, the first novel in Arabic.

Hitti, Philip K. (1886–1978): A prominent historian born in Lebanon, Hitti became a Lebanese-American professor and scholar at Princeton and Harvard University. He also taught at the American University in Beirut. An authority on Arab and Middle Eastern history, Islam, and Semitic languages, he became a giant among scholars of Arab history and Islamic studies. His many books are important sources for much serious scholarship of the region. His most popular books include two acknowledged classics: *History of the Arabs*, first published in 1937, and *The Arabs: A Short History*, first published in 1949.

Hourani, Albert (1915–1993): A leading British historian of Lebanese descent, Hourani was a teacher and an author of indispensable works of history on the Arab world. In 1958, he became the director of Oxford's Middle East Centre. In 1964, Hourani was offered a position at Harvard, but decided to stay at Oxford. At least two of Hourani's books are classics on the Middle East: *Arabic Thought in the Liberal Age* (1962) is a masterly study of Arab nationalism in the formative period from 1798 to 1939. Almost thirty years later, he published *A History of the Arab Peoples* (1991), which becoming a best-seller in the United States.

Huntington, Samuel (1927–2008): American political scientist and author, consultant to US government agencies, and an important political commentator in national debates on US foreign policy. He attended the University of Chicago, where he received a master's degree, and Harvard University, where he earned a doctorate in 1951 and joined the faculty. Emphasizing the rise of East Asia and Islam, he argued in the controversial *The Clash of Civilizations and the Remaking of World Order* (1996) that conflict between several large world civilizations was replacing conflict between states or ideologies as the dominant cleavage in international relations.

Husayn bin `Ali / Ḥusayn bin `Alī (d. 680): Younger son of `Ali bin Abi Talib who was martyred at Karbala in a massacre by the forces of Mu`awiya. Husayn's martyrdom, for Shi`ites, became a central element in their religious doctrine and theology.

Hussein, Saddam / Ḥusayn, Ṣaddām (1937–2006): President of Iraq from 1979 until 2003, when the United States invaded the country. His brutal rule was marked by costly and unsuccessful wars against neighboring countries, including Iran and Kuwait. Hussein divided the Arab world by invading Kuwait in 1990. He was captured by American forces in 2003 and executed by hanging in 2006 in a suburb outside Baghdad.

Hussein, Taha / Ḥusayn, Ṭāhā (1889–1973): Egyptian intellectual and writer who attracted a great deal of controversy for attempting to apply critical methods to determine the true age of pre-Islamic poetry and for claiming that Egypt is really part of the Western, not Eastern, world. He was also a key figure in the modernization of the Arabic language.

Ibn ʿArabi / Ibn ʿArabī (d. 1240): Greatest Sufi mystic poet of Muslim Spain.

Ibn Hazm / Ibn Ḥazm (d. 1064): Philosopher and theologian of Cordoba who wrote the well-known masterpiece *The Dove's Necklace*, an essay on the psychology, anatomy and manifestations of love in joy and sorrow.

Ibn Hisham / Ibn Hishām (d. 833): A biographer of the Prophet Muhammad, Ibn Hisham edited the previous biography of the Prophet by Ibn Ishaq, whose original work has since been lost.

Ibn Ishaq / Ibn Isḥāq (d. circa 767): The first biographer of the Prophet Muhammad, the original work of Ibn Ishaq has been lost but survives in its edited form by Ibn Hisham.

Ibn Khaldun / Ibn Khaldūn (d. 1406): One of the Arab world's most famous scholars of all time, Ibn Khaldun is considered one of humanity's first social scientists whose work strongly influenced modern sociology and history. His most famous text is the *Muqaddimah*.

Ibn Maʾmun / Ibn Maʾmūn (d. 1204): Born in Cordoba, Ibn Maʾmun was a prominent Jewish intellectual, rabbi, physician and philosopher of the Middle Ages.

Ibn Taymiyya / Ibn Taymīyyah (d. 1328): A devoted disciple of the Hanbali school who became one of the most prolific authors of Arab and Islamic history. Ibn Taymiyya's refusal to yield his political and religious positions resulted in his persecution and imprisonment, and he eventually died in a Damascus prison.

Ibrahim, Hafiz / Ibrahīm, Ḥāfiẓ (1871–1932): A neoclassical Egyptian poet who fought for social and political justice.

Idris, Suhail / Idrīs, Suhayl (1925-2008): Lebanese author and founder of influential literary periodical *al-Adaab*.

Idris, Youssef / Idrīs, Yūsuf (1927-1991): Egyptian novelist and playwright who played a major contributing role in the collective modernization of Arabic literature and language.

al-Jabiri, Mohammed ʿAbid / al-Jābirī, Muḥammad ʿĀbid (1936-2010): Moroccan philosopher and religious scholar who rejects modernist ideas that ignore Arab traditions and fundamentalist ideas based on an idealized image of the Arab past.

Jabra, Jabra Ibrahim / Jabrā, Jabrā Ibrāhīm (1920-1994): Palestinian poet and author who highly valued translation as a means of providing Arab audiences with world literature.

al-Jawahiri, Muhammad Mahdi / al-Jawāhirī, Muḥammad Mahdī (1900-1999): An Iraqi social and political justice advocate and the greatest neoclassical Arab poet of modern times.

al-Kawakibi, ʿAbd al-Rahman / al-Kawākibī, ʿAbd al-Raḥmān (1849-1902): Revolutionary Syrian thinker who promoted nationalism, secularism and social justice. See chapter 10, "Modern Arab Thought" for more details.

Khadijah / Khadījah (d. 623): The wife of the Prophet Muhammad and a crucial figure of Islamic history in her own right, Khadijah was also a successful businesswoman and a highly respected personality within her tribe of Quraysh.

al-Khal, Yusuf / al-Khāl, Yūsuf (1917-1987): Lebanese poet and co-founder, with Adonis, of influential periodical *Shiʿr* in 1957.

Khalid bin al-Walid / Khālid bin al-Walīd (d. 642): A powerful personality within the tribe of Quraysh who converted to Islam after a treaty was signed between Muhammad and Quraysh in 628. Khalid is famous for his military success in Syria and Persia.

al-Khansa' / al-Khansā' (d. 645): An Arabian poetess famous for the elegiac poems she composed for her two brothers who died in battles, and also known for her trance-like recitation style.

Khomeini, Imam Ayatollah Ruhullah / Khumaynī, Imām Āyatullāh Rūḥallāh (1902-1989): The main leader of the Iranian Revolution of 1979, Khomeini played an essential role in overthrowing the Shah of Iran and became the first Supreme Leader of the new

Islamic Republic of Iran. He was a major political and religious philosopher and thinker, and the Islamic Republic owes much of its political legitimacy to Khomeini's ability to adapt traditional Shi`ite theology and identity to the modern political systems.

Khouri, Mounah / Khūrī, Munaḥ ʿAbd Allāh (1918-1996): A Lebanese-born scholar, Khouri was hailed for both his original literary commentary and criticism.

al-Ma`arri, Abu al-`Ala' / al-Ma ʿarrī, Abū al-ʿAlā' (d. 1057): A great Arab poet of the eleventh century, al-Ma`arri wrote the influential *Risalat al-Ghufran*. He was also a philosopher.

al-Maghout, Muhammad / al-Māghūṭ, Muḥammad (1934-2006): One of Syria's most famous modern poets and writers.

al-Mahdi, Muhammad / al-Mahdī, Muḥammad (went into occultation in 874): Twelfth Shi`ite Imam who disappeared as a young child after the death of his father, the eleventh imam Hasan al-`Askari. Twelver Shi`ites believe he did not die, but rather went into occultation, and will return someday to lead a just world.

Mahfouz, Naguib / Maḥfūẓ, Najīb (1911-2006): Winner of the Nobel Prize for Literature in 1988, Mahfouz was a master at the young genre of the Arabic novel. An Egyptian national, he was impaired for the last decade of his life by a stab wound to the neck that he sustained during an assassination attempt in 1994. Mahfouz was famous for his daily attendance at his favorite coffee shop in Cairo, where he would sit and chat with friends and strangers alike.

Mahmoud, `Abd al-Rahim / Maḥmūd, ʿAbd al-Raḥīm (1913-1948): The first Arab poet-martyr of the modern era, Mahmoud died trying to free Palestine from foreign colonization.

Mahmoud, Zaki Najib / Maḥmūd, Zakī Najīb (1905-1993): Liberal Egyptian cultural and literary critic who called for rationalism and scientific thinking. See chapter 10, "Modern Arab Thought" for more details.

al-Mala'ika, Nazik / al-Malā'ikah, Nāzik (1922-2007): Born in Baghdad and one of the Arab world's most famous contemporary female poets, al-Mala'ika was a pioneer of the Arabic free verse movement.

Malik bin Anas / Mālik bin Anas (d. 796): Founder of the Maliki school of Sunni jurisprudence.

al-Ma'louf, Luis / al-Maʻlūf, Lūwīs (1867–1947): Jesuit priest and Arabic lexicographer who wrote the modern Arabic dictionary *al-Munjid*, which was first published in 1908 and has since been reprinted over fifty times.

al-Ma'mun bin Harun / al-Ma'mūn bin Hārūn (d. 833): Abbasid caliph in whose reign *Bayt al-Hikmah* was founded.

al-Manfaluti, Mustafa Lutfi / al-Manfalūṭī, Muṣṭafā Luṭfī (1876–1924): Egyptian writer who played a crucial role in modernizing the classical Arabic language.

al-Mansur, Abu Jaʻfar ʻAbdallah / al-Manṣūr, Abū Jaʻfar ʻAbd Allāh (d. 775): Second Abbasid caliph who came to power after assassinating Shiʻite Imam Jaʻfar al-Sadiq, thus rendering moot the imam's previous treaty with Mansur's father that would have made him caliph. Mansur moved the Islamic capital from Kufa to Baghdad.

Matar, Muhammad ʻAfifi / Maṭar, Muḥammad ʻAfīfī (1935–2010): Egyptian poet and editor who suffered imprisonment for his political views.

al-Mawdudi, Sayyid Abul Aʻla / al-Mawdūdī, Sayyid Abū al-Aʻlā (1903–1979): Renowned Pakistani Islamic scholar who founded the political movement Jamaʻat-e Islami in Pakistan, led the contemporary Islamic renaissance and was among the most outstanding religious thinkers of his time.

al-Mazini, Ibrahim / al-Māzinī, Ibrāhīm (1889–1949): Egyptian novelist, poet and member of the Arabic Language Academy in Cairo.

Menocal, Maria Rosa (1953–2012): Scholar of Muslim Spain and author of *The Ornament of the World: How Muslims, Jews and Christians Created a Culture of Tolerance in Medieval Spain.*

al-Misairi, Abdulwahab / al-Musayrī, ʻAbd al-Wahāb (1938–2008): Prominent Egyptian intellectual who, in May 2007, sued President Mubarak of Egypt seeking an injunction to force the President to protect the Arabic language.

Muʻawiya bin Abi Sufyan / Muʻāwiyah bin Abī Sufyān (d. 680): The first Umayyad caliph, Muʻawiya deposed ʻAli bin Abi Talib as caliph.

Muhammad / Muḥammad (570–632): Born in Mecca to the major Arabian tribe of Quraysh, the Prophet Muhammad founded Islam after receiving an initial revelation from God via the angel Gabriel. Muhammad continued receiving revelations until the end of his life, and after his death these revelations were compiled into the holy book of the Qur'an. During his life, Muhammad served not only as religious inspiration but as political leader of the Islamic community, and oversaw the early Muslims' incredible military victories. The name *Muhammad* in Arabic means "one who is highly praised."

Muhammad bin ʿAbd al-Wahab / Muḥammad bin ʿAbd al-Wahāb (d. 1792): Founder of the Wahhabi school of Sunni Islam, inspired greatly by Ibn Taymiyya and Ahmad bin Hanbal. Muhammad rejected the legitimacy of *ijmaʿ* and *qiyas* in Islamic jurisprudence. Eventually, he left the Ottoman Empire and established an independent state in central Arabia.

al-Munajjid, Salah al-Din / al-Munajjid, Ṣalāḥ al-Dīn (1920–2010): Syrian Islamic thinker who explained the Arabs' defeat in the 1967 war as a result of Muslims abandoning their faith in God.

Munif, ʿAbd al-Rahman / Munīf, ʿAbd al-Raḥmān (1933–2004): Saudi writer and one of the Arab world's greatest novelists until his death in 2004, Munif authored *Cities of Salt*.

Musa bin Nusayr / Mūsā bin Nuṣayr (d. 716): A Syrian-Arab Muslim named by the Umayyads as governor of North Africa, Musa pushed the Byzantines from the territory west of Carthage and set up the conquest of Andalusia.

Musa, Salama / Mūsā, Salāmah (1877–1958): Egyptian thinker who called for rationalism and scientific thinking. See chapter Modern Arab Thought for more details.

al-Mutanabbi, Abu al-Tayyib / al-Mutanabbī, Abū al-Ṭayyib (d. 965): A neoclassicist poet of the Abbasid era, widely regarded as the greatest Arab poet of all time.

Pahlavi, Mohammad Reza / Pahlavī, Moḥammed Reẓā (1919–1980): The last Shah of Iran and the monarchic Pahlavi dynasty, he was ousted by Imam Khomeini and the Islamic Revolution in 1979.

Pedersen, Johannes (1883–1977): A Danish linguist, theologian and scholar of ancient Arabic manuscripts.

Pound, Omar (1926–2010): Well-known translator of Arabic and Persian poetry and a poet in his own right.

Qabbani, Nizar / Qabbānī, Nizār (1923–1998): A Syrian poet, Qabbani was well-known for his championship of women's rights, his erotic love poetry, and the simple elegance of his style. He lived much of his life in self-imposed exile and died in London.

al-Qasim, Samih / al-Qāsim, Samīḥ (1939–2014): Palestinian poet heavily involved in literary resistance and social justice causes.

al-Qays, Imru' / al-Qays, Imru' (d. circa 544): Son of a king and author of one of the famous Suspended Odes (the Mu'allaqat) of pre-Islamic Arabia.

Qutb, Sayyid / Quṭb, Sayyid (1906–1966): An Islamic writer, executed by the Egyptian government, Qutb has had far-reaching effects on Islamic fundamentalist and political movements.

al-Rashid, Harun / al-Rashīd, Hārūn (d. 809): Fifth and most famous Abbasid caliph who generously supported writers, artists, musicians, philosophers, scientists and scholars.

Rida, Muhammad Rashid / Riḍā, Muḥammad Rashīd (1865–1935): Lebanese intellectual who promoted the acquisition of Western science and technology; see chapter 10, "Modern Arab Thought".

al-Rusafi, Ma'ruf / al-Ruṣāfī, Ma'rūf (1875–1945): Iraqi poet who fought for social and political justice.

Sa'ada, Antoun /Sa'ādah, Anṭūn (1904–1949): Lebanese intellectual and political activist who advocated Arab unity in the Fertile Crescent and founded the Syrian National Party. See chapter 10, "Modern Arab Thought."

al-Sadat, Anwar / al-Sādāt, Anwar (1918–1981): Egyptian army officer and politician who was president of Egypt from 1970 until his assassination by members of the Muslim Brotherhood in 1981. He was the successor to Egyptian President Jamal 'Abd al-Nasir. He initiated peace negotiations with Israel, and shared the 1978 Nobel Prize for Peace with Israeli Prime Minister Menachem Begin. Under their leadership, Egypt and Israel made peace with each other in 1979.

al-Sadiq, Ja'far / al-Ṣādiq, Ja'far (d.765): Great-grandson of Imam Husayn bin 'Ali and spiritual leader of the Shi'ite community, murdered by Caliph al-Mansur.

al-Saffah, Abu al-Abbas / al-Saffāḥ, Abū al-'Abbās (d.754): First Abbasid caliph who took over the Islamic empire after the death of the final Umayyad Caliph Marwan II.

Said, Edward / Sa'īd, Idwārd (1935–2003): Palestinian-American academic, political activist, and literary critic who examined literature in light of social and cultural politics. He was an outspoken proponent of the political rights of the Palestinian people and the creation of an independent Palestinian state. In 1978 he published *Orientalism*, his best-known work and one of the most influential scholarly books of the 20th century. In it Said examined Western scholarship of the 'Orient' specifically of the Arab Islamic world (though he was an Arab Christian), and argued that early scholarship by Westerners in that region was biased and projected a false and stereotyped vision of 'otherness' on the Islamic world that facilitated and supported Western colonial policy.

al-Sayyab, Badr Shakir / al-Sayyāb, Badr Shākir (1926–1964): A prominent Iraqi poet and pioneer of the Arabic free verse movement.

al-Sayyid, Ahmad Lutfi / al-Sayyid, Aḥmad Luṭfī (1872–1963): Liberal Egyptian intellectual who sought the freedom and liberation of women. See chapter 10, "Modern Arab Thought."

al-Shafi'i, Muhammad bin Idris / al-Shāfi'ī, Muḥammad bin Idrīs (d. 820): Founder of the Shafi'i school of Sunni jurisprudence.

Sharabi, Hisham / Sharābī, Hishām (1927–2005): A prominent Arab intellectual, he is known for his work on political and social theory and academic advocacy for women's liberation and causes. Sharabi co-founded the Center for Contemporary Arab Studies at Georgetown University.

Shari'ati, Ali / Sharī'atī, 'Alī (1933–1977): Famous Iranian religious philosopher and sociologist.

al-Sharqawi, Abdel Rahman / al-Sharqāwī, 'Abd al-Raḥmān (1920–1987): Egyptian intellectual and novelist whose novels were pioneering in style and language.

al-Shartuni, Sa'id / al-Shartūnī, Sa'īd (1849–1912): Lexicographer who compiled the modern Arabic dictionary *Aqrab al-Mawarid*.

Shawqi, Ahmad / Shawqī, Aḥmad (1868–1932): Neoclassical poet and one of Egypt's most famous artistic figures, Shawqi is sometimes known by the nickname "Prince of Poets."

Shoukri, Muhammad / Shukrī, Muḥammad (1935-2003): Well-known Moroccan novelist and author of *For Bread Alone*.

Subhi, Muhyi al-Din / Ṣubḥī, Muḥyī al-Dīn (1935-2003): A prominent Syrian literary critic and writer.

al-Tahtawi, Rifa`a Rafi` / al-Ṭahṭāwī, Rifā 'ah Rāfi ' (1801-1873): Egyptian intellectual who admired and criticized French society; see chapter 10, "Modern Arab Thought."

Tarabishi, George / Ṭarābīshī, Jūrj (1939-2016): Born in Syria and later living in Lebanon and France, Tarabishi is a leading Arab writer, translator and critic, and a respected scholar of Western and Arab ideologies.

Tariq bin Ziyad / Ṭāriq bin Ziyād (d. 720): Berber lieutenant of Musa bin Nusayr who undertook the first conquest of Andalusia and landed near the Rock of Gibraltar, which was named in Arabic after him.

Tuqan, Fadwa / Ṭūqān, Fadwah (1917-2003): Major Palestinian poet who wrote love poems in addition to her main focus on the Palestinian struggle and resistance.

Tuqan, Ibrahim / Ṭūqān, Ibrāhīm (1905-1941): A Palestinian poet who advocated political and social justice, and older brother of Fadwa Tuqan.

**`Umar bin al-Khattab / 'Umar bin al-Khaṭṭāb (d. 644):** The second Islamic caliph, `Umar greatly expanded the physical territory of the Islamic empire.

Umm Kulthoum / Umm Kulthūm (1898-1975): The most beloved singer in the Arab world, Umm Kalthoum dominated radio and television while she was alive and is still overwhelmingly popular today. She allied herself with Arab nationalist causes and then-President of Egypt Jamal `Abd al-Nasir. Her funeral was one of the largest in Egypt's history.

`Uthman bin `Affan / 'Uthmān bin 'Affān (d.656): The third Islamic caliph, Uthman directed the compilation of a canonical text of the Qur'an from previous unofficial versions. Uthman directed the continual military expansion of the growing Islamic empire.

Waraqa bin Nawfal / Waraqah bin Nawfal (d. 610): Christian monk of Mecca and cousin of Khadijah who became one of Islam's first converts.

al-Yaziji, Nasif / al-Yāzijī, Nāṣīf (1800–1871): Lebanese writer and major contributor to the modernization of the Arabic language.

al-Zahawi, Jamil Sidqi / al-Zahāwī, Jamīl Sidqī (1863–1936): Iraqi poet who advocated social and political justice.

al-Za`im, Husni / al-Za'īm, Ḥusnī (1897–1949): Syrian military colonel who took power in a military coup, dissolving the elected government. He was executed several months later in a second coup.

Zaydan, Jurji / Zaydān, Jūrjī (1861–1914): Lebanese intellectual, novelist and Arab nationalist who became a major contributor to the modernization of the Arabic language.

Zayyad, Tawfiq / Zayyād, Tawfīq (1929–1994): A Palestinian poet, Zayyad also served as mayor of Nazareth and was a prominent human rights advocate.

Zurayk, Constantine / Zurayq, Qusṭanṭīn (1909–2000): Born in Damascus, Zurayk served as president of both the University of Damascus and the American University of Beirut. He was widely regarded for his influence over many trends in national Arab thought.

ENDNOTES

CHAPTER I

1   Philip Hitti, *The Arabs: A Short History, Revised Edition* (Chicago: Second Gateway Edition, 1970), 12.
2   Hitti, *The Arabs*, 14.
3   Hitti, 14.
4   Hitti, 16.
5   Hitti, 17.
6   Hitti, 21-27.
7   Hitti, 21-27.
8   Exodus 3;1 18:10-12, as quoted in Hitti, 24.
9   Hitti, 24.
10 Hitti, 24, 25.
11 Bernard Lewis, *The Arabs in History* (New York: Harper Torchbooks, 1966), 11.
12 Lewis, *The Arabs in History*, 14.
13 Lewis, 12.
14 Lewis, 15.
15 Halim Barakat, *The Arab World: Society, Culture and State* (University of California Press, 1993), 39.
16 Albert Hourani, *A History of the Arab Peoples* (Cambridge, MA: The Belknap Press, 2002), 257.
17 Mark Allen, *Arabs* (New York: Continuum, 2006), 2.
18 Lewis, *The Arabs in History*, 9.
19 Barakat, *The Arab World: Society, Culture and State*, 33-36.
20 Edward W. Said, *The Politics of Dispossession: The Struggle for Palestinian Self-Determination, 1969-1994* (New York: Vantage Books, 1995), 388-389.
21 Albert Hourani, *Arabic Thought in the Liberal Age: 1798-1939*, 15th print. (Cambridge University Press, 2005), 1.
22 Hitti, *The Arabs: A Short History, Revised Edition*, 41-42.
23 Barakat, *The Arab World: Society, Culture and State*, 39.
24 George Tarabishi, *al-Hayat* newspaper, 3/22/2005.
25 Zurayk, *Tensions in Islamic Civilization*, 11.
26 Zurayk, 6.
27 Zurayk, 18-19.
28 Zurayk, 10-11.
29 The Qur'an 9:51.
30 Halim Barakat, *The Arab World: Society, Culture, and State* (Los Angeles: University of California Press, 1993), 191.
31 Qur'an 13:11.
32 Barakat, *The Arab World: Society, Culture, and State*, 193.
33 Abdul Wahab al-Bayati & Muhyi al-Din Subhi, *al-Bahth `an Yanabi` al-Shi`r wa al-Ru`ya [Searching for the Springs of Poetry and Vision]* (Beirut: Dar al-Tali`a, 1990), 6.
34 al-Arabiya. Available: http://www.alarabiya.net/articles/2007/06/08/35268.html#000.
35 Faysal Darraj, *al-Quds al-Arabi* newspaper, June 19, 2007.
36 Muhyi al-Din Subhi, *Malamih al-Shakhsiya al-Arabiyya* (Tunis: al-Dar al-Arabiya lil Kitab, 1978), 5.
37 James J. Zogby, *What Arabs Think: Values, Beliefs and Concerns* (Washington DC: Zogby International, The Arab Thought Foundation, 2002), 1.
38 Suha J. Sabbagh, *Sex, Lies and Stereotypes: the Image of the Arabs in American Popular Fiction* (Washington, D.C. ADC Research Institute, ADC issue paper no. 23, 1990), 11.

39 Muhammad Najib Butalib in *Surat al-Aakhar: al-Arabi Naziran wa Manzuran Ilayh*, ed. al-Tahir Labib (Beirut: Markaz Dirasat al-Wahda al-Arabiyya, 1999), 433–434.

40 Al-Tahir Labib in *Surat al-Aakhar: al-Arabi Naziran wa Manzuran Ilayh*, ed. al-Tahir Labib (Beirut: Markaz Dirasat al-Wahda al-Arabiyya, 1999), 31.

41 Marlin Nasr in *Surat al-Aakhar: al-Arabi Naziran wa Manzuran Ilayh*, ed. al-Tahir Labib (Beirut: Markaz Dirasat al-Wahda al-Arabiyya, 1999), 464.

42 Suha J. Sabbagh, *Sex, Lies and Stereotypes: the Image of the Arabs in American Popular Fiction*, 3.

43 Sabbagh, *Sex, Lies and* Stereotypes, 4.

44 Edward W. Said, *Orientalism* (NY: Pantheon Books, 1978), 286–287.

45 Raphael Patai, *The Arab Mind*, (NY: Hatherleigh Press, 2002), x.

46 Patai, *The Arab Mind*, xi.

47 Seymour Hersh, *The New Yorker*, May 24, 2004.

48 Hersh, *The New Yorker*.

49 Patai, *The Arab Mind*, 106.

50 Hersh, *The New Yorker*, May 24, 2004.

51 Emran Qureshi, *Boston Globe*, May 30, 2004. Available: http://www.boston.com/news/globe/ideas/articles/2004/05/30/misreading_the_arab_mind.

52 Qureshi, *Boston Globe*.

CHAPTER 2

1   Elizabeth Fernea, ed., *Women and Family in the Middle East* (Indiana University Press, 1985), 20.

2   Samir al-Sa`eedi, *Aslal al-`A'ila al-`Arabiyya wa Anwa` al-Zawaj al-Qadeema `ind al-`Arab* (Beirut: Dar al-Multaqa, 2000), 9–10.

3   Fernea, ed., *Women and Family in the Middle East*, 19.

4   Halim Barakat, *The Arab World: Society, Culture, and State* (University of California Press, 1993), 97–118.

5   Arab Human Development Report 2004: *Towards Freedom in the Arab World* (NY: United Nations Publications, 2005), 17.

6   Arab Human Development Report 2004: *Towards Freedom in the Arab World, 17*.

7   Barakat, *The Arab World: Society, Culture, and State*, 97–118.

8   Shereen El Feki, *Sex and the Citadel: Intimate Life in a Changing Arab World* (New York: Anchor Books, 2013), 36.

9   Hoda Rashid and Maged Osman, in *The New Arab Family*, ed. Nicholas Hopkins, (Cairo: The American University of Cairo, 2003), 20–29.

10 Arab Human Development Report 2002 (NY: United Nations Publications, 2002), 28–29.

11 Rashid and Osman, in *The New Arab Family*, ed. Nicholas Hopkins, 20–37.

12 In 2018, changes to this law were under discussion in Saudi Arabia.

13 Barakat, *The Arab World: Society, Culture, and State*, 99.

14 Barakat, *The Arab World: Society, Culture, and State*, 103.

15 http://www.worldbank.org/en/news/feature/2016/03/07/the-state-of-womens-rights-in-the-arab-world

16 Conversations with Hisham Sharabi, 2000–2001.

17 Hisham Sharabi, *Neopatriachy: A Theory of Distorted Change in Arab Society* (Oxford University Press, 1988), 41.

18 Barakat, *The Arab World: Society, Culture, and State*, 110.

19 Sharabi, *Neopatriachy: A Theory of Distorted Change in Arab Society*, 45–59.

20 Interviews with Arab young adults during the period 2005–2017.

21 Fatima, several personal interviews, 2006, 2007, 2008.

22 Hadiya, personal interview, summer 2005.

23 Majda, personal interview, January 2008.

24 Ibrahim, personal interview, summer 2005.

25 Rashid and Ja`far, personal interviews, summer 2015.

26 Shadi, personal interview, April 2017.

27 All interviewed were in agreement on this point.

CHAPTER 3

1   Edward Said, *al-Ahram* newspaper, February 2004, Issue 677. Available: http://weekly.ahram.org.eg/2004/677/cu15.htm.

2   Albert Hourani, *Arabic Thought in the Liberal Age: 1798-1939* (Cambridge University Press, 15th printing, 2005), 1.

3   Johannes Pedersen, *The Arabic Book*, trans. Geoffrey French (Princeton University Press, 1984), 16.

4   Qur'an 12:2.

5   Qur'an 20:113.

6   Qur'an 39:28.

7   Jamal al-Din bin al-Sheikh, *al-Shi`riyya al-Arabiyya* (Morocco: Dar Tubqal, 1989), 9.

8   Jaroslav Stetkevych, *The Modern Arabic Literary Language: Lexical and Stylistic Developments,* (University of Chicago Press, 1970), 61.

9   Mounh Khouri, *The Genius of Arab Civilization*, ed. John R. Hayes (Cambridge: The MIT Press, 1983), 18.

10 Jurji Zaydan, *Tarikh al-Lugha al-Arabiyya* (Beirut: Dar al-Hadatha, 1980), 110.

11 Issa Boullata, *Critical Perspectives on Modern Arabic Literature,* ed. Issa Boullata (Three Continents Press, 1980), 3.

12 Zaydan, *Tarikh al-Lugha al-Arabiyya*, 26.

13 Albert Hourani, *A History of the Arab Peoples* (Cambridge: The Belknap Press, 2002), 305.

14 Roger Allen, *The Arabic Novel: A Historical and Critical Introduction* (New York: Syracuse University Press, 1995), 65-66.

15 Faysal Darraj, *Nazariyyat al-Riwaya wa al-Riwaya al-Arabiyya* (Morocco: al-Markaz al-Thaqafi al-Arabi, 1999), 190.

16 Faysal Darraj, *Nazariyyat al-Riwaya wa al-Riwaya al-Arabiyya*, 143.

17 Emile Ya`qub, *al-Ma`ajim al-Lughawiyya al-Arabiyya: Bada`atuha wa Tatawwuruha* (Dar al-`Ilm lil Malayeen, 1981), 128.

18 Kees Versteegh, *The Arabic Language* (Edinburgh University Press, 1997), 175.

19 Barakat, *al-Mujtama` al-Arabi fi al-Qarn al-`Ishreen*, 716.

20 Edward W. Said, *al-Ahram* newspaper, February 2004, Issue 677. Available: http://weekly.ahram.org.eg/2004/677/cu15.htm.

21 Edward W. Said, *al-Ahram* newspaper, February 2004.

22 al-Jazeera. Available: http://www.aljazeera.net/NR/exeres/141558FA-92A5-492A-AE0D-8581B23208EE.htm.

23 *al-Quds al-Arabi* newspaper, May 11, 2007.

24 *al-Quds al-Arabi* newspaper, May 11, 2007.

25 Talal Salman, *Ra` Al-Yawn* newspaper, October 3, 2017.

26 Abdulla Al-Nimri, *Ra`i Al-Yawn* newspaper, October 22, 2017.

27 Faisal Al-Qasim, *Al-Quds Al-Arabi*, December 30, 2017.

28 Personal interview, May 2007.

29 al-Jazeera. Available: http://www.aljazeera.net/NR/exeres/62BBBEAA-21AE-4492-A967.

30 *al-Ahram* newspaper. Available: http://weekly.ahram.org.eg/1999/448/feature.htm.

31 *al-Ahram* newspaper. Available: http://weekly.ahram.org.eg/1999/448/feature.htm.

32 al-Jazeera. Available: http://www.aljazeera.net/NR/exeres/E8F6C225-E43D-40F7-86E1-3FD1ACA53EB2.htm.

33 *al-Ahram* newspaper. Available: http://weekly.ahram.org.eg/1999/448/feature.htm.

34 al-Jazeera. Available: http://www.aljazeera.net/NR/exeres/E8F6C225-E43D-40F7-86E1-3FD1ACA53EB2.htm.

35 al-Jazeera. Available: http://www.aljazeera.net/Channel/archive/archive?ArchiveId=90807.

36 Chronicle of Higher Education, June 19, 2012. Available: http://www.chronicle.com/article/Higher-Education-Reform-Stalls/132405

37 D. D. Guttenplan, "Battling to Preserve Arabic from English's Onslaught," *New York Times,* June 11, 2012. Available: http://www.nytimes.com/2012/06/11/world/middleeast/11iht-educle-de11.html

38 Furman, Nelly, David Goldberg, and Natalia Lusin, "Enrollments in Languages other than English in United States Institutions of Higher Education, Fall 2015." *Modern Language Association of America*. https://apps.mla.org/pdf/2013_enrollment_survey.pdf

CHAPTER 4

1   M.M. Badawi, *A Short History of Modern Arabic Literature* (Oxford: Clarendon Press, 1993), 19.
2   Jamal Eddin Bencheikh, *Arab Poetics*, trans. M. Hanoun, et al., (Morocco: Tubqal, 19976), 23.
3   Adonis, *An Introduction to Arab Poetics*, trans. Catherine Cobham (The University of Texas, Austin, 1990), 32.
4   Johannes Pedersen, *The Arabic Book*, trans. Geoffrey French (Princeton University Press, 1984), 17.
5   R.A. Nicholson, *A Literary History of the Arabs* (Cambridge University Press, 1930), 71.
6   Bencheikh, *Arab Poetics*, 74.
7   Bencheikh, *Arab Poetics*, 75.
8   Mounah Khouri, in *The Genius of Arab Civilization: Source of Renaissance*, ed. John R. Hayes (Cambridge, Massachusetts: The MIT Press, 1983), 24.
9   Mounah Khouri, *The Genius of Arab Civilization: Source of Renaissance.*, 22.
10 Adonis, *An Introduction to Arab Poetics*, 57.
11 Adonis, *An Introduction to Arab Poetics*, 57.
12 Nicholson, *A Literary History of the Arabs*, 87–88.
13 Adonis, *An Introduction to Arab Poetics*, 27.
14 Albert Hourani, *A History of the Arab Peoples* (Harvard University Press, 2002), 12.
15 Khouri, *The Genius of Arab Civilization: Source of Renaissance*, 20.
16 Hourani, *A History of the Arab Peoples*, 12.
17 Nicholson, *A Literary History of the Arabs*, 105.
18 Adonis, *Arab Poetics*, 16.
19 Khouri, *The Genius of Arab Civilization: Source of Renaissance*, 22.
20 Adonis, *An Introduction to Arab Poetics*, 57.
21 Khouri, *The Genius of Arab Civilization: Source of Renaissance*, 25.
22 Adonis, *Arab Poetics*, 16, 27.
23 Adonis, *Arab Poetics*, 16, 27.
24 Khouri, *The Genius of Arab Civilization: Source of Renaissance*, 27.
25 Imru' al-Qays, in *Translations of Ancient Arabian Poetry*, trans. Charles James Lyall (New York: Columbia University Press, 1930), 103–104.
26 Khouri, *The Genius of Arab Civilization: Source of Renaissance*, 27.
27 al-Shanfara of Azd, in *Translations of Ancient Arabian Poetry*, trans. Charles James Lyall (New York: Columbia University Press, 1930), 81.
28 Bencheikh, *Arab Poetics*, 75.
29 Khouri, *The Genius of Arab Civilization: Source of Renaissance*, 20–25.
30 al-Shareef al-Radhi, in *Lyrics from Arabia*, trans. Ghazi al-Qusaibi (Washington, D.C.: Three Continents Press, 1983), 7.
31 Bencheikh, *Arab Poetics*, 77.
32 Durayd bin Simma, in *A Literary History of the Arabs*, trans. R.A. Nicholson, (Cambridge University Press, 1930), 83.
33 Bencheikh, *Arab Poetics*, 77.
34 Badawi, *A Short History of Modern Arabic Literature*, 22.
35 Hourani, *A History of the Arab Peoples*, 13.
36 Johannes Pedersen, *The Arabic Book*, 6.
37 Johannes Pedersen, *The Arabic Book*, 17.
38 Adonis, *An Introduction to Arab Poetics*, 13–29.
39 Jawad `Ali, *al-Mufassal fi Tarikh al-Arab Qabl al-Islam* (Beirut: Dar al-`Ilm lil Malayeen, 1976), vol.1, 276.
40 Adonis, *An Introduction to Arab Poetics*, 43.
41 Bencheikh, *Arab Poetics*, 71.
42 Badawi, *A Short History of Modern Arabic Literature*, 22.

43   Khouri, *The Genius of Arab Civilization: Source of Renaissance*, 29.
44   Jamil bin Ma`mar, in *The Genius of Arab Civilization: Source of Renaissance*, trans. Mounah Khouri, 26.
45   Ibid., verses by Qays bin al-Mulawwah.
46   Shawqi Dayf, *al-`Asr al-`Abbasi al-Awwal* (Cairo: Dar al-Ma`arif, 1966), 89.
47   Khouri, *The Genius of Arab Civilization: Source of Renaissance*, 30, 36.
48   Shihab al-Din al-`Azazi, in *Muwashshah Poems from Andalusia*, trans. Arthur Wormhoudt (Oskaloosa, Iowa: William Penn College, 1985), 6.
49   Khouri, *The Genius of Arab Civilization: Source of Renaissance*, 28-37.
50   Badawi, *A Short History of Modern Arabic Literature*, 2-3.
51   Salma Khadra Jayyusi, *Modern Arabic Poetry, An Anthology* (New York: Columbia University Press, 1987), 1-7.
52   Badawi, *A Short History of Modern Arabic Literature*, 11, 24.
53   Badawi, *A Short History of Modern Arabic Literature*, 11.
54   Badawi, *A Short History of Modern Arabic Literature*, 76.
55   Jayyusi, *Modern Arabic Poetry, An Anthology*, 4.
56   Bassam Frangieh, a preface to Abdul Wahab Al-Bayati, *Love, Death, and Exile: Poems Translated from Arabic by Bassam K. Frangieh* (Georgetown University Press, 2004), 1.

CHAPTER 5

1   Constantine Zurayk, *Tensions in Islamic Civilization* (Washington, D.C.: Georgetown University, Center of Contemporary Arab Studies, 1978), 5.
2   Mohammed Arkoun, *al-Fikr al-Islami: Naqd wa Ijtihad [Islamic Thought, Criticism and Interpretation]*, trans. into Arabic by Hashim Salih (London, Dar al-Saqi, 1998), 53-54.
3   `Ali Muhammad al-Sallabi, *al-`Aqidah al-Salafiyya [Salafi Doctrine]* (United Arab Emirates, al-Sahaba Publishers, 2001), 11-12.
4   Hasan Hanafi, *al-Turath wa al-Tajdid [Heritage and Renewal]* (Beirut, Dar al-Tanwir, 1981), 131.
5   The Qur'an 34:28.
6   Qur'an 49:12.
7   Qur'an 7:33.
8   Shawqi Dayf, *Tarikh al-Adab al-Arabi: al-`Asr al-Islami [History of Arabic Literature: The Islamic Age]* (Cairo: Dar al-Ma`arif, 1963), 12-15.
9   Seyyed Hossein Nasr, *Traditional Islam in the Modern World* (London, Kegan Paul International, 1987), 76.
10   Majid Fakhry, *The History of Islamic Philosophy* (New York, Cambridge University Press, 1983), xv.
11   Zurayk, *Tensions in Islamic Civilization*, 6-7.
12   While several biographies like that of Ibn Hisham have since been written on the Prophet, the first record of Muhammad's life was written by Ibn Ishaq, and this record, although lost, can be found in Ibn Hisham's own work. See chapter 9 on the Arabic novel in this book for more details.
13   Philip K. Hitti, *History of the Arabs: From the Earliest Times to the Present*, 4th ed. (New York: The Macmillan Company, 1951), 12.
14   Qur'an 33:40.
15   Qur'an 61:6.
16   Akbar S. Ahmed, *Islam Today: A Short Introduction to the Muslim World* (London: I.B. Tauris and Company, 1999), 17.
17   John L. Esposito, *Islam: The Straight Path*, 3rd ed. (New York: Oxford University Press, 1998), 6.
18   Qur'an 97:1-4.
19   Qur'an 96:1-5.
20   Qur'an 74: 1-3.
21   Hitti, *History of the Arabs*, 113.
22   Karen Armstrong, *A History of God* (New York: Random House, 1994), 138.
23   Jalal al-Din al-Suyuti: *al-Itqan fi `Ulum al-Qur'an*, quoted in Armstrong, *A History of God*, 139.
24   Jalal al-Din al-Suyuti: *al-Itqan fi `Ulum al-Qur'an*, 140.
25   Bukhari, *Hadith* 1.3, quoted in Armstrong, *A History of God*, 139.

26 Armstrong, *A History of God*, 139, 140,155.
27 Qur'an 4:136.
28 Qur'an 16:123.
29 Zurayk, *Tension in Islamic Civilization*, 4–7.
30 Esposito, *Islam: The Straight Path*, 131.
31 Armstrong, *A History of God*, 139–145.
32 Armstrong, *A History of God*, 146.
33 Armstrong, *A History of God*, 155.
34 al-Tabari, quoted in Hitti, *History of the Arabs*, 116.
35 Armstrong, *A History of God*, 155, 165.
36 Qur'an 17:1.
37 Karen Armstrong, "Was It Inevitable," in *How Did This Happen? Terrorism and the New War*, eds. James F. Hoge and Gideon Rose (New York: Public Affairs, 2001), 57.
38 Karen Armstrong, "Was It Inevitable," 58.
39 Philip Hitti, *The Arabs: A Short History, Revised Edition* (Chicago: Second Gateway Edition, 1970), 33–38.
40 Hitti, *The Arabs: A Short History, Revised Edition*, 37.
41 Hitti, *The Arabs: A Short History, Revised Edition*, 38.
42 Hitti, *The Arabs: A Short History, Revised Edition*, 39.
43 Hitti, *The Arabs: A Short History, Revised Edition*, 39.
44 Hitti, *The Arabs: A Short History, Revised Edition*, 39.
45 Hitti, *The Arabs: A Short History, Revised Edition*, 40.
46 Albert Hourani, *A History of the Arab Peoples* (Cambridge: The Belknap Press of Harvard University Press, 2002), 147–148.
47 Qur'an 3:110.
48 Albert Hourani, *A History of the Arab Peoples* (Cambridge: The Belknap Press of Harvard University Press, 2002), 147–148.
49 Esposito, *Islam: The Straight Path*, 129.
50 Esposito, *Islam: The Straight Path*, 129.
51 Qur'an 2:143.
52 Zurayk, *Tension in Islamic Civilization*, 6–7.
53 Zurayk, *Tension in Islamic Civilization*, 8.
54 Hitti, *The Arabs: A Short History, Revised Edition*, 41–45.
55 Hitti, *The Arabs: A Short History, Revised Edition*, 41–45.
56 Hitti, *The Arabs: A Short History, Revised Edition*, 41–45.
57 The translation of the Prophet's Sermon is taken from Hitti, *History of the Arabs: From the Earliest Times to the Present*, 120 as well as from Ahmed, *Islam Today*, 21.
58 Qur'an 5:3.
59 Armstrong, *A History of God*, 140.
60 Esposito, *Islam: The Straight Path*, 12.
61 Armstrong, *A History of God*, 154.
62 Genesis 21:9–10.
63 Esposito, *Islam: The Straight Path*, 3rd ed., 20.
64 Esposito, *Islam: The Straight Path*, 20.
65 Genesis 22:1–18.
66 Esposito, *Islam: The Straight Path*, 3rd ed., 20.
67 Armstrong, *A History of God*, 155.
68 Armstrong, *A History of God*, 155.
69 Qur'an 2:135.
70 Qur'an 59:21.
71 Hitti, *The Arabs: A Short History, Revised Edition*, 41–42.
72 Qur'an 43:3.
73 Hitti, *The Arabs: A Short History, Revised Edition*, 48.
74 Hitti, quoted in Esposito, *Islam: The Straight Path*, 9.
75 Hitti, *The Arabs: A Short History, Revised Edition*, 42.
76 Fakhry, *The History of Islamic Philosophy*, xvi.
77 Armstrong, *A History of God*, 140.

78   Armstrong, *A History of God*, 140.

79   Hitti, *The Arabs: A Short History, Revised Edition*, 48.

80   Hitti, *The Arabs: A Short History, Revised Edition*, 48.

81   Qur'an 17:88.

82   Esposito, *Islam: The Straight Path*, 3rd ed., 19.

83   Armstrong, *A History of God*, 144.

84   Munzir al-Kabisi, *Lughat al-Qur'an [The Language of the Qur'an]* (Syria: al-Shahba' Publishers, 1985), 222.

85   Armstrong, *A History of God*, 144–145.

86   Armstrong, *A History of God*, 146. (quoted from Ibn Ishaq, Sira, 228).

87   The Qur'an: 72:1.

88   Muhammad Mahmoud `Abd al-`Alim, *Ahkam al-Tajweed wa Fada'il al-Qur'an* (Cairo: al-Shamarli, 2000), 3.

89   Armstrong, *A History of God*, 144.

90   Malise Ruthven, *Islam: A Very Short Introduction* (Oxford University Press, 1997), 21.

91   The Holy Qur'an, English Translation of the Meaning and Commentary (Kingdom of Saudi Arabia, al-Madina al-Munawarah: King Fahd Holy Qur'an Printing Complex), 1682.

92   Hitti, *The Arabs: A Short History, Revised Edition*, 47.

93   Qur'an 24:56.

94   Qur'an 29:45.

95   The Holy Qur'an, English Translation of the Meaning and Commentary (Kingdom of Saudi Arabia, al-Madina al-Munawarah: King Fahd Holy Qur'an Printing Complex), 281.

96   Qur'an 5:6.

97   Qur'an 2:183.

98   Qur'an 97:3–5.

99   Ahmed, *Islam Today: A Short Introduction to the Muslim World*, 36.

100   The Qur'an 41:7.

101   The Qur'an 3:96.

102   Esposito, *Islam: The Straight Path*, 91–92.

103   Armstrong, *A History of God*, 156–157.

104   Armstrong, *A History of God*, 159.

105   Ahmed, *Islam Today, A Short Introduction to the Muslim World*, 37.

106   Hesham A. Hassaballa. See: http://www.beliefnet.com.

107   Esposito, *Islam: The Straight Path*, 3rd ed., 92.

108   Muhammad Jabir al-Ansari, *Ru'ya Qur'aniyya lil-Mutaghayyirat al-Duwaliyya [Qur'anic Vision for Global Changes]* (Beirut: al-Mu'assa al-`Arabiyya lil-Dirasat wa al-Nashr, 1999), 162.

109   Kamal `Abd al-Latif, *As'ilat al-Nahda al-`Arabiyya [Questions of the Arab Renaissance]* (Beirut: Markaz Dirasat al-Wahda al-Arabiyya, 2003), 200.

110   Muhammad `Imara, *Fi Fiqh al-Muwajaha bayna al-Gharb wa al-Islam [Understanding the Conflict between the West and Islam]* (Cairo: Maktabat al-Shuruq al-Duwaliyya, 2003), 118–120.

111   Qur'an 30:22.

112   Samuel Huntington, *The Clash of Civilizations* (NY: Touchstone Edition, 1997).

113   `Imara, *Fi Fiqh al-Muwajaha bayna al-Gharb wa al-Islam*, 5–27.

114   `Abd al-Salam al-Masdi, in George Tarabishi, *Min al-Nahda ila al-Rida* (London: al-Saqi, 2000), 185.

115   Muhammad Mahfouz, *al-Islam, al-Gharb wa Hiwar al-Mustaqbal [Islam, the West and the Dialogue of the Future]* (Morocco: al-Markaz al-Thaqafi al-`Arabi, 1998), 11–28, 118–133.

116   Qur'an 2:216.

117   Qur'an 22:39.

118   `Imara, *Fi Fiqh al-Muwajaha bayna al-Gharb wa al-Islam*, 5–27.

119   Qur'an 41:34.

120   Edward W. Said, *Covering Islam* (NY, Vintage Books, 1997), I.

121   Mohammed Arkoun, *Islam, Urouba, al-Gharb [Islam, Europe and the West]*, trans. into Arabic by Hashim Salih (London, al-Saqi, 2001), 179–181.

122   Mohammed Arkoun, *Islam, Urouba, al-Gharb [Islam, Europe and the West]*, 183.

123   Mohammed Arkoun, *Islam, Urouba, al-Gharb [Islam, Europe and the West]*, 180.

CHAPTER 6

1   Albert Hourani, *A History of the Arab Peoples* (The Belknap Press of Harvard University Press, 2002), 22.
2   Karen Armstrong, *Islam: A Short History* (New York: A Modern Library Chronicles Book, Modern Library Edition, 2002), 24.
3   Ahmad Shawkat, *al-Khulafa' al-Rashidun [The Rightly-Guided Caliphs]* (Cairo: Maktabat Madbouli, 1981), 55.
4   Armstrong, *Islam: A Short History*, 25.
5   Armstrong, *Islam: A Short History*, 25.
6   Hourani, *A History of the Arab Peoples*, 22.
7   Philip K. Hitti, *The Arabs: A Short History*, Revised Edition (Chicago: Second Gateway Edition, 1970), 74.
8   Shawkat, *al-Khulafa' al-Rashidun*, 75.
9   Shawkat, *al-Khulafa' al-Rashidun*, 80.
10 Hourani, *A History of the Arab Peoples*, 23.
11 Armstrong, *Islam: A Short History*, 31.
12 Hitti, *The Arabs: A Short History*, 74.
13 Shawkat, *al-Khulafa' al-Rashidun*, 125.
14 Shawkat, *al-Khulafa' al-Rashidun*, 139–140.
15 Shawkat, *al-Khulafa' al-Rashidun*, 145.
16 Bernard Lewis, *The Arabs in History* (New York: Harper & Row, Publishers, 1966), 70.
17 Hourani, *A History of the Arab Peoples*, 25.
18 Hourani, *A History of the Arab Peoples*, 25.
19 Hussein al-Laqqiss, *Khilafat `Ali bin Abi Talib [The Caliphate of `Ali bin Abi Talib]* (Damascus: Dar al-Fikr, 1975), 29–41.
20 Mohammed Arkoun, *al-Fikr al-Islami, Naqd wa Ijtihad [Islamic Thought: Criticism and Interpretation]*, trans. into Arabic by Hashim Salih (London: Dar al-Saqi, 1998), 103.
21 Muhammad al-Hashimi, *al-Fikr al-`Arabi: Juzourah wa Thimarah*, 2nd ed. (Chicago: published in Arabic at the expense of the author, 1997), 54.
22 Armstrong, *Islam: A Short History*, 36.
23 al-Hashimi, *al-Fikr al-`Arabi: Juzourah wa Thimarah*, 58.
24 Abdallah Laroui, quoted in *Arab Human Development Report 2004: Toward Freedom in the Arab World, The United Nations Development Program* (NY: United Nations Publications, 2005), 53.
25 Moojan Momen, *An Introduction to Shi'i Islam* (New Haven: Yale University Press, 1985), 11.
26 Armstrong, *Islam: A Short History*, 43.
27 Hourani, *A History of the Arab Peoples*, 184–185.
28 Armstrong, *Islam: A Short History*, 43.
29 Akbar S. Ahmed, *Islam Today: A Short Introduction to the Muslim World*, 47.
30 Armstrong, *Islam: A Short History*, 37.
31 Lewis, *The Arabs in History*, 70.
32 Armstrong, *Islam: A Short History*, 44.
33 Hussein al-Laqqiss, *Khilafat `Ali bin Abi Talib*, 129–130.
34 Hourani, *A History of the Arab Peoples*, 36.
35 Lewis, *The Arabs in History*, 80.
36 Hourani, *A History of the Arab Peoples*, 40.
37 Lewis, *The Arabs in History*, 80.
38 Lewis, *The Arabs in History*, 81.
39 Shawkat, *al-Khulafa' al-Rashidun*, 225–240.
40 Hourani, *A History of the Arab Peoples*, 39.
41 Hourani, *A History of the Arab Peoples*, 38.
42 Maria Rosa Menocal, *The Ornament of the World: How Muslims, Jews, and Christians Created a Culture of Tolerance in Medieval Spain* (NY: Back Bay Books, 2002), 8.
43 The Umayyad dynasty existed for almost three hundred additional years after the first dynasty's defeat in Damascus, although it was not until the tenth century that the ruler took the title of Caliph. (See Hitti, *The Arabs: A Short History*, 82.)

44 John Freely, *Aladdin's Lamp: How Greek Science Came to Europe Through the Islamic World* (New York: Alfred A. Knopf, 2009).

45 Menocal, *The Ornament of the World: How Muslims, Jews, and Christians Created a Culture of Tolerance in Medieval Spain*, 8-11.

46 Hourani, *A History of the Arab Peoples*, 44.

47 Menocal, *The Ornament of the World: How Muslims, Jews, and Christians Created a Culture of Tolerance in Medieval Spain*, 8-11.

48 Began in 1009 and ended in 1031.

49 Menocal, *The Ornament of the World: How Muslims, Jews, and Christians Created a Culture of Tolerance in Medieval Spain*. 9-10, 13.

50 Hourani, *A History of the Arab Peoples*, 87.

51 Ahmed, *Islam Today: A Short Introduction to the Muslim World*, 43. (In an interview with Islamic scholar, Jamel Velji (August 3, 2017), he said that the minority communities tend to not like the term *sect* since it implies deviance from an orthodoxy).

52 Qustantin Zurayk, *Tension in Islamic Civilization* (Washington, D.C.: Center for Contemporary Arab Studies, Georgetown University, 1978), 11.

53 Farhad Khosrokhavar, *Suicide Bombers: Allah's New Martyrs*, trans. David Macey (London: Pluto Press, 2005), 22.

54 Ahmed, *Islam Today: A Short Introduction to the Muslim World*, 45-46.

55 Hourani, *A History of the Arab Peoples*, 183.

56 Moojan Momen, *An Introduction to Shi'i Islam*, 11.

57 See: How Did the Early Shi'a become Sectarian? By Marshall G. S. Hodgson, Journal of the American Oriental Society, Vol. 75, No. 1, (Jan.-Mar., 1955), American Oriental Society pp. 1-13

58 Hourani, *A History of the Arab Peoples*, 500.

59 Armstrong, *Islam: A Short History*, 56-57.

60 Armstrong, *Islam: A Short History*, 56-57.

61 Ahmed, *Islam Today: A Short Introduction to the Muslim World*, 43.

62 Moojan Momen, *An Introduction to Shi'i Islam*, 165.

63 Ahmed, *Islam Today: A Short Introduction to the Muslim World*, 48.

64 Ahmed, *Islam Today: A Short Introduction to the Muslim World*, 43-54.

65 A second Shi'ite branch is called *Zaydi*. While the defining difference between Sunni and Shia Islam pertains to a disagreement over succession to leadership over the *umma* immediately after the Prophet's death, Zaydi Islam represents a divergence within the Shi'ite tradition about three generations later. All Shi`ites recognize the fourth imam as `Ali Zayn al-`Abidin, (but not the Nizari Ismailis, according to scholar Jamel Velji), and the majority of Shi'ites including Twelvers recognize his son Muhammad al-Baqir (Imam Husayn's grandson, and the Prophet's great-great-grandson) to be the fifth imam. Zaydis share in acceptance of Ali Zayn al-`Abidin as the fourth imam, but believe that Zayn's other son (al-Baqir's brother) Zayd bin `Ali should have been the fifth imam. Zaydis are the part of the Shi'ite community that recognized Zayd as the fifth imam instead of al-Baqir; for this reason they are sometimes called Fiver Shi`ites. A Zaydi dynasty was founded in Tabaristan on the Caspian Sea of what is now northern Iran in 864, and another Zaydi imamate formed in Yemen in 893. Yemen's northern highland region has been the heart of the Zaydi community since this time.

66 Ahmed, *Islam Today: A Short Introduction to the Muslim World*, 45.

67 http://iis.ac.uk/about-us/his-highness-aga-khan

68 Ahmed, *Islam Today: A Short Introduction to the Muslim World*, 47-51.

69 Hourani, *A History of the Arab Peoples*, 183.

70 Armstrong, *Islam: A Short History*, 53.

71 Muhammad Naqshbandi, *al-Wahhabiyya [Wahhabism]* (Damascus: Dar al-Kitab, 1878), 35-37.

72 Encyclopedia of Arabic Literature, ed. Julie Scott Meisami and Paul Starkey (Routledge, 1998), 377.

73 Muhammad Arkoun, *Islam, Urouba, al-Gharb [Islam, Europe and the West]*, 188.

74 Hamid Algar, *Wahhabism: A Critical Essay* (New York: Islamic Publication International, 2002), 2.

75 John L. Esposito, *What Everyone Needs to Know About Islam* (London: Oxford University Press, 2002), 50.

76 Algar, *Wahhabism: A Critical Essay*, 1.

77 Khosrokhavar, *Suicide Bombers: Allah's New Martyrs*, 22.

78 Khosrokhavar, *Suicide Bombers: Allah's New Martyrs*, 21.

79 Ahmed, *Islam Today: A Short Introduction to the Muslim World*, 45–47.

80 Ahmed, *Islam Today: A Short Introduction to the Muslim World*, 23.

81 Hourani, *A History of the Arab Peoples*, 184–185.

82 Interview with *al-Bayader al-Siyasi*, an independent weekly news magazine published in Jerusalem, issue 940, January 5, 2008, 16–17.

CHAPTER 7

1 Adonis, *An Introduction to Arab Poetics*, translated from the Arabic by Catherine Cobham, (Austin: University of Texas Press, 1990), 15.

2 Adonis, *An Introduction to Arab Poetics*.

3 Suleman Taufiq, "Arab Music and Its Development," *Fikrun wa Fann* by Goethe-Institut e. V., November 2011.

4 Adonis, *An Introduction to Arab Poetics*, translated from the Arabic by Catherine Cobham, (Austin: University of Texas Press, 1990), 13.

5 Adonis, *An Introduction to Arab Poetics*.

6 Britannica http://www.britannica.com/eb/article-13811

7 Britannica.

8 Britannica.

9 Habib Hassan Touma, *The Music of the Arabs*, (Portland, OR: Amadeus Press, 1996), 6.

10 Habib Hassan Touma, *The Music of the Arabs.*, 7–8.

11 Suleman Taufiq, "Arab Music and Its Development," *Fikrun wa Fann* by Goethe-Institut e. V., November 2011.

12 David Muallem, *The Maqam Book: A Doorway to Arab Scales and Modes*, (Kfar Sava, Or-Tav Music Publications, 2010), 31.

13 Muallem, *The Maqam Book*, 10.

14 Muallem, *The Maqam Book*, 10.

15 Muallem, *The Maqam Book*, 10.

16 "Cities of Light: The Rise And Fall of Islamic Spain," *UPF*, retrieved from http://www.islamic-spain.tv/Arts-and-Science/The-Culture-of-Al-Andalus/Music.htm.

17 Adonis, *An Introduction to Arab Poetics*, translated from the Arabic by Catherine Cobham, (Austin: University of Texas Press, 1990), 15.

18 Adonis, *An Introduction to Arab Poetics*.

19 Adonis, *An Introduction to Arab Poetics*.

20 Suleman Taufiq, "Arab Music and Its Development," *Fikrun wa Fann* by Goethe-Institut, retrieved from http://www.goethe.de/ges/phi/prj/ffs/the/a96/en8626486.htm.

21 Touma, *The Music of the Arabs*, xix–x.

22 http://www.goethe.de/ges/phi/prj/ffs/the/a96/en8626486.htm

23 Touma, *The Music of the Arabs*, 18.

24 Andrew Hammond, *Pop Culture in the Arab World! Media, Arts and Lifestyle*, (Santa Barbara: ABC CLIO: 2005), 144.

25 http://www.goethe.de/ges/phi/prj/ffs/the/a96/en8626486.htm

26 Touma, *The Music of the Arabs*, p. 109.

27 Touma, *The Music of the Arabs.*.

28 Touma, *The Music of the Arab*, 110.

29 Touma, *The Music of the Arabs*, 123.

30 Touma, *The Music of the Arabs*, 124–30.

31 Touma, *The Music of the Arabs*.

32 Muallem, *The Maqam Book: A Doorway to Arab Scales and Modes*, 27.

33 A. J. Racy, *Making Music in the Arab World: The Culture and Artistry of Tarab*, (Cambridge, Cambridge University Press: 2003), 7–8.

34 Ghazi, *Ilya*, Part 3, Book 8, Vol. 2, 237; English trans. D. B. Macdonald, "Emotional religion in Islam as affected by music and singing," *Journal of the Royal Asiatic Society*, April (1901): 199 as quoted in Albert Hourani, *A History of the Arab Peoples* (New York: MJF Books, 1991): 199.

35   Touma, *The Music of the Arabs*, 152.

36   Touma, *The Music of the Arabs*, 153.

37   Sami Asmar, "Sheikh Hamza Shakkur Talks About Sufi Music," *Al Jadid* 7, no. 36 (Summer 2001), retrieved from http://www.aljadid.com/content/sheikh-hamza-shakkur-talks-about-sufi-music-0.

38   Sami Asmar, "Sheikh Hamza Shakkur Talks About Sufi Music."

39   "Arab Music: Folk and Traditional Styles," retrieved from http://spotlightonmusic.macmillan-mh.com/m/teachers/articles/folk-and-traditional-styles/arab-music.

40   "Arab Music: Folk and Traditional Styles."

41   "Arab Music: Folk and Traditional Styles."

42   "Arab Music: Folk and Traditional Styles."

43   "Arab Music: Folk and Traditional Styles."

44   Mubarak Altwaiji, "History of Saudi Folklore and Factors that Shaped It," *Trames* 21, no. 2 (2017): 161–171, retrieved in http://www.kirj.ee/public/trames_pdf/2017/issue_2/Trames-2017-2-161-171.pdf

45   Rebecca Torstrick, *Culture and customs of the Arab Gulf States*, (Westport, CT: Greenwood Press, 2009), 146.

46   Rebecca Torstrick, *Culture and customs of the Arab Gulf States*, 145.

47   Kay Hardy Campbell, "Saudi Folk Music: Alive and Well," *AramcoWorld* 58, no. 2 (March/April 2007), retrieved in http://archive.aramcoworld.com/issue/200702/saudi.folk.music.alive.and.well.htm

48   Alessandro Del Ben, "Malouf, Traditional Tunisian Music," *lanuvolabianca*, January 10, 2015, retrieved from https://lanuvolabianca.com/2015/01/10/malouf-traditional-tunisian-music/.

49   Dwight Reynolds, interview, *Al-Andalous 1: Europe*, Madrid, 2004, http://www.afropop.org/14235/interview-dwight-reynolds-al-andalus-1-europe/.

50   Nicole LeCorgne, "Reflections of a Time Past: The Music of Andalusia Yesterday and Today," *The Best of Habibi* 18, no. 3, retrieved from http://thebestofhabibi.com/vol-18-no-3-march-2001/music-of-andalusia/.

51   LeCorgne, "Reflections of a Time Past: The Music of Andalusia Yesterday and Today."

52   LeCorgne, "Reflections of a Time Past: The Music of Andalusia Yesterday and Today."

53   Agaila Abba, "Algerian Rai: Music of Resistance," *Thaqafa Magazine*, September 4, 2014, retrieved in https://thaqafamagazine.com/2014/09/04/algeria-rai-music/.

54   Elizabeth M. B. Woods, "Rai: The Deconstruction of a Musical Genre," p. 4, retrieved from http://www.academia.edu/7867688/Rai_The_Deconstruction_of_a_Musical_Genre

55   Suleman Taufiq, "Arab Music and Its Development," *Fikrun wa Fann* by Goethe-Institut, retrieved from http://www.goethe.de/ges/phi/prj/ffs/the/a96/en8626486.htm.

56   Sami Asmar, "Wadi al-Safi: Lebanon's Eternal Voice," *Al Jadid* 18, no. 66 (2013) retrieved from http://www.aljadid.com/content/wadi-al-safi-lebanon's-eternal-voice.

57   Sophie Frankford, "Sheikh Imam: 'A Voice of the People,'" *Ethnomusicology Review*, retrieved from http://ethnomusicologyreview.ucla.edu/content/sheikh-imam-"-voice-people".

58   "Star of the East"—The Life of Umm Kulthum, retrieved from http://albustanseeds.org/digital/kulthum/her-life/#.Wacv80qGOCc

59   Sami Asmar, "Fairouz: a Voice, a Star, a Mystery," *Al Jadid* 5, no. 27 (Spring 1999), retrieved from http://www.aljadid.com/content/fairouz-voice-star-mystery.

60   Lauren E. Bohn, "Rapping the Revolution," Foreign Policy, July 22, 2011, 3–4, retrieved at http://foreignpolicy.com/2011/07/22/rapping-the-revolution/.

61   Ramzi Salti, "Islamic Voices: Music of the Arab Spring," *Stanford Live*, September 20, 2016, retrieved from https://live.stanford.edu/blog/september-2016/islamic-voices-music-arab-spring.

62   Bohn, "Rapping the Revolution," 3.

63   Faisal Al Yafai, "A song to start something: the Arab spring's greatest hits," The National, August 27, 2001, 3, retrieved from https://www.thenational.ae/arts-culture/music/a-song-to-start-something-the-arab-spring-s-greatest-hits-1.432495.

64   Bryan Ferrell, "Hip Hop and the Arab Spring," WagingNonviolence.org, retrieved from https://wagingnonviolence.org/2011/07/hip-hop-and-the-arab-spring/.

65   Ferrell, "Hip Hop and the Arab Spring."

66   "Population Trends and Challenges in the Middle East and North Africa," PRB (Population Reference Bureau), retrieved from http://www.prb.org/Publications/Reports/2001/PopulationTrendsandChallenges intheMiddleEastandNorthAfrica.aspx.

67   Tara Mulholland, "Arab Music's Modern Voice," *The International Herald Tribune*, April 12, 2012, retrieved from http://www.nytimes.com/2012/04/13/arts/13iht-hamdan13.html?mcubz=0.

68   Suze Olbrich, "Emel Mathlouthi: 'It's Important to be out there as a creative woman from a Muslim culture,'" *The Guardian*, February 24, 2017, retrieved from https://www.theguardian.com/music/2017/feb/24/tunisian-musician-emel-mathlouthi-global-protest-pop.

69   Suleman Taufiq, "Arab Music and Its Development," *Fikrun wa Fann* by Goethe-Institut e. V., November 2011.

CHAPTER 8

1   M. M. Badawi, *A Short History of Modern Arabic Literature* (Oxford: Clarendon Press, 1993), 1.

2   Salma Khadra Jayyusi, *Modern Arabic Poetry: An Anthology* (NY: Columbia University Press, 1987).

3   Badawi, *A Short History of Modern Arabic Literature*, 85.

4   Jayyusi, *Modern Arabic Poetry: An Anthology*, 37.

5   Badawi, *A Short History of Modern Arabic Literature*, 10.

6   Jayyusi, *Modern Arabic Poetry: An Anthology*, 1.

7   Bayati, *Love, Death, and Exile: Poems of Abdul Wahab al-Bayati*, trans. from Arabic by Bassam K. Frangieh, (Georgetown University Press, 2004), 1.

8   Bassam Frangieh, "Modern Arabic Poetry: Vision and Reality," in *Tradition, Modernity, and Post-Modernity in Arabic Literature*, eds. K. Abdel-Malek and W. Hallaq (Leiden: Brill, 2000).

9   Bassam Frangieh, "Modern Arabic Poetry: Vision and Reality.".

10   Salma Jayyusi, *Anthology of Modern Palestinian Literature*, (New York: Columbia University Press, 1992), 16.

11   Albert Hourani, *A History of the Arab Peoples* (Oxford University Press, 1990), 396.

12   Naji Alloush, introduction to *The Collected Works of Badr Shakir al-Sayyab* (Beirut: Dar al-`Awda, 1986), 9.

13   Frangieh, "Modern Arabic Poetry: Vision and Reality" in *Tradition, Modernity, and Post-Modernity in Arabic Literature*.

14   Badawi, *A Short History of Modern Arabic Literature*, 58.

15   Frangieh, "Modern Arabic Poetry: Vision and Reality," in *Tradition, Modernity, and Post-Modernity in Arabic Literature*, 225.

16   Hourani, *A History of the Arab Peoples*, 401.

17   Jabra I. Jabra, *al-Hurriya wal-Tawafan* (Beirut: al-Mu'assasa al-Arabiyya lil Dirasat wal Nashr, 1982), 62.

18   Frangieh, "Modern Arabic Poetry: Vision and Reality," in *Tradition, Modernity, and Post-Modernity in Arabic Literature*.

19   Frangieh, "Modern Arabic Poetry: Vision and Reality.".

20   Kamal Abu Deeb, "Conflicts, Oppositions and Negations: Modern Arabic Poetry and The Fragmentation of Self and of Text" (unpublished manuscript, University of Sanaa, 1989–1990). And Kalimat, *Quarterly Cultural Review* (Bahrain: No. 10/11, 1989 and No. 15, 1991).

21   Muhyi al-Din Subhi, *Vision in al-Bayyati's Poetry* (Baghdad: Dar al-Shu'un al-Thaqafiya al-Ammah, 1987), 125.

22   Frangieh, "Modern Arabic Poetry: Vision and Reality," 229.

23   Frangieh, "Modern Arabic Poetry: Vision and Reality."

24   Frangieh, "Modern Arabic Poetry: Vision and Reality," 230.

25   Frangieh, "Modern Arabic Poetry: Vision and Reality," 233.

26   Frangieh, "Modern Arabic Poetry: Vision and Reality," 233.

27   Hala Khamis Nassar and Najat Rahman (eds.), *Mahmoud Darwish: Exile's Poet* (New York: Interlink, 2007).

28   Salma Jayyusi, *Trends and Movements in Modern Arabic Literature* Vol. III (Leiden, E.J. Brill, 1977), 722.

29   Issa Boullata, *Badr Shakir al-Sayyab: Hayatuh wa Shi'ruh* (Beirut: Dar al-Nahar, 1971), 96.

30   Abdul Wahab al-Bayati, *Love, Death, and Exile: Poems of Abdul Wahab al-Bayati Translated from Arabic by Bassam K. Frangieh* (Washington, D.C.: Georgetown University Press), 17–19.

31   Abdul Wahab al-Bayati, *Love, Death, and Exile*..

32   Muḥammad Badawī, *A Critical Introduction to Modern Arabic Poetry* (Cambridge: Cambridge University Press), 241.

33   Abdul Wahab al-Bayati, *Tajribati al-Shiʿriyya* (Beirut: Dar al-ʿAwda, 1972), 57.

34   Bayati, *Love, Death, and Exile: Poems of Abdul Wahab al-Bayati trans. from Arabic by Bassam K. Frangieh*, 307.

35   Rita Awad, introduction to *The Collected Works of Khalil Hawi* (Beirut: Dar al-ʿAwda, 1993), 17.

36   Mahmoud Shurayh, *Khalil Hawi wa Antoun Sa'ada* (Sweden: Dar Nelson, 1995), 43.

37   Kamal Abu Deeb, "Conflicts, Oppositions, Negations," *Kalimat* no. 10/11, 34.

38   Asʿad AbuKhalil, The Angry Arab News Service (angryarab.blogspot.com).

39   Muhammad al-Maghout, "Untitled," The Angry Arab News Service, trans. Asʿad AbuKhalil. Copyright © by The Angry Arab News Service. Reprinted with permission.

40   Muhammad al-Maghout, "Untitled," The Angry Arab News Service, trans. Asʿad AbuKhalil. Copyright © by The Angry Arab News Service. Reprinted with permission.

41   Muhammad al-Maghout, *The Fan of Swords: Poems*, trans. May Jayyusi and Naomi Shihab Nye, ed. and introduction by Salma Jayyusi (Washington, D.C.: Three Continents Press, 1991), xv.

42   Muhammad al-Maghout, *The Fan of Swords*, xvi.

43   Adonis, *al-Quds al-Arabi* newspaper, 4/6/2004.

44   Kamal Abu Deeb, "Odysseus." Available: www.library.cornell.edu/colldev/mideast/adonisc. htm.

45   Saadi Yousef, *al-Quds al-Arabi* newspaper, 4/18/2006.

46   Saadi Yousef, "America, America," trans. Khaled Mattawa, *Banipal* no. 7, (Spring 2000).

47   Nizar Qabbani, *Hal Tasmaʿin Sahil Ahzani* (Beirut: Manshurat Nizar Qabbani, 1991), 32.

48   Nizar Qabbani, *Hawamish ʿAla Daftar al-Naksah (Marginal Notes on the Book of Defeat)*, 4th ed. (Beirut: Manshurat Nizar Qabbani, 1993).

49   Frangieh, "Modern Arabic Poetry: Vision and Reality," in *Tradition, Modernity, and Post-Modernity in Arabic Literature*, 231.

50   Hala Khamis Nassar and Najat Rahman (eds.), *Mahmoud Darwish: Exile's Poet* (New York: Interlink, 2007).

51   Hala Khamis Nassar and Najat Rahman (eds.), *Mahmoud Darwish: Exile's Poet* xviii.

52   Abu al-Qasim al-Shabi, "Life's Will," poem translated by Bassam Frangieh, 1934. Original accessible: https://www.almrsal.com/post/365383

53   "Syrian uprising songwriter meets gruesome end," CBS News. July 28, 2011. Accessible: http://www.cbsnews.com/news/syrian-uprising-songwriter-meets-gruesome-end/

54   "Syria, Libya and Middle East unrest," *The Guardian*. 5 (July 2011). Accessible: https://www.theguardian.com/world/middle-east-live/2011/jul/05/syria-libya-middle-east-unrest-live

55   Hisham Sharabi, *Neopatriarchy: A Theory of Distorted Change in Arab Society* (Oxford University Press, 1988), 155.

56   Nizar Qabbani, *Arabian Love Poems*, trans. Bassam Frangieh and Clementina Brown, (Boulder: Lynne Rienner Publishers, 1999), xiv.

57   Nizar Qabbani, *Arabian Love Poems*.

58   Nizar Qabbani, *Yawmiyyat Imraʿa La Mubaliyah [Diary of an Indifferent Woman]* (Beirut: Manshurat Nizar Qabbani, 1968), 9.

59   Muhyi al-Din Subhi, *al-Kawn al-Shiʿri ʿInda Nizar Qabbani [The Poetic World of Nizar Qabbani]* (Beirut: Dar al-Taliʿa, 1977), 73.

60   Nizar Qabbani, *Complete Works*, vol. II, 5th ed. (Beirut: Manshurat Nizar Qabbani, 1993), 87–93.

61   Ihsan Abbas, *Ittijahat al-Shiʿr al-Arabi al-Hadith (Directions of Contemporary Arabic Poetry)* (Kuwait: al-Majlis al-Watani lil-Thaqafa wal-Funun wal-Adab, 1978), 176.

62   Nizar Qabbani, *al-Aʿmal al-Kamila: The Complete Works*, vol. 1 (Beirut: Manshurat Nizar Qabbani, 1983), 655.

63   Nizar Qabbani, *al-Aʿmal al-Kamila: The Complete Works*, 874.

64   Nizar Qabbani, *Qasaʿid Maghdoub ʿAlayha [Censored Poems]* (Beirut: Manshurat Nizar Qabbani, 1986), 16.

65   Qabbani, *al-Aʿmal al-Kamila: The Complete Works*, 378. From the poem "Little Things," translated by Bassam Frangieh.

66 Nizar Qabbani, interview by Muneer al-`Akash, As`ilat al-Shi`r (The Questions of Poetry) (Beirut: Arab Institute for Studies and Publications, 1979), 190.

67 Qabbani, interview by Muneer al-`Akash, 181.

68 Qabbani, interview by Muneer al-`Akash, 200.

69 Joseph Zeidan, Arab Women Novelists (NY: State University of New York Press, 1995), 5.

70 Noel Abdulahad, interview, April 30, 2007.

71 Samman, poem "A postcard from an Owl in Paris," translated by Noel Abdulahad , 2007.

72 Samman, poem "The Owl of Parting," trans. by Noel Abdulahad, 2007.

73 Ghada al-Samman, "The Lover of Blue Writing above the Sea!" Translated by Saad Ahmad and Miriam Cooke in The Poetry of Arab Women, ed. Nathalie Handal (NY: Interlink Books, 2001), 274.

74 Pauline Homsi Vinson, al-Jadid magazine 8, no. 39 (Spring 2002).

75 Homsi Vinson, al-Jadid magazine 8, no. 39 (Spring 2002).

76 Homsi Vinson, al-Jadid magazine 8, no. 39 (Spring 2002).

77 Ghada al-Samman, "The Lover of Rain in an Inkwell," translated by Miriam Cooke and Richard McKane in The Poetry of Arab Women, ed. Nathalie Handal (NY: Interlink Books, 2001), 276.

78 Joumana Haddad. www.joumanahaddad.com.

79 Joumana Haddad, "My Poem," translated by Khaled Mattawa in Invitation to a Secret Feast: Selected Poems (MA: Tupelo Press, 2008).

80 JHaddad. www.joumanahaddad.com.

81 JHaddad. www.joumanahaddad.com.

82 Joumana Haddad, "I Have a Body," translated by Issa Boullata, Kalimat: An International Periodical of Creative Writing, ed. Raghid Nahhas (Australia: December 2004), 19.

83 Haddad. www.joumanahaddad.com.

84 Suheir Daoud, al-Khataya al-`Ashr (The Ten Sins)(Jerusalem: Matba`at al-Sharq al-`Arabiyya, 1999). trans. Bassam Frangieh. Translated with permission by Suheir Daoud.

85 Daoud, al-Khataya al-`Ashr [The Ten Sins].

86 Suheir Daoud, Burtuqal al-Mada al-Aswad [Oranges of the Black Horizon] (The West Bank: Ramallah, Jefra Publication, 1997). trans. Bassam Frangieh. Translated with permission by Suheir Daoud.

87 Suheir Daoud, Burtuqal al-Mada al-Aswad [Oranges of the Black Horizon].

88 Daoud, Burtuqal al-Mada al-Aswad (Oranges of the Black Horizon).

89 Daoud, Burtuqal al-Mada al-Aswad (Oranges of the Black Horizon).

90 Qabbani, interview by Muneer al-`Akash, As`ilat al-Shi`r (The Questions of Poetry) (Beirut: Arab Institute for Studies and Publications, 1979), 185.

CHAPTER 9

1   Abdelrahman Munif, Raqabat al-Mujtama` in Mawaqif, 69 (1992): 73.

2   Abdelrahman Munif, Raqabat al-Mujtama` in Mawaqif, 69 (1992): 73.

3   Yusuf Al-Qaeed, Tajribat Jeel, in Mawaqif, 69, (1992): 131–32.

4   Hanna Mina, Al-Sayrourah wa al-Haqeeqah, in Mawaqif, 69 (1992): 84–85.

5   Gamal El-Ghitani, Al-Qalaq, al-Tajreeb, Al-Ibdaa`, in Mawaqif, 69 (1992): 109.

6   Edward Said, introduction to Days of Dust by Halim Barakat, (Washington, D.C.: Three Continents Press, 2006), xiii–xiv.

7   Ghazi Algosaibi, Lyrics from Arabia (Washington, D.C.: Three Continents Press, 1983), 101 (biographies of the poets are compiled by Bassam Frangieh).

8   Ghazi Algosaibi, Lyrics from Arabia, 76.

9   Encyclopædia Britannica.

10 Roger Allen, The Arabic Novel, An Historical and Critical Introduction, second edition (Syracuse University Press, 1995), 13.

11 Allen, The Arabic Novel, An Historical and Critical Introduction, 13.

12 Allen, The Arabic Novel, An Historical and Critical Introduction, 32.

13 M. M. Badawi, A Short History of Modern Arabic Literature (Oxford University Press, 1993), 5.

14 Albert Hourani, A History of the Arab Peoples (Cambridge: The Belknap Press, 2002), 305.

15 Allen, The Arabic Novel: A Historical and Critical Introduction, 65–66.

16 Faysal Darraj, *Nazariyyat al-Riwaya wa al-Riwaya al-Arabiyya* (Morocco: al-Markaz al-Thaqafi al-Arabi, 1999), 190.
17 Badawi, *A Short History of Modern Arabic Literature*, 97.
18 Allen, *The Arabic Novel: A Historical and Critical Introduction*, 37.
19 Halim Barakat, *al-Mujtama` al-Arabi fi al-Qarn al-`Ishreen*, (Beirut, Lebanon: Markaz dirasat Al-Wahda Al—Arabiyya, 2000), 716.
20 Naguib Mahfouz, *Chronicler of Arab Life, Dies at 94* by Robert D. McFadden. *New York Times*, AUG. 30, 2006.
21 *Les Prix Nobel. The Nobel Prizes 1988*, Editor Tore Frängsmyr, (Stockholm: Nobel Foundation, 1989). This autobiography/biography was written at the time of the award and later published in the book series *Les Prix Nobel/ Nobel Lectures/The Nobel Prizes*.
22 Naguib Mahfouz, Chronicler of Arab Life, Dies at 94 by Robert D. McFadden. *New York Times*, AUG. 30, 2006.
23 Badawi, *A Short History of Modern Arabic* Literature, 139.
24 Badawi, *A Short History of Modern Arabic Literature*.
25 Rasheed el-Anany, *Naguib Mahfouz: The Pursuit of Meaning* (Taylor & Francis, 2003), 58–59.
26 Trevor Le Gassick, *Critical Perspective on Naguib Mahfouz* (Washington, D.C.: Three Continents Press), 31.
27 Marus Deeb, *Najib Mahfuz's Midaqq Alley: A Socio-Cultural Analysis*, in *Critical Perspective on Naguib Mahfouz*, ed. Trevor Le Gassick (Washington, D.C.: Three Continents Press, 1991), 31.
28 Deeb, *Najib Mahfuz's Midaqq Alley: A Socio-Cultural Analysis*, 31.
29 Ibid.,32.
30 Ibid.,33.
31 Rasheed el-Anany, *Naguib Mahfouz: The Pursuit of Meaning* (Taylor & Francis, 2003), 56.
32 Naguib Mahfouz, *The Cairo Trilogy* (NY: Everyman's Library, 2001)
33 Badawi, *A Short History of Modern Arabic Literature*, 137.
34 Sabry Hafez, introduction to *The Cairo Trilogy* by Naguib Mahfouz (NY: Everyman's Library, 2001), vii.
35 Sabry Hafez, introduction to *The Cairo Trilogy*, xxiii.
36 Denys Johnson-Davies, *The Guardian*, Aug 30, 2006.
37 Rasheed el-Anany, *Naguib Mahfouz: The Pursuit of Meaning*, (Taylor & Francis, 2003), 81.
38 Hafez, introduction to *The Cairo Trilogy*, xxii.
39 Badawi, *A Short History of Modern Arabic Literature*, 142.
40 Trevor Le Gassick, introduction to *The Thief and the Dogs* (NY: Anchor Books, 2008), 8.
41 Le Gassick, introduction to *The Thief and the Dogs*.
42 Anders Hallengren, "Naguib Mahfouz—The Son of Two Civilizations," Nobelprize.org, Oct. 16, 2003. Accessed Aug. 11, 2017. http://www.nobelprize.org/nobel_prizes/literature/laureates/1988/mahfouz-article.html.
43 Badawi, *A Short History of Modern Arabic Literature*, 143.
44 Allen, *The Arabic Novel: A Historical and Critical Introduction*, 116.
45 Badawi, *A Short History of Modern Arabic Literature*, 144.
46 Badawi, *A Short History of Modern Arabic Literature*, 144.
47 Badawi, *A Short History of Modern Arabic Literature*, 147.
48 Rasheed el-Anany, *Naguib Mahfouz: The Pursuit of Meaning* (Taylor & Francis, 2003), 112–13.
49 Badawi, *A Short History of Modern Arabic Literature*, 148.
50 Allen, *The Arabic Novel: A Historical and Critical Introduction*.
51 Allen, *The Arabic Novel: A Historical and Critical Introduction*, 117.
52 Abdul-Hadi Jiad, "Abdul-Rahman Mounif," The *Guardian*, February 4, 2004.
53 Abdul-Hadi Jiad, "Abdul-Rahman Mounif."
54 Abdul-Hadi Jiad, "Abdul-Rahman Mounif."
55 Stefan G. Meyer, *The Experimental Arabic Novel: Postcolonial Literary Modernism in the Levant* (NY: State University of New York Press, 2001), 72.
56 Badawi, *A Short History of Modern Arabic Literature*, 203.
57 Badawi, *A Short History of Modern Arabic Literature*, 203.
58 'Abd Al-Rahman Munif, *Endings*, trans. Roger Allen (Interlink Books, 02/26/2007).
59 Badawi, *A Short History of Modern Arabic Literature*, 205.
60 Edward Said, comment in *Variations of Night and Day* by Abdulrahman Munif (First Vintage International Edition, 1994), xxv.

61   Abdul-Hadi Jiad, "Abdul-Rahman Mounif," *The Guardian*, February 4, 2004.

62   Roger Allen, review of *Cities of Salt*, World Literature Today, 63 no. 2, 250th Issue (Spring, 1989): 358–59.

63   Badawi, *A Short History of Modern Arabic Literature*, 207.

64   Roger Allen, *The Arabic Novel, An Historical and Critical Introduction*, second edition (Syracuse University Press, 1995), 145.

65   Douglas R. Magrath. "A Study of *Rijal fi al-Shams* by Ghassan Kanafani," *Journal of Arabic Literature X* (1979): 106.

66   Badawi, *A Short History of Modern Arabic Literature*, 191.

67   Hilary Kilpatrick, Introduction to *Men in the Sun* by Ghassan Kanafani, trans. by Hilary Kilpatrick (Boulder: Lynne Reiner Publishers, 1999), 15.

68   Edward Said, comment in *Variations of Night and Day* (First Vintage International Edition, 1994), xxi. Abdul-Hadi Jiad, *The Guardian*, Feb. 4, 2004

69   Allen, *The Arabic Novel, An Historical and Critical Introduction*, 159.

70   Badawi, *A Short History of Modern Arabic Literature*, 230.

71   Tayeb Salih, *Acclaimed author of Season of Migration to the North'*, The Guardian, Feb. 19, 2009.

72   Badawi, *A Short History of Modern Arabic Literature*, (Oxford University Press, 1993), 228.

73   Badawi, *A Short History of Modern Arabic Literature*.

74   Jamal Mahjoub, *The Guardian*, Feb. 19, 2009

75   Allen, *The Arabic Novel, An Historical and Critical Introduction*, second edition (Syracuse University Press, 1995), 161.

76   Badawi, *A Short History of Modern Arabic Literature*, 230.

77   Badawi, *A Short History of Modern Arabic Literature* (Oxford University Press, 1993), 230.

78   *New York Times*, Feb. 23, 2009.

79   M.M. Badawi, *A Short History of Modern Arabic Literature*, (Oxford University Press, 1993), 227.

80   Issa Boullata, review of *Sun on a Cloudy Day*, The Free Library, 1998, https://www.thefreelibrary.com/Sun+on+a+Cloudy+Day.-a020990164

81   Bassam Frangieh, preface to *Sun on a Cloudy Day* (Pueblo, Colorado: Passeggiata Press, 1997), vi.

82   Roger Allen, Introduction to *Sun on a Cloudy Day* (Pueblo, Colorado: Passeggiata Press, 1997), viii.

83   Kim Jensen, *Hanna Mina's 'Sun on a Cloudy Day': Potential of Revolt Always Present*, Translated Bassam Frangieh and Clementina Brown. Al Jadid 4, no. 24 (Summer 1998).

84   Allen, *The Arabic Novel, An Historical and Critical Introduction*, 159.

85   Halim Barakat, *Six Days*, translated into English by Bassam Frangieh and Scott McGehee (Washington, D.C.: Three Continents Press, 1990), 53.

86   Barakat, *Six Days*, 85.

87   Barakat, *Six Days*, 120.

88   Halim Barakat: *Visions of Social Reality in the Contemporary Arab Novel* (Center of Contemporary Arab Studies, Georgetown University, 1977), 37.

89   Edward Said, introduction to *Days of Dust* by Halim Barakat (Washington, D.C.: Three Continents Press, 2006), xxi.

90   Jacqui Freeman, *Socialist Review*, Moroccan Portrait, October 2006.

91   Nirvana Tanoukhi, "Rewriting Political Commitment for an International Cannon: Paul Bowles' For Bread Alone as translation of Mohamed Choukri's al-Khubz al-Hafi," *Research in African Literatures* 34, no. 2 (2003): 127–44.

92   Paul Bowles, Introduction to *For Bread Alone* by Mohamed Choukri, (London: Telegram, 1973), 6.

93   Nirvana Tanoukhi, the direct quote is from "Mohamed Choukri: Being and Place," in *The View from within: Writers and Critics on Contemporary Arabic Literature*, eds. F. Ghazoul and B. Harlow (Cairo: American University in Cairo Press, 1994) 222.

94   Paul Bowles, Introduction to *For Bread Alone* by Mohamed Choukri (London: Telegram, 1973), 5.

95   Mona El-Sherif, "Reclaiming Tangier: Mohammed Choukri's *Al-Khubz al-Ḥāfī* and Subaltern Citizenship in Urban Literature," *Research in African Literatures* 44, no. 3 (Fall 2013): 102–117.

96   Nawal El-Saadawi, *Woman at Point Zero*, trans. by Sherif Hetata (London: Zed Books, 2007), 1.

97   El-Saadawi, *Woman at Point Zero*, xii.

98 Miriam Cooke, Foreword to *Woman at Point Zero* by Nawal El-Saadawi, translated by Sherif Hetata, (London: Zed Books, 2007), viii.

99 Mona Fayad, *Woman at Point Zero": A Bid for Survival, a Review of Ghada Samman's 'Beirut Nightmares'*, Al Jadid 4, no. 23 (Spring 1998).

100 Mona Fayad, *Woman at Point Zero", a Bid for Survival, a Review of Ghada Samman's 'Beirut Nightmares'*, Al Jadid 4, no. 23 (Spring 1998).

101 Allen, *The Arabic Novel, An Historical and Critical Introduction*, 214.

102 James McDougall, "Social Memories 'in the flesh': War and Exile in Algerian Self-Writing," *Alif: Journal of Comparative Poetics* 30 (2010): 3.

103 Nuha Baaqeel, "An Interview with Ahlam Mosteghanemi," *Women: A Cultural Review* 26, nos. 1-2 (2015): 149.

104 Baaqeel, "An Interview with Ahlam Mosteghanemi," 148.

105 Jensen, Kim. "Ahlam Mostaghenemi's *Memory in the Flesh*," Al-Jadid 8, no. 39 (Spring 2002).

106 Baaqeel, "An Interview with Ahlam Mosteghanemi," 143-153.

107 Nizar Qabbani, endorsement of *Zakirat al-Jasad* by Ahlam Mostaghenemi, second print in Arabic (Beirut, Lebanon: Dar Al-Adab, 1996). The translation is mine.

108 John L. Murphy, review of *"I Killed Scheherazade: Confessions of an Angry Arab Woman,"* by Jouman Haddad, New York Journal of Books. Review. (Murphy quotes from Austrian writer Elfriede Jelinek (b. 1946).

109 Joumana Haddad, interview by Dobrina Zhekova, *ELLE*, Aug 26, 2014.

110 Review of *I Killed Scheherazade: Confessions of an Angry Arab Woman*, by Jouman Haddad, *Publishers Weekly*, June 27, 2011, Literature Resource Center, 148. https://www.publishersweekly.com/978-1-56976-840-2

111 Murphy, John L, review of *I Killed Scheherazade: Confessions of an Angry Arab Woman*, By Joumana Haddad, *New York Journal of Books*. https://www.nyjournalofbooks.com/book-review/i-killed-scheherazade-confessions-angry-arab-woman

112 Junaid Ahmed, BBC News, Sep. 13, 2010.

113 Anissa Talahite-Moodley, "Lessons from Shahrazad: Teaching about Cultural Dialogism," in *New Approaches to Teaching Folk and Fairy Tales*, eds. Christa C. Jones and Claudia Schwabe (Logan: University Press of Colorado, 2016), 122.

114 Talahite-Moodley, "Lessons from *Scheherazade*: Teaching about Cultural Dialogism," 142. January 2016. https://www.researchgate.net/publication/306261966_Lessons_from_Shahrazad_Teaching_about_Cultural_Dialogis

115 Joumana Haddad, interview by Evelyn Crunden, "Joumana Haddad, Lebanon's 'Angry Arab Woman,' Talks Feminism and Sex in a New Interview," *Muftah*, June 3, 2015. https://muftah.org/joumana-haddad-lebanons-angry-arab-woman-talks-feminism-sex-in-a-new-interview/#.WykcJqdKhhE

116 Joumana Haddad, interview by Lisa Mullins, Public Radio International, "Lebanese Writer Joumana Haddad's Call to Arab Women," November 4, 2011.

117 Joumana Haddad, interview, Public Radio International.

118 Joumana Haddad, interview by Ben East, *The National*, September 12, 2012. https://www.thenational.ae/arts-culture/books/joumana-haddad-s-book-superman-is-an-arab-lampoons-gender-politics-1.372254

119 Joumana Haddad, *I Killed Scheherazade: Confessions of an Angry Arab Woman* (Chicago, Ill: Lawrence Hill Books, 2011), 12.

120 Joumana Haddad, *I Killed Scheherazade: Confessions of an Angry Arab Woman*, 14.

121 Muhsin Jasim al-Musawi, *al-Wuqu` fi Da'irat al-Sihr: Alf Layla wa Layla fil-Naqd al-Adabi al-Inglizi: 1704-1910* (Cairo: al-Hay'a al-`Amma lil-Kitab, 1987), 8.

CHAPTER 10

1 Abdallah Laroui, *The Crisis of the Arab Intellectuals* (Berkeley: University of California Press, 1976), 1.

2 Mahmoud `Ali al-Dawid, *Ishkaliyyat al-`Alaqa al-Thaqafiyya ma`a al-Gharb* (Beirut: Center of Arab Unity Studies, 1997), 164-165.

3 Interview with Adonis. Dubai TV. March 11, 2006.

4   Ilias Khoury, *al-Quds al-Arabi* newspaper, April 5, 2006.

5   Hisham Sharabi, *Arab Intellectuals and the West* (Baltimore: The John Hopkins Press, 1970), ix.

6   Albert Hourani, *Arabic Thought in the Liberal Age: 1798-1939* (Oxford: Oxford University Press, 15th printing, 2005), v.

7   Karen Armstrong, *Islam: A Short History* (NY: Modern Library, 2002), 141.

8   Armstrong, *Islam: A Short History*, 141-142.

9   Laroui, *The Crisis of the Arab Intellectuals*, 2.

10 Armstrong, *Islam: A Short History*, 146.

11 Albert Hourani, *History of the Arab Peoples* (Cambridge: The Belknap Press, 2002), 263.

12 Armstrong, *Islam: A Short History*, 142.

13 Sharabi, *Arab Intellectuals and the West*, 2, 142-147.

14 Hourani, *Arabic Thought in the Liberal Age: 1798-1939*, v.

15 Hourani, *Arabic Thought in the Liberal Age*, 73-81.

16 Hourani, *Arabic Thought in the Liberal Age*, 110-117.

17 Hourani, *Arabic Thought in the Liberal Age*, 119, 127.

18 Hourani, *Arabic Thought in the Liberal Age*, 136-137, 149-151.

19 Hourani, *Arabic Thought in the Liberal Age*, 225-229.

20 Halim Barakat, *The Arab World : Society, Culture and State* (University of California Press, 1993), 141.

21 Barakat, *The Arab World*, 248-260.

22 Barakat, *The Arab World*, 248-260.

23 Bassam Frangieh, *Banipal* (London: Summer 2000), 33.

24 Hourani, *Arabic Thought in the Liberal Age*, 185-186.

25 Hourani, *Arabic Thought in the Liberal Age*, 189.

26 Barakat, *The Arab World*, 253.

27 Frangieh, *Banipal*, 33.

28 Hourani, *Arabic Thought in the Liberal Age*, 330.

29 Hourani, *Arabic Thought in the Liberal Age*, 330.

30 Mona Mikhail, *Encyclopedia of Arabic Literature*, ed. Julie Scott Meisami and Paul Starkey (London: Routledge, 1998), 554-555.

31 Barakat, *The Arab World*, 258.

32 *al-Jadid fi `Alam al-Kutub wa al-Maktabat* (Amman: Summer 1994).

33 Richard P Mitchell, *The Society of the Muslim Brothers* (Oxford: Oxford University Press, 1969), 1-7.

34 Brynjar Lia, *The Society of the Muslim Brothers in Egypt: The Rise of an Islamic Mass Movement, 1928-1942* (England: Ithaca Press, 1998), 24.

35 Barakat, *The Arab World*, 255.

36 Emmanuel Sivan, *Radical Islam: Medieval Theology and Modern Politics* (New Haven: Yale University Press,1990), 44-46.

37 Encyclopedia of Arabic Literature, 332.

38 Barakat, *The Arab World*, 255.

39 Barakat, *The Arab World*, 254.

40 Ibrahim al-`Aris, *al-Hayat* newspaper, 4/17/2005.

41 Barakat, *The Arab World*, 354.

42 Kemal Karpart, *Political and Social Thought in the Contemporary Middle East* (NY: Praeger, 1982), 138-140.

43 Barakat, *The Arab World*, 255.

44 Youssef Choueiri, *Arab Nationalism: A History* (Blackwell Publishers, 2000), 157.

45 Hourani, *Arabic Thought in the Liberal Age*, 402.

46 Subhi Ghandour, al-arabia.net., 9/30/2005.

47 Jay Murphy, ed., *For Palestine* (NY: Writers 7 Readers, 1993), 2.

48 Hourani, *Arabic Thought in the Liberal Age*, 407.

49 Barakat, *The Arab World*, 257.

50 Hourani, *History of the Arab Peoples*, 444.

51 Dartmouth College Office of Public Affairs, 01/18/06.

52 Barakat, *The Arab World*, 265.

53 Barakat, *The Arab World* , 258.

54 Barakat, *The Arab World* , 260.

55 Muhannad Mubaidin, *Democratic Front for Peace and Equality*. www.aljabha.org. 4/22/2006.

56 Hourani, *History of the Arab Peoples*, 444.
57 Barakat, *The Arab World*, 260.
58 Barakat, *The Arab World* , 264.
59 Armstrong, *Islam: A Short History*, 168.

CHAPTER II

1 John R. Bradley, *After the Arab Spring: How Islamists Hijacked the Middle East Revolts* (New York: Palgrave MacMillan, 2012), 2.
2 Mark Lynch, *The Arab Uprising: The Unfinished Revolutions in the New Middle East* (New York: PublicAffairs, 2012), 30.
3 Mark Lynch, *The Arab Uprising*, 44–45.
4 Mark Lynch, *The Arab Uprising*.
5 Mark Lynch, *The Arab Uprising*, 68.
6 Rex Brynan, Pete W. Moore, Bassel F. Salloukh, and Marie-Joelle Zahar, *Beyond the Arab Spring: Authoritarianism & Democratization in the Arab World* (Boulder: Lynne Rienner Publishers, 2012), 233.
7 Dana Hochman Rand, *Roots of the Arab Spring: Contested Authority and Political Change in the Middle East* (Philadelphia: University of Pennsylvania Press, 2013), 38.
8 Michele Penner Angrist, "Understanding the Successful Mass Civic Protest in Tunisia," *Middle East Journal*, 64, no. 4 (Autumn 2013): 547.
9 Sidney G. Tarrow, *Power in Movement: Social Movements and Contentious Politics*, 3rd ed., (Cambridge University Press, 2011), 16.
10 "Tunisian Revolution," Al Jazeera English. Accessed June 10, 2017. http://www.aljazeera.com/indepth/inpictures/2015/12/tunisian-revolution-151215102459580.html.
11 "Tunisian Revolution." Al Jazeera English.
12 Shelly Culbertson, *The Fires of Spring*, (Cambridge: St. Martin's Press, 2016), 17.
13 George Joffe, "The Arab Spring in North Africa: origins and prospects," *Journal of North African Studies*, 16 no. 4 ((2011): 519.
14 Lynch, *The Arab Uprising, 30*.
15 Brynan, *Beyond the Arab Spring*, 233.
16 Faisal Al Yafai, "A song to start something: The Arab spring's greatest hits," *The National*, Aug. 27, 2011. Accessible: https://www.thenational.ae/arts-culture/music/a-song-to-start-something-the-arab-spring-s-greatest-hits-1.432495.
17 Nobelprize.org, "The Nobel Peace Prize for 2015." Accessible: https://www.nobelprize.org/nobel_prizes/peace/laureates/2015/press.html.
18 Culbertson, *The Fires of Spring*, 62–63.
19 Culbertson, *The Fires of Spring*, 69.
20 Jon Armajani, *Modern Islamic Movements: History, Religion and Politics* (Wiley-Blackwell, 2012). Accessed online as e-book.
21 Mehran Kamrava, *The Modern Middle East: A Political History since the First World War* (Berkeley: University of California Press, 2013), 134.
22 Kamrava, *The Modern Middle East*, 217.
23 Lynch, *The Arab Uprising*, 57.
24 Khalil Al-Anani, "Upended: The Rise and Fall of the Muslim Brotherhood," *Middle East Journal* 69, no. 4 (Autumn, 2015): 529.
25 Brynan et al., *Beyond the Arab Spring*, 233.
26 Rand, *Roots of the Arab Spring*, 65.
27 Rand, *Roots of the Arab Spring*, 65..
28 Lynch, *The Arab Uprising* 68.
29 Lynch, *The Arab Uprising*, 85.
30 Culbertson, *The Fires of Spring*, 304.
31 Lynch, *The Arab Uprising*,. 90.
32 Tarrow, *Power in Movement: Social Movements and Contentious Politics*, 16.
33 Faisal Al Yafai, "A song to start something: The Arab spring's greatest hits," *The National*, August 27, 2011. Accessible: https://www.thenational.ae/arts-culture/music/a-song-to-start-something-the-arab-spring-s-greatest-hits-1.432495.

34   Paul Amar, *Dispatches from the Arab Spring: Understanding the New Middle East*, (Minneapolis: University of Minnesota Press, 2013), 31–33.

35   Al-Anani, "Upended: The Rise and Fall of the Muslim Brotherhood," *Middle East Journal* 69, no. 4 (Autumn, 2015): 532.

36   Al-Anani, "Upended: The Rise and Fall of the Muslim Brotherhood."

37   Al-Anani, "Upended: The Rise and Fall of the Muslim Brotherhood," 538.

38   Al-Anani, "Upended: The Rise and Fall of the Muslim Brotherhood," 533.

39   "Arab uprising: Country by country—Egypt." BBC News. December 16, 2013. Accessed June 11, 2017. http://www.bbc.com/news/world-12482293.

40   Election Guide, Arab Republic of Egypt, Accessible: http://www.electionguide.org/countries/id/65/.

41   "The World Bank in Egypt." Accessible: https://data.worldbank.org/country/egypt-arab-rep.

42   Amar, *Dispatches from the Arab Spring: Understanding the New Middle East*, 160.

43   Amar, *Dispatches from the Arab Spring: Understanding the New Middle East*, 160.

44   Amar, *Dispatches from the Arab Spring: Understanding the New Middle East*, 160.

45   "LibGuides: Arab Spring: A Research & Study Guide * الربيع العربي: Libya," Libya—Arab Spring: A Research & Study Guide * الربيع العربي—LibGuides at Cornell University. Accessed June 11, 2017. http://guides.library.cornell.edu/c.php?g=31688&p=200752.

46   "LibGuides: Arab Spring: A Research & Study Guide * الربيع العربي: Libya."

47   Amar, *Dispatches from the Arab Spring: Understanding the New Middle East*.

48   Zineb Abdessadok, "Libya Today: From Arab Spring to failed state," Libya | Al Jazeera, May 30, 2017. Accessed June 11, 2017. http://www.aljazeera.com/indepth/features/2017/04/happening-libya-today-170418083223563.html.

49   Abdessadok, "Libya Today: from Arab Spring to failed state."

50   Abdessadok, "Libya Today: from Arab Spring to failed state."

51   R. M., "Will the new peace deal end the conflict in Libya?" *The Economist*, July 31, 2017, retrieved from https://www.economist.com/blogs/economist-explains/2017/08/economist-explains?zid=304&ah=e5690753dc78ce91909083042ad12e30.

52   Lynch, *The Arab Uprising*, 178.

53   Lynch, *The Arab Uprising*, 178.

54   Amar, *Dispatches from the Arab Spring: Understanding the New Middle East*, 216.

55   Amar, *Dispatches from the Arab Spring: Understanding the New Middle East*.,

56   Lynch, *The Arab Uprising*, 180.

57   "LibGuides: Arab Spring: A Research & Study Guide * الربيع العربي: Syria." Syria—Arab Spring: A Research & Study Guide * الربيع العربي—LibGuides at Cornell University. Accessed June 11, 2017. http://guides.library.cornell.edu/c.php?g=31688&p=200753.

58   Lynch, *The Arab Uprising*, 119.

59   Amar, *Dispatches from the Arab Spring: Understanding the New Middle East*, 248.

60   Amar, *Dispatches from the Arab Spring: Understanding the New Middle East*, 248..

61   Amar, *Dispatches from the Arab Spring: Understanding the New Middle East* 249.

62   Lynch, *The Arab Uprising*, 180.

63   Lynch, *The Arab Uprising*, 181.

64   Curtis R. Ryan, "Five Years after Arab Uprisings, Security Trumps Reforms in Jordan," *Washington Post*, March 4, 2016.

65   Nuri Yesilyurt, "Jordan and the Arab Spring: Challenges and Opportunities," *Perceptions: Journal of International Affairs* 19, no. 4 (Winter 2014): 169–94.

66   Sarah A. Tobin, "Jordan's Arab Spring: The Middle Class and Anti-Revolution," *Middle East Policy Council* 19, no. 1 (March 14, 2012).

67   Curtis R. Ryan, "Five Years after Arab Uprisings, Security Trumps Reforms in Jordan," *Washington Post*, March 4, 2016.

68   Nuri Yesilyurt, "Jordan and the Arab Spring: Challenges and Opportunities," *Perceptions: Journal of International Affairs* 19, no. 4 (Winter 2014): 169–94..

69   Tariq Tell, "Early Spring in Jordan: The Revolt of the Military Veterans," Carnegie Middle East Center, November 4, 2015.

70   Alexandra Francis, "Jordan's Refugee Crisis," Carnegie Endowment for International Peace, September 21, 2015.

71   Alexandra Francis, "Jordan's Refugee Crisis."

72   "U.S. Humanitarian Assistance in Response to the Syrian Crisis," Fact Sheet, U.S. Department of State, April 5, 2017, retrieved from https://www.state.gov/j/prm/releases/factsheets/2017/269469.htm.

73   "U.S. Security Cooperation with Jordan," Fact Sheet, U.S. Department of State, January 20, 2017. Accessible at: https://www.state.gov/t/pm/rls/fs/2017/266863.htm.

74   Country Report (March 2015 – April 2017), EU-Jordan Partnership, High Representative of the Union for Foreign Affairs and Security Policy, European Commission, June 13, 2017, retrieved from https://eeas.europa.eu/sites/eeas/files/2017_report_on_eu-jordan_relations_2015-2017.pdf.

75   Country Report, https://eeas.europa.eu/sites/eeas/files/2017_report_on_eu-jordan_relations_2015-2017.pdf.

76   Ibrahim Fraihat, *Unfinished Revolutions: Yemen, Libya, and Tunisia after the Arab Spring.* Yale University Press, 2016. 39

77   Amar, *Dispatches from the Arab Spring: Understanding the New Middle East,* 104.

78   Ibrahim Fraihat, *Unfinished Revolutions: Yemen, Libya, and Tunisia after the Arab Spring.* Yale University Press, 2016. 54.

79   "LibGuides: Arab Spring: A Research & Study Guide * الربيع العربي: Yemen," Yemen—Arab Spring: A Research & Study Guide * الربيع العربي—LibGuides at Cornell University. Accessed June 11, 2017. http://guides.library.cornell.edu/c.php?g=31688&p=200752.

80   "LibGuides: Arab Spring: A Research & Study Guide * الربيع العربي: Yemen."

81   "LibGuides: Arab Spring: A Research & Study Guide * الربيع العربي: Yemen."

82   Noel Brehony, "Yemen and the Huthis: Genesis of the 2015 Crisis," *Asian Affairs* 46, no. 2 (2015): 232–50.

83   Brehony, "Yemen and the Huthis: Genesis of the 2015 Crisis."

84   Ibrahim Fraihat, *Unfinished Revolutions: Yemen, Libya, and Tunisia after the Arab Spring.* Yale University Press, 2016. 57

85   "The World Bank in Yemen," The World Bank, retrieved from http://www.worldbank.org/en/country/yemen.

86   Toby Matthiesen, "The Sectarian Gulf vs. the Arab Spring," Foreign Policy. October 8, 2013.

87   Toby Matthiesen, "The Sectarian Gulf vs. the Arab Spring," 69.

88   Amar, *Dispatches from the Arab Spring: Understanding the New Middle East,* 77.

89   Amar, *Dispatches from the Arab Spring: Understanding the New Middle East,* 70.

90   Amar, *Dispatches from the Arab Spring: Understanding the New Middle East,* 71.

91   Amar, *Dispatches from the Arab Spring: Understanding the New Middle East,* 71.

92   Amar, *Dispatches from the Arab Spring: Understanding the New Middle East,* 94.

93   Culbertson, *The Fires of Spring: A Post-Arab Spring Journey through the Turbulent New Middle East,* (New York: St. Martin's Press, 2016), 206.

94   Lynch, *The Arab Uprising,* 113.

95   Sean L. Yom, "The Survival of Arab Monarchies," *Foreign Policy,* Nov. 12, 2012.

96   Cornell University Library. "Arab Spring: A Research and Study Guide: Bahrain."

97   John R. Bradley, Foreign Affairs. "Saudi Arabia's Invisible Hand in the Arab Spring," *Foreign Affairs,* Oct. 13, 2011.

98   James Worrall, "Oman: The 'Forgotten' Corner of the Arab Spring," *Middle East Policy Council* 19, no. 3 (September 17, 2012).

99   Culbertson, *The Fires of Spring,* 120.

100   Culbertson, *The Fires of Spring,* 211.

101   Sam Razavi, "Qatar and the Arab Spring," review of *Qatar and the Arab Spring,* by Kristen Coates Ulrichsen, Middle East Policy Council, 2014. https://www.mepc.org/qatar-and-arab-spring

102   Razavi, "Qatar and the Arab Spring, review.

103   BBC "Arab Uprising: Country by Country - Kuwait." December 16, 2013.

104   Ingo Forstenlechner, Emilie Rutledge, and Rashed Salem Alnuaimi, "The UAE, the 'Arab Spring,' and Different Types of Dissent," Middle East Policy Council 19, no. 4 (Winter).

105   Forstenlechner et al., "The UAE, the 'Arab Spring,' and Different Types of Dissent."

106   Forstenlechner et al., "The UAE, the 'Arab Spring,' and Different Types of Dissent."

107   Sean L. Yom, "The Survival of Arab Monarchies," Foreign Policy, November 12, 2012.

108   BBC "Arab Uprising: Country by Country—Saudi Arabia." December 16, 2013.

109   James Worrall, "Oman: The 'Forgotten' Corner of the Arab Spring," *Middle East Policy Council* 19, no. 3(September 17, 2012).

110   Worrall, "Oman: The 'Forgotten' Corner of the Arab Spring."

111   Sean L. Yom, "The Survival of Arab Monarchies," Foreign Policy, November 12, 2012.

112   Kelly McEvers, "Bahrain: The Revolution that Wasn't," NPR, January 5, 2012.

113   Toby Matthiesen, "The Sectarian Gulf vs. the Arab Spring," Foreign Policy. October 8, 2013.

114   Matthiesen, "The Sectarian Gulf vs. the Arab Spring."

115   Matthiesen, "The Sectarian Gulf vs. the Arab Spring."

116   Matthiesen, "The Sectarian Gulf vs. the Arab Spring."

117   Matthiesen, "The Sectarian Gulf vs. the Arab Spring."

118   Perry Cammack, Michele Dunne, Amr Hamzawy, Marc Lynch, Marwan Muasher, Yezid Sayich, Maha Yahya "Arab Fractures: Citizens, States and Social Contracts," Carnegie Endowment for International Peace, December, 2016, Accessible: http://carnegieendowment.org/2017/02/01/arab-fractures-citizens-states-and-social-contracts-pub-66612.

119   Perry Cammrack and Marwan Muasher, "Arab Voices on the Challenges in the New Middle East," Carnegie Endowment for International Peace, February 3, 2016. Accessible: http://carnegieendowment.org/2016/02/12/arab-voices-on-challenges-of-new-middle-east-pub-62721. 120: David Ignatius, "A look at the Arab Spring, six years later," *The Washington Post*, February 6, 2017. Accessible: https://www.washingtonpost.com/blogs/post-partisan/wp/2017/02/06/a-look-at-the-arab-spring-six-years-later/?utm_term=.9add86ca0b94.

120   Alfred Stepan and Juan J. Linz, *Journal of Democracy* 24, no. 2(April 2013), National Endowment for Democracy and The Johns Hopkins University Press, 2013.

CHAPTER 12

1   Antonio Guterres, "Struggle of the Middle East Refugees," *The Cairo Review of Global Affairs*, spring 2013.

2   Hoffman, Sophia. *Iraqi Migrants in Syria: The Crisis before the Storm*. Syracuse (New York: Syracuse University Press, 2016).

3   Hoffman, Sophia, *Iraqi Migrants in Syria: The Crisis before the* Storm.

4   Antonio Guterres, "Struggle of the Middle East Refugees," *The Cairo Review of Global Affairs*, spring 2013.

5   Avi Melamed, *Inside the Middle East: Making Sense of the Most Dangerous and Complicated Region on Earth* (New York: Skyhorse Publishing, 2016), 56.

6   Syrian Refugees.eu, Updated September 2016. Syria Regional Refugee Response, Operational Data Portal, UNHCR. Accessible: http://data.unhcr.org/syrianrefugees/regional.php—http://www.unhcr.org/en-us/syria-emergency.html

7   Tahir Zaman, *Islamic Traditions of Refuge in the Crises of Iraq and Syria* (Palgrave Macmillan, 2016).

8   Antonio Guterres, "Struggle of the Middle East Refugees," *The Cairo Review of Global Affairs*, spring 2013.

9   Antonio Guterres, "Struggle of the Middle East Refugees," *The Cairo Review of Global Affairs*, spring 2013.

10   Omer Karasapan, "The Internally Displaced in the Middle East and North Africa: Harbingers of Future Conflict," Brookings Institution, July 5, 2017.

11   Ben White, Simone Haysom, Eleanor Davey, "Refugees, Host States, and Internal Displacement in the Middle East: an Enduring Challenge," Humanitarian Practice Network, November 2013.

12   Tamarice Fakhoury, "Migration, Conflict, and Security in the post-2011 Landscape," The Middle East Institute, April 13, 2016.

13   Soner Cagaptay, Oya Aktas, and Cagatay Ozdemir, "The Impact of Syrian Refugees on Turkey," Washington Institute, August 25, 2016.

14   Cagaptay, "The Impact of Syrian Refugees on Turkey."

15   Shelly Culbertson and Louay Constant, *Education of Syrian Refugee Children: Managing the Crisis in Turkey, Lebanon, and Jordan* (RAND Corporation, 2015).

16   Soner Cagaptay, Oya Aktas, and Cagatay Ozdemir, "The Impact of Syrian Refugees on Turkey," Washington Institute, August 25, 2016.

17   Cagaptay, "The Impact of Syrian Refugees on Turkey."

18   Tahir Zaman, *Islamic Traditions of Refuge in the Crises of Iraq and Syria* (Palgrave Macmillan, 2016).

19   Tahir Zaman, *Islamic Traditions of Refuge in the Crises of Iraq and Syria.*

20   European Parliament Think Tank. "Syria Crisis: Impact on Lebanon," March 3, 2017.

21   Elias al-Araj, "How the War in Syria Left its Mark," Al-Monitor, May 13, 2016.

22   Zeinab Cherri, Pedro Acros Gonzalez, and Rafael Castro Delgado, "The Lebanese-Syrian Crisis: Impact of Influx of Syrian Refugees to an Already Weak State," National Center for Biotechnology Information, July 14, 2016.

23   Zeinab Cherri, "The Lebanese-Syrian Crisis."

24   Julia Craig Romero, "Humanitarian Crisis: Impact of Syrian Refugees in Lebanon," Woodrow Wilson Center, October 29, 2013.

25   Zeinab Cherri, Pedro Acros Gonzalez, and Rafael Castro Delgado, "The Lebanese-Syrian Crisis: Impact of Influx of Syrian Refugees to an Already Weak State," National Center for Biotechnology Information, July 14, 2016.

26   European Parliament Think Tank, "Syrian Crisis: Impact on Jordan," July 2, 2017.

27   Alexandra Francis, "Jordan's Refugee Crisis," Carnegie Endowment for International Peace, September 21, 2015.

28   Oxfam International. "Life in Za'atari Refugee Camp, Jordan's Fourth Biggest City," July 18, 2017.

29   Suleiman Al-Khalidi, "In Jordan, a Syrian Refugee Camp Withers," Reuters, November 22, 2016.

30   Amy Guttman, "World's largest Syrian Refugee Camp has Developed its own Economy," PBS, June 18, 2016.

31   http://data.unhcr.org/syrianrefugees/settlement.php?id=224&country=107&region=73

32   Adam Rasmi, "A Tale of Two Refugee Cities," Al Jazeera, September 23, 2013.

33   UNHCR, "Syria Regional Refugee Response," July 3, 2017. http://data.unhcr.org/syrianrefugees/settlement.php?id=251&country=107&region=73

34   Bill Neely and Ziad Jaber, "ISIS Infiltrates the Rukban Refugee Camp at Jordan-Syria Border," NBC, May 8, 2017.

35   Tim Hume, "75,000 Trapped in Refugee Camp on Jordan-Syria Border, Amnesty Warns," CNN, September 16, 2016.

36   King Abdullah II of Jordan, interview with Wolf Blitzer, CNN, Jan. 13, 2016. Full Transcript Accessible: http://cnnpressroom.blogs.cnn.com/2016/01/13/king-abdullah-ii-of-jordan-on-syrian-refugees-we-cant-ignore-them-and-just-keep-refugees-isolated/

37   King Abdullah II of Jordan, interview with Wolf Blitzer, CNN, Jan. 13, 2016.

38   Alexandra Francis, "Jordan's Refugee Crisis," Carnegie Endowment for International Peace, September 21, 2015.

39   European Parliament Think Tank, "Syrian Crisis: Impact on Jordan," July 2, 2017.

40   Alexandra Francis, "Jordan's Refugee Crisis," Carnegie Endowment for International Peace, September 21, 2015.

41   Francis, "Jordan's Refugee Crisis."

42   Francis, "Jordan's Refugee Crisis."

43   Francis, "Jordan's Refugee Crisis."

44   Francis, "Jordan's Refugee Crisis."

45   Francis, "Jordan's Refugee Crisis."

46   Francis, "Jordan's Refugee Crisis."

47   European Parliament Think Tank. "Syrian Crisis: Impact on Jordan," July 2, 2017.

48   Alexandra Francis, "Jordan's Refugee Crisis," Carnegie Endowment for International Peace, September 21, 2015.

49   Omer Karasapan, "The Internally Displaced in the Middle East and North Africa: Harbingers of Future Conflict," Brookings Institution, July 5, 2017.

50   Omer Karasapan, "The Internally Displaced in the Middle East and North Africa: Harbingers of Future Conflict."

51   Antonio Guterres, "Struggle of the Middle East Refugees," *The Cairo Review of Global Affairs*, spring 2013.

52   Omer Karasapan, "The Tragedy of Migrants in Libya," Brookings Institution, May 15, 2017.

53   Omer Karasapan, "The Tragedy of Migrants in Libya."

54   Omer Karasapan, "The Internally Displaced in the Middle East and North Africa: Harbingers of Future Conflict," Brookings Institution, July 5, 2017.

55   Omer Karasapan, "The Tragedy of Migrants in Libya," Brookings Institution, May 15, 2017.

56   ibid

57   Omer Karasapan, "The Internally Displaced in the Middle East and North Africa: Harbingers of Future Conflict," Brookings Institution July 5, 2017.

58   Omer Karasapan, "The Internally Displaced in the Middle East and North Africa: Harbingers of Future Conflict."

59   Antonio Guterres, "Struggle of the Middle East Refugees," The Cairo Review of Global Affairs, spring 2013.

60   BBC, "How is the Migrant Crisis Dividing EU Countries?" March 4. 2016.

61   BBC, "How is the Migrant Crisis Dividing EU Countries?"

62   BBC, "How is the Migrant Crisis Dividing EU Countries?"

63   BBC, "How is the Migrant Crisis Dividing EU Countries?"

64   BBC, "How is the Migrant Crisis Dividing EU Countries?"

65   Office of the Federal Chancellor. Speech by Angela Merkel at G20 Africa Partnership conference, Berlin, 12 June 2017. Accessible: https://www.bundeskanzlerin.de/Content/EN/Reden/2017/2017-06-12-bk-merkel-g20-africa-conference_en.html

66   BBC, "How is the Migrant Crisis Dividing EU Countries?" March 4, 2016.

67   BBC, "How is the Migrant Crisis Dividing EU Countries?"

68   Accessible: http://news.bbc.co.uk/1/shared/bsp/hi/pdfs/000000.pdf

69   Andrew Geddes and Peter Scholten, *The Politics of Migration and Immigration in Europe* (SAGE Publications, 2016).

70   William J. Parker III, "Addressing the Refugee Crisis and Terrorism Simultaneously and Immediately," EastWest Institute, June 23, 2017.

71   William J. Parker III, "Addressing the Refugee Crisis and Terrorism Simultaneously and Immediately."

72   Shelly Culbertson and Louay Constant. *Education of Syrian Refugee Children: Managing the Crisis in Turkey, Lebanon, and Jordan* (RAND Corporation, 2015).

73   Julia Craig Romero, "Humanitarian Crisis: Impact of Syrian Refugees in Lebanon," Woodrow Wilson Center, October 29, 2013.

74   Shelly Culbertson and Louay Constant, *Education of Syrian Refugee Children: Managing the Crisis in Turkey, Lebanon, and Jordan* (RAND Corporation, 2015).

75   Shelly Culbertson and Louay Constant, *Education of Syrian Refugee Children.*

76   Shelly Culbertson and Louay Constant, *Education of Syrian Refugee Children.*

77   Kemal Kirisci, "To Really Improve the Lives of Syrian Refugees, Turkey and the World Must Cooperate Better," Brookings, June 9, 2016.

78   Kirisci, "To Really Improve the Lives of Syrian Refugees, Turkey and the World Must Cooperate Better."

79   Cherri Zeinab, Pedro Acros Gonzalez, and Rafael Castro Delgado, "The Lebanese-Syrian Crisis: Impact of Influx of Syrian Refugees to an Already Weak State," National Center for Biotechnology Information, July 14, 2016.

80   Elias al-Araj, "How the War in Syria Left its Mark," Al-Monitor, May 13, 2016.

81   USAID, "Addressing Impacts of the Syria Complex Crisis," May 23, 2017.

82   USAID, "Addressing Impacts of the Syria Complex Crisis," May 23, 2017.

83   Alexandra Francis, "Jordan's Refugee Crisis," Carnegie Endowment for International Peace, September 21, 2015.

84   King Abdullah II of Jordan, interview with Wolf Blitzer, CNN, Jan. 13, 2016. Full Transcript Accessible: http://cnnpressroom.blogs.cnn.com/2016/01/13/king-abdullah-ii-of-jordan-on-syrian-refugees-we-cant-ignore-them-and-just-keep-refugees-isolated.

CHAPTER 13

1   Khalid Yahya Blankinship, *The End of the Jihad State, the Reign of Hisham Ibn ʿAbd-al Malik and the collapse of the Umayyad,* (State University of New York Press, 1994), 37.

2   M. M. Badawi, *A Short History of Modern Arabic Literature* (Oxford: Clarendon Press, 1993), 19.

3   Mahmoud Amin al-`Alim, *al-Thaqafa al-Arabiyya: As'ilat al-Tatawwur wa al-Mustaqbal [Arab Culture: Questions on Development and the Future]* (Beirut: Center for Arab Unity Studies, 2000), 11–14.

4   Muta` Safadi article, *al-Quds al-`Arabi* newspaper, June 5, 2006.

5   Muta` Safadi article.

6   Muta` Safadi article.

7   Muta` Safadi, *al-Quds al-`Arabi* newspaper, July 3, 2006.

8   Albert Hourani, *A History of the Arab Peoples*, 419.

9   Ilias Khouri, *al-Quds al-`Arabi* newspaper, April 4, 2006 and July 25, 2005.

10 Albert Hourani, *A History of the Arab Peoples*, 417–23.

11 Hourani, *A History of the Arab Peoples*, 419.

12 Hourani, *A History of the Arab Peoples*, 422–24.

13 Hourani, *A History of the Arab Peoples*.

14 Khouri, *al-Quds al-`Arabi* newspaper, April 6, 2004.

15 Sadiq Jalal al-`Azm, interview by Larissa Bender and Mona Naggar, Qantara.de, trans. Samira Kawer, April, 2003.

16 `Abdul Wahab al-Bayati and Muhyi al-Din Subhi, *al-Bahth `an Yanabi` al-Shi`r wa al-Ru'ya [Searching for the Springs of Poetry and Vision]* (Beirut: Dar al-Tali`a, 2000), 6–15.

17 `Abdul Wahab al-Bayati and Muhyi al-Din Subhi, *al-Bahth `an Yanabi` al-Shi`r wa al-Ru'ya*, 7–8.

18 `Abdul Wahab al-Bayati and Muhyi al-Din Subhi, *al-Bahth `an Yanabi` al-Shi`r wa al-Ru'ya*, 421.

19 Fouad Ajami, "Retreat from Economic Nationalism: The Political Economy of Sadat's Egypt," *Journal of Arab Affairs* (October 31, 1981): 27.

20 "Saudi Arabia—Openness to and Restriction on Foreign Investment," Export.gov, accesses at https://www.export.gov/article?id=Saudi-Arabia-openness-to-foreign-investment.

21 Hilal Khashan, "Saudi Arabia's Flawed 'Vision 2030,'" *Middle East Quarterly*, (Winter 2017), accessed at http://www.meforum.org/6397/saudi-arabia-flawed-vision-2030.

22 Rex Brynan et al., *Beyond the Arab Spring: Authoritarianism and Democratization in the Arab World* (Boulder: Lynne Rienner Publishers, 2012), 223.

23 Shelly Culbertson, *The Fires of Spring: A Post-Arab Spring Journey Through the Turbulent Middle East* (New York: St. Martins Press, 2016), 177.

24 Safadi, *al-Quds al-`Arabi* newspaper, July 3, 2006

25 Safadi, *al-Quds al-`Arabi*.

26 Burhan Ghalioun, *Aljazeera. Net*, December 25, 2005.

27 Hisham Sharabi, Burhan Ghalioun, and Khalid Harb, Special Program on *Azmat al-Muthaqqafin al-`Arab [The Crisis of Arab Intellectuals]*, aljazeera.net., April 17, 2005.

28 Sharabi, *Azmat al-Muthaqqafin al-`Arab [The Crisis of Arab Intellectuals]*.

29 Sharabi, *Azmat al-Muthaqqafin al-`Arab [The Crisis of Arab Intellectuals]*.

30 Ghalioun, *Azmat al-Muthaqqafin al-`Arab [The Crisis of Arab Intellectuals]*.

31 Sharabi, *Azmat al-Muthaqqafin al-`Arab [The Crisis of Arab Intellectuals]*.

32 Khouri, *al-Quds al-`Arabi* newspaper, April 4, 2006.

33 United Nations Arab Human Development Report 2016, available: http://www.undp.org/content/undp/en/home/presscenter/pressreleases/2016/11/29/arab-human-development-report-2016-enabling-youth-to-shape-their-own-future-key-to-progress-on-development-and-stability-in-arab-region-.html.

34 `Alim, *al-Thaqafa al-`Arabiyya: As'ilat al-Tatawwur wa al-Mustaqbal*, 12.

35 Khalid Harb, "The Crisis of Arab Intellectuals," Special Program on *Azmat al-Muthaqqafin al-`Arab [The Crisis of Arab Intellectuals]*, by Hisham Sharabi, Burhan Ghalioun, and Khalid Harb, aljazeera.net, April 4, 2005.

36 Harb, "The Crisis of Arab Intellectuals," Special Program on *Azmat al-Muthaqqafin al-`Arab*.

37 Ghalioun, "The Crisis of Arab Intellectuals," Special Program on *Azmat al-Muthaqqafin al-`Arab [The Crisis of Arab Intellectuals]*, by Hisham Sharabi, Burhan Ghalioun and Khalid Harb, aljazeera.net, April 4, 2005.

38 Khouri, *al-Quds al-`Arabi* newspaper, June 5, 2006.

39 Khouri, *al-Quds al-`Arabi*.

40   Adonis, *al-Hayat* newspaper, February 23, 2005.

41   Khouri, *al-Quds al-'Arabi* newspaper, May 10, 2005 and February 2, 2005.

42   The United Nations Arab Human Development Report (New York, The United Nations Publications, 2005), 5.

43   The United Nations Arab Human Development Report.

44   The United Nations Arab Human Development Report.

45   The United Nations Arab Human Development Report (New York, The United Nations Publications, 2005), 129–30.

46   Rex Brenyn et al., *Beyond the Arab Spring: Authoritarianism and Democratization in the Arab World* (Boulder: Lynne Reinner Publishers, 2012), 291.

47   Samir Amin, *al-Amrikiyyun Yuridun lana Dimoqratiya bila Taqaddum wa Wataniyyuna Taqadduman bila Dimoqratiya* [*The Americans Want for Us Democracy Without Progress and Our Patriots Want for Us Progress Without Democracy*], al-hayat.net, January 23, 2006.

48   Amin, *al-Amrikiyyun Yuridun lana Dimoqratiya bila Taqaddum wa Wataniyyuna Taqadduman bila Dimoqratiya.*

49   Amin, *al-Amrikiyyun Yuridun lana Dimoqratiya bila Taqaddum wa Wataniyyuna Taqadduman bila Dimoqratiya.*

50   Amin, *al-Amrikiyyun Yuridun lana Dimoqratiya bila Taqaddum wa Wataniyyuna Taqadduman bila Dimoqratiya.*

51   Amin, *al-Amrikiyyun Yuridun lana Dimoqratiya bila Taqaddum wa Wataniyyuna Taqadduman bila Dimoqratiya.*

52   Sharabi, ibid.

53   Halim Barakat, *The Arab World: Society, Culture, and State* (Berkeley: University of California Press, 1993), xii.

54   Adam Hanieh, "Inequalities in the Arab Region," *World Social Science Report 2016* (UNESCO), 101. http://unesdoc.unesco.org/images/0024/002459/245947e.pdf

55   Elena Ianchovichina, "How Unequal are Arab Countries?" Brookings Institute, February 4, 2015.

56   Adam Hanieh, "Inequalities in the Arab Region," *World Social Science Report 2016* (UNESCO), 101–3. http://unesdoc.unesco.org/images/0024/002459/245947e.pdf

57   Hakam al-Baba, *al-Quds al-'Arabi* newspaper, August 7, 2006.

58   Ned Lamont, "Changing Media Landscape in the Arab World," *The Nation*, Deb. 14, 2007, http://nedlamont.com/news/2253/changing-media-landscape-in-the-arab-world. Ned Lamont was the 2006 Connecticut Democratic nominee for the US Senate and is the founder of Lamont Digital Systems, now known as Campus Televideo.

59   Shelly Culbertson, *The Fires of Spring: A Post-Arab Spring Journey Through the Turbulent Middle East* (New York: St. Martins Press, 2016), 271.

60   Lina Atallah, "Egypt's Government Can't Crush Independent Journalism," *The New York Times*, June 4, 2017, accesed at https://www.nytimes.com/2017/06/04/opinion/egypt-journalism-mada-masr.html?mcubz=0&_r=0.

61   Interview with Ibrahim Fraihat, May 2013.

62   Rex Brenyn et al., *Beyond the Arab Spring: Authoritarianism and Democratization in the Arab World*, (Boulder: Lynne Reinner Publishers, 2012), 233.

63   Brenyn et al., *Beyond the Arab* Spring, 234.

64   Brenyn et al., *Beyond the Arab Spring*, 251.

65   Tawakkol Karman, interview with WAN-IFRA, "In the absence of a free press, there is no democracy," accessed at http://www.wan-ifra.org/articles/2012/05/02/in-the-absence-of-a-free-press-there-is-no-democracy-a-wan-ifra-interview-with-t.

66   Vincent Romani, "The Politics of Higher Education in the Middle East: Problems and Prospects," Crown Center for Middle East Studies no. 36 (Brandeis University, May 2009): 1–6.

67   Vincent Romani, "The Politics of Higher Education in the Middle East: Problems and Prospects," Crown Center for Middle East Studies no. 36 (Brandeis University, May 2009): 1–6.

68   Abdeljalil Akkari, "Education in the Middle East and North Africa: The Current Situation and Future Challenges," *International Education Journal* 5, no. 2 (2004), 144.

69   Akkari, "Education in the Middle East and North Africa," 151.

70   Akkari, "Education in the Middle East and North Africa."

71   Abdeljalil Akkari, "Education in the Middle East and North Africa," 151.

72 Akkari, "Education in the Middle East and North Africa."

73 Vincent Romani, "The Politics of Higher Education in the Middle East: Problems and Prospects," *Crown Center for Middle East Studies* no. 36 (Brandeis University, May 2009): 2.

74 Abdeljalil Akkari, "Education in the Middle East and North Africa: The Current Situation and Future Challenges," *International Education Journal* 5, no. 2 (2004): 144–151.

75 `Alim, *al-Thaqafa al-`Arabiyya: As'ilat al-Tatawwur wa al-Mustaqbal*, 20.

76 Emma C. Murphy, "Problematizing Arab Youth: Generational Narratives of Systemic Failure," *Mediterranean Politics* 17, no. 1 (March 2012): 5–22.

77 United Nations Arab Human Development Report 2016, available: http://www.undp.org/content/undp/en/home/presscenter/pressreleases/2016/11/29/arab-human-development-report-2016-enabling-youth-to-shape-their-own-future-key-to-progress-on-development-and-stability-in-arab-region-.html.

78 Murphy, "Problematizing Arab Youth: Generational Narratives of Systemic Failure."

79 M. Booth, "Arab Adolescents Facing the Future: Enduring Ideals and Pressures to Change," in *The World's Youth: Adolescence in Eight Regions of the Globe*, eds. B. Bradford Brown, Reed W. Larson and T.S. Saraswathi (Cambridge: Cambridge University Press, 2002), 207–42.

80 M. Booth, "Arab Adolescents Facing the Future: Enduring Ideals and Pressures to Change."

81 Jad Chaaban, "Youth and Development in the Arab Countries: The Need for a Different Approach," *Middle Eastern Studies* 45, no. 1(2009): 33–55

82 Murphy, "Problematizing Arab Youth: Generational Narratives of Systemic Failure."

83 Murphy, "Problematizing Arab Youth: Generational Narratives of Systemic Failure," 15.

84 United Nations Arab Human Development Report 2016, available: http://www.undp.org/content/undp/en/home/presscenter/pressreleases/2016/11/29/arab-human-development-report-2016-enabling-youth-to-shape-their-own-future-key-to-progress-on-development-and-stability-in-arab-region-.html.

85 Abd al-Wahab al-Bayati, *Love, Death, and Exile: Poems Translated from Arabic by Bassam Frangieh*, (Georgetown University Press, 1991), 29.

INDEX

CPSIA information can be obtained
at www.ICGtesting.com
Printed in the USA
FSHW021851181120
76048FS